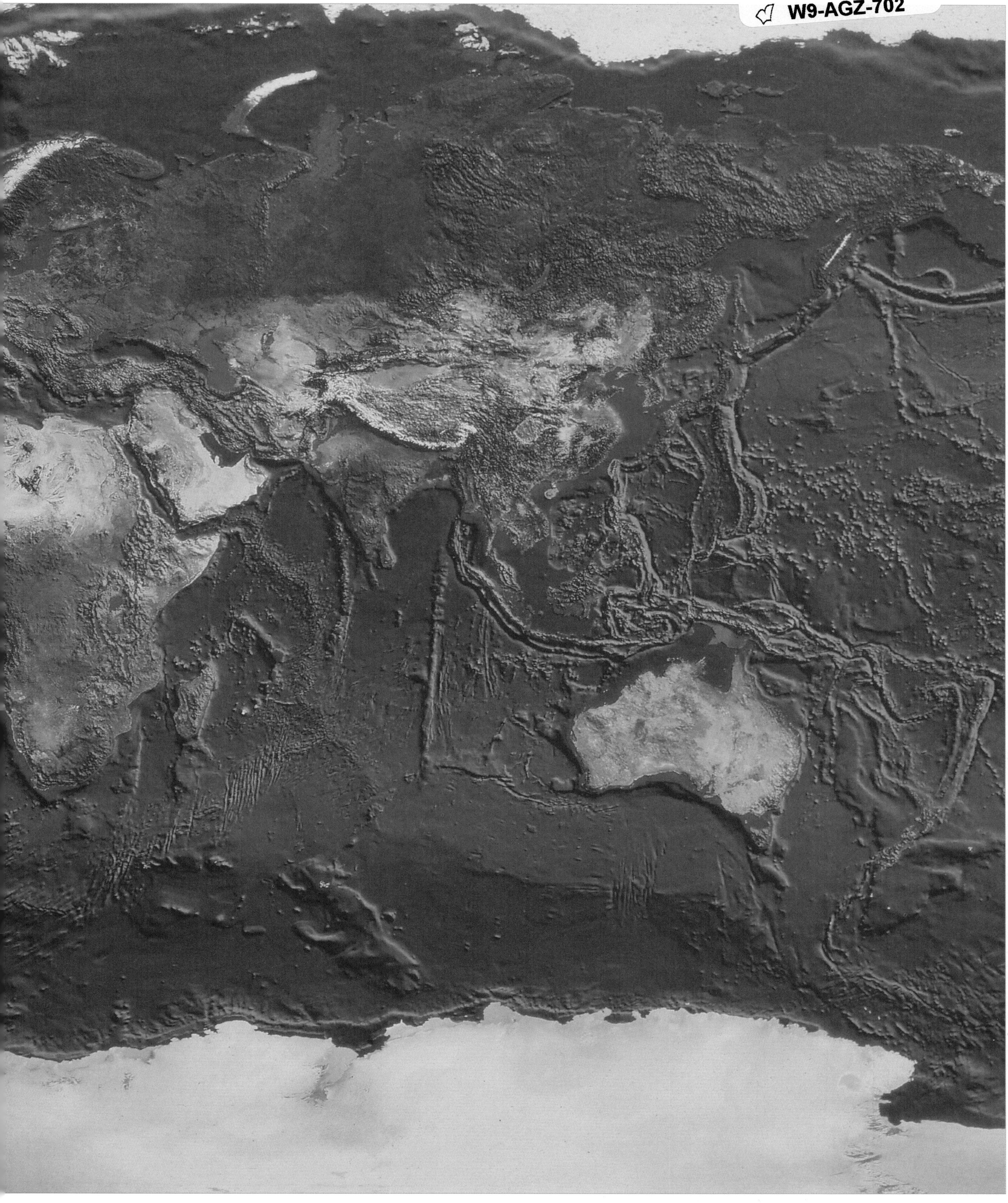

SATELLITE
WORLD
ATLAS

Produced by AND Cartographic Publishers Ltd.,
Alberto House, Hogwood Lane,
Finchampstead, Berks, RG40 4RF,
United Kingdom

First published as the 2 in 1 Atlas of the World © 1999 by AND Cartographic Publishers Ltd., Finchampstead, UK
Copyright © 2000 by AND Cartographic Publishers Ltd., Finchampstead, UK
Copyright © 1999 by WorldSat International Inc., Ontario, Canada
Copyright © 1998 SPOT Image, Toulouse, France

This edition published by MetroBooks, an imprint of Friedman/Fairfax Publishers

ISBN 1-58663-069-5

987654321

Cover design by Paul Taurins
Preliminary section design by Phil Jacobs

Cartographic production, design and layout:
AND Cartographic Publishers Ltd., Finchampstead, UK

Consultants: Simon Butler, Nigel Bradley
Editorial: Craig Asquith, Veronica Beattie, John Watkins
Cartography: Ben Brown, Ross Clode, Dave Edwards
Rachel Hopper, Adam Meara, Lee Rowe, Glyn Rozier, James Smith
DTP: Richard Fox
Production Coordinator: Caroline Beckley

Production of satellite imagery:
Robert Stacey, WorldSat International Inc.,
Ontario, Canada; Jim Knighton
Satellite data: NOAA
Ocean floor bathymetry by NOAA courtesy of USGS
Images on pages 58, 68, 70, 72 based on the
Resurs satellite imagery, provided by SSC/Satellitbild of Kiruna, Sweden

Printed in Spain

PACIFIC

SATELLITE
WORLD
ATLAS

TWO STUNNING VIEWS OF OUR WORLD

MetroBooks

CONTENTS

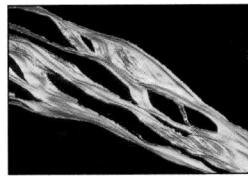 
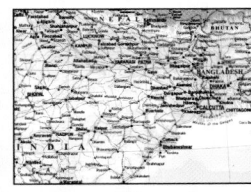 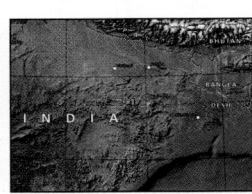

Africa

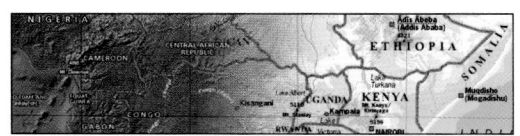

Asia

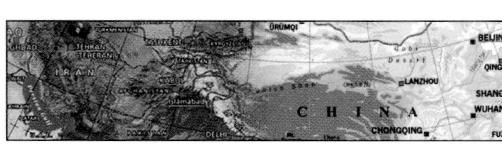

Oceania

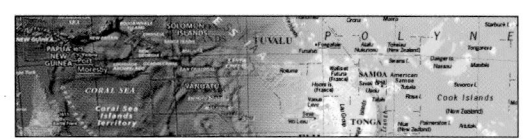

North America

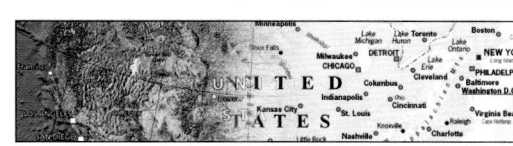

South America

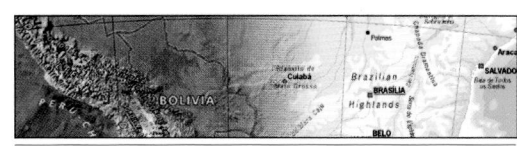

Polar Regions

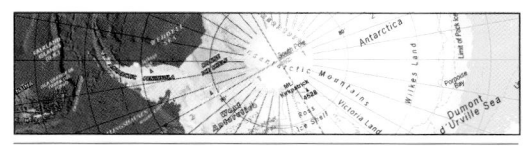

Statistics and Index

Endpapers

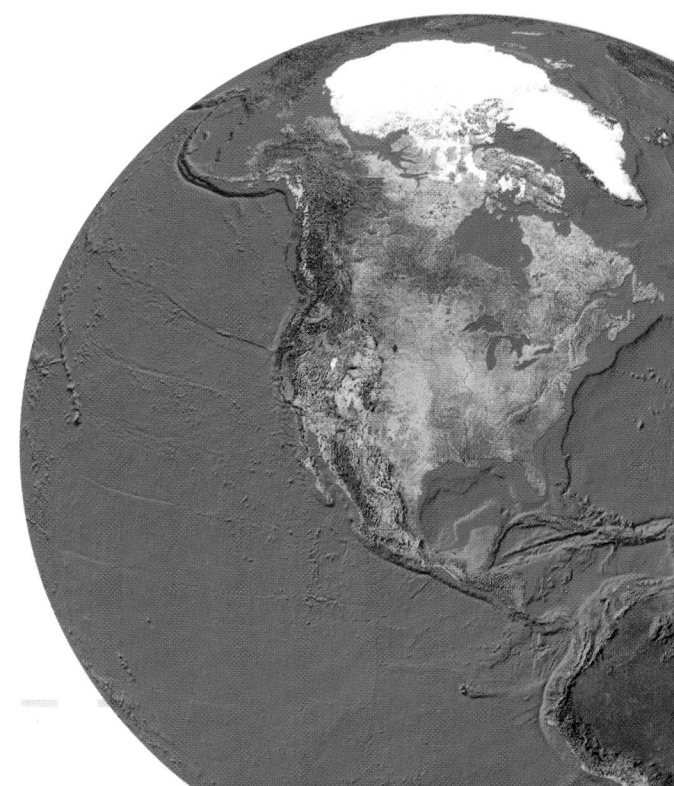

HOW TO USE THIS BOOK

THE ILLUSTRATION shows the different items of information presented in this atlas. Below it is the key to all the symbols used on the maps and satellite pictures.

Scale

Scale is the ratio between distance on the map and distance on the Earth's surface. A scale of 1:12,000,000 means that the distance on the map is 12 million times smaller than the actual distance measured on the Earth's surface. For example, one inch on the map represents 12,000,000 inches, or 189 miles, in reality.

Place location

The grid of lines on maps—the graticule—represent longitude (measured east or west of the Greenwich meridian) and latitude (measured north or south of the Equator). These lines are used by cartographers to accurately pinpoint locations. A similar network system has been used in this atlas, though here the longitudinal and latitudinal references have been replaced with letters and figures respectively. The grid reference A2, for example, signifies that the feature you are looking for lies in the "square" made by the intersection of Column A with Row 2.

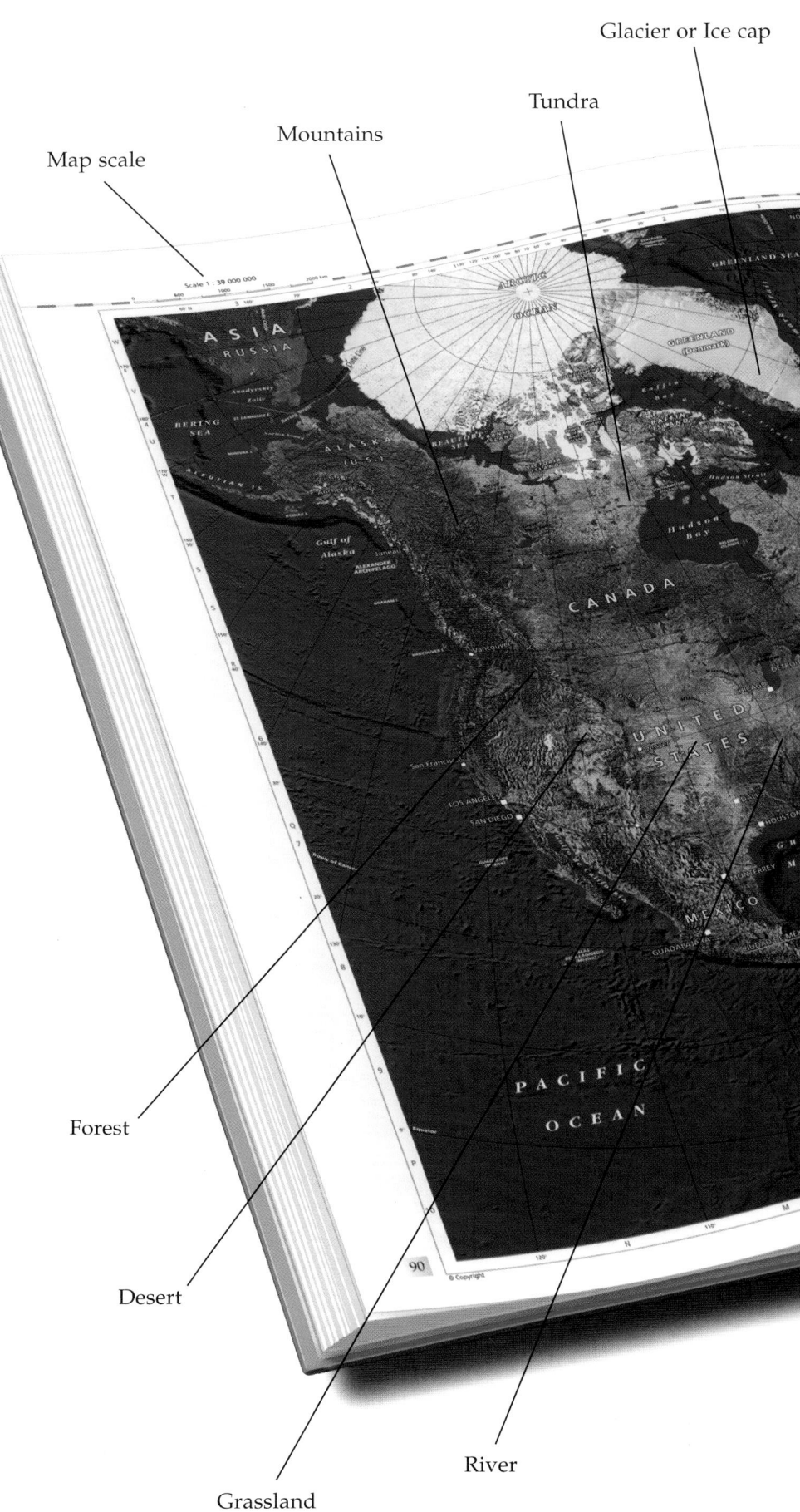

Map scale

Mountains

Tundra

Glacier or Ice cap

Forest

Desert

Grassland

River

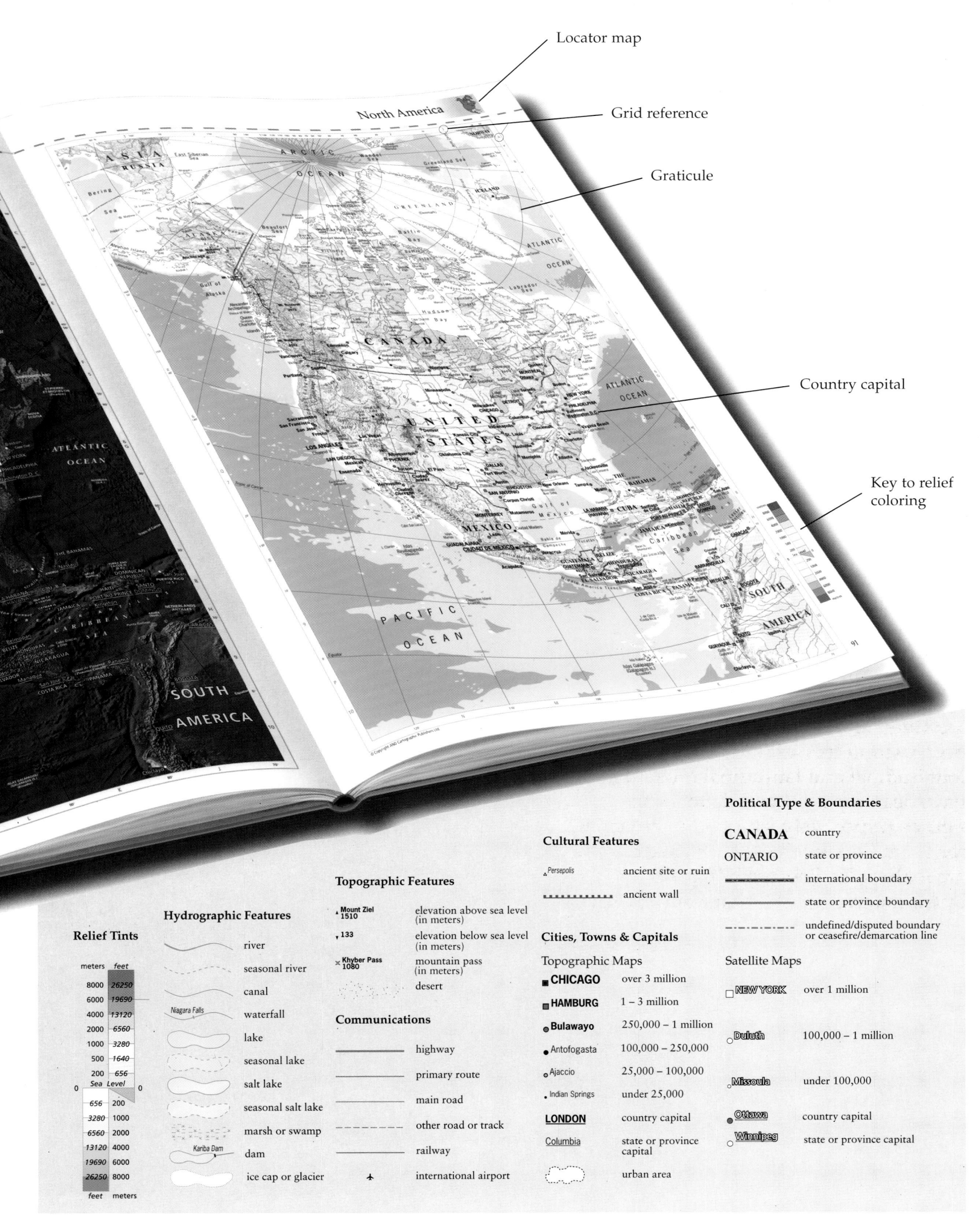

Locator map

North America

Grid reference

Graticule

Country capital

Key to relief coloring

Relief Tints

meters	feet
8000	26250
6000	19690
4000	13120
2000	6560
1000	3280
500	1640
200	656
0 Sea Level	0
656	200
3280	1000
6560	2000
13120	4000
19690	6000
26250	8000

feet   meters

Hydrographic Features

river

seasonal river

canal

Niagara Falls   waterfall

lake

seasonal lake

salt lake

seasonal salt lake

marsh or swamp

Kariba Dam   dam

ice cap or glacier

Topographic Features

Mount Ziel 1510   elevation above sea level (in meters)

, 133   elevation below sea level (in meters)

Khyber Pass 1080   mountain pass (in meters)

desert

Communications

highway

primary route

main road

other road or track

railway

✈   international airport

Cultural Features

Persepolis   ancient site or ruin

ancient wall

Cities, Towns & Capitals

Topographic Maps

■ CHICAGO   over 3 million

■ HAMBURG   1 – 3 million

● Bulawayo   250,000 – 1 million

● Antofagasta   100,000 – 250,000

○ Ajaccio   25,000 – 100,000

. Indian Springs   under 25,000

LONDON   country capital

Columbia   state or province capital

urban area

Political Type & Boundaries

CANADA   country

ONTARIO   state or province

international boundary

state or province boundary

undefined/disputed boundary or ceasefire/demarcation line

Satellite Maps

□ NEW YORK   over 1 million

○ Duluth   100,000 – 1 million

○ Missoula   under 100,000

● Ottawa   country capital

○ Winnipeg   state or province capital

INDEX TO MAP PAGES

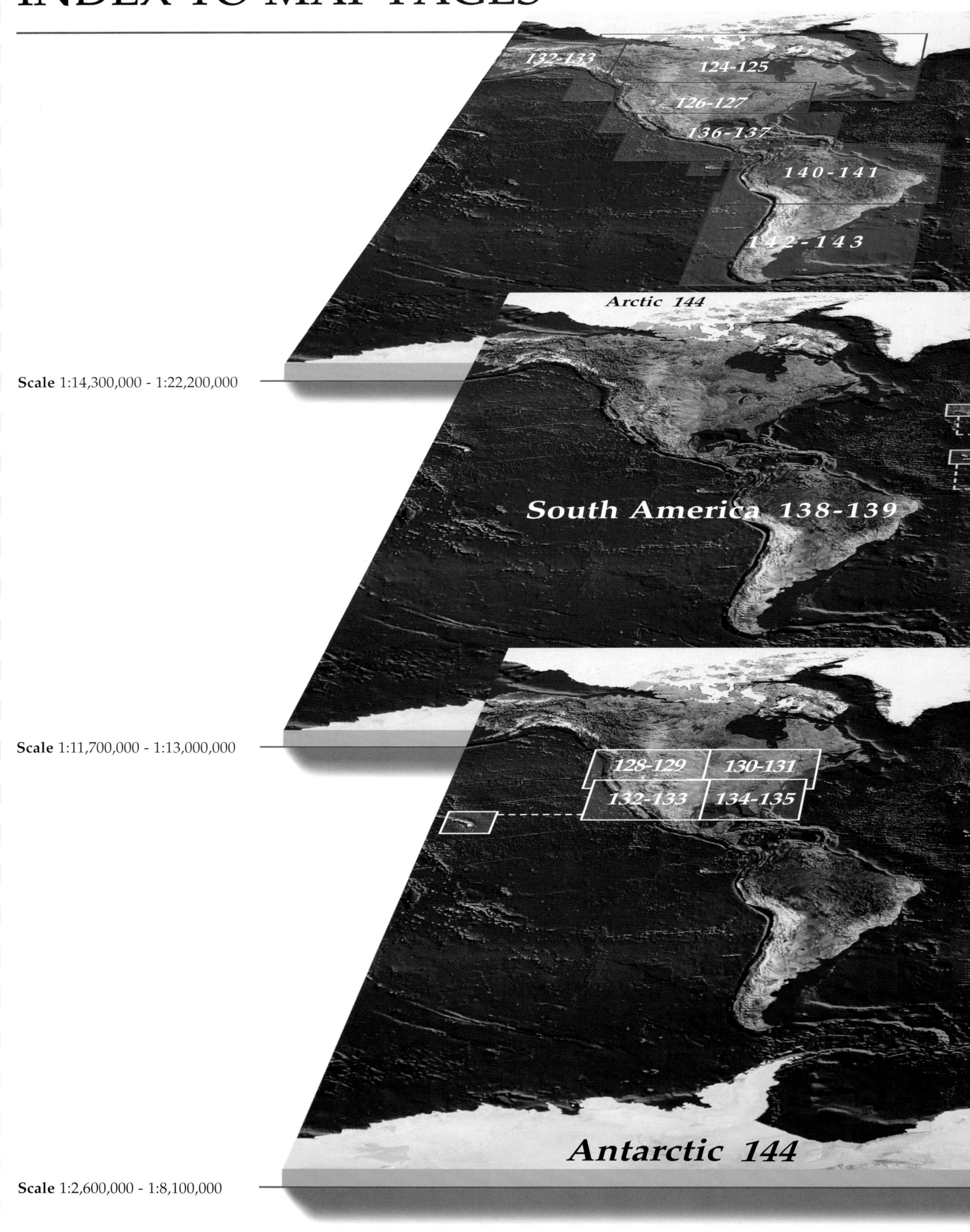

132-133

124-125

126-127

136-137

140-141

142-143

Arctic 144

Scale 1:14,300,000 - 1:22,200,000

South America 138-139

Scale 1:11,700,000 - 1:13,000,000

128-129   130-131

132-133   134-135

Antarctic 144

Scale 1:2,600,000 - 1:8,100,000

102-103

104-105

84-85

Africa 88-89

Oceania 116-117

118-119

62-63

Asia 100-101

110-111

90-91 92-93

106-107 108-109

4-95

114 115

96-97

98-99

Europe 56-57

82-83

112-113

86

87

Europe

120-121

60-61

68-69

66-67

64-65

70-71 7 -75

78-79

72-73

76-77

MAPPING THE EARTH

THERE ARE MANY HUNDREDS of man-made satellites orbiting the Earth. The majority are communication satellites, receiving and sending signals for radio, television and telecommunications. But a significant minority of satellites are used solely for observation. Not only do these retrieve information for espionage, weather forecasting and studying the universe, they provide mapmakers with vital data about the surface of our planet.

There are two main ways in which mapping satellites study the Earth. Some use optical scanners. These, while often extremely accurate, are limited by factors such as low light levels, cloud cover and atmospheric blurring. Moreover, they collect only visible light—just one part of what is known as the electromagnetic spectrum. The electromagnetic spectrum comprises waves which vary in size and have different properties. Yet while these are invisible to the naked eye, they can be detected and converted into images by electronic scanners. A scanner using microwaves, for example, can penetrate clouds and "see in the dark"—a distinct advantage over optical scanners.

ELECTROMAGNETIC RADIATION

All wavelengths collected by a satellite, whether they are visible light or belong to the invisible part of the electromagnetic radiation spectrum, "bounce" off the surface or object being viewed. Electromagnetic radiation used in mapping can come from a number of sources such as visible and infrared light from the sun, and thermal infrared (heat) from the Earth. The way an electromagnetic radiation wave bounces off an object is called its "spectral signature," because it gives a characteristic reading when detected. This enables technicians to process data for creating maps.

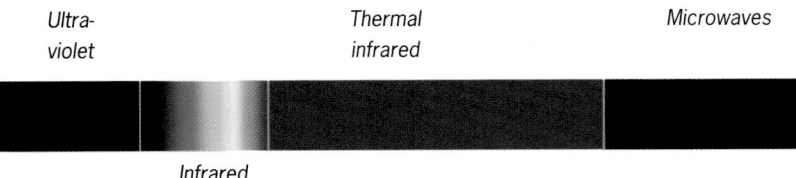

Ultra-violet | Infrared | Thermal infrared | Microwaves

The result is that an electronic scanner can extract geological and geographical information such as changes in elevation, differences in land cover and variations in temperature.

But whatever the comparative virtues of optical and electronic scanners, the combination of both methods results in maps that are both informative and extremely useful.

"Polar orbiting" satellites such as Landsat and Spot observe a different strip or "track" of the Earth after every rotation of the planet. In this way a complete picture of the surface can be compiled.

Aboard the satellite as it orbits the Earth, the scanner views a track of the surface and constantly photographs it.

The European Space Agency Satellite ERS–2, which generates its own microwaves. The radiation "bounced" off the Earth's surface is converted into the data needed to produce a computer-generated map.

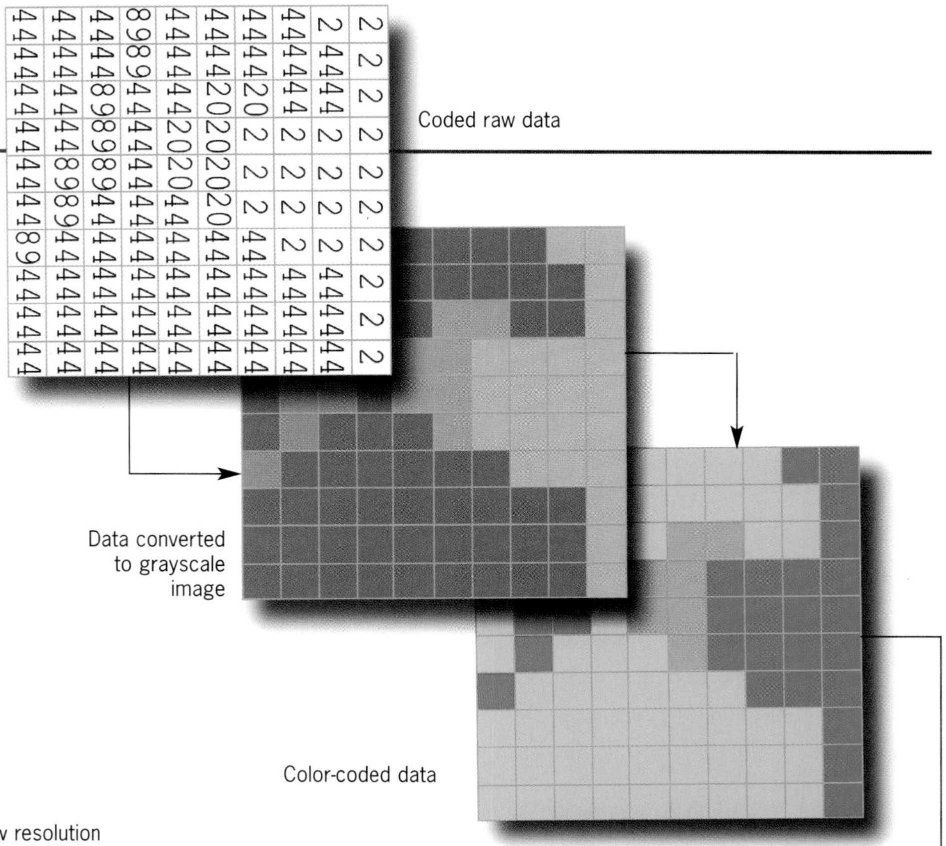

Coded raw data

Data converted to grayscale image

Color-coded data

Low resolution

Medium resolution

High resolution

IMAGE ENHANCEMENT

The data collected by the satellite's scanner is processed by computers into binary code—a series of ones and zeros. This code is translated to supply the pixels (dots which form an electronic picture) with separate digital numbers, each of which represents a tonal value. Such information is used initially to generate gray scale images with 256 possible tones. Computer processing can be used to group pixels with similar spectral signatures in order to make maps of environmental phenomena such as land use or geology.

A CLEAR VIEW

Electronic images derived from scanners vary in detail and clarity depending on their spatial resolution. Just like a picture on a TV screen, electronic images are made up of rows and columns of dots that are assigned different colors or shades of gray. These dots are known as pixels. The spatial resolution of the image is the area that the pixel represents on the Earth's surface. For mapping and monitoring the entire globe, spatial resolutions of $.39mi^2$ are commonly used; however, for detailed mapping of the Earth's resources, spatial resolutions of between 5.5 and 33 yards are more appropriate. In the near future, satellite imagery with a spatial resolution of 1.1 yard or less will become available and this will revolutionize large-scale mapping.

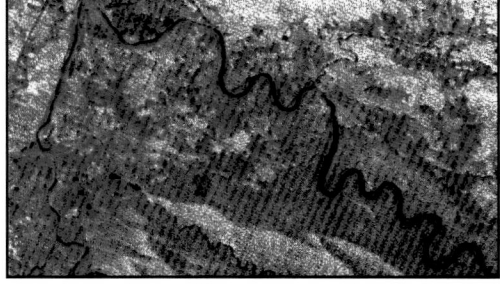

False color image

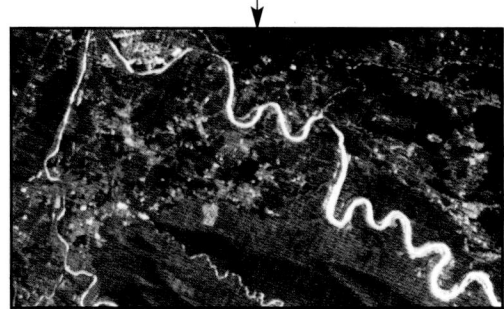

True-color image

THE FINAL STEPS

Raw data has to be processed before being used to generate images. Atmospheric disturbances, faults with scanning sensors and flaws in transmission are among the possible causes of distorted or incomplete data. Overlap of scanned tracks and the problem of converting data about a curved surface into a flat format also have to be overcome. By comparing two or more similar scans, however, accurate images can soon be created.

The accentuation of certain parts of the pictures with artificial colors results in "false color" images. These can be used for specialized applications such as monitoring the depletion of rainforests or aiding geological prospecting. A further intriguing development has been their use in identifying archeological sites.

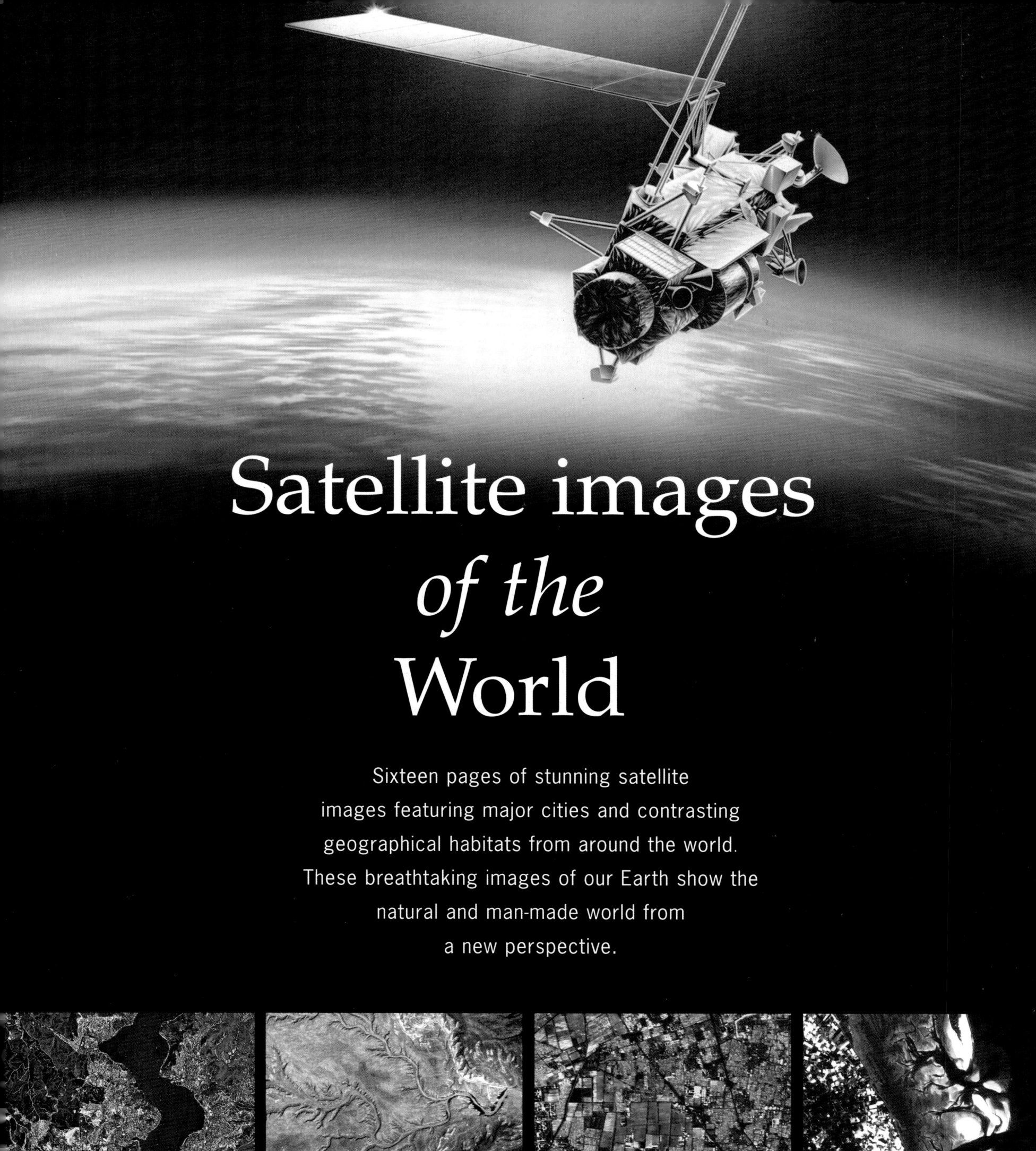

Satellite images
of the
World

Sixteen pages of stunning satellite
images featuring major cities and contrasting
geographical habitats from around the world.
These breathtaking images of our Earth show the
natural and man-made world from
a new perspective.

CLEARLY SPOTTED. An extremely detailed infrared image of New York, taken by the French Spot I satellite. The image resolution is so high that roads, stadiums, bridges and even boats and jetties are all visible. The very small oval island (lower right of center) is Liberty Island, and the white speck at its eastern end is the Statue of Liberty.

MUD AND WATER. This infrared Landsat image shows the mouth of the Mahakam River in Indonesian Borneo. The river is 400 miles long and exits into the Makassar Strait through a wide delta. Roads in this image can be seen as straight lines between the sinuous curves of the river tributaries. The red color indicates dry land whilst the brown is swamp.

SOUTH AMERICAN MOONSCAPE. The true-color image above shows the Atacama region of Chile. In the center two snow-capped volcanic cones can be seen and to the top right a high altitude salt-pan. Flowing from top left to top right is a river which is being fed by tributaries of melt water from the snow line. This a rare occurrence as rain has never been recorded in much of the region.

SHOWING ITS TRUE COLORS. A near-true color image taken by the French Spot I satellite of Sydney and its environs. The city's Parramatta River is crossed by the Sydney Harbor Bridge at the point where it flows into Port Jackson. On the white promontory just east of the bridge stands the Sydney Opera House. South of the city is Botany Bay, with Sydney Airport extending from its northern shore.

CARIBBEAN ISLAND. An infrared image of Eleuthera in the Bahamas. Off the east coast (top), parallel rows of waves can be seen approaching the shore, blown by winds across the Atlantic. This is in marked contrast to their total absence in the very shallow, sheltered water to the west. Wave action on the western tip of the island's southern end has caused the offshore deposition of a spectacular series of sandbanks.

CROWDED CAPITAL. This infrared image offers an excellent view of one of the world's largest cities, Beijing. Over five million people live in the city's central area—registered here as a slate blue-gray. In the middle of the image lie the palaces and lakes of the Forbidden City, while to the south lies the vast space of Tiananmen Square.

MEANDERING RIVER. This image shows part of the Paraná river in Argentina. Large areas of braiding can be seen on either side of the river, indicating that it has gradually changed course over many years. Toward the top of the image, left of the smaller river, an oxbow lake is visible; this occurs when a loop, or meander, has been pinched off as the river pursues a shorter course.

ICE MEETS OCEAN. An infrared image of the Exmouth peninsula, part of the Parque Nacional Bernardo O'Higgins in southern Chile. Glaciers, formed at altitudes of more than 3300 yards, can be seen as they gradually edge into the Pacific Ocean. At the edge of the right-hand glacier can be seen crevasses, where the ice is starting to break up as it melts into the sea.

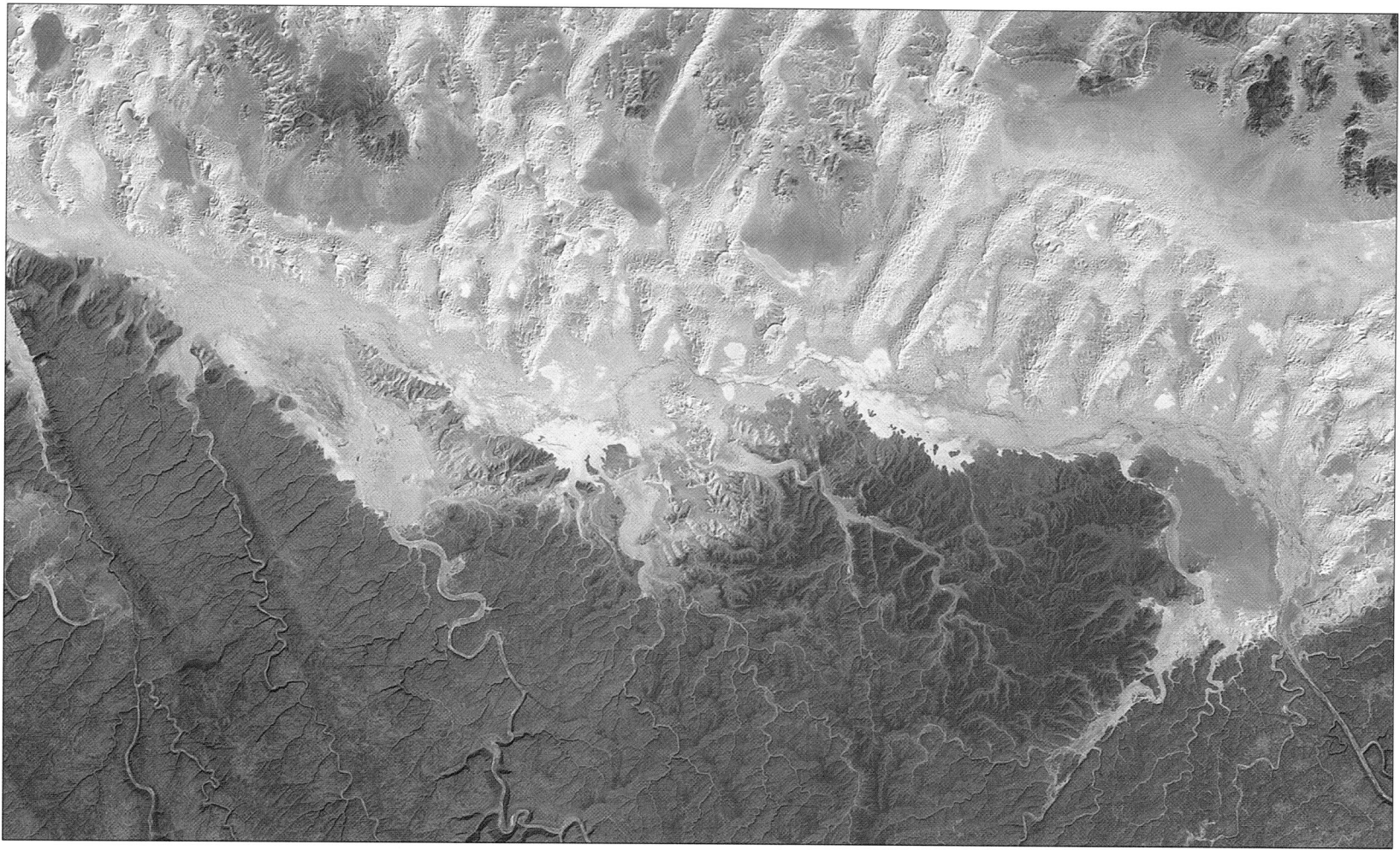

Two worlds collide. This true-color image starkly reveals the dramatic landscape of the Algerian Sahara. Part of the Sahara Desert can be seen across the top of the photograph. The remaining area shows the Saharan Atlas mountains, cut into by sharply defined gullies in which water would have only infrequently flowed. These mountains are ancient and worn unlike the much younger ones to the north.

Cultivated floodplains. This image shows the mouth of the Guadalquivir River in southern Spain. The white streaks indicate where a coastal spit has formed, and behind this are the marshy areas of Las Marismas. The red checkerboard effect at the top denotes an area of cultivated land, where drainage on the river's floodplain has been improved by the presence of a series of canals.

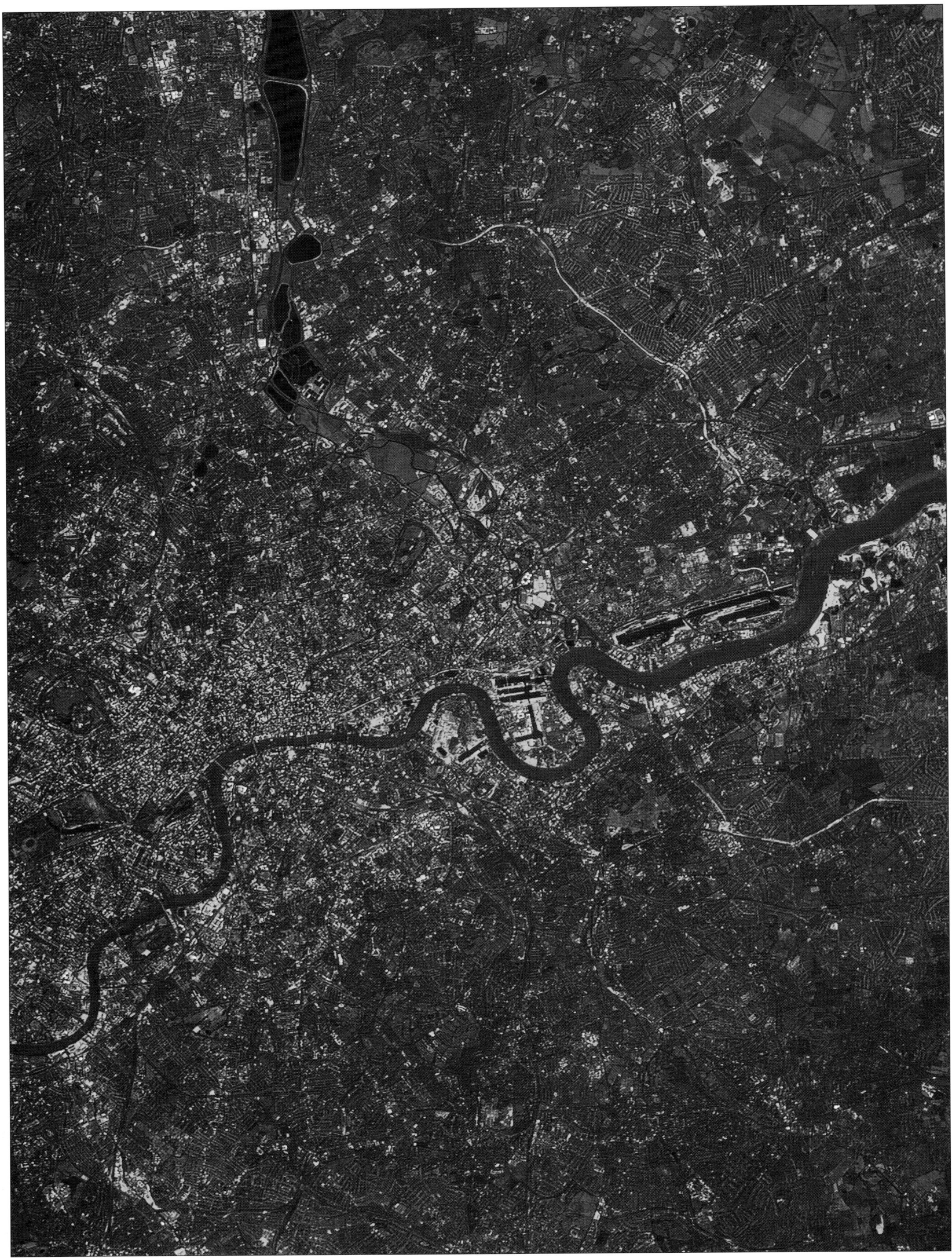

LONDON TOWN. An infrared image of Great Britain's capital, taken by the French Spot II satellite. The River Thames winds its way through the city to Docklands, clearly visible in the center of the image. The black spaces (top) represent the reservoirs that provide some of London's drinking water. Areas of open land—such as Hyde Park, Regent's Park and Buckingham Palace grounds—all show up as red and are visible to the north of the river (left).

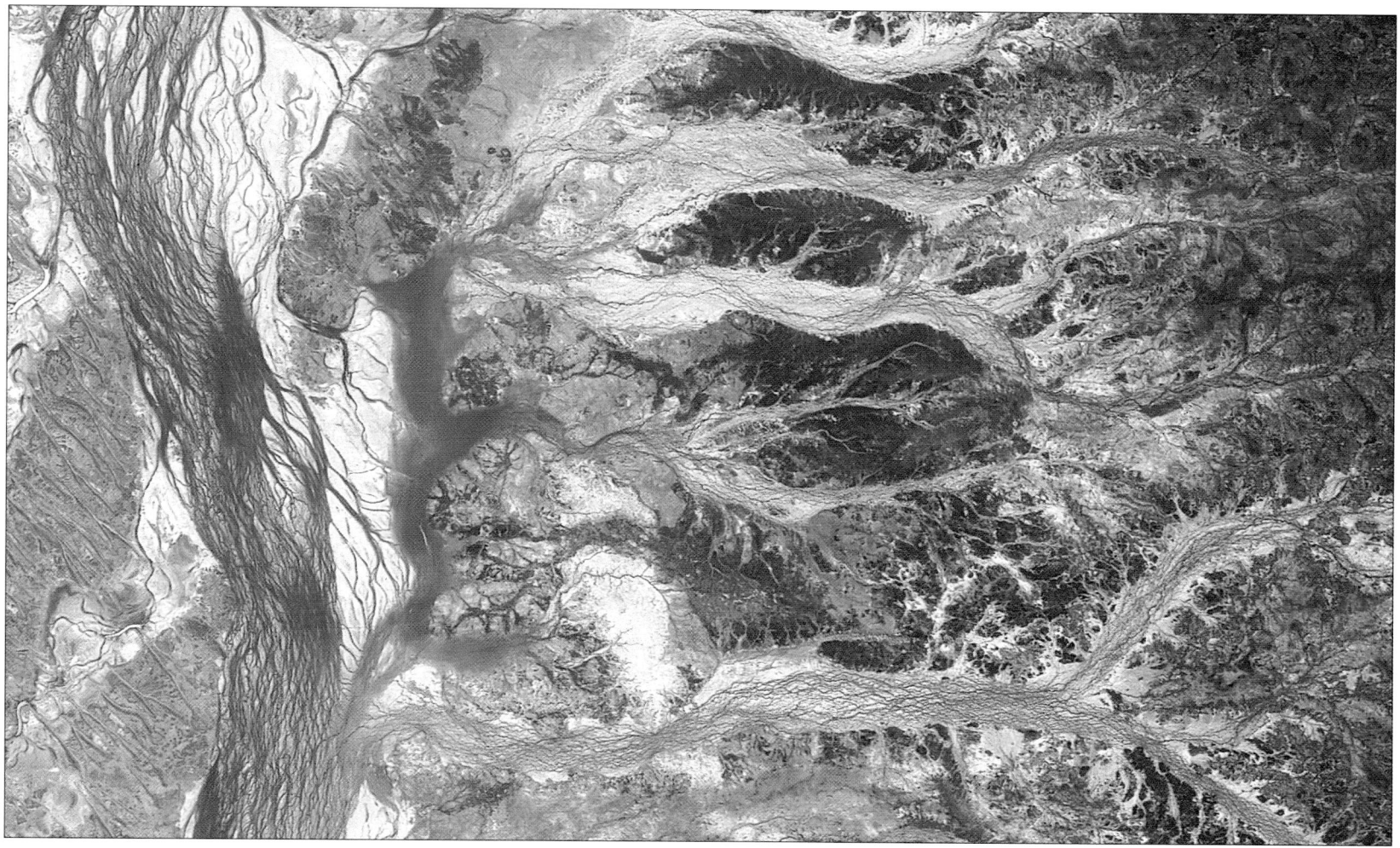

GONE IN A MOMENT. This image shows the ghostly arteries of a long dried-up river, the Diamantina in South Australia. This intermittent river can discharge water at rates varying from over 50,000 cubic feet per second when it is in flood, to nothing at all in dry years. The area is known as Channel Country, evidenced by the number of river channels shown in the photograph.

HIGHLAND LANDSCAPE. An image of the Highlands and islands of Scotland. The oval island at left is Scalpay, and south of this is Skye, where the Cuillin Hills are clearly visible. Several lochs can be seen forming deep indentations in the coastline of the mainland; the rivers that flow into these wind back up through the glens to their sources in the snow-covered mountains.

MARCHING SANDS. This almost abstract image of part of the Sahara Desert highlights the way that sand dunes form and creep across the underlying ground. These are barchan dunes, formed by particles of sand being consistently blown in one direction. The separation between the dunes is dependent on the wind speed and the way in which the winds spiral.

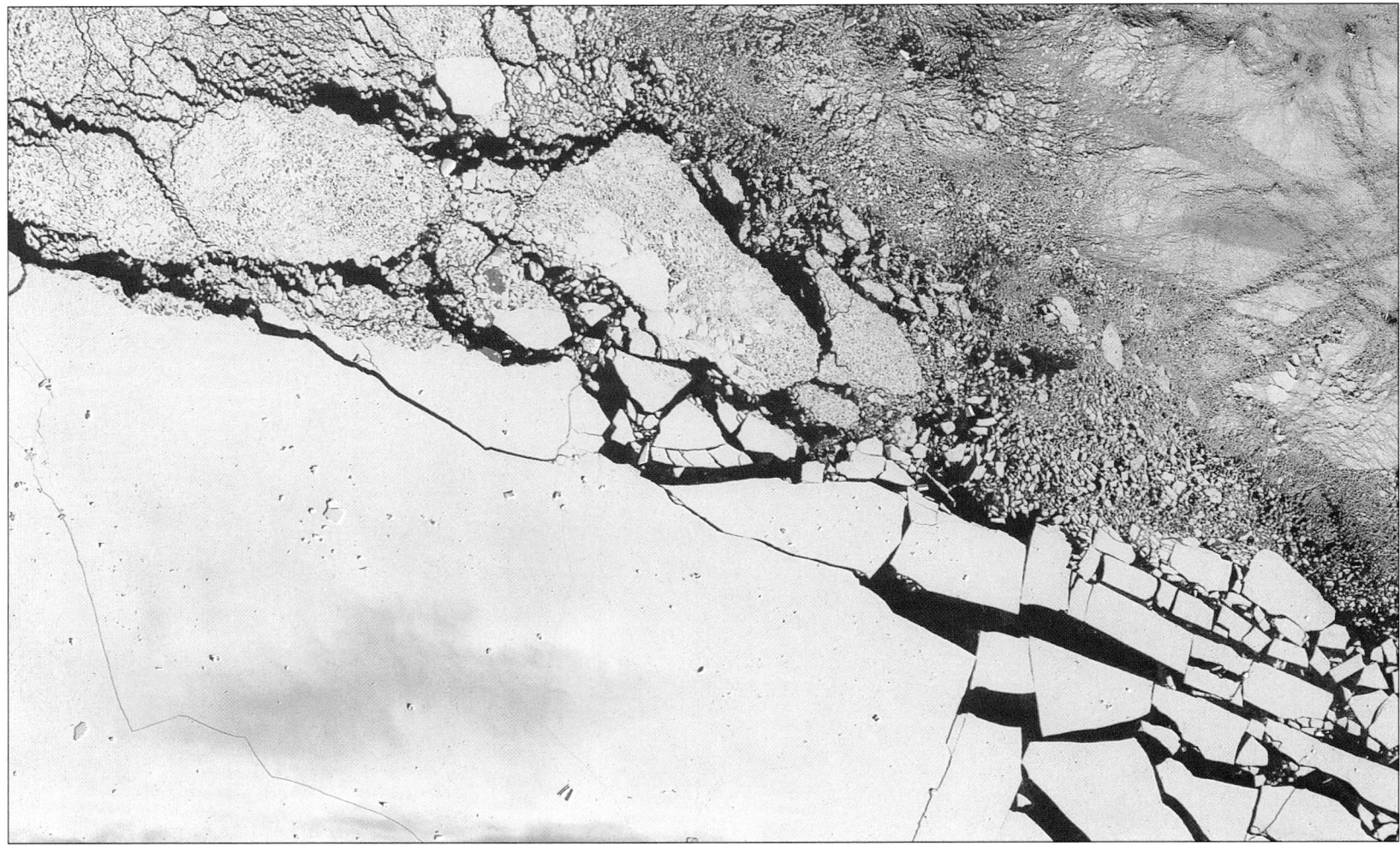

ICEBERG MAKER. The crumbling edge of the Antarctic Ice Shelf is graphically caught by this Landsat image. A split can be seen in the Shelf, lower left. This crack will split and split again forming myriad small icebergs. Occasionally, as in March 2000, a massive berg will split off. That single iceberg was over 170 miles long and 25 miles wide, making it nearly as large as the state of Connecticut.

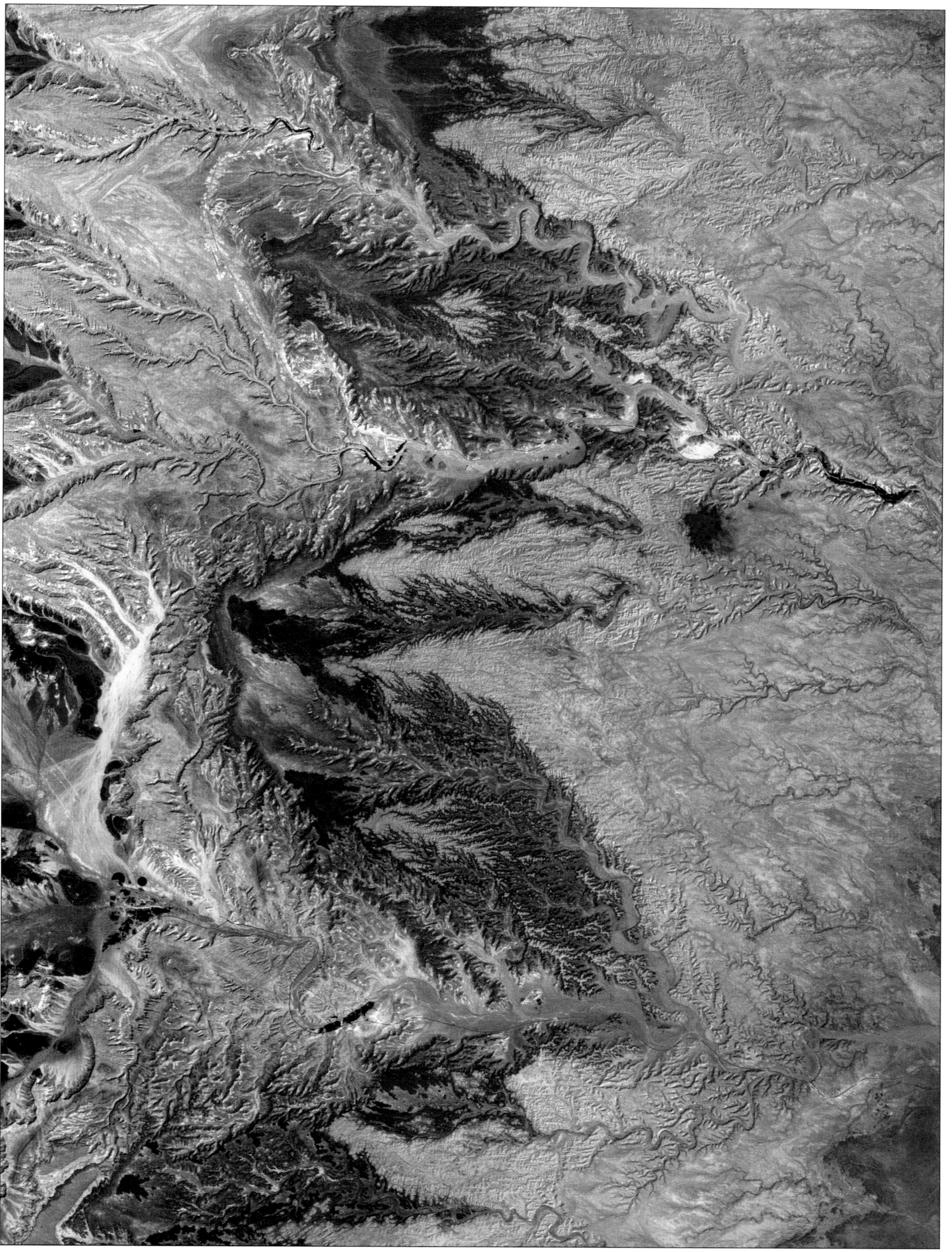

DESERT LANDS. This false-color image of the Arabian Desert provides a vivid record of the desertification process. Two distinct kinds of terrain are shown. The pink area is an arid, windswept plateau, while the coppery-green one is a great plain scored with dried-up watercourses, or *wadis*. If every wadi was once a river running off the plateau, this desert must once have been a truly rich, fertile land.

SOUTH AMERICAN CITY. The compact city of Neuquén is on the right of this infrared image, lying in a fertile valley watered by two rivers, the Limay and the Neuquén. The city is a market-center for the neighboring fruit-growing area and in recent years has become the home of many wine cellars, as Argentina's wine export trade becomes increasingly more important.

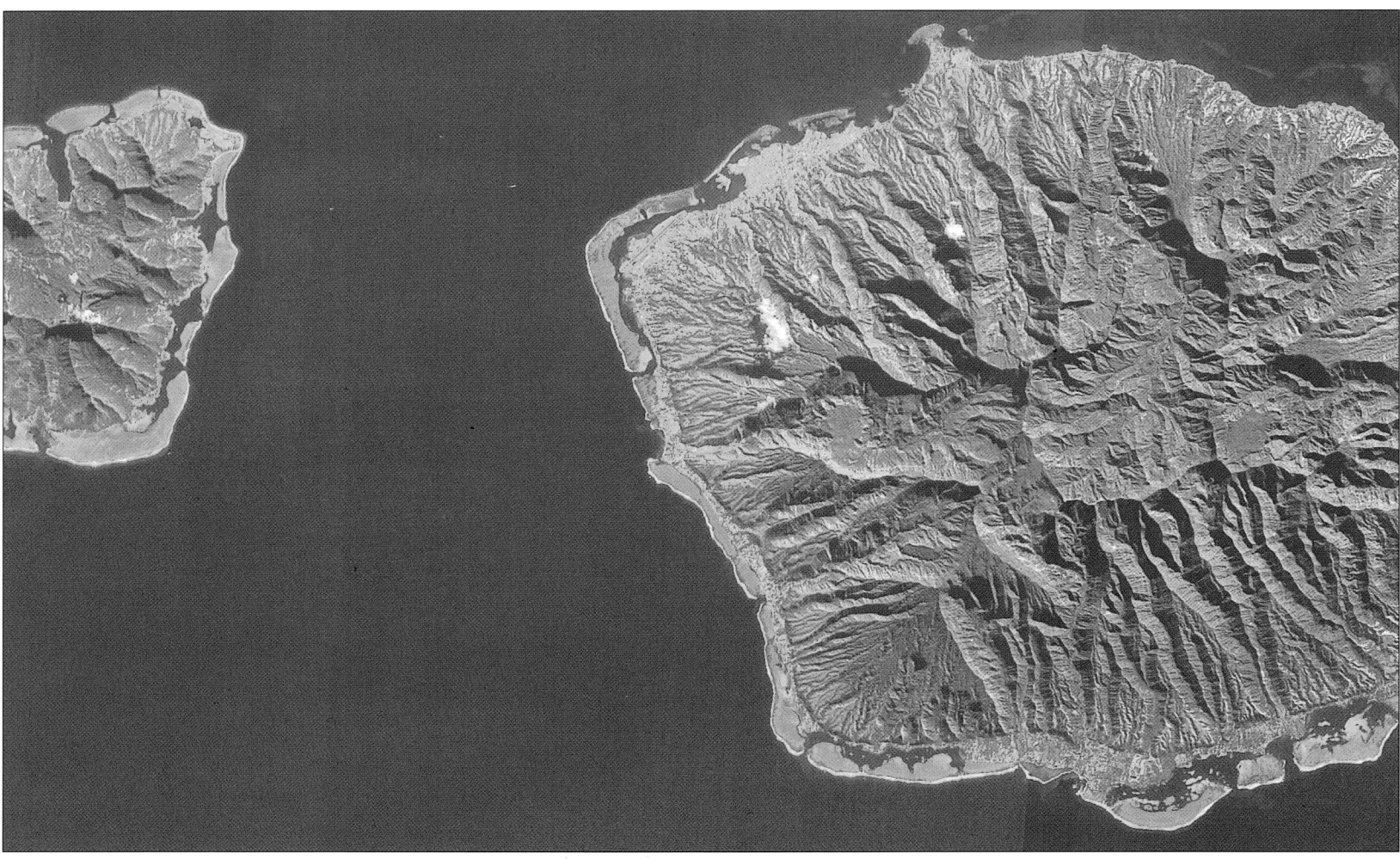

CORAL JEWELS. The true-color image shown above is of Tahiti, on the right, and Moorea in the Pacific Ocean. Together with other adjacent islands they form the Windward Group of the Society Islands in French Polynesia. Volcanic in origin, both islands have high-sided, forest-clad mountains, though Moorea is older and has more rounded contours. Surrounding both islands are blue-colored coral reefs.

THE BOLIVIAN ANDES. Only about one-third of Bolivia lies within the Andean mountain chain: even so it is regarded as a highland country and as this image shows, the valleys and peaks form formidable barriers to communication. Bolivia is rich in history, being part of the ancient Inca Empire. It is an underdeveloped country and has a mainly agricultural economy.

PACIFIC PARADISE. Straddling the Equator, the Isla Isabela is the largest of the Galapogos Islands. It has five volcanic craters reaching altitudes of over 5,000 feet; two of the volcanoes are still active. Superbly imaged in this Landsat picture is the most southerly volcano with small white clouds hovering over the flank of its lava field. The hills are covered with vines and forests.

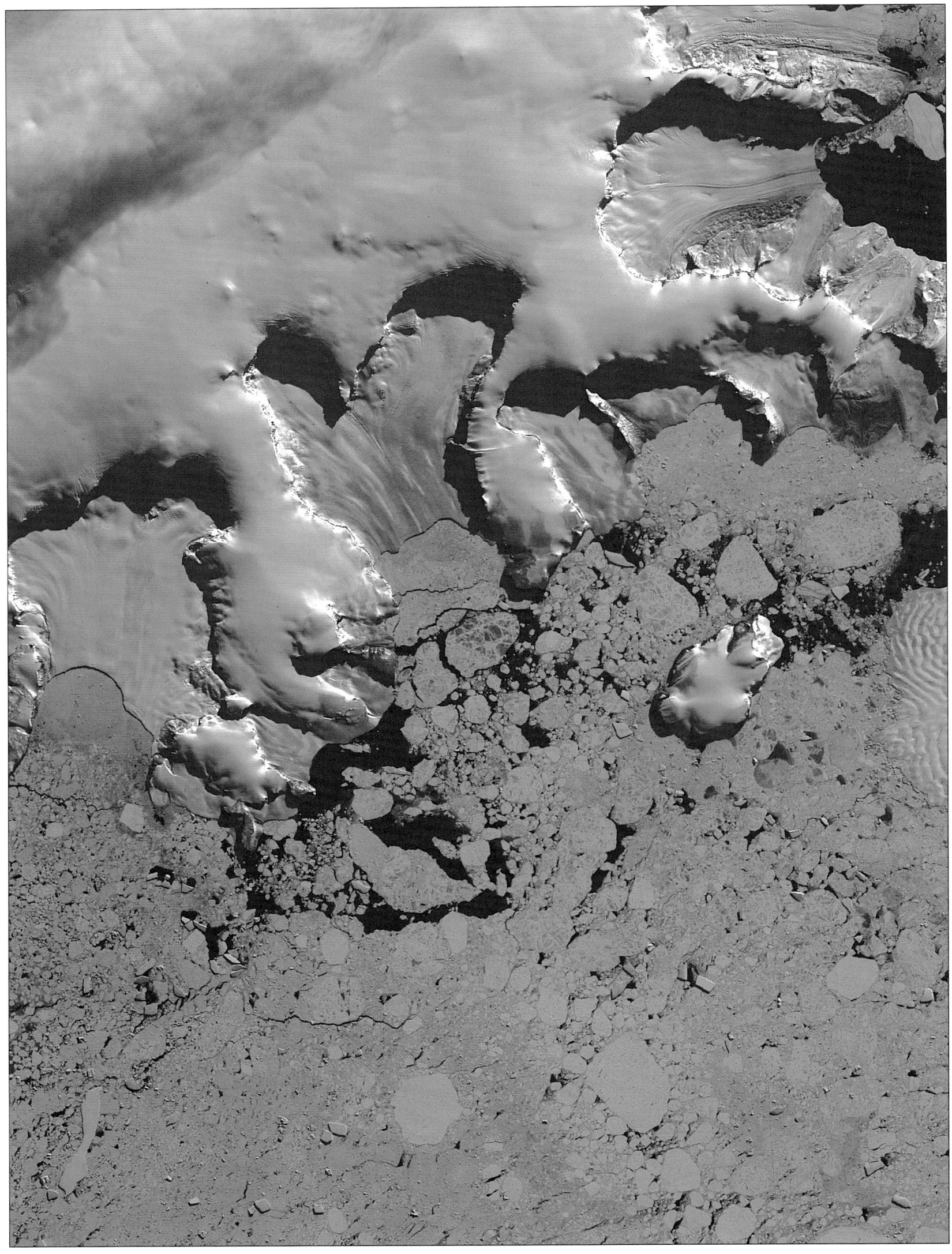

POLAR REGIONS. A crystal-clear view of Antarctica, demonstrating yet another aspect of satellite technology. Images such as this enable scientists to monitor long-term changes in ice landscapes, such as the movements of iceberg fields and the retreat of glaciers. In this way, forecasts can be made of the possible climatic effects of global warming.

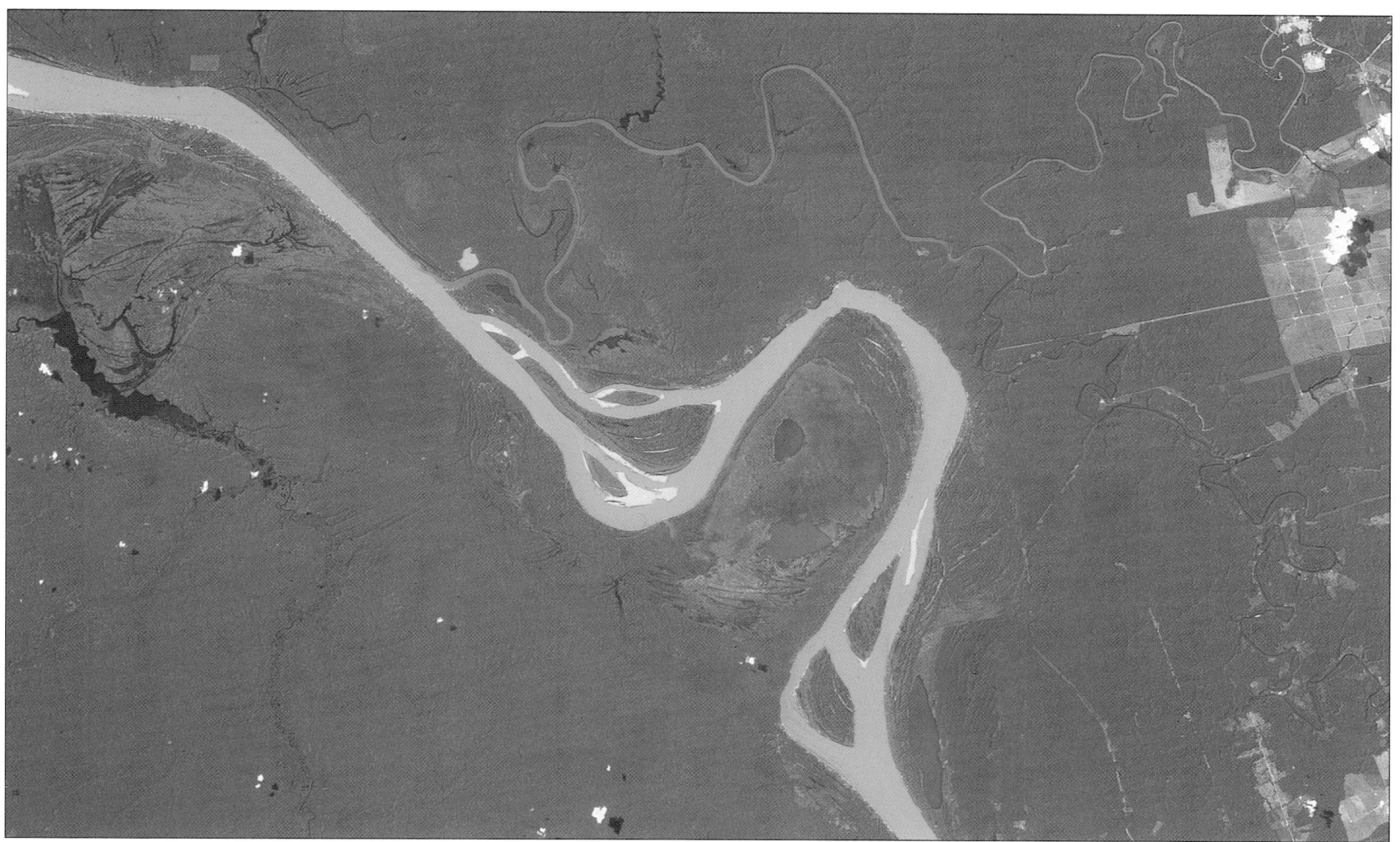

A GREAT RIVER. The winding band of azure-colored water crossing the infrared image is the Río Grande de Santiago. It winds some 225 miles through Mexico to exit into the Pacific Ocean 10 miles northwest of San Blas. The river is not navigable as it has many rapids and waterfalls, but the long valley through which it runs for most of its length is of great economic importance.

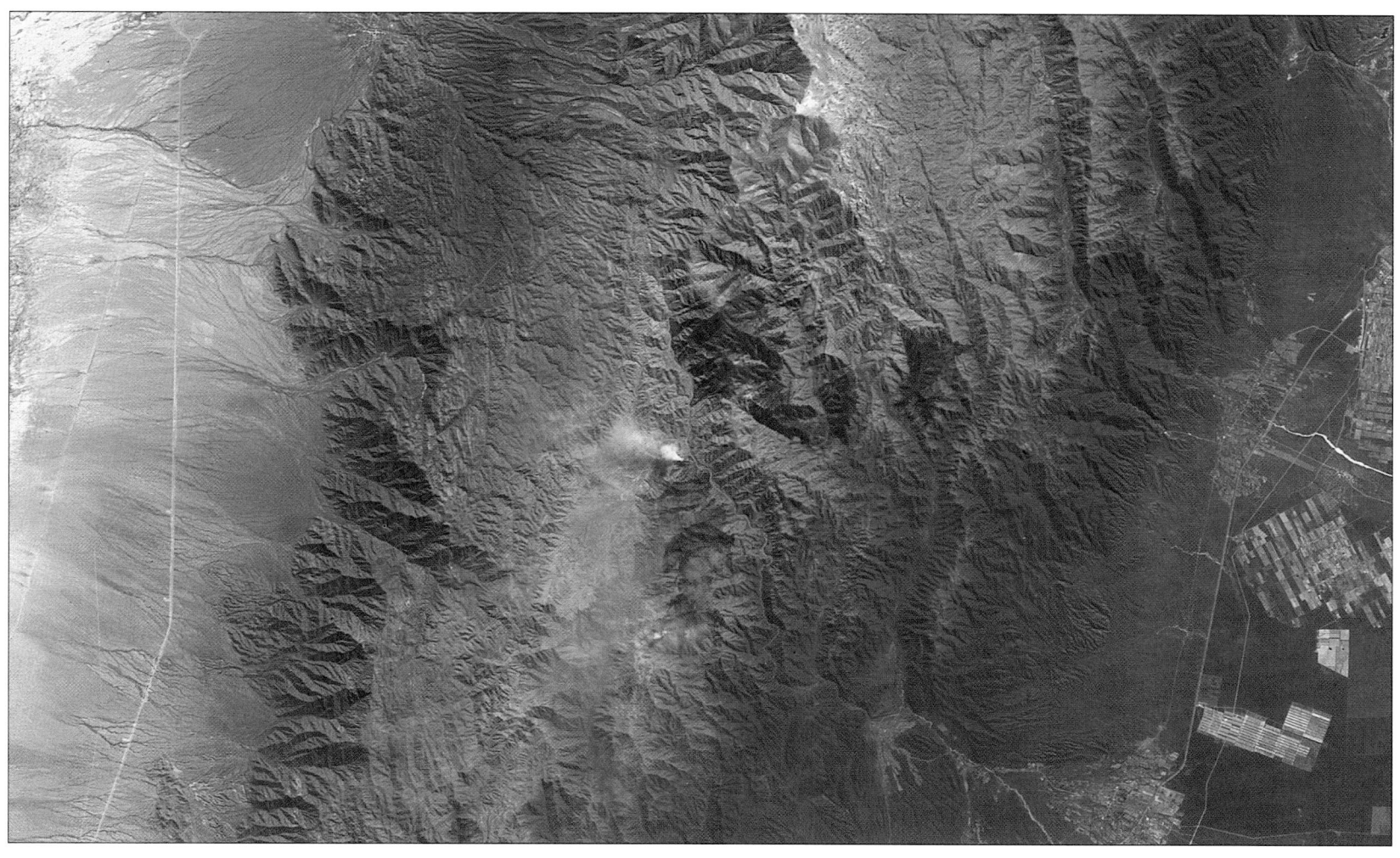

A SOUTH AMERICAN SAHARA. Catamarca city is in the northwestern part of Argentina and is shown here lying in the foothills on the right of the Andean mountain range, which runs down the center of the photograph. To the left of the picture lies the Sierre del Aconquija, a desert area also known as the Argentine Sahara.

LOST IN SPACE. The Gibson Desert in Western Australia, shown in this Landsat image, is an arid, windswept and inhospitable place. It is covered with sandhills and patches of Trioda desert grass. The area now constitutes the Gibson Desert Nature Reserve and is named after Alfred Gibson, who was lost here whilst looking for water in 1876.

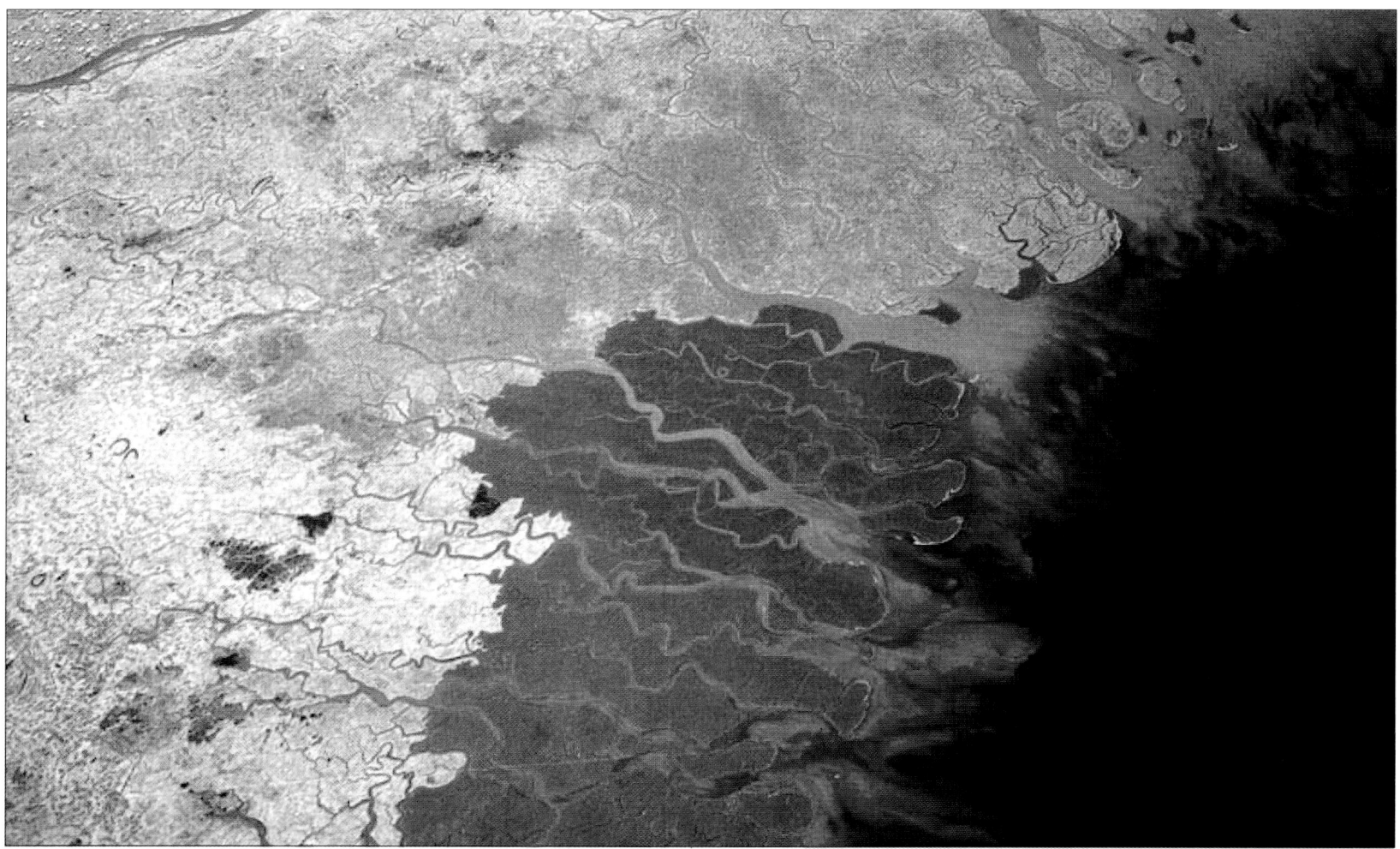

A BENGALI VENICE. Seen from the Space Shuttle, the Ganges Delta in northwest India is a network of myriad small interconnecting channels running off the main river Ganges. Each year from June to October the river overflows its banks and inundates the countryside with a fertile silt. The delta is scattered with small villages and hamlets which in this area of climatic extremes can be swept away by rising river water or rain from tropical storms.

BETWEEN EAST AND WEST. Istanbul sits astride the Bosporus Strait, the narrow waterway separating Europe (left) from Asia (right) and connecting the Black Sea (top) and the Aegean Sea (bottom). Founded as Byzantium in 667 BC, the city's name was changed to Constantinople in 330 AD and became Istanbul following its conquest by the Turks in 1453.

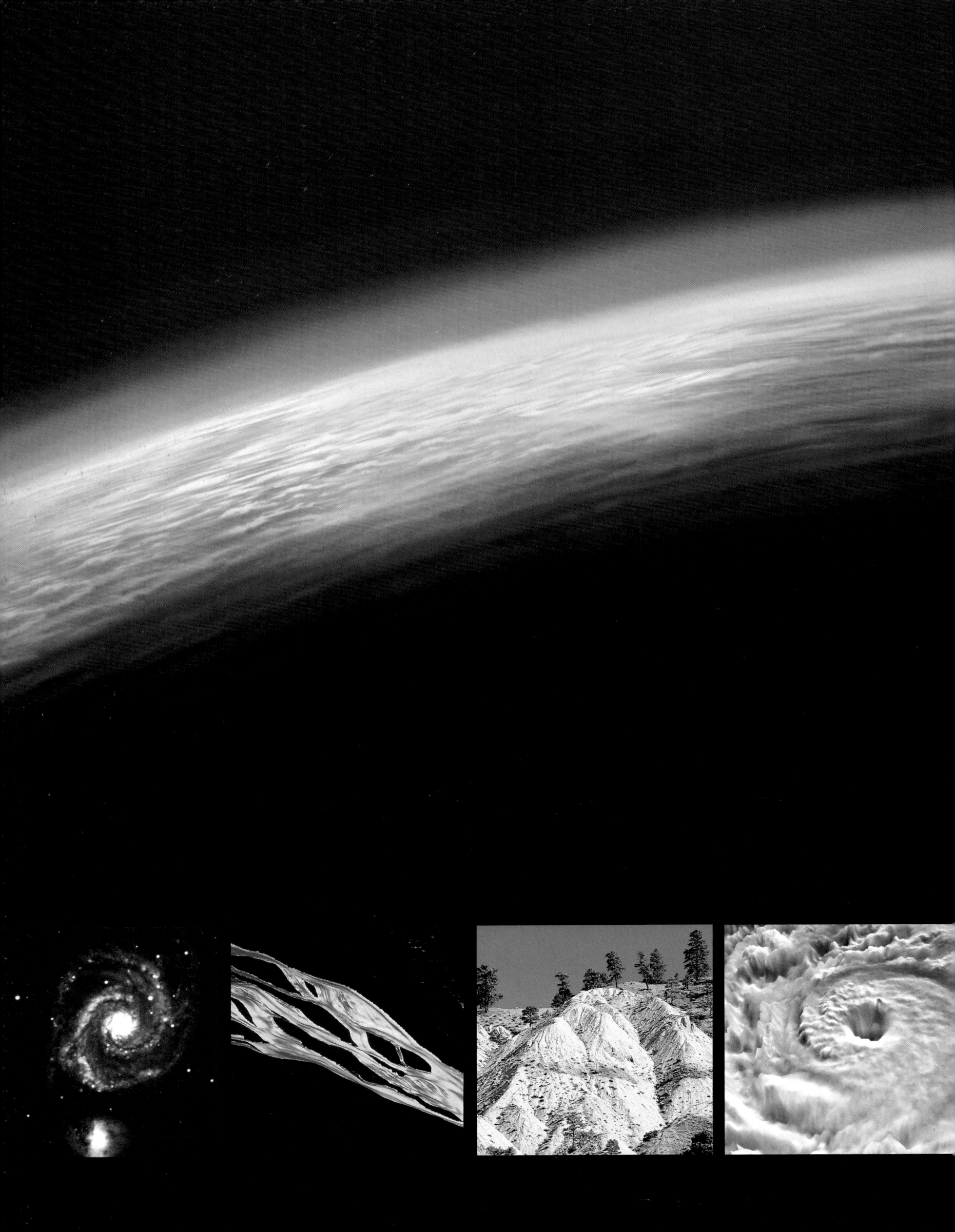

An introduction
to our
World

This section gives a broad overview of our planet and
the way it developed, from a mass of molten space
debris to the wind-blown and water-sculpted Earth of
today. Man's impact is also highlighted, as is
transportation, religion and the ever increasing
problems of population growth.

OUR STAR AND OUR NEIGHBORS

THE EARTH IS ONE MEMBER OF A SOLAR SYSTEM of nine planets orbiting our local star—the Sun. All these bodies formed from a single cloud of gas and dust around 4.5 billion years ago as it was compressed, possibly by shockwaves from a giant supernova explosion. The center of the cloud collapsed most rapidly, becoming denser and attracting more material until eventually it reached a point so hot and dense that nuclear reactions began inside it. These reactions continue today and are the source of the sunlight that heats our planet and sustains life. The Sun is critical to the regulation of our climate and environment—fine alterations in Earth's orbit are thought to cause periodic ice ages, so we are fortunate that the Sun is not likely to change drastically for another 5 billion years.

On a shorter scale, the Sun's output does have slight fluctuations. A cycle of sunspot formation (comparatively cool regions of the Sun's surface caused by magnetic activity), reaches a maximum every 11 years. From 1645–1705 almost no sunspots were seen, a dip in solar activity which coincided with a "mini-Ice Age" of unusually low temperatures on Earth.

Once the Sun had formed, a disk of material would have been left outside the newly-formed star, which condensed to form the planets. Particles in the gas and dust cloud collided and stuck together, becoming increasingly larger bodies. Eventually these "proto-planets" were pulled into a spherical shape by their increasing gravity.

The Solar System we see today reflects the composition of that gas and dust cloud, and divides into two regions. The inner portion contains the four terrestrial (Earth-like) planets—from Mercury orbiting close to the Sun, through Venus and Earth, to Mars. Beyond the orbit of Mars lies the asteroid belt, a ring of rocky debris, outside which are the gas giants, enormous planets created where the cloud bulged with huge quantities of gas.

The inner rocky worlds

The terrestrial planets are all very different. Mercury is a small, baking world, quite similar to our own Moon, and covered in craters. Venus is shrouded in a thick atmosphere of carbon

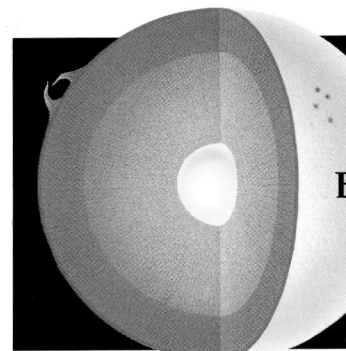

▶ THE SUN
The Sun is a massive ball of hydrogen gas **[B]**, *0.86 million mi. across. Energy is generated at its heart, where temperatures exceed 59 million°F, by nuclear fusion—the joining together through a chain reaction of two hydrogen atoms to form one helium. In the process, a large amount of excess energy is released, carried to the surface of the Sun in giant convection cells, and then radiated across the Solar System from the top of* the "photosphere"—the visible disk of the Sun, with a temperature of 9932°F.

◀ THE SOLAR SYSTEM
The Solar System consists of 9 planets **[A]**: *Pluto* [1], *the smallest, is the furthest away from the Sun, though once in every 248.6 years its orbit crosses inside Neptune's path. Neptune* [2], *the outermost of the gas giants, has a* diameter of 30,697mi. and orbits every 164.8 years.

Uranus [3] *is similar in size to Neptune and orbits every 84 years. All the gas giants have ring systems, but Uranus's are second only to Saturn's. The planet is tilted at over 98° to the plane of the*

A

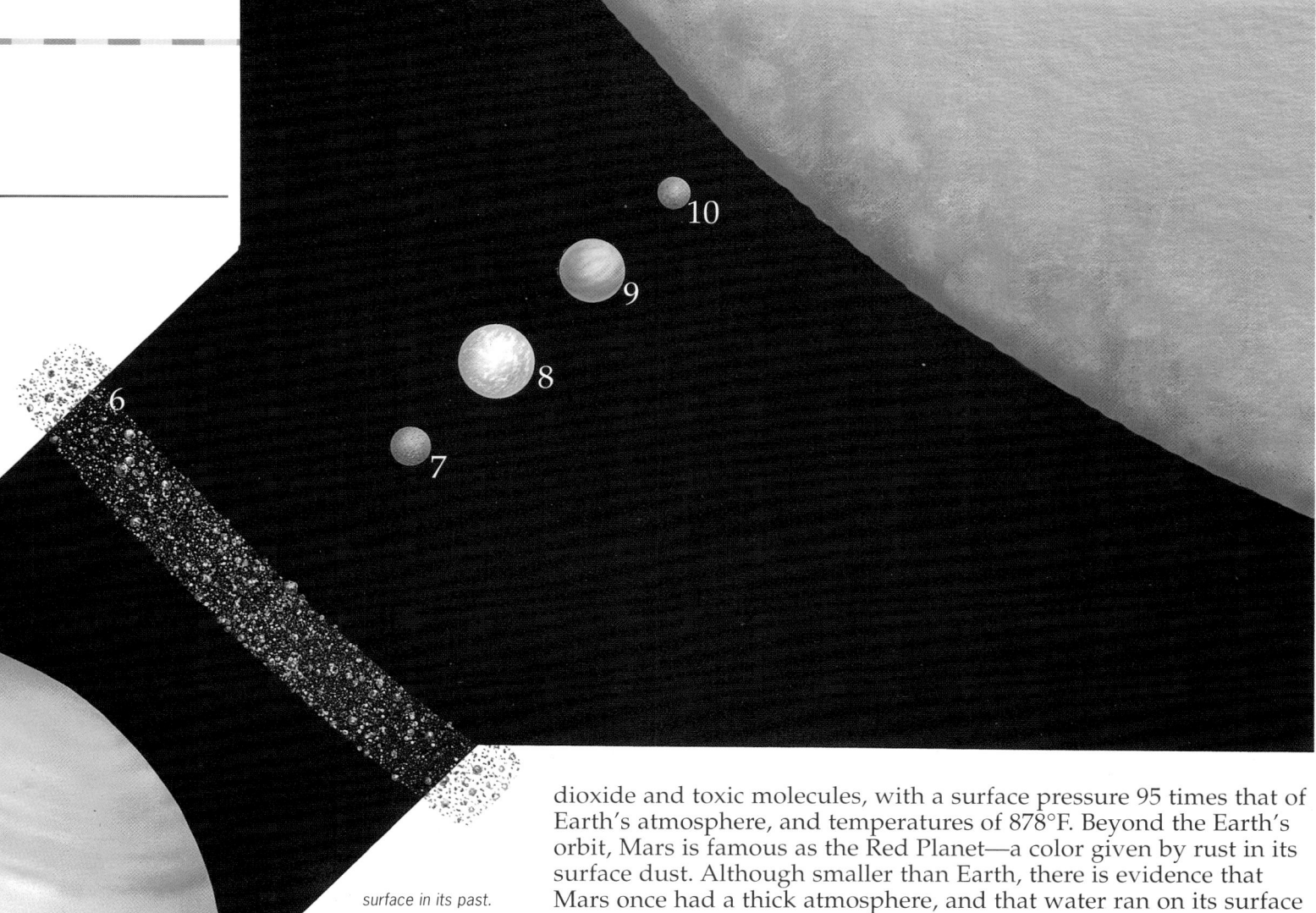

dioxide and toxic molecules, with a surface pressure 95 times that of Earth's atmosphere, and temperatures of 878°F. Beyond the Earth's orbit, Mars is famous as the Red Planet—a color given by rust in its surface dust. Although smaller than Earth, there is evidence that Mars once had a thick atmosphere, and that water ran on its surface —although now it is frozen into polar ice caps.

The gas giants

The outer Solar System contains worlds quite different from those nearer the Sun—the gas giants. Largest of these is Jupiter, more massive than all the other planets in the Solar System put together, with churning weather systems that include the Great Red Spot, a storm large enough to engulf Earth. Beyond Jupiter lies Saturn, with its spectacular ring system of icy particles, and then the smaller giants Uranus and Neptune. Space probes have shown that Jupiter, Uranus and Neptune also have thin ring systems, although these are nothing to match Saturn's spectacle.

All four of these worlds have large families of moons orbiting round them. Jupiter has a vast family of moons, including Io, the most volcanic body in the Solar System, whose eruptions launch yellow plumes of sulphur into space, scarring its surface with streaks. The most interesting member of Uranus's satellite system is Miranda—a small, deeply-cratered world which displays so many variations in terrain that it must have suffered some great cataclysm in the past. Neptune's giant satellite, Triton, has active geysers shooting water, ammonia and methane 5 miles above its surface.

surface in its past. Next in toward the Sun is our own blue planet, Earth [8], with a diameter of 7892 mi. Within the orbit of Earth lies its near twin Venus [9], circling the Sun in 225 days, and with a diameter of 7519 mi. The atmosphere of Venus, however, is a poisonous mixture of carbon dioxide and other gases, with clouds of sulphuric acid.

Mercury [10] is the second smallest planet with a diameter of only 3032 mi, and a solar orbit that lasts 88 days. Its proximity to the Sun (36 million mi) makes it a scorched world with no atmosphere, and a cratered surface similar to that of the Moon. It orbits the Sun once every 88 days.

Solar System, so it seems to roll around its orbit. Saturn [4] is noted for its spectacular ring system— the planet has a diameter of 65,247 mi, while the rings stretch out to 186,300 mi. It orbits the Sun every 29.5 years, and has a huge family of satellites.

Jupiter [5] orbits the Sun every 11.9 years. With a diameter of 85,380 mi it is the largest planet in the Solar System. It has complex weather systems, including the Great Red Spot, a storm with a diameter larger than the Earth's.

Between Jupiter and Mars is the asteroid belt [6], rocky debris left over from the Solar System's formation. Inside it lie the terrestrial planets. Mars [7], the red planet, circles the Sun in 1.9 years, and has a diameter of 4219 mi. Its surface is scoured by massive dust storms, and it shows evidence of running water on the

◀ The Sun is just one of over 200 billion stars in the vast spiral of the Milky Way galaxy, like every other star that we see with the naked eye in the night sky. It lies roughly two-thirds of the way toward the edge of the galactic disc, orbiting the center at a speed of 155 miles per second, taking 200 million years to complete each revolution. This view is what the galaxy would look like to an observer outside. But because of our position in the plane, we see the dense star clouds as a pale band across the sky.

THE EARTH AND THE MOON

The Earth's satellite, the Moon, is so large by comparison with our own world (at 2328 mi, it is over one-quarter the Earth's diameter) that astronomers consider the two together as a "double planet." This massive size and proximity means that the Moon has a great influence on the Earth itself, for example through the tides.

The origins of the Moon are open to debate—some believe that the Moon is a chunk of debris flung off when the still-molten Earth collided with another body the size of Mars, in the early days of the Solar System. Since then, the two bodies have had very different histories. The Moon's small size meant that it cooled more quickly and its low gravity made it unable to hold onto an atmosphere—the factor which has been crucial in shaping our own planet's terrain. In fact, the Moon has altered so little that it provides valuable information about the history of the early Solar System. The lack of an atmosphere also means that, unlike Earth, the Moon is not shielded from the extremes of heat from the Sun. Temperatures at noon climb to 302°F, while at night they can plummet to -328°F. These acute differences can even cause moonquakes as the surface stretches and contracts.

A familiar face

The Moon's surface divides into two distinct types of terrain, which can be easily distinguished with the naked eye from Earth. The bright highlands are highly cratered areas created more than 4 billion years ago during an era of bombardment by rock particles from space. The numbers of these particles dwindled until only a few massive chunks were left, which created enormous impact basins as they crashed into the Moon's surface. The gnarled highlands contrast sharply with the smoother, darker Maria (from the Latin for seas). After the cratering had died away, the Moon seems to have undergone a brief period of intense volcanic activity. Red-hot fissures opened up across its surface, out of which huge volumes of lava poured, flooding low-lying areas. These lava lakes solidified to form the Maria, marked by only a few, very small craters.

Lunar attraction

The changing direction of the Sun and Moon from Earth cause our monthly cycle of tides. Twice a month, at full and new moon, the high Spring Tides occur, with Moon and Sun lined up, or directly opposed, so the tidal effect is at its strongest. Such tidal effects have influenced the Earth-Moon system as a whole. Over millions of years, the friction of the ocean's movement has slowed the lunar "day," so it now lasts exactly as long as the time the Moon takes to orbit Earth, with the result that it always keeps

B

▶ **STRUCTURE OF THE MOON**
The Earth's satellite, the Moon [B], has a structure that reflects its different size, and possibly origin. Because it is a much smaller body—around one-twentieth the volume of the Earth—it has a higher surface area to volume ratio. It cooled down more rapidly early in the history of the Solar System, and is now inactive. The lunar crust [1] is actually thicker than Earth's — an average of 43 mi, though it is *thinner on the Earth-facing side, possibly due to the tidal effects of the Earth's gravity. This could be a possible explanation of why the smooth "seas" are found far more on this side, formed from* *eruptions of lava through the thin crust. Beneath this lie layers of solidified, cold rock, which decrease in rigidity. At the center there may be a cold core [2], although its existence is still debated.*

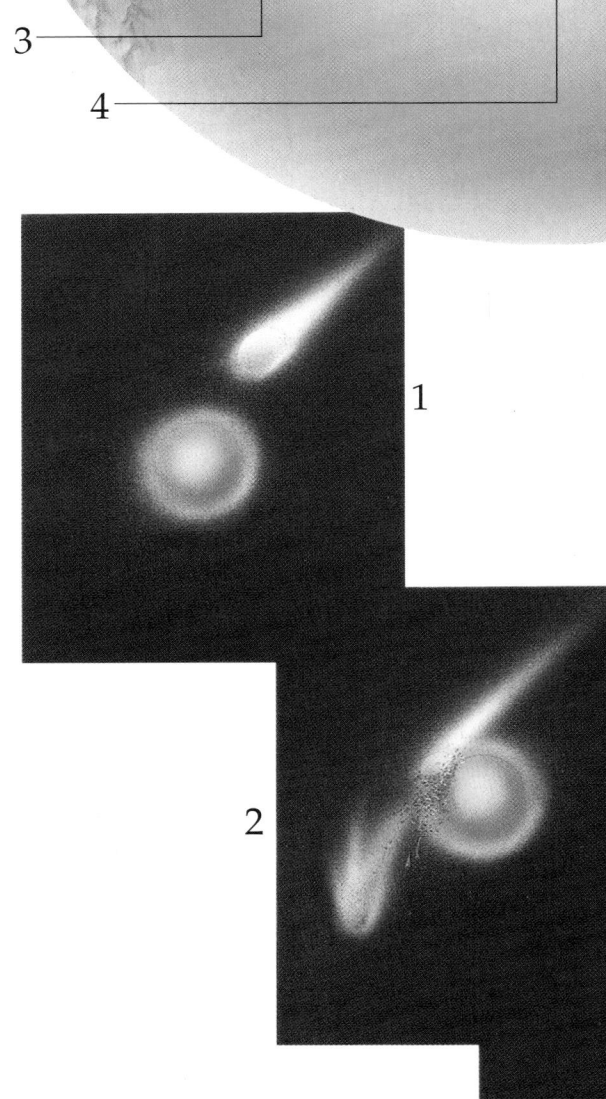

THE STRUCTURE OF THE EARTH

The Earth has the shape of a squashed ball or a spheroid [A]. It has a diameter at the poles of 7894mi., but is wider at the Equator, thrown outward by the rapid daily spin which causes a "bulge." The crust [1], on which lie the continents and oceans, is a thin layer of rock varying in depth between 6.2 and 12.4 mi. Below this lies a mantle [2], divided into two regions. The upper mantle extends down to 1864 mi, and divides into the mainly solid lithosphere and the mostly molten aesthenosphere. Beyond this, the molten rock of the upper and lower mantle extends down toward the molten outer [3] and solid inner [4] cores of iron and nickel, around 4350 mi across, at the center of the Earth. It is the rotation of this core that is believed to generate the Earth's magnetic field, in an effect similar to that of a dynamo.

THE EARTH'S SEASONS

The Poles of the Earth are tilted at 23.5° [D]. As it orbits the Sun, different parts of the globe receive a varying amount of sunlight through the year-long cycle of the seasons [3]. For six months of the year, the Northern Hemisphere is tilted toward the Sun, which therefore appears higher in the sky, giving warmer temperatures and longer days [1]. Six months later, when the Northern Hemisphere is tilted in the other direction, the days are shorter and the Sun stays closer to the horizon [2]. The situation is reversed in the Southern Hemisphere. The Tropics of Cancer and Capricorn are lines around the globe at the lines of latitude +/- 23.5°. They mark the northernmost and southern-most points where the Sun appears directly overhead.

the same face turned toward us. Fossil records show that there were once 400 days in each Earth year, so the same effect must also be slowing its rotation as well. Hence in the distant future, the spin of the Earth could be so slow that its day and year are equal, so that one scorched side of the planet will permanently face the Sun.

Complete coverage

Very occasionally, as the Moon orbits around the Earth and it in turn moves around the Sun, all three bodies—Sun, Earth and Moon—line up exactly and an eclipse is seen. If the Earth blocks out the Sun shining onto the full Moon, a rather unspectacular lunar eclipse happens. Far more spectacular are solar eclipses, when the new Moon passes right across the face of the Sun. By chance the Moon and Sun are discs in the sky that are almost the same size. This means that total solar eclipses can only be seen for short periods of time from tiny regions of the Earth. The effect is breathtaking as the Moon covers the bright central disk of the Sun, and reveals the wispy white corona of gas streaming out from the Sun's surface.

HOW THE MOON BEGAN

The Moon orbits too far from the Earth to be a captured asteroid. Instead, it is thought to have been formed when a body the size of Mars collided with the still-molten Earth during the formation of the Solar System, some 5 billion years ago [1].

The collision resulted in a stream of debris being thrown off into orbit around the Earth [2], and this eventually condensed to form the Moon [3]. The iron-rich cores of the two original bodies combined and remained within the Earth, becoming its very dense central region, while the Moon formed from the two lighter outer sections. This may explain why the Earth is thought to have a more complicated structure than the Moon, and also the lack of iron in Moon rock.

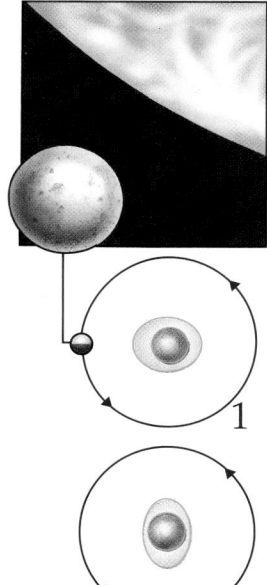

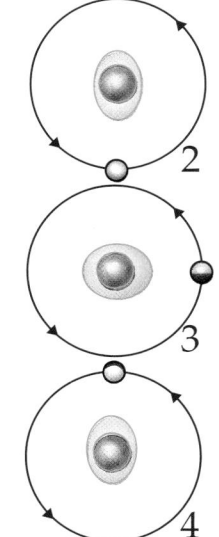

HOW THE MOON AFFECTS THE EARTH'S TIDES

The proximity of the Moon to the Earth, coupled with its size, causes strong gravitational forces between the two worlds, which is shown in the tides [E].

As the Moon exerts a gravitational pull on the Earth, it draws the seas toward it, and creates a bulge in the seawater on one side of the planet. At the same time, the Earth itself is attracted toward the Moon, pulling it away from the sea on the opposite side of the globe and creating a smaller tidal bulge on the opposite side. Because the Moon is relatively slow-moving, the tidal bulges in the sea remain in almost the same place, while the Earth rotates under them [1, 2, 3, 4]. As each bulge passes a point on the Earth roughly once each day, seashores experience two high and two low tides each day (although the shape of an inlet can alter their spacing). As the Moon circles the Earth once a month, the tides occur at different times each day.

During the brief minutes of the eclipse, the corona of the Sun can be seen.

Normally this is an invisible halo, made up of two distinct regions of gas which overlap, the K-corona and the F-corona. The latter reaches out many millions of miles from the Sun's surface while the K-corona extends for a mere 46,605 mi.

A WORLD IN MOTION

W E THINK OF THE GROUND AS BEING STEADY AND IMMOVABLE: in fact the surface of the Earth is in a constant state of movement, propelled by the intense heat of the interior. Although our planet is 7,892 mi. wide, the crust on which the continents and oceans lie is only a few tens of miles thick at its deepest. This thin crust is broken into slabs or plates, which float on top of an inner molten layer, the mantle. Where these plates collide with each other or slowly draw apart are areas of violent activity, subject to earthquakes and studded with volcanoes. This drama is not restricted to dry land: satellite photography has shown that the two-thirds of Earth's surface under the ocean is just as fascinating, with features such as chains of volcanic mountains that stretch for 37,284 mi. around the globe.

The idea that the continents are slowly moving was first put forward to explain how the coastlines of different continents appear to fit together like pieces of a jigsaw puzzle. For example, the eastern coast of South America nestles snugly into the western coast of Africa. Such continental drifts can be traced back to a point around 250 million years ago, when all the land masses on Earth were joined into a supercontinent called Pangaea (from the Greek for "all earth"), surrounded by a single vast sea, the Tethys Ocean. This supercontinent slowly disintegrated into the major land masses we know today.

Geologists call their model for the movements of the Earth's crust plate tectonics. This describes the surface, both continents and ocean floor, as being split into plates whose movements are driven by the churning of the molten rock in the inner mantle. The largest plates are as wide as the Pacific Ocean, while others are much smaller. Their thickness varies from around 6.2 mi. beneath the oceans, to 19 mi. under major land masses, and up to 37 mi. where a plate has to support the weight of a mountain range. In general, ocean floor plates are made of dense basaltic rocks, while the continents are formed from less dense granite.

Earthquakes

Most of the areas where plates are separating are hidden beneath the ocean. At the fault between the plates molten rock wells up through a fissure and solidifies, creating new ocean floor. Only in a few places can this process be seen on dry land, notably in the volcanoes of Iceland, which sits on a fault called the Mid-Atlantic Ridge.

Plates can meet in a number of ways. At earthquake zones they grind past each other in opposite directions, being compressed so that they store huge amounts of energy. This is released in calamitous movements of the ground—earthquakes. The most famous earthquake zone of all, the San Andreas Fault in California, is a region where the North American and Pacific Plates are moving past each other. Earthquake prediction hinges on the theory that major quakes are preceded by "quiet" periods during which the plates lock together, and store up the energy. Not all the plate boundaries are earthquake or volcano zones—the Himalayas are the result of a head-on collision between the relatively fast-moving Indo-Australian Plate, and the Eurasian Plate. These two continental plates buckled upward, forming the mountain

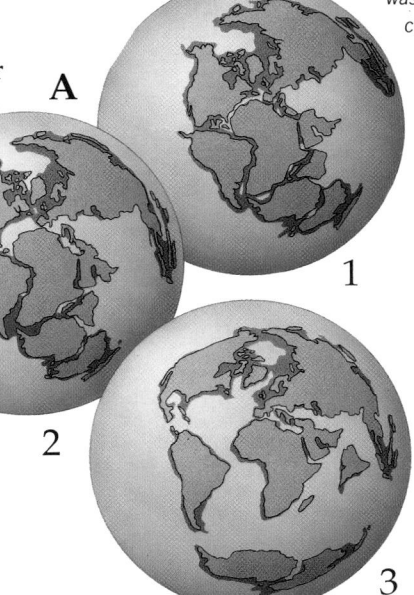

▼ PANGAEA

The continents of the world have not always looked as they do today [A]. The process of plate tectonics means that they have migrated across the surface of the Earth. 200 million years ago, in the Jurassic era, all the land masses were joined in a single supercontinent, Pangaea [1].

Eventually, 120 million years ago, Pangaea split in two, the northern Laurasia made up of present-day North America and Eurasia, and the southern Gondwana, comprising South America, Africa, Australia and India [2].

By 40 million years ago the world had taken on a familiar look, although India had yet to collide with Eurasia (and create the Himalayas in the process) and Australia was still located very close to Antarctica [3].

▼ PLATE TECTONICS

The processes of plate tectonics can be seen most clearly on a section of ocean floor [B]. At a subduction zone [1], an oceanic plate meets a much thicker continental plate and is forced down into the Earth's upper mantle. The heat in this zone melts the upper basalt layer of the oceanic plate, forming liquid magma which then rises to the surface and is vented through volcanoes.

At a mid-oceanic ridge [2] new crust is constantly being generated where two plates are separating. Magma rises up from the Earth's mantle, forcing its way through cracks in the crust, and solidifying.

As the cracks expand, a striated ocean floor is formed. When the new crust solidifies, traces of iron in it align with the Earth's magnetic field and so preserve a record of the various reversals in the field over millions of years.

A hot spot volcano [3] forms where the crust thins above a hot plume rising from the inner mantle. It is only the latest in a string of volcanoes that form as the oceanic plate moves over the stationary plume. The earlier volcanoes become extinct, subsiding to volcanic islands with coral fringes, and eventually become atolls, where only the ring of coral remains above the surface of the ocean.

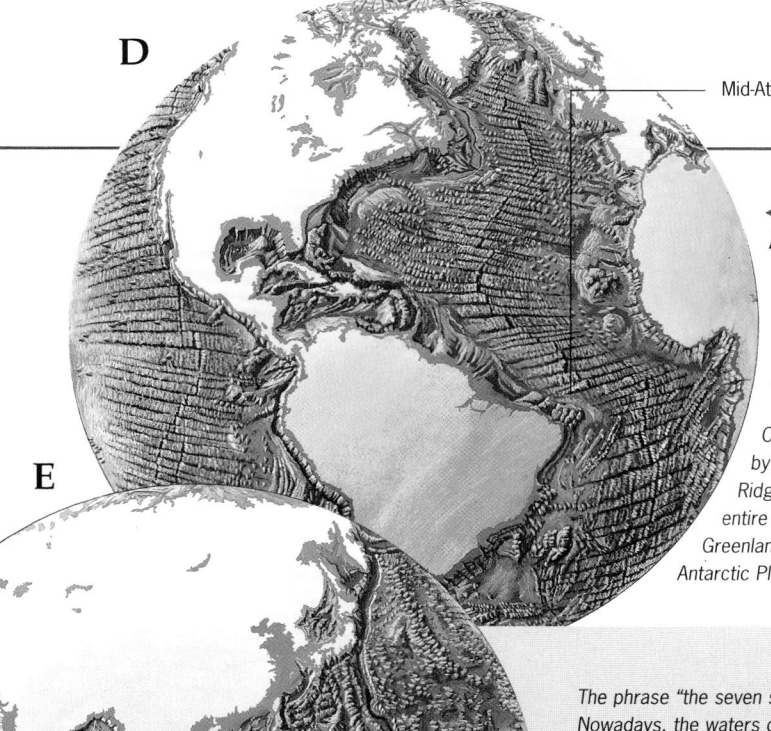

Mid-Atlantic Ridge

D

E

◀ THE ATLANTIC AND THE PACIFIC

The floors of the two largest oceans reveal important differences in their structures.

The Atlantic Ocean [D] is divided by the Mid-Atlantic Ridge that runs for its entire length, from Greenland down to the Antarctic Plate. This is a region where the Earth's crust is stretching, new floor being pumped out so that the Atlantic is gradually widening. As the rock is pulled apart, large slabs sink, creating the series of rifts that run parallel to the ridge along its length. Only in a few places does the ridge emerge above the sea, most spectacularly in Iceland, the shape of which is constantly being redefined by volcanic activity.

In contrast, the floor of the Pacific Ocean [E] shows signs of many different seismic activities. It is surrounded by the so-called "ring of fire"— volcanic zones where the oceanic plates dive below continental ones and create volcanoes. At other places, oceanic plates converge, creating trenches where one plate dives below the other, such as the Marianas Trench, the deepest place on Earth.

Marianas Trench

THE SEVEN SEAS

The phrase "the seven seas" dates back to the seas known to Muslim voyagers before the fifteenth century. Nowadays, the waters of the world are divided into seven oceans—the North Pacific, the South Pacific, the North Atlantic, the South Atlantic, the Indian, the Arctic and the Antarctic. But divisions such as these are in reality arbitrary, as all these waters can just as easily be considered as parts of one continuous global ocean.

The Pacific Ocean
Water Area:
69,500,000 square miles
Volume:
174,000,000 cubic miles
Average Depth: 4310 yards

The Atlantic Ocean
Water Area:
40,900,000 square miles
Volume:
85,200,000 cubic miles
Average Depth: 3620 yards

The Indian Ocean
Water Area:
29,000,000 square miles
Volume:
70,100,000 cubic miles
Average Depth: 4200 yards

▼ SEA CHANGE

A coastal region [C] is shaped by the forces of longshore drift. Sand is pushed along the shore by ocean currents to build up spits [1], bars [2] and sometimes enclosing bays to form lagoons.

A river carries vast amounts of sediment out to sea, which is deposited to form a delta [3]. Under the sea, the accumulation of sediment forms the continental shelf [4], a region that slopes gently out from the coastline for about 47 mi, to depths of 110-220 yards. In places it is cut through by submarine gorges, formed either by rivers when the sea level was lower or by the undercutting effect of river currents flowing out to sea. The shelf gives way to the steep continental slope, which dives to depths of several miles. From the base of the slope, the continental rise extends up to 621 mi. from the coast into the ocean.

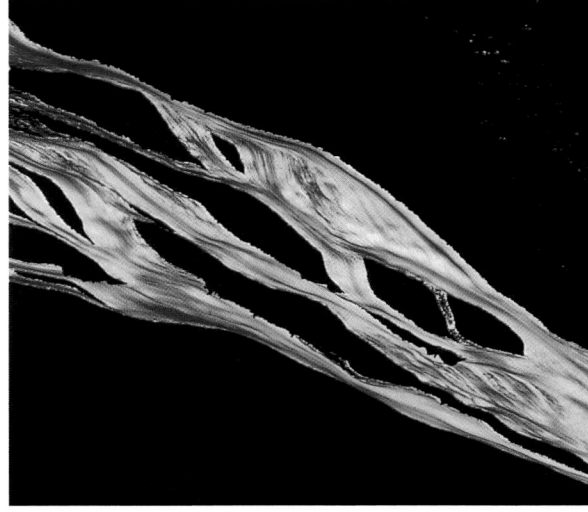

◀ Lava which erupts from the earth's surface can take on a number of forms. Aa, or block lava, is runny, and quickly forms a hard pastry-like crust when it cools. Pahoehoe lava has a sheen to it like satin and often consolidates in rope-like forms. When this kind of lava comes into contact with the sea it takes on the form of a jumbled heap of pillows, hence its name pillow lava.

C

range, and halting the Indo-Australian plate's movement. Conversely, not all volcanoes are at plate boundaries. The volcanic Hawaiian Islands, for instance, lie in the middle of the Pacific Plate. This chain of volcanic mountains is caused by a semi-permanent "hot spot" where molten magma rises from the depths of the mantle through the crust, and spews out of a volcano. Although the hot spot in the mantle is stationary, the Pacific Plate, and with it the volcano, is continually moving. Hawaii itself is only the most recent in a chain of 107 volcanic vents formed by the plume. As the plate moves on, each volcano becomes extinct, and a new one forms further along the chain. Many thousands of these "hot spot" volcanoes are known—mostly beneath the ocean surface—so there must be hundreds of hot plumes in the mantle to have created them all.

While plates are being destroyed in the subduction zones where they collide, new plate material is being produced all the time deep beneath the ocean surface. The sea floor is just as geologically fascinating as the continental land surface, and is still awaiting full exploration.

Occasionally, the volcanic activity of the mid-oceanic ridges reaches the surface, and forms islands. At other places, hot gases venting from the depths of the Earth create pools of warmth on the ocean floor, where life can flourish.

SHAPING THE EARTH

OVER BILLIONS OF YEARS, THE HARSH landscape created by geological activity such as plate tectonics and volcanism has been softened and sculpted by the eroding forces of ice, water and air. Glaciers have ground out valleys, and rivers have carved huge gorges, including America's Grand Canyon. At the same time the steady pounding of the seas and oceans eats away at and remodels coastlines.

Studies of the changing climate in the past show that the Earth has gone through periodic "ice ages" when the ice-caps pushed into temperate regions closer to the Equator. These periods were critical in shaping the landscape that we see today—during the last Ice Age, which ended 10,000 years ago, an ice sheet covered most of Northern Europe, Asia and North America. The ice ages can be dated by drilling out an ice core from a polar cap. Each year a layer of new ice is laid down, which in colder years—during ice ages—is thicker. These records surprisingly reveal that over the last 4 million years, successive ice ages have gripped Earth for longer than the warmer periods in between.

Variations in the Earth's climate are thought to be the result of cyclical changes in its orbit, which becomes more, then less, elongated. According to these models the Earth's average temperature should currently be on the increase—which means that the measured increases in temperature cited as evidence of global warming and the greenhouse effect may have a natural cause.

Getting in shape

During the ice ages, massive glaciers formed across the globe. As these vast, slow-moving rivers of ice rolled forward, the sheer weight of ice ground down rocks in their paths, leaving a softened, altered landscape once they had retreated. These forces are still at work today: on Greenland and in Antarctica there are many glaciers which eventually find their way to the sea, where they break up into icebergs.

Although glaciers are the most dramatic form of erosion, there are others: over longer periods, rivers and seas can cut through rock and carve out valleys. Even rain has a profound cumulative effect on rock. Raindrops dissolve gases from the atmosphere and become dilute acid, chemically attacking igneous rocks formed from volcanic lava. In time, the particles broken off build up to great depths and are converted by pressure and heat into sedimentary rocks such as limestone. When these are subjected to the intense heat of the Earth's crust they become metamorphic rocks, such as marble and slate.

▶ **EARTH SCRAPER**
Glaciers [A] are dramatic rivers of ice slowly creeping down valleys and carving mountain ranges into a series of sharp peaks. They usually originate where ice or hard-packed snow builds up in a cirque [1], a basin near a mountain top. After a sufficient mass has built up, it will start to move under its own gravity, wearing down rocks by pressure, scraping and frost action, to form glacial spoil called "moraines." The boulders of moraine underneath the glacier act as abrasives, scouring the landscape. Lateral moraines [2] are rocks cut away and pulled along at the sides of the glacier. Where two ice-rivers meet, the lateral moraines can join to form a medial moraine [3]—a stripe of rubble down the center of the glacier. As the glacier grinds along over rocks and boulders, the stresses induced can open up deep and jagged splits called crevasses [4]. A glacier terminates at a snout [5] which may empty into the sea, or a great lake. On dry land the shape of the snout depends on the climatic conditions, and especially the rate at which the snout melts compared with the rate at which the glacier advances. If the the two rates are exactly balanced, the snout

▼ **A WOBBLING WORLD**
The climate of the Earth is not constant but gradually varies over time in cycles of thousands of years [B]. The shape of the Earth's orbit around the Sun can vary between an almost perfect circle [1] and a pronounced ellipse [2] over a cycle of around 100,000 years. When the orbit is more elliptical, the climate of the Earth is more extreme. At the same time, another cycle changes the angle of tilt of the planet between a minimum 21.8° and a maximum 24.4° [C]. At the maximum inclination, every 22,000 years, the climate is most extreme, and the seasons are especially marked, with the Poles pointing further away from the Sun during winter. When the effects of these cycles are combined, they lead to ice ages of varying severity, the last of which ended around 10,000 years ago.

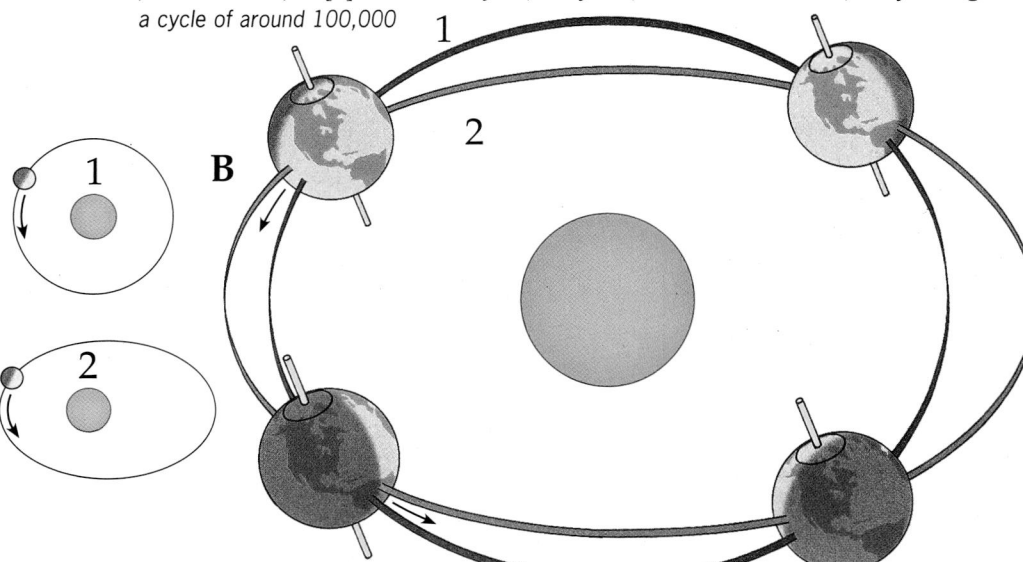

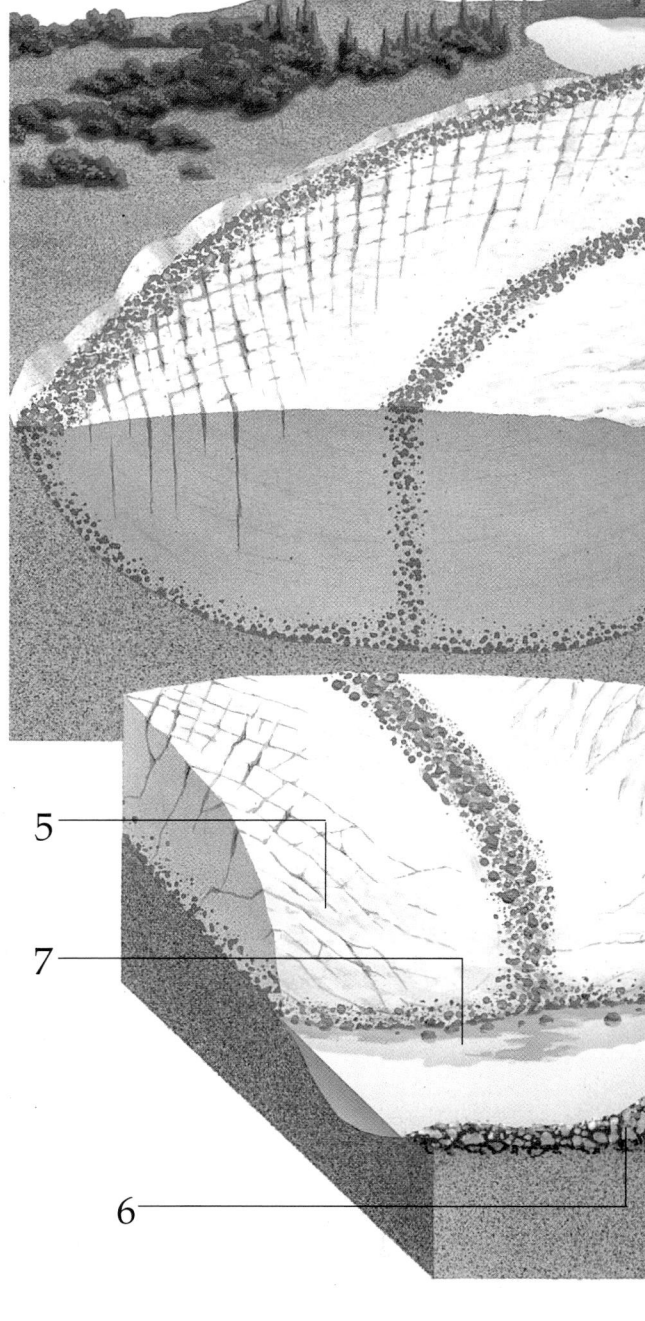

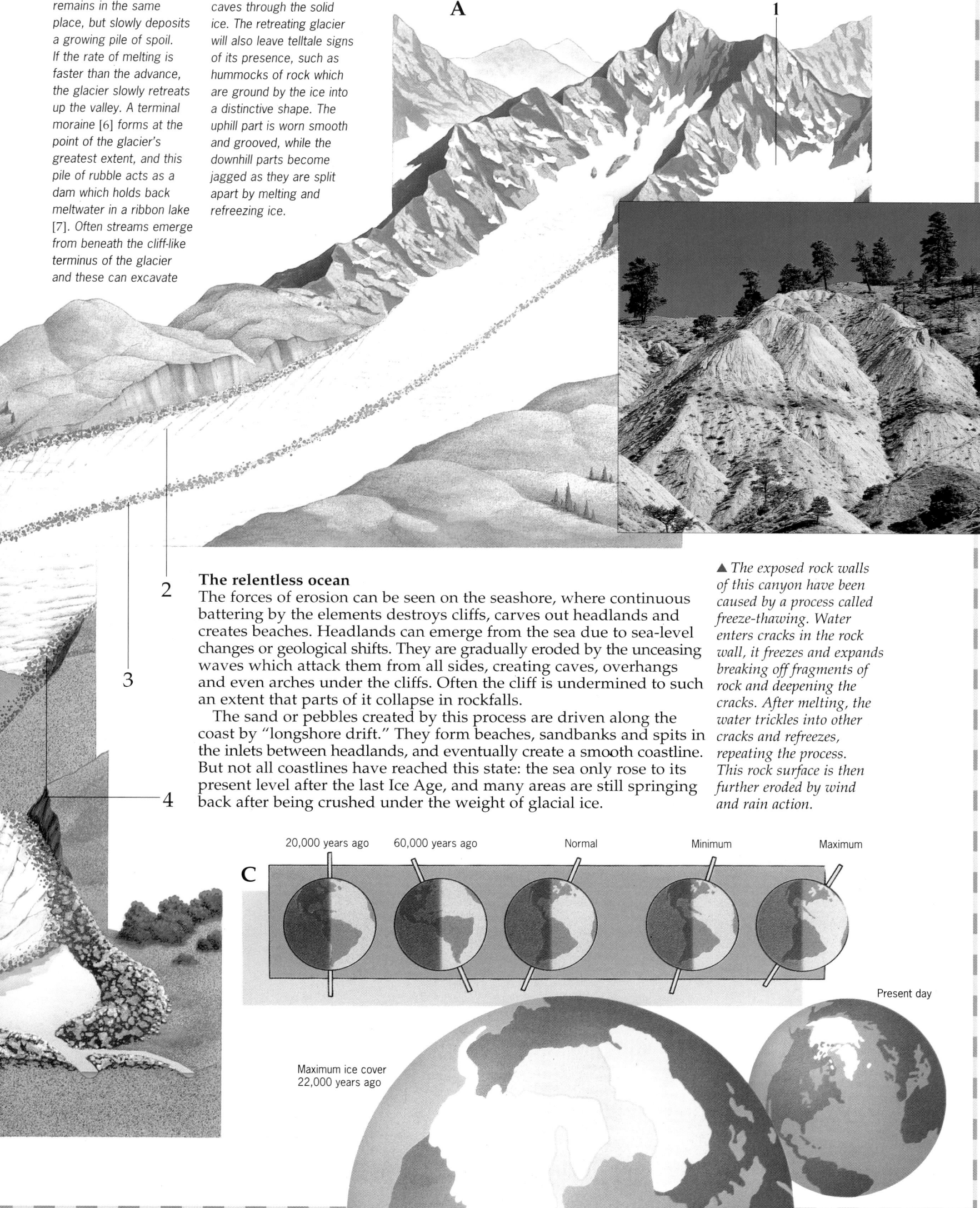

remains in the same place, but slowly deposits a growing pile of spoil. If the rate of melting is faster than the advance, the glacier slowly retreats up the valley. A terminal moraine [6] forms at the point of the glacier's greatest extent, and this pile of rubble acts as a dam which holds back meltwater in a ribbon lake [7]. Often streams emerge from beneath the cliff-like terminus of the glacier and these can excavate caves through the solid ice. The retreating glacier will also leave telltale signs of its presence, such as hummocks of rock which are ground by the ice into a distinctive shape. The uphill part is worn smooth and grooved, while the downhill parts become jagged as they are split apart by melting and refreezing ice.

A

1

2

3

4

The relentless ocean

The forces of erosion can be seen on the seashore, where continuous battering by the elements destroys cliffs, carves out headlands and creates beaches. Headlands can emerge from the sea due to sea-level changes or geological shifts. They are gradually eroded by the unceasing waves which attack them from all sides, creating caves, overhangs and even arches under the cliffs. Often the cliff is undermined to such an extent that parts of it collapse in rockfalls.

The sand or pebbles created by this process are driven along the coast by "longshore drift." They form beaches, sandbanks and spits in the inlets between headlands, and eventually create a smooth coastline. But not all coastlines have reached this state: the sea only rose to its present level after the last Ice Age, and many areas are still springing back after being crushed under the weight of glacial ice.

▲ The exposed rock walls of this canyon have been caused by a process called freeze-thawing. Water enters cracks in the rock wall, it freezes and expands breaking off fragments of rock and deepening the cracks. After melting, the water trickles into other cracks and refreezes, repeating the process. This rock surface is then further eroded by wind and rain action.

C

20,000 years ago 60,000 years ago Normal Minimum Maximum

Present day

Maximum ice cover
22,000 years ago

CONTRASTING CONDITIONS

We TALK SO MUCH ABOUT THE WEATHER because of its infinite changeability. As the Sun's radiation heats up the Equatorial zones of the planet much more than the Polar regions, it creates wide temperature contrasts. The hottest places on Earth can be a blistering 122°F in the shade, while in the depths of an Antarctic winter, levels as low as -94°F have been recorded. This variable heat produces hot air at the Equator, which rises, while cooler air further north and south sinks under it, producing wind patterns that stretch across the globe. These in turn create swirling eddies of air that can absorb water vapor over the sea, forming clouds, and deposit it as rain over land. Such air currents couple with the variable heat of the Sun to produce the wide variety of climates found on Earth, ranging from hot, rainless deserts to cool, wet, temperate coastal regions.

The atmosphere of the Earth just after it formed was an unbreatheable mixture of hydrogen and helium. In time this was replaced by an equally unbreatheable mixture belched out from volcanoes, which in turn has been modified by life forms to the air we breathe today. This is made up of 78 per cent nitrogen, 21 per cent oxygen, and a small proportion of carbon dioxide, which plants then recycle into oxygen. The remainder of the atmosphere is water vapor and small traces of other gases. The balance is a delicate one, perfectly suited to life as it has evolved, and the entire planet —both living things and minerals—is needed to maintain it.

The outer limits of the atmosphere stretch 1491 miles above the surface, but the lower 9 miles, the troposphere, is the densest, holding nearly all the atmosphere's water vapor—which condenses under different conditions to create clouds. Beyond this region, up to 25 mi. high, lies the stratosphere, which contains a thin ozone layer that blocks out harmful ultraviolet radiation.

Hadley cell

A

Climate types
Land near the Equator has weather patterns typified by those of southern Asia. For six months of the year cold dry winds blow from the land out to sea, giving arid conditions and little rain. In the summer the wind reverses direction and starts to blow warm air off the ocean. This air is heavy with water vapor and triggers torrential rainstorms over land.

Weather in the temperate latitudes of northern Europe is dominated by the jet stream, a band of high winds at altitudes of about 7 mi. It forms where warm air from the tropics meets cold Polar air, creating a jet of air traveling at speeds around 124mph in summer, 249mph in winter. The jet stream's direction develops in a similar way to a slowly flowing river, meandering and forming eddies. These are seen as high-pressure anticyclones, wind systems that create clear, dry weather, or low-pressure depressions with associated clouds and weather fronts.

The circulation patterns of the oceans are just as important in

▲ CREATING WINDS
The amount of heat absorbed at the Equator is much greater than at the Poles. The temperature difference creates giant circulation cells which transfer heat from the Equator to the Poles [A]. The Hadley cell is driven by hot air rising from the Equator which cools and returns to the surface at 30° latitude. Some of this returning air is drawn back toward the Equator, creating the trade winds. The Ferrel cell guides warm air toward the Poles, creating winds which

the Earth's rotation skews to become the Westerlies. Where these winds meet cold air blowing directly from the Poles, frontal depressions form, giving unsettled weather. At the cell boundaries jet streams form—channels of high winds which encircle the planet. This circulation from the Equator to the Poles is complicated by the Earth's rotation, creating the Coriolis force which bends winds to the right in the Northern Hemisphere, and to the left in the Southern Hemisphere.

▶ Deserts can be created in many ways, and they may be hot or cold. The Antarctic, being one of the driest places in the world, is classed as a cold desert. The Sahara and the Arabian Deserts are classic examples of hot deserts. The photograph shows a sand dune system in the Namib Desert in Southern Africa. Winds blowing over the land constantly shift dunes in ever-changing patterns.

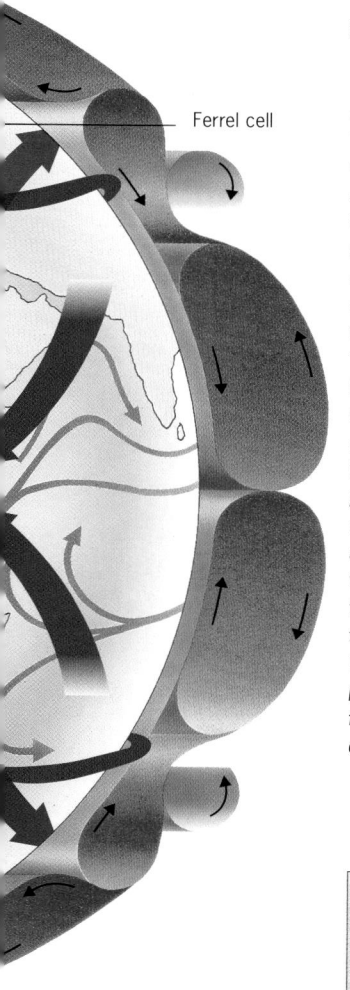

Ferrel cell

▶ A tornado can form during a very severe thunderstorm **[C]**. Hot air evaporating off land or sea rises rapidly through the atmosphere, condensing to form clouds. As surface air rushes into the low pressure at the center of the storm, the spin of the Earth makes the whole complex spin, producing a typhoon or hurricane (right). Tornadoes occur when the fast-rising thermals, which create a storm, begin to spin even more quickly, perhaps in response to the local geography. As the thermal winds up on itself, it draws a funnel of cloud down from the bottom of the storm toward the ground, where the winds often exceed 124mph. The extreme low pressure sucks up material from the ground, flinging it out at the top of the tornado, sometimes to land several miles away. Waterspouts are similar vortices that form over water.

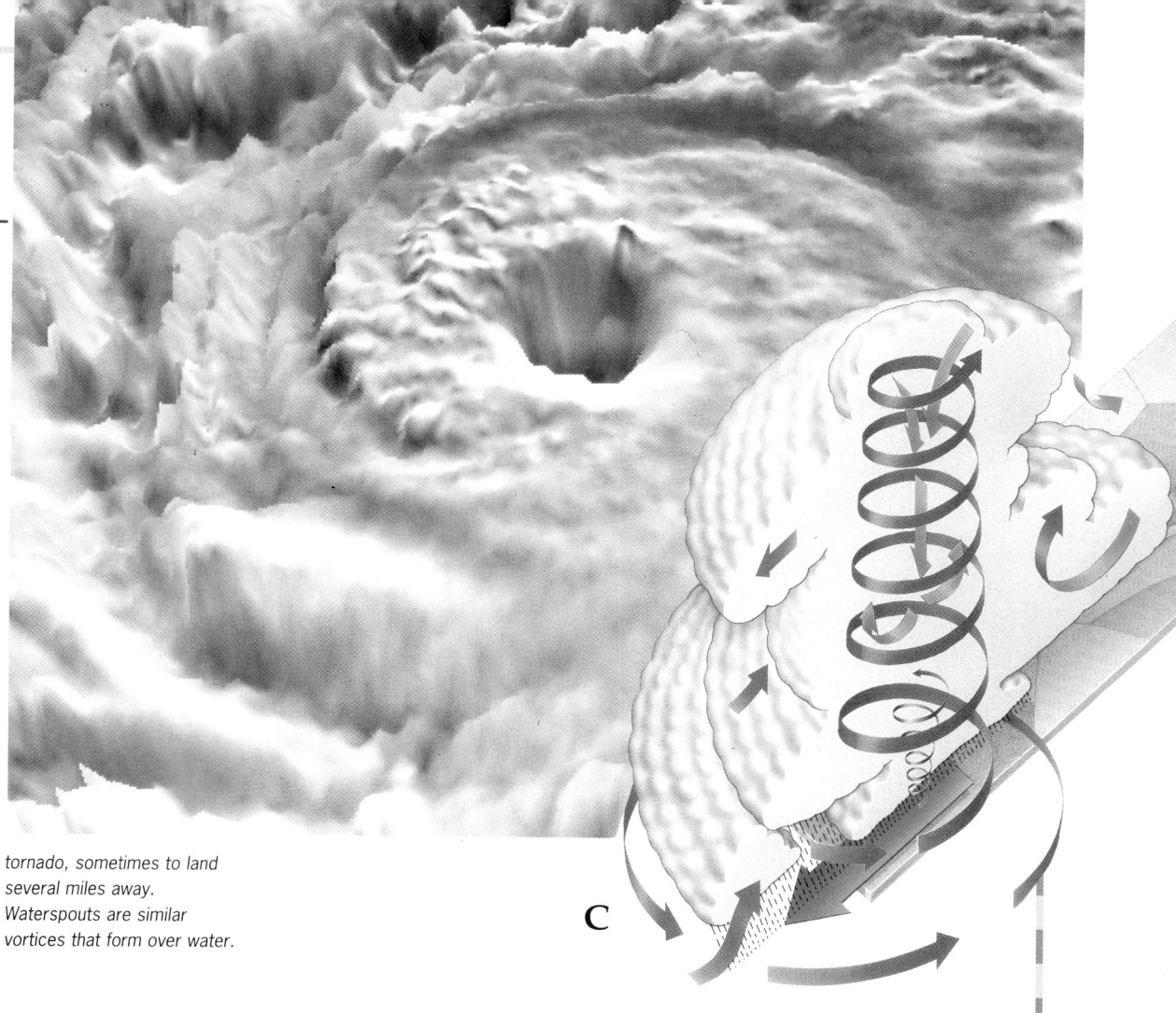

C

▶ **VARIETY OF CLIMATE**
The patterns of rainfall and temperature around the world divide the Earth into different regions of vegetation **[B]**. Seven cities around the world illustrate the wide variety of weather these produce.

New York has an east coast continental climate, with cold winters, hot summers and steady rainfall all year round. London's climate is marine west coast, similarly wet to New York's but with less variation between summer and winter temperatures. Omsk has typical steppe climate, with low rainfall and very cold winters followed by hot summers. Singapore's tropical climate gives almost constant hot and very wet weather. Manaus in Brazil's region of tropical savanna has constant high temperatures, with very dry summer months. A desert climate like that of Alice Springs has very high average temperatures (with a slight dip during the southern winter months), but almost no rain throughout the year. The Nigerian capital, Lagos, has a constantly hot tropical rainforest climate, characterized by its extremely wet summer months.

B

New York | London | Omsk | Singapore
Rainfall cm: 45 40 35 30 25 20 15 10 5
Temperature C: 40 30 20 10 0 −10

Manaus | Alice Springs | Lagos
Rainfall cm: 45 40 35 30 25 20 15 10 5
Temperature C: 40 30 20 10 0 −10

○ Deciduous forest
○ Steppe
○ Evergreen forest
○ Tropical rainforest
○ Tropical savanna
○ Desert
○ Tundra

regulating climate. In general, the oceans circulate in large eddies, clockwise in the Northern Hemisphere, counterclockwise in the Southern. One of the best-known currents is the Gulf Stream, which crosses the Atlantic toward northern Europe, moderating the climate with warm water carried from the Gulf of Mexico, counteracting the Polar air blowing over the rest of the continent.

Another example of the oceanic effect on the weather is El Niño. Normally, the circulation of the Pacific Ocean creates cold, dry weather on the west coast of South America, and rain on the east coast of Australia. Air and water currents circulate warm surface water westward to Australia, raising sea levels and creating an upwelling of deep cold water off South America. But as the warm water spreads eastward it destabilizes the trade winds, which reverse their direction. The ocean circulation reverses as well, with warm water off South America preventing the cold upwelling which brings up nutrients vital to fish stocks. On land, Australia experiences drought, and South America suffers torrential rain. Such drastic climatic changes show how delicate the balance is between climate and the environment.

Major volcanic eruptions can also affect the climate, throwing dust particles high into the upper atmosphere, where they block out sunlight. Sudden climate changes are believed to have caused mass extinction of life on Earth in the past, and as yet there is little humanity can do to counter, or even predict, these changes.

PEOPLING THE GLOBE

THE ORIGINS OF HUMANKIND ARE VERY HARD TO DETERMINE. The fossil record of our ancestors is very patchy, and thus the story involves large amounts of guesswork. Archaeologists believe that between 7 and 10 million years ago, a human ancestor, called *Ramapithecus*, developed from the same stock as chimpanzees and gorillas. The route from these creatures to modern man can be traced in terms of changing skeletons. Bipedal motion required a sturdy pelvis, while the increasing intelligence of these progenitors can be followed through increasing brain capacities. *Ramapithecus* was succeeded by *Australopithecus*, whose later form is named *Homo habilis*, the handy man, because fossil evidence shows that it used simple tools.

Homo erectus appeared in Africa 1.7 million years ago and spread to the rest of the world roughly 1 million years ago. They were almost as tall as modern humans, with skull capacities twice as large as *Homo habilis*. This species lived longer in Asia than in Africa—it includes Peking Man, who lived 250,000 years ago. It was gradually succeeded by our species, *Homo sapiens*, which appeared in Africa more than 500,000 years ago. The expansion was a slow drift as bands of hunter-gatherers followed prey animals. There can have been no population pressure: 10,000 years ago the world population was between 5 and 10 million, about the population of New York City today. As people settled in various places, climate and food sources led them to evolve differently. For example, those in very hot Equatorial countries kept a dark skin to protect them from ultraviolet sunlight; those in colder climates developed lighter skins to maximize the effect of a weaker sun—vitamin D, essential to bone growth, is gained from sunlight.

At first only Africa, Asia and the warmer parts of Europe were colonized: America and Australia remained empty for thousands of years. Movement between continental land masses was made possible by climate changes. During the last Ice Age, much of the world's water was locked into the ice caps. Sea levels dropped dramatically, what is now the Bering Strait became a land passage, and vast stretches of ocean became navigable by small boats.

Hunters to farmers
For two million years, human ancestors lived as hunter-gatherers, following a nomadic pattern of life, with a

THE ICE AGE
In the Ice Age, parts of Europe were covered in glacial sheets and the North Sea was a great plain [A]. The climate and terrain were very like Alaska today, and herds of reindeer roamed the area. These were a main food source for groups of hunter-gatherers, traces of whom have been found in Europe, mostly in the warmer areas (southern Spain, south-west France and along main rivers). These people followed the deer herds on their grazing migrations, augmenting their diet with small game as well as vegetables, berries and grains. As the climate became warmer various groups settled near coasts to become fisher-gatherers.

A

● Hunter-gatherers
● Fisher-gatherers

HOMO SAPIENS
From central and southern Africa *Homo sapiens* spread out to populate the whole world [B]. The first migration spread from Africa eastward across to Asia. Routes branched off to northern Africa and southern Europe. A second wave occurred 15,000 years ago, when glaciation provided a land bridge across the Bering Strait, allowing movement from northern Asia to the Americas.

B

● Evidence of *Homo sapiens*
▲ Prehistoric Americans

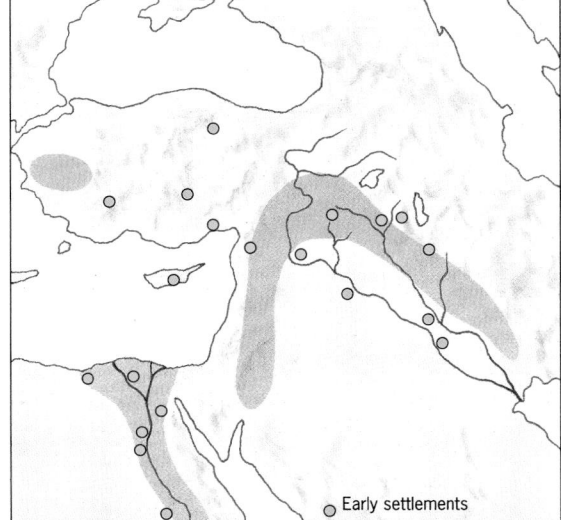

C

● Early settlements

THE FIRST FARMERS
The first farming settlements, which developed into the first cities, were probably founded around 10,000 years ago in the "Fertile Crescent" [C], a band of land stretching from the Mediterranean to the rivers Tigris and Euphrates, in modern Jordan, Lebanon, Syria, Turkey and Iraq. Civilization also flowered along the banks of the river Nile, similarly suited to agriculture. From simple farmsteads grew villages, towns, cities and eventually whole civilizations.

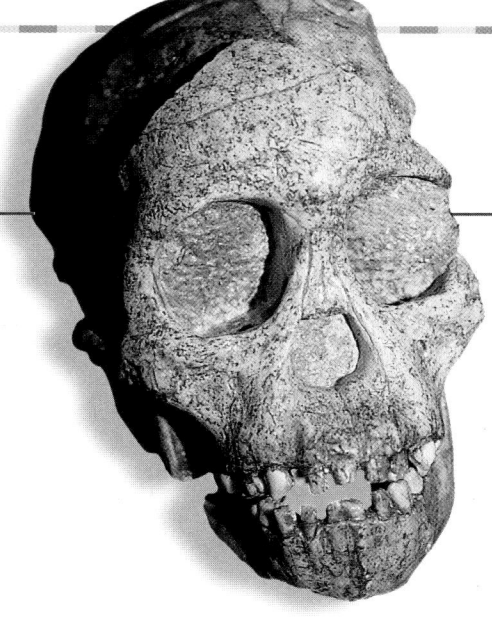

diet of animals and seasonal fruits. This changed between 20,000 and 10,000 years ago with the development of agriculture. About 15,000 years ago, as temperatures rose, primitive farming practices began to appear wherever the climate allowed it. The most important of these were Mesopotamia, the crescent between the rivers Tigris and Euphrates in modern Iraq, southeastern Turkey and eastern Syria, the Nile Valley, Central America and northeast China. Once wandering groups settled down the population soared, increasing from 5 to 300 million in 8000 years.

Small farming settlements developed into villages, then towns, then cities. Social and political organizations developed to control large groups of people. Gradually, the great civilizations grew, in the fertile fields of these first settlements. Along the Nile Valley, the Egyptians started to build a sophisticated culture around 3000 BC, at the same time as the Sumerians were developing a system of city-states in Mesopotamia. Similar civilizations appeared in China and Central America. Influences from these civilizations rippled outward, laying down the pattern for the shape of the modern world.

▲ *This skull of* Australopithecus africanus *is over 2 million years old.* Africanus *was the first hominid to leave the forest for the open plain.*

► **OUT OF AFRICA**
It is now considered that the ancestors of humankind first appeared in Africa [D]. As well as indications of early Homo sapiens, the evidence for Africa's claims to be the cradle of humanity comes from fossils of Australopithecus and Homo erectus found in South Africa, Olduvai Gorge in Kenya, and Ethiopia. These are older than any others so far discovered in the world and so it seems likely that the human beings who evolved in Africa gradually spread out to other parts of the world. This is corroborated by fossils of a later date found in India, Java and China which indicate the direction of migration out of Africa. Early Homo sapiens fossils have also been found in China, southern Europe, North and South America and the Middle East. In Europe, the fossils found so far are confined to early forms of Homo sapiens and Neanderthal man, whose traces have been found in Germany, Hungary, France, Belgium, Greece, Czechoslovakia, Russia and the Middle East.

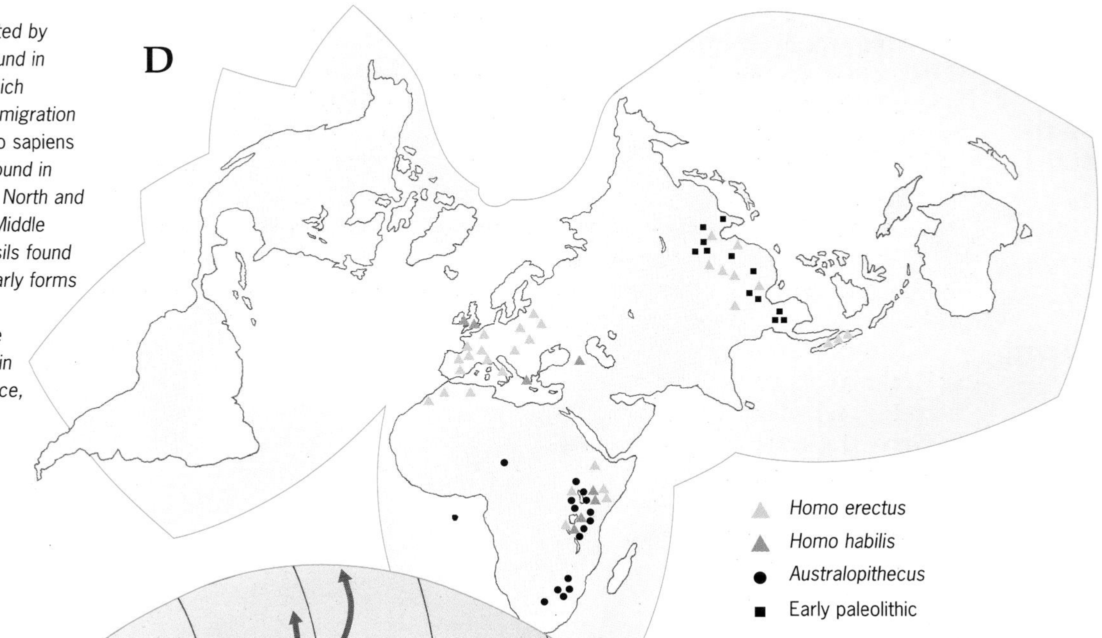

D

▲ Homo erectus
▲ Homo habilis
● Australopithecus
■ Early paleolithic

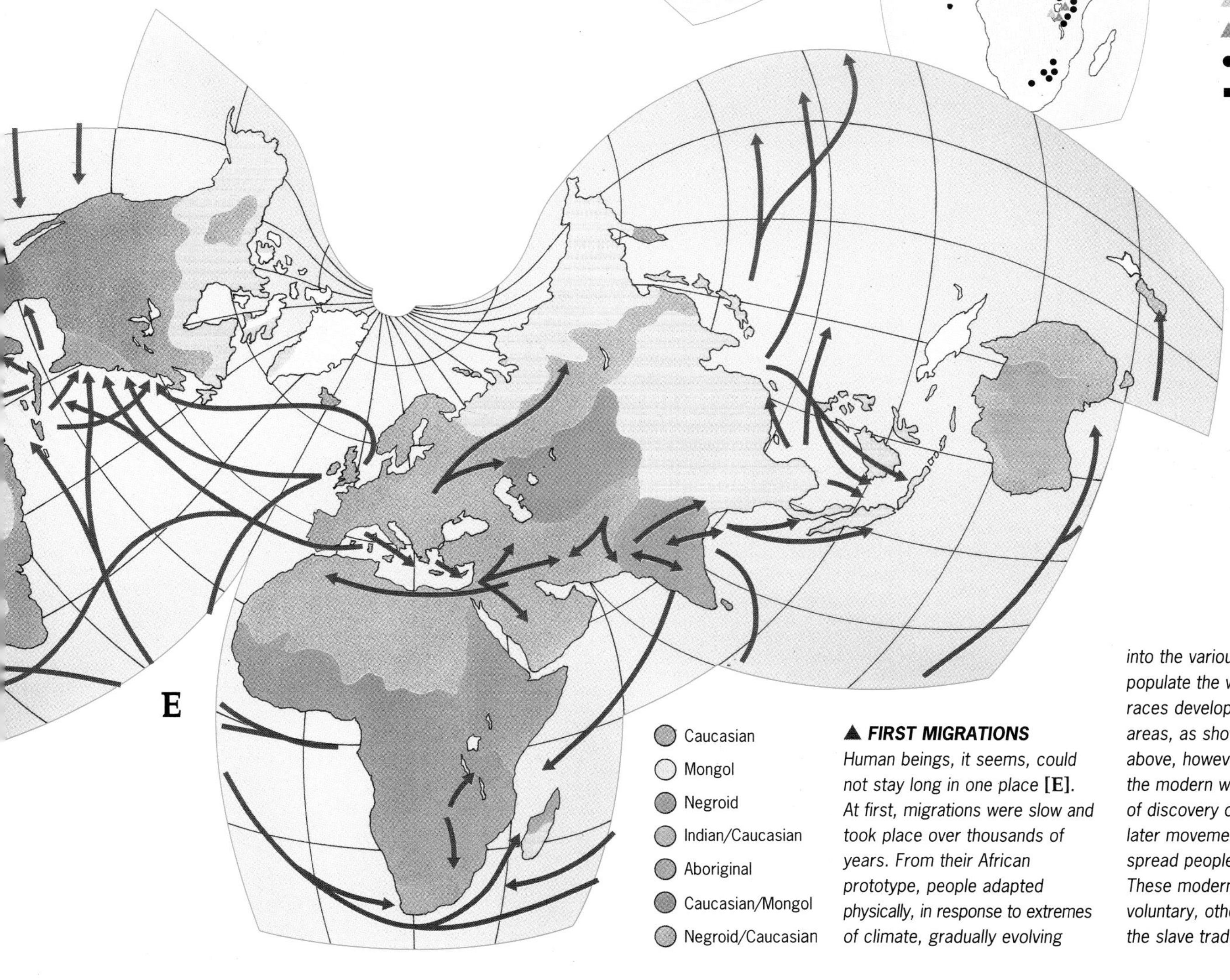

E

Caucasian
Mongol
Negroid
Indian/Caucasian
Aboriginal
Caucasian/Mongol
Negroid/Caucasian

▲ **FIRST MIGRATIONS**
Human beings, it seems, could not stay long in one place [E]. At first, migrations were slow and took place over thousands of years. From their African prototype, people adapted physically, in response to extremes of climate, gradually evolving into the various races that populate the world today. These races developed in certain areas, as shown on the map above, however, the forces of the modern world from the age of discovery onward created later movements that have spread people around the world. These modern migrations, some voluntary, others enforced, as in the slave trade, are also shown.

THE POPULATION EXPLOSION

THERE ARE 6 BILLION PEOPLE IN THE WORLD TODAY. This figure is rising at a rate of 140 million each year, an increase of more than the population of Japan. But until comparatively recently, the rate of increase of the world population was low. Two thousand years ago, there were an estimated 300 million people on Earth; by 1650 this had increased to a mere 500 million. Then in only 200 years this number had doubled, and in the 150 years since then it has increased fivefold. In spite of recurrent famine and war, the world population seems set on an inexorable upward curve, doubling every 39 years.

This population explosion is a result of social developments since the Industrial Revolution. Proportionally there are the same number of births each year—or perhaps fewer. But the advances of improved sanitation and nutrition made possible by the industrial and scientific advances of the 18th and 19th centuries meant that fewer babies died at birth and that people lived longer.

At first these changes were confined to the countries of the developed world, in Europe and America, but as they have spread around the world, the population has ballooned. Now in most European countries the population remains stable, mainly because of the availability of reliable contraception. Indeed, in some countries the birth rate has fallen below the number needed to maintain stability; this will result in a top-heavy "age pyramid," with too many grandparents and not enough grandchildren to support them. Some countries, such as France and Sweden, have tried to encourage people to have more babies through maternity payments and tax discounts for large families.

In the developing world the situation is different. There are many cultural and religious objections to the use of contraception. In a traditional agricultural community, too, a large family was desirable. As well as ensuring that the parents would have surviving children to look after them, many children provided a workforce to farm the land. But fewer people now live on the land, as farming becomes mechanized; and a large family in an urban industrialized setting just creates more mouths to feed. China, the most populated country in the world, has solved the problem, rationing families to one child each.

The rush to the cities

All over the world, more people live in cities than in the country, because it is no longer possible to make a living working on the land. As a consequence cities have proliferated. The process is not a new one: after the Industrial Revolution industrial towns gradually expanded until they merged to form huge conurbations. In terms of population density, a vast swathe of

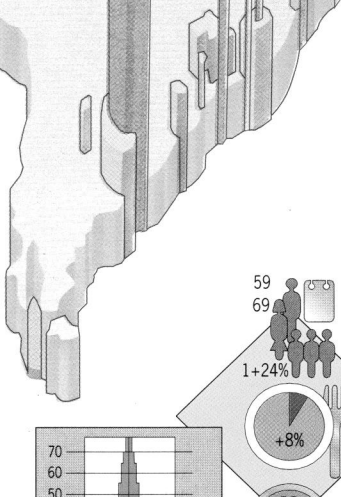

United States

VS $ 28.020

B

	No of people per sq. km.
>100	
11-100	
8-10	
<2	

A

Brazil

VS $ 4.400

▲ GLOBAL POPULATION

The global population is distributed in clumps and clusters around the world. In hotter countries, most people live on a narrow ribbon along the coast, leaving vast arid inner tracts of land underpopulated. In cooler countries, the population is able to spread itself more evenly about the landmass. The map makes clear the huge numbers of people living all across China and India, in contrast with the comparatively sparse population of much of the United States. The graphics around illustration [A] show for each continent the rate of population growth, the average longevity of men and women, the gross national product per capita (a measure of wealth), and the calorific intake per head as a percentage of an adult's average daily requirement. These illustrate the gap in health and wealth between the developed world and the developing nations.

1750

1900

2000

D

▲ GROWTH 1750–2000

The growth of the human population can be shown [D] by demonstrating the number of people that would occupy each 0.8 mi² of land of the Earth's surface at various eras: 1750, 1900 and an estimation of the figure for the year 2000.

▶ POPULATION GROWTH

The Earth's population has swollen from a mere 250 million 1000 years ago (roughly the present-day population of the United States) to 6 billion today.

For most of the intervening period growth was very slow, and there were even slight declines caused by plagues

such as the Black Death. However, from about the time of the Industrial Revolution the rate of growth increased, accelerating further with each improvement in hygiene and health care.

A graph of world population growth over the past 300 years [C] can be split to show how the relative increases in

each continent have been staggered. Throughout recorded history, the population of Asia has been greater than that of all the other continents combined. However, during the 19th century the population of Europe grew at twice the rate of Asia's, thanks mainly to the improvements in living conditions brought about by

scientific advances and the Industrial Revolution. This rate of growth has slowed in Europe this century, whereas that of Asia has accelerated spectacularly—its population seems likely to have tripled in the fifty years from 1950. Over the last two centuries the populations of North and South America have been

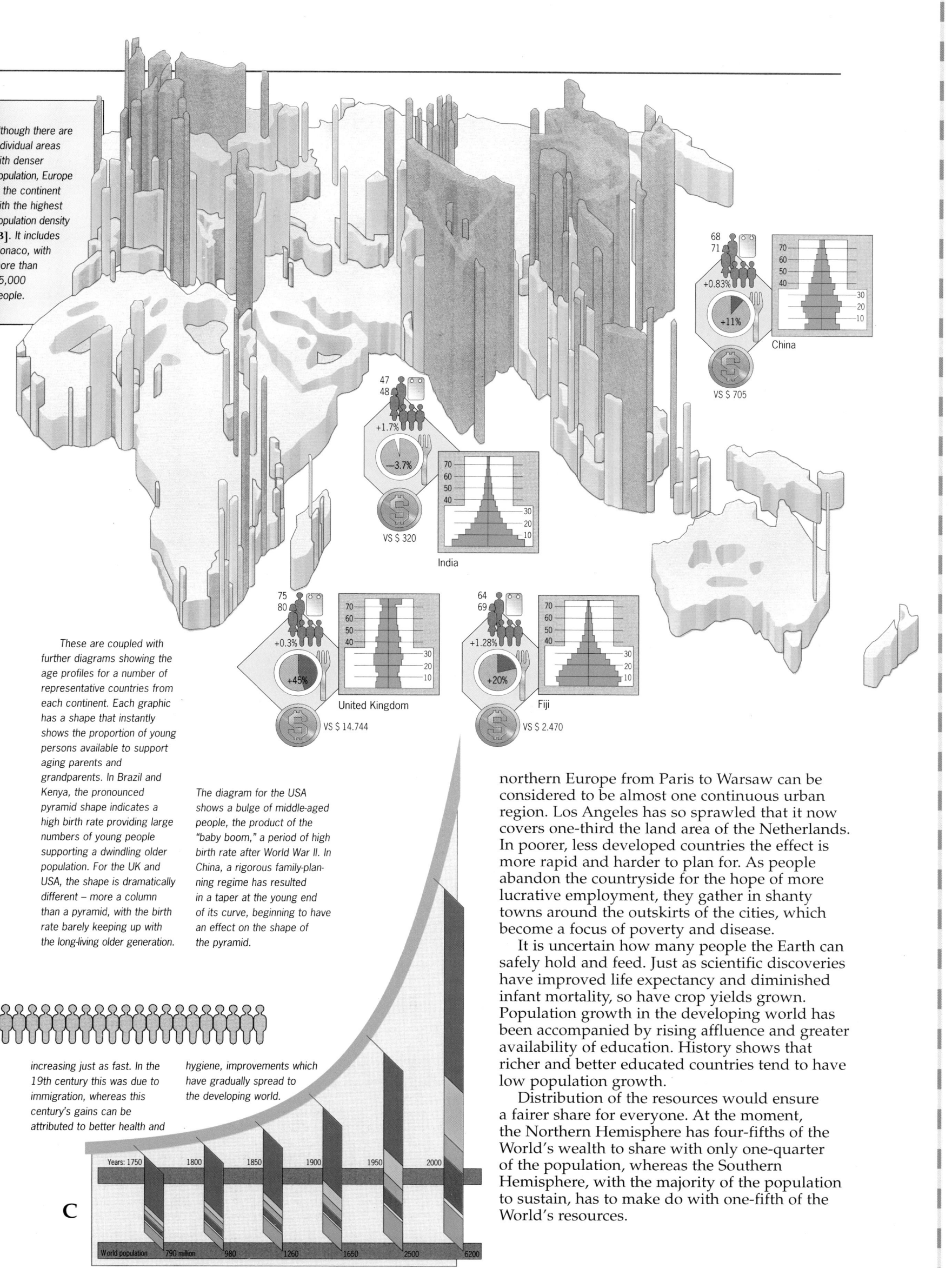

Although there are individual areas with denser population, Europe [the continent with the highest population density B]. It includes Monaco, with more than 25,000 people.

68
71
+0.83%
+11%
China
VS $ 705

47
48
+1.7%
−3.7%
VS $ 320
India

75
80
+0.3%
+45%
United Kingdom
VS $ 14.744

64
69
+1.28%
+20%
Fiji
VS $ 2.470

These are coupled with further diagrams showing the age profiles for a number of representative countries from each continent. Each graphic has a shape that instantly shows the proportion of young persons available to support aging parents and grandparents. In Brazil and Kenya, the pronounced pyramid shape indicates a high birth rate providing large numbers of young people supporting a dwindling older population. For the UK and USA, the shape is dramatically different – more a column than a pyramid, with the birth rate barely keeping up with the long-living older generation.

The diagram for the USA shows a bulge of middle-aged people, the product of the "baby boom," a period of high birth rate after World War II. In China, a rigorous family-planning regime has resulted in a taper at the young end of its curve, beginning to have an effect on the shape of the pyramid.

northern Europe from Paris to Warsaw can be considered to be almost one continuous urban region. Los Angeles has so sprawled that it now covers one-third the land area of the Netherlands. In poorer, less developed countries the effect is more rapid and harder to plan for. As people abandon the countryside for the hope of more lucrative employment, they gather in shanty towns around the outskirts of the cities, which become a focus of poverty and disease.

It is uncertain how many people the Earth can safely hold and feed. Just as scientific discoveries have improved life expectancy and diminished infant mortality, so have crop yields grown. Population growth in the developing world has been accompanied by rising affluence and greater availability of education. History shows that richer and better educated countries tend to have low population growth.

Distribution of the resources would ensure a fairer share for everyone. At the moment, the Northern Hemisphere has four-fifths of the World's wealth to share with only one-quarter of the population, whereas the Southern Hemisphere, with the majority of the population to sustain, has to make do with one-fifth of the World's resources.

increasing just as fast. In the 19th century this was due to immigration, whereas this century's gains can be attributed to better health and

hygiene, improvements which have gradually spread to the developing world.

C

| Years: 1750 | 1800 | 1850 | 1900 | 1950 | 2000 |

| World population | 790 million | 980 | 1260 | 1650 | 2500 | 6200 |

45

BELIEF AND UNDERSTANDING

ODERN COUNTRIES HAVE BEEN SHAPED POLITICALLY by many forces and movements, the most important being religion and language. Religion has been a central aspect of human society since before the earliest written records—fertility sculptures dating from the Ice Age indicate a need to recognize and pacify a spirit that brought forth the sun and rain, made crops grow and ensured a plentiful supply of food. The ancient Near Eastern civilizations, particularly Egypt, had a multitude of different gods for each aspect of human life or death. This polytheism was continued in the Greek and Roman traditions, in contrast with monotheism, belief in a single all-powerful god, exemplified by Judaism and first recorded around 1200 BC.

Today there are eleven major formal religions in the world: Christianity; Judaism; Islam; Hinduism; Buddhism and Jainism; Zoroastrianism; Confucianism; Taoism; Shinto and Sikhism. Of these Christianity is the most widespread, with over a billion followers. It has three major divisions: Roman Catholic, Protestant and Greek Orthodox, and 300 different denominations.

Christianity staked a political claim very early in the history of the developed world, being adopted as the official religion of the Roman Empire in AD 324 by the emperor Constantine. The religion instantly changed from being a local Near Eastern cult to the majority religion of Europe. It became more widespread over 1000 years later through the zeal of European colonists. The Portuguese and Spanish took Catholicism to South America, while the French, English and Dutch brought a variety of denominations to North America. The British took Anglicanism to Africa, India and China and the Dutch took Calvinism to South Africa and Malaysia.

More than words

There are over 3000 spoken languages in the world, a figure that does not include dialects. Of these, just over 100 have more than a million speakers, and only 13 have over 50 million speakers. Some of these are spoken by very large numbers of people (more than 800 million people speak Mandarin Chinese) concentrated in one country. Others—notably Portuguese, Spanish and English—are spoken in many places as a result of the colonial past. Just as explorers brought their religion with them, they also brought their language. Languages spread across the world through different mechanisms today. The growth of international trade has meant that a few languages—mostly English, and to a lesser extent French, Spanish and German—have become standard for business. The film, television and music industries have been instrumental in making American English understood almost worldwide. American English is also the language of electronics and computing. As electronic communication grows through the Internet and other networks, it is interesting to speculate on what will happen to language in the freedom of cyberspace; perhaps a new, worldwide *lingua franca* of the Internet will emerge, allowing everyone to communicate as long as they have the technology.

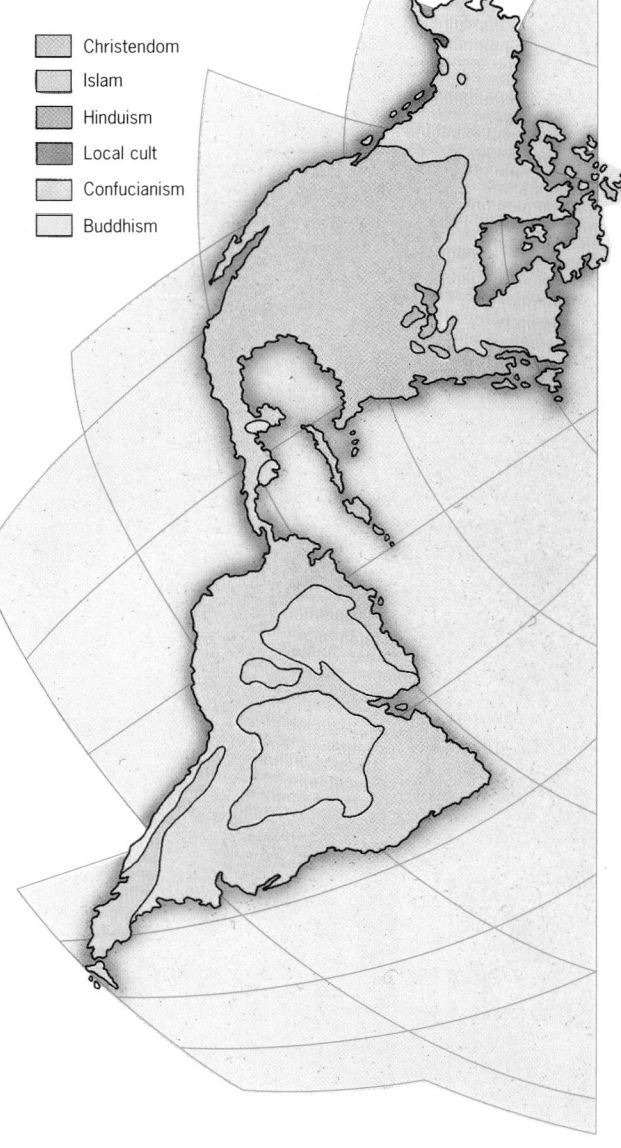

Christendom
Islam
Hinduism
Local cult
Confucianism
Buddhism

▲ **MAIN BELIEF SYSTEMS**
The main illustration shows the distribution of the adherents to the main belief systems of the world [**A**]. The areas that carry no shading are not dominated by any of these main systems of belief: this does not mean that they are free of religion, merely that they are dominated by local or tribal traditions.

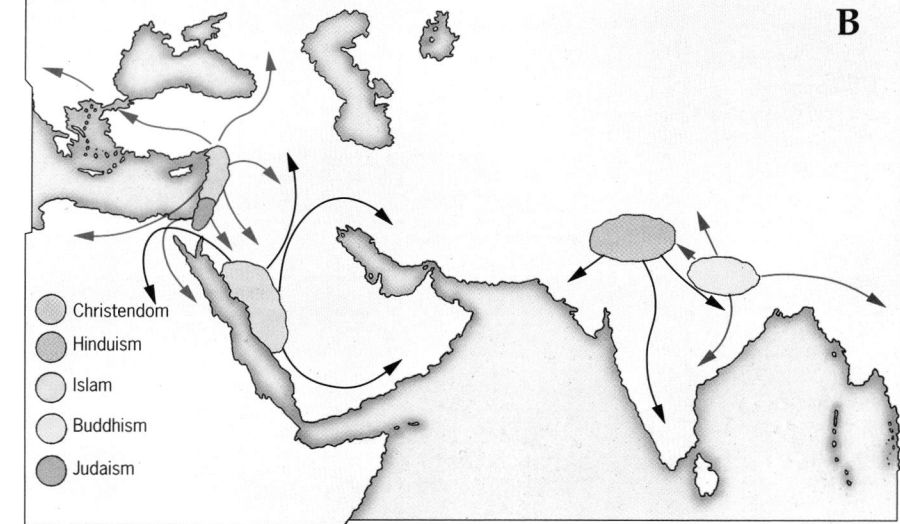

Christendom
Hinduism
Islam
Buddhism
Judaism

B

▶ **SPREAD OF RELIGIONS**
The great religions all originated in a comparatively small area of the globe [**B**], but have spread in different directions to be practiced by the majority of the world's population.

Hinduism and Buddhism are the world's oldest religions. Hinduism arose in prehistoric India. Strictly speaking it is not a single religion, but a group of different bodies of belief. Today there are roughly 733 million Hindus worldwide.

Buddhism was founded in the 6th century BC, also in India, but spread eastward and is now practiced in various forms all over East Asia with large numbers of adherents in Tibet, China and Japan. The number of Buddhists in the world has been estimated at 315 million.

Judaism can be traced from before 1200 BC. Jewish people have spread worldwide from Israel, partly driven by periodic persecution. In particular, during the Nazi Holocaust, 6 million Jews perished. Today Jews number 18 million world-wide.

Islam was was created in Arabia in the 7th century, and spread through migration, conversion and conquest.

There are an estimated 1 billion Muslims worldwide.

Christianity, which also began in Palestine as a Jewish sect, has spread most around the world, through conquest and conversion. Today it is the most popular religion worldwide, the different denominations numbering 1.8 billion adherents.

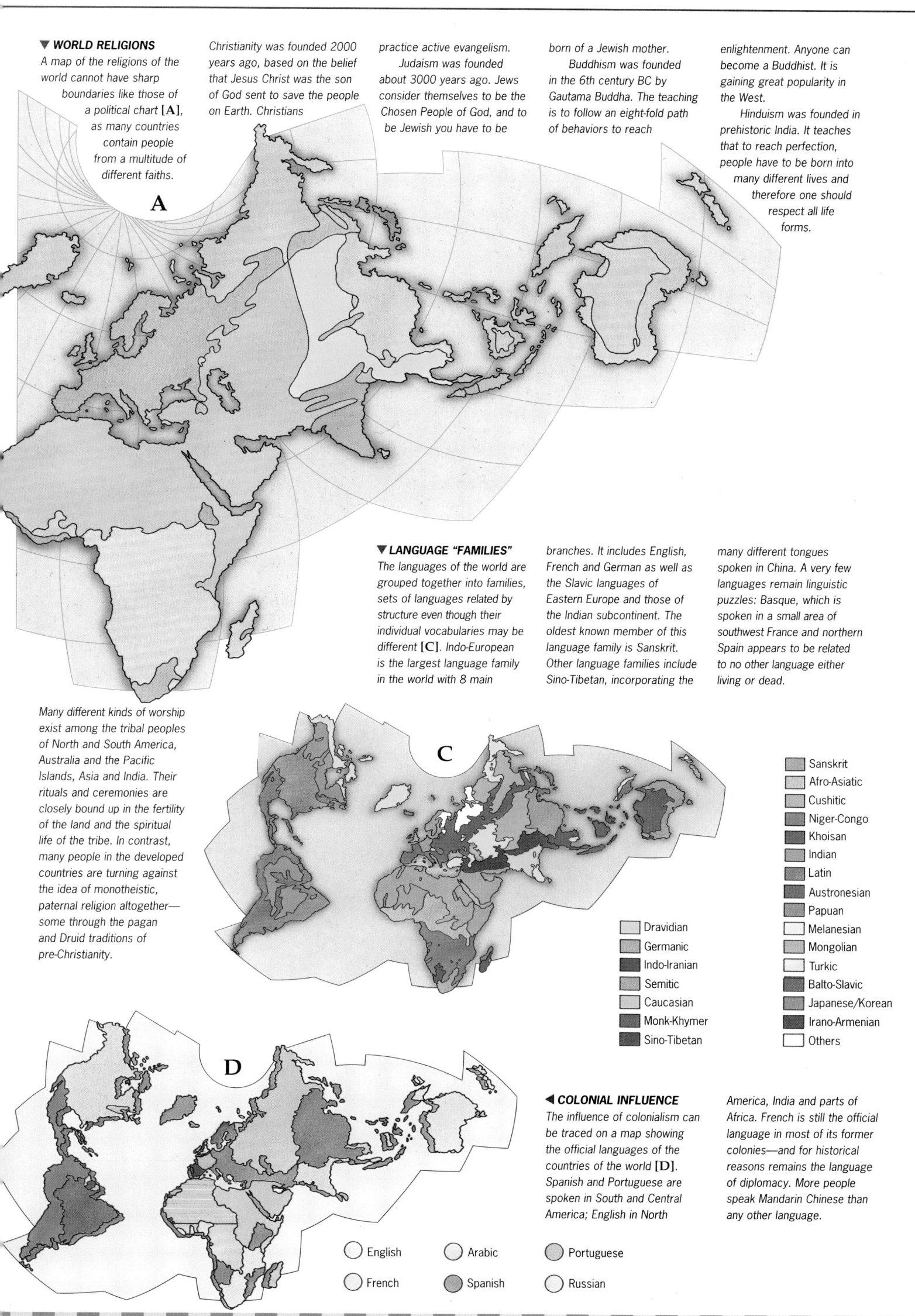

▼ WORLD RELIGIONS

A map of the religions of the world cannot have sharp boundaries like those of a political chart [A], as many countries contain people from a multitude of different faiths.

A

Christianity was founded 2000 years ago, based on the belief that Jesus Christ was the son of God sent to save the people on Earth. Christians practice active evangelism.

Judaism was founded about 3000 years ago. Jews consider themselves to be the Chosen People of God, and to be Jewish you have to be born of a Jewish mother.

Buddhism was founded in the 6th century BC by Gautama Buddha. The teaching is to follow an eight-fold path of behaviors to reach enlightenment. Anyone can become a Buddhist. It is gaining great popularity in the West.

Hinduism was founded in prehistoric India. It teaches that to reach perfection, people have to be born into many different lives and therefore one should respect all life forms.

Many different kinds of worship exist among the tribal peoples of North and South America, Australia and the Pacific Islands, Asia and India. Their rituals and ceremonies are closely bound up in the fertility of the land and the spiritual life of the tribe. In contrast, many people in the developed countries are turning against the idea of monotheistic, paternal religion altogether—some through the pagan and Druid traditions of pre-Christianity.

▼ LANGUAGE "FAMILIES"

The languages of the world are grouped together into families, sets of languages related by structure even though their individual vocabularies may be different [C]. Indo-European is the largest language family in the world with 8 main branches. It includes English, French and German as well as the Slavic languages of Eastern Europe and those of the Indian subcontinent. The oldest known member of this language family is Sanskrit. Other language families include Sino-Tibetan, incorporating the many different tongues spoken in China. A very few languages remain linguistic puzzles: Basque, which is spoken in a small area of southwest France and northern Spain appears to be related to no other language either living or dead.

C

Dravidian
Germanic
Indo-Iranian
Semitic
Caucasian
Monk-Khmer
Sino-Tibetan

Sanskrit
Afro-Asiatic
Cushitic
Niger-Congo
Khoisan
Indian
Latin
Austronesian
Papuan
Melanesian
Mongolian
Turkic
Balto-Slavic
Japanese/Korean
Irano-Armenian
Others

◄ COLONIAL INFLUENCE

The influence of colonialism can be traced on a map showing the official languages of the countries of the world [D]. Spanish and Portuguese are spoken in South and Central America; English in North America, India and parts of Africa. French is still the official language in most of its former colonies—and for historical reasons remains the language of diplomacy. More people speak Mandarin Chinese than any other language.

D

English   Arabic   Portuguese

French   Spanish   Russian

THE WORLD AT WORK

THE DEVELOPMENT OF SOCIETY can be looked at as a series of industrial revolutions, as man has learned to use the Earth's resources. Ancient history divides up into three such stages: the Stone Age, when humans first learned to make stone tools and began to practice agriculture; the Bronze Age, when pure metals were first refined and used; and the Iron Age, when man discovered how to extract iron from rock and cast or forge it into tools and weapons.

The greatest industrial leaps have come in the past three centuries. New scientific discoveries led to the construction of the first steam engines, which transformed industry as well as transport. Iron was then overtaken by steel, and the chemical and electrical industries developed. Plastics, electrical transistors and silicon chips became part of everyday life. Each new wave of industries has had a far-reaching effect on society: employment rises and falls, new methods of transport become available and global trade opens up. With each "revolution" a world economy is brought closer, fueling an ever-increasing demand for energy.

The source of power

The first Industrial Revolution depended on coal to produce the iron and fire the steam engines. Today, the vast majority of the world's energy still comes from fossil fuels such as coal, oil and natural gas which are a finite resource. Coal is still burnt to generate electricity, supplying about 28 per cent of our total energy needs. The internal combustion engine has created an insatiable demand for petroleum. Today, oil reserves supply 40 per cent of the world's energy, and natural gas 20 per cent. As well as being a finite resource, fossil fuels are a major source of pollution, contributing to the greenhouse effect and the global warming that it brings. In the long term, other sources of energy will have to be found.

Energy alternatives

Nuclear power comes from the splitting of heavy uranium atoms, accompanied by the release of energy in a process called "fission." In many countries this energy has been harnessed for electricity needs, but there are many problems, particularly the long-term storage of waste products. Research continues into nuclear fusion, the process which powers the Sun. Although much more difficult to achieve, this could be a cleaner way of generating cheap energy. There are pollution-free energy sources. Hydroelectric power is used in countries such as Switzerland, where water provides more than half of all energy requirements, but it can have a great impact on the environment, flooding valleys and destroying ecosystems. Tidal power exploits the energy of the sea in a similar way. Windmills were one of our earliest sources of power. Today, wind-farms are sited on exposed coasts or on offshore spits, and some countries hope to be able to generate 10 to 20 percent of energy needs in this way in the next decade or so. California, for instance, has tens of thousands of wind turbines.

The demand for energy is highest in the USA and western Europe, which are heavily industrialized and also have large consumer societies. At the same time, increasing consumption of oil has led to the rise in power and wealth of Middle Eastern countries where two-thirds of the world's reserves are located. The Industrial

A

○	<10%
○	11-25%
○	26-50%
○	51-74%
○	<75%

▲ **THE GLOBAL ECONOMY**
The engine-houses of today's global economy are those countries that produce the most consumer goods. Map A is shaded according to the percentage of each country's total exports that are manufactured goods. It clearly demonstrates that the most successful manufacturing economies are concentrated in the richer northern hemisphere of the world. Almost the whole of Europe and North America have figures over 50%, but the best performers are in Central Europe and the Far East. These include traditionally industrial nations, such as Germany and Japan, as well as fast-growing economies like Korea, Taiwan and the

Czech Republic.

The world's biggest producers of food are its largest countries in terms of area and population. However, although there is an overall excess of food, some countries, particularly in Africa, are still susceptible to famine. The reasons for this are both political and environmental. Traditionally farmed areas of land are often cleared to make way for so-called "cash crops," and instead of using the land for self-sufficiency, an export-driven economy is created, with newly-displaced farmers to support. At the other extreme, the United States farms staple crops successfully on a massive scale, producing surpluses which can then be sold to smaller countries.

◄ **ENERGY**
The driving force of an economy is energy [B], so the balance between the energy a country produces—in the form of coal, oil and other fuels—and the amount it consumes is vital. This table shows the ratio for the main regions of the world. In many areas the balance is even, but some, such as Europe, produce 12% of world energy, but consume 17%.

▲ Wind turbines, pictured here in Palm Springs, California, are being viewed as an increasingly viable way of producing energy. Europe, especially Holland and Germany, has a number of these eco-friendly farms.

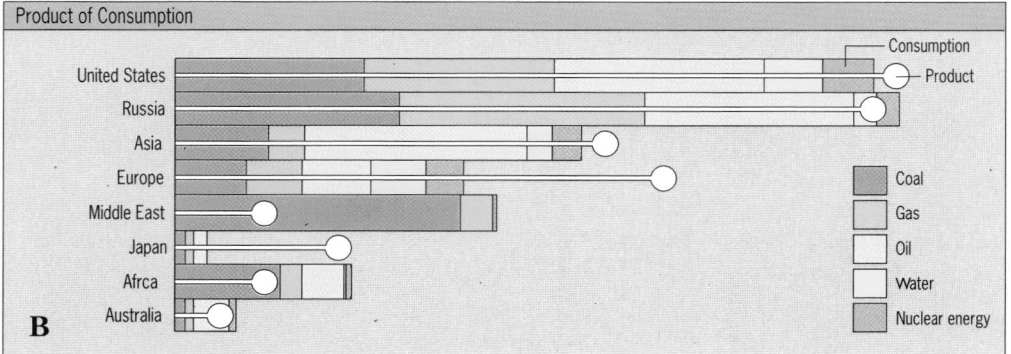

Product of Consumption

- United States
- Russia
- Asia
- Europe
- Middle East
- Japan
- Afrca
- Australia

B

- ○ Consumption
- ○ Product

- Coal
- Gas
- Oil
- Water
- Nuclear energy

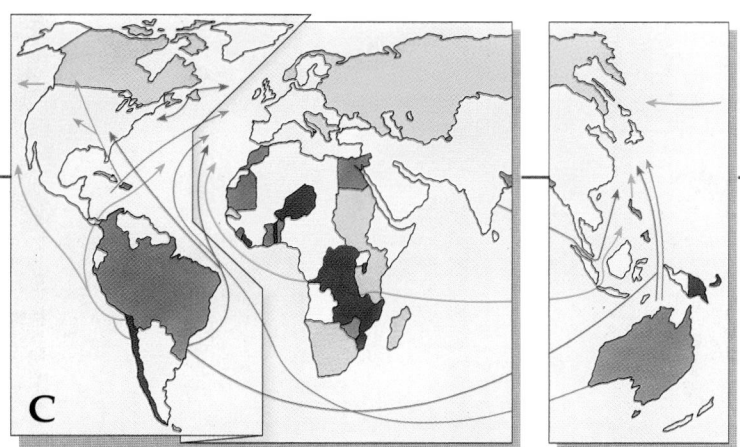

Copper
Iron
Bauxite

- 5-9%
- >5%
- >50%
- 10-49%

C

▲ MINERALS

Mineral deposits can often be the key to a nation's economy [C]. Jamaica has extensive bauxite and alumina deposits —the raw material for the production of aluminium— which account for almost half the country's total exports.

Mineral deposits are not only valued for their practical

uses: gemstones can also bring in considerable income. Central and Southern Africa were the world's largest producers but are now threatened by the deposits in Australia, and those in Russia which have yet to be fully exploited, but which could flood and destabilize the market. If in the future the

market is flooded with Russian diamonds, the market could collapse.

Many other minerals and metal ores are concentrated only in rocks which have undergone extensive weathering, or around mountain ranges, which have seen intense metamorphic processes in the past.

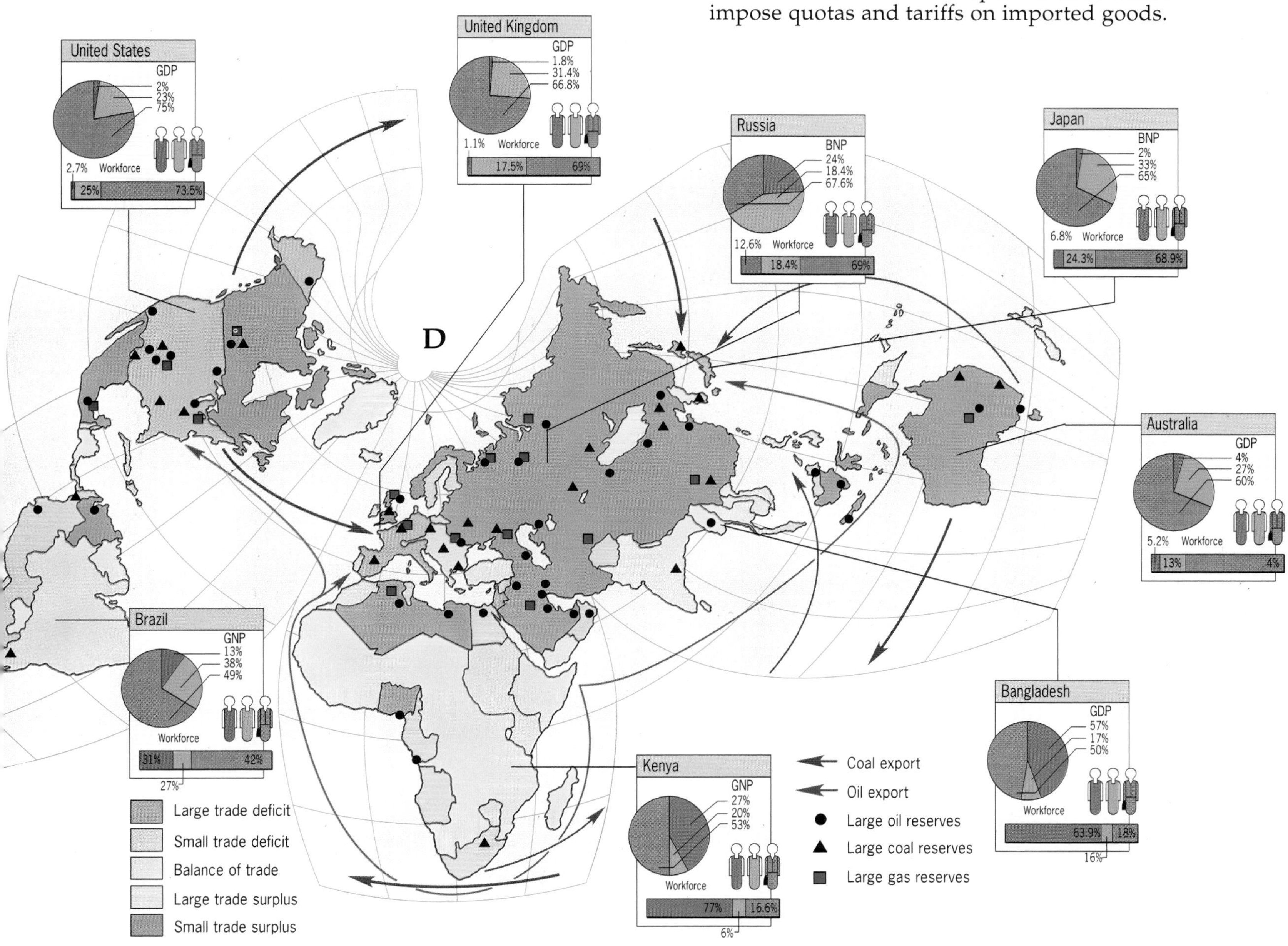

Revolution, which·began in Britain, soon spread through the rest of Europe. Apart from America, the industrialization of the rest of the world was the result of investment by colonial European powers, taking advantage of cheap labor and raw materials, and faster, cheaper transport which turned the world into a single complex economy.

In the last fifty years the rest of the world has also developed major industries, overtaking the West. Japan became one of the world's great economic powers by heavy investment in new technology, and other nations are following its example. The pattern is now reversed as Far Eastern companies open manufacturing plants in the West to provide goods for the lucrative consumer markets. Often, these plants assemble imported components, but they also provide access to the major economic blocs, such as the United States and the European Union, which impose quotas and tariffs on imported goods.

United States
GDP
2%
23%
75%
2.7% Workforce
25%   73.5%

United Kingdom
GDP
1.8%
31.4%
66.8%
1.1% Workforce
17.5%   69%

Russia
BNP
24%
18.4%
67.6%
12.6% Workforce
18.4%   69%

Japan
BNP
2%
33%
65%
6.8% Workforce
24.3%   68.9%

Australia
GDP
4%
27%
60%
5.2% Workforce
13%   4%

D

Brazil
GNP
13%
38%
49%
Workforce
31%   42%
27%

Kenya
GNP
27%
20%
53%
Workforce
77%   16.6%
6%

Bangladesh
GDP
57%
17%
50%
Workforce
63.9%   18%
16%

- Coal export
- Oil export
- ● Large oil reserves
- ▲ Large coal reserves
- ■ Large gas reserves

- Large trade deficit
- Small trade deficit
- Balance of trade
- Large trade surplus
- Small trade surplus

▲ THE LABOR FORCE

The relative economic development of various countries can be seen by comparing the numbers of people employed in different types of work, and the contribution to the gross domestic product (GDP) made by each [D]. Developing

countries such as Bangladesh have a high proportion of labor involved in agriculture, which is responsible for a comparatively high proportion of GDP. Nigeria is similar, but its extensive oil reserves account for a higher industrial contribution to GDP.

As countries make more use of natural resources, more of the population is employed in heavy industry, creating more wealth, while improvements in agriculture lead to increased efficiency, and a reduction in the numbers employed. The agricultural output tends to

remain steady, so that its contribution as a percentage of GDP decreases. In the most developed nations the majority of the workforce is employed in the manufacture and service sectors.

The graphics in the illustration [C] show the labor

forces of several countries. The bar at the bottom gives the percentage involved in the agricultural (brown), industrial (blue) and service (gray) sectors, while the pie chart shows the contribution that each of these sectors makes to the GDP of that country.

ON THE MOVE

Once the majority of humanity had settled down into permanent villages, towns and cities, they began to devise ways to travel between them to trade and treaty. It was quickly realized that whoever controlled trade routes or devised the quickest means of transport would be at an advantage. Just as today, communications were all-important.

At first, people could only move as far as they could walk in a day, at most 20 mi. Around 8000 years ago, as farming was becoming established, some domesticated animals were employed as a means of transport. This did not make travel much faster, but enabled more goods to be carried or pulled along on sleds.

The great transportation breakthrough was of course the wheel, which was invented about 5000 years ago somewhere in the eastern Mediterranean. The earliest known example of wheeled transport is an Egyptian chariot, built about 2000 BC. Horse-drawn chariots formed a rapid transport communications network in all the great empires and kingdoms, where rulers needed to know what was going on all over their territory.

Chariots could go faster if they had straight roads to run along. The first road network was established around 1122 BC in China under the emperor Chou, but the most famous road system, traces of which still exist today, was established in the Roman Empire. In engineering terms, probably the most impressive road system was built by the Incas of Peru. Built entirely of dry stone, the 2983 mi. system wound over the steep slopes of the western Andes. These roads were for messengers on horse or foot: the Incas never used the wheel for transport.

Ships and the sea

The development of sea travel parallels that of roads. Empires that needed good internal communications along roads also needed to reach trading partners quickly and efficiently by sea. The oar was developed around the same time and in the same part of the world as the wheel. At once a propellant and a steering device, the oar made it possible to control speed and direction. The Phoenicians, a people from the eastern Mediterranean, combined oars with sail power in the galley, a long ship powered by a row of oars along each side. This eventually developed into the the Greek and Roman *trireme*, with three rows of oars on each side, which needed 200 rowers to power it.

Between the 14th and the 17th centuries ships and sea trading shaped the world. In 1300 northern European shipbuilders invented the rudder: before that, ships had been steered by a set of oars at the stern. In the mid-1400s, the Portuguese developed the three-masted ship, which at once increased sail-power, but kept the sails small enough to be easily handled. From the 15th to 17th centuries, these ships were used and developed by many nations, and oceans were crisscrossed by Portuguese, Dutch, Spanish and English ships claiming new colonies and discovering new trade routes.

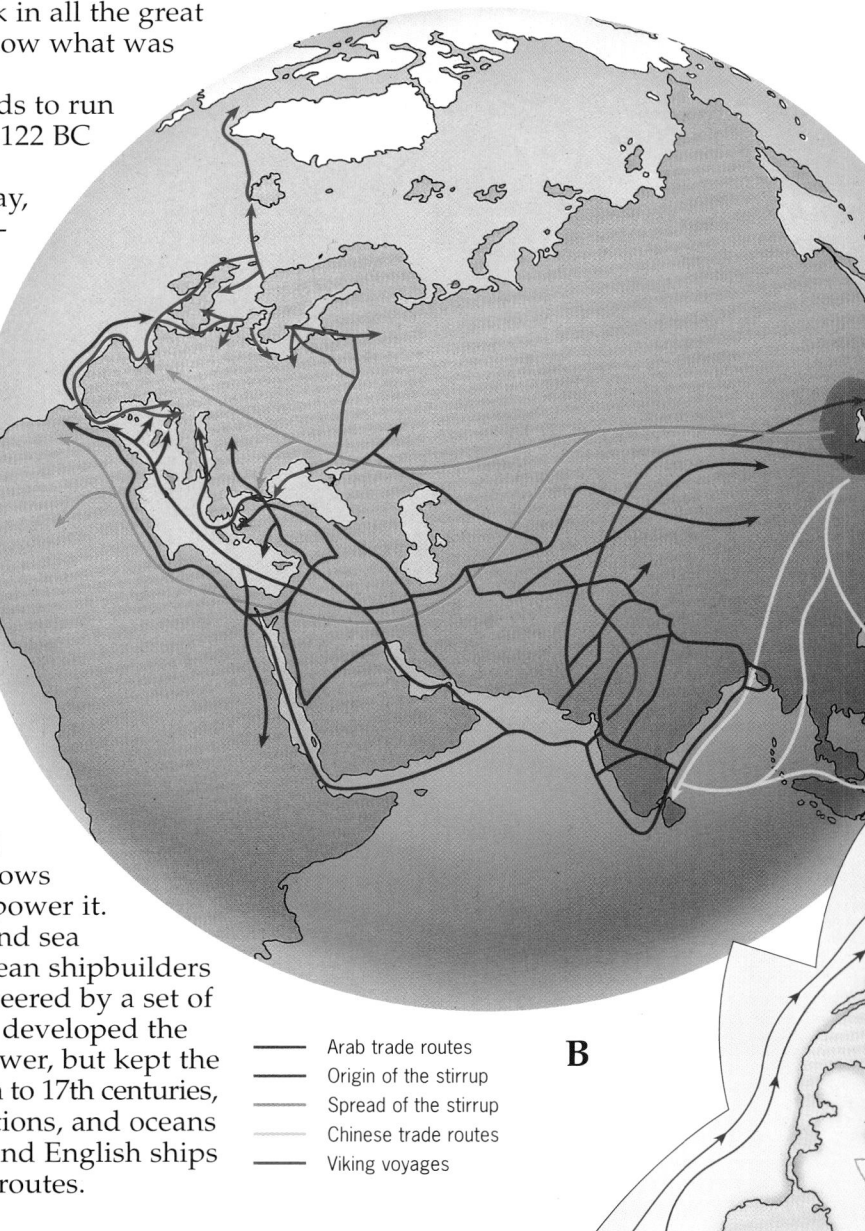

A

Great Wall

Silk Road

Trade routes

— Roman roads
■ Roman Empire
■ Chinese Empire

▲ **EARLY ROAD SYSTEMS**
In the first few centuries of the Christian era, the landmass of Eurasia was dominated by empires at its east and west extremes [A]. Transport was central to both these realms. In Europe, the Romans built an extensive network of roads which allowed troops, administrators, tax collectors and traders to travel quickly from one end of the empire to the other.

Under the Han Dynasty, China began extensive trade. As well as extensive sea-trading routes, there was the old Silk Road linking oases across the deserts of central Asia, along which caravans carried China's silks and spices as far as the Greek and Roman worlds.

— Arab trade routes
— Origin of the stirrup
— Spread of the stirrup
— Chinese trade routes
— Viking voyages

B

▲ **THE DARK AGES**
The fall of the Roman Empire was a signal for mass movement across the known world. Arab traders opened trade routes that extended from Spain to China.

During the Dark Ages, both Europe and Asia were subject to raids by the Mongols, whose use of the stirrup gave them a mastery of warfare on horseback. The invention of the stirrup had spread from India to the Mongols by the 4th century, and to Europe three centuries later [B]. The Mongolian war bands swept eastward toward Europe, displacing Huns, Vandals, Goths, Ostrogoths, Visigoths and Alans who moved into the western part of Europe, in turn displacing the Franks who moved from what is now

Germany into France. The native Gauls and Celts were pushed up into the corners of Brittany.

The Vikings used their ocean-going longboats to raid many European coastal areas as well as penetrating inland along the great rivers. Some may have even reached the coast of North America.

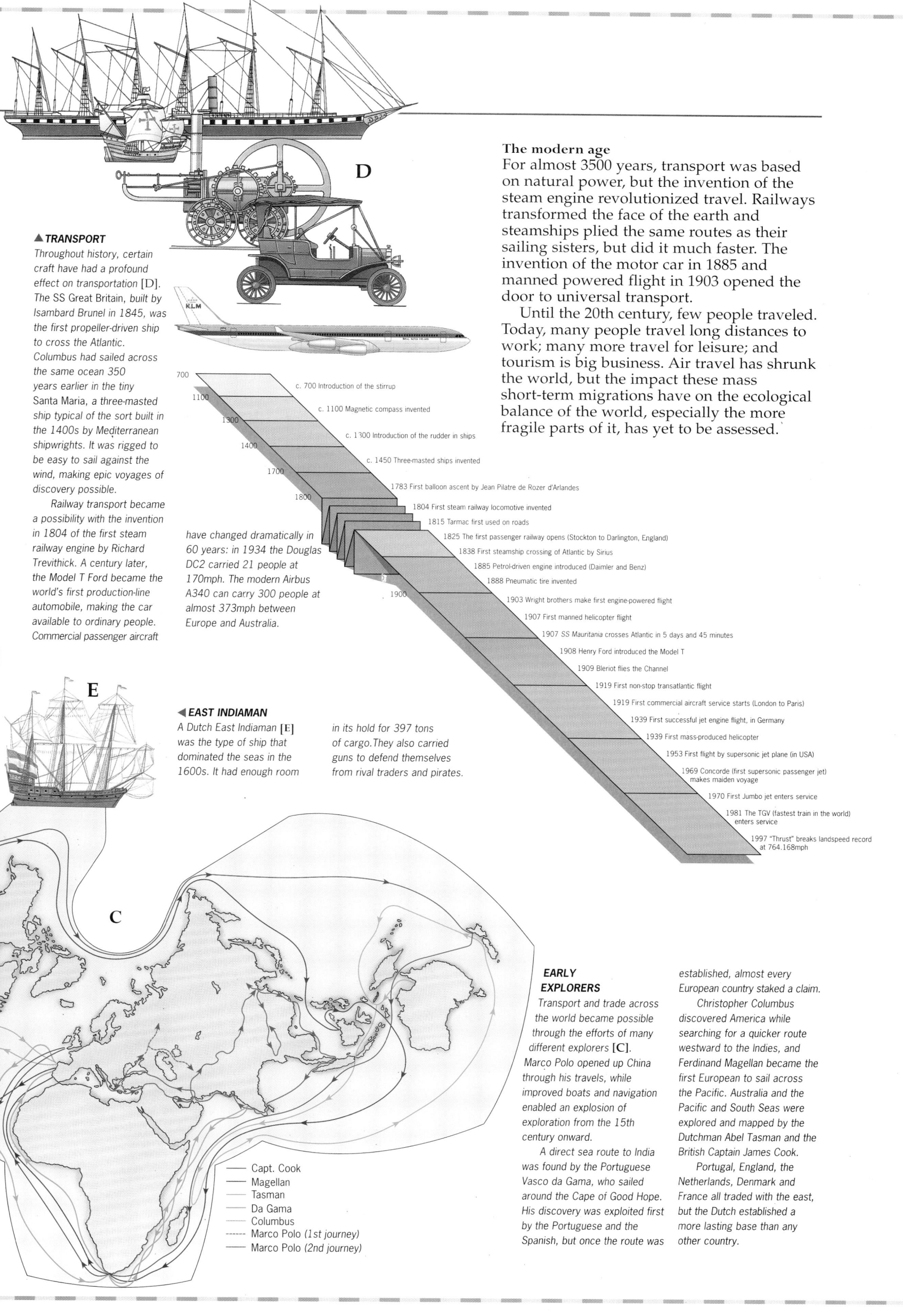

▲ TRANSPORT

Throughout history, certain craft have had a profound effect on transportation [D]. The SS Great Britain, built by Isambard Brunel in 1845, was the first propeller-driven ship to cross the Atlantic. Columbus had sailed across the same ocean 350 years earlier in the tiny Santa Maria, a three-masted ship typical of the sort built in the 1400s by Mediterranean shipwrights. It was rigged to be easy to sail against the wind, making epic voyages of discovery possible.

Railway transport became a possibility with the invention in 1804 of the first steam railway engine by Richard Trevithick. A century later, the Model T Ford became the world's first production-line automobile, making the car available to ordinary people. Commercial passenger aircraft

have changed dramatically in 60 years: in 1934 the Douglas DC2 carried 21 people at 170mph. The modern Airbus A340 can carry 300 people at almost 373mph between Europe and Australia.

The modern age

For almost 3500 years, transport was based on natural power, but the invention of the steam engine revolutionized travel. Railways transformed the face of the earth and steamships plied the same routes as their sailing sisters, but did it much faster. The invention of the motor car in 1885 and manned powered flight in 1903 opened the door to universal transport.

Until the 20th century, few people traveled. Today, many people travel long distances to work; many more travel for leisure; and tourism is big business. Air travel has shrunk the world, but the impact these mass short-term migrations have on the ecological balance of the world, especially the more fragile parts of it, has yet to be assessed.

c. 700 Introduction of the stirrup
c. 1100 Magnetic compass invented
c. 1300 Introduction of the rudder in ships
c. 1450 Three-masted ships invented
1783 First balloon ascent by Jean Pilatre de Rozer d'Arlandes
1804 First steam railway locomotive invented
1815 Tarmac first used on roads
1825 The first passenger railway opens (Stockton to Darlington, England)
1838 First steamship crossing of Atlantic by Sirius
1885 Petrol-driven engine introduced (Daimler and Benz)
1888 Pneumatic tire invented
1903 Wright brothers make first engine-powered flight
1907 First manned helicopter flight
1907 SS Mauritania crosses Atlantic in 5 days and 45 minutes
1908 Henry Ford introduced the Model T
1909 Bleriot flies the Channel
1919 First non-stop transatlantic flight
1919 First commercial aircraft service starts (London to Paris)
1939 First successful jet engine flight, in Germany
1939 First mass-produced helicopter
1953 First flight by supersonic jet plane (in USA)
1969 Concorde (first supersonic passenger jet) makes maiden voyage
1970 First Jumbo jet enters service
1981 The TGV (fastest train in the world) enters service
1997 "Thrust" breaks landspeed record at 764.168mph

◄ EAST INDIAMAN

A Dutch East Indiaman [E] was the type of ship that dominated the seas in the 1600s. It had enough room in its hold for 397 tons of cargo. They also carried guns to defend themselves from rival traders and pirates.

EARLY EXPLORERS

Transport and trade across the world became possible through the efforts of many different explorers [C]. Marco Polo opened up China through his travels, while improved boats and navigation enabled an explosion of exploration from the 15th century onward.

A direct sea route to India was found by the Portuguese Vasco da Gama, who sailed around the Cape of Good Hope. His discovery was exploited first by the Portuguese and the Spanish, but once the route was

established, almost every European country staked a claim.

Christopher Columbus discovered America while searching for a quicker route westward to the Indies, and Ferdinand Magellan became the first European to sail across the Pacific. Australia and the Pacific and South Seas were explored and mapped by the Dutchman Abel Tasman and the British Captain James Cook.

Portugal, England, the Netherlands, Denmark and France all traded with the east, but the Dutch established a more lasting base than any other country.

— Capt. Cook
— Magellan
— Tasman
— Da Gama
— Columbus
- - - Marco Polo (1st journey)
— Marco Polo (2nd journey)

THE LEGACY OF INDUSTRY

MODERN INDUSTRIAL SOCIETY PLACES GREAT DEMANDS on the Earth's natural resources and the environment, constantly increasing demand for materials and energy. Not only is our way of life diminishing our planet's resources rapidly, but industry often produces harmful by-products. One of the best-known examples is the hole in the ozone layer. Aerosol spray cans were invented in the 1950s, using chlorofluorocarbons (CFCs) as propellants. The harmful effect on the environment was only realized after the discovery of a hole forming in the ozone layer high above the Antarctic. Ozone exists mainly at high altitudes where it absorbs harmful ultraviolet light from the Sun—radiation so intense that it would render the Earth uninhabitable if it reached the surface unchecked. CFC molecules break down the ozone molecules, but remain unaltered themselves, so that one CFC molecule can destroy many ozone molecules. An international agreement has now banned the manufacture of CFCs, but it will be several more years before the expansion of the ozone hole comes to a halt.

Global greenhouse

Industrialization and our increasingly energy-hungry society have lead to the production of high levels of carbon dioxide (CO_2). The major effect is to trap heat near the Earth's surface, and prevent its reflection into space. The average temperature of the planet may rise, melting some of the Polar ice caps and raising sea levels, posing major problems for low-lying countries in the next century. First predictions suggested that the sea level would rise up to 24in. in the next century, compared to around 6in. this century.

Ironically, these predictions are now being revised downward because of a newly-discovered "benefit" of a different industrial pollutant. Oxides of sulphur in the atmosphere, a by-product of coal burning, actually have a cooling effect on the Earth, but they create another major problem—acid rain. Many industrial processes produce oxides of sulphur and nitrogen, which rise high into the atmosphere and are carried over great distances by the wind. Acid rain forms when the molecules come into contact with water, falling on land up to 621 mi. away. It can slowly poison and kill entire forests and wipe out fish stocks in lakes.

The Scandinavian countries have been particularly affected by this problem—prevailing winds from heavily industrialized countries such as Britain blow the pollution toward them. Evergreen forests have been badly damaged as the acid rainfall not only acidifies the soil, but also increases the uptake of alkaline molecules, draining the soil even more. Nutrients are washed out of the acidified soil, and poisonous metals released. Because the

▼ **CAUSE AND EFFECT**
The effects of human activity on a landscape can be seen by examining the changes in a fictional town over two centuries of industrialization [A]. Where there was once a village on a riverbank [1] there is now an urban sprawl, suffering from

pollution. This comes from many sources: industrial effluent and gas emissions; agricultural run-off of pesticides and fertilizers into the water course; exhaust emissions from road transport; the waste of the chemical and oil industries; and the possible radioactive poisoning of the environment from nuclear power stations.

At sea and in ports, oil spills are common. Even in the air, jet aircraft can leave lingering trails of exhaust gas, as well as habitually dumping unused fuel over built-up areas. And they add to a further taint of urban life—all-pervading noise pollution.

Agriculture
- Pesticides and herbicides can affect farmers' health and leave residues on food.
- Fertilizers percolate through to ground water, raising nitrate levels in tap water.

Transportation
- Gas engines produce roughly 330 million tons of poisonous carbon monoxide each year.
- Diesel engines create particulates, tiny granules of soot that can cause respiratory problems.

Chemical Industry
- Oil slicks are visible in every ocean and along the coast of most continents.
- Most plastics do not break down readily. Beaches covered with plastic flotsam are now a familiar but unwelcome sight.

Nuclear Power
- Each year nuclear power stations in the USA produce 16,534 tons of high-level waste, which needs to be stored for 10,000 years before it is safe—longer than any human civilization has lasted.

Industrial pollution
- Carbon dioxide emissions contribute to the Greenhouse effect.
- Poisonous heavy metals from industrial processes flow into rivers and enter the food chain.

A

▲ *Smoke pours out of an industrial complex and pollutes the atmosphere. Governments across the globe have brought in legislation in an attempt to control them but there is little success, especially in Asia.*

▶ **THE GREENHOUSE EFFECT**
Carbon dioxide (CO_2), makes up only 0.035% of the Earth's atmosphere but is an important component as it traps the heat of the Sun in the Greenhouse effect [B]. Of incoming sunlight, 25% is reflected back into space by gases in the upper atmosphere [1]. A further 25% of the radiation is reflected back or absorbed by clouds [2]. Roughly 5% is immediately reflected by the Earth's surface [3], leaving 45% which is absorbed. The sunlight enters the atmosphere as relatively short wavelength ultraviolet and visible radiation, to which CO_2 is transparent. It is re-emitted by the Earth as longer wavelength infrared radiation, which CO_2 does absorb. This means that only 12% of the re-emitted radiation escapes into space [4] but 88% is reflected back to the ground, conserving the planet's heat [5]. The graph [C] shows how the average surface temperature of the

Earth has been increasing over the last few years [D], an effect that some scientists attribute to the increasing amount of CO_2 in the atmosphere due to the burning of fossil fuels. The warming may simply be part of a natural cycle, and could be countered by the cooling effects of other pollutants.

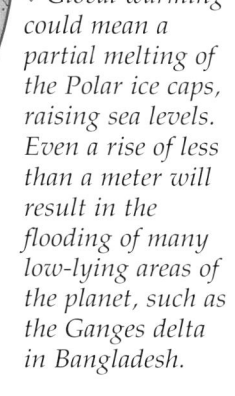

▲ **THE OZONE HOLE**
In 1985 it was discovered that the level of protective ozone in the stratosphere above Antarctica had dropped dramatically. This "hole" was caused by refrigerants called CFCs, whose production has now been banned.

B

C

C°
4°
3°
2°
1°
Temperature

CO_2
Surface temp.

1875 1900 1925 1950 1975 2000

D

1
2
3
4

5

▼ *Global warming could mean a partial melting of the Polar ice caps, raising sea levels. Even a rise of less than a meter will result in the flooding of many low-lying areas of the planet, such as the Ganges delta in Bangladesh.*

acidity affects the soil first, the effects can spread through an entire forest before they start to show up in dying trees.

Water tables and rivers can be tainted either by leakage from industrial sites, or by "run-off" of pesticides and fertilizers from agricultural land. Ground water is particularly vulnerable. In some places rainwater soaks into the ground and collects in underground reservoirs called aquifers. Aquifers provide a large proportion of water supplies, but can easily absorb agricultural chemicals, sewage or industrial waste soaking into the ground. Once polluted, they are difficult to clean up.

Not all ecological problems are caused by heavy industry. Across the world, deserts are spreading, not just because of changing climate, but because of the increasing needs of farmers who depend on the land that borders them. Constant grazing and cropping without ever giving the soil a chance to recover saps it of nutrients and moisture. Winds then blow away the topsoil, leaving an arid, infertile wasteland, which in turn prevents cloud formation and rain in the area. The deforestation of the rain forests also leaves topsoil which can only be farmed for a short time before becoming exhausted.

A hopeful future
We are still discovering many of the side effects of modern industry. But recognizing the problems is the first step towards solving them through methods such as recycling and the development of alternative energy sources and manufacturing processes.

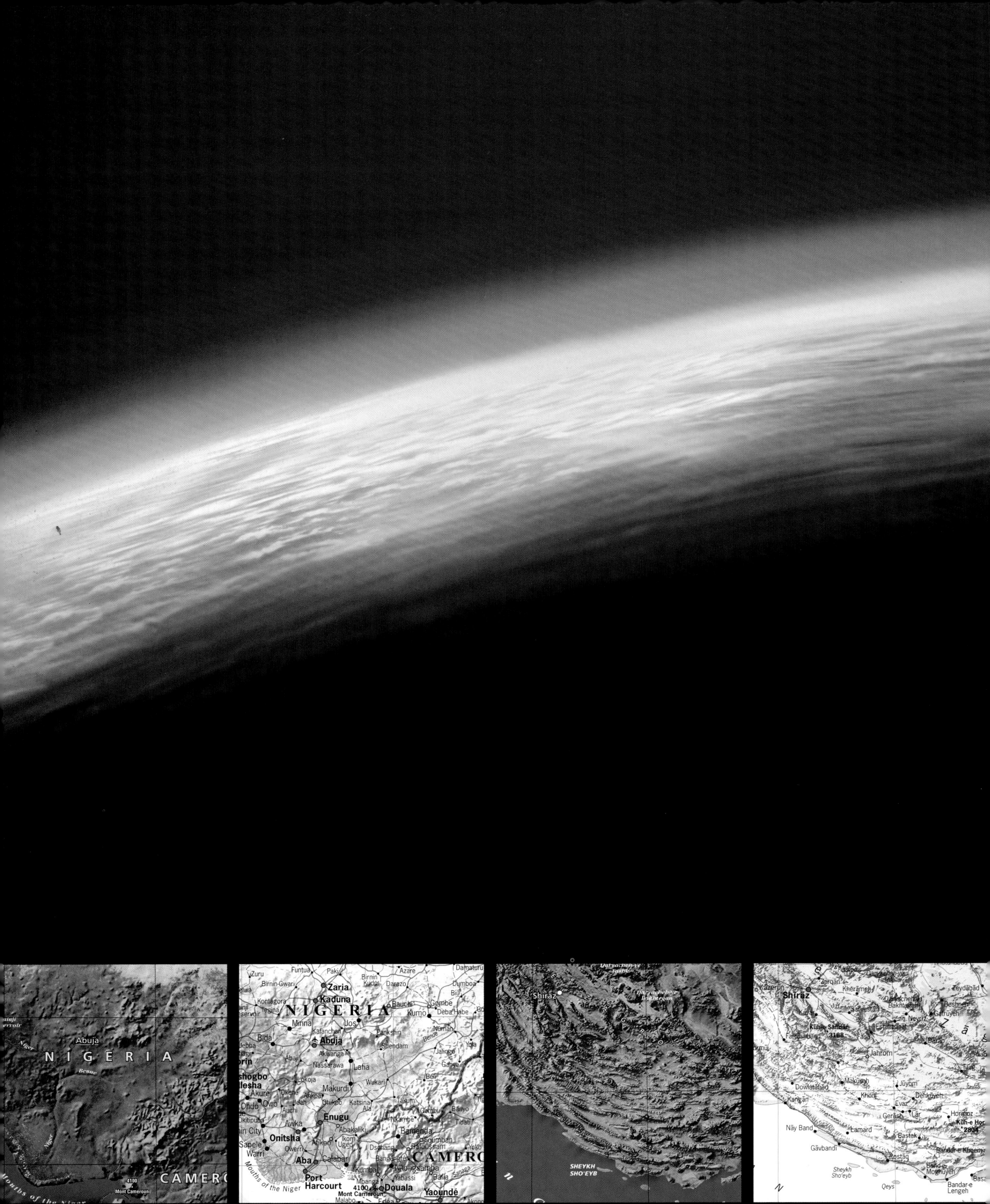

Maps
of the
World

Forty-eight pairs of full color satellite images and maps covering the world. Each pair created to the same projection for easy comparison. Each satellite image enhanced with elevation data, plus a layer of cartographic information related directly to the detail on the map. The following pages provide a unique view of our Earth—lines and symbols of traditional maps seen for the first time alongside images of the world as seen from space.

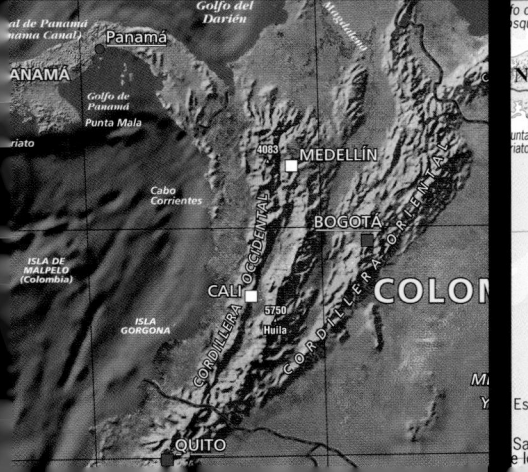

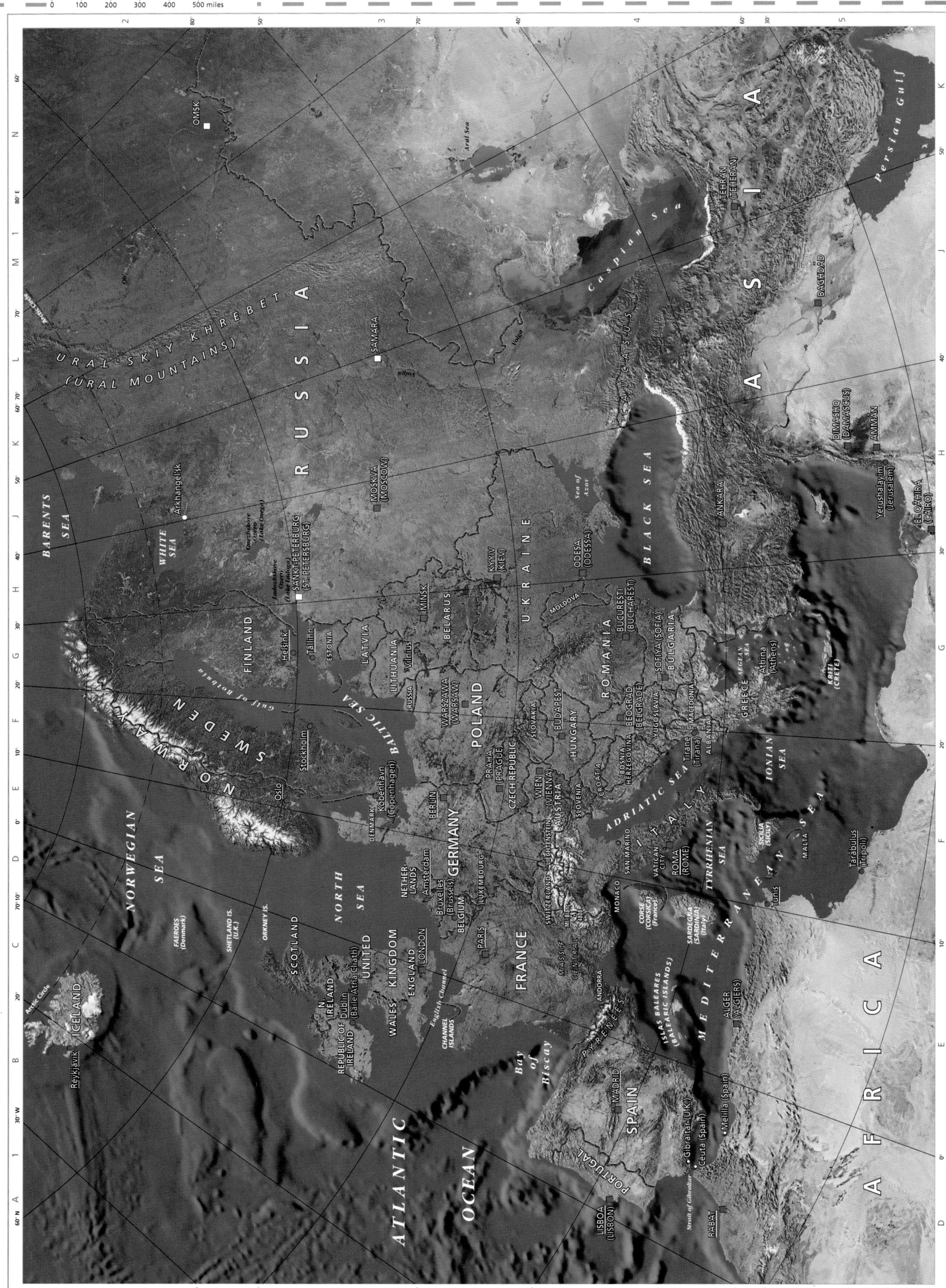

Scale 1 : 22 700 000

56

© Copyright

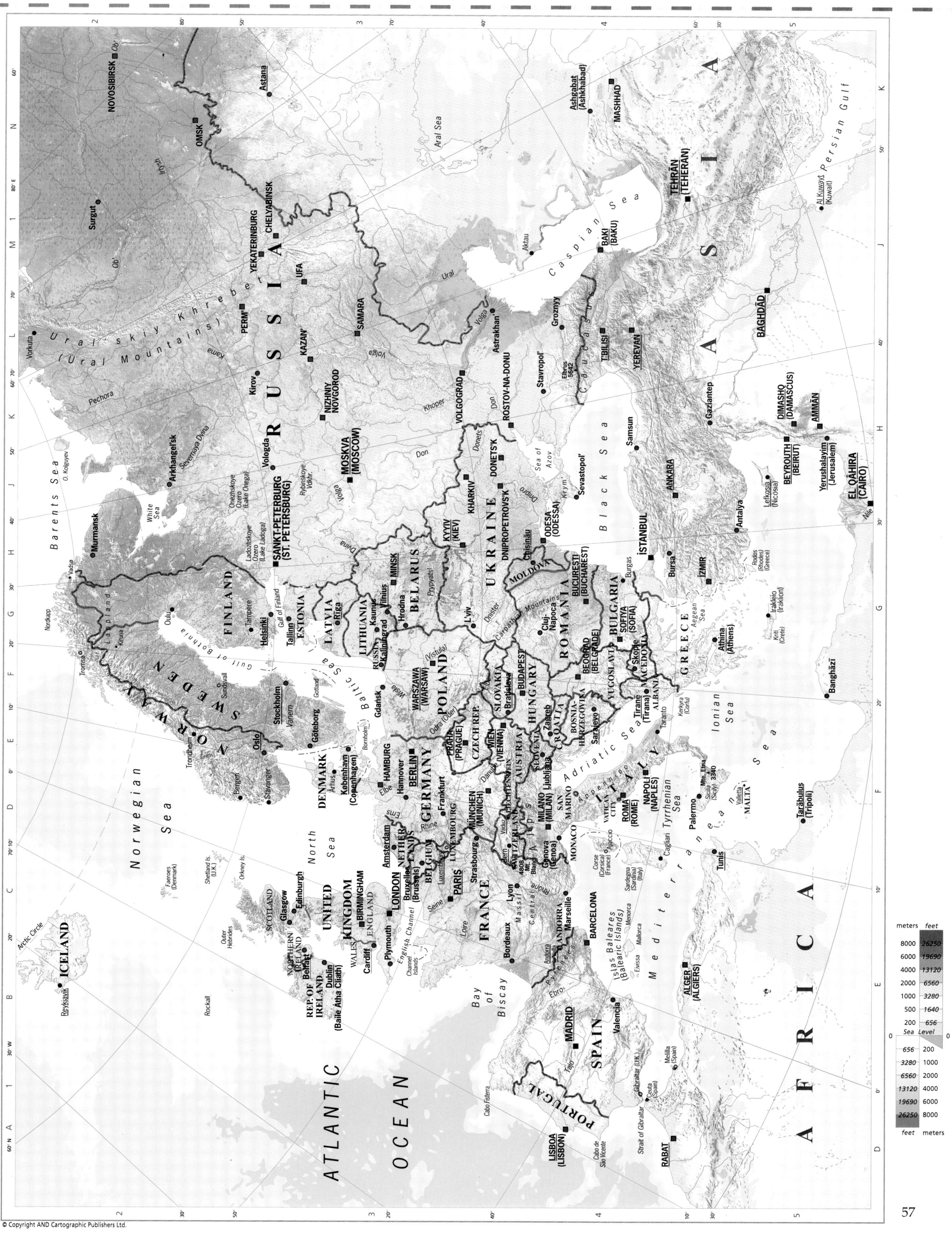

RUSSIA

NOVOSIBIRSK
Astana
OMSK
Surgut
Vorkuta

Barents Sea

Murmansk
White Sea

Arkhangel'sk

Ural'skiy Khrebet
(Ural Mountains)
Pechora
Severnaya Dvina

Onezhskoye
Ozero (Lake Onega)
Vologda

PERM'
YEKATERINBURG
CHELYABINSK
UFA

Kirov
KAZAN'
SAMARA

NIZHNIY
NOVGOROD

Volga

Aral Sea

Aktau

Caspian Sea

Ashgabat
(Ashkhabad)
MASHHAD

TEHRĀN
(TEHERĀN)

Al Kuwayt
(Kuwait)

Persian Gulf

A S I A

BĀKŪ
(BAKU)

Grozny

BAGHDĀD

Elbrus
5642
Caucasus

TBILISI

YEREVAN

Gaziantep

DIMASHQ
(DAMASCUS)
AMMĀN

ANKARA

BEYROUTH
(BEIRUT)

Yerushalayim
(Jerusalem)

EL QĀHIRA
(CAIRO)

Nile

MOSKVA
(MOSCOW)

Astrakhan'

VOLGOGRAD

ROSTOV-NA-DONU

Stavropol'

Sevastopol'

Sea of Azov

Samsun

Antalya

İZMIR

İSTANBUL

Bursa

Rodos
(Rhodes)
(Greece)

Irakleio
(Iraklion)

Lefkosia
(Nicosia)

SANKT-PETERBURG
(ST. PETERSBURG)

Ladozhskoye
Ozero (Lake Ladoga)

FINLAND
Tampere
Helsinki

KYYIV
(KIEV)

U K R A I N E

KHARKIV

DNIPROPETROVS'K

ODESA
(ODESSA)

DONETS'K

Chisinau

MOLDOVA

BUCUREŞTI
(BUCHAREST)

ROMANIA

Cluj-
Napoca

Black Sea

Burgas

SOFIYA
(SOFIA)

BULGARIA

İstanbul

Aegean Sea

GREECE

Athina
(Athens)

Krit
(Crete)

Bangħāzī

NORWAY

SWEDEN

Tromsø
Narvik

Lapland
Kiruna

Oulu

Bodø

Trondheim

Sundsvall

Gulf of Bothnia

Tallinn
ESTONIA

Riga
LATVIA

Vilnius
LITHUANIA

Kaunas
RUSSIA
Kaliningrad

Hrodna

MINSK
BELARUS

Pripyats'

Lviv

Dnestr

Carpathian Mountains

MOLDOVA

Danube

Oslo
Stockholm
Vänern
Göteborg

Baltic Sea

Gdansk
Bornholm

WARSZAWA
(WARSAW)

POLAND

Wisła

Odra (Oder)

Reykjavík

ICELAND

Faeroes
(Denmark)

Shetland Is.
(U.K.)

Orkney Is.

DENMARK
København
(Copenhagen)
Århus

HAMBURG
Hanover
BERLIN
GERMANY
Elbe
Frankfurt

PRAHA
(PRAGUE)
CZECH REP.

SLOVAKIA
Bratislava

WIEN
(VIENNA)
AUSTRIA

BUDAPEST
HUNGARY

Zagreb

Ljubljana
SLOVENIA

CROATIA

BOSNIA
HERZEGOVINA
Sarajevo

BEOGRAD
(BELGRADE)

YUGOSLAVIA

Skopje
MACEDONIA

Tirane
(Tirana)
ALBANIA

Kerkyra
(Corfu)

Ionian Sea

Taranto

Adriatic Sea

Outer
Hebrides

SCOTLAND
Glasgow
Edinburgh

NORTHERN
IRELAND
Belfast

REP. OF
IRELAND
Dublin
(Baile Átha Cliath)

UNITED
KINGDOM
ENGLAND
BIRMINGHAM

WALES
Cardiff

Plymouth

LONDON

North Sea

Amsterdam
NETHERLANDS
Bruxelles
(Brussels)
BELGIUM
LUXEMBOURG

PARIS

Strasbourg

MÜNCHEN
(MUNICH)

Rhine

SWITZERLAND
Bern

Mt.
4808
Mont
Blanc

MILANO
(MILAN)
Genova
(Genoa)

MONACO

VATICAN
CITY
ROMA
(ROME)

SAN
MARINO

NAPOLI
(NAPLES)

Palermo

Mte. Etna
(Sicily) 3340

Valletta
MALTA

TUNIS

Tyrrhenian Sea

English Channel

Channel
Islands

FRANCE

Lyon
Bordeaux

Marseille

Massif
Central

*Bay of
Biscay*

Loire

Seine

Cabo Fisterra

ANDORRA
Andorra

BARCELONA

*Islas Baleares
(Balearic Islands)*

Menorca

Mallorca

Eivissa

ALGER
(ALGIERS)

MADRID
SPAIN

Valencia

Ebro

Tajo

PORTUGAL

LISBOA
(LISBON)

Cabo de
São Vicente

Melilla
(Spain)

Ceuta
(Spain)

Strait of Gibraltar

RABAT

A F R I C A

Tarābulus
(Tripoli)

Mediterranean Sea

ATLANTIC OCEAN

Norwegian Sea

Arctic Circle

Rockall

Faeroes
(Denmark)

meters	feet
8000	26250
6000	19690
4000	13120
2000	6560
1000	3280
500	1640
200	656
0	Sea Level 0

656	200
3280	1000
6560	2000
13120	4000
19690	6000
26250	8000

feet   meters

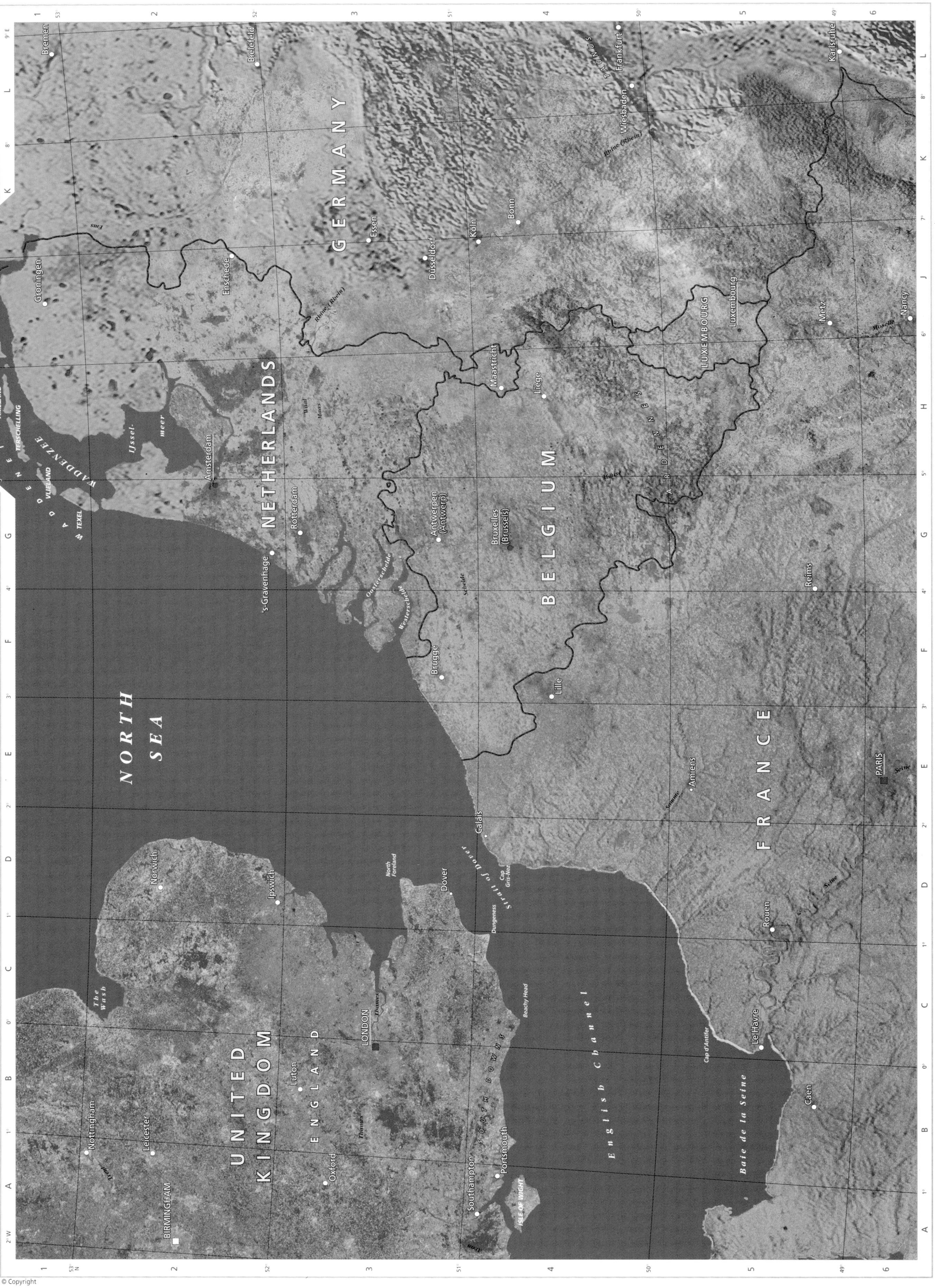

NORTH

SEA

UNITED KINGDOM

ENGLAND

GERMANY

NETHERLANDS

BELGIUM

LUXEMBOURG

FRANCE

English Channel

Bremen
Bielefeld
Frankfurt
TAUNUS
Wiesbaden
Karlsruhe
Rhine (Rhein)
Essen
Köln
Bonn
Düsseldorf
Enschede
Groningen
BORKUM
WADDENZEE
SCHIERMONNIKOOG
AMELAND
TERSCHELLING
VLIELAND
TEXEL
Ijssel-meer
Ijssel
Waal
Maas
Amsterdam
Maastricht
Liège
Luxembourg
Metz
Nancy
Moselle
A R D E N N E S
Sambre
's-Gravenhage
Rotterdam
Antwerpen (Antwerp)
Bruxelles (Brussels)
Oosterschelde
Westerschelde
Schelde
Brugge
Lille
Reims
Amiens
Somme
PARIS
Seine
Calais
Cap Gris-Nez
Strait of Dover
Dungeness
Beachy Head
North Foreland
Dover
Le Havre
Cap d'Antifer
Baie de la Seine
Caen
Rouen
Seine
Norwich
The Wash
Ipswich
Nottingham
Leicester
Luton
Oxford
LONDON
Thames
Southampton
Portsmouth
ISLE OF WIGHT
BIRMINGHAM
Ems

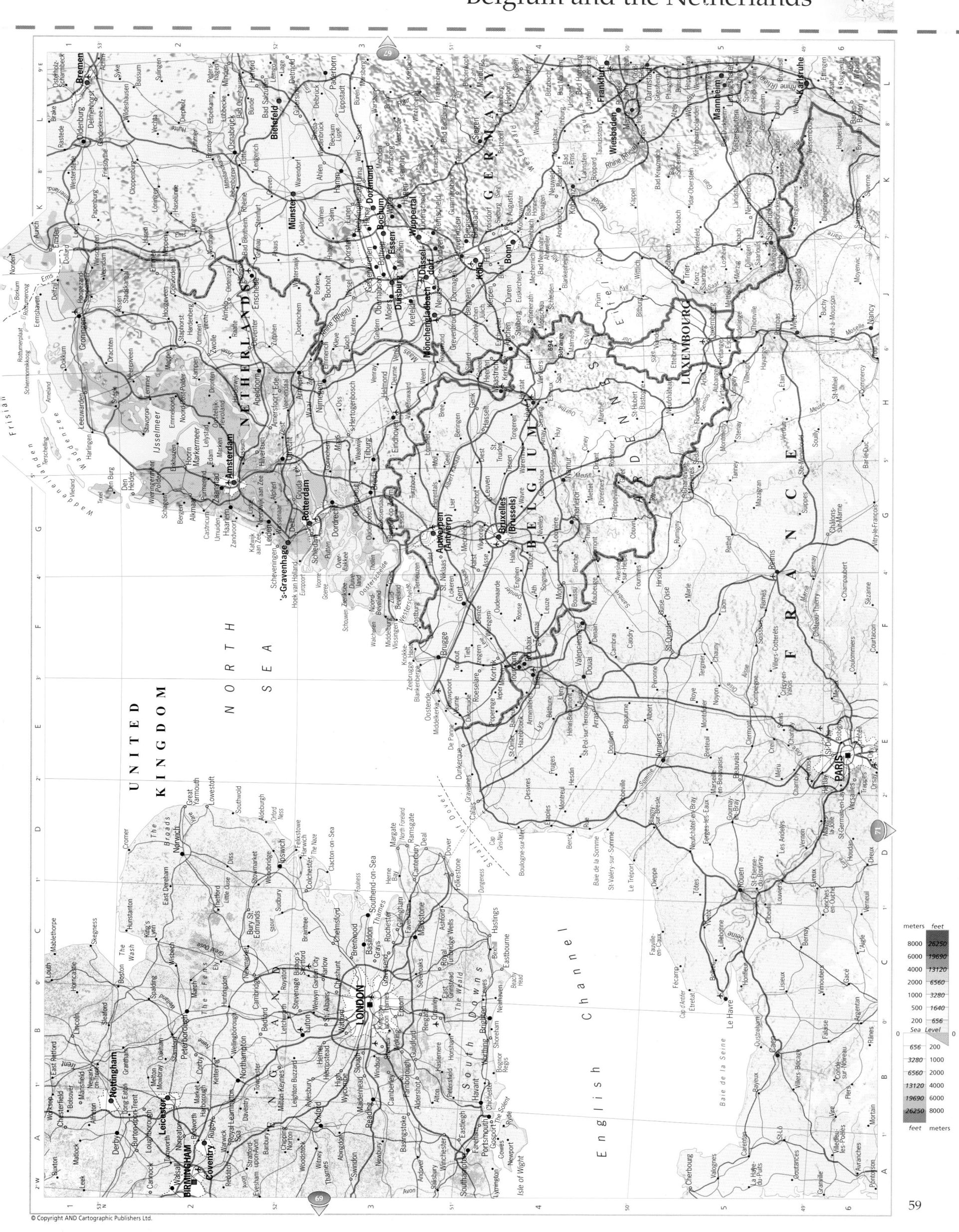

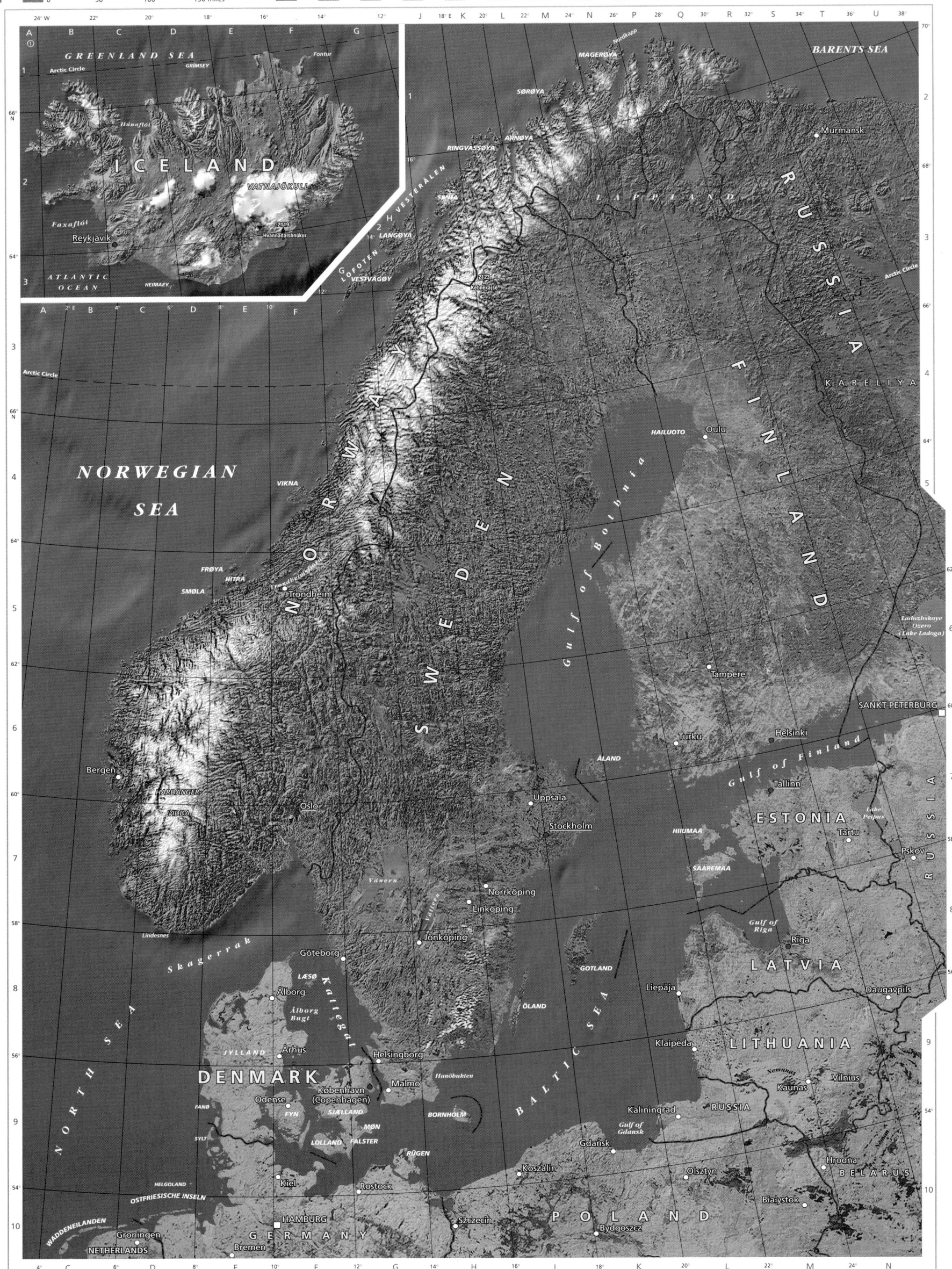

Scale 1 : 6 500 000

100   200   300 km

50   100   150 miles

GREENLAND SEA

Arctic Circle   GRIMSEY   Fontur

Húnaflói

ICELAND

VATNAJÖKULL

Faxaflói

Reykjavik   2119   Hvannadalshnúkur

ATLANTIC OCEAN   HEIMAEY

MAGERØYA   Nordkapp   **BARENTS SEA**

SØRØYA

Murmansk

ARNØYA

RINGVASSØYA   **RUSSIA**

SENJA   **LAPPLAND**

VESTERÅLEN

LANGØYA   2123   Kebnekaise

LOFOTEN   **KARELIYA**

VESTVÅGØY

Arctic Circle

NORWEGIAN

SEA

NORWAY   **FINLAND**

VIKNA

SWEDEN

HAILUOTO   Oulu

FRØYA

HITRA   Ladozhskoye Ozero (Lake Ladoga)

SMØLA   Trondheim

Tampere

SANKT-PETERBURG

Turku   Helsinki

Bergen   ÅLAND   **Gulf of Finland**

HARDANGER   Tallinn   **ESTONIA**   Lake Peipus

VIDDA   Uppsala   Tartu

Oslo   Stockholm   HIIUMAA   Pskov   **RUSSIA**

Vänern   SAAREMAA

Norrköping

Vättern   Linköping   **Gulf of Riga**

Lindesnes   Jönköping   Rīga

Skagerrak   Göteborg   **LATVIA**

GOTLAND

LÆSØ   Daugavpils

Ålborg   Liepāja

Ålborg Bugt   Kattegat   ÖLAND

JYLLAND   Århus   Klaipėda   **LITHUANIA**

Helsingborg   Hanöbukten

DENMARK   **BALTIC SEA**   Nemunas

København (Copenhagen)   Malmö   Vilnius

FANØ   Odense   Kaunas

FYN   SJÆLLAND   BORNHOLM   Kaliningrad   **RUSSIA**

SYLT   MØN   Gulf of Gdansk

LOLLAND FALSTER   Gdansk   Hrodna

HELGOLAND   RÜGEN   **BELARUS**

OSTFRIESISCHE INSELN   Kiel   Rostock   Koszalin   Olsztyn   Białystok

WADDENEILANDEN   HAMBURG   Szczecin   **POLAND**

Groningen   Bremen   Bydgoszcz

NETHERLANDS   **GERMANY**

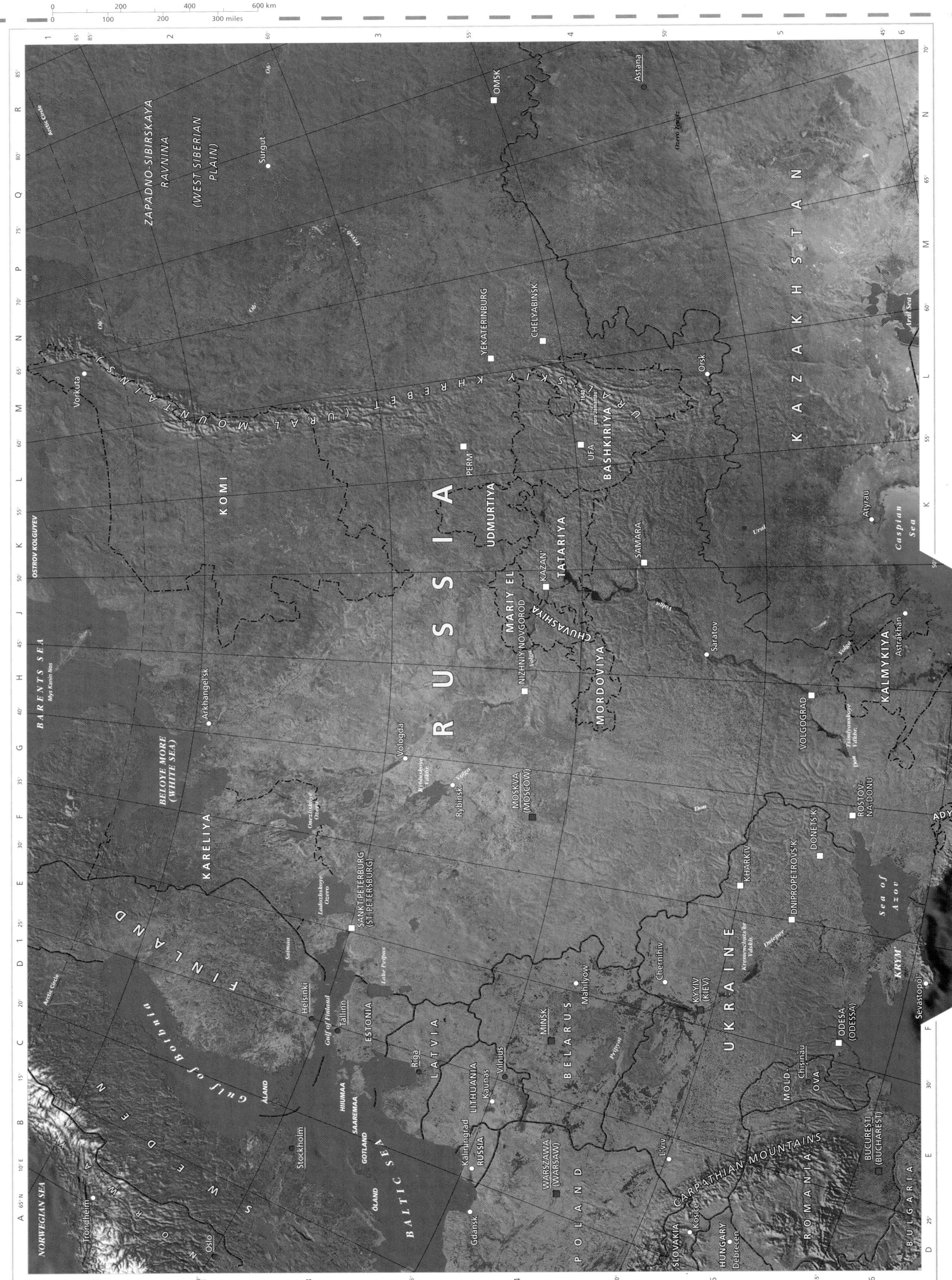

Scale 1 : 11 700 000

© Copyright

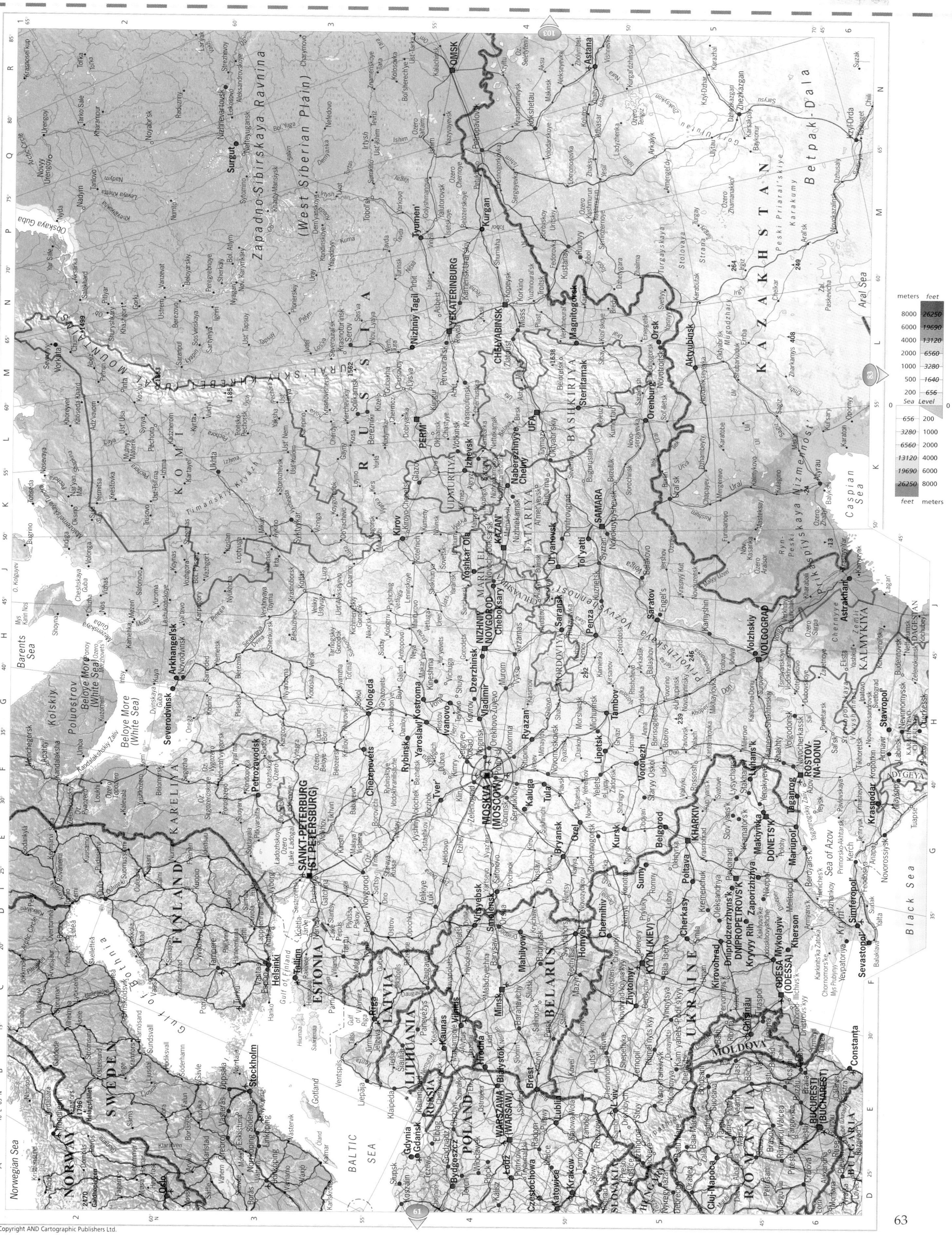

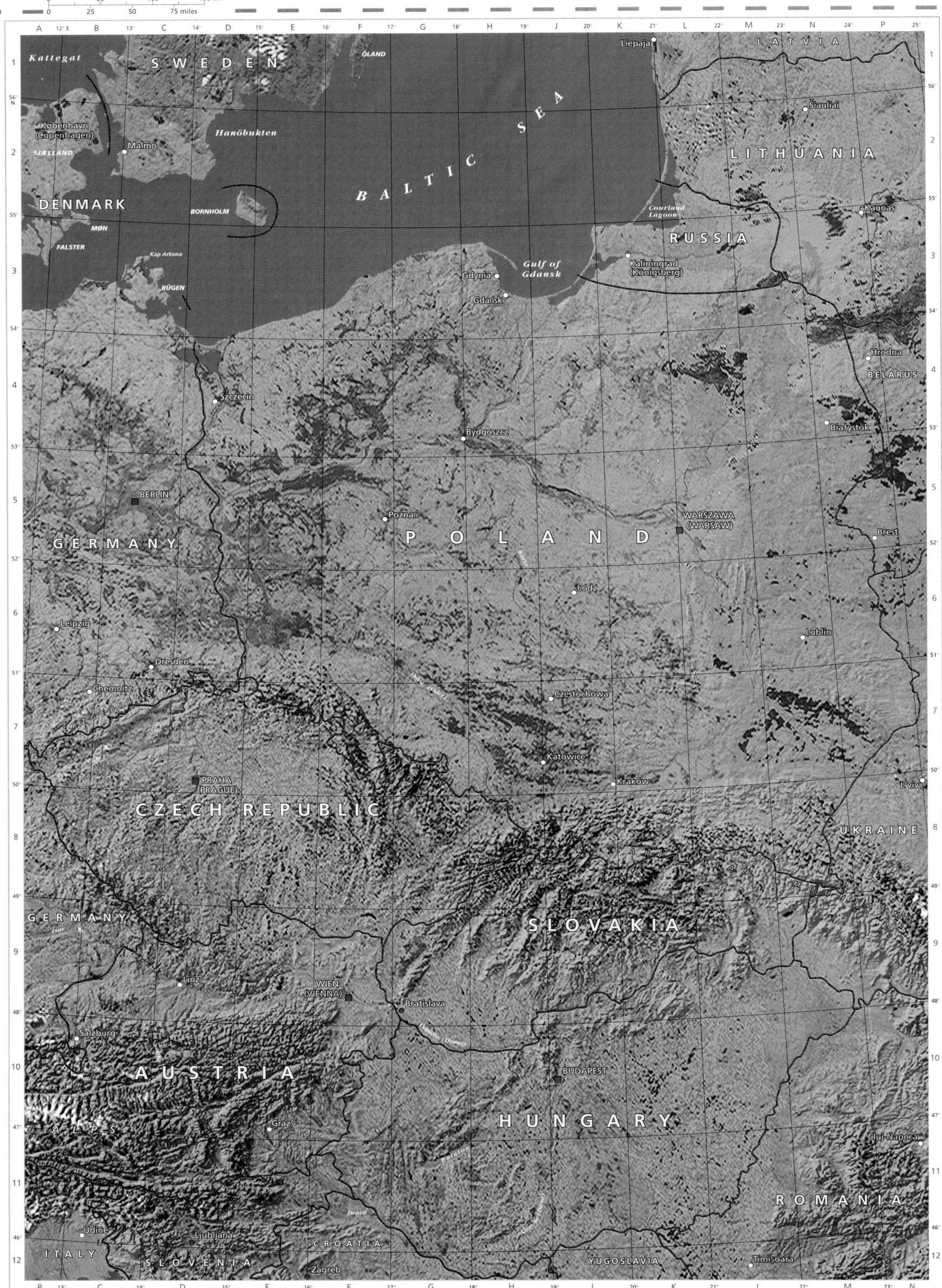

Scale 1 : 3 900 000

0	50	100	150 km
0	25	50	75 miles

Kattegat

SWEDEN

ÖLAND

København
(Copenhagen)

Malmö

Hanöbukten

BALTIC SEA

Liepāja

LATVIA

Šiauliai

LITHUANIA

SJÆLLAND

DENMARK

MØN

BORNHOLM

*Courland
Lagoon*

Kaunas

FALSTER

Kap Arkona

RÜGEN

Gdynia

*Gulf of
Gdansk*

Kaliningrad
(Königsberg)

RUSSIA

Gdańsk

Szczecin

Hrodna

BELARUS

Bydgoszcz

Białystok

BERLIN

Poznań

P O L A N D

WARSZAWA
(WARSAW)

Brest

GERMANY

Łódź

Leipzig

Lublin

Dresden

Chemnitz

ERZGEBIRGE

Odra (Oder)

Częstochowa

Katowice

L'viv

PRAHA
(PRAGUE)

Kraków

UKRAINE

C Z E C H   R E P U B L I C

CARPATHIAN   MOUNTAINS

GERMANY

Isar

S L O V A K I A

Linz

WIEN
(VIENNA)

Bratislava

Danube (Donau)

Salzburg

BUDAPEST

A U S T R I A

A L P S

Graz

H U N G A R Y

Cluj Napoca

Udine

Drava

ITALY

SLOVENIA

Ljubljana

C R O A T I A

YUGOSLAVIA

Timișoara

R O M A N I A

Zagreb

64

© Copyright

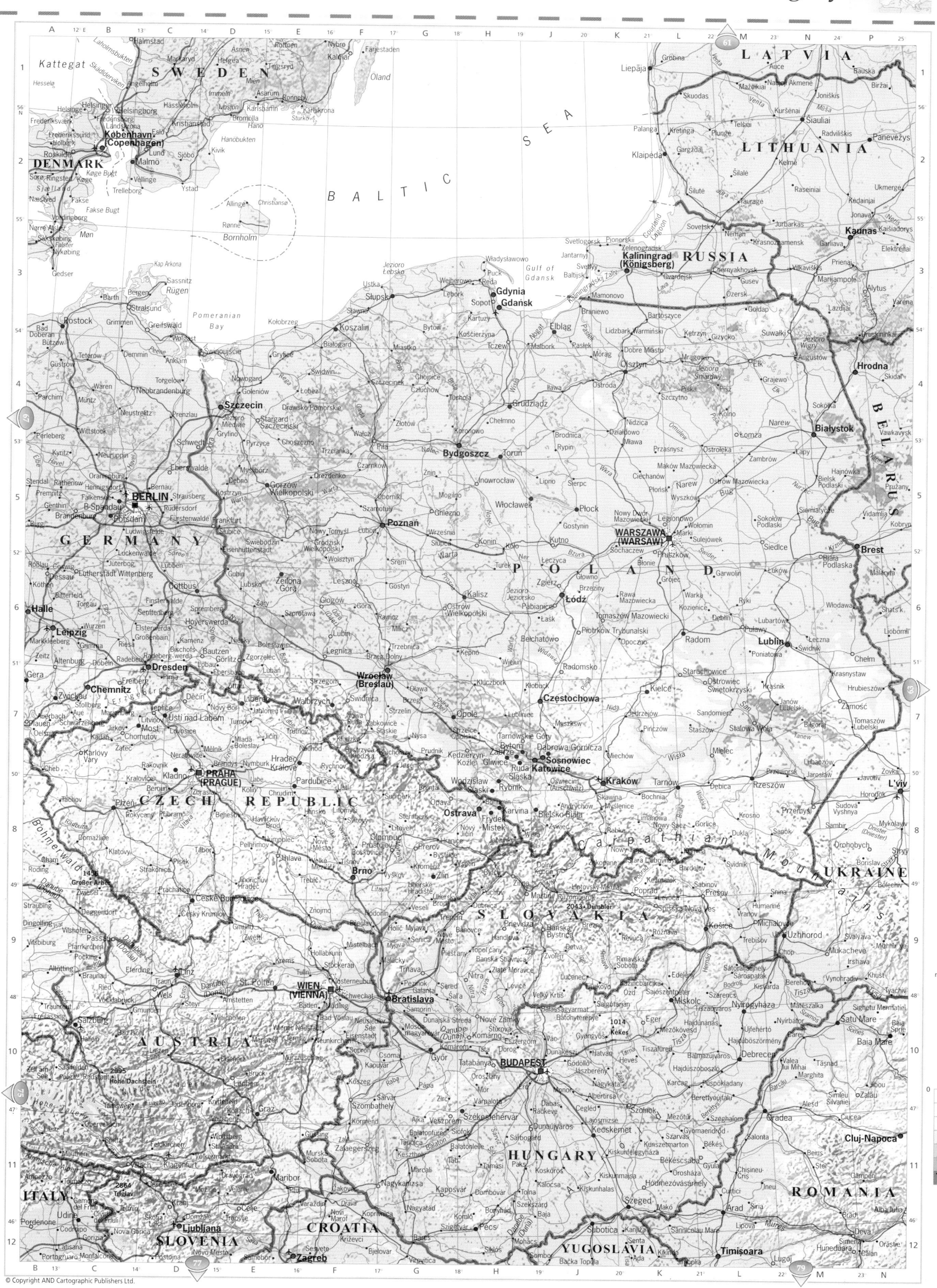

NORTH SEA

DENMARK

SWEDEN

BORNHOLM

BALTIC

SEA

FYN

SJÆLLAND

Odense

Storebælt

SYLT

ALS

MØN

ÆRØ

FALSTER

LANGELAND

Kap Arkona

HELGOLAND

LOLLAND

HIDDENSEE

RÜGEN

NORDFRIESISCHE INSELN

FÖHR

Helgoländer
Bucht

FEHMARN

Greifswalder
Bodden

Kiel

Mecklenburger
Bucht

Rostock

WADDENEILANDEN

OSTFRIESISCHE INSELN

NORDERNEY

LANGEOOG

WANGEROOG

Müritz

Szczecin

TERSCHELLING

AMELAND

SCHIERMONNIKOOG

BORKUM

HAMBURG

Groningen

WADDENZEE

Bremen

Weser

IJssel-
meer

BERLIN

POLA

NETHERLANDS

Hannover

Braunschweig

Enschede

Magdeburg

Arnhem

Bielefeld

Münster

Ems

Cottbus

Essen

Dortmund

Halle

Krefeld

Leipzig

Düsseldorf

G E R M A N Y

Maastricht

Köln

Dresden

Liège

Bonn

ERZGEBIRGE

BELGIUM

THÜRINGER WALD

Frankfurt

CZECH REPUBLIC

Wiesbaden

Main

PRA
(PRA

LUXEMBOURG

Luxembourg

Mannheim

Nürnberg

Heidelberg

Rhine (Rhein)

Karlsruhe

Stuttgart

SCHWÄRZWALD

Strasbourg

Rhine (Rhein)

SCHWÄBISCHE ALB

Danube (Donau)

FRANCE

Isar

1424
Grand Ballon

MÜNCHEN
(MUNICH)

AUSTRIA

Salzburg

Lake
Constance

Basel

SWITZERLAND

AUSTRIA

Zürich

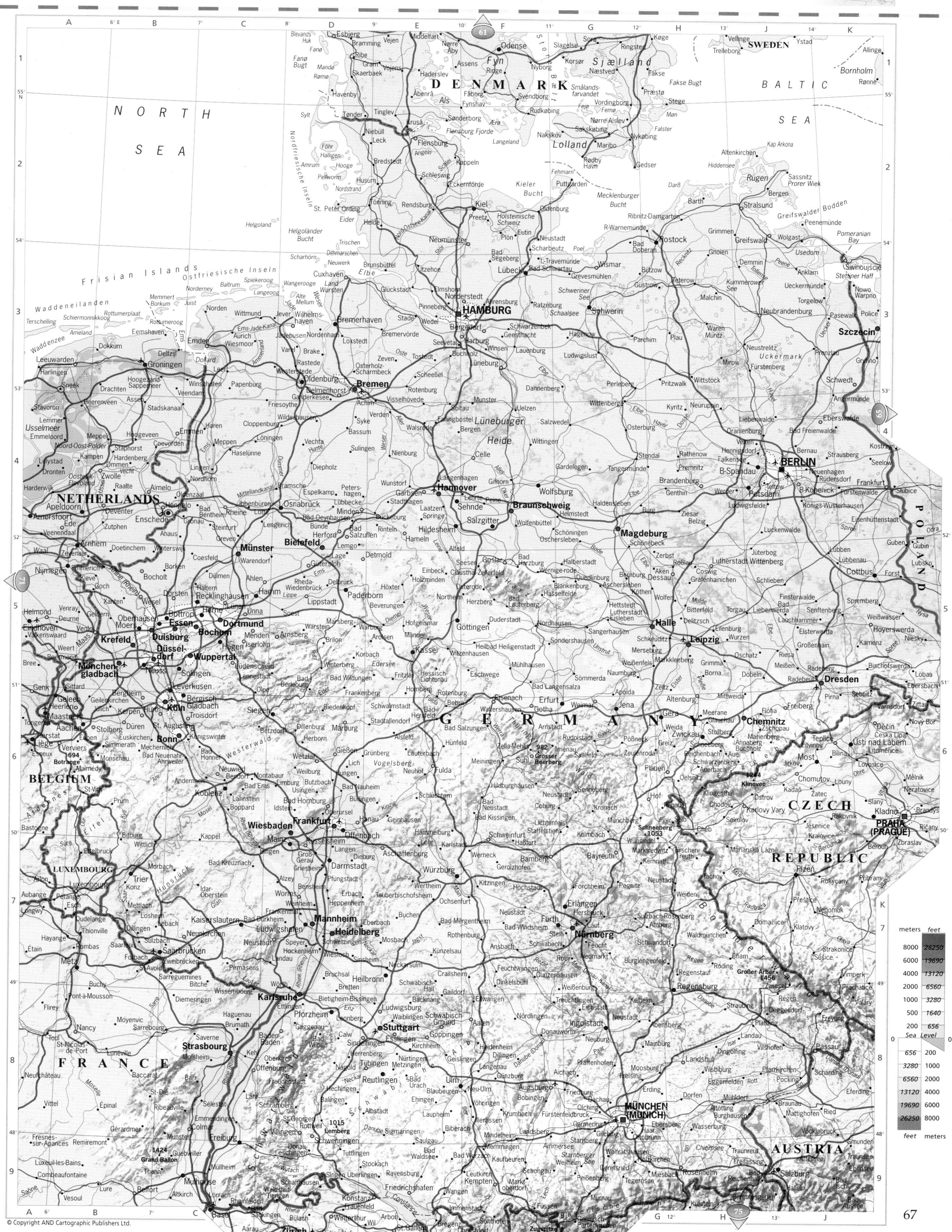

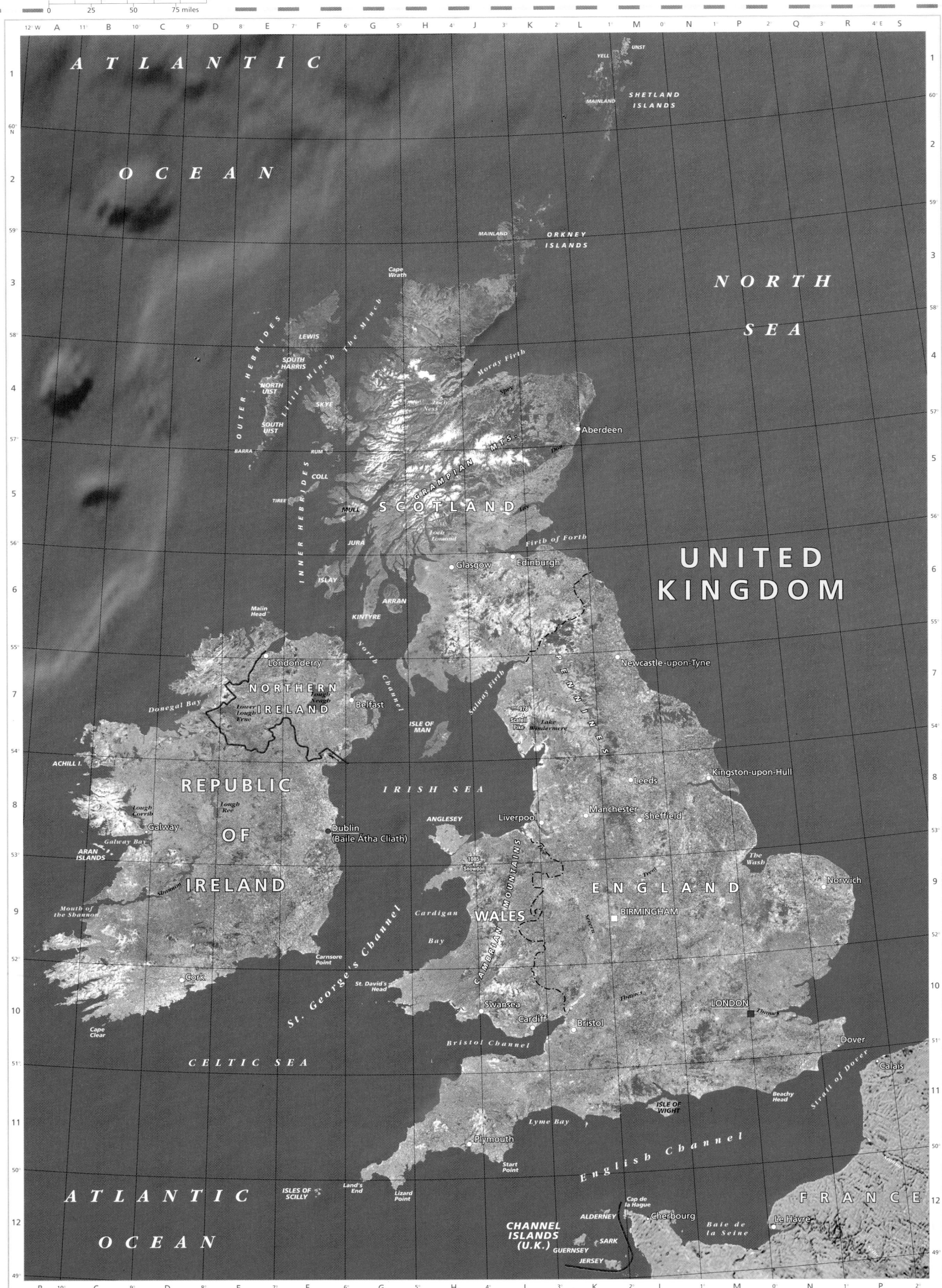

ATLANTIC

OCEAN

NORTH

SEA

UNITED

KINGDOM

SHETLAND
ISLANDS

YELL
UNST

MAINLAND

ORKNEY
ISLANDS

MAINLAND

Cape
Wrath

OUTER HEBRIDES

LEWIS

SOUTH
HARRIS

NORTH
UIST

SKYE

SOUTH
UIST

BARRA

RUM

COLL

TIREE

MULL

JURA

ISLAY

INNER HEBRIDES

Little Minch   The Minch

Moray Firth

Spey

Loch
Ness

GRAMPIAN MTS.

SCOTLAND

Aberdeen

Dee

Tay

Loch
Lomond

Firth of Forth

Glasgow   Edinburgh

ARRAN

KINTYRE

Malin
Head

North Channel

Newcastle-upon-Tyne

Londonderry

NORTHERN
IRELAND

Lower
Lough
Erne

Lough
Neagh

Belfast

Solway Firth

PENNINES

Donegal Bay

ISLE OF
MAN

978
Scafell
Pike

Lake
Windermere

ACHILL I.

REPUBLIC

OF

IRELAND

Lough
Corrib

Lough
Ree

IRISH SEA

Leeds

Kingston-upon-Hull

Galway

Galway Bay

ARAN
ISLANDS

Shannon

Dublin
(Baile Átha Cliath)

ANGLESEY

Liverpool

Manchester   Sheffield

Mouth of
the Shannon

1085
Snowdon

CAMBRIAN MOUNTAINS

WALES

ENGLAND

BIRMINGHAM

Trent

The Wash

Norwich

Cardigan
Bay

Severn

Cork

Carnsore
Point

St. David's
Head

St. George's Channel

Swansea

Cardiff

Bristol

Thames

LONDON

Thames

Dover

Cape
Clear

CELTIC SEA

Bristol Channel

Beachy
Head

Strait of Dover

Calais

ISLE OF
WIGHT

Lyme Bay

English Channel

ATLANTIC

ISLES OF
SCILLY

Land's
End

Lizard
Point

Plymouth

Start
Point

Cap de
la Hague

Cherbourg

Baie de
la Seine

Le Havre

FRANCE

CHANNEL
ISLANDS
(U.K.)

ALDERNEY

SARK

GUERNSEY

JERSEY

OCEAN

© Copyright

69

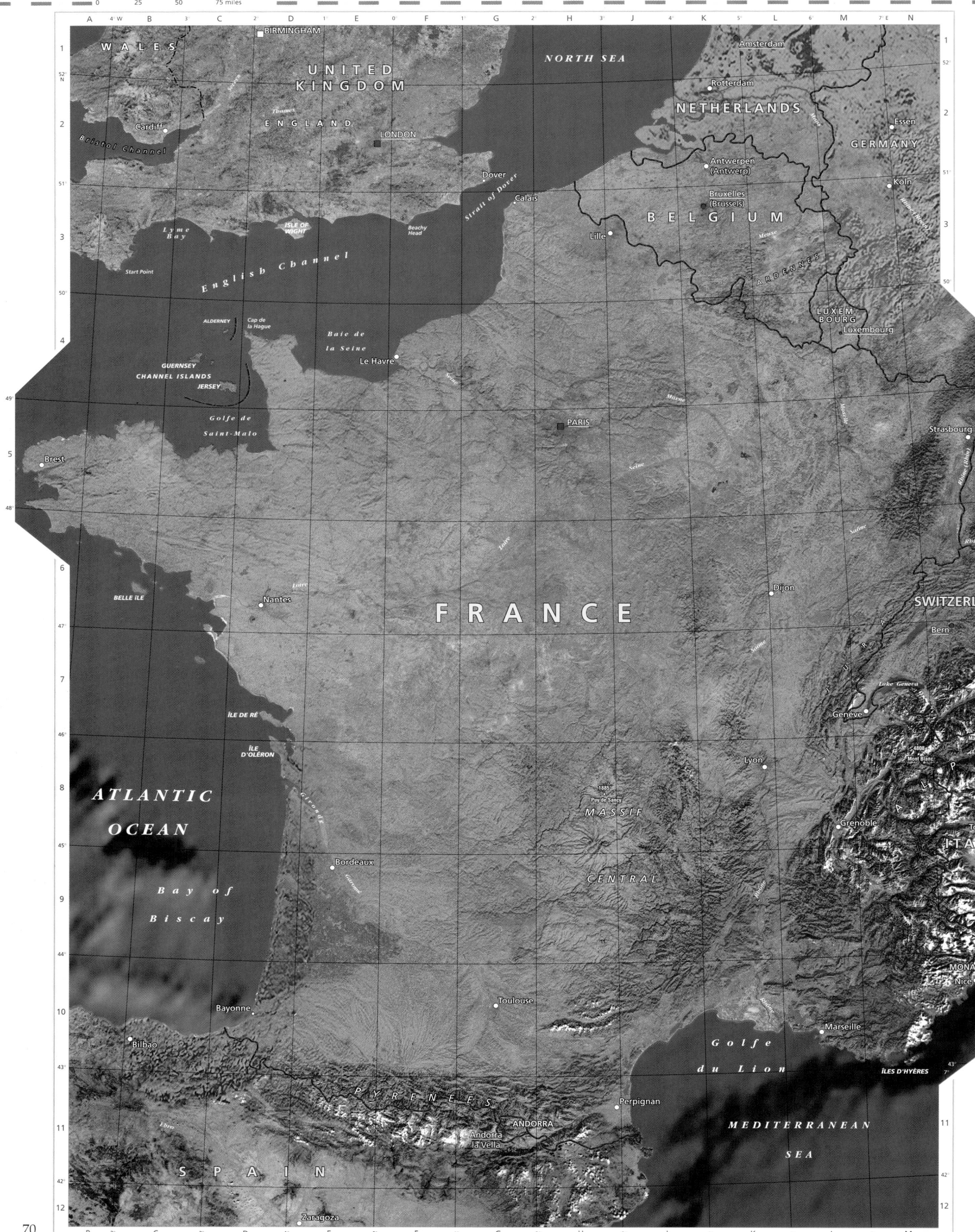

0   50   100   150 km
0   25   50   75 miles

A   4° W   B   3°   C   2°   D   1°   E   0°   F   1°   G   2°   H   3°   J   4°   K   5°   L   6°   M   7° E   N

W A L E S
BIRMINGHAM
UNITED
KINGDOM
NORTH SEA
Amsterdam
52°
N
Rotterdam
NETHERLANDS
Essen
GERMANY
Cardiff
E N G L A N D
Bristol Channel
LONDON
Antwerpen
(Antwerp)
Köln
51°
Dover
Bruxelles
(Brussels)
Calais
B E L G I U M
Lyme
Bay
ISLE OF
WIGHT
Beachy
Head
Strait of Dover
Lille
Meuse
A R D E N N E S
50°
Start Point
English Channel
LUXEM-
BOURG
Luxembourg
4
ALDERNEY
Cap de
la Hague
Baie de
la Seine
GUERNSEY
CHANNEL ISLANDS
JERSEY
Le Havre
Seine
Marne
49°
Golfe de
Saint-Malo
PARIS
Strasbourg
5
Brest
Seine
48°
Moselle
Saône
Rhine (Rhein)
Loire
Rhine
BELLE ÎLE
Loire
Nantes
F R A N C E
Dijon
SWITZERLA
47°
Bern
7
ÎLE DE RÉ
J
U
R
A
Lake Geneva
46°
ÎLE
D'OLÉRON
Genève
4806
Mont Blanc
Matter
8
ATLANTIC
1885
Puy de Sancy
MASSIF
Lyon
A
L
P
Grenoble
ITAL
OCEAN
45°
Bordeaux
Garonne
C E N T R A L
Bay of
Biscay
9
Rhône
44°
MONAC
Nice
Bayonne
Toulouse
10
Bilbao
Marseille
Golfe
du Lion
43°
ÎLES D'HYÈRES
P Y R E N E E S
Perpignan
MEDITERRANEAN
11
Ebro
S P A I N
Andorra
la Vella
ANDORRA
SEA
42°
12
Zaragoza

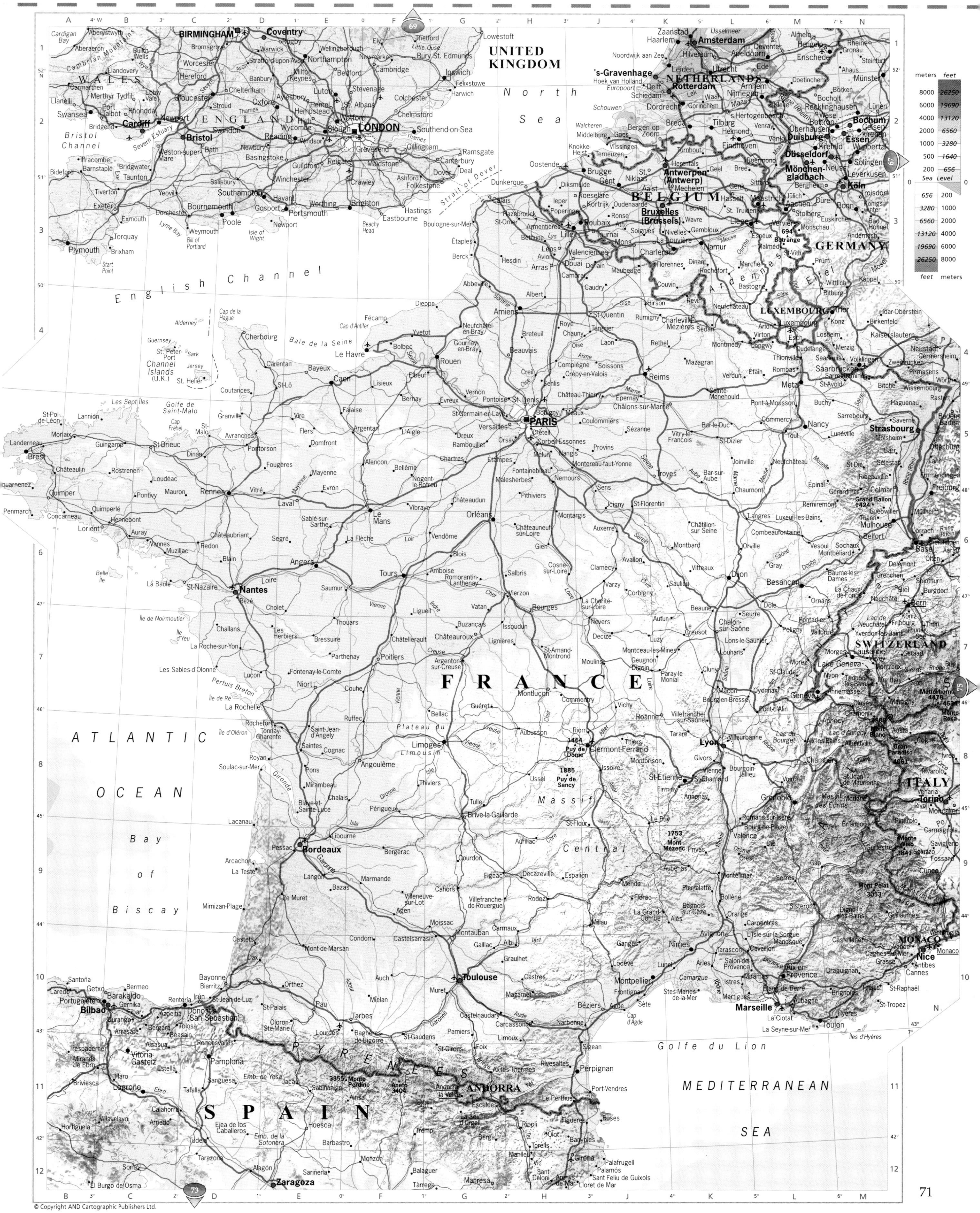

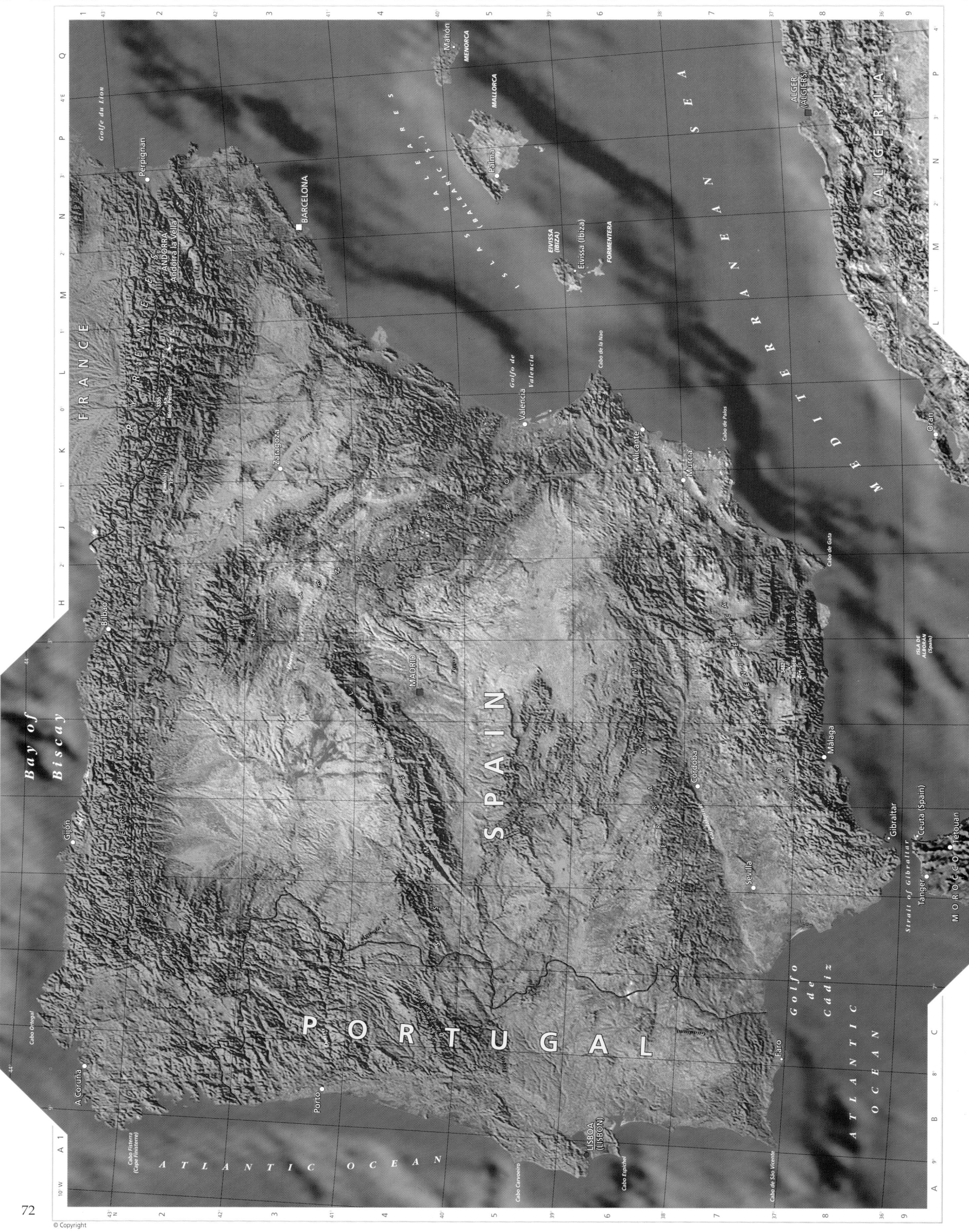

0   50   100   150 km

0   25   50   75 miles

FRANCE

Golfe du Lion

Perpignan

ANDORRA
Andorra la Vella

BARCELONA

P Y R E N E E S

Mahón

MENORCA

MALLORCA

Palma

I S L A S   B A L E A R E S
(I L L E S   B A L E A R S)

EIVISSA
(IBIZA)

Eivissa (Ibiza)

FORMENTERA

M E D I T E R R A N E A N   S E A

ALGER
(ALGIERS)

A L G E R I A

Zaragoza

Ebro

3355
Monte Perdido

Golfo de
Valencia

Valencia

Cabo de la Nao

Cabo de Palos

Cabo de Gata

Orán

Bilbao

S I S T E M A   I B É R I C O

S P A I N

MADRID

Tajo

ISLA DE
ALBORÁN
(Spain)

Melilla (Spain)

Bay of
Biscay

Gijón

Cabo Ortegal

Córdoba

Málaga

Sevilla

Gibraltar

Strait of Gibraltar

Ceuta (Spain)

Tánger

Tetouan

M O R O C C O

A Coruña

Cabo Fisterra
(Cabo Finisterre)

Porto

P O R T U G A L

Faro

Golfo
de
Cádiz

A T L A N T I C   O C E A N

LISBOA
(LISBON)

Cabo Carvoeiro

Cabo Espichel

Cabo de São Vicente

A T L A N T I C   O C E A N

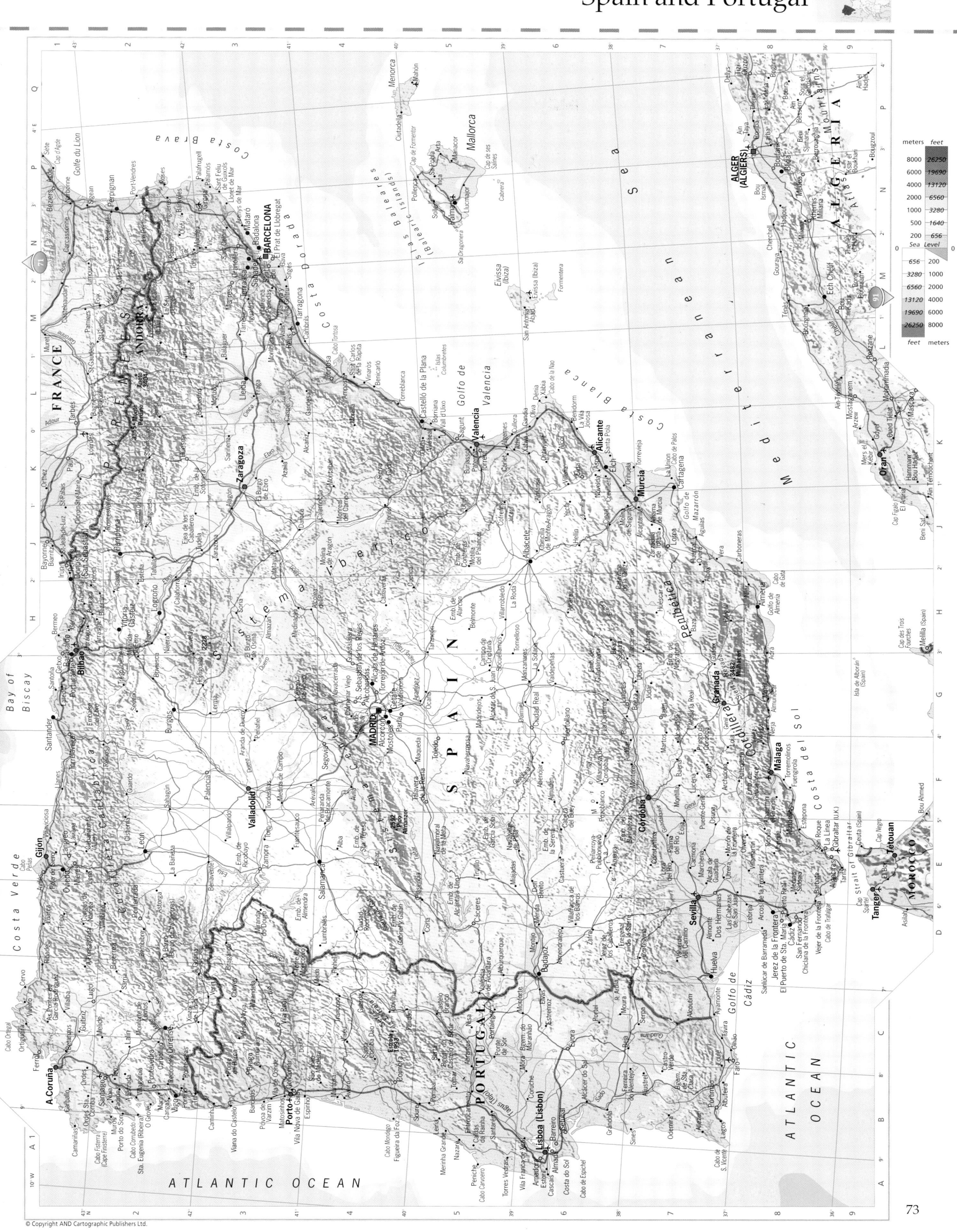

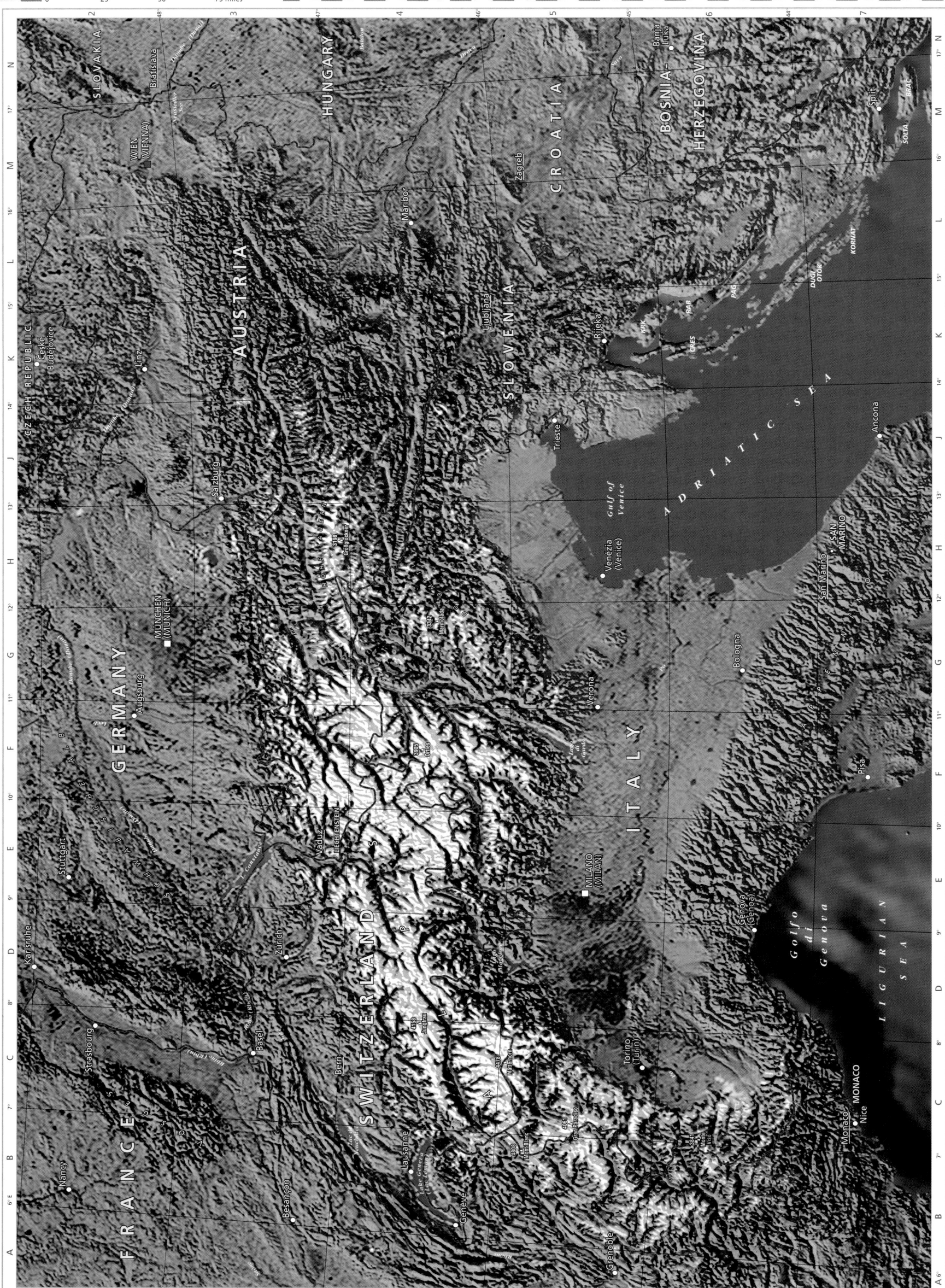

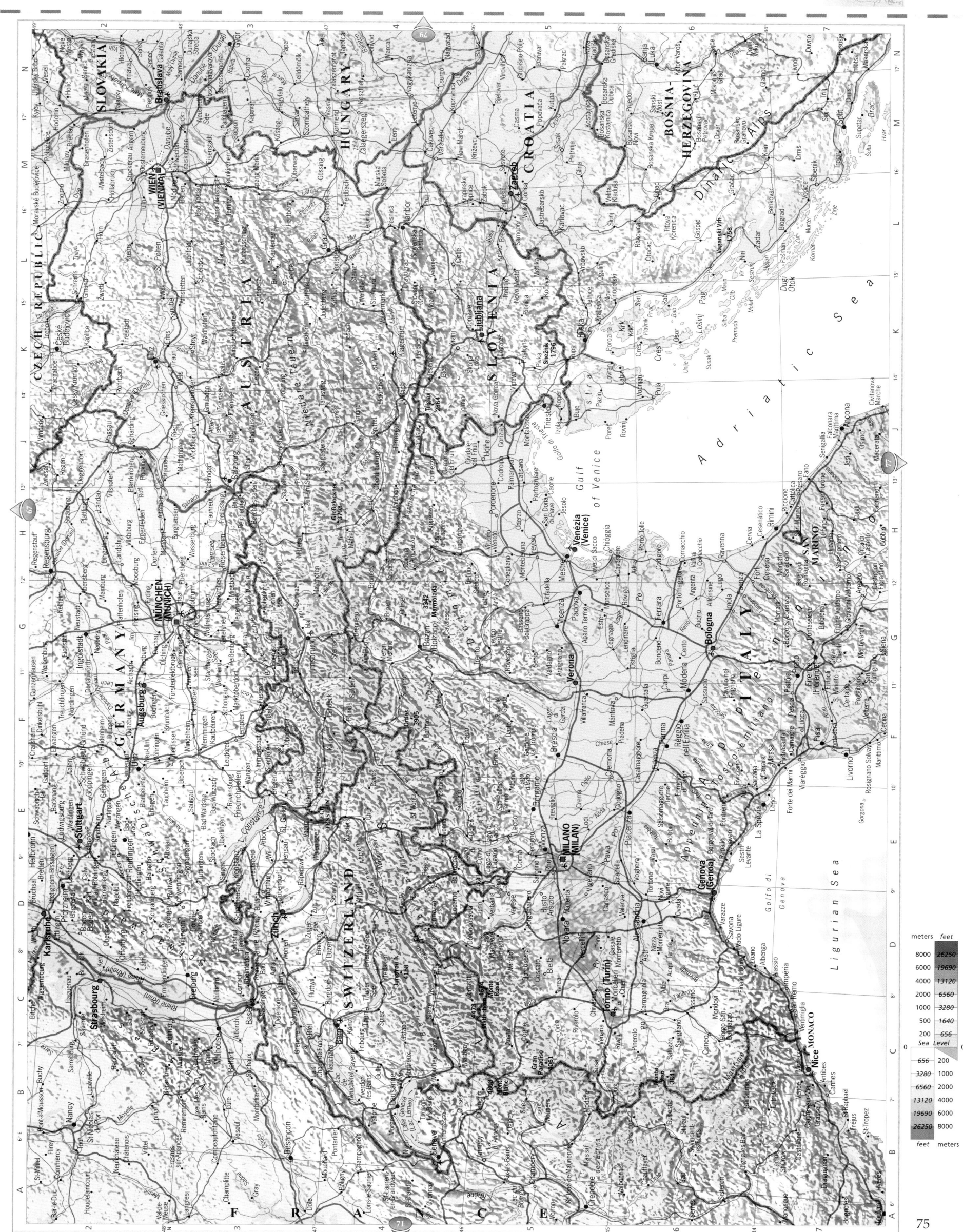

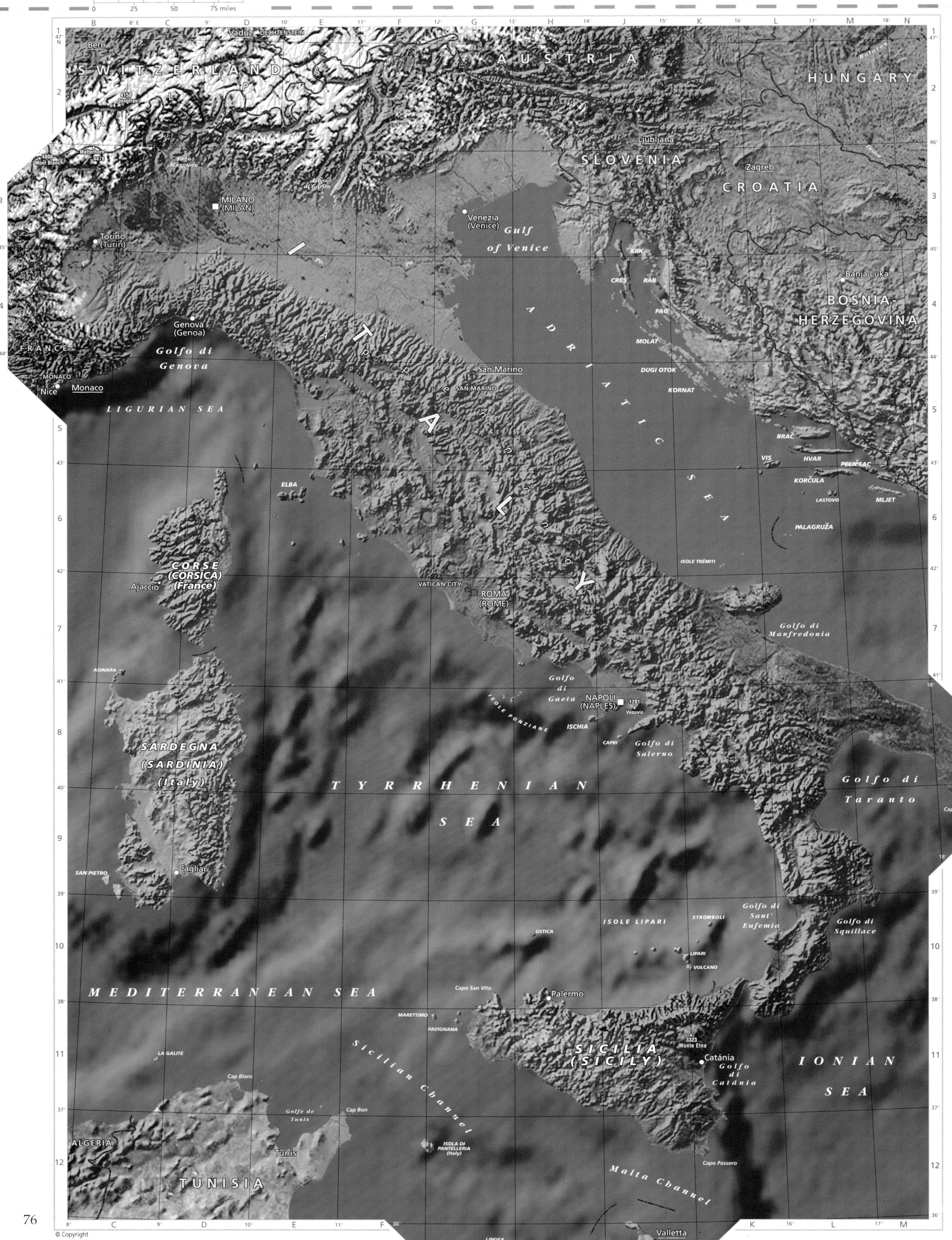

0   50   100   150 km
0   25   50   75 miles

B   8° E   C   9°   D   10°   E   11°   F   12°   G   13°   H   14°   J   15°   K   16°   L   17°   M   18°   N

Vaduz LIECHTENSTEIN

Bern

S W I T Z E R L A N D

4158 Jungfrau

4600 Mont Blanc

4478 Matterhorn

A U S T R I A

H U N G A R Y

Lago Maggiore

Lago di Garda

MILANO (MILAN)

Torino (Turin)

Po

Po

I

T

A

P

P

E

N

I

N

E

S

L

Y

Venezia (Venice)

Gulf of Venice

Ljubljana

S L O V E N I A

Zagreb

C R O A T I A

KRK

CRES   RAB

PAG

MOLAT

Banja Luka

B O S N I A - HERZEGOVINA

Genova (Genoa)

FRANCE

Golfo di Genova

MONACO

Nice   Monaco

L I G U R I A N   S E A

San Marino

SAN MARINO

DUGI OTOK

KORNAT

BRAČ

VIS   HVAR   PELJEŠAC

KORČULA

LASTOVO   MLJET

PALAGRUŽA

ELBA

ISOLE TRÉMITI

CORSE (CORSICA) (France)

Ajaccio

VATICAN CITY

ROMA (ROME)

Golfo di Manfredonia

ASINARA

Golfo di Gaeta

NAPOLI (NAPLES)   1281 Vesuvio

ISOLE PONZIANE

ISCHIA

CAPRI

Golfo di Salerno

Capo San di L

SARDEGNA (SARDINIA) (Italy)

T Y R R H E N I A N

S E A

Golfo di Taranto

SAN PIETRO

Cagliari

ISOLE LIPARI

STRÓMBOLI

Golfo di Sant' Eufemia

Golfo di Squillace

ÚSTICA

LIPARI

VULCANO

M E D I T E R R A N E A N   S E A

Capo San Vito

Palermo

I O N I A N

S E A

MARETTIMO

FAVIGNANA

Sicilian Channel

SICILIA (SICILY)

3325 Monte Etna

Catánia

Golfo di Catánia

LA GALITE

Cap Blanc

Golfe de Tunis

Cap Bon

ISOLA DI PANTELLERIA (Italy)

Capo Passero

ALGERIA

Tunis

T U N I S I A

LINOSA (Italy)

Malta Channel

Valletta

MALTA

B   8°   C   9°   D   10°   E   11°   F 36°   G   13°   H   14°   J 15°   K   16°   L   17°   M

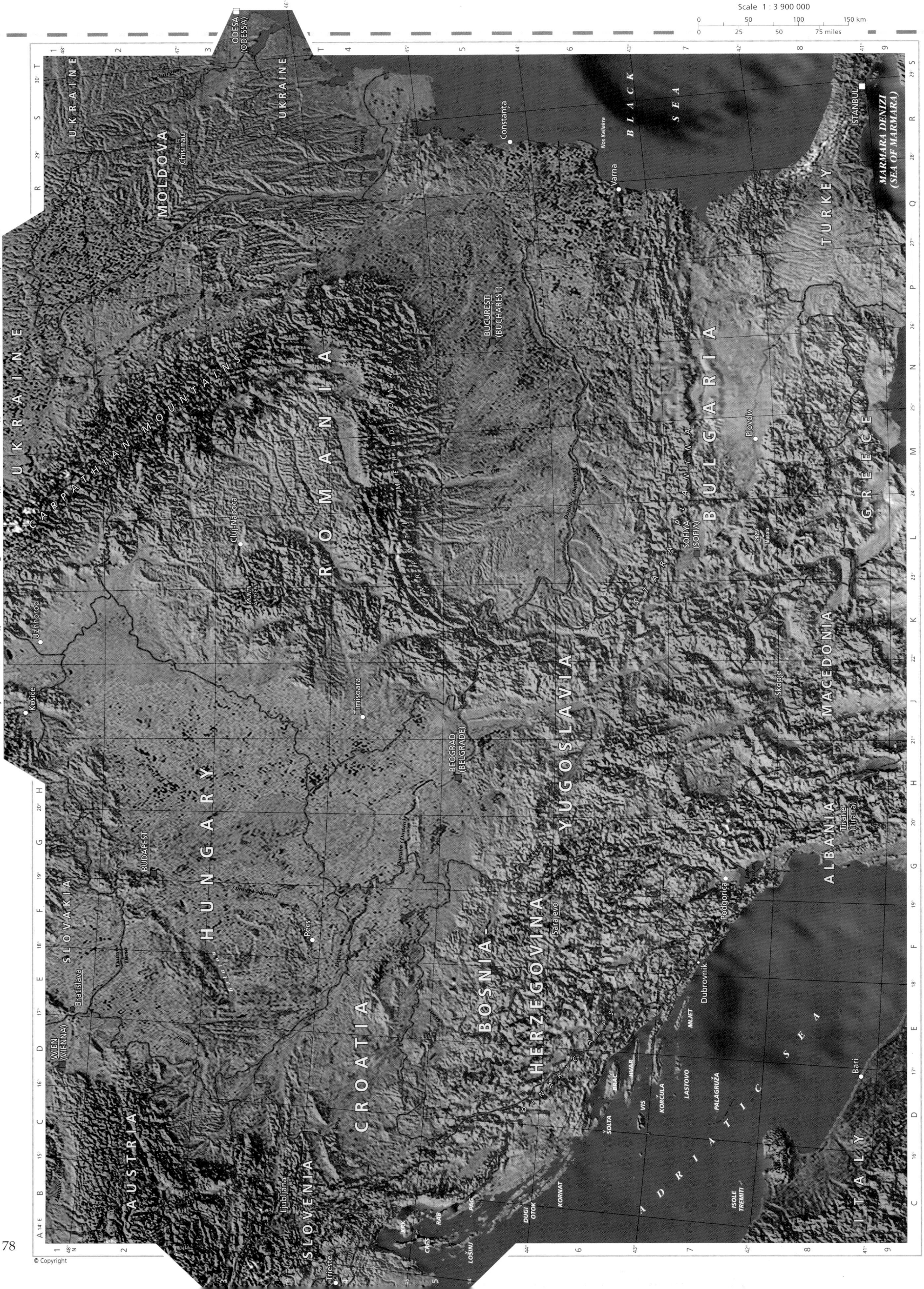

0   50   100   150 km
0   25   50   75 miles

ODESA
(ODESSA)

UKRAINE

MOLDOVA

Chişinău

UKRAINE

B L A C K   *S E A*

Constanţa

Nos Kaliakra

Varna

BUCUREŞTI
(BUCHAREST)

R O M A N I A

TURKEY

MARMARA DENIZI
(SEA OF MARMARA)

İSTANBUL

Cluj-Napoca

CARPATHIAN MOUNTAINS

Munții
APUSENI

Plovdiv

B U L G A R I A

SOFIYA
(SOFIA)

G R E E C E

Uzhhorod

Košice

Timişoara

Skopje

MACEDONIA

BEOGRAD
(BELGRADE)

Y U G O S L A V I A

BUDAPEST

H U N G A R Y

SLOVAKIA

Pécs

Podgorica

Sarajevo

B O S N I A -
H E R Z E G O V I N A

C R O A T I A

ALBANIA

Tiranë
(Tirana)

Bratislava

WIEN
(VIENNA)

A U S T R I A

Ljubljana

S L O V E N I A

Trieste

Dubrovnik

MLJET

HVAR

BRAČ

VIS

KORČULA

LASTOVO

PALAGRUŽA

ŠOLTA

A D R I A T I C   *S E A*

ISOLE
TREMITI

Bari

I T A L Y

KORNAT

DUGI
OTOK

PAG

RAB

CRES

LOŠINJ

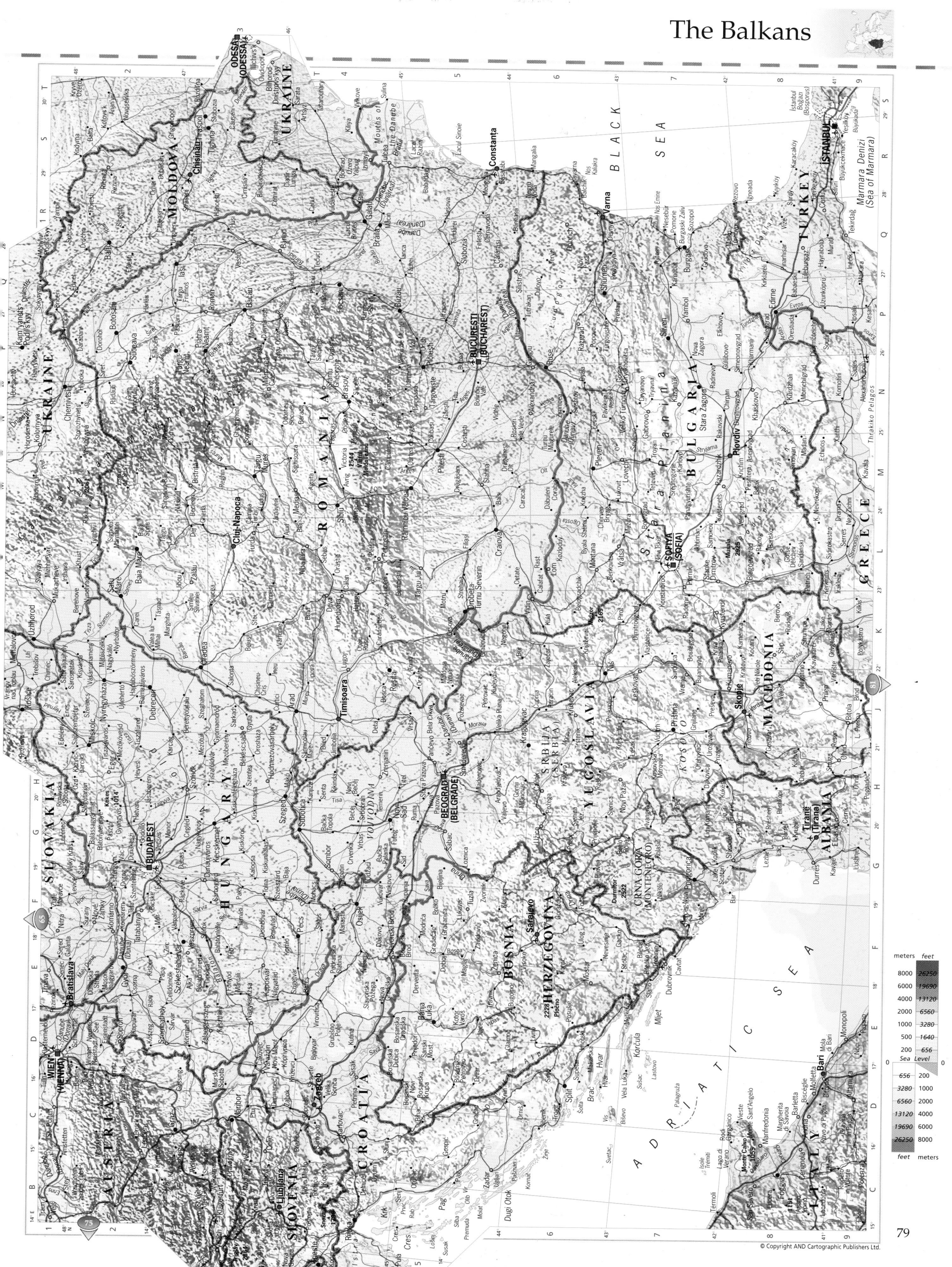

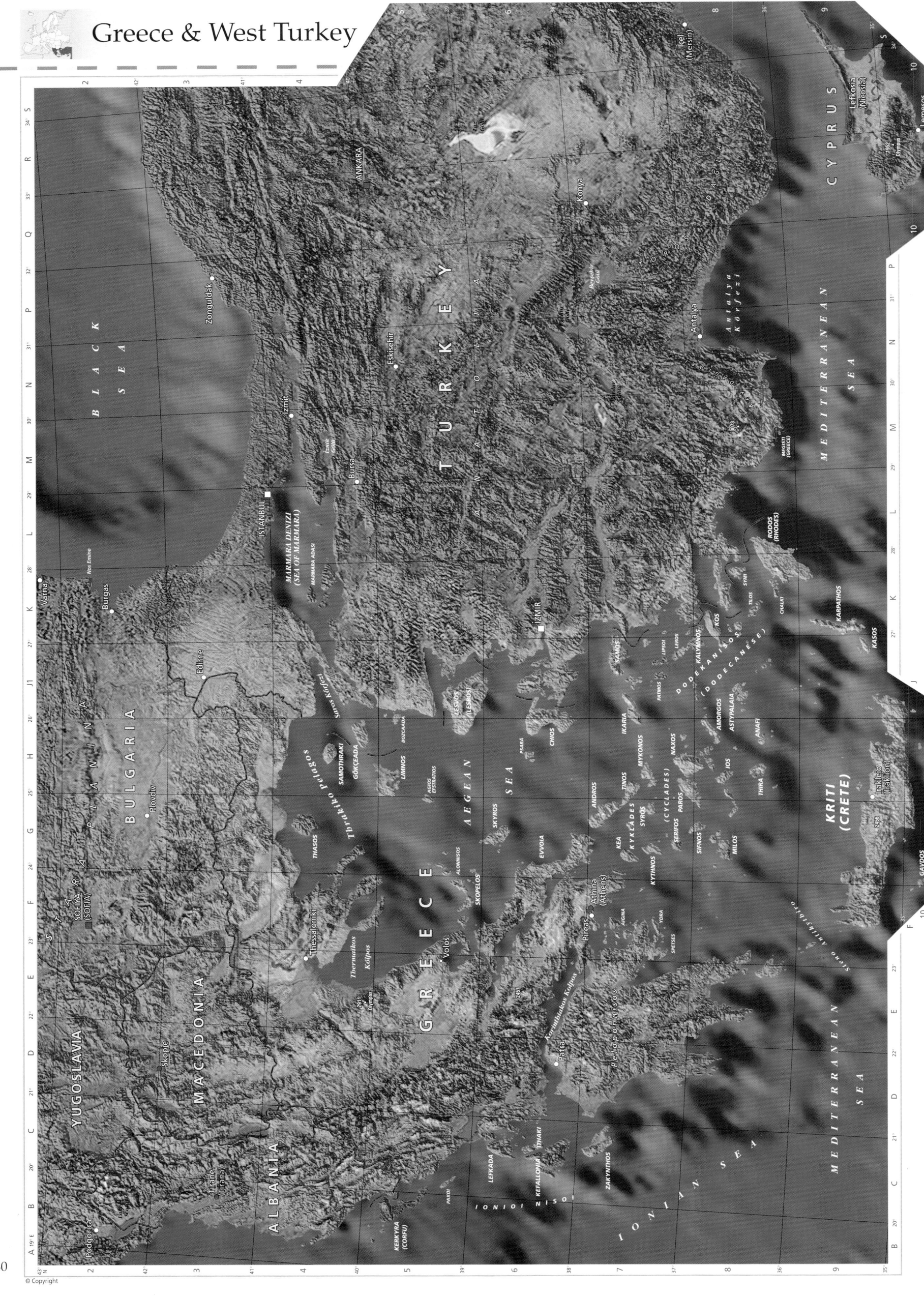

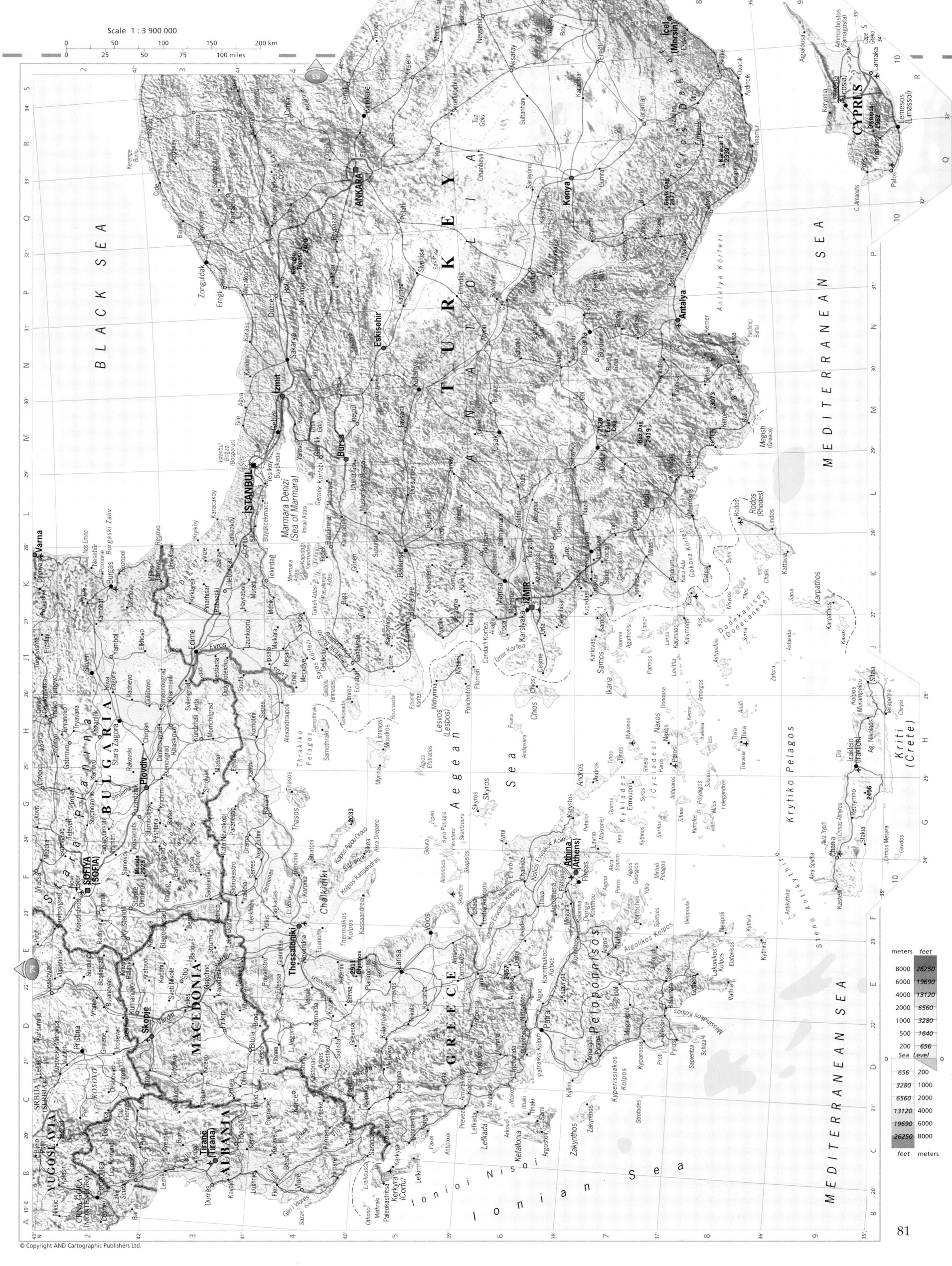

Scale 1 : 3 900 000

0   50   100   150   200 km
0   25   50   75   100 miles

81

© Copyright AND Cartographic Publishers Ltd.

meters	feet
8000	26250
6000	19690
4000	13120
2000	6560
1000	3280
200	656
0 Sea Level	0
656	200
3280	1000
6560	2000
13120	4000
19690	6000
26250	8000
feet	meters

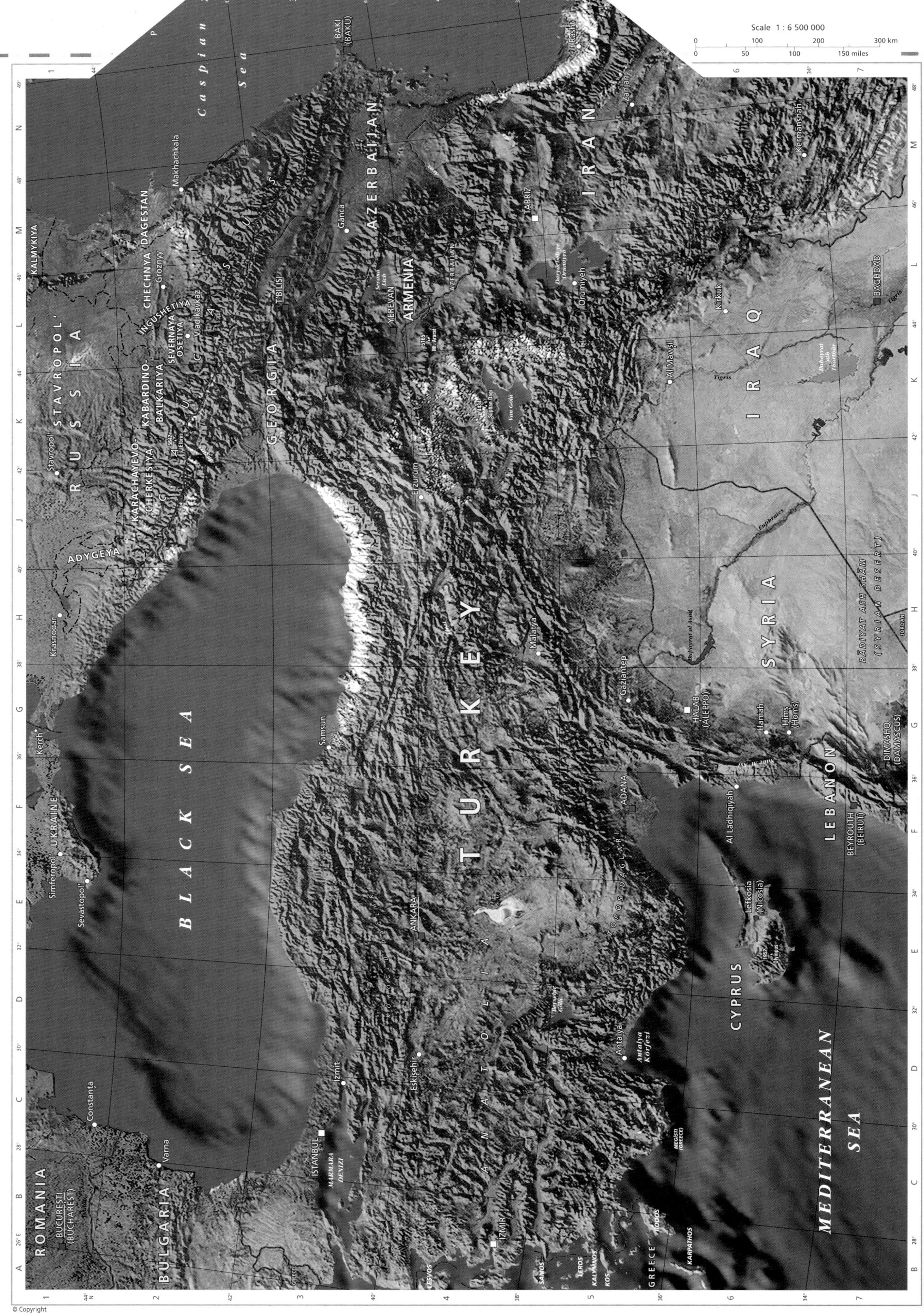

BLACK SEA

Caspian Sea

MEDITERRANEAN SEA

ROMANIA

BUCUREŞTI
(BUCHAREST)

BULGARIA

Varna

Constanta

UKRAINE

Simferopol'

Sevastopol'

Kerch

RUSSIA

STAVROPOL'

Krasnodar

Stavropol'

KALMYKIYA

Makhachkala

ADYGEYA

KARACHAYEVO-
CHERKESIYA

KABARDINO-
BALKARIYA

SEVERNAYA
OSETIYA

INGUSHETIYA

CHECHNYA

DAGESTAN

Vladikavkaz

Grozniy

El'brus

GEORGIA

TBILISI

AZERBAIJAN

Gäncä

ARMENIA

YEREVAN

Mt. Ararat

Sevana
Lich

BAKI
(BAKU)

IRAN

Zanjan

TABRIZ

Daryächeh-ye
Orumiyeh

Orūmīyeh

Kermānshāh

Van Gölü

Süphan Dag

Erzurum

TURKEY

Samsun

İzmit

İSTANBUL

MARMARA
DENIZI

Eskişehir

ANKARA

ANATOLIA

TOROS DAGLARI

ADANA

Antalya

Antalya
Körfezi

İZMİR

LESVOS
GREECE

KOS
GREECE

KALÍMNOS

SAMOS

MEGISTI
(GREECE)

RODOS

KARPATHOS

CYPRUS

Lefkosia
(Nicosia)

Malatya

Gaziantep

HALAB
(ALEPPO)

Ḥamāh

Ḥimş
(Homs)

Al Ladhiqiyah

LEBANON

BEYROUTH
(BEIRUT)

DIMASHQ
(DAMASCUS)

SYRIA

BĀDIYAT ASH SHĀM
(SYRIAN DESERT)

Buḥayrat al Asad

Euphrates

IRAQ

Al Mawşil

Kirkūk

BAGHDAD

Tigris

Buḥayrat
ath Tharthār

JORDAN

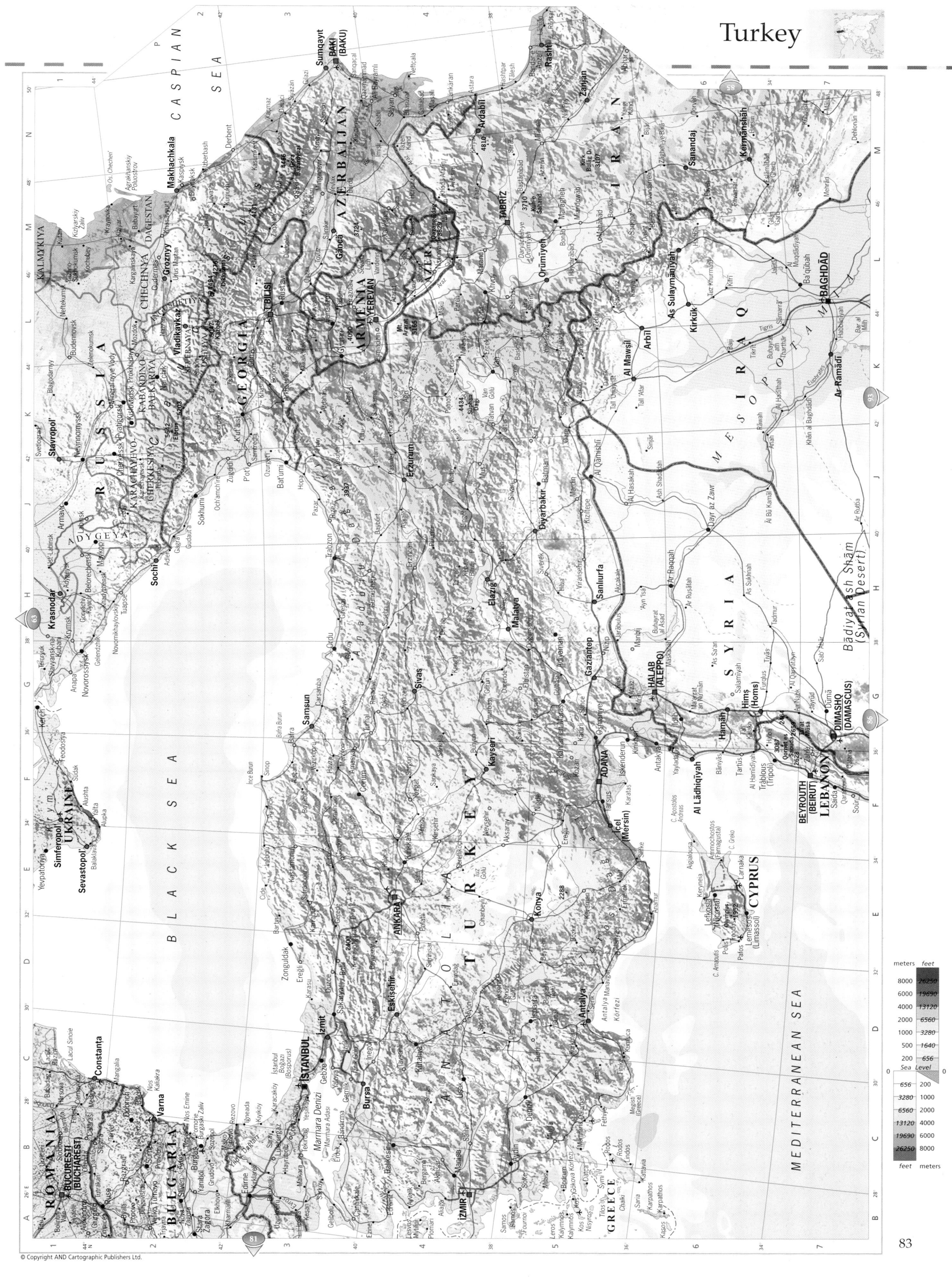

Turkey

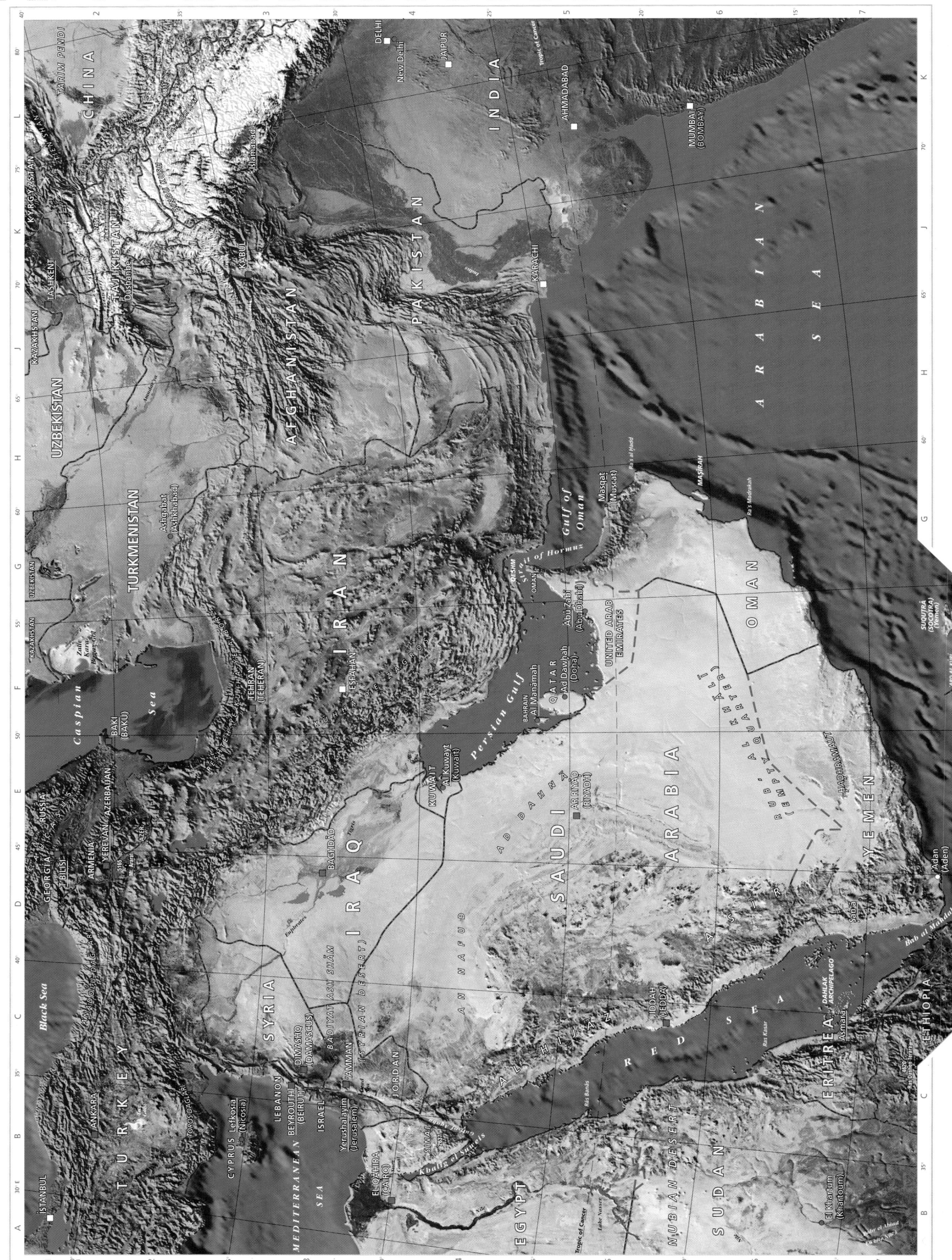

Scale 1 : 14 300 000

0   200   400   600 km
0   100   200   300 miles

CHINA

TARIM PENDI

KYRGYZSTAN

KAZAKHSTAN

TASHKENT

UZBEKISTAN

TAJIKISTAN

Dushanbe

Islamabad

KABUL

DELHI

New Delhi

JAIPUR

AHMADABAD

INDIA

Tropic of Cancer

MUMBAI
(BOMBAY)

A R A B I A N

S E A

TURKMENISTAN

AFGHANISTAN

PAKISTAN

KARACHI

Ashgabat
(Ashkhabad)

UZBEKISTAN

KAZAKHSTAN

Zaliv
Kara-
Bogaz-Gol

Caspian

Sea

BAKI
(BAKU)

I R A N

TEHRAN
(TEHERAN)

ESPAHAN

ZAGROS

QESHM

Strait of Hormuz

OMAN

Gulf of
Oman

Masqat
(Muscat)

Ra's al Hadd

MASIRAH

Ra's Madrakah

SUQUTRA
(SOCOTRA)
(Yemen)

ABD AL KURI

Abū Dhabī
(Abu Dhabi)

UNITED ARAB
EMIRATES

BAHRAIN
QATAR
Al Manamah
Ad Dawhah
(Doha)

Persian Gulf

Al Kuwayt
(Kuwait)

KUWAIT

O M A N

RUB' AL KHALI

RUB' AL QUARTER
(EMPTY QUARTER)

HADRAMAUT

YEMEN

GEORGIA

RUSSIA

T'bilisi

ARMENIA

AZERBAIJAN

YEREVAN

AZER.

5165
Mt. Ararat

BAGHDAD

I R A Q

Tigris

AD DAHNA

AR RIYAD
(RIYADH)

S A U D I

A R A B I A

AN NAFUD

Euphrates

BADIYAT ASH SHAM
(SYRIAN DESERT)

SYRIA

DIMASHQ
(DAMASCUS)

DAMMAN

JORDAN

LEBANON

BEYROUTH
(BEIRUT)

ISRAEL

Yerushalayim
(Jerusalem)

CYPRUS Lefkosia
(Nicosia)

ANKARA

T U R K E Y

ISTANBUL

TOROSDAGLARI

MEDITERRANEAN

SEA

Black Sea

SINAI

Khalig el Suweis

EL QAHIRA
(CAIRO)

E G Y P T

Tropic of Cancer

NUBIAN DESERT

SUDAN

El Khartum
(Khartoum)

Lake Nasser

Nile

AL HIJAZ

JIDDAH
(JEDDA)

Ras Kasar

R E D

S E A

DAHLAK
ARCHIPELAGO

Ras Banas

ERITREA

Asmara

ETHIOPIA

Adan
(Aden)

Bab al Mandab

DJIBOUTI

Saba

84

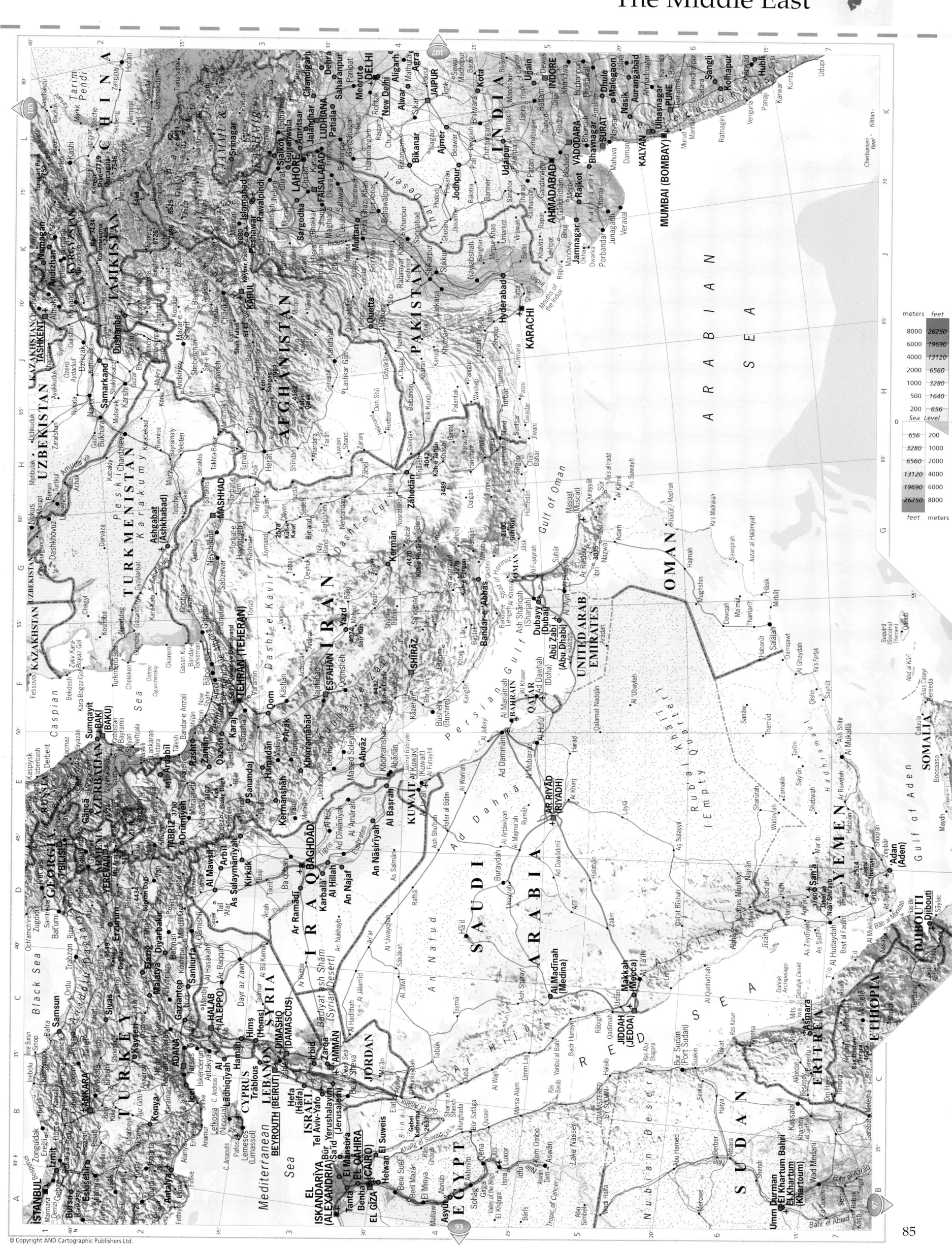

Scale 1 : 3 200 000

0   50   100   150 km
0   25   50   75 miles

meters	feet
8000	26250
6000	19690
4000	13120
2000	6560
1000	3280
500	1640
200	656
Sea Level	0

feet	meters
656	200
3280	1000
6560	2000
13120	4000
19690	6000
26250	8000

SYRIA • JORDAN • SAUDI ARABIA • LEBANON • ISRAEL • EGYPT • CYPRUS

Bādiyat ash Shām (Syrian Desert)

Hamāh • Hims (Homs) • DIMASHQ (DAMASCUS) • BEYROUTH (BEIRUT) • Trâblous (Tripoli) • AMMAN • Zarqa' • Irbid • Yerushalayim (Jerusalem) • Tel Aviv-Yafo • Hefa (Haifa) • Eilat • Gaza • GAZA STRIP • WEST BANK • NEGEV • SINAI • Dead Sea • Lerkosia (Nicosia) • Lemesos (Limassol)

MEDITERRANEAN SEA • Gulf of Aqaba • Wādi as Sirhān

The Gulf States

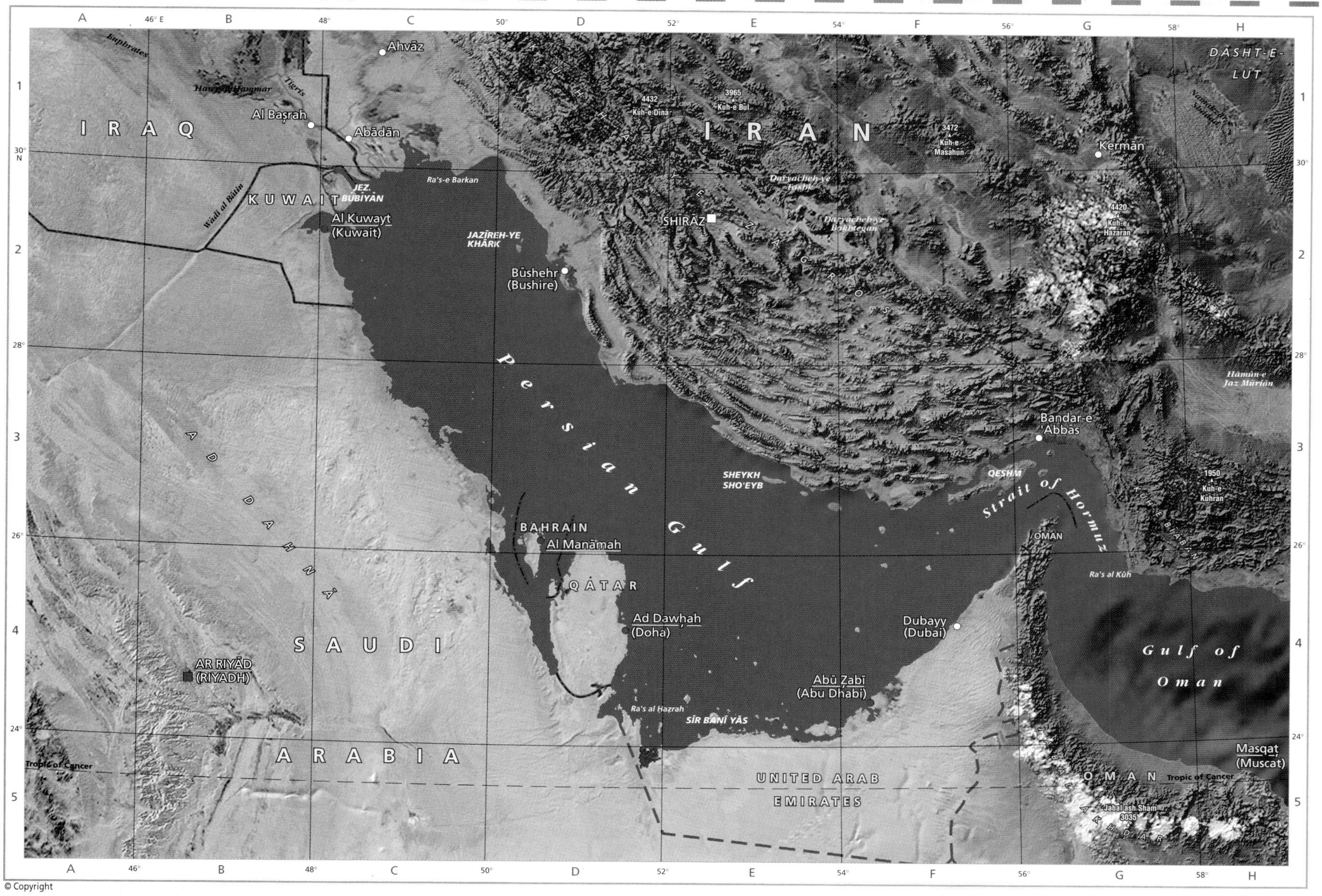

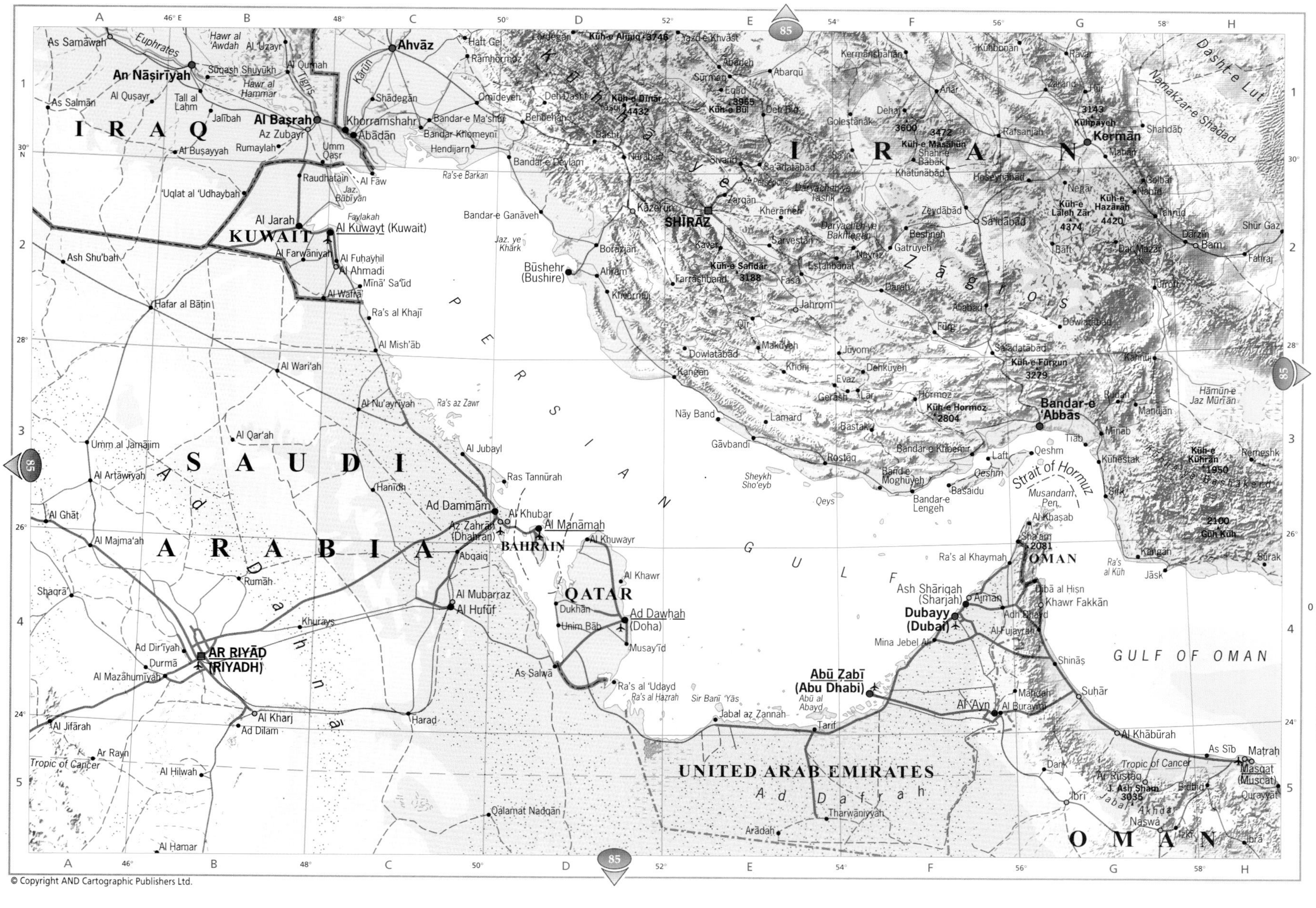

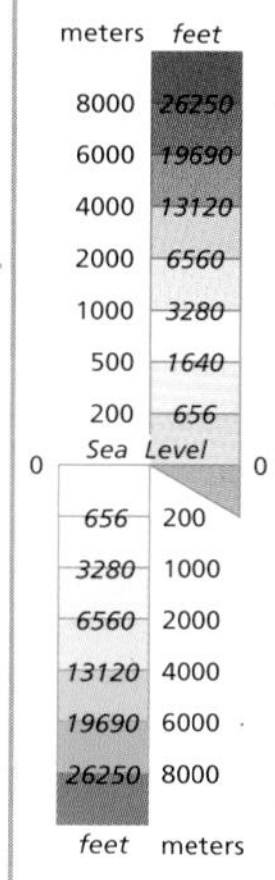

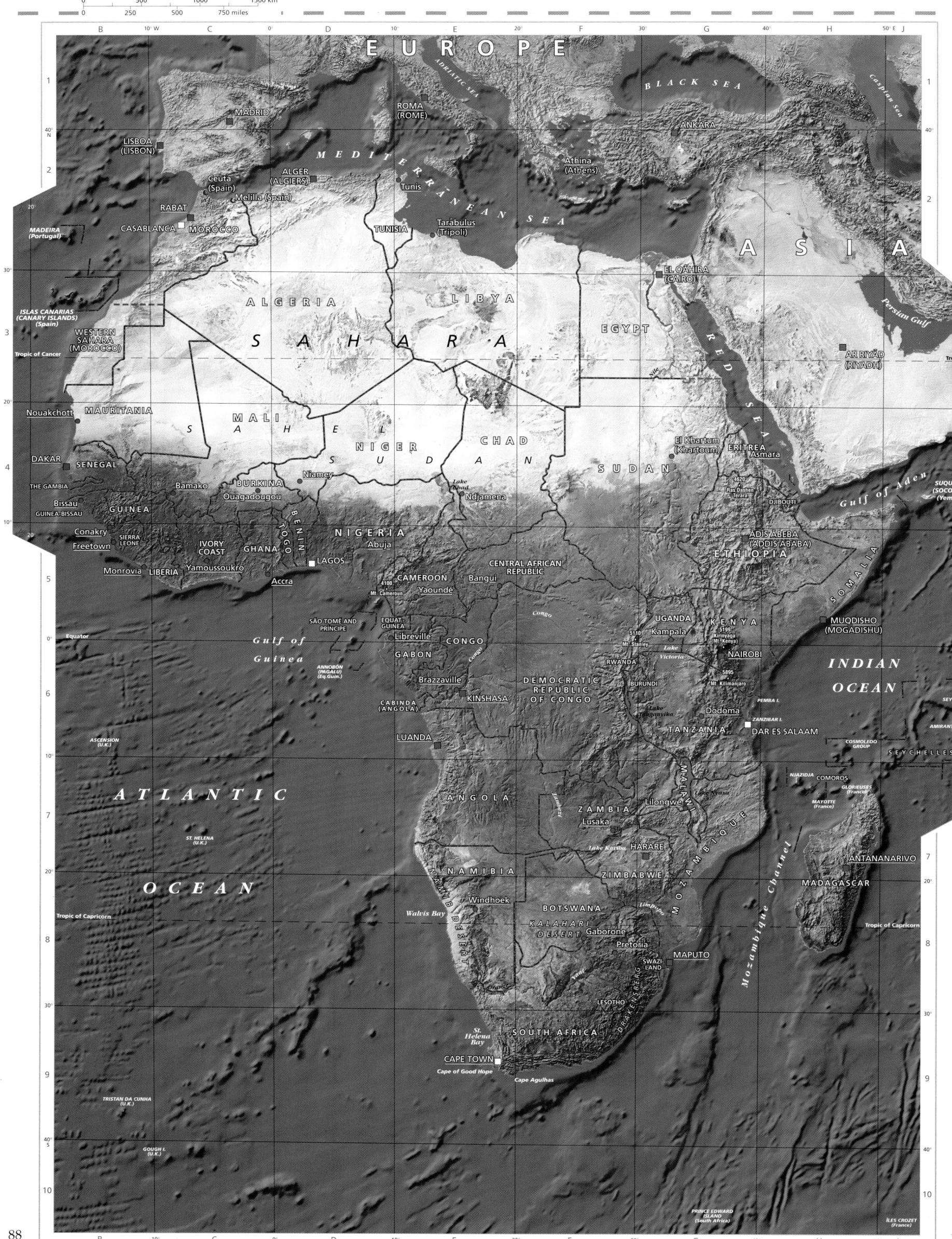

0   500   1000   1500 km
0   250   500   750 miles

EUROPE

ALPS
ADRIATIC SEA
BLACK SEA
CAUCASUS
Caspian Sea

MADRID
ROMA
(ROME)
ANKARA

LISBOA
(LISBON)
MEDITERRANEAN SEA
Athina
(Athens)

Ceuta
(Spain)
ALGER
(ALGIERS)
Tunis
ASIA

Melilla (Spain)
RABAT
TUNISIA
Tarābulus
(Tripoli)
EL QÂHIRA
(CAIRO)

CASABLANCA
MOROCCO

MADEIRA
(Portugal)

Persian Gulf

ISLAS CANARIAS
(CANARY ISLANDS)
(Spain)
WESTERN
SAHARA
(MOROCCO)
ALGERIA
LIBYA
EGYPT
AR RIYĀD
(RIYADH)

Tropic of Cancer
S   A   H   A   R   A
Tropic of Cancer

Nile

Nouakchott
MAURITANIA
MALI
S   A   H   E   L
CHAD
El Khartum
(Khartoum)
ERITREA
Asmara

DAKAR
SENEGAL
NIGER
SUDAN
SUDAN
4620
Ras Dashen
Terara
DJIBOUTI
SUQUTRĀ
(SOCOTRA)
(Yemen)

THE GAMBIA
Bamako
Niamey
Ndjamena
Gulf of Aden

Bissau
GUINEA-BISSAU
BURKINA
Ouagadougou
Lake
Chad
ADIS ABEBA
(ADDIS ABABA)

Conakry
Freetown
GUINEA
SIERRA
LEONE
IVORY
COAST
GHANA
TOGO
BENIN
NIGERIA
Abuja
ETHIOPIA
SOMALIA

Monrovia
LIBERIA
Yamoussoukro
Accra
LAGOS
CAMEROON
CENTRAL AFRICAN
REPUBLIC
Bangui

Equator
SÃO TOMÉ AND
PRÍNCIPE
4100
Mt. Cameroun
Yaoundé
Congo
UGANDA
KENYA
MUQDISHO
(MOGADISHU)

Gulf of
Guinea
EQUAT.
GUINEA
Libreville
CONGO
5110
Mt. Stanley
5199
Kirinyaga
(Mt. Kenya)
Kampala
Lake
Victoria
Equator

ANNOBÓN
(PAGALU)
(Eq.Guin.)
GABON
Congo
RWANDA
NAIROBI
INDIAN
OCEAN
SEYCHELLES

Brazzaville
BURUNDI
5895
Mt. Kilimanjaro
AMIRANTE IS.

ASCENSION
(U.K.)
CABINDA
(ANGOLA)
KINSHASA
DEMOCRATIC
REPUBLIC
OF CONGO
Lake
Tanganyika
PEMBA I.
Dodoma
ZANZIBAR I.
COSMOLEDO
GROUP
SEYCHELLES

LUANDA
TANZANIA
DAR ES SALAAM

A   T   L   A   N   T   I   C
ANGOLA
Zambezi
Lake
Nyasa
Lilongwe
ZAMBIA
MALAWI
NJAZIDJA
COMOROS
GLORIEUSES
(France)
ANTANANARIVO

ST. HELENA
(U.K.)
Lusaka
MOZAMBIQUE
MAYOTTE
(France)

O   C   E   A   N
NAMIBIA
Lake Kariba
HARARE
ZIMBABWE
MADAGASCAR

Tropic of Capricorn
Windhoek
KALAHARI
DESERT
BOTSWANA
Limpopo
Mozambique Channel
Tropic of Capricorn

Walvis Bay
ZAMBEZI DESERT
Gaborone
SWAZI-
LAND
MAPUTO

Pretoria
DRAKENSBERG
Orange
LESOTHO

St.
Helena
Bay
SOUTH AFRICA

CAPE TOWN
Cape of Good Hope
Cape Agulhas

TRISTAN DA CUNHA
(U.K.)

GOUGH I.
(U.K.)

PRINCE EDWARD
ISLAND
(South Africa)
ÎLES CROZET
(France)

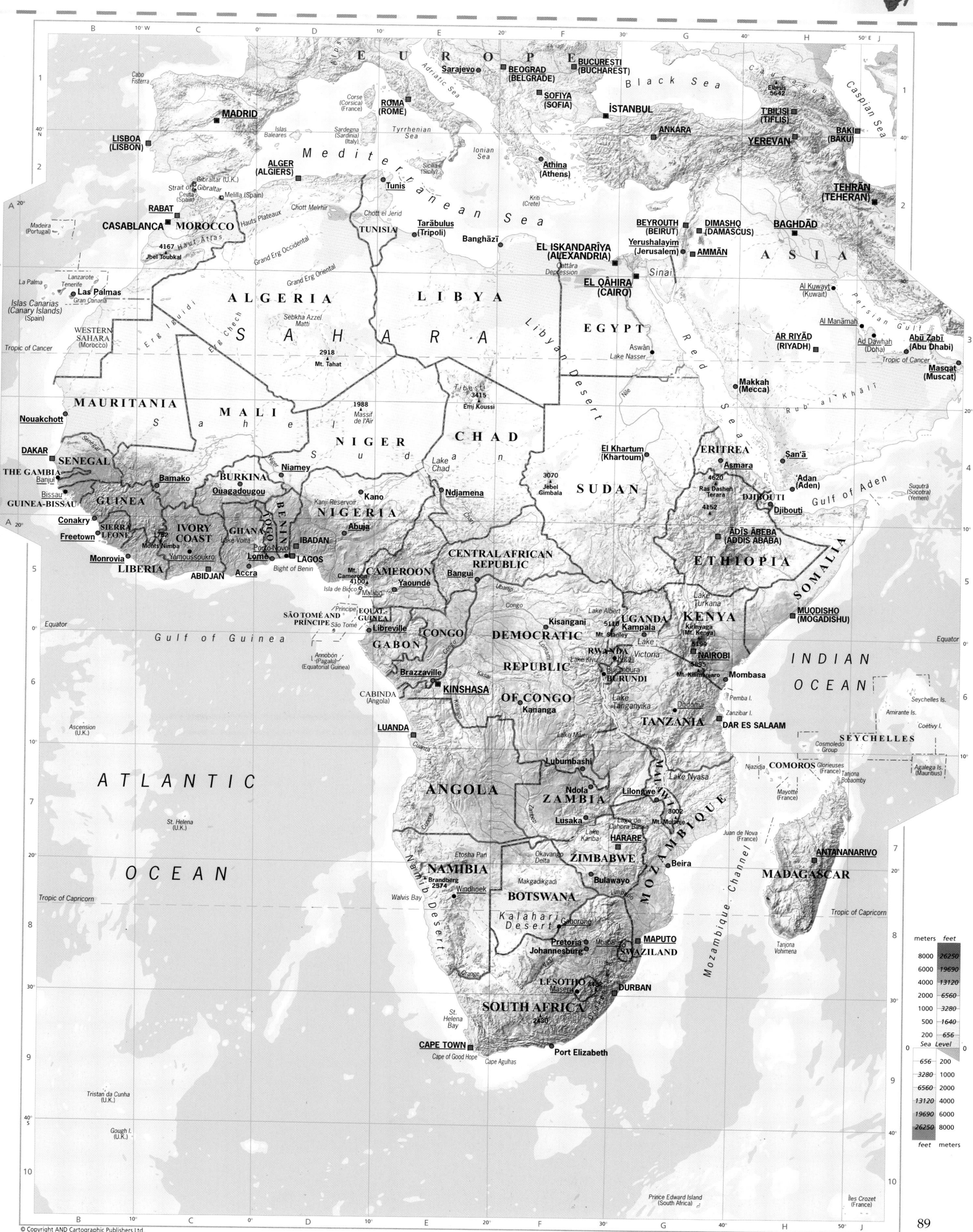

Africa

© Copyright AND Cartographic Publishers Ltd.

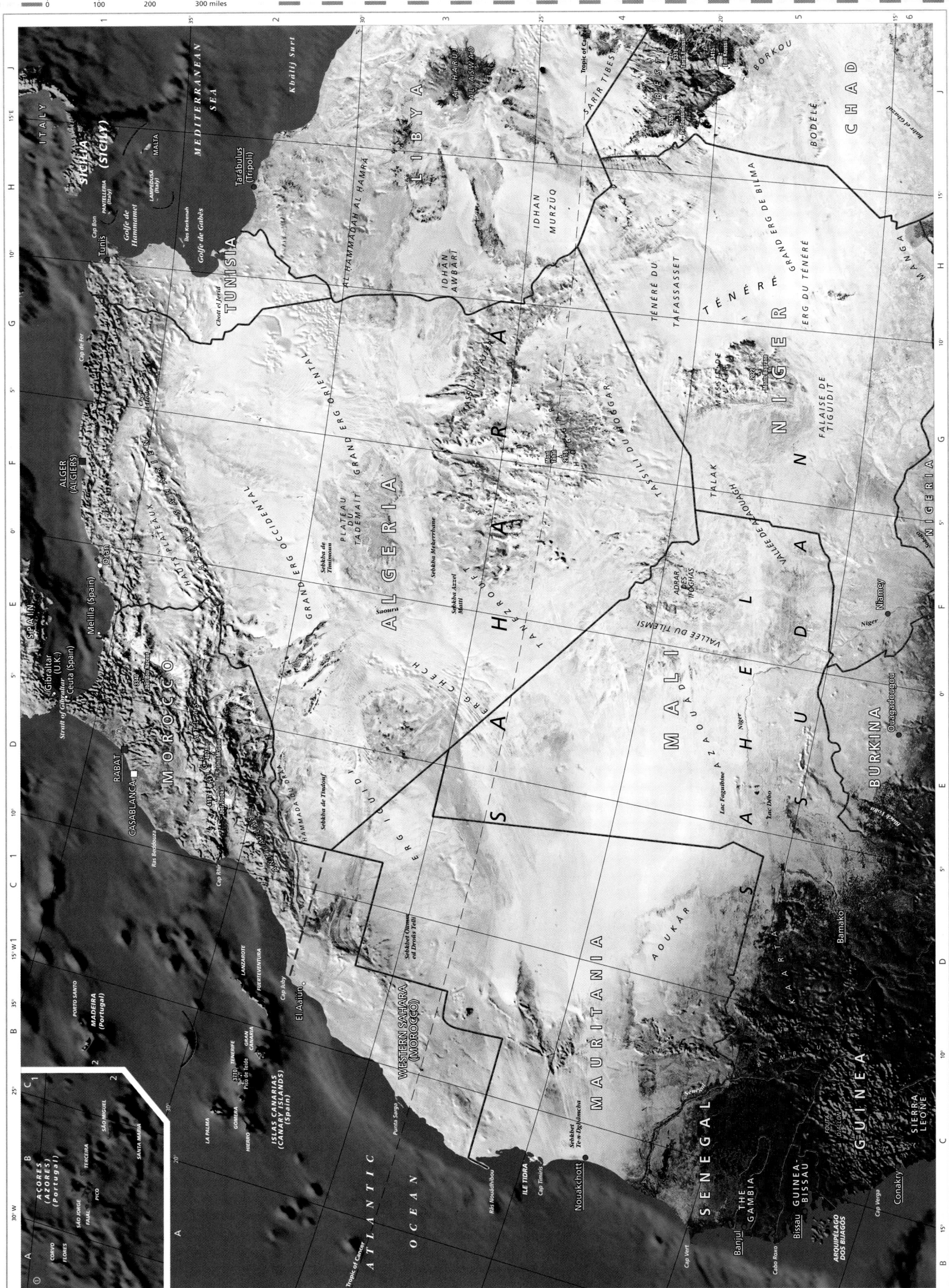

Scale 1 : 13 000 000

© Copyright

90

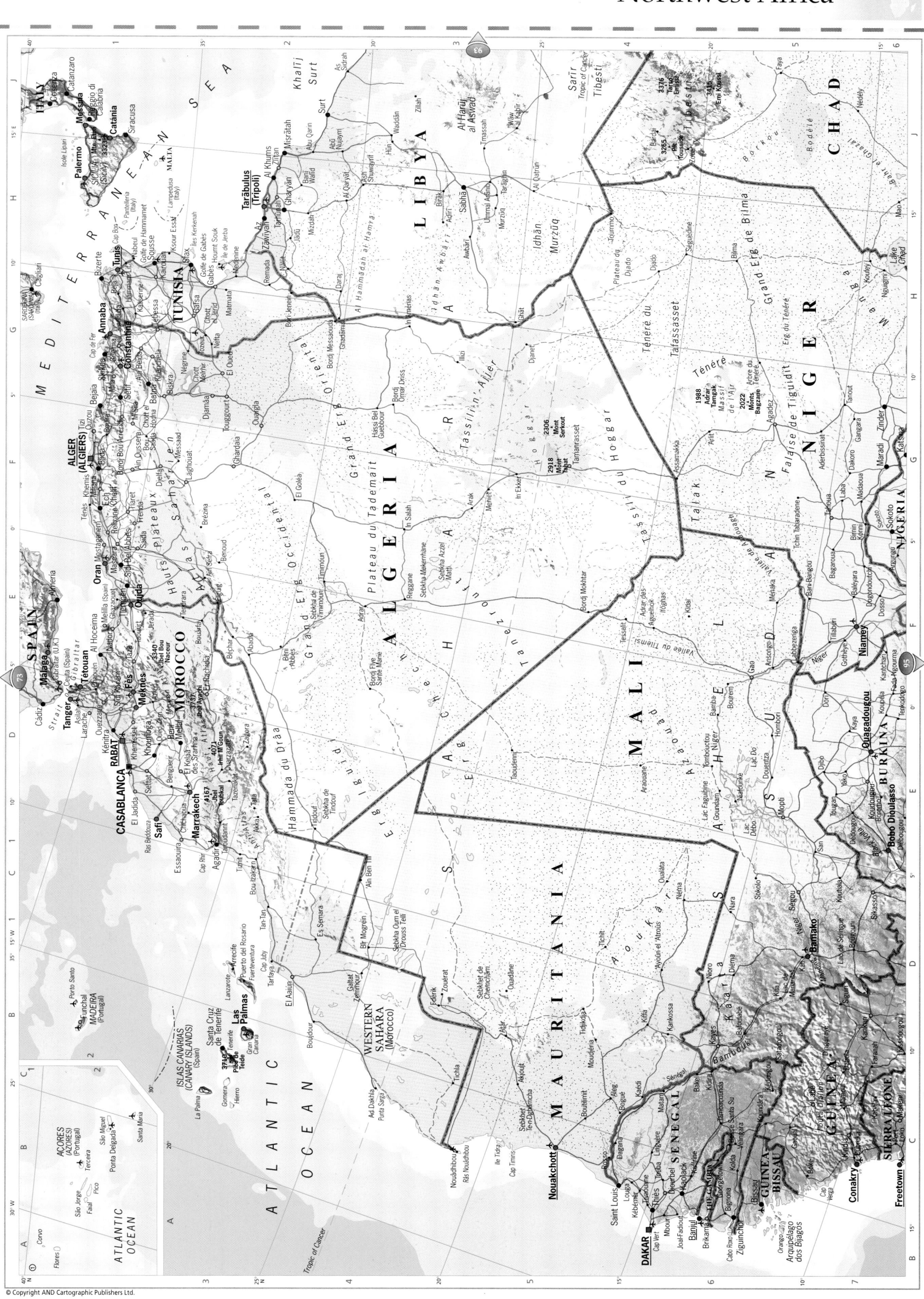

91

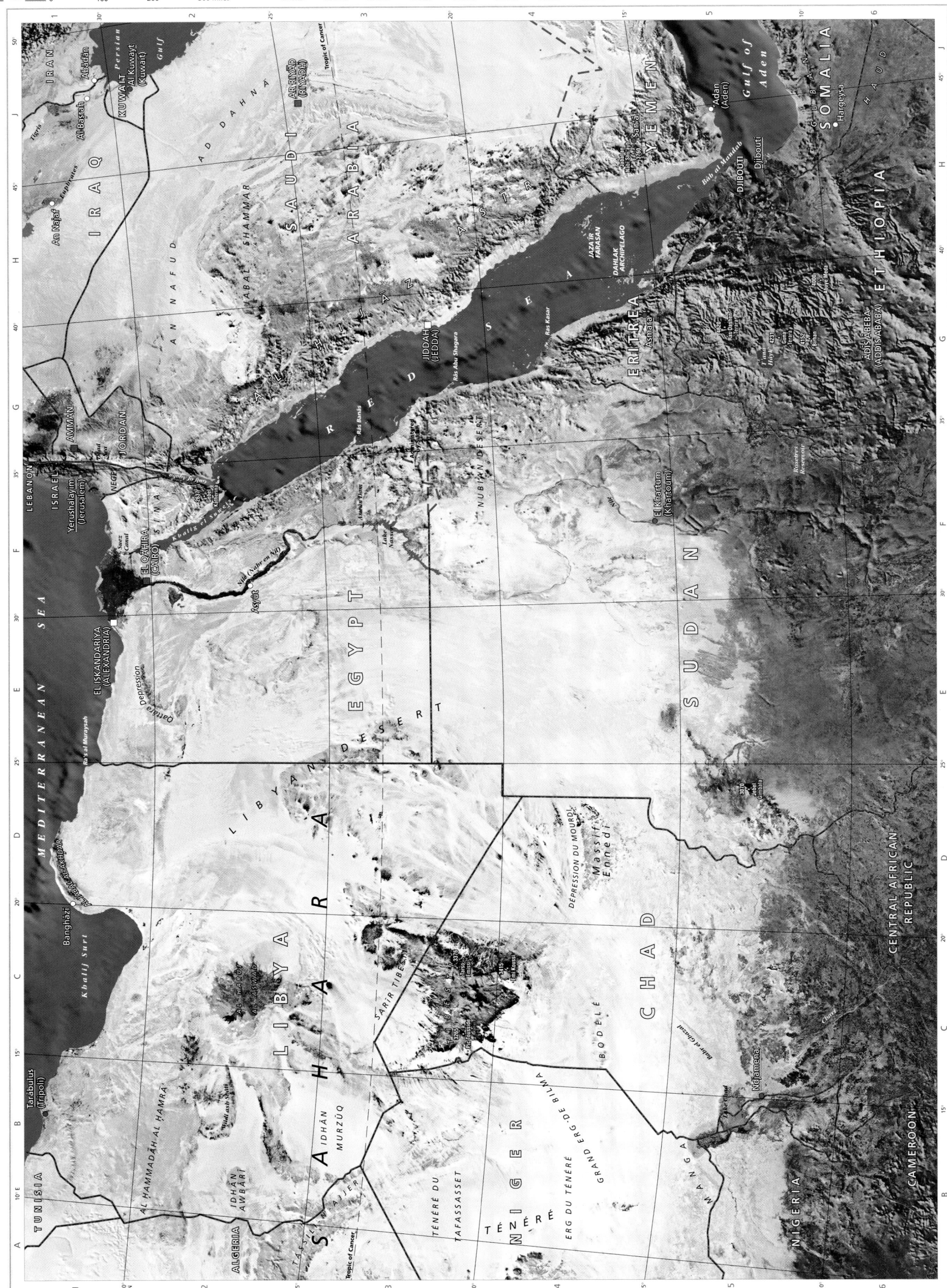

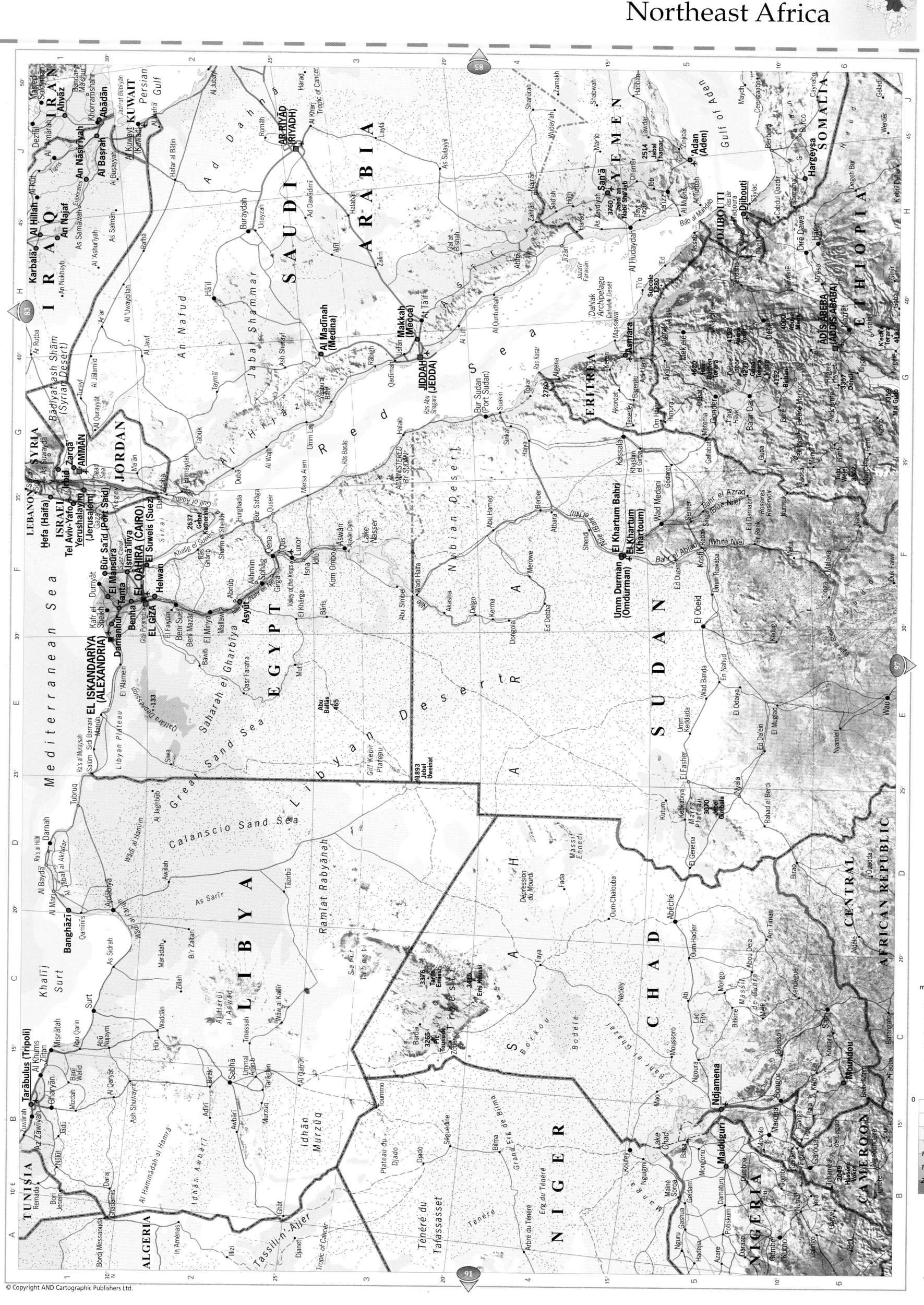

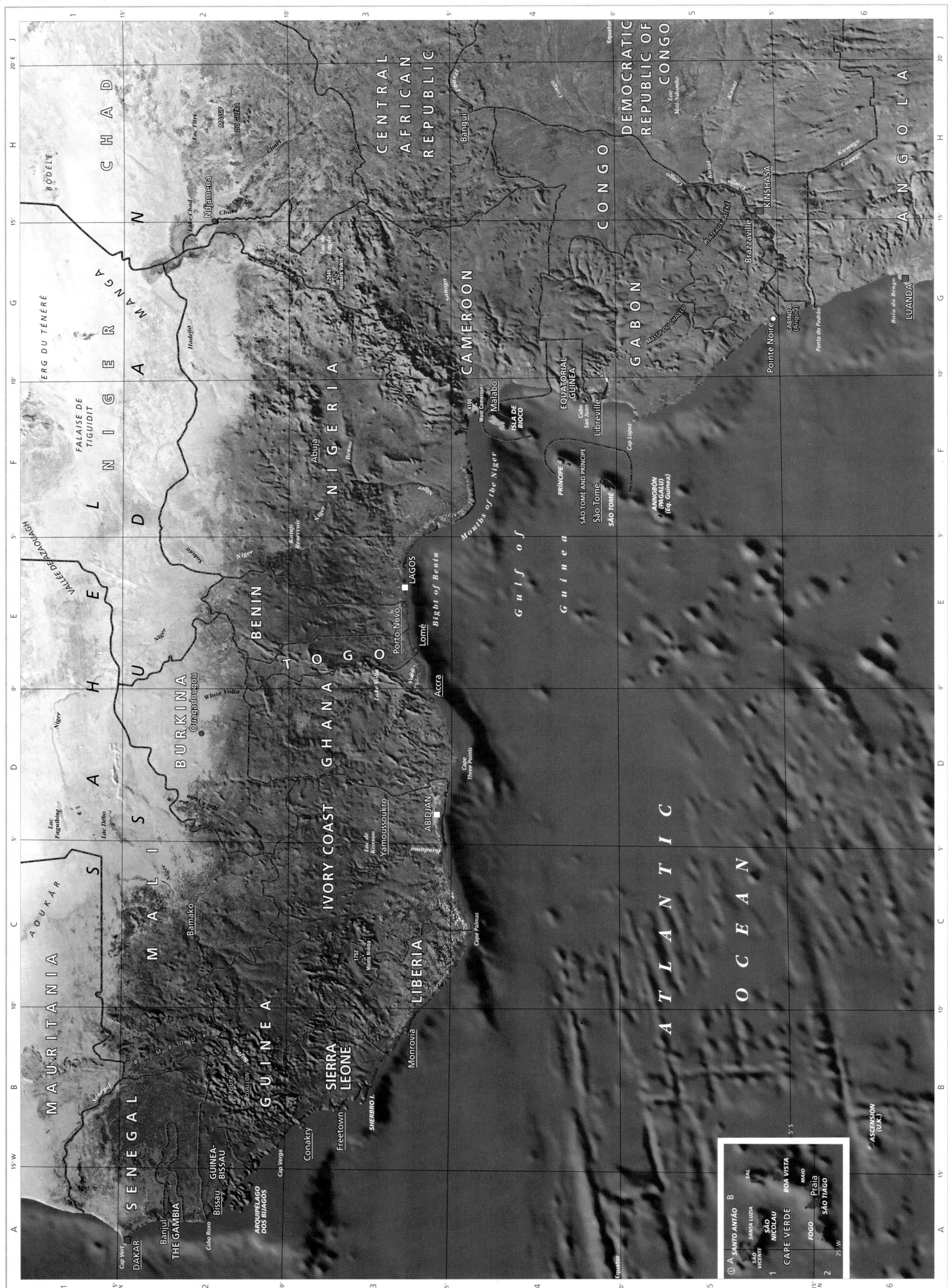

Scale 1 : 13 000 000

200   400   600 km

100   200   300 miles

94

© Copyright

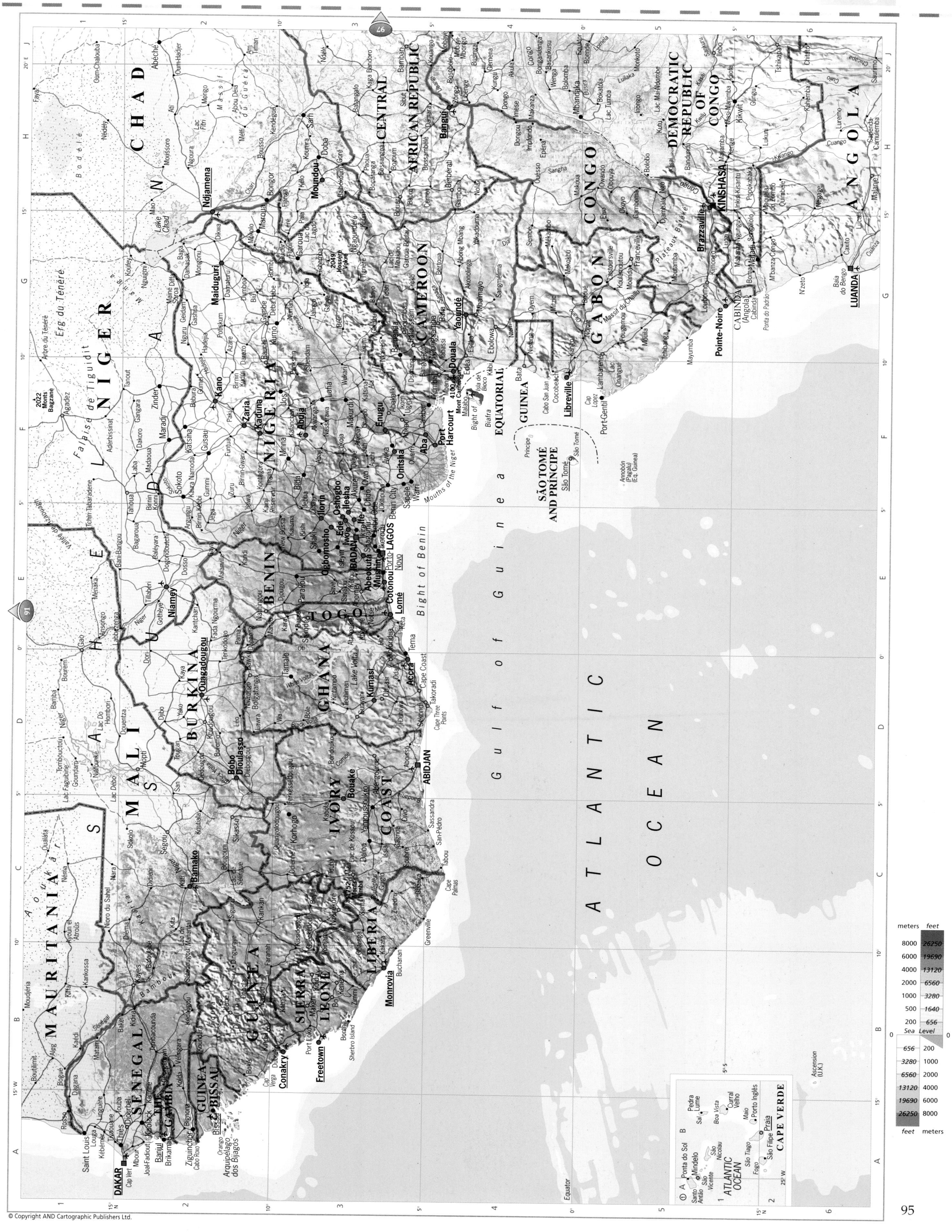

CHAD

NIGER

NIGERIA

MALI

MAURITANIA

SENEGAL

GUINEA

GUINEA-BISSAU

SIERRA LEONE

LIBERIA

IVORY COAST

GHANA

BURKINA

BENIN

TOGO

CENTRAL AFRICAN REPUBLIC

CAMEROON

EQUATORIAL GUINEA

GABON

CONGO

DEMOCRATIC REPUBLIC OF CONGO

ANGOLA

SÃO TOMÉ AND PRÍNCIPE

CAPE VERDE

Gulf of Guinea

ATLANTIC OCEAN

Bight of Benin

Bight of Biafra

Mouths of the Niger

Lake Chad

DAKAR · Njamena · Kano · Abuja · LAGOS · Yaoundé · Bangui · Brazzaville · KINSHASA · LUANDA · Libreville · Pointe-Noire · Port Harcourt · Douala · Cotonou · Lomé · Accra · Kumasi · ABIDJAN · Monrovia · Freetown · Conakry · Bamako · Ouagadougou · Niamey · Maiduguri · Ibadan

meters	feet
8000	26250
6000	19690
4000	13120
2000	6560
1000	3280
500	1640
200	656
Sea Level	
656	200
3280	1000
6560	2000
13120	4000
19690	6000
26250	8000
feet	meters

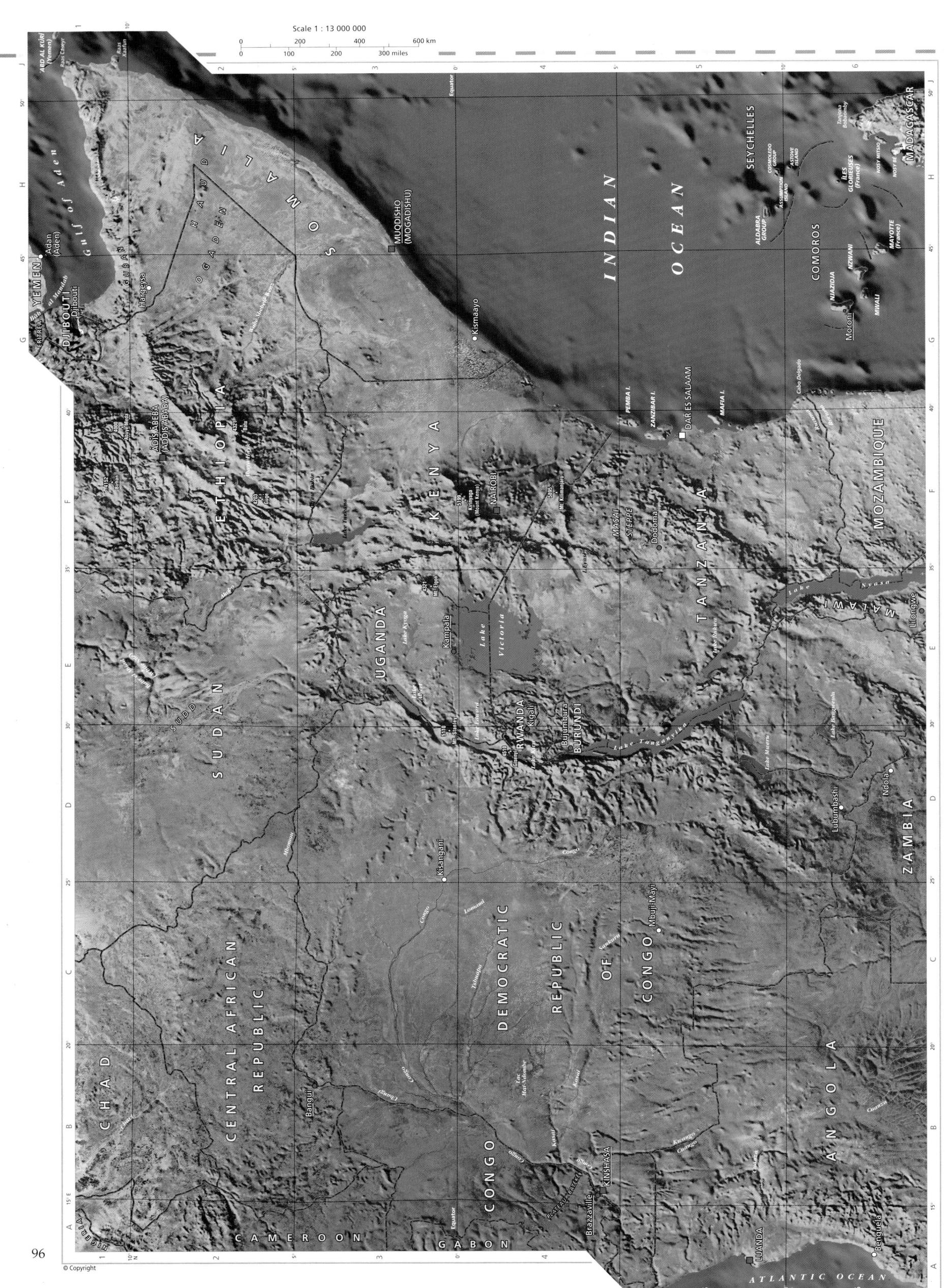

Scale 1 : 13 000 000

0   200   400   600 km
0   100   200   300 miles

ARD AL KŪRĪ
(Yemen)
Raas Caseyr
Raas Xaafuun

YEMEN
Adan
(Aden)
Bāb al Mandab
Gulf of Aden

ERITREA
DJIBOUTI
Djibouti

Hargeysa

SOMALIA

GUBAN

HAUD

OGADEN

Wabi Shabeelle

ETHIOPIA

ADĪS ĀBEBA
(ADDIS ABABA)

4192
Jīmā

4203
Giɓe

Ākobo

Lake Turkana

4321
Batu

Prograde Zone

SUDAN

SUDD

Lake Turkana

UGANDA

Kampala

Lake Kyoga

4321
Mt. Elgon

Lake Albert

Lake Edward

5110
Mt. Stanley

4510
Geno

Lake Kivu

RWANDA
Kigali

BURUNDI
Bujumbura

Lake Tanganyika

Kilimanjaro
(Mount Kenya)
5199

NAIROBI

5895
Mt. Kilimanjaro

KENYA

MUQDISHO
(MOGADISHU)

Kismaayo

INDIAN   OCEAN

Equator

SEYCHELLES

COSMOLEDO
GROUP

ASSUMPTION
ISLAND

ASTOVE
ISLAND

ALDABRA
GROUP

ÎLES
GLORIEUSES
(France)

NOSY MITSIO

NOSY BE

Tanjona
Bobaomby

MADAGASCAR

COMOROS

NJAZIDJA

NZWANI

MWALI

MAYOTTE
(France)

Moroni

PEMBA I.

ZANZIBAR I.

DAR ES SALAAM

MAFIA I.

Cabo Delgado

TANZANIA

Dodoma

MASAI
STEPPE

Livasai

Lake Eyasi

Lake Rukwa

Lake Natron

MALAWI

Lake Nyasa

Lilongwe

MOZAMBIQUE

Congo

Lomami

Lualaba

Lake Mweru

Lake Bangweulu

Lubumbashi

Ndola

ZAMBIA

DEMOCRATIC

REPUBLIC

OF

CONGO

Kisangani

Uele

Mbuji Mayi

Sankuru

Tshuapa

CENTRAL AFRICAN
REPUBLIC

CHAD

Mbomou

Uele

Lac
Mai-Ndombe

Bangui

Ubangi

Congo
(Zaire)

Kwilu

Kasai

Sankuru

Kwango

ANGOLA

Kasai

Kwango

Cuango

LUANDA

Benguela

Cuanza

Cuanza

CONGO

Brazzaville

KINSHASA

PLATEAU DES BATÉKÉ

GABON

CAMEROON

Equator

ATLANTIC   OCEAN

96

© Copyright

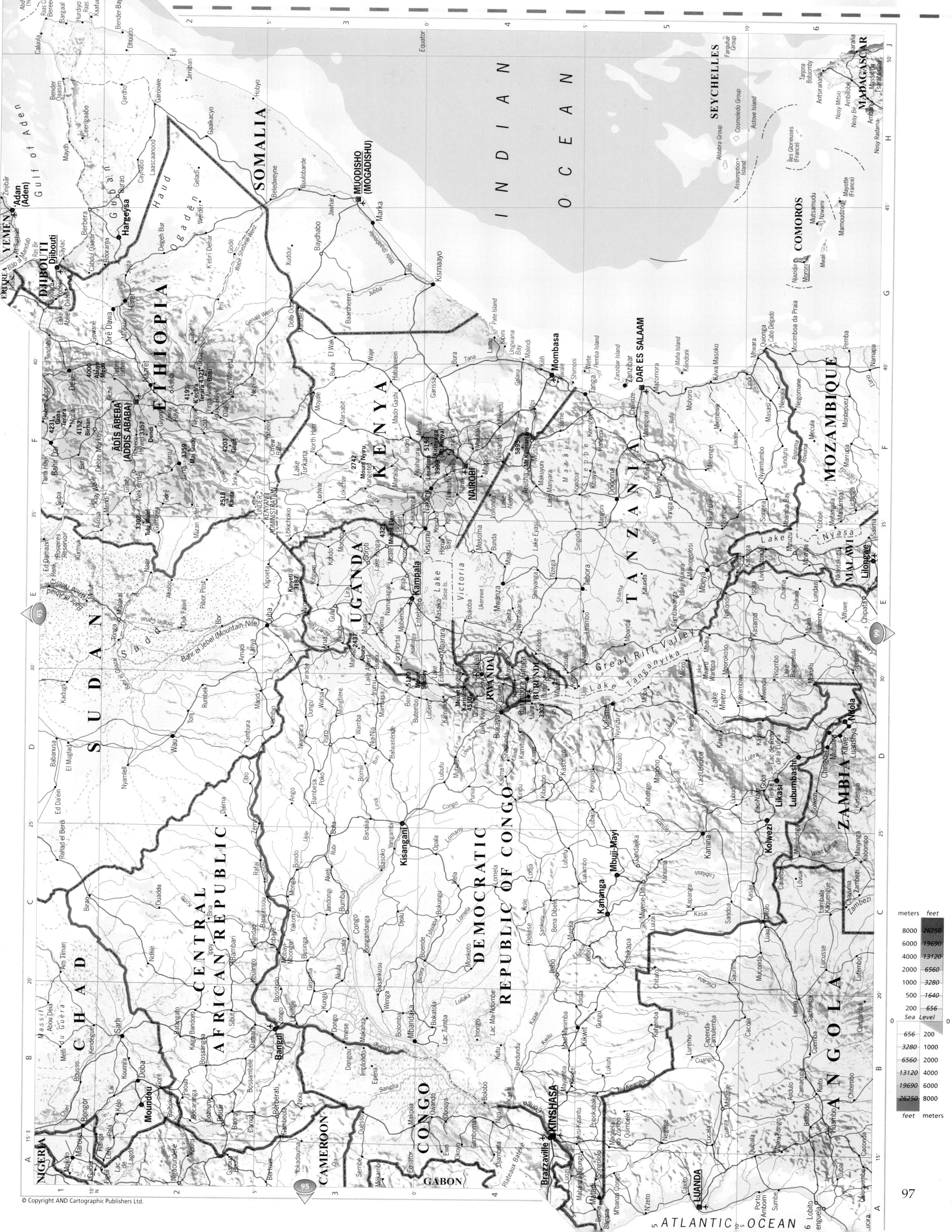

YEMEN
'Adan (Aden)
Gulf of Aden
DJIBOUTI
ERITREA
Hargeysa
SOMALIA
ETHIOPIA
ADĪS ABEBA (ADDIS ABEBA)
MUQDISHO (MOGADISHU)
SUDAN
UGANDA
Kampala
KENYA
NAIROBI
Lake Victoria
RWANDA
BURUNDI
TANZANIA
Lake Tanganyika
Great Rift Valley
DAR ES SALAAM
SEYCHELLES
COMOROS
MADAGASCAR
INDIAN OCEAN
CENTRAL AFRICAN REPUBLIC
CHAD
NIGERIA
CAMEROON
CONGO
GABON
Brazzaville
KINSHASA
DEMOCRATIC REPUBLIC OF CONGO
Kisangani
Kananga
Mbuji-Mayi
ZAMBIA
Lubumbashi
Likasi
Kolwezi
Ndola
ANGOLA
LUANDA
MALAWI
Lilongwe
MOZAMBIQUE
Lake Nyasa
Mombasa
ATLANTIC OCEAN

meters	feet
8000	26250
6000	19690
4000	13120
2000	6560
1000	3280
500	1640
200	656
Sea Level	

feet	meters
656	200
3280	1000
6560	2000
13120	4000
19690	6000
26250	8000

97

Scale 1 : 13 000 000

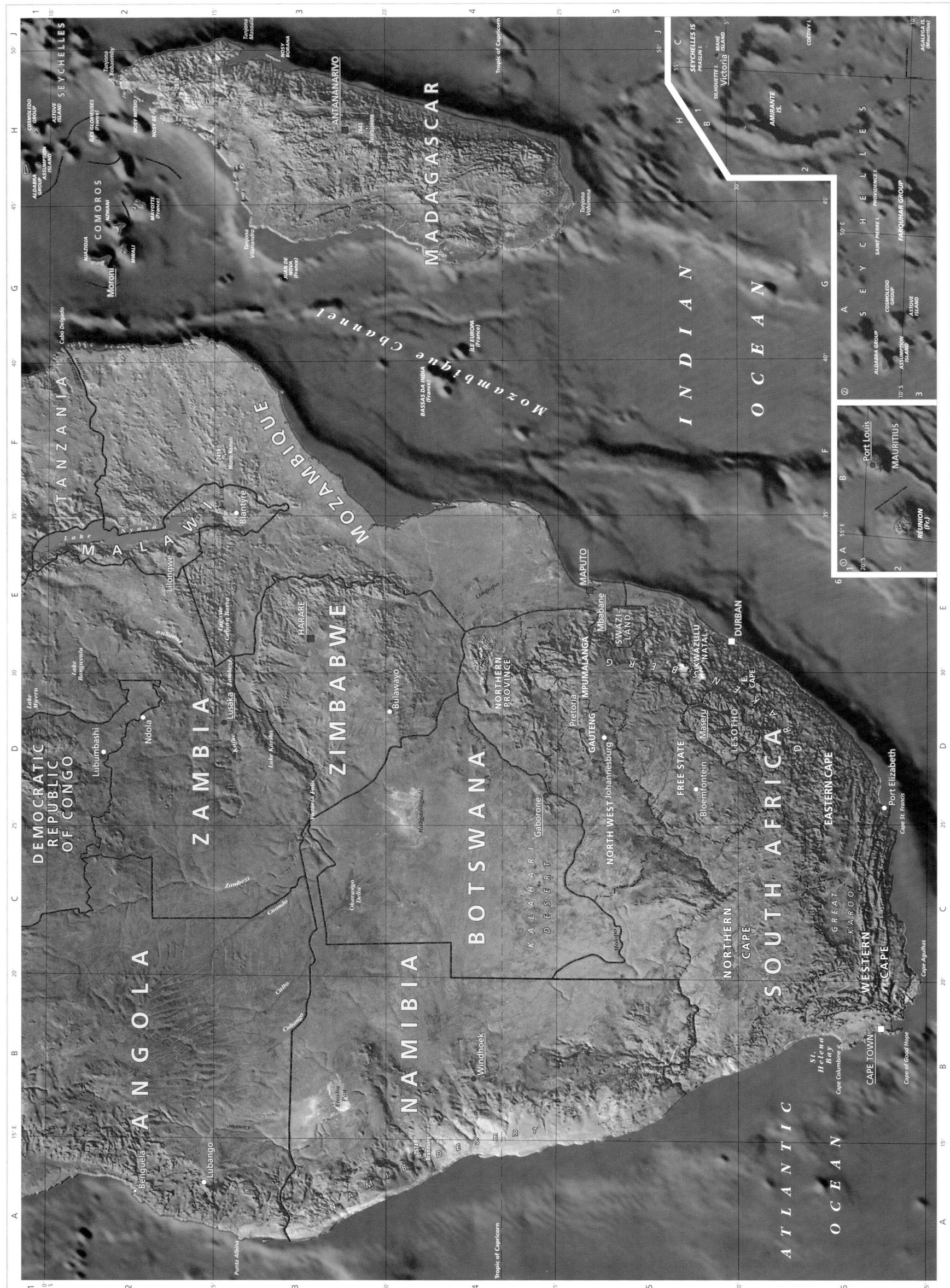

© Copyright

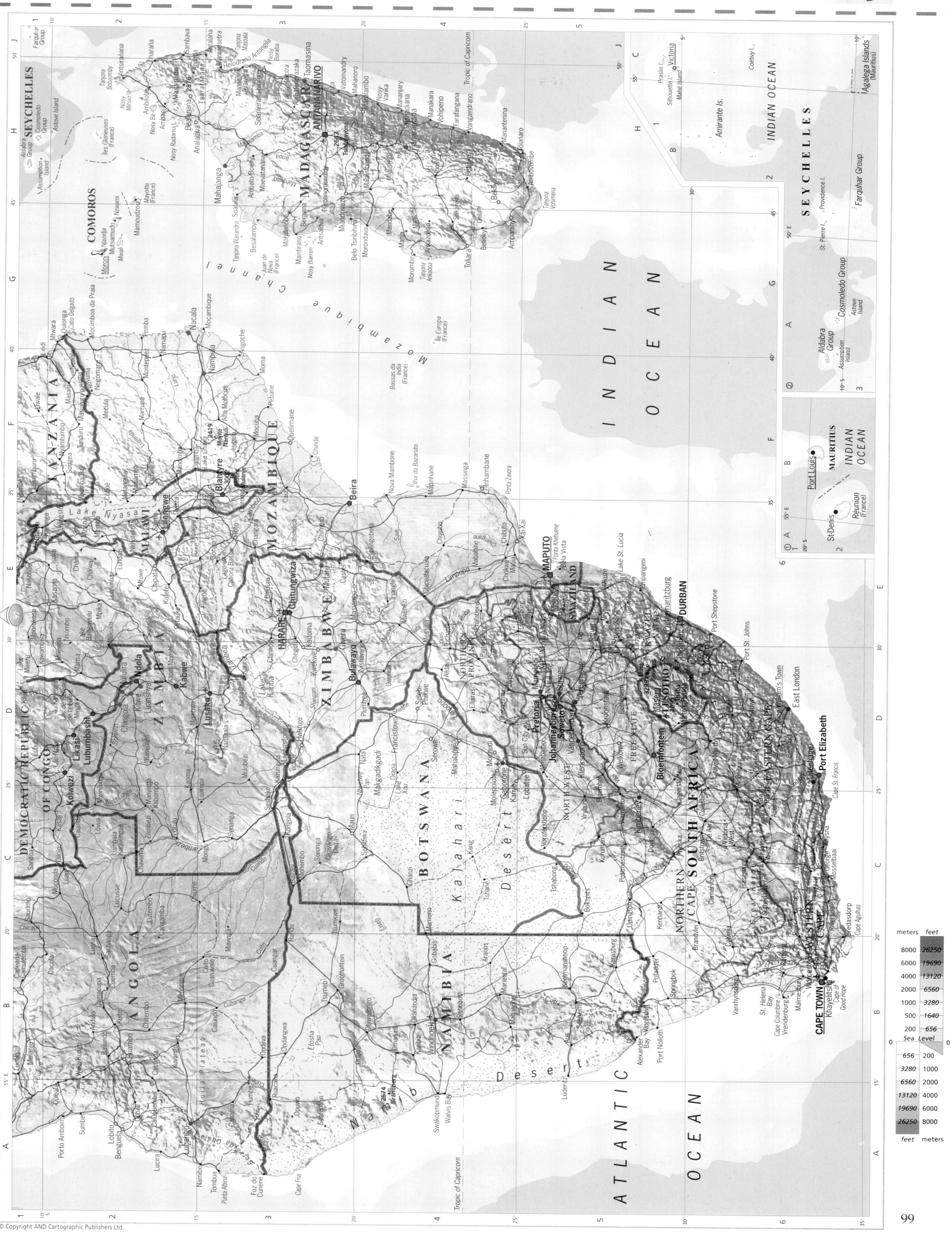

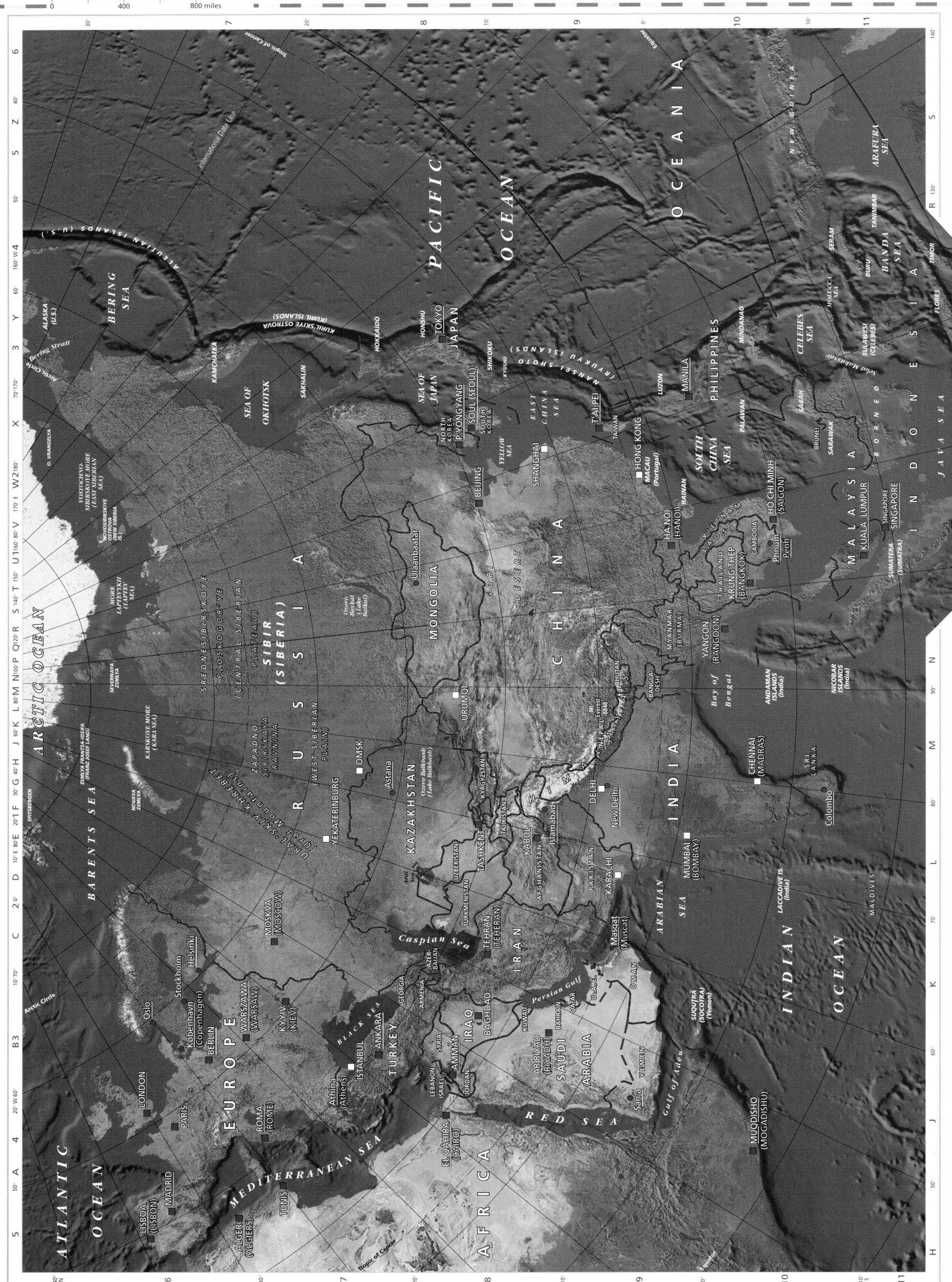

Scale 1 : 37 000 000

0   400   800   1200   1600 km
0   400   800 miles

ATLANTIC OCEAN

ARCTIC OCEAN

PACIFIC OCEAN

OCEANIA

International Date Line

BERING SEA

ALASKA (U.S.)

ALEUTIAN ISLANDS (U.S.)

Bering Strait

Arctic Circle

KAMCHATKA

VOSTOCHNO-SIBIRSKOYE MORE (EAST SIBERIAN SEA)

SEA OF OKHOTSK

SAKHALIN

MORE LAPTEVYKH (LAPTEV SEA)

KURIL'SKIYE OSTROVA (KURIL ISLANDS)

HOKKAIDO

HONSHU

TOKYO

JAPAN

SEA OF JAPAN

SHIKOKU

NANSEI-SHOTO (RYUKYU ISLANDS)

O. VRANGELYA

NOVOSIBIRSKIYE OSTROVA (NEW SIBERIA IS.)

NORTH KOREA

PYONGYANG

SOUL (SEOUL)

SOUTH KOREA

EAST CHINA SEA

TAIPEI

TAIWAN

MANILA

LUZON

PHILIPPINES

SOUTH CHINA SEA

MINDANAO

CELEBES SEA

SULAWESI (CELEBES)

Selat Makasar

SERAM

BURU

BANDA SEA

TANIMBAR

ARAFURA SEA

MALACCA SEA

SABAH

BRUNEI

SARAWAK

BORNEO

JAVA SEA

INDONESIA

TIMOR

FLORES

NEW GUINEA

Equator

SPITSBERGEN

ZEMLYA FRANTSA-IOSFA (FRANZ JOSEF LAND)

NOVAYA ZEMLYA

BARENTS SEA

KARSKOYE MORE (KARA SEA)

SEVERNAYA ZEMLYA

SREDNESIBIRSKOYE PLOSKOGOR'YE (CENTRAL SIBERIAN PLATEAU)

SIBIR (SIBERIA)

R U S S I A

Ozero Baykal (Lake Baykal)

Ulaanbaatar

MONGOLIA

GOBI DESERT

C H I N A

BEIJING

SHANGHAI

YELLOW SEA

HONG KONG

MACAU (Portugal)

HAINAN

HA NOI (HANOI)

VIETNAM

LAOS

HO CHI MINH (SAIGON)

CAMBODIA

Phnum Penh

THAILAND

KRUNG THEP (BANGKOK)

MYANMAR (BURMA)

YANGON (RANGOON)

ANDAMAN ISLANDS (India)

NICOBAR ISLANDS (India)

Bay of Bengal

KUALA LUMPUR

MALAYSIA

SINGAPORE

SUMATERA (SUMATRA)

JAKARTA

ZAPADNO SIBIRSKAYA RAVNINA (WEST SIBERIAN PLAIN)

URAL'SKIY KHREBET (URAL MOUNTAINS)

YEKATERINBURG

OMSK

Astana

KAZAKHSTAN

Ozero Balkhash (Lake Balkhash)

URUMQI

KYRGYZSTAN

TASHKENT

UZBEKISTAN

TURKMENISTAN

TAJIKISTAN

Mt. Everest 8848

H I M A L A Y A

BHUTAN

BANGLA DESH

NEPAL

DELHI

New Delhi

I N D I A

CHENNAI (MADRAS)

SRI LANKA

Colombo

LACCADIVE IS. (India)

MALDIVES

INDIAN OCEAN

MOSKVA (MOSCOW)

Helsinki

Stockholm

Oslo

København (Copenhagen)

BERLIN

WARSZAWA (WARSAW)

KYYIV (KIEV)

BLACK SEA

ISTANBUL

ANKARA

TURKEY

Athina (Athens)

GEORGIA

ARMENIA

AZER- BAIJAN

Caspian Sea

TEHRAN (TEHERAN)

IRAN

Masqat (Muscat)

OMAN

U.A.E.

QATAR

BAHRAIN

Persian Gulf

KUWAIT

ARRIYAD (RIYADH)

SAUDI ARABIA

ARABIAN SEA

MUMBAI (BOMBAY)

KARACHI

PAKISTAN

Islamabad

KABUL

AFGHANISTAN

EUROPE

Kobenhavn

LONDON

PARIS

MADRID

LISBOA (LISBON)

ROMA (ROME)

TUNIS

ALGER (ALGIERS)

MEDITERRANEAN SEA

EL QÂHIRA (CAIRO)

AFRICA

LEBANON

ISRAEL

SYRIA

JORDAN

AMMAN

IRAQ

BAGHDAD

YEMEN

Sana

Gulf of Aden

RED SEA

SUQUTRÁ (SOCOTRA) (Yemen)

MUQDISHO (MOGADISHU)

Tropic of Cancer

Tropic of Cancer

Arctic Circle

Equator

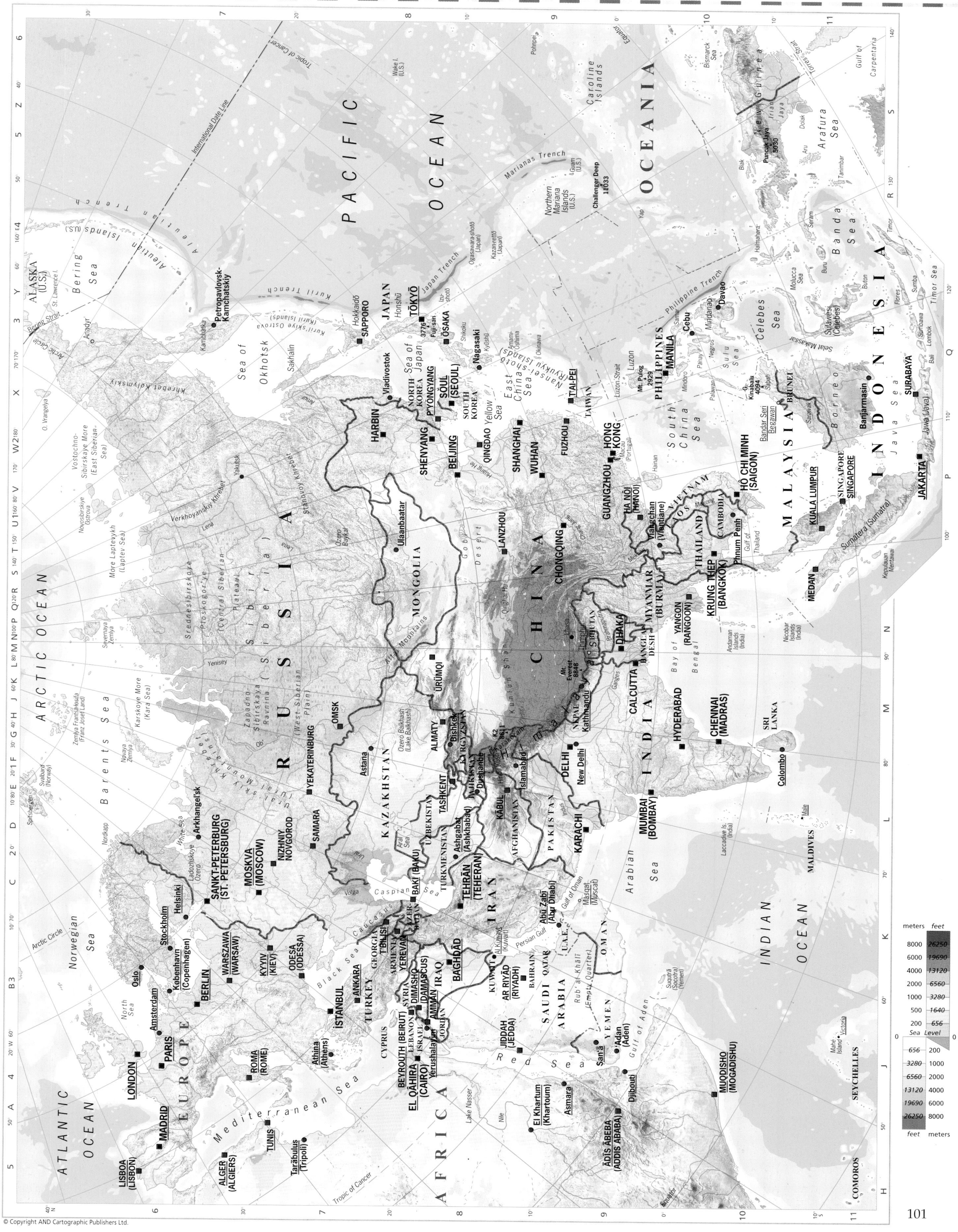

Scale 1 : 15 500 000

| 0 | 200 | 400 | 600 km |

| 0 | 100 | 200 | 300 miles |

B A R E N T S   S E A

MORE LAPTEVYKH
(LAPTEV SEA)

ZEMLYA FRANTSA-IOSIFA
(FRANZ JOSEF LAND)

SEVERNAYA ZEMLYA

OSTROV
BOL'SHOY
BEGICHEV

NORWAY

Murmansk

KARSKOYE MORE
(KARA SEA)

Ostrov Belyy

Ozero
Taymyr

SAKHA

Arctic Circle

Mys Kanin Nos

OSTROV
KOLGUYEV

OSTROV
VAYGACH

Noril'sk

S R E D N E   S I B I R S K O Y E

BELOYE MORE
(WHITE SEA)

Pechorskoye
More

Yenisey

P L O S K O G O R ' Y E

Arkhangel'sk

Vorkuta

Ob'

KOMI

Ob'

Z A P A D N O - S I B I R S K A Y A
R A V N I N A
(W E S T   S I B E R I A N
P L A I N)

Surgut

R U S S I A

Bratsk

MARIY EL
UDMURTIYA
PERM

CHUVASHIYA
KAZAN

Yenisey
Ob'

Krasnoyarsk

TATARIYA

YEKATERINBURG

Tyumen'

U R A L ' S K I Y   K H R E B E T
(U R A L   M O U N T A I N S)

UFA

CHELYABINSK

OMSK

NOVOSIBIRSK

SAMARA

BASHKIRIYA

Irtysh

KHAKASIYA

Barnaul

TYVA

Uvs Nuur

ALTAY

Orsk

Astana

Ozero Tengiz

Aktyubinsk

Semipalatinsk

MONGOLIA

PRIKASPIYSKAYA NIZMENNOST'

Karaganda

Altay

K A Z A K H S T A N

Ozero Zaysan

A L T A Y   M O U N T A I N S

Caspian
Sea

Ozero Balkhash

Ozero
Alakol'

Aktau

KHR. TARBAGATAY

4925
Karlik Shan

Aral Sea

Shihezi

URUMQI

Kara
Bogaz Gol

Syrdar'ya

T I A N   S H A N

Korla

ALMATY

Bosten Hu

UZBEKISTAN

Zhambyl

Ysyk-Köl

Aksu

Bishkek

7439
Pik Pobedy

TASHKENT

KYRGYZSTAN

C H I N A

TURKMENISTAN

Andizhan

Kashi

Peski Karakumy

TARIM PENDI

Samarkand

Ashgabat
(Ashkhabad)

Qarqan He

Dushanbe

7495
Pik Kommunizma

IRAN

MASHHAD

7546
Muztagata

TAJIKISTAN

Mazar-e Sharif

AFGHANISTAN

PAKISTAN

0   200   400   600 km
0   100   200   300 miles

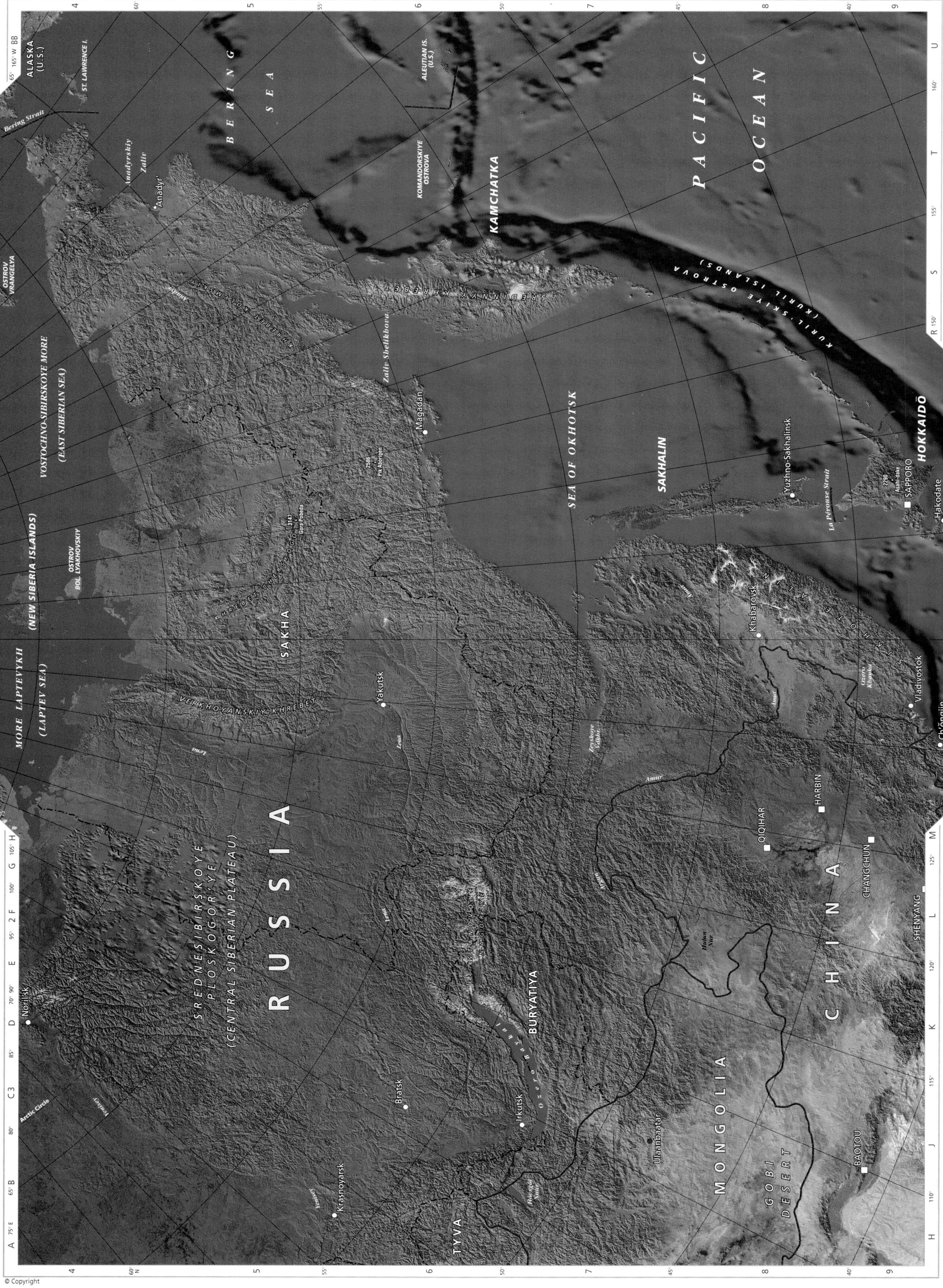

ALASKA (U.S.)

ST. LAWRENCE I.

Bering Strait

Arctic Circle

ALEUTIAN IS. (U.S.)

KOMANDORSKIYE OSTROVA

B E R I N G   S E A

Anadyrskiy Zaliv

Anadyr'

OSTROV VRANGELYA

KAMCHATKA

P A C I F I C   O C E A N

NOVOSIBIRSKIYE OSTROVA
(NEW SIBERIA ISLANDS)

VOSTOCHNOSIBIRSKOYE MORE
(EAST SIBERIAN SEA)

OSTROV BOL. LYAKHOVSKIY

MORE LAPTEVYKH
(LAPTEV SEA)

SREDINNYY KHREBET

Zaliv Shelikhova

Magadan

KURIL'SKIYE OSTROVA
(KURIL ISLANDS)

SEA OF OKHOTSK

SAKHALIN

HOKKAIDO

JAPAN

SAPPORO

Asahi-dake

Hakodate

La Pérouse Strait

Yuzhno-Sakhalinsk

SREDNESIBIRSKOYE PLOSKOGOR'YE
(CENTRAL SIBERIAN PLATEAU)

VERKHOYANSKIY KHREBET

KHREBET CHERSKOGO

SAKHA

Yakutsk

Lena

Aldan

Amur

Khabarovsk

Ozero Khanka

SEA OF JAPAN

Vladivostok

Chŏngjin

NORTH KOREA

R U S S I A

Norilsk

Arctic Circle

Yenisey

Krasnoyarsk

Bratsk

Irkutsk

Angara

OZERO BAYKAL

BURYATIYA

TYVA

Ulaanbaatar

Hōvsgōl Nur

M O N G O L I A

GOBI DESERT

BAOTOU

C H I N A

QIQIHAR

HARBIN

CHANGCHUN

SHENYANG

104

© Copyright

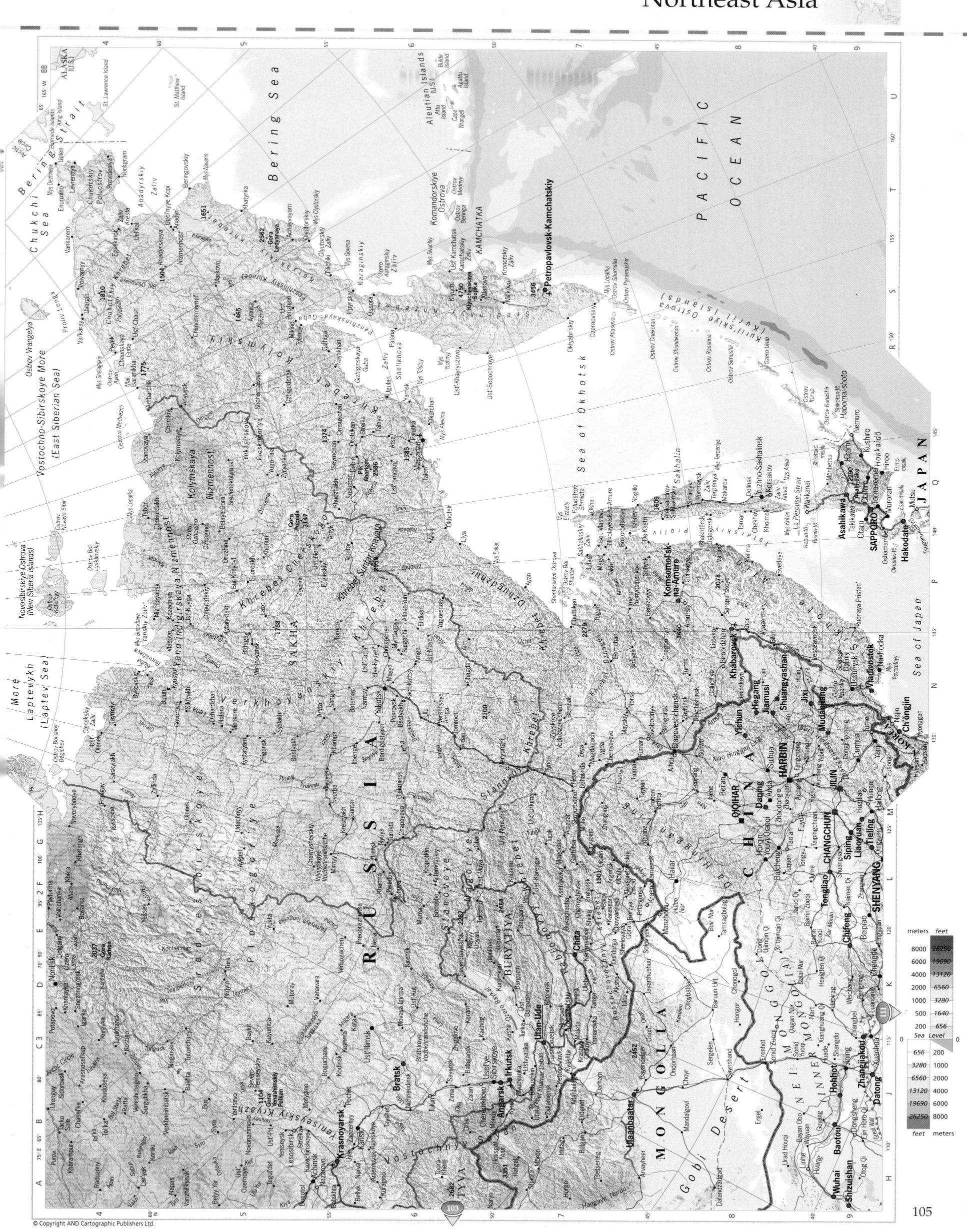

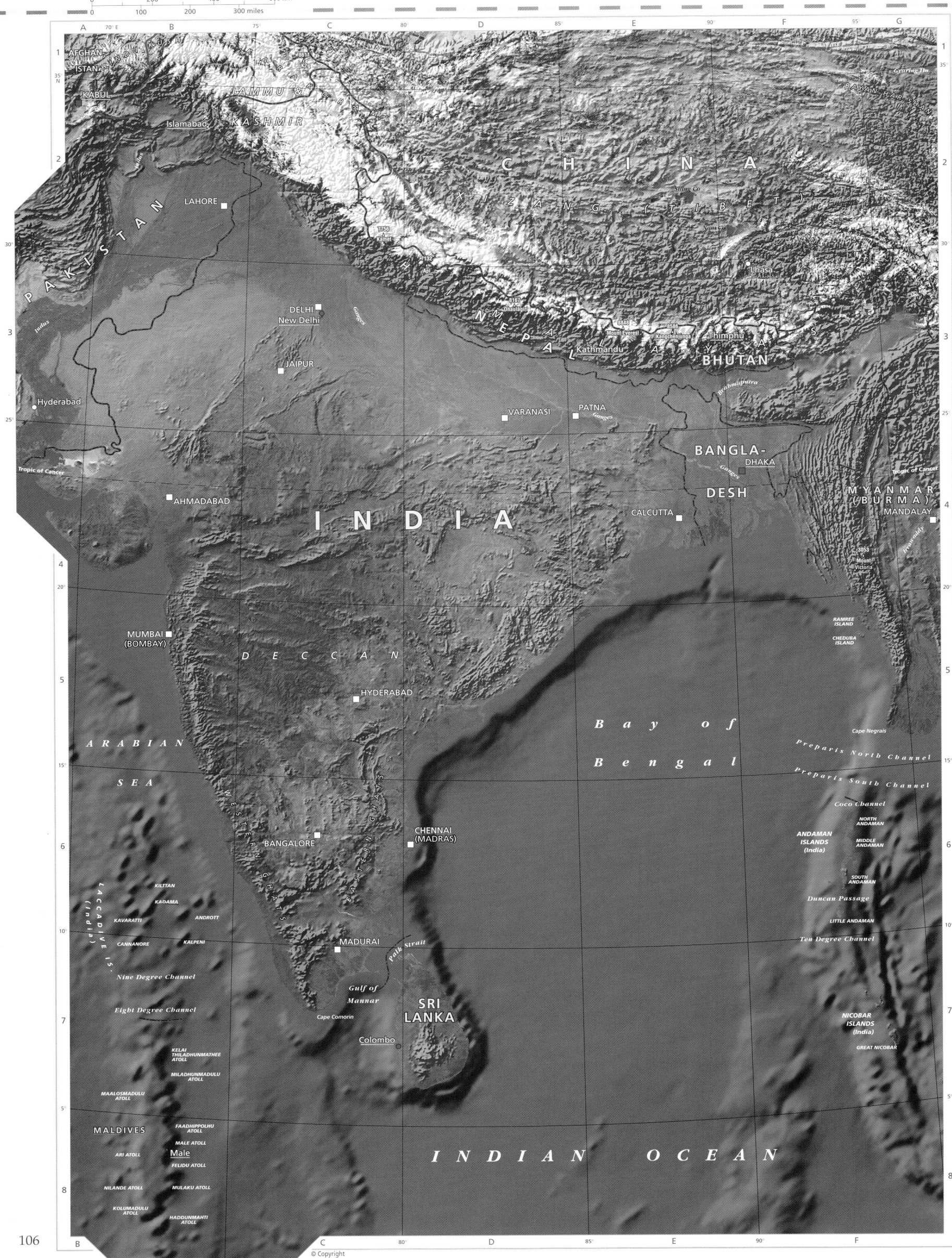

Scale 1 : 13 000 000

© Copyright

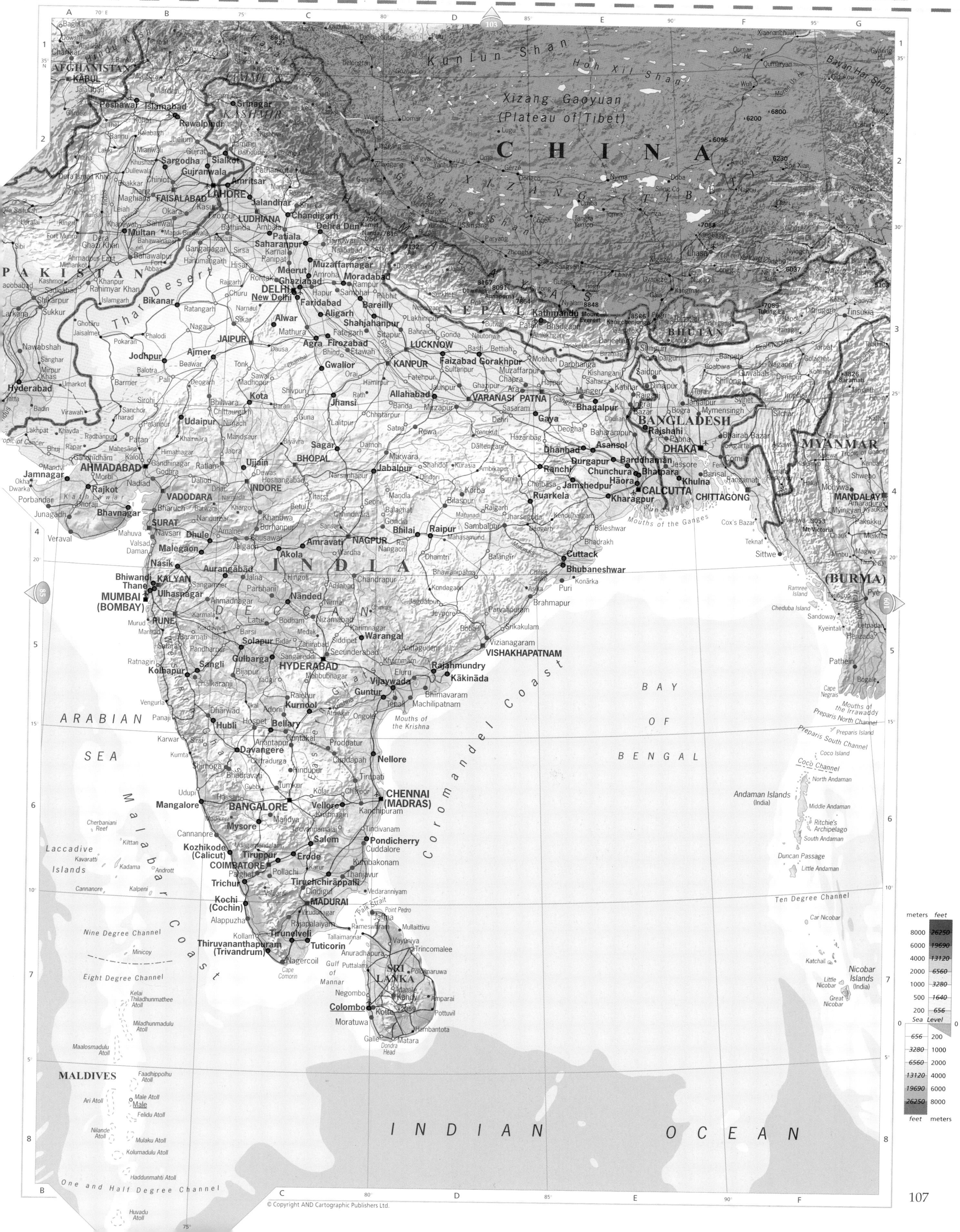

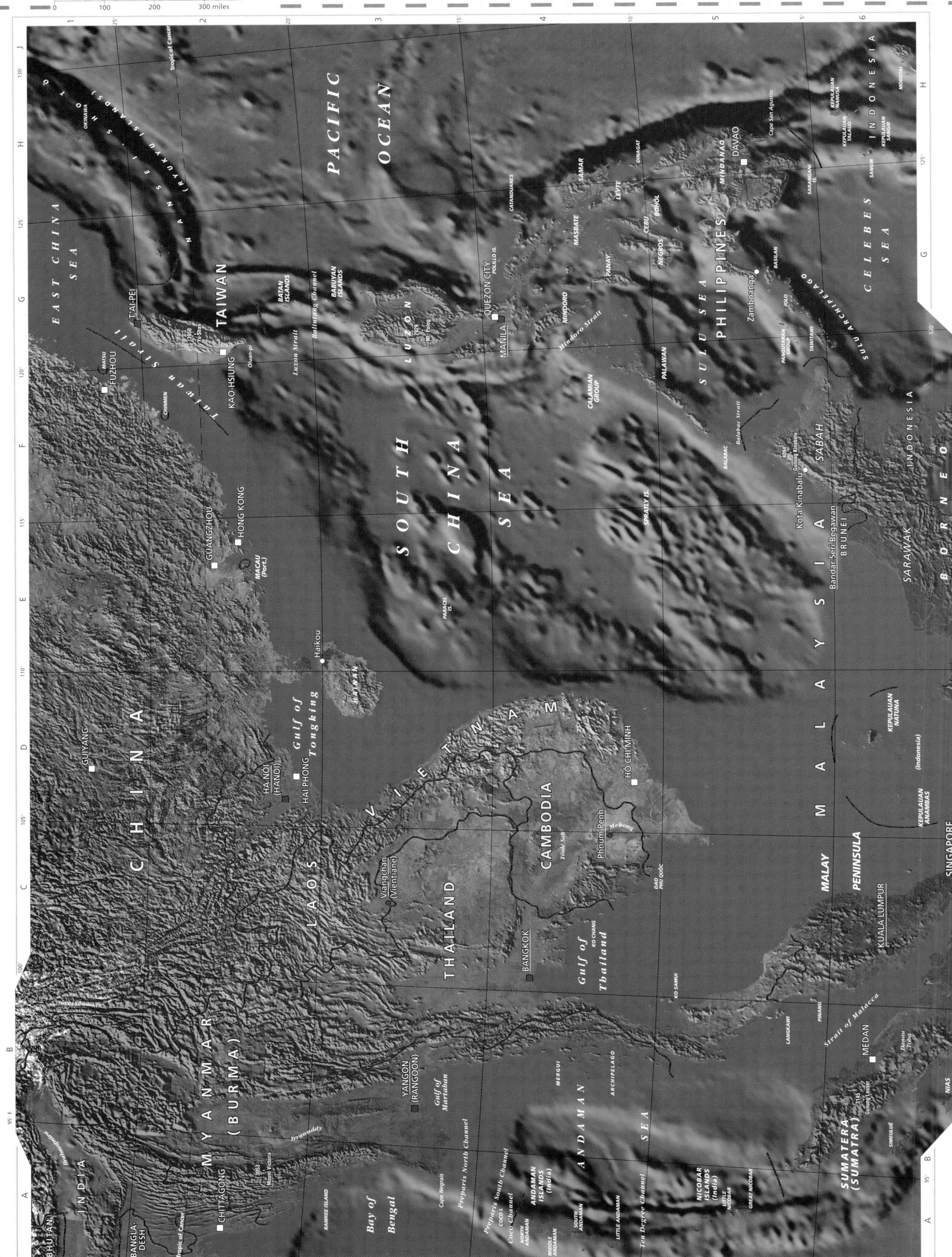

0   200   400   600 km

0   100   200   300 miles

PACIFIC

OCEAN

EAST CHINA

SEA

TAIWAN

TAI-PEI

MATSU

FUZHOU

KAO-HSIUNG

CHIMMEN

Oluan-pi

BATAN
ISLANDS

BABUYAN
ISLANDS

Balintang Channel

Luzon Strait

L U Z O N

POLILLO IS.

CATANDUANES

SAMAR

LEYTE

DINAGAT

Cape San Agustin

MINDANAO

DAVAO

KEPULAUAN
TALAUD

KEPULAUAN
SANGIR

SANGIR

I N D O N E S I A

KEPULAUAN
NANUSA

MOROTAI

CELEBES

SEA

QUEZON CITY

MANILA

MINDORO

PANAY

MASBATE

CEBU

NEGROS

BOHOL

BASILAN

Zamboanga

JOLO

PANGUTARAN
GROUP

TAWITAWI

SULU SEA

PHILIPPINES

SULU ARCHIPELAGO

CALAMIAN
GROUP

PALAWAN

SPRATLY IS.

Balabac Strait

BALABAC

Mindoro Strait

S O U T H

C H I N A

S E A

PARACEL
IS.

Kota Kinabalu

Gunung Kinabalu

SABAH

BRUNEI

Bandar Seri Begawan

SARAWAK

B O R N E O

M A L A Y S I A

I N D O N E S I A

KEPULAUAN
NATUNA
(Indonesia)

KEPULAUAN
ANAMBAS
(Indonesia)

GUANGZHOU

HONG KONG

MACAU
(Port.)

C H I N A

GUIYANG

Haikou

HAINAN

Gulf of
Tongking

HAI PHONG

HA NOI
(HANOI)

L A O S

V I E T N A M

HO CHI MINH

CAMBODIA

Phnum Penh

Tonle Sab

Mekong

DAO
PHU QUOC

Viangchan
(Vientiane)

T H A I L A N D

BANGKOK

Gulf of
Thailand

KO CHANG

KO SAMUI

MALAY

PENINSULA

KUALA LUMPUR

SINGAPORE

PINANG

LANGKAWI

Strait of Malacca

MEDAN

SUMATERA
(SUMATRA)

NIAS

SIMEULUE

Danau Toba

Gunung Leuser

3145

M Y A N M A R
(B U R M A)

YANGON
(RANGOON)

Gulf of
Martaban

Irrawaddy

MERGUI

ARCHIPELAGO

A N D A M A N

S E A

ANDAMAN
ISLANDS
(India)

NORTH
ANDAMAN

MIDDLE
ANDAMAN

SOUTH
ANDAMAN

LITTLE
ANDAMAN

NICOBAR
ISLANDS
(India)

LITTLE
NICOBAR

GREAT NICOBAR

Ten Degree Channel

Preparis North Channel

Preparis South Channel

COCO I.

Cape Negrais

RAMREE ISLAND

Bay of
Bengal

Tropic of Cancer

I N D I A

BHUTAN

CHITTAGONG

BANGLA-
DESH

Mount Victoria

3053

Tropic of Cancer

Tropic of Cancer

NANSEI-SHOTO (RYUKYU ISLANDS)

OKINAWA

Taiwan Strait

Yü-Shan

3950

Mt Pulog

2929

4101

108

© Copyright

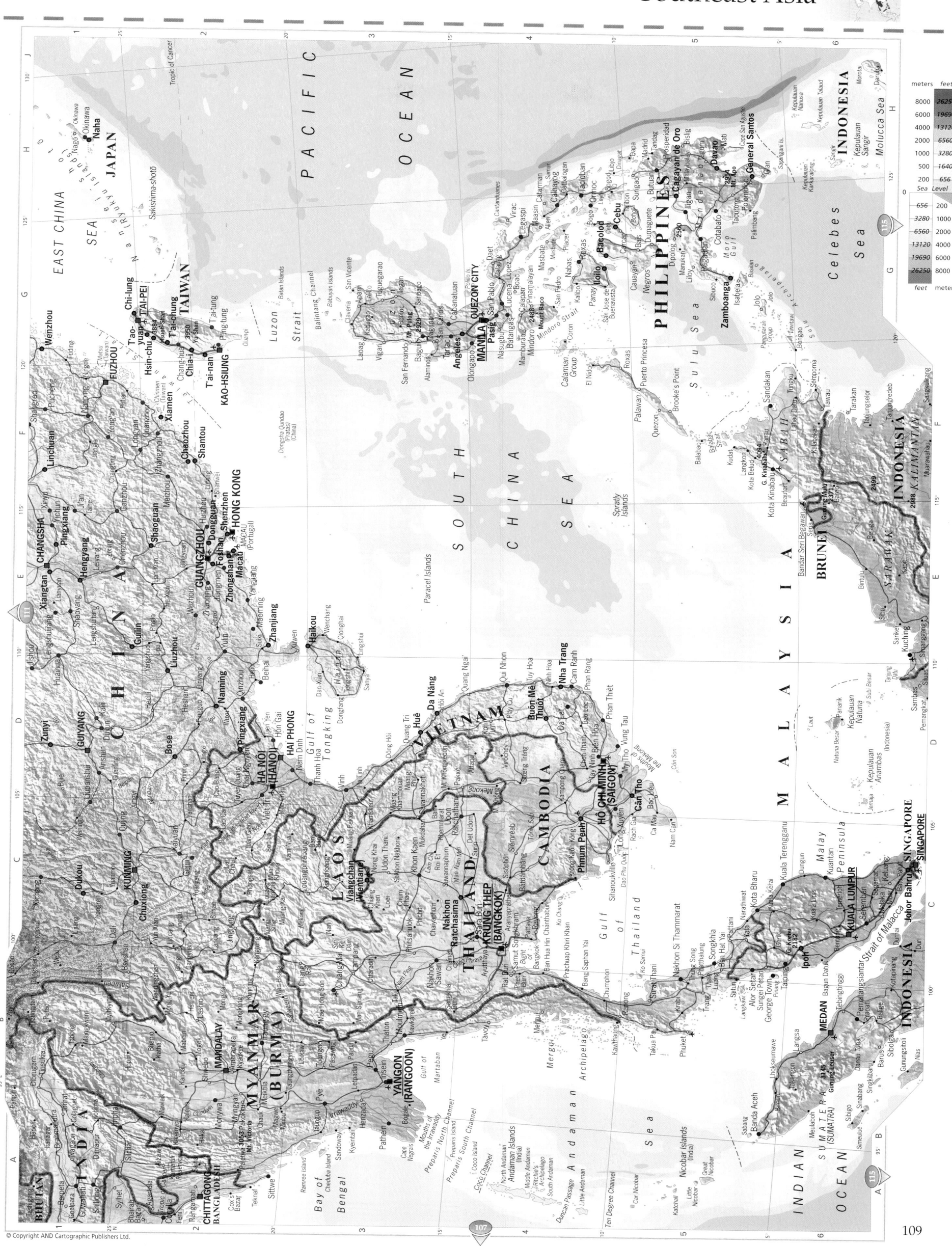

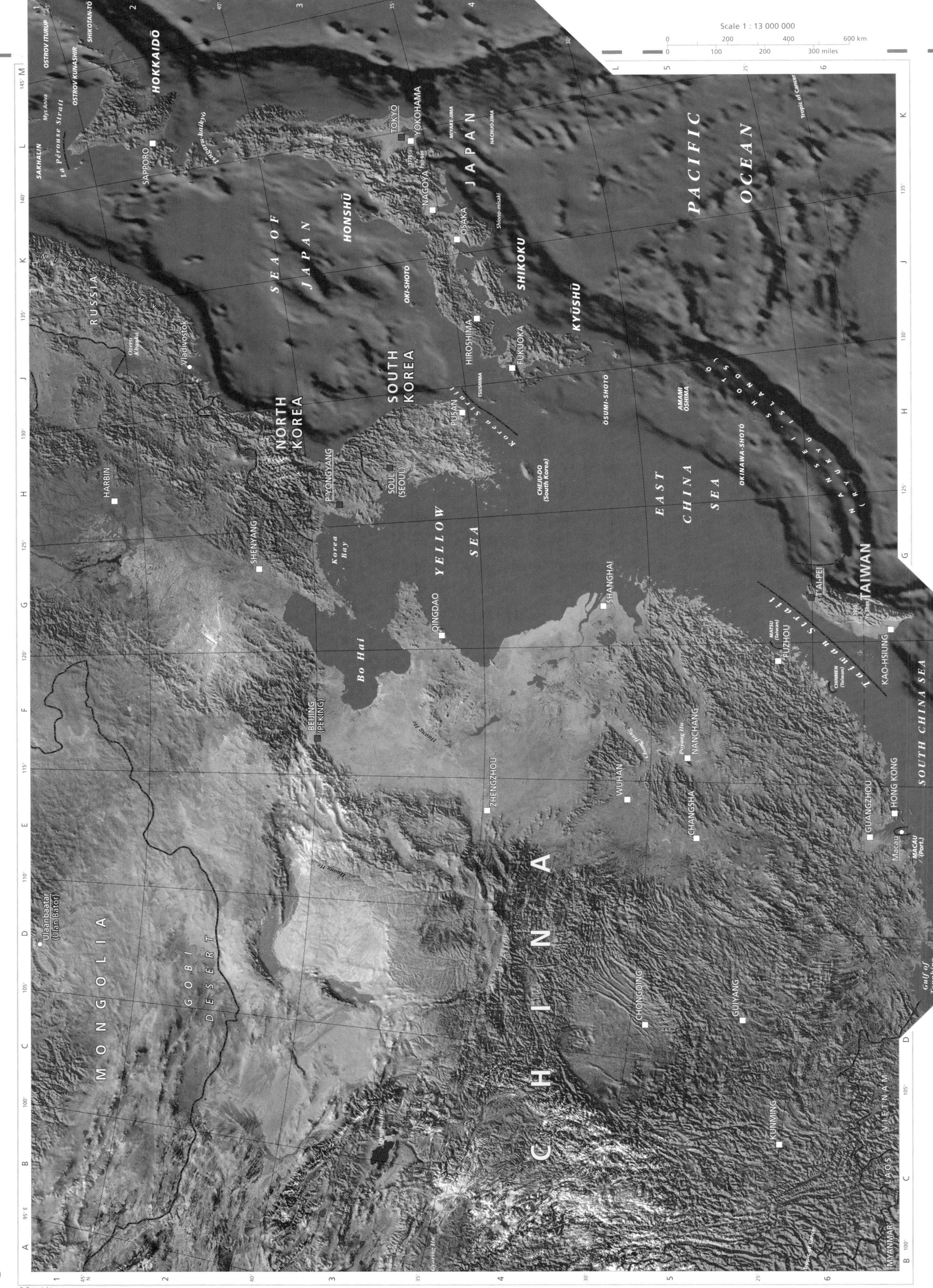

Scale 1 : 13 000 000

| 0 | 200 | 400 | 600 km |

| 0 | 100 | 200 | 300 miles |

RUSSIA

MONGOLIA

Ulaanbaatar
(Ulan Bator)

GOBI   DESERT

C H I N A

SAPPORO

HOKKAIDŌ

OSTROV ITURUP
OSTROV KUNASHIR
SHIKOTAN-TO
SAKHALIN
La Pérouse Strait
Mys Aniva

SEA OF JAPAN

HONSHŪ

JAPAN

TOKYO
YOKOHAMA
NAGOYA
OSAKA
MIYAKE-JIMA
HACHIJO-JIMA
Fuji-san
Shiono-misaki

SHIKOKU

HIROSHIMA
FUKUOKA
KYŪSHŪ
OKI-SHOTO

ŌSUMI-SHOTO
AMAMI
ŌSHIMA

NORTH KOREA

SOUTH KOREA

PYONGYANG
SOUL
(SEOUL)
PUSAN
TSUSHIMA
Korea Strait
CHEJU-DO
(South Korea)

HARBIN

SHENYANG

Korea Bay

BEIJING
(PEKING)

Bo Hai

YELLOW SEA

QINGDAO

Huang He
(Yellow River)

ZHENGZHOU

Huang He

EAST CHINA SEA

SHANGHAI

Yangtze

WUHAN
NANCHANG
Poyang Hu
CHANGSHA

TAIWAN

TAIPEI
MATSU
(Taiwan)
CHINMEN
(Taiwan)
FUZHOU
Taiwan Strait

PACIFIC OCEAN

Tropic of Cancer

RYUKYU ISLANDS

NANSEI-SHOTO

OKINAWA-SHOTO

CHONGQING

GUIYANG

GUANGZHOU
HONG KONG
Macau
MACAU
(Port.)
KAO-HSIUNG

SOUTH CHINA SEA

Gulf of Tonking

KUNMING

MYANMAR

LAOS

VIETNAM

Vladivostok

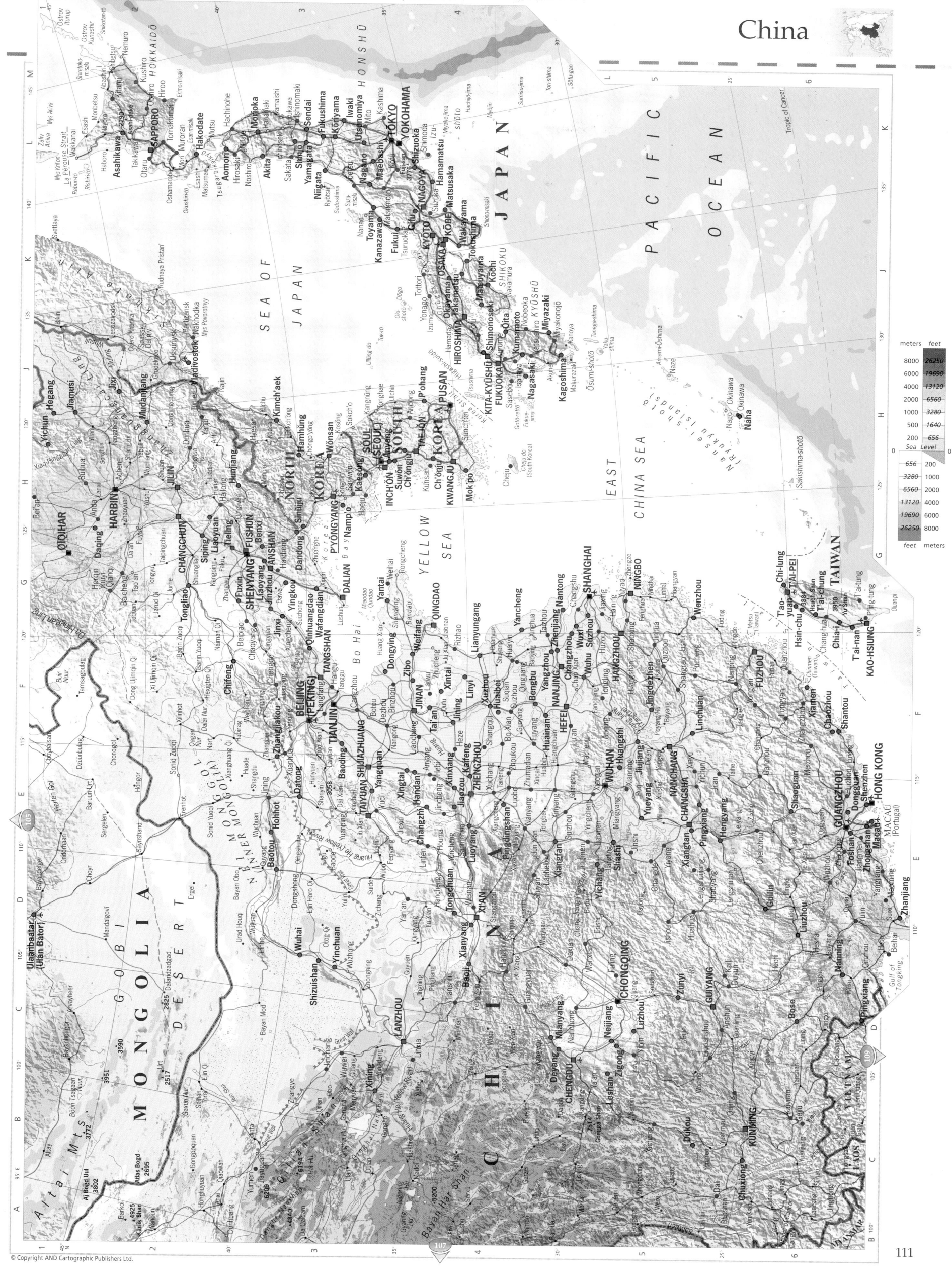

China

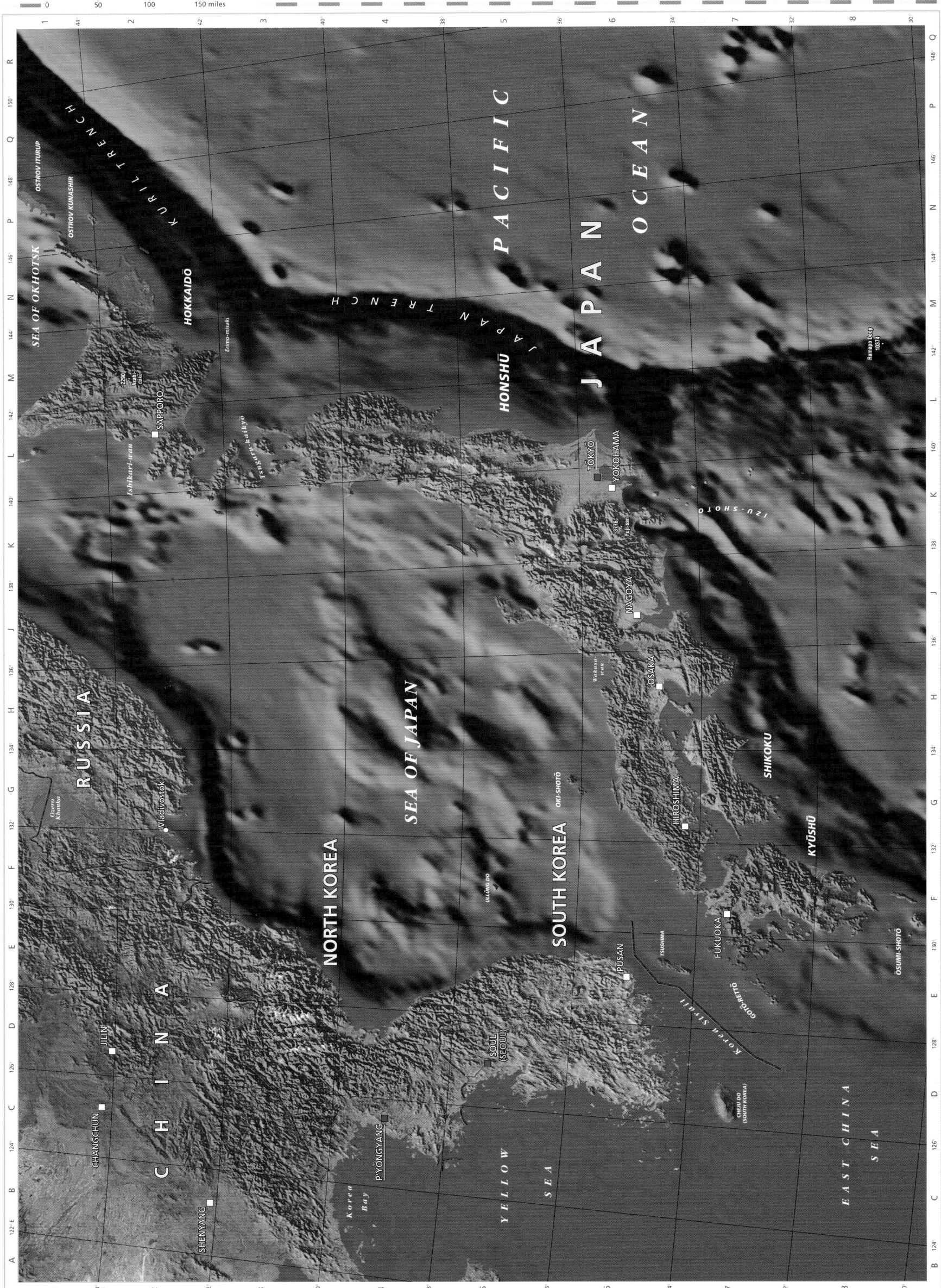

Scale 1 : 6 500 000

RUSSIA

CHINA

NORTH KOREA

SOUTH KOREA

SEA OF JAPAN

YELLOW SEA

EAST CHINA SEA

SEA OF OKHOTSK

PACIFIC

JAPAN

OCEAN

HOKKAIDŌ

HONSHŪ

SHIKOKU

KYŪSHŪ

KURIL TRENCH

JAPAN TRENCH

IZU-SHOTŌ

CHANGCHUN

SHENYANG

JILIN

P'YŎNGYANG

SŎUL (SEOUL)

PUSAN

VLADIVOSTOK

SAPPORO

TŌKYŌ

YOKOHAMA

NAGOYA

ŌSAKA

HIROSHIMA

FUKUOKA

OSTROV ITURUP

OSTROV KUNASHIR

Erimo-misaki

Ishikari-wan

Asahi-dake 2290

Tsugaru-kaikyō

Fuji-san 3776

Wakasa-wan

OKI-SHOTŌ

ULLŬNG DO

TSUSHIMA

Korea Strait

GOTŌ-RETTŌ

CHEJU DO (SOUTH KOREA)

ŌSUMI-SHOTŌ

Ramapo Deep 10374

Korea Bay

Ozero Khanka

112

© Copyright

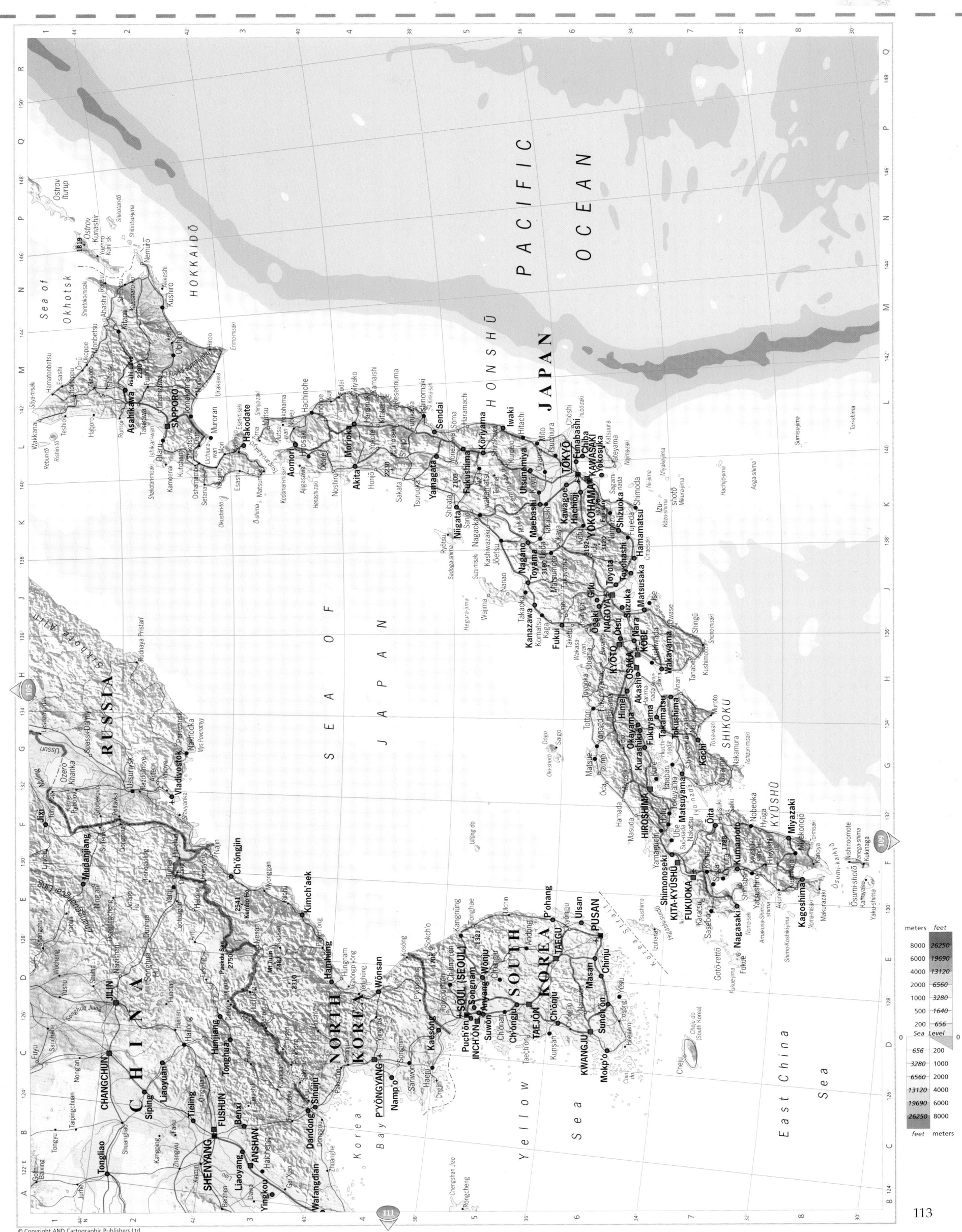

Scale 1 : 13 000 000

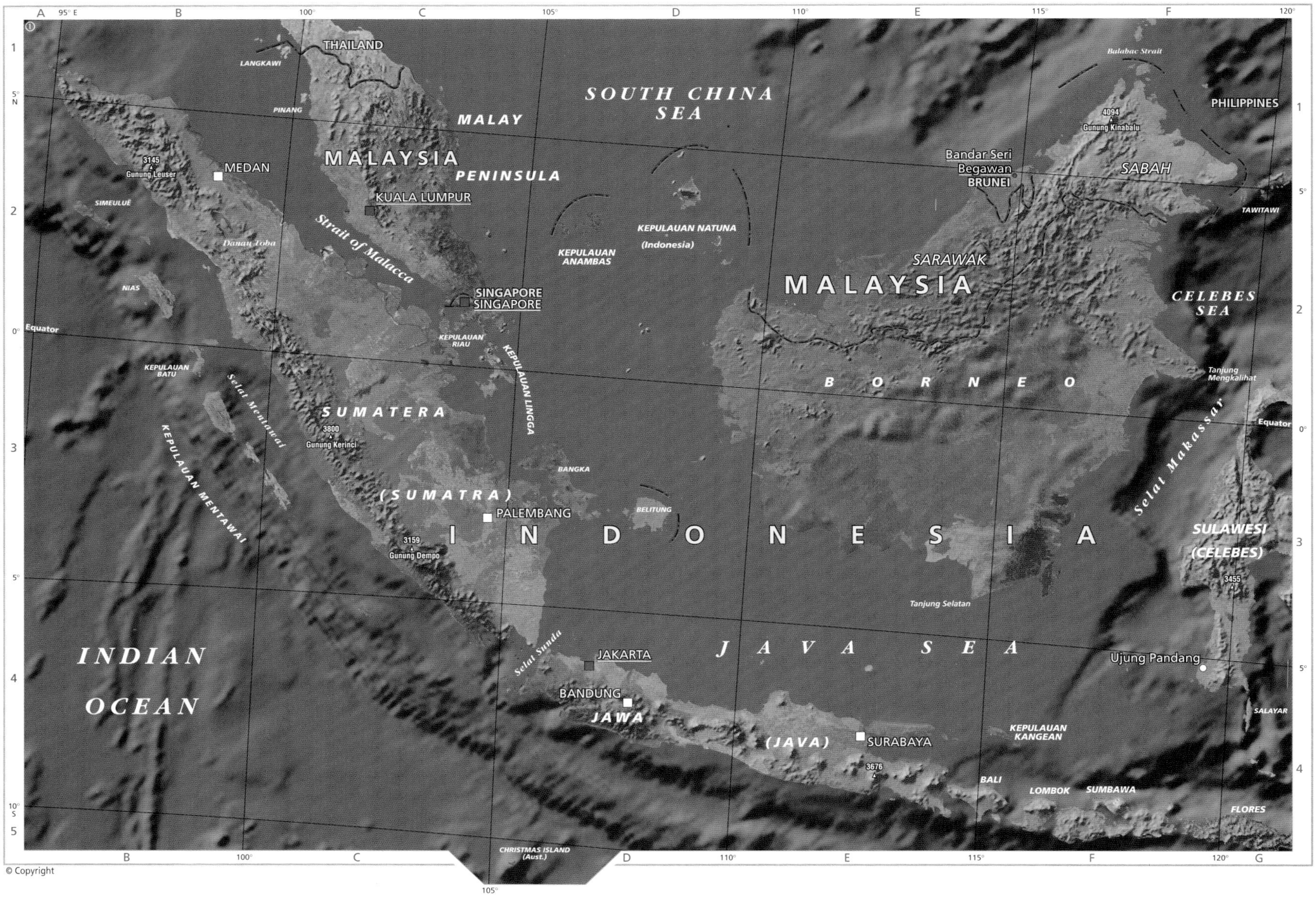

0 200 400 600 km
0 100 200 300 miles

A 95° E B 100° C 105° D 110° E 115° F 120°

THAILAND
LANGKAWI
PINANG
MALAY
SOUTH CHINA SEA
Balabac Strait
PHILIPPINES
MALAYSIA
PENINSULA
Gunung Kinabalu 4094
SABAH
3145 Gunung Leuser
MEDAN
KUALA LUMPUR
Bandar Seri Begawan
BRUNEI
TAWITAWI
SIMEULUE
KEPULAUAN NATUNA (Indonesia)
SARAWAK
MALAYSIA
Strait of Malacca
Danau Toba
KEPULAUAN ANAMBAS
NIAS
SINGAPORE SINGAPORE
CELEBES SEA
KEPULAUAN BATU
KEPULAUAN RIAU
BORNEO
Tanjung Mengkalihat
Equator
SELAT MENTAWAI
SUMATERA
KEPULAUAN LINGGA
KEPULAUAN MENTAWAI
3800 Gunung Kerinci
BANGKA
Equator
(SUMATRA)
PALEMBANG
BELITUNG
INDONESIA
SULAWESI (CELEBES)
3159 Gunung Dempo
3455
Tanjung Selatan
INDIAN OCEAN
Selat Sunda
JAKARTA
JAVA SEA
Ujung Pandang
BANDUNG
JAWA
KEPULAUAN KANGEAN
SALAYAR
(JAVA)
SURABAYA
3676
BALI
LOMBOK
SUMBAWA
FLORES

CHRISTMAS ISLAND (Aust.)

© Copyright

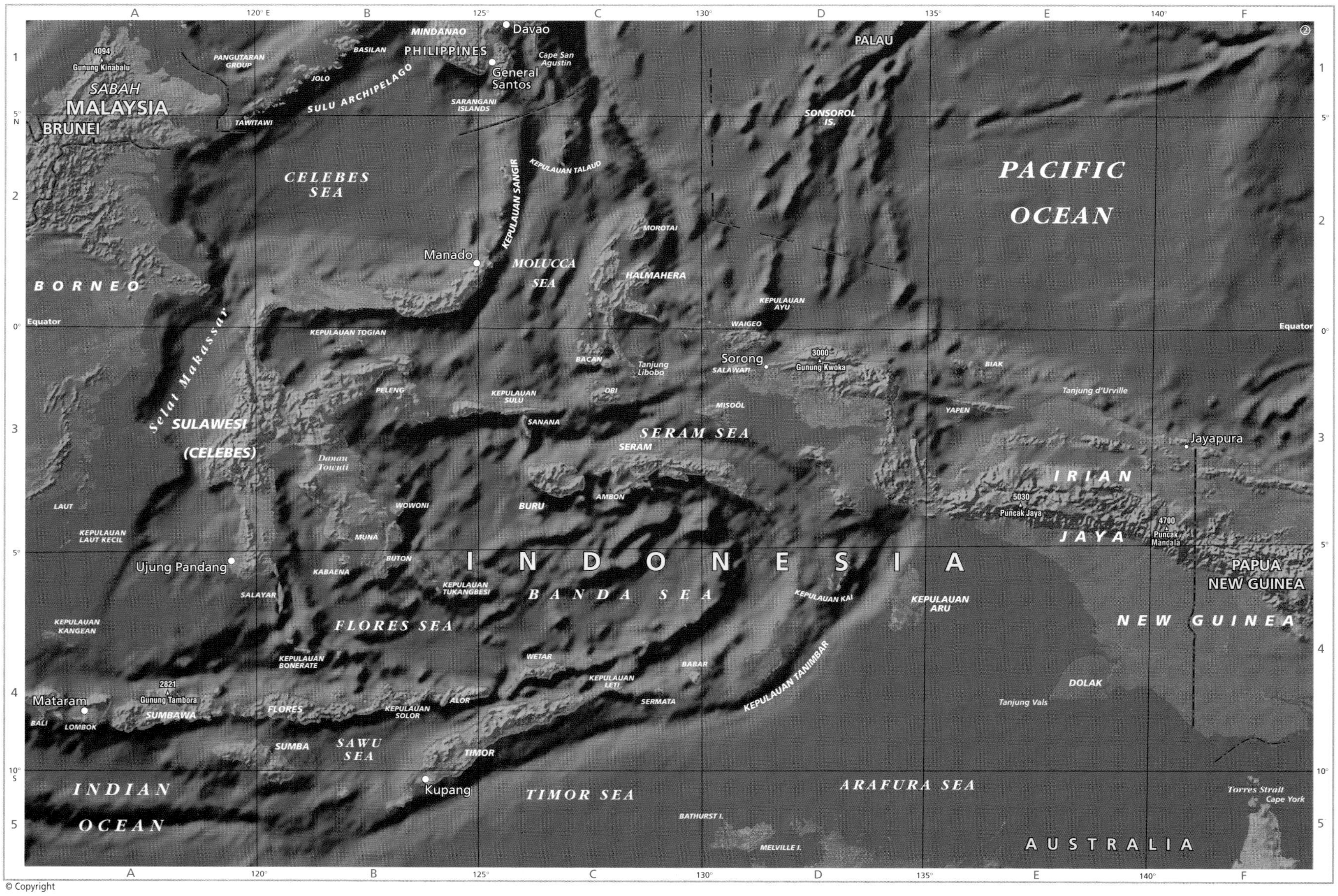

A 120° E B 125° C 130° D 135° E 140° F

4094 Gunung Kinabalu
PANGUTARAN GROUP
MINDANAO
PHILIPPINES
Davao
PALAU
BASILAN
Cape San Agustin
SABAH MALAYSIA
JOLO
SULU ARCHIPELAGO
General Santos
BRUNEI
TAWITAWI
SARANGANI ISLANDS
SONSOROL IS.
PACIFIC OCEAN
CELEBES SEA
KEPULAUAN SANGIR
KEPULAUAN TALAUD
MOROTAI
BORNEO
Manado
MOLUCCA SEA
HALMAHERA
KEPULAUAN AYU
WAIGEO
Equator
KEPULAUAN TOGIAN
BACAN
Tanjung Libobo
Sorong
SALAWATI
3000 Gunung Kwoka
BIAK
Equator
PELENG
KEPULAUAN SULU
OBI
MISOÖL
Tanjung d'Urville
SULAWESI
SANANA
SERAM SEA
YAPEN
(CELEBES)
Danau Towuti
SERAM
Jayapura
WOWONI
BURU
AMBON
IRIAN
LAUT
MUNA
5030 Puncak Jaya
4700 Puncak Mandala
KEPULAUAN LAUT KECIL
BÜTON
INDONESIA
JAYA
Ujung Pandang
KABAENA
KEPULAUAN TUKANGBESI
BANDA SEA
KEPULAUAN KAI
KEPULAUAN ARU
PAPUA NEW GUINEA
KEPULAUAN KANGEAN
SALAYAR
KEPULAUAN BONERATE
WETAR
NEW GUINEA
FLORES SEA
KEPULAUAN LETI
BABAR
Mataram
2821 Gunung Tambora
FLORES
ALOR
SERMATA
KEPULAUAN TANIMBAR
DOLAK
BALI
LOMBOK
SUMBAWA
KEPULAUAN SOLOR
Tanjung Vals
SUMBA
SAWU SEA
TIMOR
INDIAN OCEAN
Kupang
TIMOR SEA
ARAFURA SEA
Torres Strait
Cape York
BATHURST I.
AUSTRALIA
MELVILLE I.

114

© Copyright

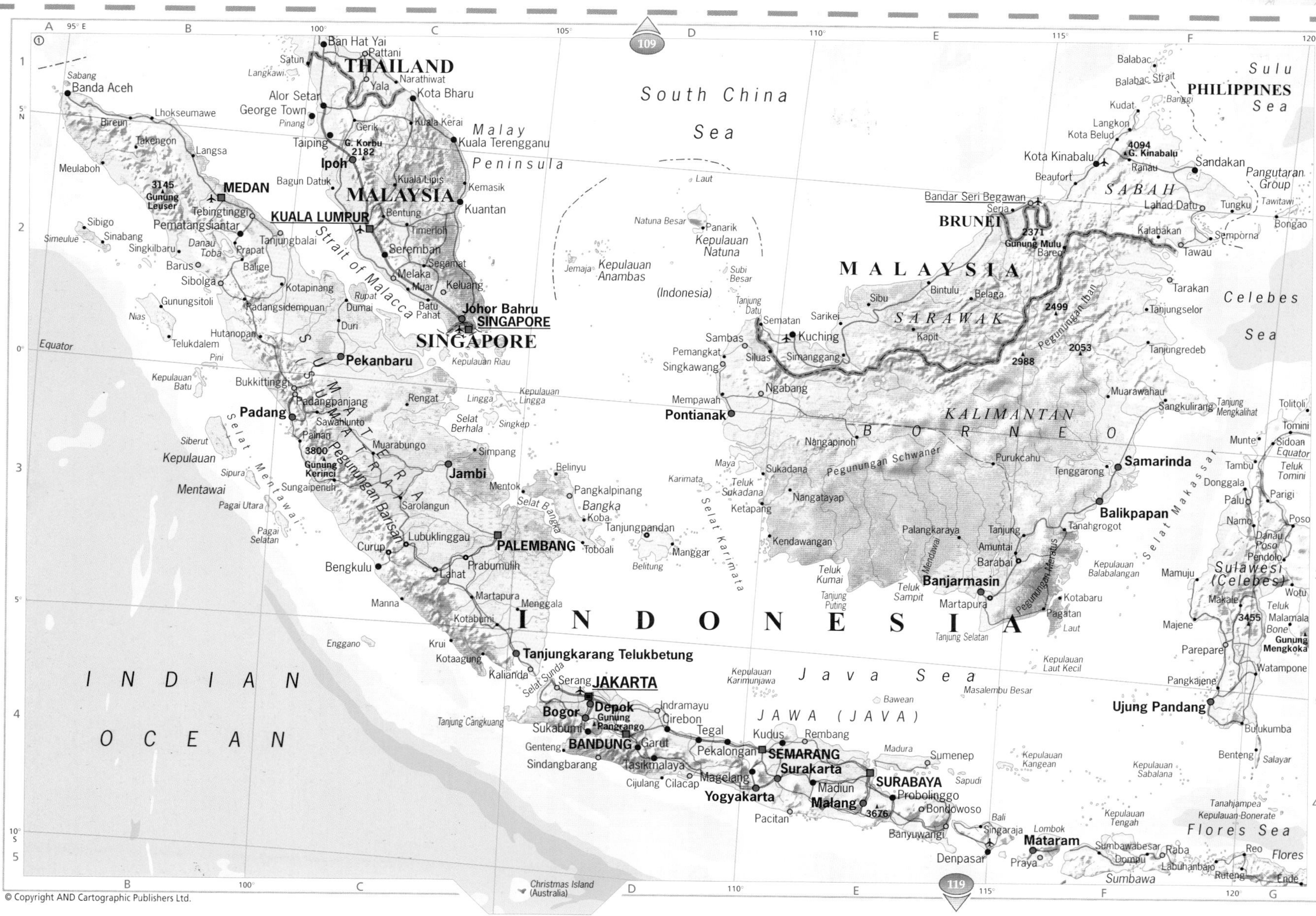

Map 1 (upper)

THAILAND
Ban Hat Yai
Pattani
Satun
Narathiwat
Yala
Langkawi
Alor Setar
Kota Bharu
Sabang
Banda Aceh
Bireun
Lhokseumawe
George Town
Pinang
Gerik
Kuala Kerai
Takengon
Langsa
Taiping
Kuala Terengganu
Kuala Lipis
G. Korbu 2182
Ipoh
MALAYSIA
Kemasik
Kuantan
Meulaboh
3145 Gunung Leuser
MEDAN
Tebingtinggi
Pematangsiantar
KUALA LUMPUR
Bentung
Timerloh
Seremban
Sibigo
Sinabang
Prapat
Danau Toba
Balige
Kotapinang
Tanjungbalai
Melaka
Muar
Segamat
Keluang
Simeulue
Singkilbaru
Barus
Sibolga
Gunungsitoli
Padangsidempuan
Duri
Batu Pahat
Johor Bahru
SINGAPORE
Nias
Hutanopan
Dumai
SINGAPORE
Telukdalam
Pini
Pekanbaru
Kepulauan Riau
Bukittinggi
Kepulauan Batu
SUMATERA
Padangpanjang
Rengat
Lingga
Kepulauan Lingga
Siberut
Padang
Sawahlunto
Painan
Pegunungan Barisan
Muarabungo
Simpang
Belinyu
Pangkalpinang
Kepulauan Mentawai
Pagai Utara
Sungaipenuh
3800 Gunung Kerinci
Jambi
Sarolangun
Mentok
Bangka
Koba
Tanjungpandan
Pagai Selatan
Lubuklinggau
Curup
PALEMBANG
Toboali
Belitung
Manggar
Enggano
Bengkulu
Lahat
Prabumulih
Manna
Kotabumi
Menggala
Martapura
Krui
Kotaagung
Tanjungkarang Telukbetung
Kalianda
Serang
JAKARTA
Bogor
Depok
Gunung Pangrango
Indramayu
Qirebon
Sukabumi
Tegal
Kudus
Rembang
Genteng
BANDUNG
Garut
Pekalongan
SEMARANG
Surakarta
Sumenep
Madura
Sindangbarang
Tasikmalaya
Cijulang
Cilacap
Magelang
Madiun
SURABAYA
Yogyakarta
Pacitan
Malang
Probolinggo
Bondowoso
3676
Banyuwangi
Bali
Singaraja
Lombok
Mataram
Denpasar
Praya
Sumbawabesar
Dompu
Raba
Reo
Flores
Sumbawa
Ruteng
Ende

JAWA (JAVA)
INDONESIA

INDIAN OCEAN

South China Sea
Malay Peninsula
Natuna Besar
Kepulauan Natuna
Panarik
Kepulauan Anambas (Indonesia)
Jemaja
Subi Besar
Tanjung Datu
Sambas
Pemangkat
Singkawang
Mempawah
Ngabang
Pontianak
Kuching
Sarikei
Sibu
Bintulu
Belaga
2499
BRUNEI
Bandar Seri Begawan
Seria
2371 Gunung Mulu Bareo
Miri
Pegunungan Iban
Kota Kinabalu
4094 G. Kinabalu
Beaufort
Kudat
Kota Belud
Langkon
SABAH
Sandakan
Pangutaran Group
Lahad Datu
Tungku
Tawau
Semporna
Bongao
PHILIPPINES
Sulu Sea
Balabac
Balabac Strait

MALAYSIA
SARAWAK
2988
2053
Nangapinoh
Muarawahau
Sangkulirang
Tarakan
Tanjungselor
Tanjungredeb
Celebes Sea
KALIMANTAN
BORNEO
Maya
Sukadana
Nangatayap
Ketapang
Teluk Sukadana
Palangkaraya
Purukcahu
Tenggarong
Samarinda
Balikpapan
Kendawangan
Pegunungan Schwaner
Tanjung
Tanahgrogot
Amuntai
Barabai
Banjarmasin
Martapura
Pagatan
Tanjung Selatan
Teluk Kumai
Tanjung Puting
Teluk Sampit
Kepulauan Laut Kecil
Kepulauan Balabalangan
Mamuju
Donggala
Palu
Parigi
Poso
Namo
Danau Poso
Pendolo
Sidoan
Tolitoli
Equator
Tomini
Munte
Tambu
Sulawesi (Celebes)
Wotu
3455 Gunung Mengkoka
Majene
Parepare
Pangkajene
Ujung Pandang
Bulukumba
Benteng
Salayar
Teluk Bone
Teluk Malamala

Selat Malacca
Strait of Malacca
Selat Mentawai
Selat Berhala
Selat Bangka
Selat Karimata
Selat Makassar
Java Sea
Kepulauan Karimunjawa
Bawean
Masalembu Besar
Kepulauan Kangean
Kepulauan Sabalana
Kepulauan Tengah
Kepulauan Laut Kecil
Sapudi
Kepulauan Bonerate
Tanahjampea
Flores Sea
Laut
Christmas Island (Australia)

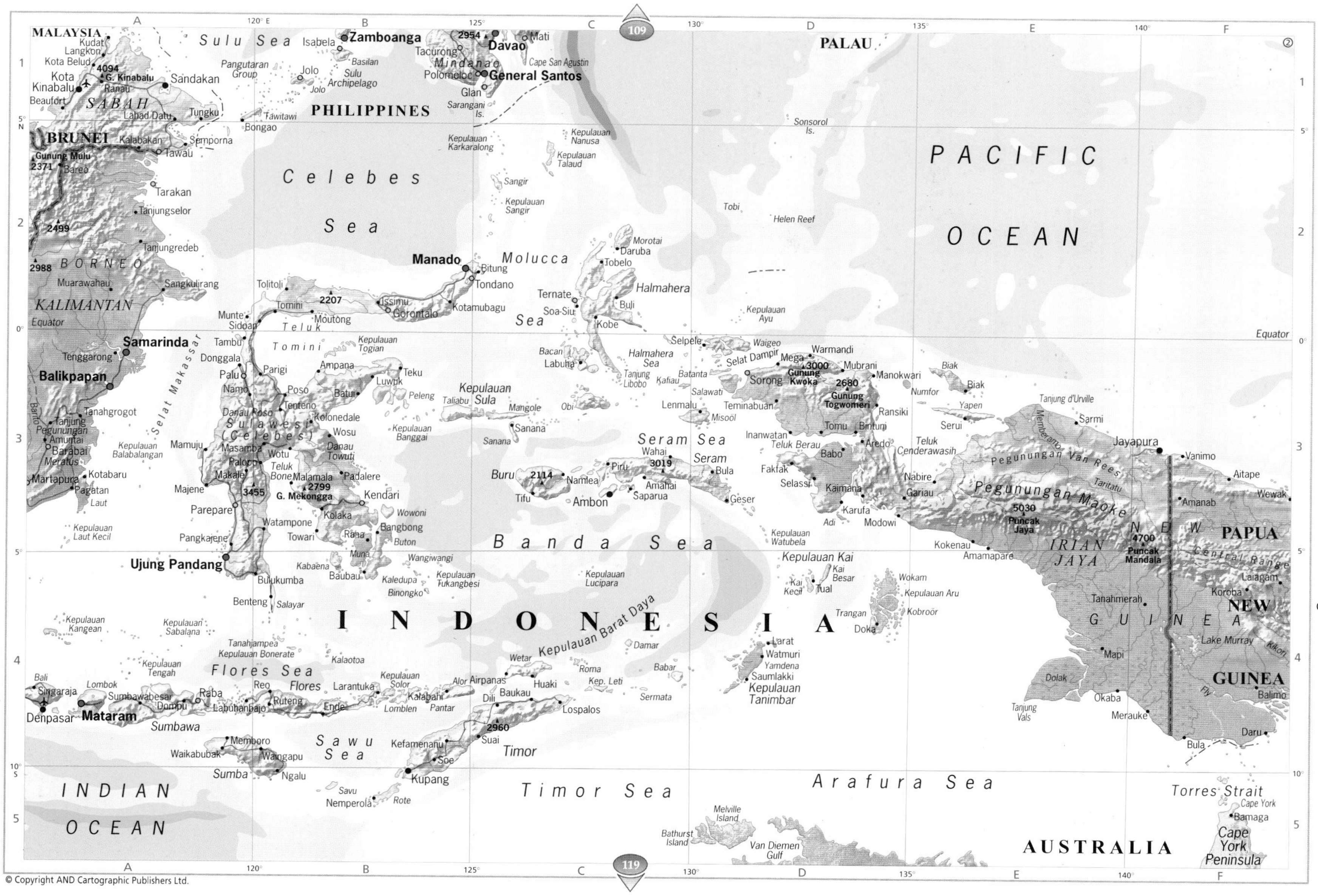

Map 2 (lower)

MALAYSIA
Kudat
Langkon
Kota Belud
4094 G. Kinabalu
Ranau
Kota Kinabalu
Beaufort
Sandakan
Labad Datu
SABAH
Tungku
Tawitawi
Bongao
BRUNEI
Gunung Mulu 2371 Bareo
Kalabakan
Semporna
Tawau
Tarakan
Tanjungselor
2499
2988
BORNEO
Muarawahau
Sangkulirang
KALIMANTAN
Equator
Samarinda
Tenggarong
Balikpapan
Tanahgrogot
Pegunungan Meratus
Barabai
Amuntai
Martapura
Kotabaru
Pagatan
Kepulauan Laut Kecil
Majene
Mamuju
Masamba
Palopo
Wotu
3455 G. Mekongga
2799
Kolaka
Kendari
Parepare
Pangkajene
Ujung Pandang
Bulukumba
Benteng
Salayar
Kepulauan Kangean
Kepulauan Sabalana
Kepulauan Bonerate
Kalaotoa
Bali
Singaraja
Lombok
Denpasar
Mataram
Sumbawabesar
Dompu
Raba
Reo
Flores
Sumbawa
Waikabubak
Memboro
Wanggau
Ngalu
Savu
Nemperola
Sumba
Rote
Kupang
Soe
Kefamenanu
Suai
2960
Timor
Baukau
Lospalos
Dili
Atapupu

Sulu Sea
Isabela
Zamboanga
Tacurong
Davao
Mati
Cape San Agustin
Pangutaran Group
Jolo
Sulu Archipelago
Basilan
Mindanao
Polomolac
General Santos
Glan
Sarangani Is.
PHILIPPINES
Bongao
Kepulauan Nanusa
Kepulauan Karkaralong
Kepulauan Talaud
Sonsorol Is.
PALAU
Tobi
Helen Reef
Sangir
Kepulauan Sangir
Manado
Bitung
Tondano
Celebes Sea
Tolitoli
2207
Tissimu
Gorontalo
Moutong
Teluk Tomini
Molucca Sea
Ternate
Soa-Siu
Kobe
Kotamubagu
Morotai
Daruba
Tobelo
Halmahera
Buli
PACIFIC OCEAN
Selpele
Waigeo
Mega 3000
Warmandi
Sorong
Gunung Kwoka
Manokwari
Biak
Numfor
Yapen
Serui
Tanjung d'Urville
Sarmi
Jayapura
Vanimo
Aitape
Wewak
Amanab

Sulawesi (Celebes)
Palu
Parigi
Poso
Ampana
Teku
Peleng
Banggai
Kepulauan Banggai
Kepulauan Sula
Taliabu
Mangole
Obi
Bacan
Labuha
Sanana
Sanana
Tifu
Buru
2114
Namlea
Piru
Wahai
3019
Seram
Bula
Amahai
Saparua
Ambon
Fakfak
Kaimana
Nabire
Enarotali
Teluk Cenderawasih
Babo
Bintuni
Teluk Berau
Tomu
Inanwatan
Teminabuan
Kaiana
Misool
Salawati
Lenmalu
Kofiau
Batanta
Seram Sea
Banda Sea
Kendari
Raha
Buton
Wangiwangi
Kabaena
Kaledupa
Binongko
Kepulauan Tukangbesi
Watampone
Towari
Bone
Malamala
Padalere
Towori
Wowoni
Muna
Bangbong
Kolaka
Wosu
Danau Towuti
Danau Poso
Tentena
Luwuk
Lawele

Halmahera Sea
Selat Dampir
5030 Puncak Jaya
4700 Puncak Mandala
Pegunungan Van Rees
Taritatu
IRIAN JAYA
Pegunungan Maoke
N E W G U I N E A
Kokenau
Amamapare
Tanahmerah
Lake Murray
Mapi
Dolak
Kobroor
Kepulauan Aru
Trangan
Dobo
Okaba
Merauke
Daru
Bula
Balimo
PAPUA
NEW GUINEA
Lalagam
Laiagam
Cape York Peninsula
Bamaga
Cape York
Torres Strait

Banda Sea
Kepulauan Kai
Kai Besar
Kai Kecil
Wokam
Watubela
Kepulauan Lucipara
Damar
Babar
Wetar
Kepulauan Barat Daya
Alor
Airpanas
Solor
Kalabahi
Huaki
Roma
Leti
Kep. Leti
Sermata
Lomblen
Pantar
Larantuka
Flores
Ende
Maumere
Watmuri
Yamdena
Larat
Saumlakki
Kepulauan Tanimbar
Tanjung Vals
Arafura Sea
Timor Sea
Melville Island
Bathurst Island
Van Diemen Gulf
AUSTRALIA

INDONESIA

INDIAN OCEAN

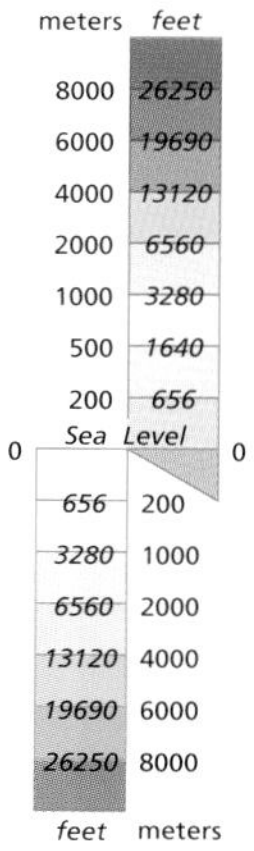

meters	feet
8000	26250
6000	19690
4000	13120
2000	6560
1000	3280
500	1640
200	656
Sea Level	
656	200
3280	1000
6560	2000
13120	4000
19690	6000
26250	8000
feet	meters

115

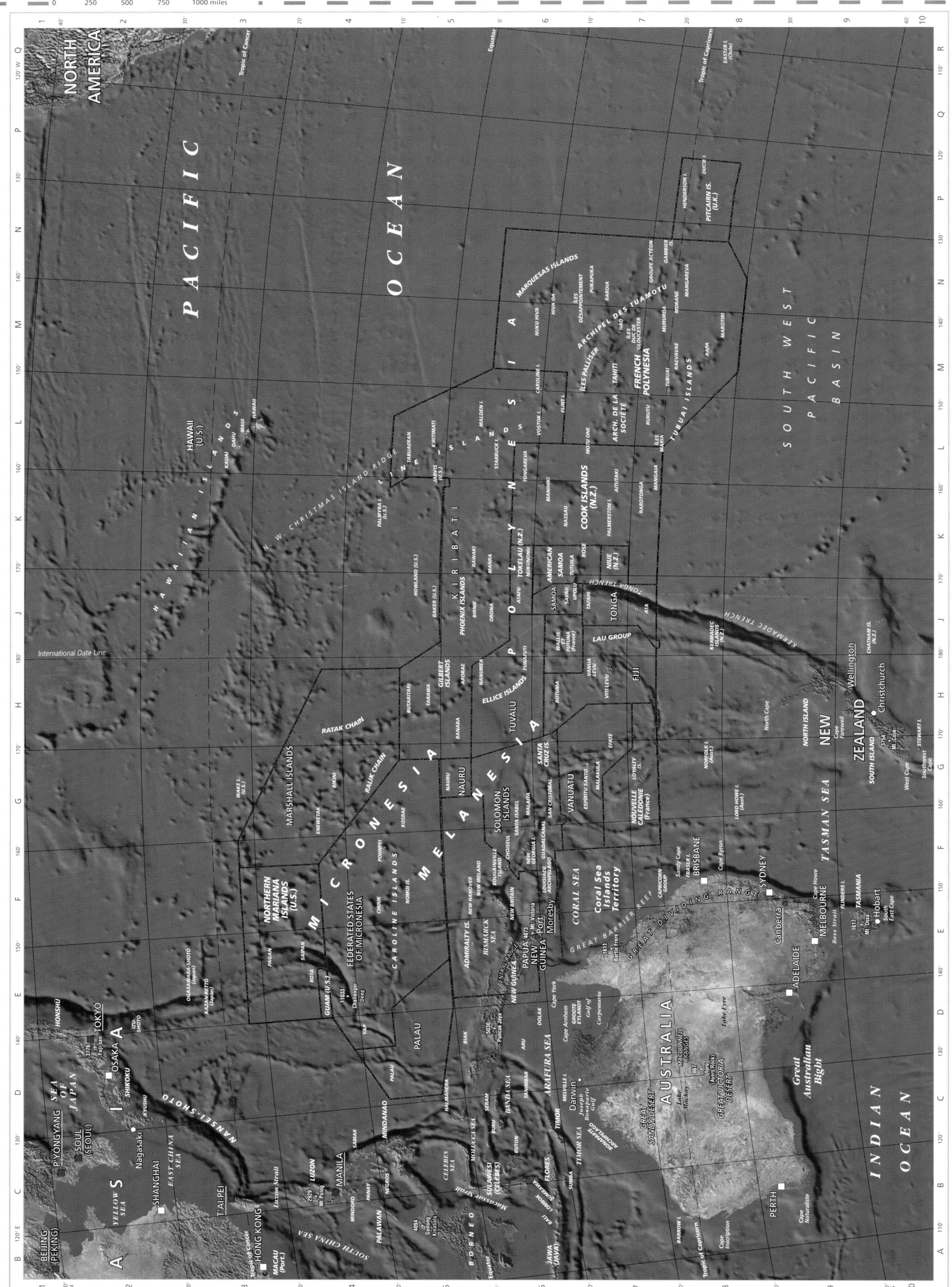

0   500   1000   1500   2000 km
0   250   500   750   1000 miles

NORTH AMERICA

PACIFIC OCEAN

POLYNESIA

MICRONESIA

MELANESIA

MARQUESAS ISLANDS

French Polynesia

International Date Line

COOK ISLANDS (N.Z.)

SOUTH WEST PACIFIC BASIN

HAWAIIAN ISLANDS

HAWAII (U.S.)

KIRIBATI

PHOENIX ISLANDS

GILBERT ISLANDS

ELLICE ISLANDS

TUVALU

NAURU

MARSHALL ISLANDS

RATAK CHAIN

RALIK CHAIN

NORTHERN MARIANA ISLANDS (U.S.)

GUAM (U.S.)

FEDERATED STATES OF MICRONESIA

CAROLINE ISLANDS

PALAU

SOLOMON ISLANDS

VANUATU

NOUVELLE CALÉDONIE (France)

FIJI

TONGA

SAMOA

AMERICAN SAMOA

NIUE (N.Z.)

TOKELAU (N.Z.)

WALLIS ET FUTUNA (France)

LAU GROUP

TONGA TRENCH

KERMADEC TRENCH

KERMADEC ISLANDS (N.Z.)

PITCAIRN IS. (U.K.)

ARCHIPEL DES TUAMOTU

TUBUAI ISLANDS

PAPUA NEW GUINEA

BISMARCK SEA

ADMIRALTY IS.

CORAL SEA

Coral Sea Islands Territory

GREAT BARRIER REEF

GREAT DIVIDING RANGE

AUSTRALIA

Great Australian Bight

GREAT VICTORIA DESERT

GREAT SANDY DESERT

ARAFURA SEA

TIMOR SEA

Gulf of Carpentaria

TASMAN SEA

TASMANIA

NEW ZEALAND

NORTH ISLAND

SOUTH ISLAND

CHATHAM IS. (N.Z.)

Wellington

Christchurch

BRISBANE

SYDNEY

Canberra

MELBOURNE

ADELAIDE

PERTH

Hobart

Darwin

INDIAN OCEAN

BORNEO

JAWA (JAVA)

CELEBES SEA

SOUTH CHINA SEA

EAST CHINA SEA

YELLOW SEA

SEA OF JAPAN

PHILIPPINES

MANILA

LUZON

MINDANAO

PALAWAN

TAI-PEI

HONG KONG

MACAU (Port.)

SHANGHAI

BEIJING (PEKING)

PYONGYANG

SEOUL (SOUL)

TOKYO

OSAKA

Nagasaki

HONSHU

SHIKOKU

KYUSHU

JAPAN

NANSEI-SHOTO

116

© Copyright

© Copyright AND Cartographic Publishers Ltd.

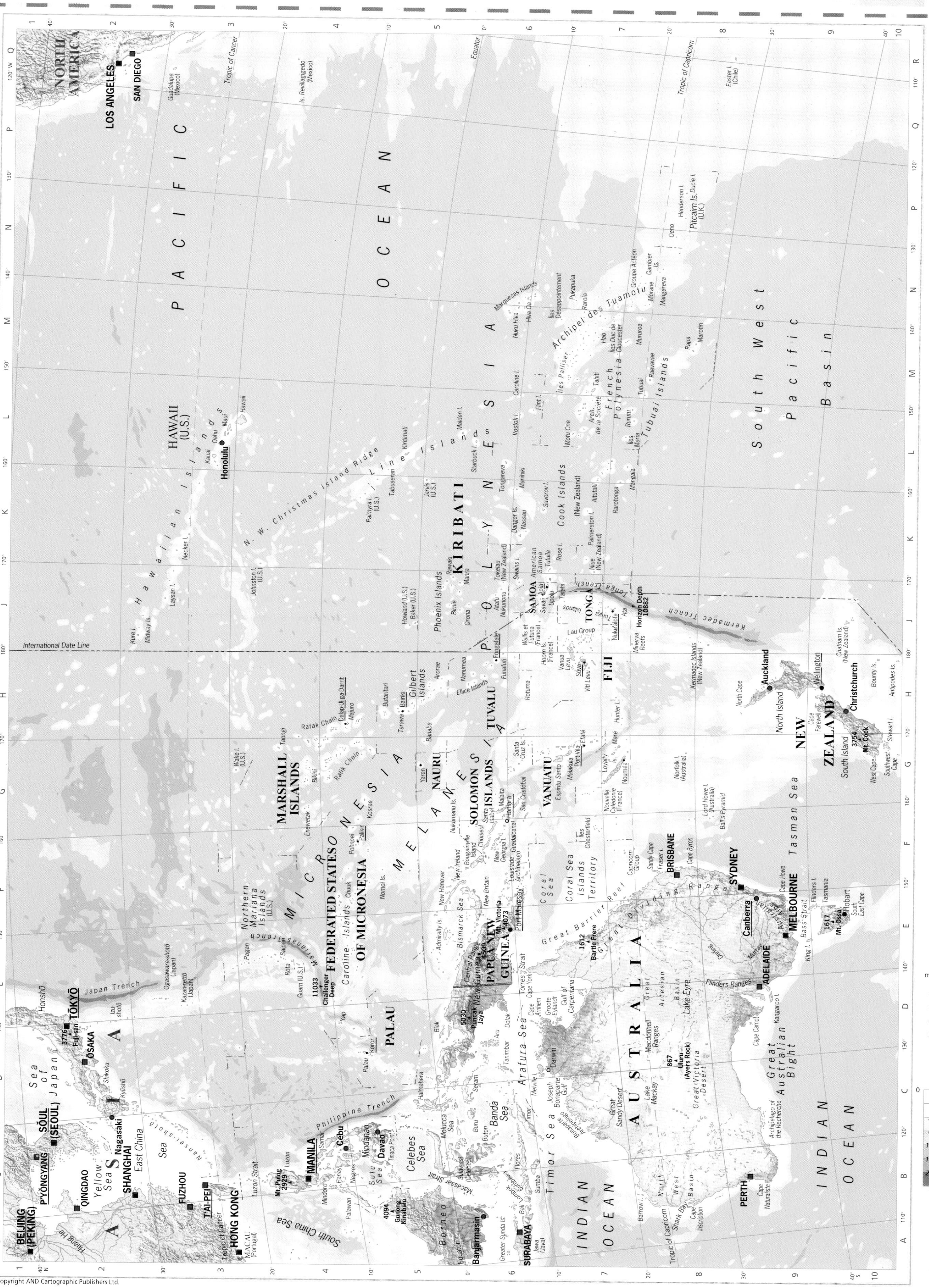

200   400   600 km

100   200   300 miles

INDONESIA

SUMBA

TIMOR

SAVU

ROTE

INDIAN OCEAN

PAPUA NEW GUINEA

Port Moresby

CORAL SEA ISLANDS TERRITORY

CORAL SEA

PACIFIC OCEAN

Tropic of Capricorn

GREAT BARRIER REEF

OSPREY REEF
BOUGAINVILLE REEF
DIANE BANK
HOLMES REEFS
HERALD CAYS
WILLIS GROUP
MAGDELAINE CAYS
DIAMOND ISLETS
FLINDERS REEFS
TREGOSSE ISLETS
MALAY REEF

CATO I.

SWAIN REEFS

CAPRICORN GROUP

Hervey Bay   Sandy Cape

FRASER I.

CURTIS I.

BREAKSEA Spit

Broad Sound

Repulse Bay

THE WHITSUNDAYS

HOOK I.

HINCHINBROOK I.

Halifax Bay

Mount Bartle Frere 1612

MORETON I.
NORTH STRADBROKE I.

BRISBANE

Mt Roberts 4597

Cape Byron

ARAFURA SEA

TIMOR SEA

MELVILLE ISLAND
BATHURST ISLAND

Darwin

Van Diemen Gulf

CROKER ISLAND

Cape Arnhem

WESSEL ISLANDS

ARNHEM LAND

GROOTE EYLANDT

SIR EDWARD PELLEW GROUP

BICKERTON ISLAND

WELLESLEY IS.

MORNINGTON I.

BENTINCK I.

Gulf of Carpentaria

Cape Wessel

DALY TABLELAND

NORTHERN TERRITORY

TANAMI DESERT

Lake Woods

CAPE YORK PENINSULA

Cape York

PRINCE OF WALES

Torres Strait

MOA (BANKS ISLAND)

MULGRAVE I.

Duifken Point

Albatross Bay

Cape Grenville

Princess Charlotte Bay

Cape Melville

GREAT DIVIDING RANGE

QUEENSLAND

AUSTRALIA

KIMBERLEY PLATEAU

Cape Londonderry

Cape Scott

Joseph Bonaparte Gulf

BONAPARTE ARCHIPELAGO

Collier Bay

King Sound

Cape Leveque

GREAT SANDY DESERT

Lake Gregory

Lake Mackay

Lake White

Lake Wills

Lake Hopkins

MACDONNELL RANGES

Mount Zeil 1531
Mount Liebig 1510

Lake Neale

Lake Amadeus

Uluru (Ayers Rock) 867

MUSGRAVE RANGES

Mount Woodroffe 1440

GIBSON DESERT

TANAMI DESERT

Lake Disappointment

WESTERN AUSTRALIA

GREAT VICTORIA DESERT

Lake Carnegie

Mount Vernon 810

HAMERSLEY RANGE

Mount Bruce 1251

Mount Meharry 1249

MONTE BELLO IS.

BARROW I.

North West Cape

Tropic of Capricorn

Cape Inscription

Dirk Hartog I.

Shark Bay

Cape Naturaliste

Cape Leeuwin

PERTH

Lake Moore

Lake Barlee

Lake Austin

Lake MacLeod

Mount Magnet 1106

SOUTH AUSTRALIA

SIMPSON DESERT

STURT STONY DESERT

Lake Eyre North

Lake Eyre South

Lake Torrens

Lake Gairdner

Lake Frome

Lake Blanche

Lake Callabonna

NULLARBOR PLAIN

Lake Maurice

Lake Gairdner

Lake Everard

Yeo Lake

Rason Lake

Lake Carey

Lake Darlot

FLINDERS RANGES

GAWLER RANGES

ADELAIDE

Spencer Gulf

Cape Carnot

Investigator Strait

KANGAROO I.

INVESTIGATOR GROUP

ARCHIPELAGO OF THE RECHERCHE

Esperance Bay

Cape Arid

Point Culver

Twilight Cove

Head of Bight

Great Australian Bight

NEW SOUTH WALES

Darling

Murrumbidgee

Murray

Lake Eucumbene

Lake Eildon

SYDNEY

AUSTRALIAN CAPITAL TERRITORY

Canberra

The Black Stump 1334

Mount Kosciuszko 2228

GREAT DIVIDING RANGE

AUSTRALIAN ALPS

VICTORIA

MELBOURNE

Wilsons Promontory

Cape Howe

Cape Nelson

Cape Jaffa

Lacepede Bay

LORD HOWE I.

BALL'S PYRAMID

TASMAN SEA

Bass Strait

KING ISLAND

FURNEAUX GROUP

FLINDERS I.

CAPE BARREN I.

Banks Strait

TASMANIA

Mount Ossa 1617

HOBART

South East Cape

INDIAN OCEAN

115° E   120°   125°   130°   135°   140°   145°   150°   155°   160°

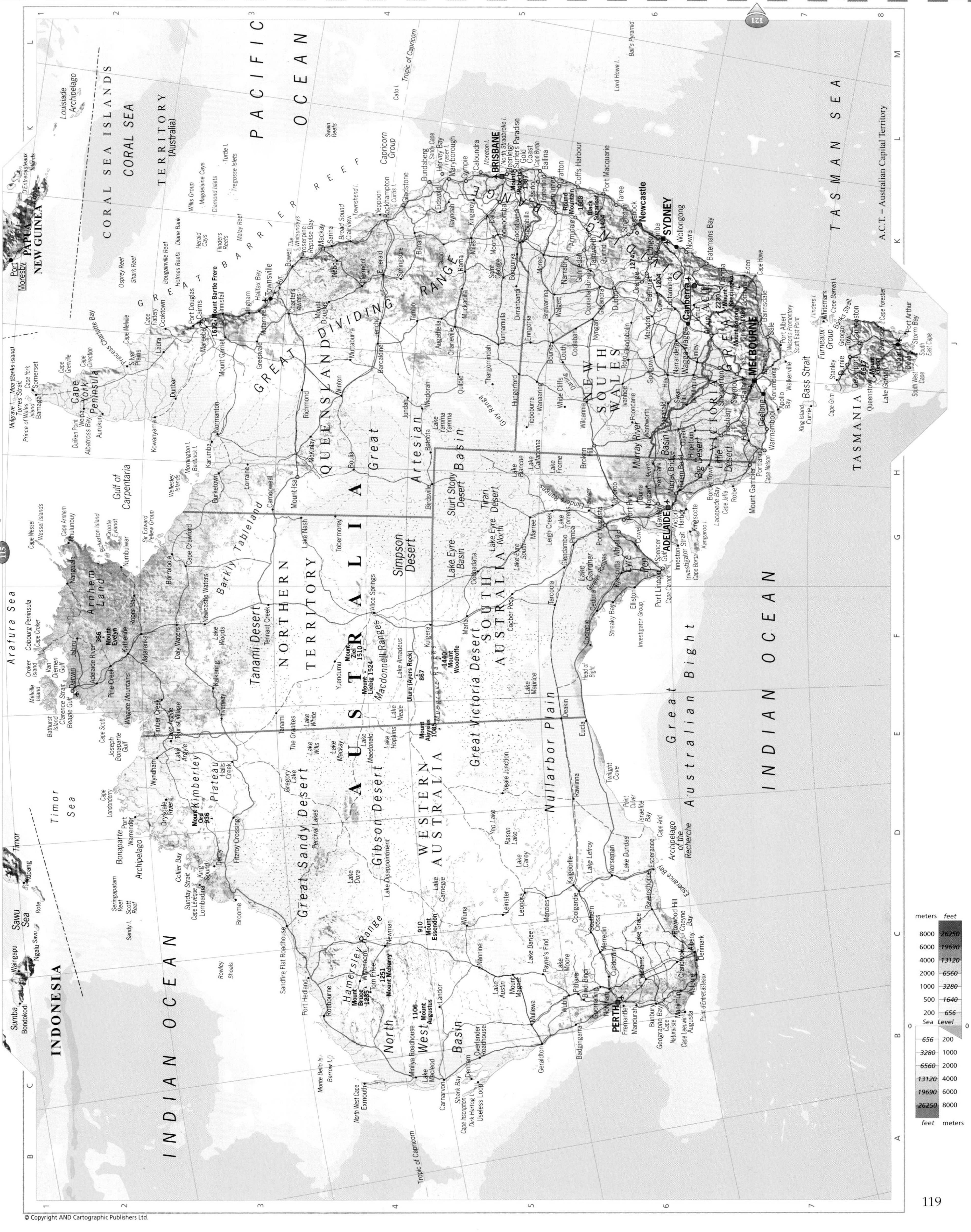

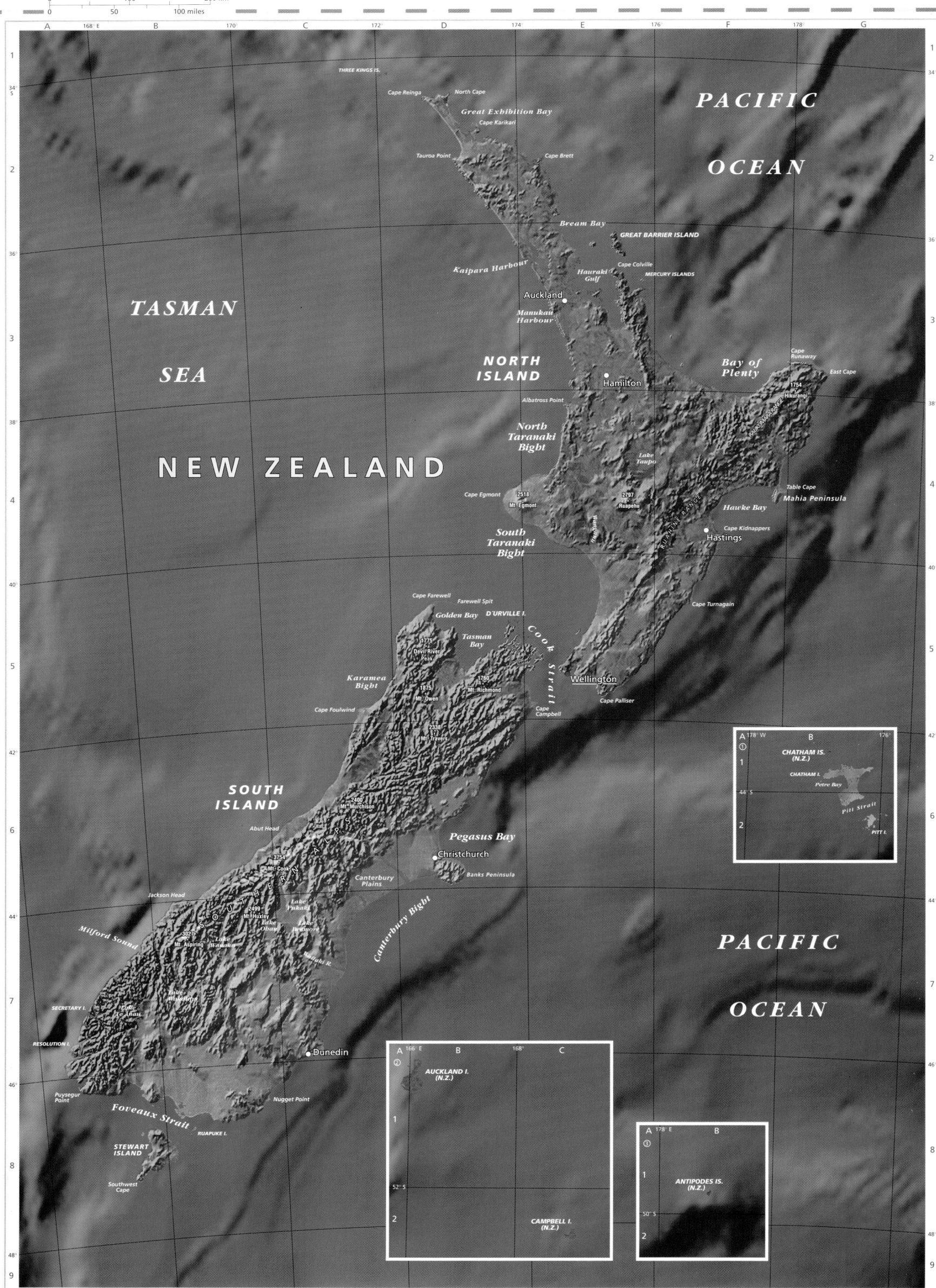

Scale 1 : 5 200 000

| 0 | 100 | 200 km |
| 0 | 50 | 100 miles |

PACIFIC

OCEAN

THREE KINGS IS.

Cape Reinga
North Cape
Great Exhibition Bay
Cape Karikari

Tauroa Point
Cape Brett

TASMAN

Bream Bay
GREAT BARRIER ISLAND

Kaipara Harbour
Cape Colville
Hauraki Gulf
MERCURY ISLANDS

SEA

Auckland

Manukau Harbour

NORTH ISLAND

Hamilton

Bay of Plenty
Cape Runaway
East Cape
1754 Hikurangi

Albatross Point

NEW ZEALAND

North Taranaki Bight

Lake Taupo

Table Cape
Mahia Peninsula

Cape Egmont
2518 Mt. Egmont
2797 Ruapehu

Hawke Bay
Cape Kidnappers
Hastings

South Taranaki Bight

Cape Turnagain

Cape Farewell
Farewell Spit
Golden Bay
D'URVILLE I.

1775 Devil River Peak
Tasman Bay

Karamea Bight
1875 Mt. Owen
1760 Mt. Richmond

Cape Foulwind
2338 Mt. Travers

Cook Strait

Wellington
Cape Palliser
Cape Campbell

A 178° W *B* 176°
CHATHAM IS. (N.Z.)
CHATHAM I.
Petre Bay
Pitt Strait
PITT I.

SOUTH ISLAND

2400 Mt. Murchison

Abut Head

Pegasus Bay

Christchurch

3764 Mt. Cook

Canterbury Plains

Banks Peninsula

Jackson Head

2499 Mt. Huxley
Lake Pukaki
Lake Ohau
Lake Benmore
3027 Mt. Aspiring
Lake Wanaka

Canterbury Bight

Waitaki R.

PACIFIC

SECRETARY I.
Lake Te Anau

Milford Sound

RESOLUTION I.

Dunedin

OCEAN

Puysegur Point
Nugget Point

Foveaux Strait
RUAPUKE I.

STEWART ISLAND

Southwest Cape

A 166° E *B* 168° *C*
AUCKLAND I. (N.Z.)

52° S
CAMPBELL I. (N.Z.)

A 178° E *B*
ANTIPODES IS. (N.Z.)

50° S

© Copyright

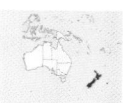

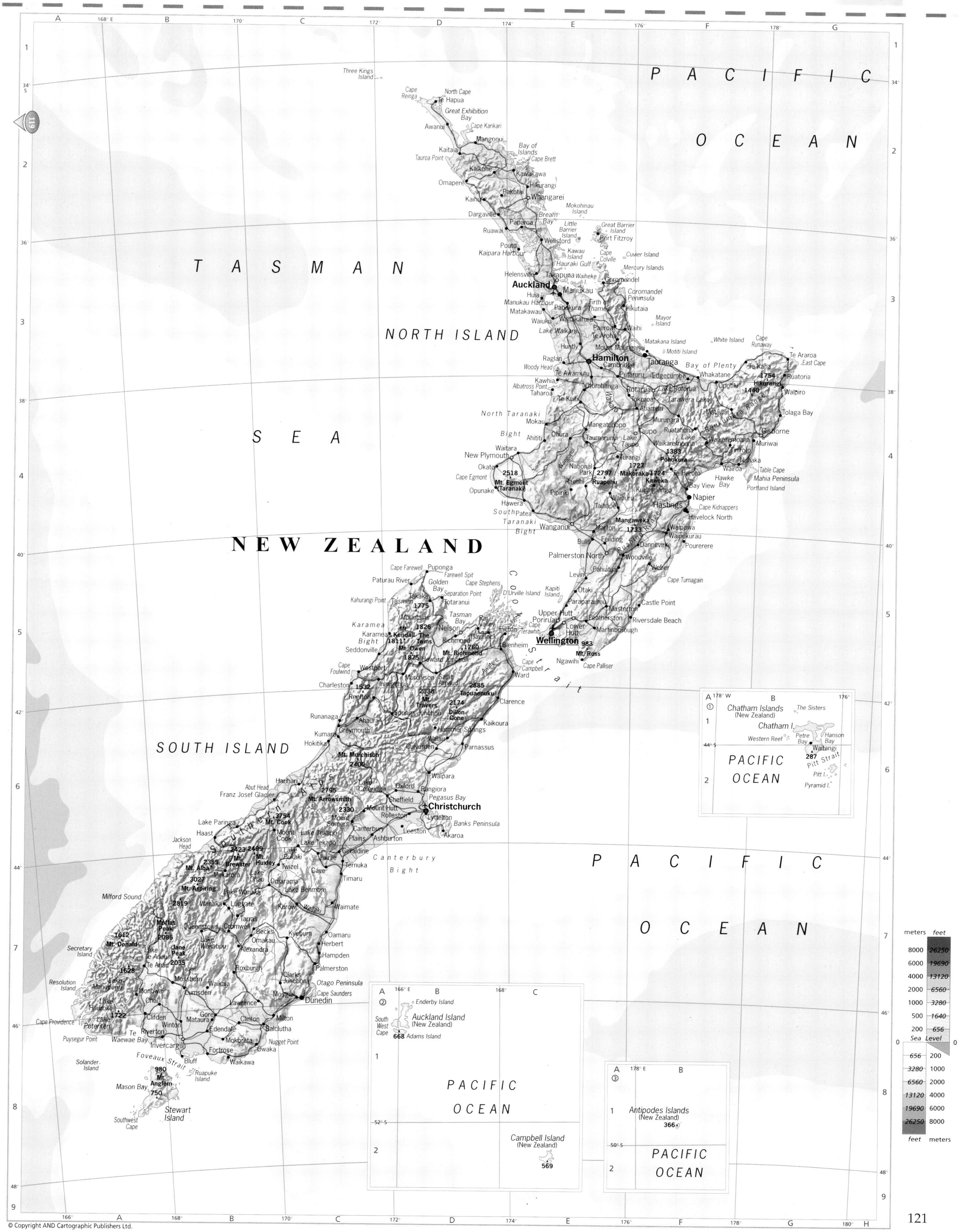

Scale 1 : 39 000 000

0   500   1000   1500   2000 km
0   500   1000 miles

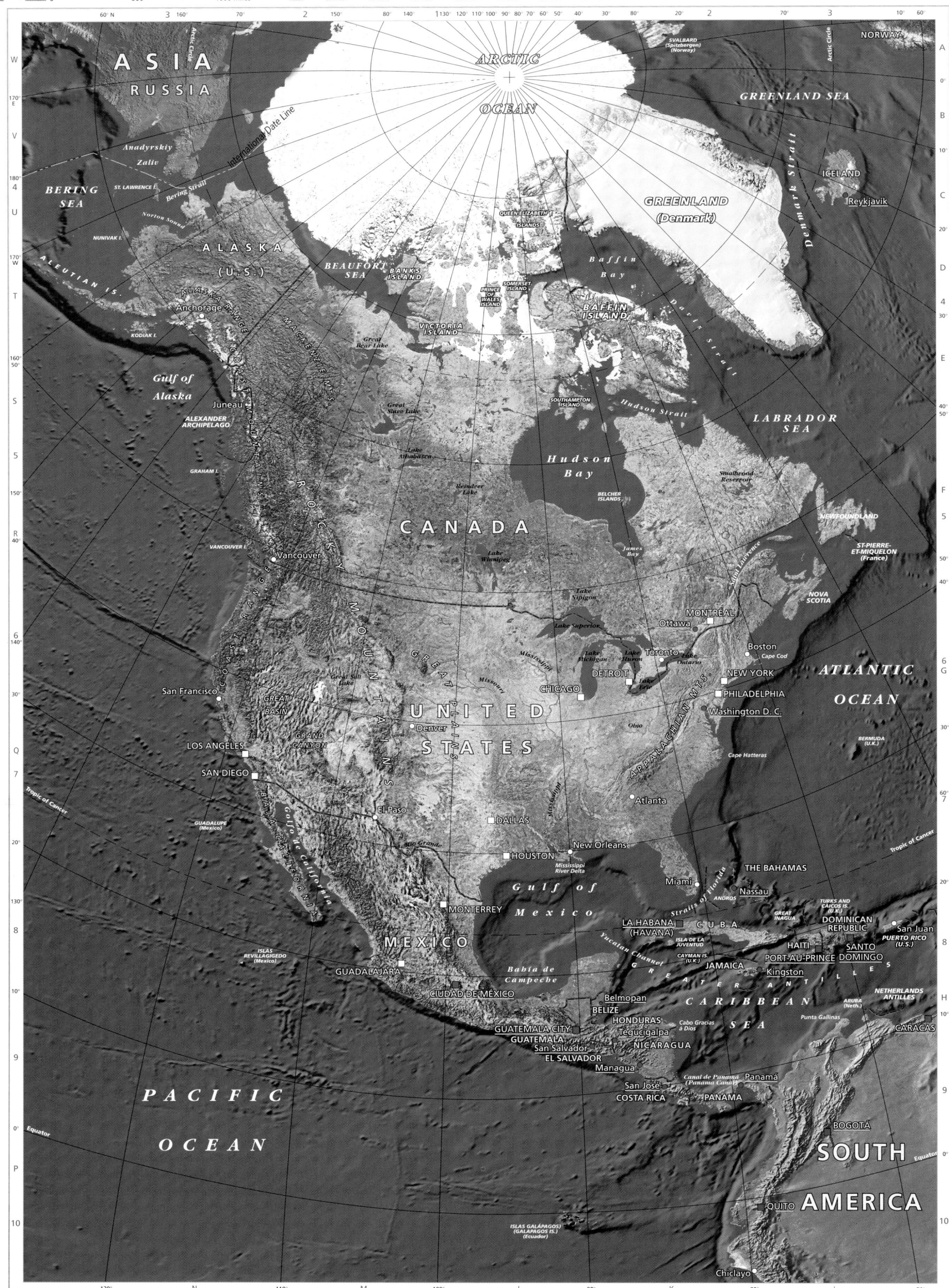

60° N   3   160°   70°   2   150°   80°   1   130° 120° 110° 100° 90° 80°   50°   40°   2   30°   80°   2   70°   3   10°   60°

ASIA
RUSSIA

ARCTIC
OCEAN

GREENLAND SEA

SVALBARD
(Spitsbergen)
(Norway)

NORWAY

Anadyrskiy
Zaliv

BERING
SEA

ST. LAWRENCE I.

Bering Strait

Norton Sound

NUNIVAK I.

ALEUTIAN IS.

ALASKA
(U.S.)

BEAUFORT
SEA

BANKS
ISLAND

PRINCE
OF
WALES
ISLAND

SOMERSET
ISLAND

QUEEN ELIZABETH
ISLANDS

GREENLAND
(Denmark)

Baffin
Bay

ICELAND

Reykjavik

Denmark Strait

Arctic Circle

VICTORIA
ISLAND

BAFFIN
ISLAND

Davis Strait

Great
Bear Lake

Anchorage

KODIAK I.

ALASKA RANGE

Gulf of
Alaska

Juneau

ALEXANDER
ARCHIPELAGO

GRAHAM I.

Great Slave Lake

Lake
Athabasca

Reindeer
Lake

SOUTHAMPTON
ISLAND

Hudson Strait

Hudson
Bay

LABRADOR
SEA

Smallwood
Reservoir

NEWFOUNDLAND

VANCOUVER I.

Vancouver

CANADA

Lake
Winnipeg

BELCHER
ISLANDS

James
Bay

St. Lawrence

ST-PIERRE-
ET-MIQUELON
(France)

NOVA
SCOTIA

COAST RANGE

MACKENZIE MTS.

ROCKY MOUNTAINS

GREAT PLAINS

Lake
Nipigon

Lake Superior

MONTRÉAL

Ottawa

Toronto

Lake
Michigan

Lake
Huron

Lake
Ontario

Lake
Erie

DETROIT

Boston
Cape Cod

NEW YORK

PHILADELPHIA

Washington D. C.

ATLANTIC
OCEAN

San Francisco

GREAT
BASIN

Great Salt
Lake

Denver

Mississippi

Missouri

CHICAGO

UNITED
STATES

Ohio

APPALACHIAN MTS.

BERMUDA
(U.K.)

LOS ANGELES

GRAND
CANYON

SAN DIEGO

Cape Hatteras

Tropic of Cancer

GUADALUPE
(Mexico)

El Paso

DALLAS

Atlanta

Rio Grande

Mississippi

HOUSTON

New Orleans

Mississippi
River Delta

Miami

THE BAHAMAS

Straits of Florida

Nassau

ANDROS

Tropic of Cancer

ISLAS
REVILLAGIGEDO
(Mexico)

BAJA CALIFORNIA

Golfo de California

MONTERREY

Gulf of
Mexico

LA HABANA
(HAVANA)

ISLA DE LA
JUVENTUD

CUBA

GREAT
INAGUA

TURKS AND
CAICOS IS.
(U.K.)

DOMINICAN
REPUBLIC

San Juan

PUERTO RICO
(U.S.)

MEXICO

Bahía de
Campeche

Yucatan Channel

CAYMAN IS.
(U.K.)

JAMAICA

HAITI

PORT-AU-PRINCE

SANTO
DOMINGO

GUADALAJARA

Kingston

GREATER ANTILLES

NETHERLANDS
ANTILLES

CIUDAD DE MÉXICO

BELMOPAN
BELIZE

HONDURAS

Cabo Gracias
á Dios

CARIBBEAN
SEA

ARUBA
(Neth.)

Punta Gallinas

CARACAS

GUATEMALA CITY
GUATEMALA

Tegucigalpa

NICARAGUA

San Salvador
EL SALVADOR

Managua

Canal de Panamá
(Panama Canal)

Panamá

PACIFIC

San José
COSTA RICA

PANAMA

BOGOTÁ

OCEAN

Equator

SOUTH

QUITO

AMERICA

Equator

ISLAS GALÁPAGOS
(GALAPAGOS IS.)
(Ecuador)

Chiclayo

120°   N   110°   M   100°   L   90°   K   80°   J   70°

International Date Line

170°
E

180°
4

170°
W

160°
50°

150°

140°
6

130°

120°

W

V

U

T

S

R
40°

Q

7

8

9

10

A

0°

B

10°

C

20°

D

4

30°

E

40°
50°

F

5

50°

G

6

30°

20°

H

10°

0°

P

10°

122

© Copyright

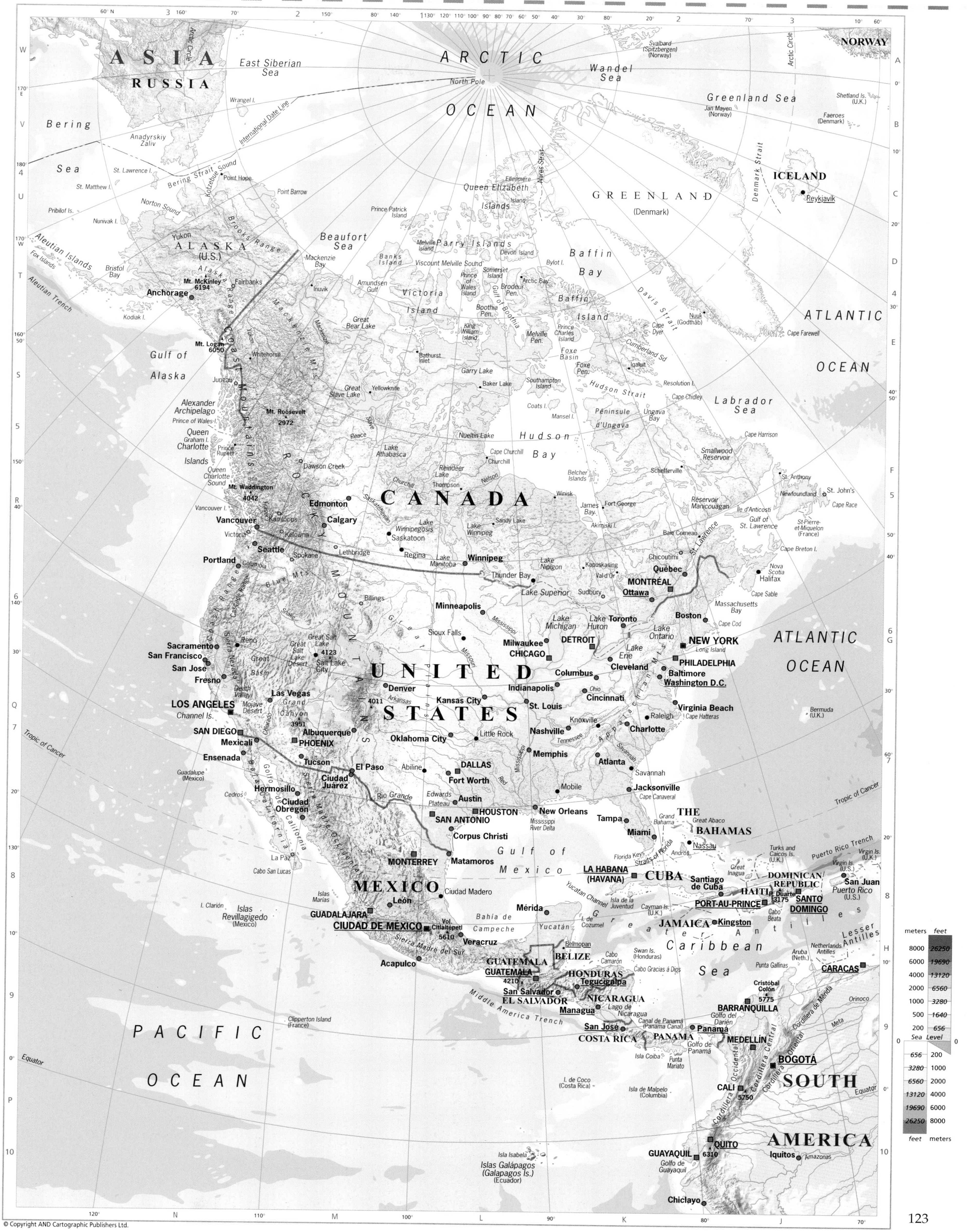

Scale 1 : 15 500 000

200   400   600 km

100   200   300 miles

ATLANTIC OCEAN

GREENLAND (Denmark)

BAFFIN BAY

Davis Strait

DISKO

LABRADOR SEA

NEWFOUNDLAND AND LABRADOR

Gander

NEWFOUNDLAND

ST-PIERRE-ET-MIQUELON (France)

SABLE I.

Gulf of St. Lawrence

Cabot Strait

CAPE BRETON ISLAND

NOVA SCOTIA

Cape Sable

ATLANTIC OCEAN

ÎLE D'ANTICOSTI

PRINCE EDWARD ISLAND

Halifax

Bay of Fundy

NEW BRUNSWICK

Fredericton

MAINE

Augusta

Cape Cod

Boston

Providence

NEW HAMP-SHIRE

MASS.

R.I.

CONN.

White Bay

BAFFIN ISLAND

Cape Mercy

RESOLUTION I.

LAKPIT0K I.

Ungava Bay

QUÉBEC

Québec

Montréal

Ottawa

VERMONT

NEW YORK

Albany

Hudson

NEW YORK

LONG I.

PENNSYLVANIA

Baffin Bay

Lancaster Sound

Foxe Basin

PRINCE CHARLES ISLAND

BYLOT I.

Foxe Channel

Lake Nipigon

Buffalo

Niagara Falls

Lake Erie

DEVON ISLAND

SOMERSET ISLAND

Gulf of Boothia

COATS I.

MANSEL I.

SOUTHAMPTON ISLAND

BELCHER ISLANDS

AKIMISKI I.

James Bay

Hudson Bay

ONTARIO

Lake Huron

Toronto

Hamilton

London

DETROIT

Lake Ontario

Lake Michigan

MICHIGAN

Thunder Bay

Lake Superior

BATHURST I.

CORNWALLIS I.

Viscount Melville Sound

PRINCE OF WALES ISLAND

MELVILLE I.

McClintock Channel

NUNAVUT

Lake Winnipeg

Lake Winnipegosis

Winnipeg

Lake of the Woods

St. Paul

Minneapolis

WISCONSIN

N

MINNESOTA

VICTORIA ISLAND

BANKS ISLAND

Amundsen Gulf

Coronation Gulf

NORTHWEST TERRITORIES

Great Slave Lake

Great Bear Lake

Yellowknife

Lake Athabasca

MANITOBA

G R E A T   P L A I N S

NORTH DAKOTA

SOUTH DAKOTA

MONTANA

WYOMING

UNITED STATES

BEAUFORT SEA

Mackenzie

Mackenzie

MACKENZIE MOUNTAINS

Arctic Circle

YUKON TERRITORY

ALBERTA

Edmonton

Calgary

SASKATCHEWAN

ALASKA (U.S.)

Anchorage

Juneau

Gulf of Alaska

ALEXANDER ARCHIPELAGO

PRINCE OF WALES I.

BRITISH COLUMBIA

R O C K Y   M O U N T A I N S

Vancouver

VANCOUVER ISLAND

Cape Flattery

Seattle

Mt. Rainier 4380 m

WASHINGTON

Portland

OREGON

IDAHO

Boise

Great Salt Lake

Salt Lake City

NEVADA

Reno

Dixon Entrance

Hecate Strait

Queen Charlotte Sound

QUEEN CHARLOTTE IS.

124

© Copyright

Canada

125

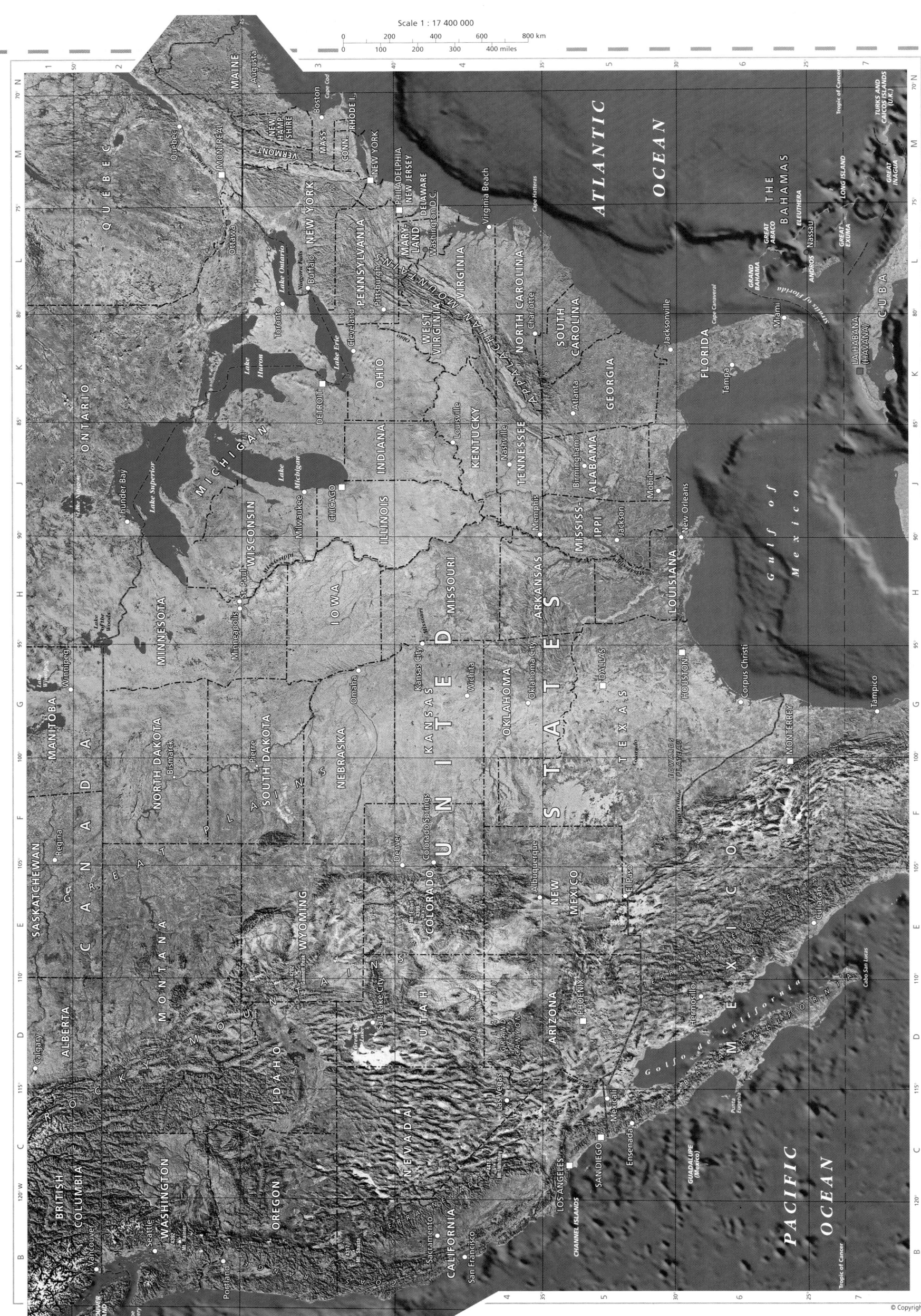

0	200	400	600	800 km
0	100	200	300	400 miles

ATLANTIC OCEAN

PACIFIC OCEAN

Gulf of Mexico

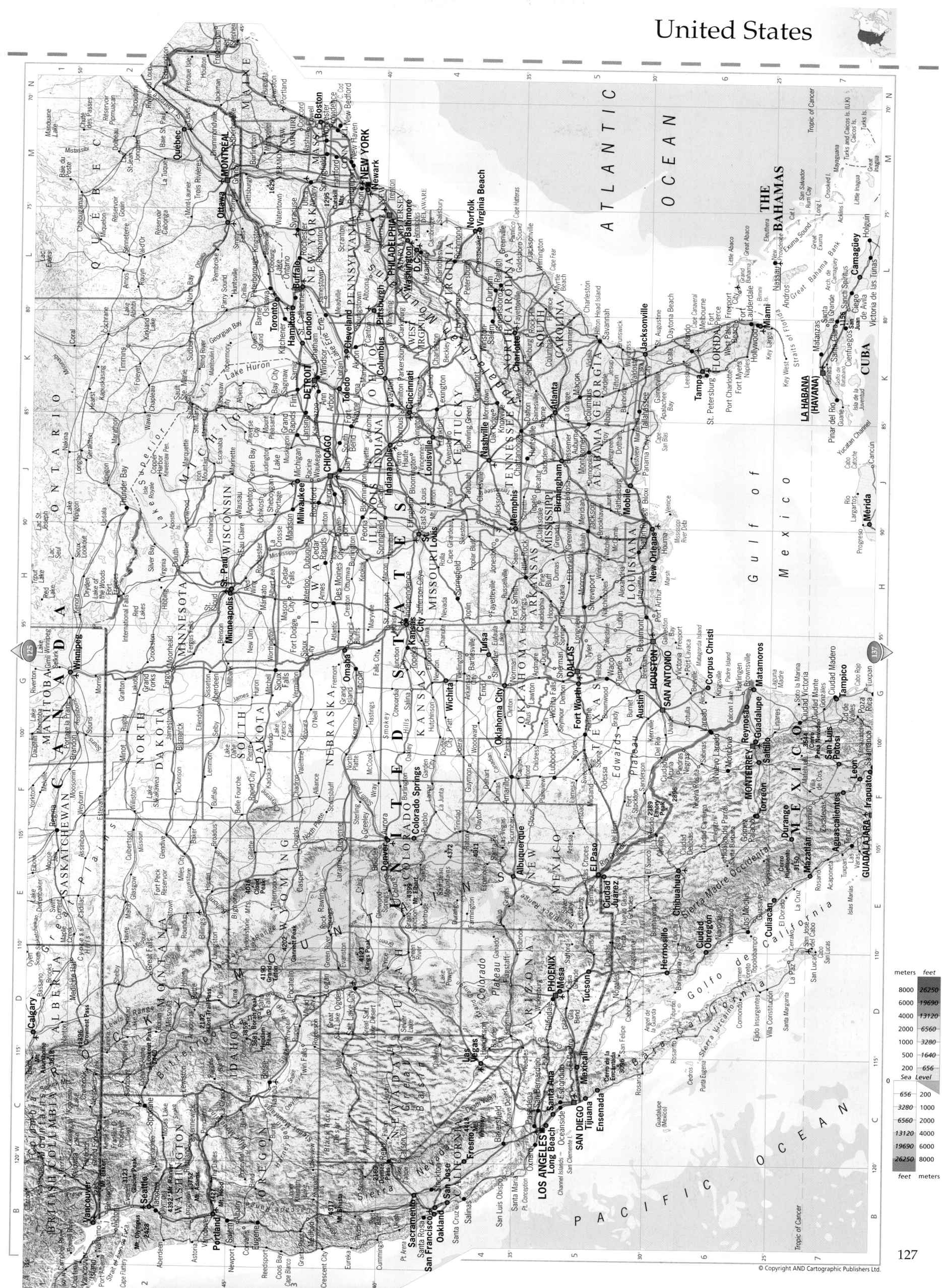

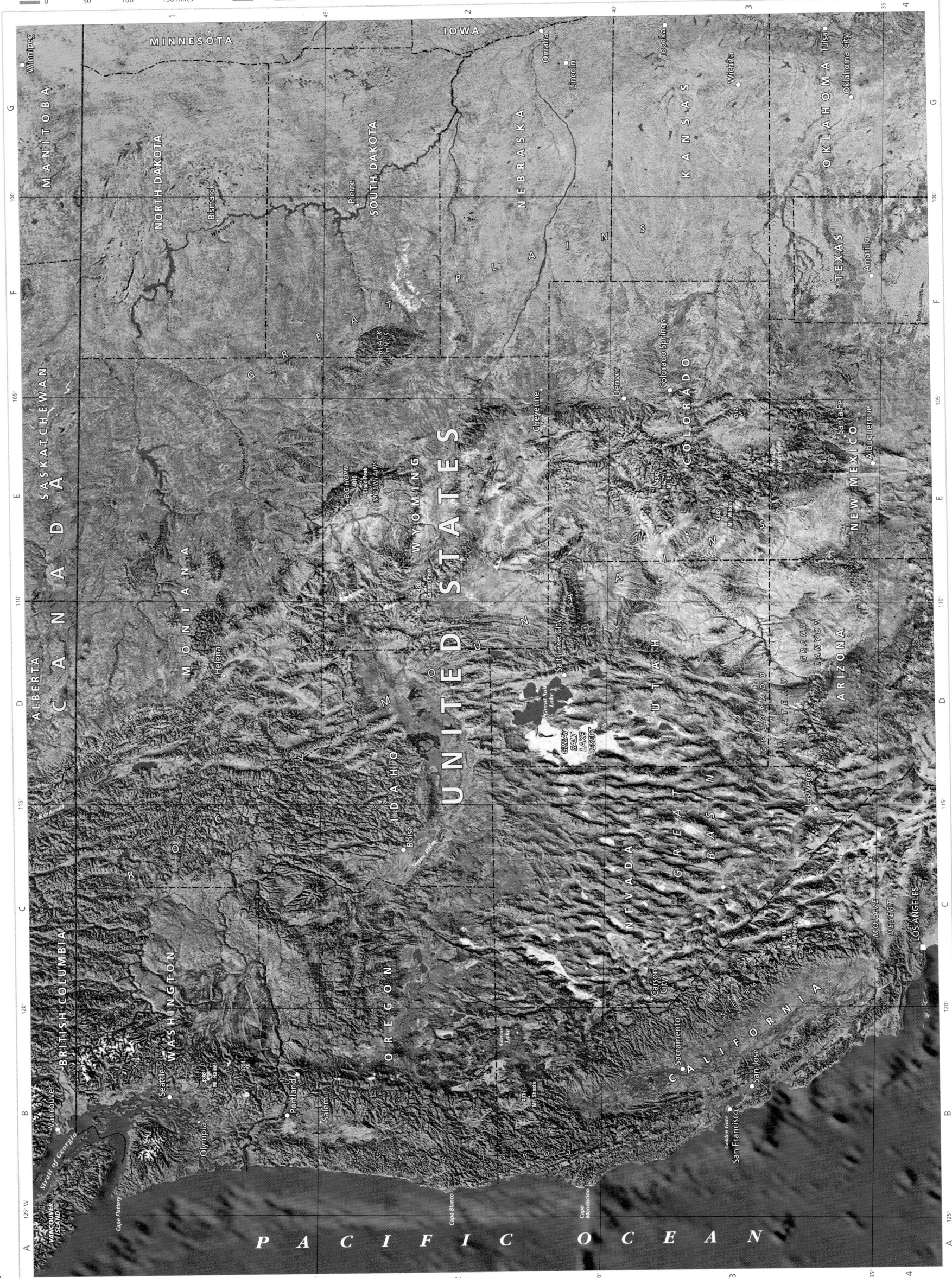

MANITOBA

MINNESOTA

IOWA

Winnipeg

NORTH DAKOTA

SOUTH DAKOTA

NEBRASKA

Omaha

Lincoln

Topeka

KANSAS

Wichita

OKLAHOMA

Tulsa

Oklahoma City

Bismarck

Pierre

BLACK HILLS

Cheyenne

Denver

Colorado Springs

COLORADO

TEXAS

Amarillo

Santa Fe

Albuquerque

NEW MEXICO

CANADA

SASKATCHEWAN

ALBERTA

BRITISH COLUMBIA

MONTANA

WYOMING

UNITED STATES

BIGHORN MOUNTAINS

IDAHO

Helena

Boise

Salt Lake City

GREAT SALT LAKE DESERT

UTAH

GRAND CANYON

COLORADO PLATEAU

ARIZONA

Las Vegas

NEVADA

GREAT BASIN

MOJAVE DESERT

LOS ANGELES

ROCKY MOUNTAINS

GREAT PLAINS

Vancouver

VANCOUVER ISLAND

Strait of Georgia

Cape Flattery

Seattle

WASHINGTON

Olympia

Portland

Salem

OREGON

Cape Blanco

Cape Mendocino

Sacramento

San Francisco

Golden Gate

San Jose

CALIFORNIA

Carson City

SIERRA NEVADA

Mt Shasta

Crater Lake

Snake River

Missouri

P A C I F I C   O C E A N

128

© Copyright

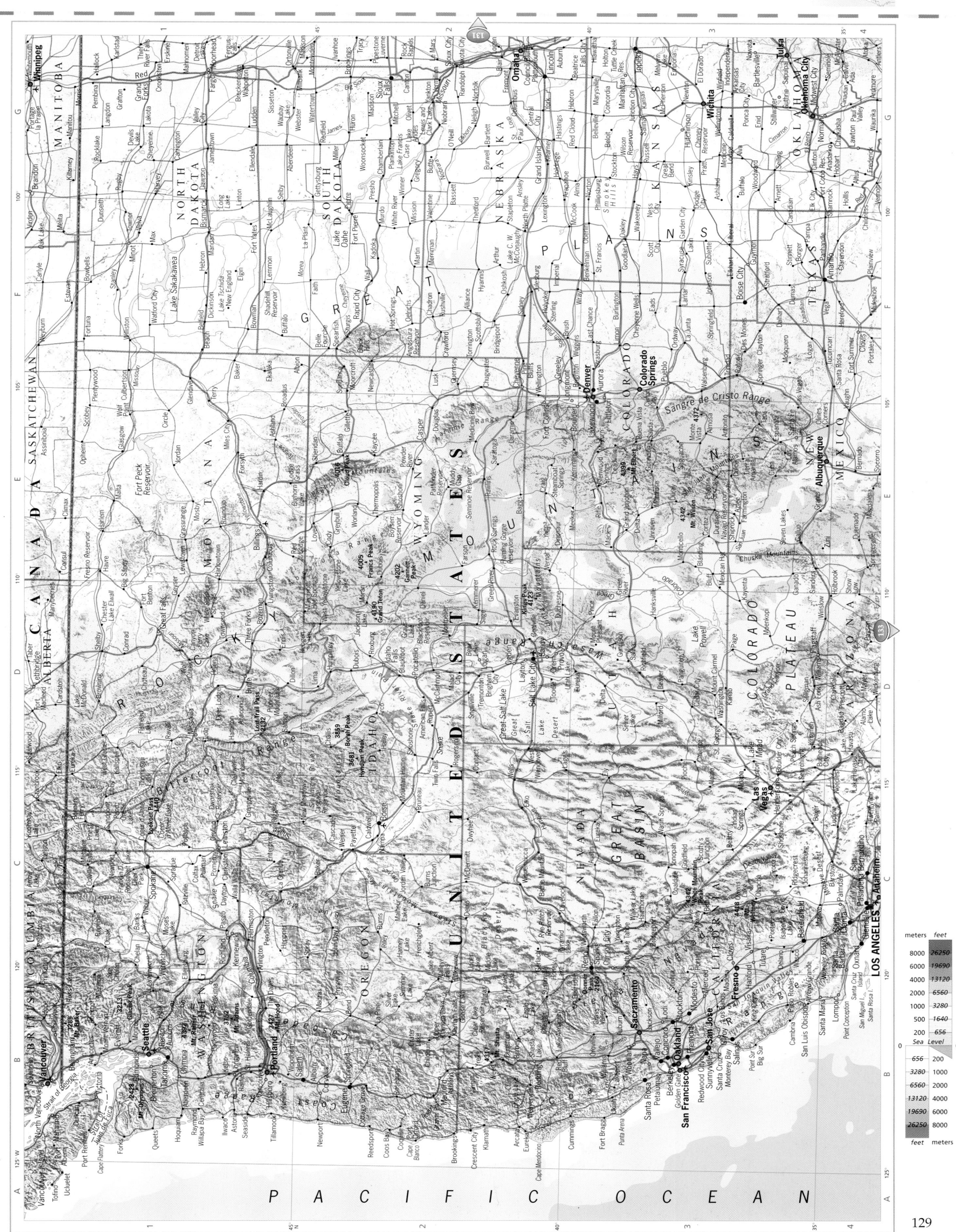

PACIFIC OCEAN

meters / feet

meters	feet
8000	26250
6000	19690
4000	13120
2000	6560
1000	3280
500	1640
200	656
Sea Level	0
656	200
3280	1000
6560	2000
13120	4000
19690	6000
26250	8000

feet / meters

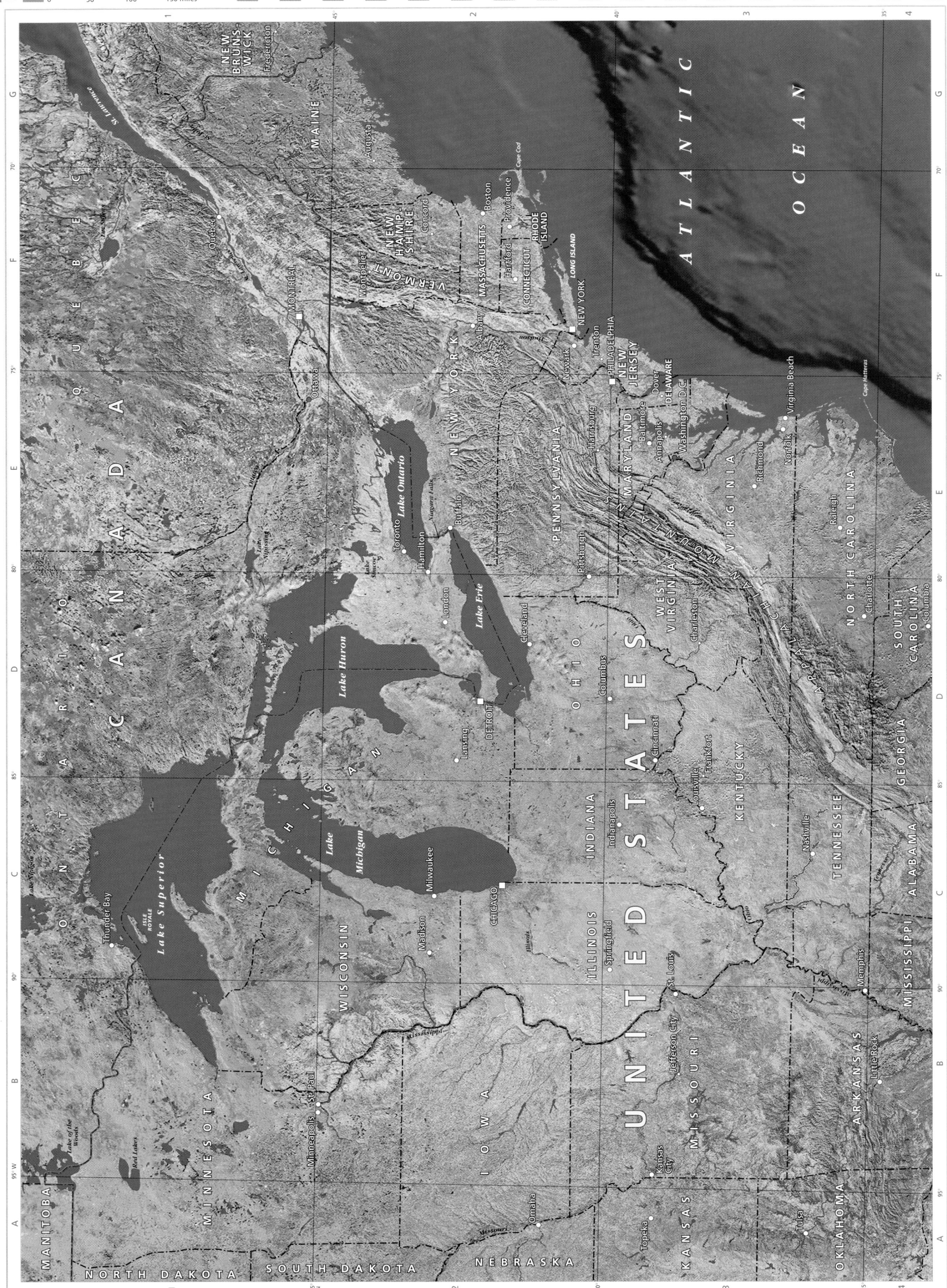

0   100   200   300 km
0   50   100   150 miles

MANITOBA

NORTH DAKOTA   SOUTH DAKOTA   NEBRASKA

MINNESOTA

95° W

Lake of the Woods

Red Lakes

Thunder Bay

ISLE ROYALE

Lake Superior

St. Louis

Minneapolis   St. Paul

IOWA

WISCONSIN

Madison

Milwaukee

CHICAGO

Springfield

ILLINOIS

MICHIGAN

Lake Michigan

Lansing

DETROIT

Lake Huron

Lake Simcoe

ONTARIO

CANADA

QUEBEC

Lac Saint-Jean

St. Lawrence

Québec

Ottawa

MONTREAL

Lake Nipissing

Toronto

Hamilton

Lake Ontario

Buffalo

Niagara Falls

London

Lake Erie

Cleveland

NEW YORK

Albany

VERMONT

Montpelier

NEW HAMP-SHIRE

Concord

MAINE

Augusta

NEW BRUNS-WICK

Fredericton

Boston

MASSACHUSETTS

Providence

RHODE ISLAND

Hartford

CONNECTICUT

LONG ISLAND

NEW YORK

Newark

Trenton

NEW JERSEY

PHILADELPHIA

Dover

DELAWARE

Harrisburg

PENNSYLVANIA

Pittsburgh

OHIO

Columbus

INDIANA

Indianapolis

KANSAS

Topeka

Kansas City

MISSOURI

Jefferson City

St. Louis

Mississippi

Missouri

Omaha

OKLAHOMA

Tulsa

ARKANSAS

Little Rock

MISSISSIPPI

Memphis

TENNESSEE

Nashville

KENTUCKY

Louisville

Frankfort

Cincinnati

WEST VIRGINIA

Charleston

Columbia

SOUTH CAROLINA

GEORGIA

ALABAMA

NORTH CAROLINA

Charlotte

Raleigh

VIRGINIA

Richmond

Norfolk

Virginia Beach

Cape Hatteras

MARYLAND

Baltimore

Annapolis

Washington D.C.

APPALACHIAN MOUNTAINS

UNITED STATES

ATLANTIC OCEAN

Cape Cod

45°

70°

75°

80°

85°

90°

95°

70°

75°

80°

85°

90°

95° W

45° N

40°

35°

A   B   C   D   E   F   G

1   2   3   4

130

© Copyright

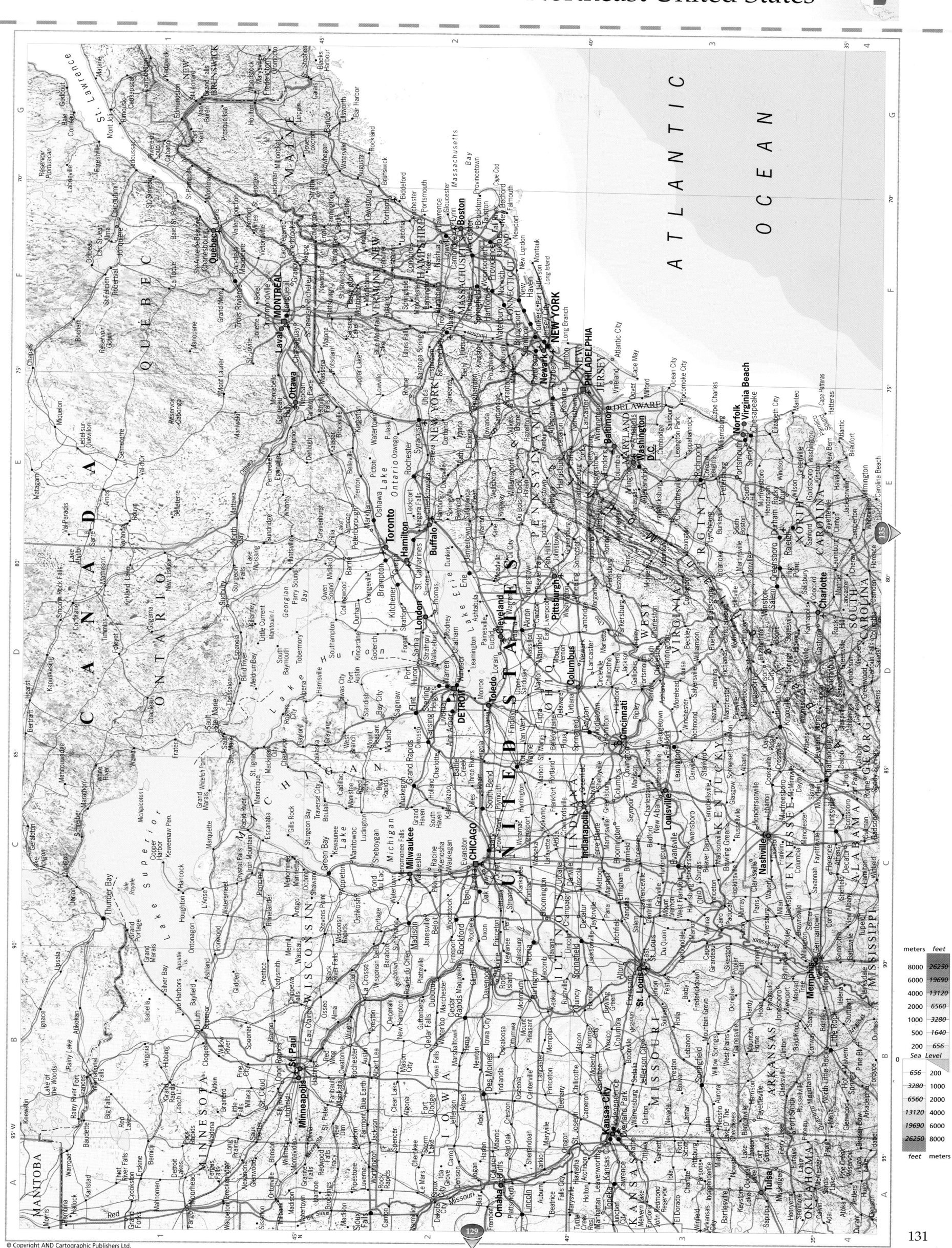

131

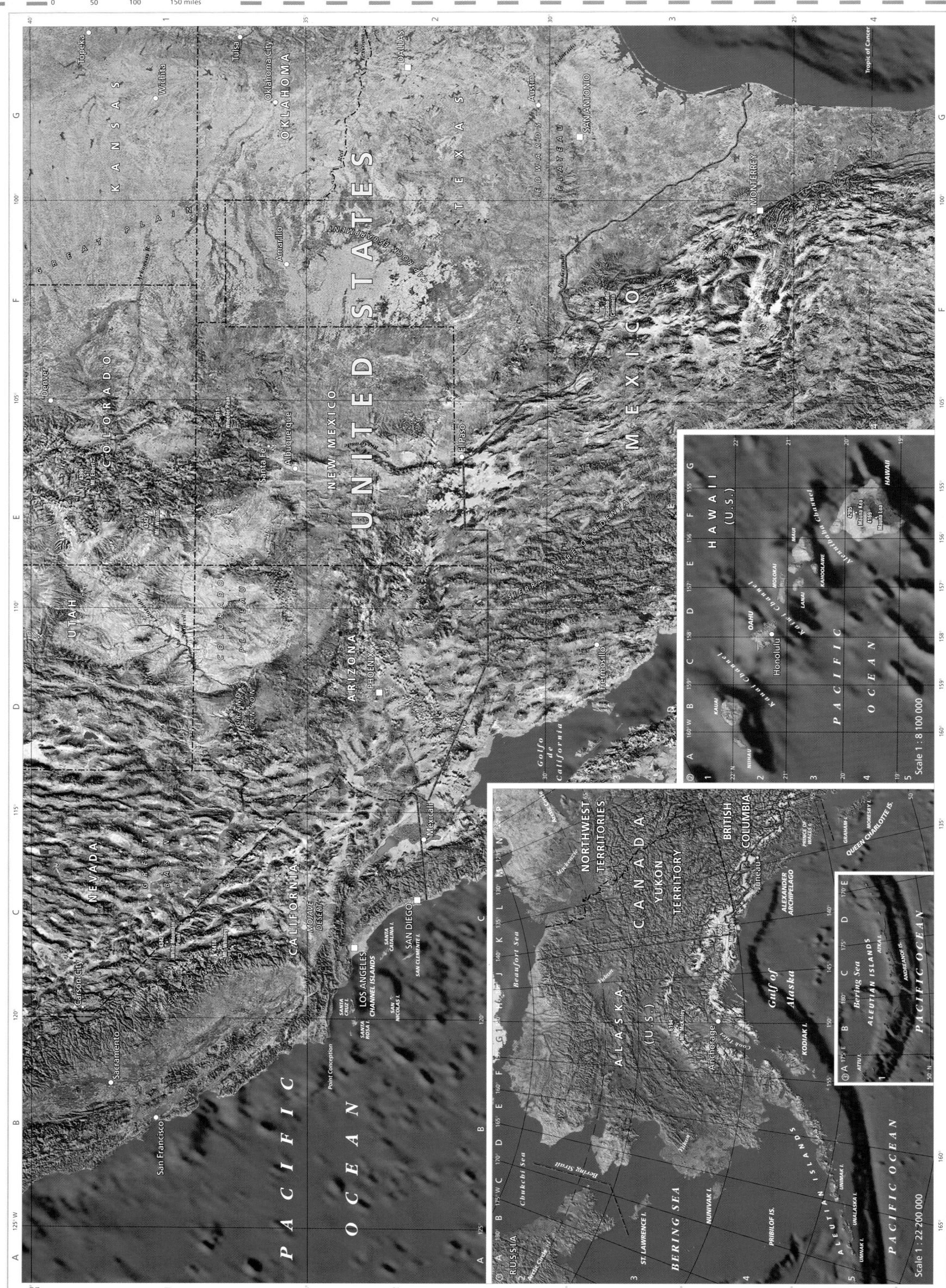

Scale 1 : 8 100 000

| 100 | 200 | 300 km |
| 50 | 100 | 150 miles |

GREAT PLAINS

KANSAS

Topeka

Wichita

Tulsa

Oklahoma City

OKLAHOMA

DALLAS

TEXAS

Austin

SAN ANTONIO

UNITED STATES

EDWARDS PLATEAU

MONTERREY

SIERRA MADRE ORIENTAL

MEXICO

Amarillo

CAP ROCK ESCARPMENT

COLORADO

Denver

Wheeler Peak

Santa Fe

Albuquerque

NEW MEXICO

El Paso

UTAH

Mt. Elbert
Mt. Wilson

COLORADO PLATEAU

GRAND CANYON

ARIZONA

PHOENIX

SIERRA MADRE OCCIDENTAL

Hermosillo

Golfo de California

NEVADA

Carson City

GREAT BASIN

MOJAVE DESERT

Mexicali

CALIFORNIA

Sacramento

San Francisco

Point Conception

LOS ANGELES

CHANNEL ISLANDS

SANTA CRUZ I.

SANTA ROSA I.

SAN NICOLAS I.

SANTA CATALINA I.

SAN CLEMENTE I.

SAN DIEGO

PACIFIC

OCEAN

HAWAII (U.S.)

KAUAI

NIIHAU

OAHU

Honolulu

MOLOKAI

Kaiwi Channel

LANAI

KAHOOLAWE

MAUI

Alenuihaha Channel

Kauai Channel

MAUNA KEA
Mauna Loa

HAWAII

PACIFIC OCEAN

Scale 1 : 8 100 000

NORTHWEST TERRITORIES

CANADA

YUKON TERRITORY

BRITISH COLUMBIA

Juneau

ALEXANDER ARCHIPELAGO

PRINCE OF WALES I.

GRAHAM I.

QUEEN CHARLOTTE IS.

MORESBY I.

ALASKA (U.S.)

Anchorage

Cook Inlet

Gulf of Alaska

KODIAK I.

Beaufort Sea

Bering Sea

ST. LAWRENCE I.

NUNIVAK I.

Chukchi Sea

Bering Strait

RUSSIA

PRIBILOF IS.

UNIMAK I.

UNALASKA I.

ALEUTIAN ISLANDS

PACIFIC OCEAN

Scale 1 : 22 200 000

ALEUTIAN ISLANDS

ATTU I.

AGATTU I.

ANDREANOF IS.

ADAK I.

Bering Sea

PACIFIC OCEAN

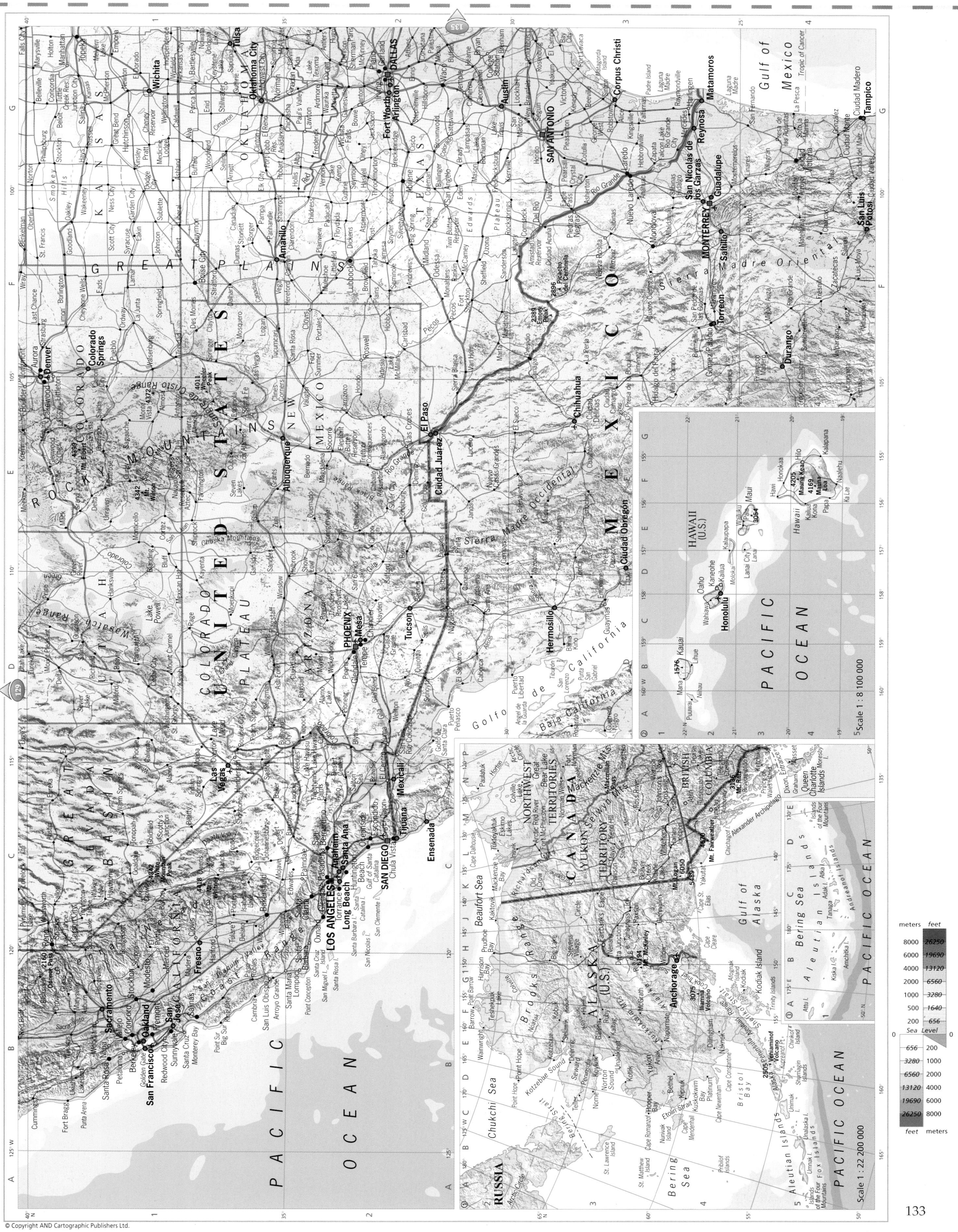

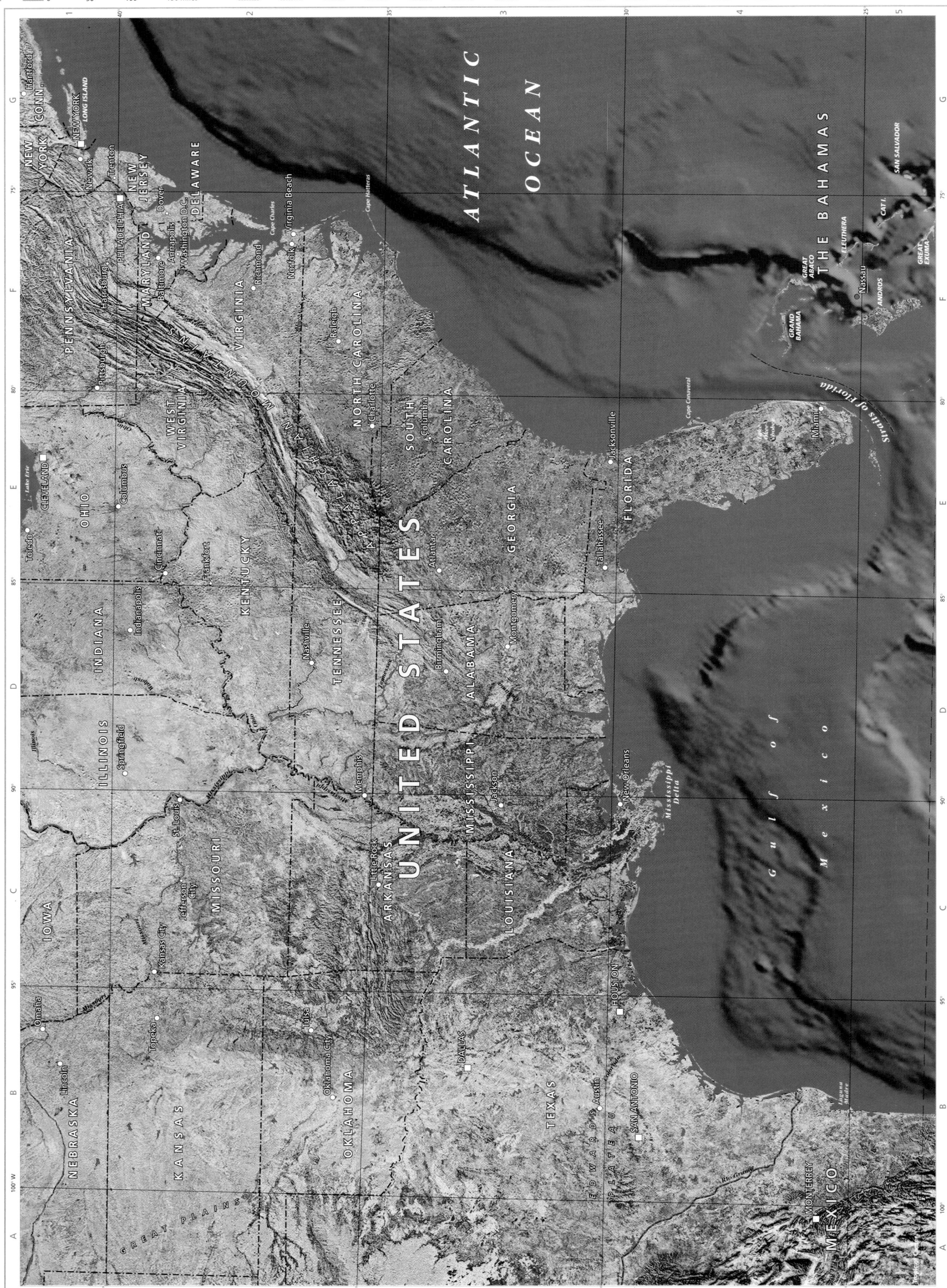

Scale 1 : 8 100 000

| 0 | 100 | 200 | 300 km |

0   50   100   150 miles

ATLANTIC

OCEAN

THE BAHAMAS

GREAT ABACO

GRAND BAHAMA

ELEUTHERA

San Salvador

CAT I.

Nassau

ANDROS

GREAT EXIMA

UNITED STATES

NEW YORK

CONN

Hartford

NEW YORK

LONG ISLAND

Newark

Trenton

NEW JERSEY

PHILADELPHIA

Dover

DELAWARE

Harrisburg

PENNSYLVANIA

MARYLAND

Baltimore

Annapolis

Washington D.C.

Pittsburgh

WEST VIRGINIA

VIRGINIA

Richmond

Norfolk

Virginia Beach

Cape Charles

Cape Hatteras

Cleveland

Lake Erie

CLEVELAND

OHIO

Columbus

Toledo

Cincinnati

Frankfort

KENTUCKY

Indianapolis

INDIANA

Nashville

TENNESSEE

NORTH CAROLINA

Charlotte

Raleigh

SOUTH CAROLINA

Columbia

APPALACHIAN MOUNTAINS

Atlanta

GEORGIA

ALABAMA

Birmingham

Montgomery

Tallahassee

FLORIDA

Jacksonville

Cape Canaveral

Miami

Straits of Florida

Gulf of Mexico

ILLINOIS

Springfield

Ohio

MISSOURI

St. Louis

Jefferson City

Kansas City

IOWA

NEBRASKA

Lincoln

Omaha

Topeka

KANSAS

GREAT PLAINS

OKLAHOMA

Oklahoma City

Tulsa

Little Rock

ARKANSAS

Memphis

MISSISSIPPI

Jackson

LOUISIANA

New Orleans

Mississippi Delta

TEXAS

DALLAS

Austin

SAN ANTONIO

HOUSTON

EDWARDS PLATEAU

Rio Grande

Laguna Madre

MONTERREY

MEXICO

134

© Copyright

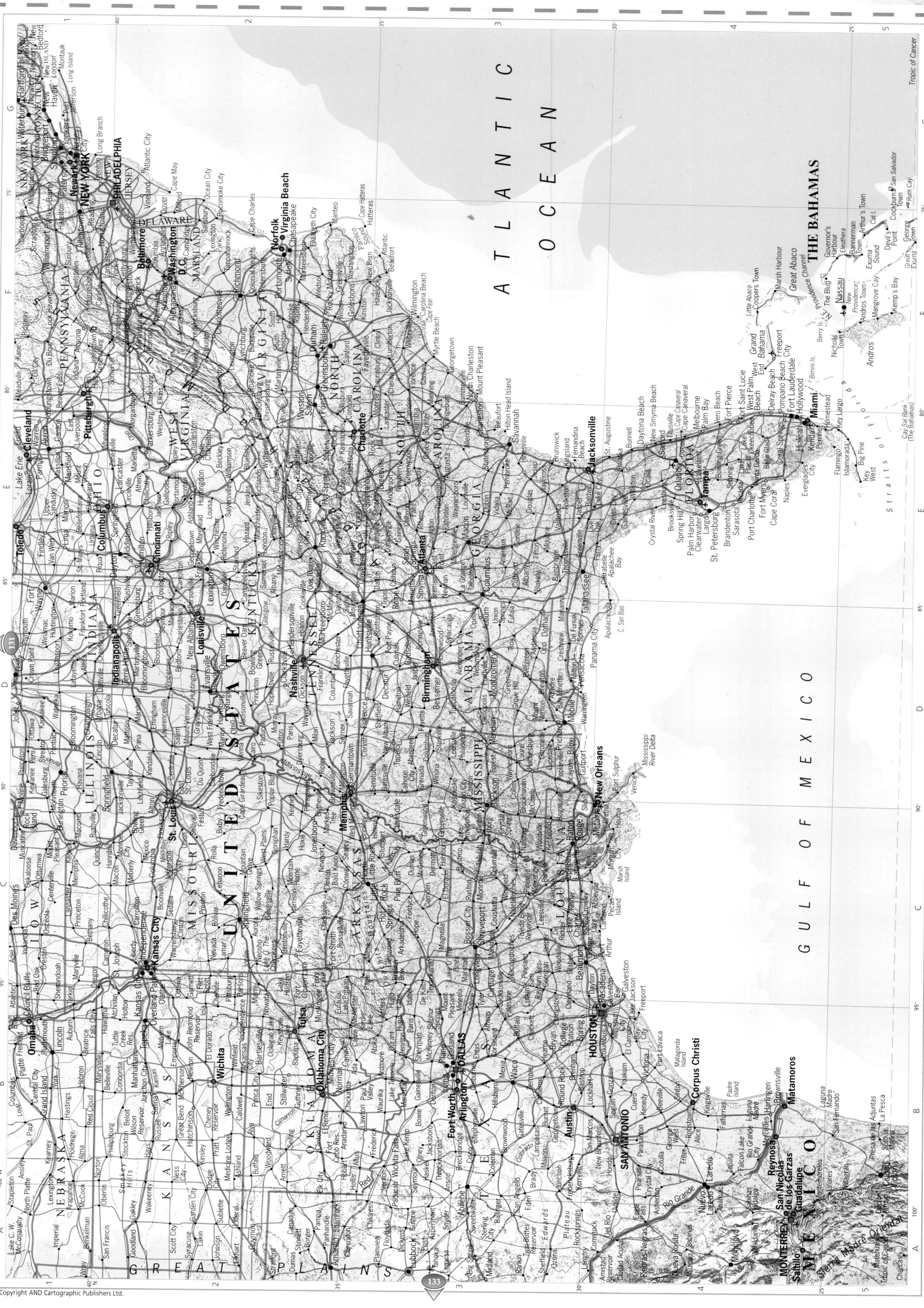

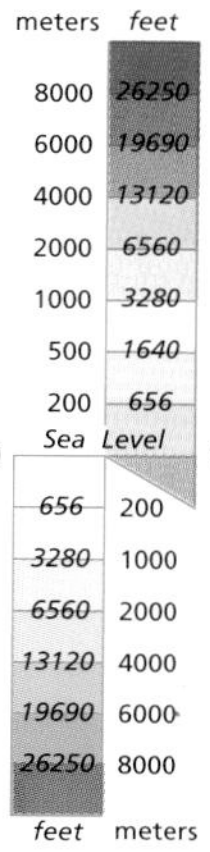

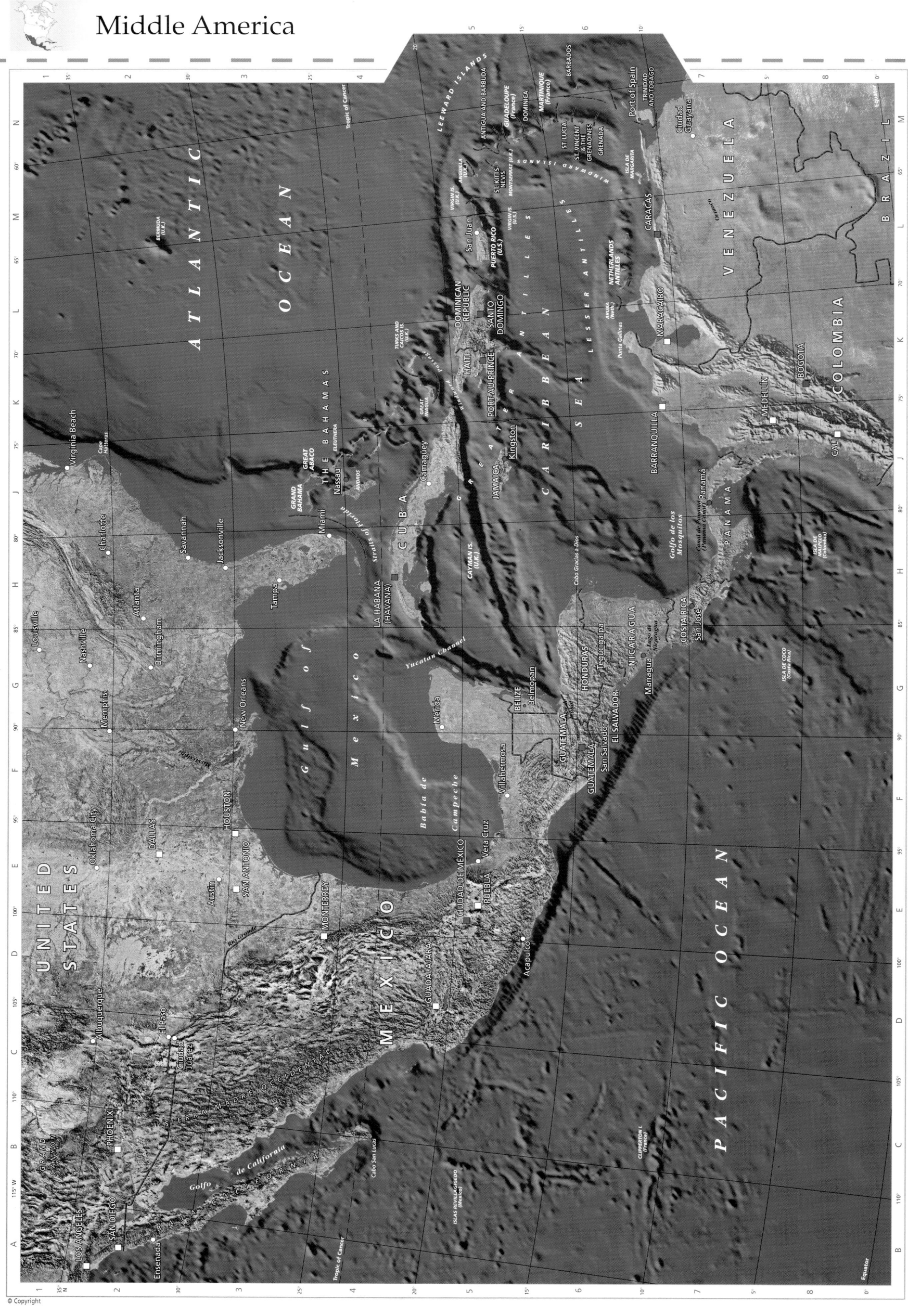

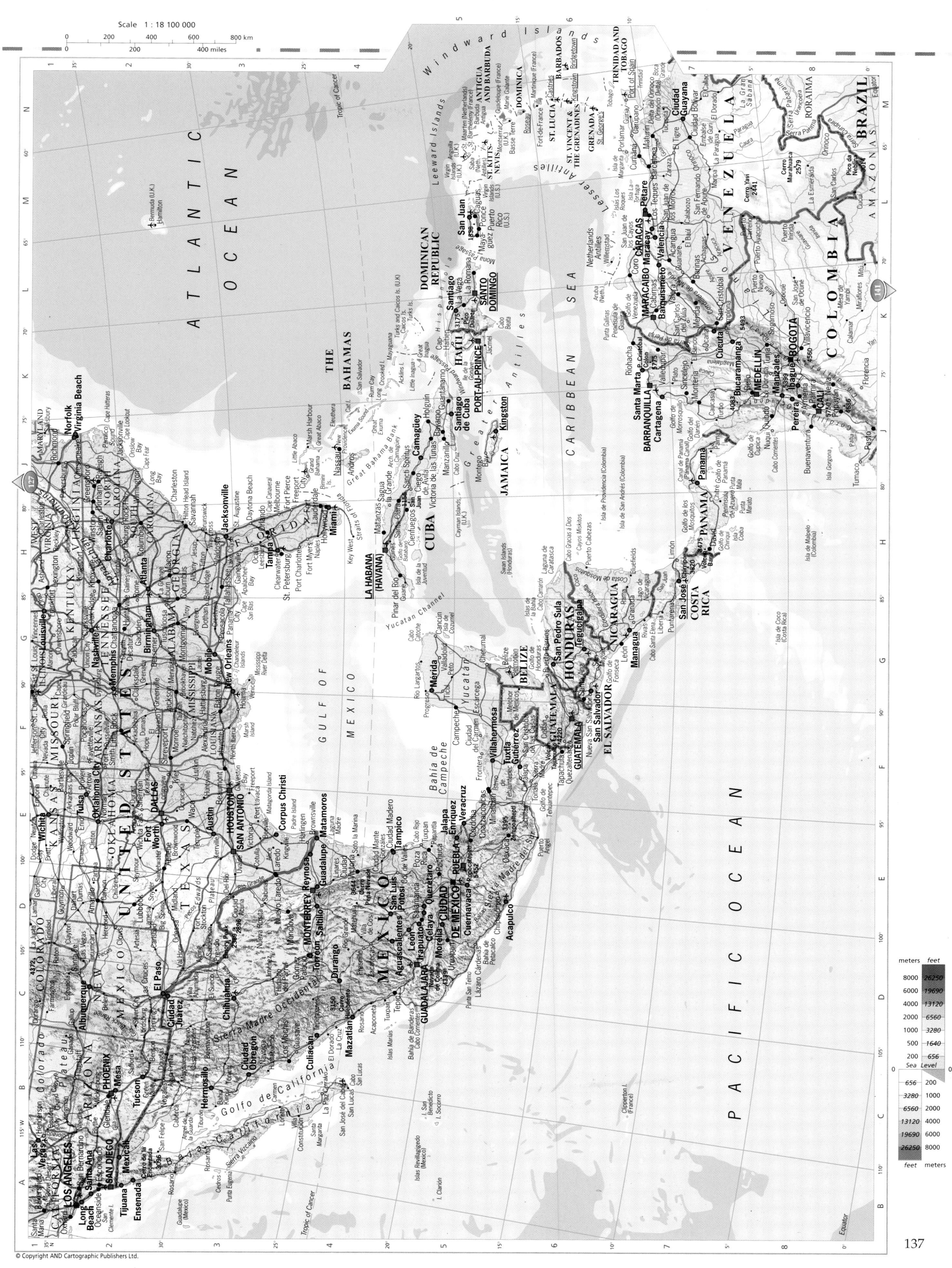

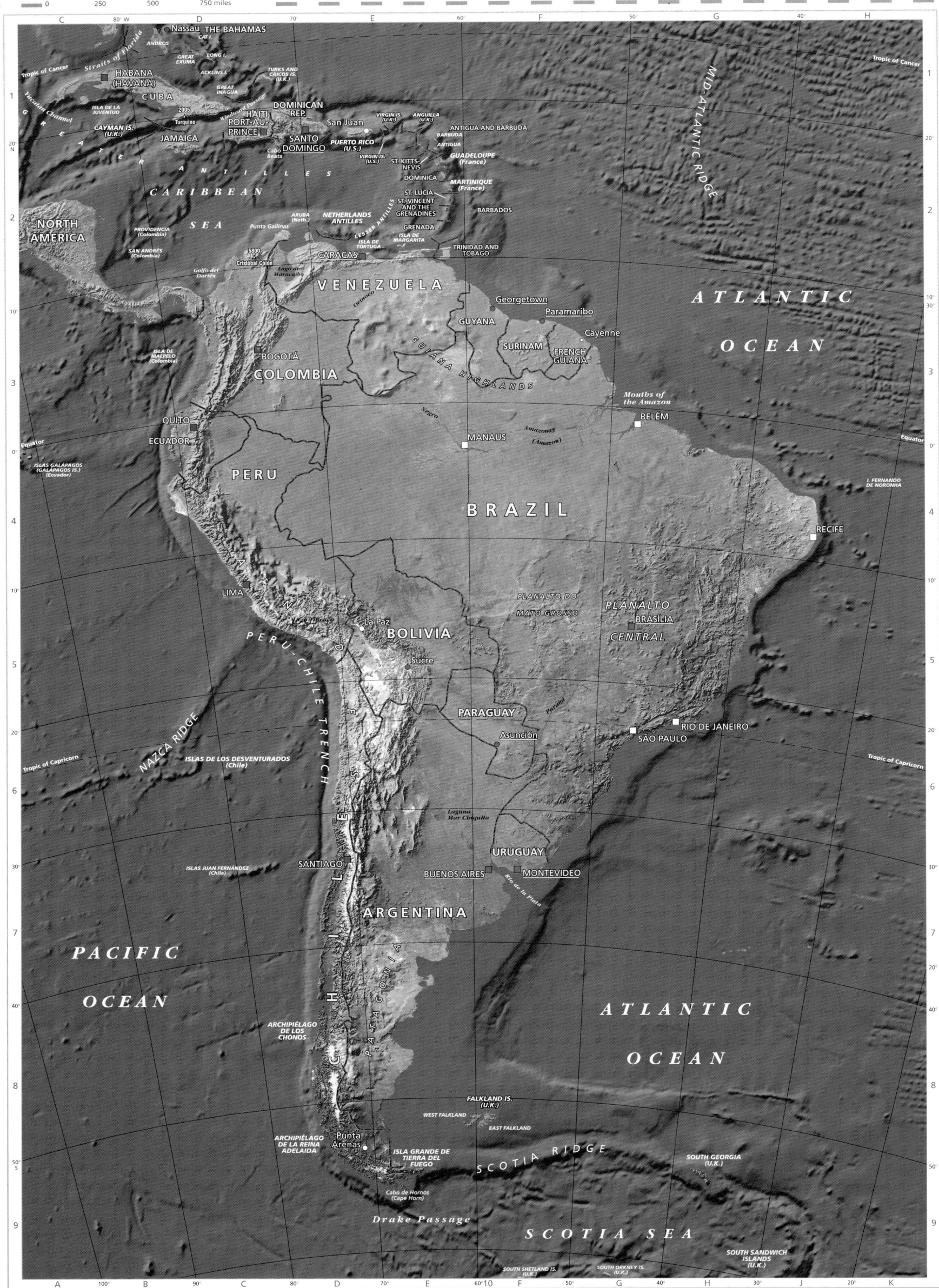

Scale 1 : 31 500 000

© Copyright

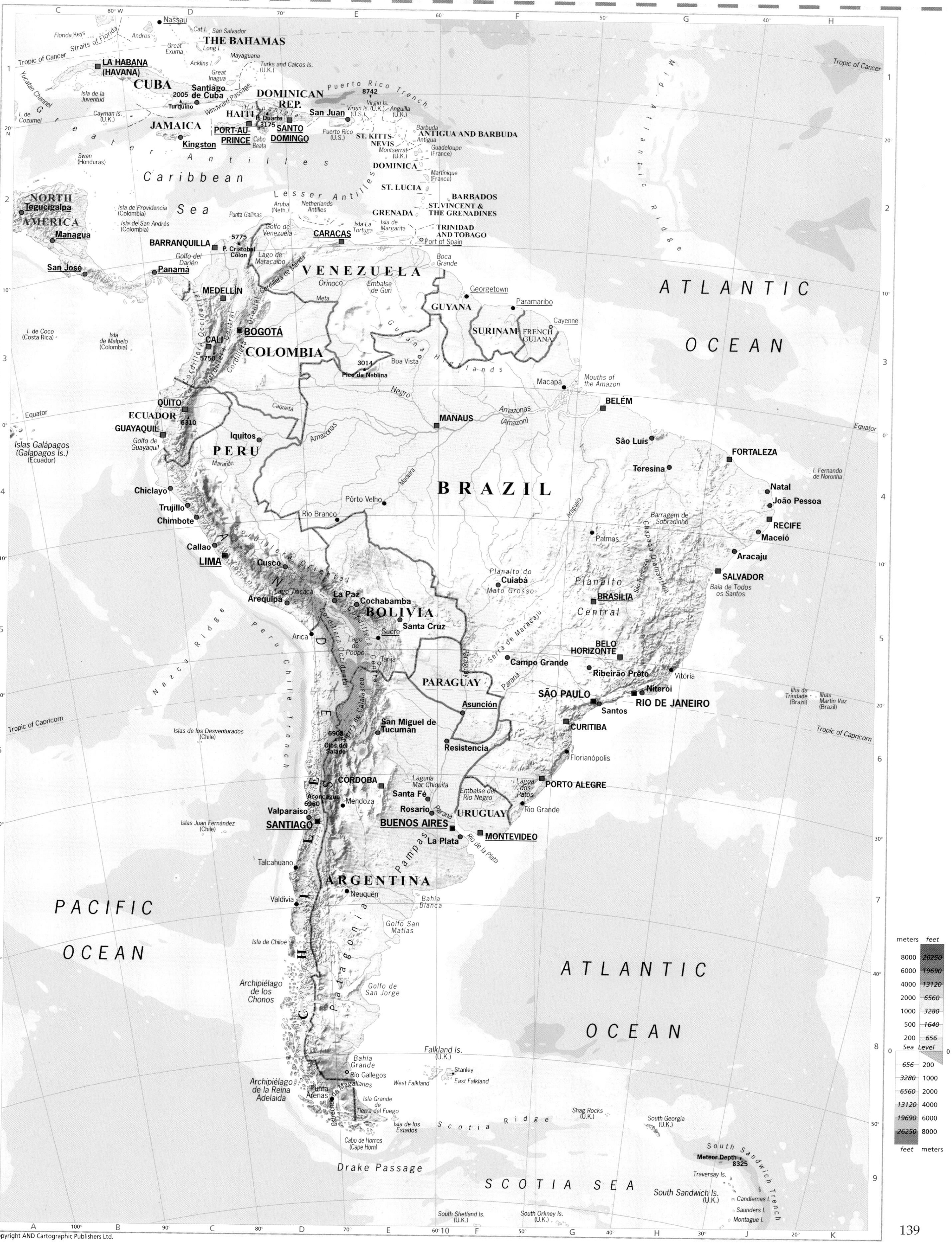

South America

139

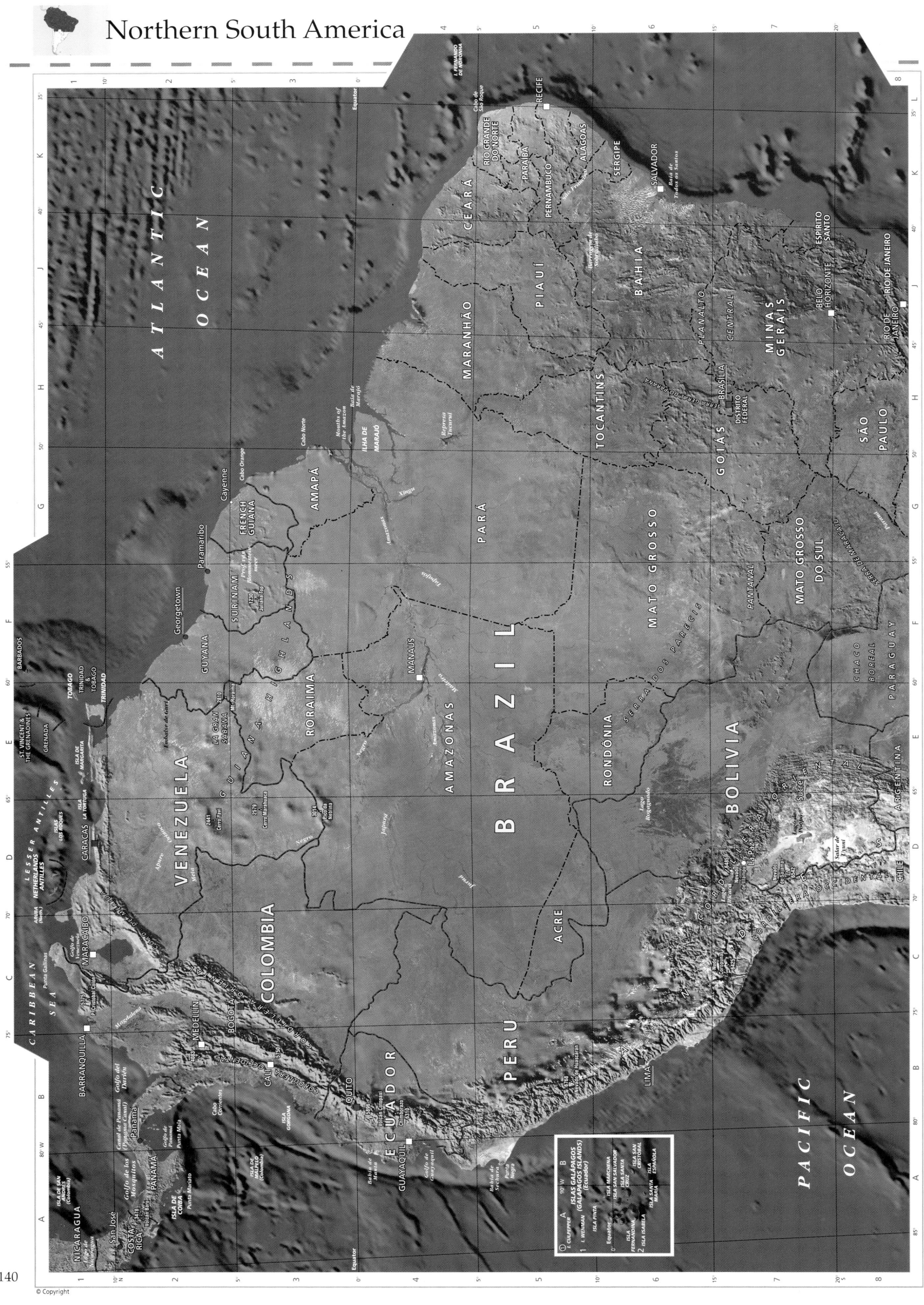

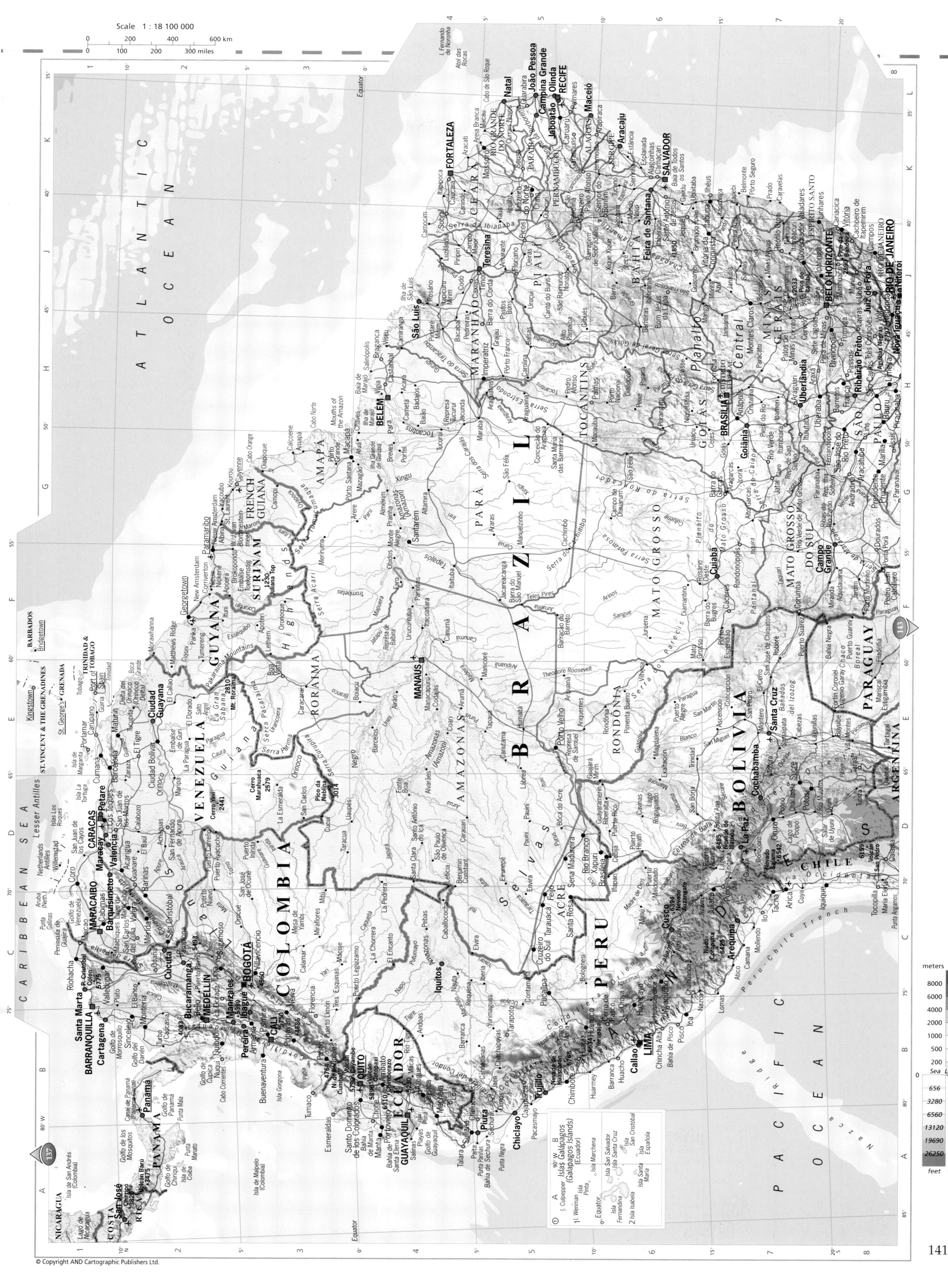

141

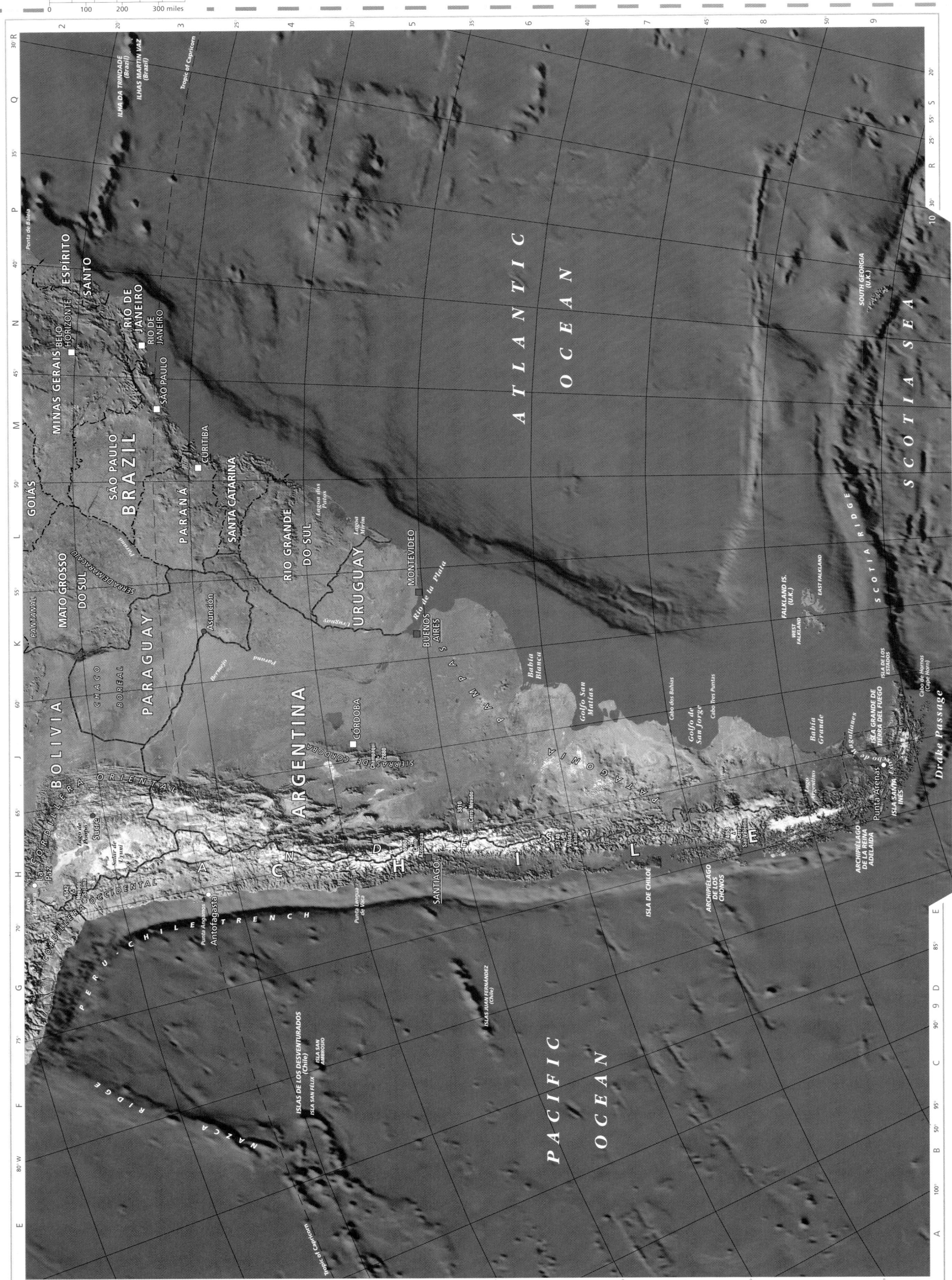

Scale 1 : 18 100 000

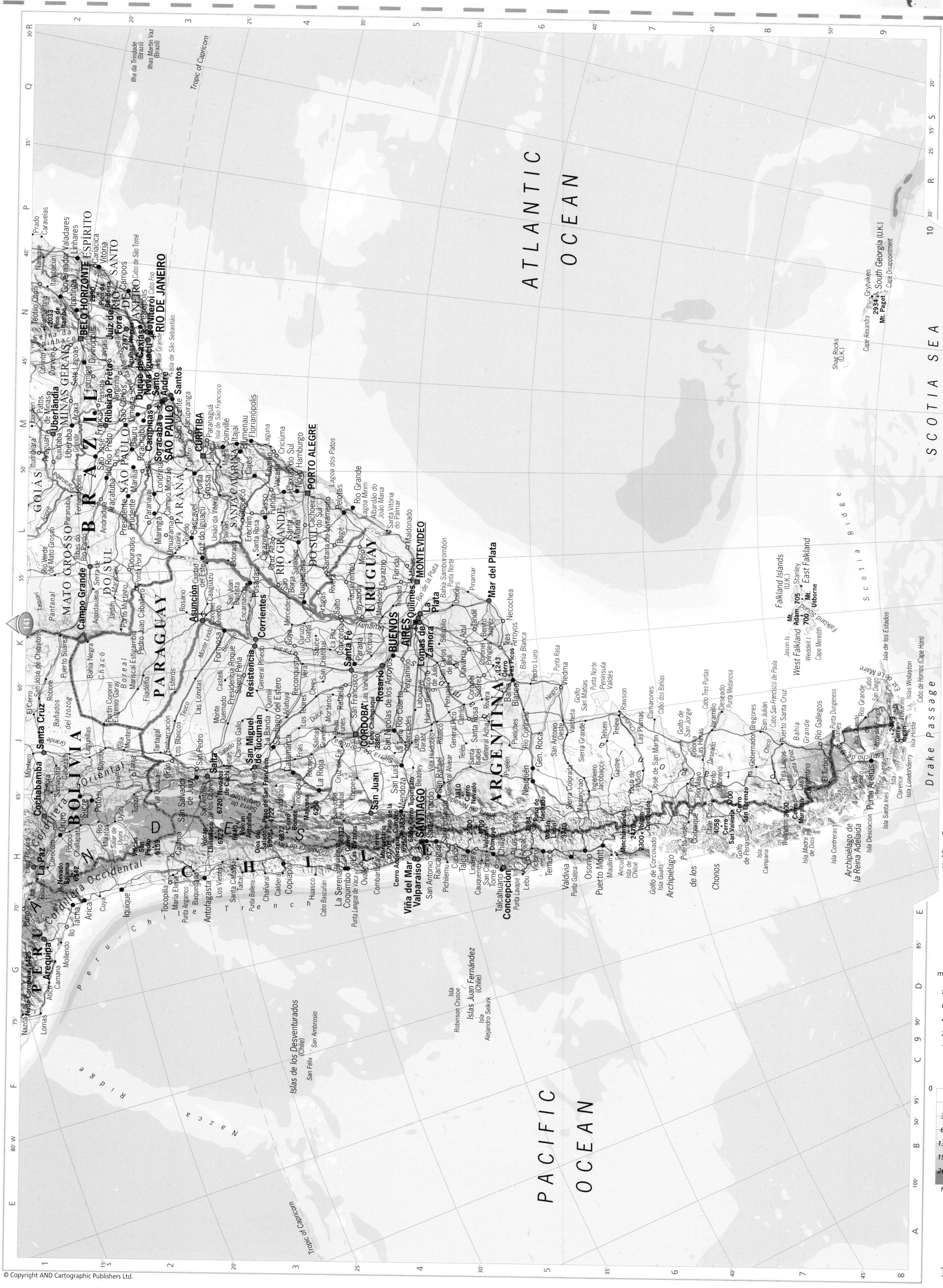

ATLANTIC OCEAN

PACIFIC OCEAN

SCOTIA SEA

Drake Passage

Tropic of Capricorn

BRAZIL

BOLIVIA

PARAGUAY

URUGUAY

ARGENTINA

CHILE

PERU

South Georgia (U.K.)

Falkland Islands (U.K.)

RIO DE JANEIRO
SÃO PAULO
CURITIBA
PORTO ALEGRE
BELO HORIZONTE
MONTEVIDEO
BUENOS AIRES
SANTIAGO
ASUNCIÓN
CÓRDOBA
Rosario
Santa Fe
Mar del Plata
Valparaíso
Viña del Mar
Concepción
La Paz
Sucre
Cochabamba
Santa Cruz
Arequipa
Salta
San Miguel de Tucumán
San Juan
Mendoza
Resistencia
Corrientes
Campo Grande

meters	feet
8000	26250
6000	19690
4000	13120
2000	6560
1000	3280
500	1640
200	656
Sea Level	

feet	meters
656	200
3280	1000
6560	2000
13120	4000
19690	6000
26250	8000

Scale 1 : 57 000 000

0 500 1000 1500 2000 km
0 250 500 750 1000 miles

Map 1 — Arctic (relief)

RUSSIA
UKRAINE
KYYIV (KIEV)
POLAND
BELARUS
LITHUANIA
LATVIA
ESTONIA
GERMANY
DENMARK
SWEDEN
NORWAY
FINLAND
Helsinki
Stockholm
Oslo
MOSKVA (MOSCOW)
Arkhangel'sk
Murmansk
UNITED KINGDOM
Dublin (Baile Átha Cliath)
REP. OF IRELAND
Reykjavik
ICELAND

North Sea
Baltic Sea
Gulf of Bothnia
Norwegian Sea
Volga
Ladozhskoye Ozero (Lake Ladoga)
Onezhskoye Ozero

Barents Sea
Novaya Zemlya
Zemlya Frantsa-Iosifa (Franz Josef Land) (Russia)
Svalbard (Norway)
Spitsbergen
Jan Mayen (Norway)
Nordaustlandet
Greenland Sea
Denmark Strait
GREENLAND (Denmark)
Gunnbjørns Field 3700
Nuuk (Godthåb)
Davis Strait
Baffin Bay
Baffin I.
Foxe Basin
Hudson Strait
Hudson Bay
Ellesmere I.
Queen Elizabeth Islands
Devon I.
Melville I.
Victoria I.
Banks I.
Great Bear Lake
Great Slave Lake
Labrador Sea
ATLANTIC OCEAN
Limit of Drift Ice

Arctic Ocean
North Pole

RUSSIA
Arctic Circle
Yenisey
Lena
Ob'
Severnaya Zemlya
Novosibirskiye Ostrova (New Siberian Islands)
More Laptevykh (Laptev Sea)
Vostochno-Sibirskoye More (East Siberian Sea)
Ostrov Vrangelya
Chukchi Sea
Karskoye More (Kara Sea)

Sea of Okhotsk
Sakhalin
Kuril'skiye Ostrova
Kamchatka
Klyuchevskaya Sopka 4750
Komandorskiye Ostrova
Attu Island
Aleutian Islands
Bering Sea
International Dateline
Bering Strait
St. Lawrence I.
Norton Sound
Nunivak
Bristol Bay
Kodiak
Gulf of Alaska

ALASKA (U.S.)
Mt. McKinley 6194
Anchorage
Mt. Logan 6050
Brooks Range
Mackenzie
Mackenzie Mountains
Coast Mountains
CANADA
Beaufort Sea
Limit of Pack Ice
Alexander Archipelago
Queen Charlotte Islands
PACIFIC OCEAN

Elevation key

meters	feet
8000	26250
6000	19690
4000	13120
2000	6560
1000	3280
500	1640
200	656
0 Sea Level	0
656	200
3280	1000
6560	2000
13120	4000
19690	6000
26250	8000

feet / meters

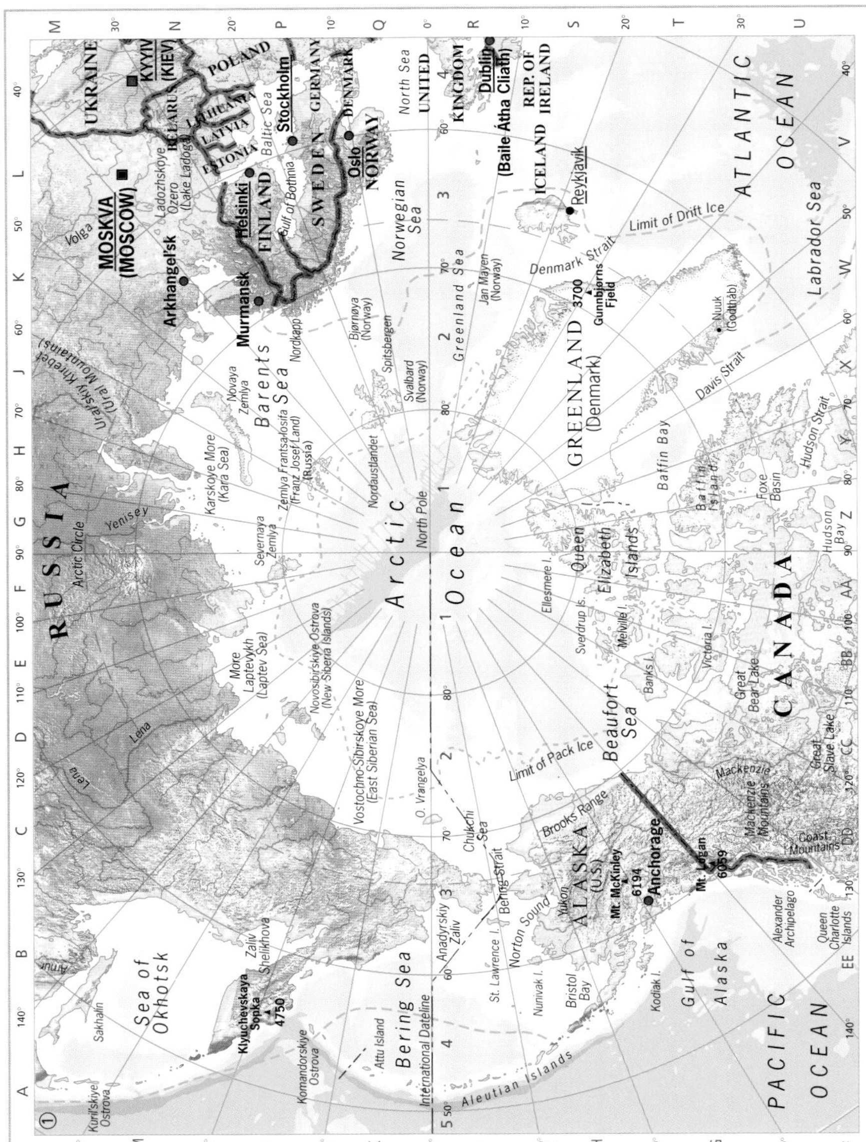

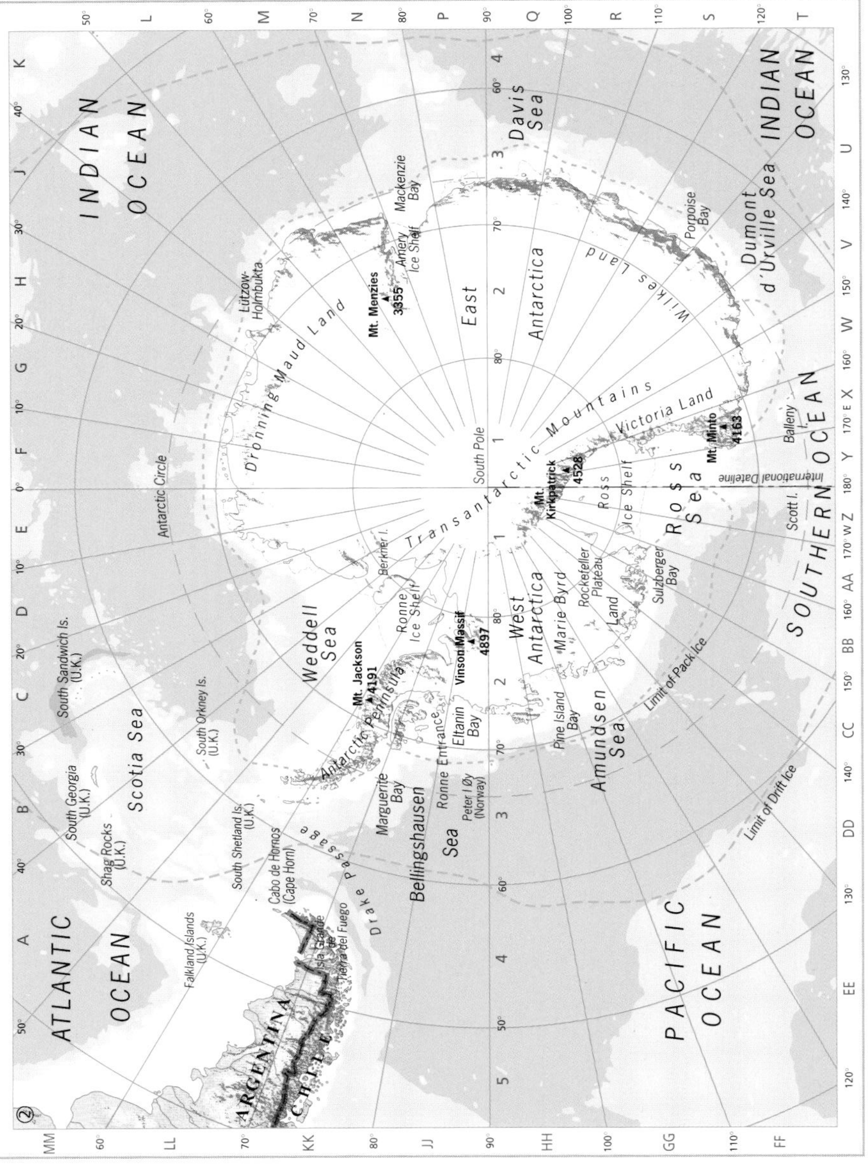

Map 2 — Antarctic (relief)

INDIAN OCEAN
Davis Sea
Mackenzie Bay
Porpoise Bay
Dumont d'Urville Sea
Wilkes Land
East Antarctica
Antarctica
Dronning Maud Land
Lützow-Holmbukta
Amery Ice Shelf
Mt. Menzies 3355
South Pole
Transantarctic Mountains
Victoria Land
Mt. Minto 4163
Mt. Kirkpatrick 4528
Ross Ice Shelf
Ross Sea
Ballery I.
Scott I.
International Dateline
Rockefeller Plateau
Marie Byrd Land
West Antarctica
Vinson Massif 4897
Mt. Jackson 4191
Antarctic Peninsula
Ronne Ice Shelf
Ronne Entrance
Berkner I.
Weddell Sea
Antarctic Circle
Peter I Øy (Norway)
Amundsen Sea
Bellingshausen Sea
Marguerite Bay
Eltanin Bay
Pine Island Bay
Sulzberger Bay
Limit of Pack Ice
Limit of Drift Ice
SOUTHERN OCEAN
PACIFIC OCEAN

South Sandwich Is. (U.K.)
South Orkney Is. (U.K.)
South Georgia (U.K.)
Shag Rocks (U.K.)
South Shetland Is. (U.K.)
Scotia Sea
Falkland Islands (U.K.)
Cabo de Hornos (Cape Horn)
Tierra del Fuego
Drake Passage
ARGENTINA
ATLANTIC OCEAN

© Copyright AND Cartographic Publishers Ltd.

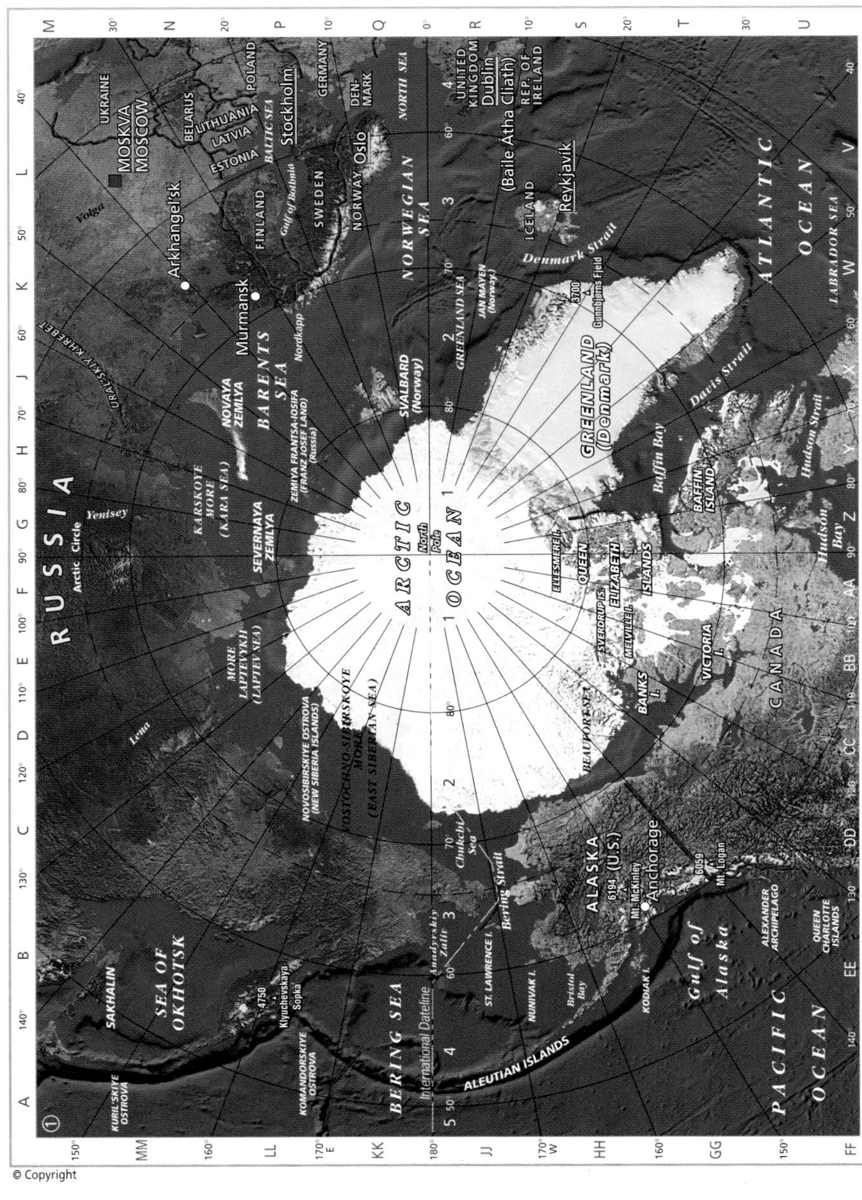

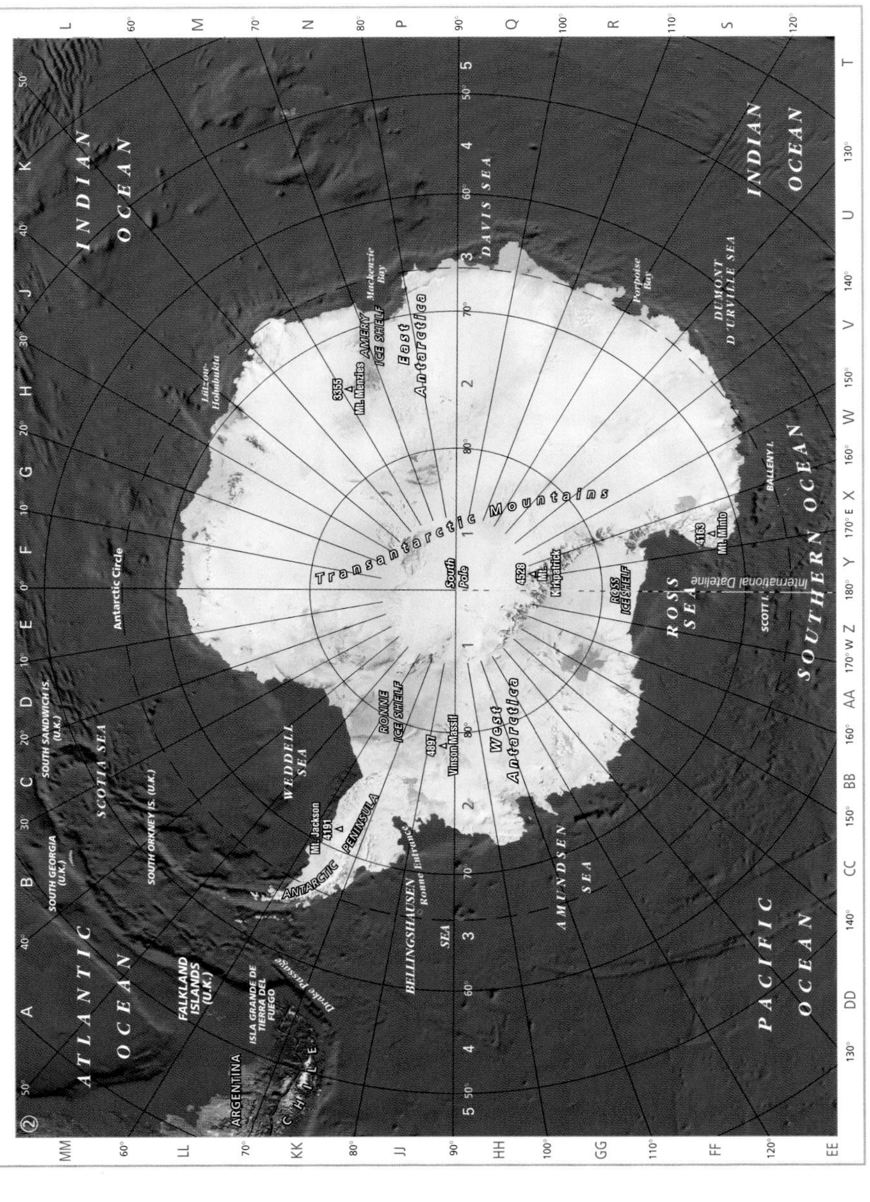

© Copyright

GLOSSARY

This is an alphabetically arranged glossary of the geographical terms used on the maps and in this index. The first column shows the map form, the second the language of origin and the third the English translation.

A

açude	Portuguese	reservoir
adası	Turkish	island
akra	Greek	peninsula
alpen	German	mountains
alpes	French	mountains
alpi	Italian	mountains
älven	Swedish	river
archipiélago	Spanish	archipelago
arquipélago	Portuguese	archipelago

B

bab	Arabic	strait
bahía	Spanish	bay
bahir, bahr	Arabic	bay, lake, river
baia	Portuguese	bay
baie	French	bay
baja	Spanish	lower
bandar	Arabic, Somalian, Malay, Persian	harbor, port
baraji	Turkish	dam
barragem	Portuguese	reservoir
ben	Gaelic	mountain
Berg(e)	German	mountain(s)
boğazı	Turkish	strait
Bucht	German	bay
buḥayrat	Arabic	lake
burnu, burun	Turkish	cape

C

cabo	Spanish	cape
canal	French, Spanish	canal, channel
canale	Italian	canal, channel
cerro	Spanish	mountain
chott	Arabic	marsh, salt lake
co	Tibetan	lake
collines	French	hills
cordillera	Spanish	range

D

dağ(ı)	Turkish	mountain
dağlar(ı)	Turkish	mountains
danau	Indonesian	lake
daryacheh	Persian	lake
dasht	Persian	desert
djebel	Arabic	mountain(s)
-do	Korean	island

E

embalse	Spanish	reservoir
erg	Arabic	sandy desert
estrecho	Spanish	strait

F

feng	Chinese	mountain
-fjördur	Icelandic	fjord
-flói	Icelandic	bay

G

Gebirge	German	range
golfe	French	bay, gulf
golfo	Italian, Portuguese, Spanish	bay, gulf
göl, gölü	Turkish	lake
gora	Russian	mountain
gory	Russian	mountains
gunong	Malay	mountain
gunung	Indonesian	mountain

H

hai	Chinese	lake, sea
hāmūn	Persian	lake, marsh
hawr	Arabic	lake
hu	Chinese	lake, reservoir

I

île(s)	French	island(s)
ilha(s)	Portuguese	island(s)
isla(s)	Spanish	island(s)

J

jabal	Arabic	mountain(s)
-järvi	Finnish	lake
jaza'īr	Arabic	islands
jazīrat	Arabic	island
jbel	Arabic	mountain
jebel	Arabic	mountain
jezero	Serbo-Croatian	lake
jezioro	Polish	lake
jiang	Chinese	river
-jima	Japanese	island
-joki	Finnish	river
-jökull	Icelandic	glacier

K

kepulauan	Indonesian	islands
khrebet	Russian	mountain range
-ko	Japanese	lake
kolpos	Greek	bay, gulf
körfezi	Turkish	bay, gulf
kryazh	Russian	ridge
kūh(ha)	Persian	mountain(s)

L

lac	French	lake
lacul	Romanian	lake
lago	Italian, Portuguese, Spanish	lake
lagoa	Portuguese	lagoon
laguna	Spanish	lagoon, lake
limni	Greek	lake
liqeni	Albanian	lake
loch, lough	Gaelic	lake

M

massif	French	mountains
-meer	Dutch	lake, sea
mont	French	mount
monte	Italian, Portuguese, Spanish	mount
montes	Portuguese, Spanish	mountains
monts	French	mountains
muntii	Romanian	mountains
mys	Russian	cape

N

nafud	Arabic	desert
nevado	Spanish	snow-capped mountain
nuruu	Mongolian	mountains
nuur	Mongolian	lake

O

| ostrov(a) | Russian | island(s) |
| ozero | Russian | lake |

P

pegunungan	Indonesian	mountains
pelagos	Greek	sea
pendi	Chinese	basin
pesky	Russian	sandy desert
pic	French	peak
pico	Portuguese, Spanish	peak
planalto	Portuguese	plateau
planina	Bulgarian	mountains
poluostrov	Russian	peninsula
puerto	Spanish	harbor, port
puncak	Indonesian	peak
punta	Italian, Spanish	point
puy	French	peak

Q

| qundao | Chinese | archipelago |

R

ras, râs, ra's	Arabic	cape
represa	Portuguese	dam, reservoir
-rettō	Japanese	archipelago
rio	Portuguese	river
río	Spanish	river

S

sahra	Arabic	desert
salar	Spanish	salt flat
-san	Japanese, Korean	mountain
-sanmaek	Korean	mountains
sebkha	Arabic	salt flat
sebkhet	Arabic	salt marsh
See	German	lake
serra	Portuguese	range
severnaya, severo-	Russian	northern
shan	Chinese	mountain(s)
-shima	Japanese	island
-shotō	Japanese	islands
sierra	Spanish	range

T

tanjona	Malagasy	cape
tanjung	Indonesian	cape
teluk	Indonesian	bay, gulf
ténéré	Berber	desert
-tō	Japanese	island

V

vârful	Romanian	mountain
-vesi	Finnish	lake
vodokhranilishche	Russian	reservoir
volcán	Spanish	volcano

W

| wādī | Arabic | watercourse |
| Wald | German | forest |

Z

| -zaki | Japanese | cape |
| zaliv | Russian | bay, gulf |

WORLD FACTS AND FIGURES

Dimensions of the Earth

Circumference of the Equator 24,903 mi.

Total surface area of the Earth 196,949,970 mi^2

Area of dry land (29.2%) 57,686,646 mi^2

Area of sea (70.8%) 139,263,324 mi^2

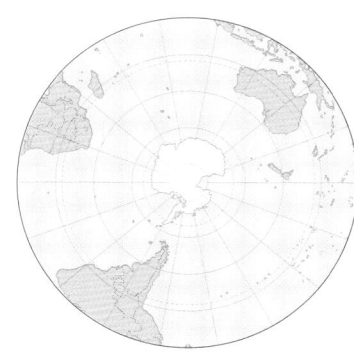

Continental Land Surface

1.   Asia 16,837,048 mi^2

2.   Africa 11,712,344 mi^2

3.   North America 9,787,249 mi^2

4.   South America 6,799,607 mi^2

5.   Antarctica 5,150,574 mi^2

6.   Europe 4,053,278 mi^2

7.   Australia and Oceania 3,448,170 mi^2

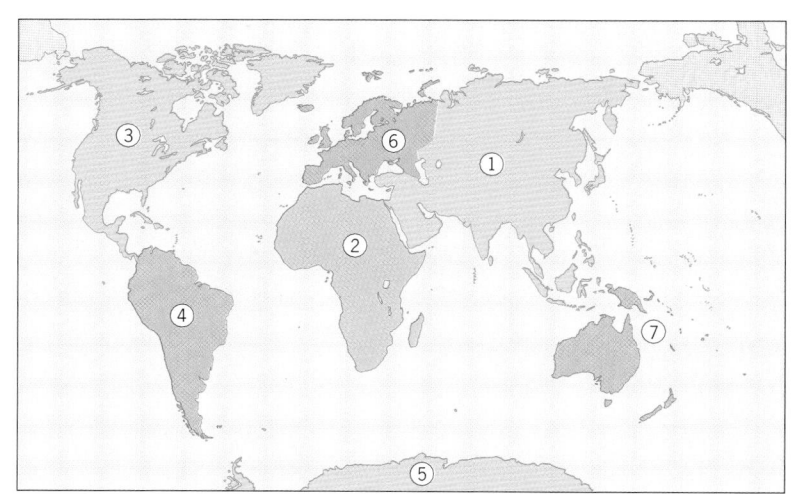

Largest Countries according to area

1.   Russia 6,602,310 mi^2

2.   Canada 3,851,787 mi^2

3.   China 3,696,128 mi^2

4.   United States 3,615,118 mi^2

5.   Brazil 3,286,482 mi^2

6.   Australia 2,966,136 mi^2

7.   India 1,222,713 mi^2

8.   Argentina 1,073,394 mi^2

9.   Sudan 967,494 mi^2

10.   Algeria 919,590 mi^2

Oceans and largest inland waters

1.   Caspian Sea (Salt) (Asia) 143,243 mi^2

2.   Lake Superior (N. America) 32,151 mi^2

3.   Lake Victoria (Africa) 26,564 mi^2

4.   Lake Huron (N. America) 23,436 mi^2

5.   Lake Michigan (N. America) 22,402 mi^2

6.   Aral Sea (Salt) (Asia) 13,900 mi^2

7.   Lake Tanganyika (Africa) 12,703 mi^2

8.   Great Bear Lake (N. America) 12,274 mi^2

9.   Lake Baikal (Asia) 11,776 mi^2

10.   Great Slave Lake (N. America) 10,981 mi^2

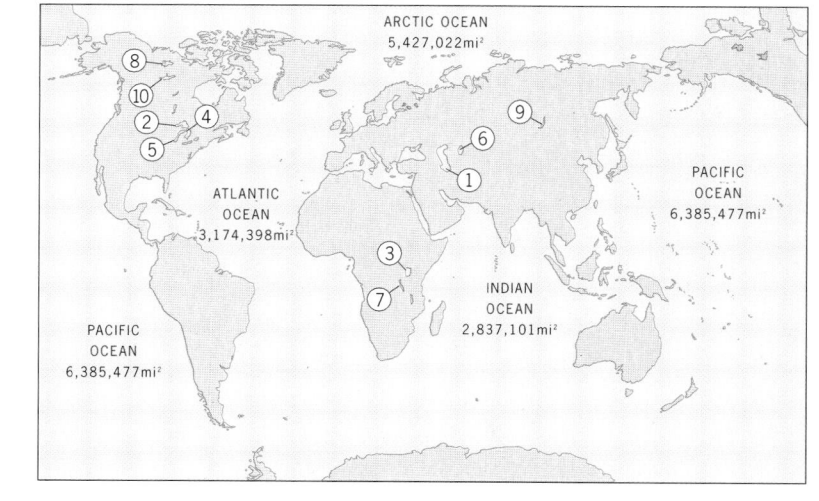

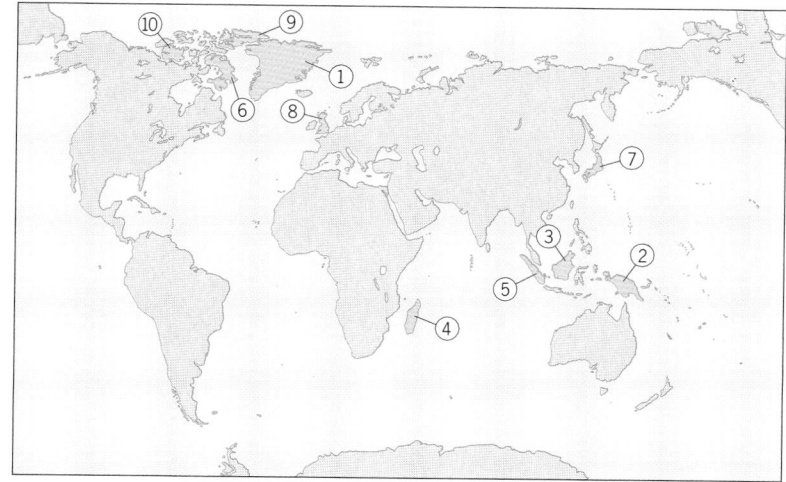

Largest islands of the world

1.	Greenland 839,999 mi²
2.	New Guinea 312,166 mi²
3.	Borneo 292,297 mi²
4.	Madagascar 229,413 mi²
5.	Sumatra 202,355 mi²
6.	Baffin Island 183,811 mi²
7.	Honshu 88,979 mi²
8.	Great Britain 88,753 mi²
9.	Ellesmere Island 82,120 mi²
10.	Victoria Island 81,930 mi²

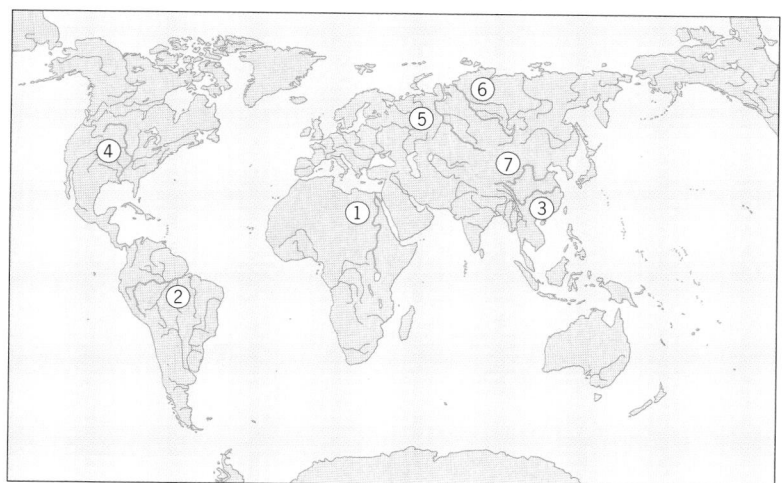

Longest rivers of the world

1.	Nile (Africa) 4,160 mi.
2.	Amazon (S. America) 4,048 mi.
3.	Chang-Jiang/Yangtze (Asia) 3,965 mi.
4.	Mississippi-Missouri (N. America) 3,740 mi.
5.	Ob-Irtysh (Asia) 3,461 mi.
6.	Jenisey-Angara (Asia) 3,449 mi.
7.	Huang He-Yellow River (Asia) 3,395 mi.

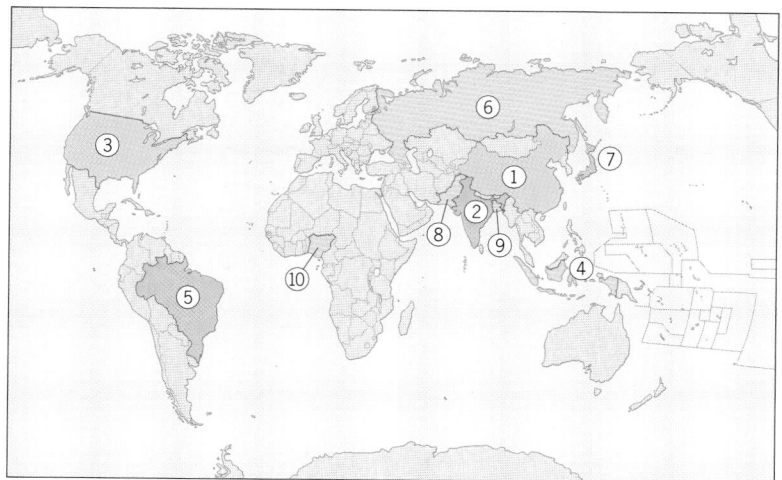

Largest countries according to population

1.	China 1,185,000,000
2.	India 903,000,000
3.	United States 257,000,000
4.	Indonesia 188,000,000
5.	Brazil 159,000,000
6.	Russia 150,000,000
7.	Japan 124,900,000
8.	Pakistan 122,400,000
9.	Bangladesh 122,280,000
10.	Nigeria 92,800,000

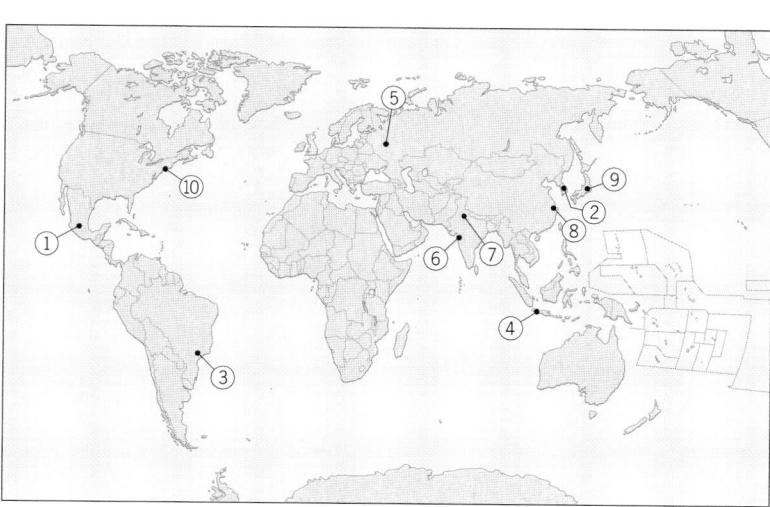

Largest cities of the world

1.	Mexico City 15,047,000
2.	Seoul 10,628,000
3.	Sao Paulo 9,480,427
4.	Jakarta 9,000,000
5.	Moscow 8,967,000
6.	Bombay 8,400,000
7.	Delhi 8,380,000
8.	Shanghai 8,214,436
9.	Tokyo 7,976,000
10.	New York 7,322,564

WORLD FLAGS AND STATISTICS

NORTH AND CENTRAL AMERICA

Antigua and Barbuda
Area: 171 sq. mi.
Population: 67,000
Capital: St John's (*pop:* 22,342)
Religions: Protestant, Roman Catholic
Languages: English, Creole
Political system: Constitutional monarchy
Economy: Tourism, fishing
GNP per capita: US$7,380
Currency: East Caribbean dollar

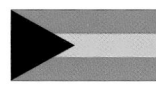

Bahamas, The
Area: 5,358 sq. mi.
Population: 296,000
Capital: Nassau (*pop:* 172,196)
Religions: Protestant, Roman Catholic
Languages: English, Creole
Political system: Constitutional monarchy
Economy: Tourism, banking
GNP per capita: US$11,940
Currency: Bahamian dollar

Barbados
Area: 166 sq. mi.
Population: 268,000
Capital: Bridgetown (*pop:* 108,000)
Religions: Protestant, Roman Catholic
Languages: English, Creole
Political system: Constitutional monarchy
Economy: Sugar, tourism
GNP per capita: US$6,560
Currency: Barbados dollar

Belize
Area: 8,763 sq. mi.
Population: 230,000
Capital: Belmopan (*pop:* 44,087)
Religion: Christian
Languages: English, Spanish, Creole
Political system: Constitutional monarchy
Economy: Agriculture, tourism
GNP per capita: US$2,740
Currency: Belize dollar

Canada
Area: 3,849,674 sq. mi.
Population: 30,563,000
Capital: Ottawa (*pop:* 1,010,288)
Religions: Roman Catholic, Protestant
Languages: English, French
Political system: Constitutional monarchy
Economy: Light industries
GNP per capita: US$19,290
Currency: Canadian dollar

Costa Rica
Area: 19,730 sq. mi.
Population: 3,841,000
Capital: San José (*pop:* 1,186,417)
Religion: Roman Catholic
Languages: Spanish, English, Creole
Political system: Republic
Economy: Agriculture, coffee
GNP per capita: US$2,640
Currency: Costa Rican colón

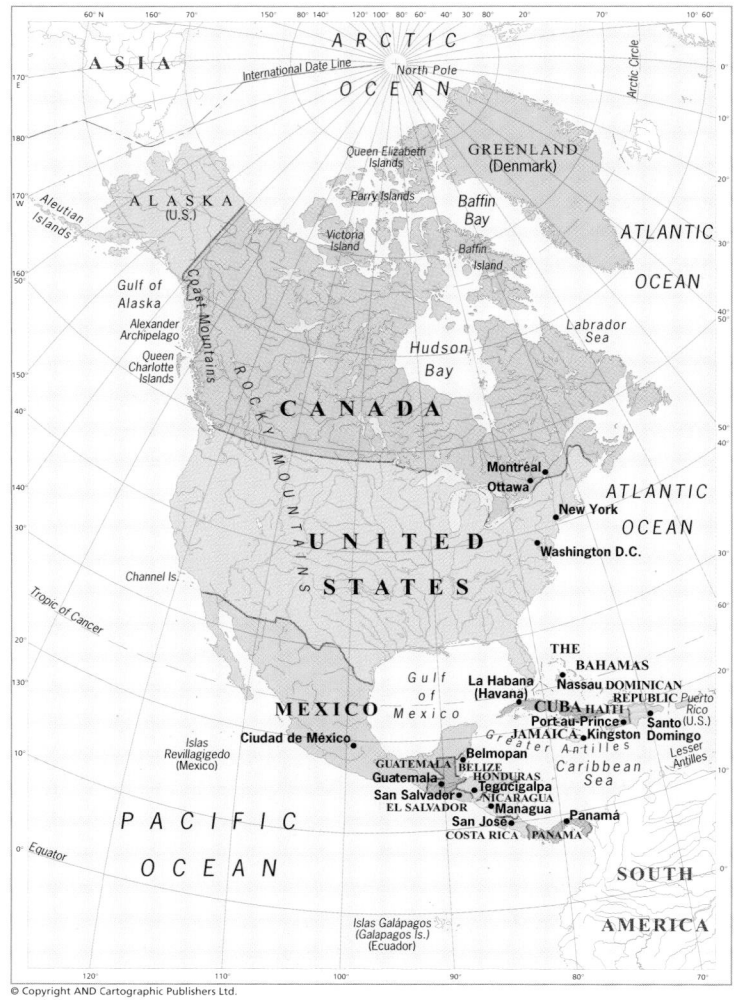

© Copyright AND Cartographic Publishers Ltd.

Cuba
Area: 42,804 sq. mi.
Population: 11,116,000
Capital: Havana (*pop:* 2,175,888)
Religion: Roman Catholic
Languages: Spanish, English
Political System: Republic
Economy: Sugar
GNP per capita: US$1,250
Currency: Cuban peso

Dominica
Area: 290 sq. mi.
Population: 71,000
Capital: Roseau (*pop:* 16,243)
Religions: Roman Catholic, Protestant
Languages: English, Creole
Political system: Republic
Economy: Bananas, tourism
GNP per capita: US$3,120
Currency: East Caribbean dollar

Dominican Republic
Area: 18,816 sq. mi.
Population: 8,232,000
Capital: Santo Domingo (*pop:* 2,134,779)
Religions: Roman Catholic, Protestant
Main language: Spanish
Political system: Republic
Economy: Mining, sugar
GNP per capita: US$1,670
Currency: Dominican Republic peso

El Salvador
Area: 8,124 sq. mi.
Population: 6,032,000
Capital: San Salvador (*pop:* 422,570)
Religions: Roman Catholic, Protestant
Main language: Spanish
Political system: Republic
Economy: Coffee, foreign aid
GNP per capita: US$1,810
Currency: El Salvador colón

Grenada
Area: 133 sq. mi.
Population: 93,000
Capital: St George's (*pop:* 4,788)
Religions: Roman Catholic, Protestant
Languages: English, Creole
Political system: Constitutional monarchy
Economy: Spices, cocoa
GNP per capita: US$3,000
Currency: East Caribbean dollar

Guatemala
Area: 42,042 sq. mi.
Population: 10,801,000
Capital: Guatemala City (*pop:* 1,675,589)
Religion: Christian
Languages: Spanish, Indian languages
Political system: Republic
Economy: Agriculture, sugar
GNP per capita: US$1,500
Currency: Quetzal

Haiti
Area: 10,714 sq. mi.
Population: 7,952,000
Capital: Port-au-Prince (*pop:* 690,168)
Religions: Roman Catholic, Protestant
Languages: Creole, French
Political system: Republic
Economy: Dependent on foreign aid
GNP per capita: US$330
Currency: Gourde

Honduras
Area: 43,277 sq. mi.
Population: 6,147,000
Capital: Tegucigalpa (*pop:* 670,000)
Religions: Roman Catholic, others
Languages: Spanish, English
Political system: Republic
Economy: Bananas, coffee
GNP per capita: US$700
Currency: Lempira

Jamaica
Area: 4,243 sq. mi.
Population: 2,538,000
Capital: Kingston (*pop:* 103,962)
Religions: Christian, others
Languages: English, Creole
Political system: Constitutional monarchy
Economy: Bauxite, tourism
GNP per capita: US$1,560
Currency: Jamaican dollar

Mexico
Area: 756,066 sq. mi.
Population: 95,831,000
Capital: Mexico City (*pop:* 15,047,685)
Religions: Roman Catholic, Protestant
Languages: Spanish, Indian languages
Political system: Republic
Economy: Oil, cash crops
GNP per capita: US$3,680
Currency: Peso

Nicaragua
Area: 50,193 sq. mi.
Population: 4,807,000
Capital: Managua (*pop:* 608,020)
Religions: Roman Catholic, others
Languages: Spanish, English
Political system: Republic
Economy: coffee, sugar
GNP per capita: US$410
Currency: Córdoba

Panama
Area: 29,157 sq. mi.
Population: 2,767,000
Capital: Panama City (*pop:* 445,902)
Religions: Roman Catholic, others
Languages: Spanish, Creole
Political system: Republic
Economy: Banking, insurance
GNP per capita: US$3,080
Currency: Balboa

National populations: UN, Population Division, Dept. of Economic & Social Affairs, 1998. Capital city population figures reflect greater metropolitan areas

St Kitts-Nevis

Area: 101 sq. mi.
Population: 39,000
Capital: Basseterre (pop: 14,161)
Religion: Protestant
Languages: English, Creole
Political system: Constitutional monarchy
Economy: Sugar, tourism
GNP per capita: US$6,160
Currency: East Caribbean dollar

St Lucia

Area: 240 sq. mi.
Population: 150,000
Capital: Castries (pop: 56,000)
Religions: Roman Catholic, others
Languages: English, Creole
Political system: Constitutional monarchy
Economy: Agriculture
GNP per capita: US$3,620
Currency: East Caribbean dollar

St Vincent and the Grenadines

Area: 150 sq. mi.
Population: 112,000
Capital: Kingstown (pop: 33,694)
Religions: Protestant, Roman Catholic
Languages: English, Creole
Political system: Constitutional monarchy
Economy: Agriculture
GNP per capita: US$2,500
Currency: East Caribbean dollar

Trinidad and Tobago

Area: 1,981 sq. mi.
Population: 1,283,000
Capital: Port of Spain (pop: 50,878)
Religions: Christian, Hindu, Muslim
Main language: English
Political system: Republic
Economy: Oil, gas
GNP per capita: US$4,230
Currency: Trinidad and Tobago dollar

United States

Area: 3,615,276 sq. mi.
Population: 274,028,000
Capital: Washington DC (pop: 7,051,495)
Religions: Protestant, Roman Catholic, Jewish
Languages: English, Spanish
Political system: Republic
Economy: Manufacturing, agriculture
GNP per capita: US$28,740
Currency: US dollar

SOUTH AMERICA

Argentina

Area: 1,073,518 sq. mi.
Population: 36,123,000
Capital: Buenos Aires (pop: 10,686,163)
Religions: Roman Catholic, Jewish, others
Languages: Spanish, English
Political system: Republic
Economy: Beef, wheat
GNP per capita: US$8,570
Currency: Peso

Bolivia

Area: 424,165 sq. mi.
Population: 7,957,000
Capital: Sucre (pop: 144,994)
Religions: Roman Catholic, others
Languages: Spanish, Quechua, Aymará
Political system: Republic
Economy: Mining, oil
GNP per capita: US$950
Currency: Boliviano

Brazil

Area: 3,300,171 sq. mi.
Population: 165,851,000
Capital: Brasilia (pop: 1,601,094)
Religion: Christian
Main language: Portuguese
Political system: Republic
Economy: Mining industry
GNP per capita: US$4,720
Currency: Real

Chile

Area: 292,135 sq. mi.
Population: 14,824,000
Capital: Santiago (pop: 5,257,937)
Religions: Roman Catholic, Protestant
Languages: Spanish, Indian languages
Political system: Republic
Economy: Copper, wine
GNP per capita: US$5,020
Currency: Chilean peso

Colombia

Area: 439,737 sq. mi.
Population: 40,803,000
Capital: Bogotá (pop: 8,000,000)
Religions: Roman Catholic, others
Languages: Spanish, Indian languages
Political system: Republic
Economy: Coffee, coal
GNP per capita: US$2,280
Currency: Colombian peso

Ecuador

Area: 109,484 sq. mi.
Population: 12,175,000
Capital: Quito (pop: 1,387,887)
Religions: Roman Catholic, others
Languages: Spanish, Quechua
Political system: Republic
Economy: Bananas, oil
GNP per capita: US$1,590
Currency: Sucre

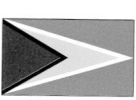

Guyana

Area: 83,000 sq. mi.
Population: 850,000
Capital: Georgetown (pop: 250,000)
Religions: Christian, Hindu, Muslim
Languages: English, Creole
Political system: Republic
Economy: Bauxite, gold
GNP per capita: US$800
Currency: Guyana dollar

Paraguay

Area: 157,048 sq. mi.
Population: 5,222,000
Capital: Asuncion (pop: 718,690)
Religions: Roman Catholic, other
Languages: Spanish, Guaraní
Political system: Republic
Economy: Agriculture, electricity
GNP per capita: US$2,010
Currency: Guaraní

Peru

Area: 496,225 sq. mi.
Population: 24,797,000
Capital: Lima (pop: 6,483,901)
Religions: Roman Catholic, others
Languages: Spanish, Quechua, Aymará
Political system: Republic
Economy: Minerals, fishing
GNP per capita: US$2,460
Currency: New Sol

Surinam

Area: 63,037 sq. mi.
Population: 414,000
Capital: Paramaribo (pop: 200,970)
Religions: Christian, Hindu, Muslim
Languages: Dutch, Sranang Tongo, Hindi
Political system: Republic
Economy: Aluminium, bauxite
GNP per capita: US$1,240
Currency: Surinam guilder

Uruguay

Area: 68,500 sq. mi.
Population: 3,289,000
Capital: Montevideo (pop: 1,383,660)
Religions: Roman Catholic, Protestant, Jewish
Main language: Spanish
Political system: Republic
Economy: Agriculture, livestock
GNP per capita: US$6,020
Currency: New Uruguayan peso

Venezuela

Area: 352,145 sq. mi.
Population: 23,242,000
Capital: Caracas (pop: 2,784,042)
Religions: Roman Catholic, Protestant
Languages: Spanish, Indian languages
Political system: Republic
Economy: Oil, coal, bauxite
GNP per capita: US$3,450
Currency: Bolívar

© Copyright AND Cartographic Publishers Ltd.

EUROPE

Albania
Area: 11,099 sq. mi.
Population: 3,119,000
Capital: Tirana (*pop:* 244,153)
Religions: Muslim, Greek Orthodox
Languages: Albanian, Greek
Political system: Republic
Economy: Oil, gas
GNP per capita: US$750
Currency: Lek

Andorra
Area: 175 sq. mi.
Population: 72,000
Capital: Andorra la Vella (*pop:* 16,151)
Religions: Roman Catholic, others
Languages: Catalan, French, Spanish
Political system: Constitutional principality
Economy: Tourism, banking, commerce
GNP per capita: US$14,000
Currency: French franc, Spanish peseta

Austria
Area: 32,378 sq. mi.
Population: 8,140,000
Capital: Vienna (*pop:* 1,806,737)
Religions: Roman Catholic, Protestant
Main language: German
Political system: Republic
Economy: Manufacturing industry
GNP per capita: US$27,980
Currency: Schilling

Belarus
Area: 80,155 sq. mi.
Population: 10,315,000
Capital: Minsk (*pop:* 1,687,400)
Religions: Russian Orthodox, Roman Catholic
Languages: Belarusian, Russian
Political system: Republic
Economy: Food processing
GNP per capita: US$2,150
Currency: Rouble

Belgium
Area: 11,783 sq. mi.
Population: 10,141,000
Capital: Brussels (*pop:* 960,324)
Religions: Roman Catholic, others
Languages: Flemish, French
Political system: Constitutional monarchy
Economy: Steel, glassware
GNP per capita: US$26,490
Currency: Belgian franc

Bosnia-Herzegovina
Area: 19,741 sq. mi.
Population: 3,675,000
Capital: Sarajevo (*pop:* 415,631)
Religion: Muslim
Languages: Serbo-Croat, Croato-Serb
Political system: Republic
Economy: Manufacturing industry
GNP per capita: US$2,600
Currency: Convertible marka

Bulgaria
Area: 42,823 sq. mi.
Population: 8,336,000
Capital: Sofia (*pop:* 1,188,563)
Religions: Christian, Muslim, Jewish
Languages: Bulgarian, Turkish
Political system: Republic
Economy: Agriculture, wine
GNP per capita: US$1,140
Currency: Lev

Croatia
Area: 34,022 sq. mi.
Population: 4,481,000
Capital: Zagreb (*pop:* 867,717)
Religions: Roman Catholic, Protestant
Languages: Croato-Serb, Serbo-Croat
Political system: Republic
Economy: Manufacturing
GNP per capita: US$4,610
Currency: Kuna

Czech Republic
Area: 30,450 sq. mi.
Population: 10,282,000
Capital: Prague (*pop:* 1,216,568)
Religions: Roman Catholic, Protestant
Languages: Czech, Slovak
Political system: Republic
Economy: Heavy industry
GNP per capita: US$5,200
Currency: Koruna

Denmark
Area: 16,639 sq. mi.
Population: 5,270,000
Capital: Copenhagen (*pop:* 1,353,333)
Religions: Evangelical, Lutheran, others
Main language: Danish
Political system: Constitutional monarchy
Economy: Industry, agriculture
GNP per capita: US$32,500
Currency: Kroner

Estonia
Area: 17,413 sq. mi.
Population: 1,429,000
Capital: Tallinn (*pop:* 447,672)
Religions: Evangelical, Lutheran
Languages: Estonian, Russian
Political system: Republic
Economy: Machinery, shipping
GNP per capita: US$3,330
Currency: Kroon

Finland
Area: 130,559 sq. mi.
Population: 5,154,000
Capital: Helsinki (*pop:* 1,016,291)
Religions: Evangelical, Lutheran, Greek Orthodox
Languages: Finnish, Swedish
Political system: Republic
Economy: Engineering
GNP per capita: US$24,080
Currency: Markka

 **France**
Area: 212,935 sq. mi.
Population: 58,683,000
Capital: Paris (*pop:* 9,319,367)
Religions: Roman Catholic, Protestant
Main language: French
Political system: Republic
Economy: Steel, chemicals
GNP per capita: US$26,050
Currency: Franc

 **Germany**
Area: 137,735 sq. mi.
Population: 82,133,000
Capital: Berlin
(*pop:* 3,472,009)
Religions: Protestant, Roman Catholic
Main language: German
Political system: Republic
Economy: Cars, engineering
GNP per capita: US$28,260
Currency: Deutsche mark

 **Greece**
Area: 50,949 sq. mi.
Population: 10,600,000
Capital: Athens (*pop:* 3,027,922)
Religions: Greek Orthodox, Muslim
Main language: Greek
Political system: Republic
Economy: Tourism, shipping
GNP per capita: US$12,010
Currency: Drachma

 **Hungary**
Area: 35,920 sq. mi.
Population: 10,116,000
Capital: Budapest (*pop:* 2,002,121)
Religions: Roman Catholic, Protestant
Languages: Magyar, German
Political system: Republic
Economy: Industry, agriculture
GNP per capita: US$4,430
Currency: Forint

 **Iceland**
Area: 39,769 sq. mi.
Population: 276,000
Capital: Reykjavik
(*pop:* 153,210)
Religions: Evangelical, Lutheran, others
Languages: Icelandic, Danish
Political system: Republic
Economy: Fishing
GNP per capita: US$27,580
Currency: Icelandic króna

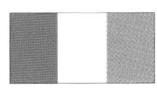 **Ireland, Republic of**
Area: 27,137 sq. mi.
Population: 3,681,000
Capital: Dublin (*pop:* 952,700)
Religions: Roman Catholic, Protestant
Languages: English, Irish
Political system: Republic
Economy: Agriculture
GNP per capita: US$18,280
Currency: Punt

 **Italy**
Area: 116,320 sq. mi.
Population: 57,369,000
Capital: Rome (*pop:* 2,693,383)
Religions: Roman Catholic, other
Main language: Italian
Political system: Republic
Economy: Industry design, textiles
GNP per capita: US$20,120
Currency: Lira

 **Latvia**
Area: 24,942 sq. mi.
Population: 2,424,000
Capital: Riga (*pop:* 847,976)
Religions: Evangelical, Lutheran, others
Languages: Latvian, Russian
Political system: Republic
Economy: Transport, defence equipment
GNP per capita: US$2,430
Currency: Lats

 **Liechtenstein**
Area: 62 sq. mi.
Population: 32,000
Capital: Vaduz (*pop:* 5,072)
Religions: Roman Catholic, Protestant
Main language: German
Political system: Constitutional monarchy
Economy: Banking, dental products
GNP per capita: US$33,500
Currency: Swiss franc

 **Lithuania**
Area: 25,174 sq. mi.
Population: 3,694,000
Capital: Vilnius (*pop:* 581,500)
Religions: Roman Catholic, others
Languages: Lithuanian, Russian
Political system: Republic
Economy: Textiles, engineering
GNP per capita: US$2,230
Currency: Litas

 **Luxembourg**
Area: 998 sq. mi.
Population: 422,000
Capital: Luxembourg
(*pop:* 76,446)
Religions: Roman Catholic, others
Languages: Letzebuergesch, French,
German
Political system: Constitutional monarchy
Economy: Steel-making
GNP per capita: US$45,440
Currency: Luxembourg franc

 **Macedonia**
Area: 9,928 sq. mi.
Population: 1,999,000
Capital: Skopje (*pop:* 448,229)
Religions: Christian, Muslim
Languages: Macedonian, Serbo-Croat
Political system: Republic
Economy: Reliant on foreign aid
GNP per capita: US$1,090
Currency: Dinar

 **Malta**
Area: 122 sq. mi.
Population: 384,000
Capital: Valletta (*pop:* 9,144)
Religions: Roman Catholic, Anglican
Languages: Maltesse, English
Political system: Republic
Economy: Tourism
GNP per capita: US$11,000
Currency: Maltese lira

 **Moldova**
Area: 13,012 sq. mi.
Population: 4,378,000
Capital: Chisinau (*pop:* 667,100)
Religions: Romanian Orthodox, Jewish
Languages: Moldovan, Russian
Political system: Republic
Economy: Wine, tobacco, cotton
GNP per capita: US$540
Currency: Leu

 Monaco
Area: 0.4 sq. mi.
Population: 33,000
Capital: Monaco (*pop:* 27,063)
Religions: Roman Catholic, others
Languages: French, Italian
Political system: Constitutional monarchy
Economy: Tourism, gambling
GNP per capita: US$16,000
Currency: French franc

 **Netherlands**
Area: 15,770 sq. mi.
Population: 15,678,000
Capital: Amsterdam
(*pop:* 1,100,764)
Religions: Roman Catholic, Protestant,
others
Main language: Dutch
Political system: Constitutional monarchy
Economy: Machinery, chemicals
GNP per capita: US$25,820
Currency: Guilder

 **Norway**
Area: 125,050 sq. mi.
Population: 4,419,000
Capital: Oslo (*pop:* 758,949)
Religions: Evangelical, Lutheran, others
Main language: Norwegian
Political system: Constitutional monarchy
Economy: Oil, gas
GNP per capita: US$36,090
Currency: Krone

 **Poland**
Area: 124,808 sq. mi.
Population: 38,718,000
Capital: Warsaw (*pop:* 1,643,203)
Religions: Roman Catholic, others
Main language: Polish
Political system: Republic
Economy: Heavy industry
GNP per capita: US$3,590
Currency: Zloty

 **Portugal**
Area: 35,514 sq. mi.
Population: 9,869,000
Capital: Lisbon (*pop:* 2,561,225)
Religions: Roman Catholic, Protestant
Main language: Portuguese
Political system: Republic
Economy: Agriculture, wine
GNP per capita: US$10,450
Currency: Escudo

 **Romania**
Area: 92,043 sq. mi.
Population: 22,474,000
Capital: Bucharest (*pop:* 2,060,551)
Religions: Romanian Orthodox,
Roman Catholic
Main language: Romanian
Political system: Republic
Economy: Heavy industry
GNP per capita: US$1,420
Currency: Leu

 **Russia**
Area: 6,592,850 sq. mi.
Population: 147,434,000
Capital: Moscow (*pop:* 8,663,142)
Religions: Russian Orthodox,
Jewish, Muslim
Main language: Russian
Political system: Republic
Economy: Oil, gas
GNP per capita: US$2,740
Currency: Rouble

 San Marino
Area: 24 sq. mi.
Population: 26,000
Capital: San Marino (*pop:* 4,251)
Religions: Roman Catholic, Protestant
Main language: Italian
Political system: Republic
Economy: Tourism, light industry
GNP per capita: US$20,000
Currency: Italian lira

 **Slovakia**
Area: 18,924 sq. mi.
Population: 5,377,000
Capital: Bratislava (*pop:* 451,272)
Religions: Roman Catholic, Protestant
Languages: Slovak, Hungarian, Czech
Political system: Republic
Economy: Heavy industry
GNP per capita: US$3,700
Currency: Koruna

 **Slovenia**
Area: 7,821 sq. mi.
Population: 1,993,000
Capital: Ljubljana (*pop:* 330,000)
Religions: Roman Catholic, Muslim
Languages: Slovene, Hungarian, Italian
Political system: Republic
Economy: Manufacturing, tourism
GNP per capita: US$9,680
Currency: Tolar

Spain
Area: 195,365 sq. mi.
Population: 39,628,000
Capital: Madrid (*pop:* 3,084,673)
Religions: Roman Catholic, others
Languages: Spanish, Basque
Political system: Constitutional monarchy
Economy: Agriculture, industry
GNP per capita: US$14,510
Currency: Peseta

Sweden
Area: 173,732 sq. mi.
Population: 8,875,000
Capital: Stockholm (*pop:* 1,532,803)
Religions: Evangelical, Lutheran, Roman Catholic
Main language: Swedish
Political system: Constitutional monarchy
Economy: Car industry, electronics
GNP per capita: US$26,220
Currency: Swedish krona

Switzerland
Area: 15,940 sq. mi.
Population: 7,299,000
Capital: Bern (*pop:* 321,932)
Religions: Roman Catholic, Protestant
Languages: German, French, Italian
Political system: Republic
Economy: Banking, tourism
GNP per capita: US$44,430
Currency: Swiss franc

Ukraine
Area: 233,090 sq. mi.
Population: 50,861,000
Capital: Kiev (*pop:* 2,646,100)
Religions: Ukrainian Orthodox, others
Languages: Ukrainian, Russian
Political system: Republic
Economy: Heavy industry
GNP per capita: US$1,040
Currency: Hryvna

United Kingdom
Area: 94,248 sq. mi.
Population: 58,649,000
Capital: London (*pop:* 6,962,319)
Religions: Protestant, Roman Catholic, others
Main language: English
Political system: Constitutional monarchy
Economy: Financial services, defence
GNP per capita: US$20,710
Currency: Pound

Vatican City
Area: 0.2 sq. mi.
Population: 1,000
Capital: Vatican City (*pop:* 480)
Religion: Roman Catholic
Main language: Italian
Political system: Absolute rule
Economy: Investment
GNP per capita: not available
Currency: Italian lira

Yugoslavia
Area: 39,449 sq. mi.
Population: 10,635,000
Capital: Belgrade (*pop:* 1,136,786)
Religions: Orthodox Catholic, Muslim
Languages: Serbo-Croat, Albanian, Hungarian
Political system: Republic
Economy: Largely barter
GNP per capita: US$1,400
Currency: New dinar

AFRICA

Algeria
Area: 919,595 sq. mi.
Population: 30,081,000
Capital: Algiers (*pop:* 3,250,000)
Religions: Muslim, Christian
Languages: Arabic, Berber, French
Political system: Republic
Economy: Oil, gas
GNP per capita: US$1,490
Currency: Algerian dinar

Angola
Area: 481,354 sq. mi.
Population: 12,092,000
Capital: Luanda (*pop:* 475,328)
Religions: Roman Catholic, Protestant
Main language: Portuguese
Political system: Republic
Economy: Oil, diamonds
GNP per capita: US$340
Currency: Readjusted kwanza

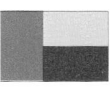
Benin
Area: 43,484 sq. mi.
Population: 5,781,000
Capital: Porto Novo (*pop:* 179,138)
Religions: Traditional beliefs, Muslim
Languages: French, Fon, Bariba, Yoruba
Political system: Republic
Economy: Subsistence farming
GNP per capita: US$380
Currency: Franc CFA

Botswana
Area: 224,607 sq. mi.
Population: 1,570,000
Capital: Gaborone (*pop:* 133,468)
Religions: Traditional beliefs, Anglican
Languages: Setswana, English
Political system: Republic
Economy: Diamonds, copper
GNP per capita: US$3,260
Currency: Pula

Burkina
Area: 105,792 sq. mi.
Population: 11,305,000
Capital: Ouagadougou (*pop:* 634,479)
Religions: Traditional beliefs, Muslim
Languages: French, Mossi, Fulani, Tuareg
Political system: Republic
Economy: Agriculture
GNP per capita: US$240
Currency: Franc CFA

Burundi
Area: 10,747 sq. mi.
Population: 6,457,000
Capital: Bujumbura (*pop:* 235,440)
Religions: Roman Catholic, traditional beliefs
Languages: Kirundi, French, Kiswahili
Political system: Republic
Economy: Agriculture
GNP per capita: US$180
Currency: Burundi franc

Cameroon
Area: 183,569 sq. mi.
Population: 14,305,000
Capital: Yaoundé (*pop:* 653,670)
Religions: Traditional beliefs, Christian
Languages: French, English
Political system: Republic
Economy: Oil, timber, cocoa
GNP per capita: US$650
Currency: Franc CFA

Cape Verde
Area: 1,557 sq. mi.
Population: 408,000
Capital: Praia (*pop:* 80,000)
Religions: Roman Catholic, Protestant
Languages: Portuguese, Creole
Political system: Republic
Economy: Subsistence farming
GNP per capita: US$1,090
Currency: Escudo

Central African Republic
Area: 240,535 sq. mi.
Population: 3,485,000
Capital: Bangui (*pop:* 473,817)
Religions: Christian, traditional beliefs
Languages: French, Sango
Political system: Republic
Economy: Subsistence farming, gold
GNP per capita: US$320
Currency: Franc CFA

Chad
Area: 495,755 sq. mi.
Population: 7,270,000
Capital: Ndjamena (*pop:* 179,000)
Religions: Muslim, Christian
Languages: French, Arabic, Sara
Political system: Republic
Economy: Subsistence farming
GNP per capita: US$240
Currency: Franc CFA

Comoros
Area: 863 sq. mi.
Population: 658,000
Capital: Moroni (*pop:* 17,267)
Religions: Muslim, Roman Catholic
Languages: French, Arabic, Comoran
Political system: Republic
Economy: Subsistence farming
GNP per capita: US$400
Currency: Comorian franc

[Map of Africa showing countries, capitals, and surrounding seas and oceans including EUROPE, ASIA, the Mediterranean Sea, Black Sea, Caspian Sea, Red Sea, Atlantic Ocean, Indian Ocean, and Gulf of Guinea. Labeled countries include MOROCCO, WESTERN SAHARA (Morocco), ALGERIA, TUNISIA, LIBYA, EGYPT, MAURITANIA, MALI, NIGER, CHAD, SUDAN, ERITREA, DJIBOUTI, ETHIOPIA, SOMALIA, SENEGAL, THE GAMBIA, GUINEA-BISSAU, GUINEA, SIERRA LEONE, LIBERIA, IVORY COAST, BURKINA, GHANA, TOGO, BENIN, NIGERIA, CAMEROON, CENTRAL AFRICAN REPUBLIC, EQUAT. GUINEA, SÃO TOMÉ AND PRÍNCIPE, GABON, CONGO, DEMOCRATIC REPUBLIC OF CONGO, CABINDA (Angola), UGANDA, KENYA, RWANDA, BURUNDI, TANZANIA, ANGOLA, ZAMBIA, MALAWI, MOZAMBIQUE, ZIMBABWE, NAMIBIA, BOTSWANA, SWAZILAND, LESOTHO, SOUTH AFRICA, MADAGASCAR, COMOROS, SEYCHELLES.]

© Copyright AND Cartographic Publishers Ltd.

 **Congo**
Area: 132,047 sq. mi.
Population: 2,785,000
Capital: Brazzaville (*pop:* 596,200)
Religions: Roman Catholic, traditional beliefs
Languages: French, Lingala, Kikongo
Political system: Republic
Economy: Oil, sugar, coffee
GNP per capita: US$660
Currency: Franc CFA

 **Congo, Democratic Republic of**
Area: 905,355 sq. mi.
Population: 49,139,000
Capital: Kinshasa (*pop:* 2,664,309)
Religions: Christian, traditional beliefs
Languages: Swahili, Lingala, French
Political system: Republic
Economy: Minerals
GNP per capita: US$110
Currency: Congolese franc

 **Djibouti**
Area: 8,958 sq. mi.
Population: 623,000
Capital: Djibouti (*pop:* 340,700)
Religions: Christian, others
Languages: Arabic, French, Somali
Political system: Republic
Economy: Sea trade
GNP per capita: US$1,000
Currency: Djibouti franc

 **Egypt**
Area: 386,662 sq. mi.
Population: 65,978,000
Capital: Cairo (*pop:* 13,000,000)
Religions: Muslim, others
Main language: Arabic
Political system: Republic
Economy: Oil, gas
GNP per capita: US$1,180
Currency: Egyptian pound

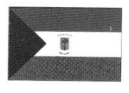 **Equatorial Guinea**
Area: 10,831 sq. mi.
Population: 431,000
Capital: Malabo (*pop:* 30,418)
Religions: Roman Catholic, others
Languages: French, Spanish
Political system: Republic
Economy: Timber, cocoa, oil
GNP per capita: US$1,050
Currency: Franc CFA

 **Eritrea**
Area: 45,406 sq. mi.
Population: 3,577,000
Capital: Asmara (*pop:* 358,100)
Religions: Coptic Christian, Muslim, others
Languages: English, Arabic
Political system: Republic
Economy: Subsistence farming, gold
GNP per capita: US$210
Currency: Nakfa

 **Ethiopia**
Area: 426,373 sq. mi.
Population: 59,649,000
Capital: Addis Ababa (*pop:* 2,316,400)
Religions: Muslim, Christian
Languages: Amharic, English, Arabic
Political system: Republic
Economy: Subsistence farming
GNP per capita: US$110
Currency: Ethiopian birr

 **Gabon**
Area: 103,347 sq. mi.
Population: 1,167,000
Capital: Libreville (*pop:* 251,000)
Religions: Roman Catholic, Protestant
Languages: French, Fang, Eshira
Political system: Republic
Economy: Oil, timber, cocoa
GNP per capita: US$4,230
Currency: Franc CFA

 **Gambia, The**
Area: 4,361 sq. mi.
Population: 1,229,000
Capital: Banjul (*pop:* 109,986)
Religions: Muslim, Christian
Languages: English, Mandinka, Fula, Wollof
Political system: Republic
Economy: Agriculture, fishing
GNP per capita: US$350
Currency: Dalasi

 **Ghana**
Area: 92,098 sq. mi.
Population: 19,162,000
Capital: Accra (*pop:* 738,498)
Religions: Traditional beliefs, Muslim
Languages: English, Twi, Fanti
Political system: Republic
Economy: Cocoa, timber, gold
GNP per capita: US$370
Currency: Cedi

 **Guinea**
Area: 94,926 sq. mi.
Population: 7,337,000
Capital: Conakry (*pop:* 763,000)
Religions: Muslim, Christian
Languages: French, Susu, Malinké
Political system: Republic
Economy: Cash crops
GNP per capita: US$570
Currency: Guinea franc

 **Guinea-Bissau**
Area: 13,948 sq. mi.
Population: 1,161,000
Capital: Bissau (*pop:* 109,214)
Religions: Traditional beliefs, Muslim
Languages: Portuguese, Creole
Political system: Republic
Economy: Subsistence farming
GNP per capita: US$240
Currency: Franc CFA

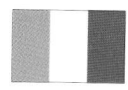 **Ivory Coast**
Area: 124,504 sq. mi.
Population: 14,292,000
Capital: Yamoussoukro (*pop:* 126,191)
Religions: Traditional beliefs, Muslim
Main language: French
Political system: Republic
Economy: Cash crops, timber
GNP per capita: US$690
Currency: Franc CFA

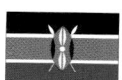 **Kenya**
Area: 224,081 sq. mi.
Population: 29,008,000
Capital: Nairobi (*pop:* 1,400,000)
Religions: Roman Catholic, Protestant
Languages: Swahili, English
Political system: Republic
Economy: Tourism, tea
GNP per capita: US$330
Currency: Kenya shilling

 **Lesotho**
Area: 11,720 sq. mi.
Population: 2,062,000
Capital: Maseru (*pop:* 288,951)
Religions: Roman Catholic, Protestant
Languages: Sesotho, English
Political system: Constitutional monarchy
Economy: Subsistence farming
GNP per capita: US$670
Currency: Loti

 **Liberia**
Area: 43,000 sq. mi.
Population: 2,666,000
Capital: Monrovia (*pop:* 421,053)
Religions: Traditional beliefs, Muslim
Languages: English, many ethnic languages
Political system: Republic
Economy: Unstable
GNP per capita: US$850
Currency: Liberian dollar

 **Libya**
Area: 679,362 sq. mi.
Population: 5,339,000
Capital: Tripoli (*pop:* 1,000,000)
Religions: Muslim, others
Languages: Arabic, Tuareg
Political system: Republic
Economy: Oil
GNP per capita: US$7,000
Currency: Libyan dinar

 **Madagascar**
Area: 226,658 sq. mi.
Population: 15,057,000
Capital: Antananarivo (*pop:* 377,600)
Religions: Traditional beliefs, Christian
Languages: Malagasy, French
Political system: Republic
Economy: Coffee, vanilla
GNP per capita: US$250
Currency: Franc malgache

 **Malawi**
Area: 45,747 sq. mi.
Population: 10,346,000
Capital: Lilongwe (*pop:* 233,973)
Religions: Protestant, traditional beliefs
Languages: Chichewa, English
Political system: Republic
Economy: Tobacco, tea
GNP per capita: US$220
Currency: Kwacha

 **Mali**
Area: 478,841 sq. mi.
Population: 10,694,000
Capital: Bamako (*pop:* 658,275)
Religions: Muslim, traditional beliefs
Languages: French, Bambara, Fulani
Political system: Republic
Economy: Farming, herding, fishing
GNP per capita: US$260
Currency: Franc CFA

 **Mauritania**
Area: 395,956 sq. mi.
Population: 2,529,000
Capital: Nouakchott (*pop:* 850,000)
Religion: Muslim
Languages: Arabic, French, Pulaar
Political system: Republic
Economy: Agriculture, mining
GNP per capita: US$450
Currency: Ouguiya

 **Mauritius**
Area: 788 sq. mi.
Population: 1,141,000
Capital: Port Louis (*pop:* 144,776)
Religions: Hindu, Roman Catholic, Muslim
Languages: Creole, English, French, Hindi
Political system: Republic
Economy: Sugar, tourism
GNP per capita: US$3,800
Currency: Mauritius rupee

 **Morocco**
Area: 172,414 sq. mi.
Population: 27,377,000
Capital: Rabat (*pop:* 1,220,000)
Religion: Muslim
Languages: Arabic, Berber, French, Spanish
Political system: Constitutional monarchy
Economy: Phosphates, tourism
GNP per capita: US$1,250
Currency: Dirham

 **Mozambique**
Area: 309,496 sq. mi.
Population: 18,880,000
Capital: Maputo (*pop:* 882,601)
Religions: Traditional beliefs, Christian
Main language: Portuguese
Political system: Republic
Economy: Foreign aid
GNP per capita: US$90
Currency: Metical

 **Namibia**
Area: 318,261 sq. mi.
Population: 1,660,000
Capital: Windhoek (*pop:* 147,056)
Religions: Christian, others
Languages: English, Afrikaans, German
Political system: Republic
Economy: Uranium, diamonds
GNP per capita: US$2,220
Currency: Namibian dollar

 Niger
Area: 489,191 sq. mi.
Population: 10,078,000
Capital: Niamey (*pop:* 392,169)
Religions: Muslim, traditional beliefs
Languages: French, Hausa, Djerma, Fulani
Political system: Republic
Economy: Uranium
GNP per capita: US$200
Currency: Franc CFA

 **Nigeria**
Area: 356,669 sq. mi.
Population: 106,409,000
Capital: Abuja (*pop:* 378,671)
Religions: Muslim, Christian
Languages: English, Hausa, Yoruba, Ibo
Political system: Republic
Economy: Oil
GNP per capita: US$260
Currency: Naira

 **Rwanda**
Area: 10,169 sq. mi.
Population: 6,604,000
Capital: Kigali (*pop:* 156,000)
Religions: Roman Catholic, traditional beliefs
Languages: Kinyarwanda, French, English
Political system: Republic
Economy: Coffee, oil, gas
GNP per capita: US$210
Currency: Rwanda franc

 **São Tomé and Príncipe**
Area: 372 sq. mi.
Population: 141,000
Capital: São Tomé (*pop:* 43,420)
Religions: Roman Catholic, others
Languages: Portuguese, Creole
Political system: Republic
Economy: Cocoa, coffee, palm oil
GNP per capita: US$270
Currency: Dobra

 **Senegal**
Area: 75,955 sq. mi.
Population: 9,003,000
Capital: Dakar (*pop:* 1,641,358)
Religions: Muslim, traditional beliefs
Languages: French, Wolof, Fulani, Serer
Political system: Republic
Economy: Farming, mining
GNP per capita: US$550
Currency: Franc CFA

 **Seychelles**
Area: 176 sq. mi.
Population: 76,000
Capital: Victoria (*pop:* 24,324)
Religions: Roman Catholic, others
Languages: French, English, Creole
Political system: Republic
Economy: Tourism
GNP per capita: US$6,880
Currency: Rupee

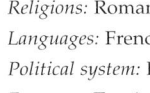 **Sierra Leone**
Area: 27,699 sq. mi.
Population: 4,568,000
Capital: Freetown (*pop:* 469,776)
Religions: Traditional beliefs, Muslim
Languages: English, French, Krio
Political system: Republic
Economy: Subsistence farming
GNP per capita: US$200
Currency: Leone

 **Somalia**
Area: 246,201 sq. mi.
Population: 9,237,000
Capital: Mogadishu (*pop:* 1,000,000)
Religions: Sunni Muslim, others
Languages: Somali, Arabic, English
Political system: Republic
Economy: Foreign aid
GNP per capita: US$500
Currency: Somali shilling

 **South Africa**
Area: 471,445 sq. mi.
Population: 39,357,000
Capital: Pretoria (*pop:* 525,583)
Religions: Protestant, Roman Catholic, others
Languages: English, Afrikaans, Zulu, Xhosa
Political system: Republic
Economy: Manufacturing, agriculture
GNP per capita: US$3,400
Currency: Rand

 **Sudan**
Area: 967,500 sq. mi.
Population: 28,292,000
Capital: Khartoum (*pop:* 924,505)
Religions: Muslim, traditional beliefs
Languages: Arabic, English
Political system: Republic
Economy: Cash crops
GNP per capita: US$280
Currency: Sudanese dinar

 **Swaziland**
Area: 6,704 sq. mi.
Population: 952,000
Capital: Mbabane (*pop:* 38,290)
Religions: Protestant, others
Languages: Siswati, English
Political system: Absolute monarchy
Economy: Cash crops, asbestos
GNP per capita: US$1,440
Currency: Lilangeni

 **Tanzania**
Area: 341,217 sq. mi.
Population: 32,102,000
Capital: Dodoma (*pop:* 88,474)
Religions: Traditional beliefs, Muslim
Languages: Swahili, English
Political system: Republic
Economy: Agriculture, cash crops
GNP per capita: US$210
Currency: Shilling

 **Togo**
Area: 21,925 sq. mi.
Population: 4,397,000
Capital: Lomé (*pop:* 366,476)
Religions: Traditional beliefs, Christian
Languages: French, Ewe
Political system: Republic
Economy: Agriculture, coffee
GNP per capita: US$330
Currency: Franc CFA

 **Tunisia**
Area: 63,170 sq. mi.
Population: 9,335,000
Capital: Tunis (*pop:* 1,394,749)
Religions: Muslim, Christian
Languages: Arabic, French, English
Political system: Republic
Economy: Oil, gas
GNP per capita: US$2,090
Currency: Tunisian dinar

 **Uganda**
Area: 93,065 sq. mi.
Population: 20,554,000
Capital: Kampala (*pop:* 750,000)
Religions: Roman Catholic, Protestant, others
Languages: English, Swahili
Political system: Republic
Economy: Coffee, mining
GNP per capita: US$330
Currency: Uganda shilling

 Zambia
Area: 290,587 sq. mi.
Population: 8,781,000
Capital: Lusaka (*pop:* 982,362)
Religions: Christian, traditional beliefs
Languages: English, Nyanja, Tonga, Beruba
Political system: Republic
Economy: Subsistence farming
GNP per capita: US$380
Currency: Kwacha

 **Zimbabwe**
Area: 150,872 sq. mi.
Population: 11,377,000
Capital: Harare (*pop:* 1,189,103)
Religions: Christian, traditional beliefs
Languages: English, Shona, Ndebele
Political system: Republic
Economy: Self-sufficient
GNP per capita: US$750
Currency: Zimbabwe dollar

ASIA

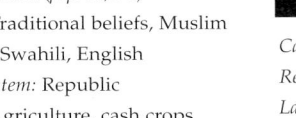 **Afghanistan**
Area: 251,773 sq. mi.
Population: 21,354,000
Capital: Kabul (*pop:* 1,424,400)
Religions: Sumi, Muslim
Languages: Dari, Pushtu
Political system: Republic
Economy: Agriculture
GNP per capita: US$300
Currency: Afghani

 **Armenia**
Area: 11,506 sq. mi.
Population: 3,536,000
Capital: Yerevan (*pop:* 1,254,000)
Religions: Armenian Apostolic, others
Languages: Armenian, Russian
Political system: Republic
Economy: Mining, agriculture
GNP per capita: US$530
Currency: Dram

 **Azerbaijan**
Area: 33,436 sq. mi.
Population: 7,669,000
Capital: Baku (*pop:* 1,149,000)
Religions: Muslim, Armenian Apostolic
Languages: Azerbaijani, Russian
Political system: Republic
Economy: Oil, gas
GNP per capita: US$510
Currency: Manat

 **Bahrain**
Area: 268 sq. mi.
Population: 595,000
Capital: Manama (*pop:* 140,401)
Religions: Shi'a Muslim, Christian
Languages: Arabic, English
Political system: Constitutional monarchy
Economy: Oil, gas
GNP per capita: US$7,840
Currency: Bahraini dinar

 **Bangladesh**
Area: 55,598 sq. mi.
Population: 124,774,000
Capital: Dhaka (*pop:* 3,397,187)
Religions: Muslim, Hindu
Languages: Bengali, English
Political system: Republic
Economy: Foreign aid, jute
GNP per capita: US$270
Currency: Taka

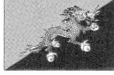 **Bhutan**
Area: 18,147 sq. mi.
Population: 2,004,000
Capital: Thimphu (*pop:* 15,000)
Religions: Buddhist, Hindu
Languages: Dzongkha, English
Political system: Absolute monarchy
Economy: Subsistence farming
GNP per capita: US$400
Currency: Ngultrum

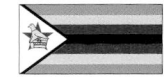

Brunei
Area: 2,226 sq. mi.
Population: 315,000
Capital: Bandar Seri Begawan (*pop:* 49,902)
Religions: Muslim, Buddhist, Christian
Languages: Malay, English
Political system: Absolute monarchy
Economy: Oil, gas
GNP per capita: US$14,500
Currency: Brunei dollar

Cambodia
Area: 69,898 sq. mi.
Population: 10,716,000
Capital: Phnom Penh (*pop:* 832,000)
Religions: Buddhist, Muslim
Languages: Khmer, Chinese, Vietnamese
Political system: Constitutional monarchy
Economy: Rubber, timber
GNP per capita: US$300
Currency: Riel

China
Area: 3,705,408 sq. mi.
Population: 1,240,658,000
Capital: Beijing (*pop:* 7,362,426)
Religions: Confucian, Buddhist
Languages: Mandarin Chinese, Cantonese
Political system: Republic
Economy: Agriculture, industry
GNP per capita: US$860
Currency: Yuan

Cyprus
Area: 3,572 sq. mi.
Population: 771,000
Capital: Nicosia (*pop:* 188,800)
Religions: Greek Orthodox, Muslim
Languages: Greek, Turkish
Political system: Republic
Economy: Tourism, shipping
GNP per capita: US$11,500
Currency: Cyprus pound

Georgia
Area: 26,911 sq. mi.
Population: 5,059,000
Capital: Tbilisi (*pop:* 1,268,000)
Religion: Georgian Orthodox
Languages: Georgian, Russian, Armenian
Political system: Republic
Economy: Food processing
GNP per capita: US$840
Currency: Lari

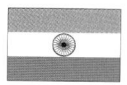
India
Area: 1,269,346 sq. mi.
Population: 982,223,000
Capital: New Delhi (*pop:* 301,297)
Religions: Hindu, Muslim, Christian
Languages: Hindi, English, others
Political system: Republic
Economy: High-tech industry, clothing
GNP per capita: US$390
Currency: Indian rupee

Indonesia
Area: 735,358 sq. mi.
Population: 206,338,000
Capital: Jakarta
(*pop:* 9,160,500)
Religions: Muslim, Christian, others
Languages: Bahasa Indonesian, Dutch, English
Political system: Republic
Economy: Timber, minerals
GNP per capita: US$1,110
Currency: Rupiah

Iran
Area: 630,577 sq. mi.
Population: 65,758,000
Capital: Tehran (*pop:* 6,750,043)
Religion: Shi'a Muslim
Languages: Persian, Turkish, Kurdish, Arabic
Political system: Republic
Economy: Oil
GNP per capita: US$1,780
Currency: Rial

Iraq
Area: 169,235 sq. mi.
Population: 21,800,000
Capital: Baghdad (*pop:* 3,841,268)
Religion: Shi'a Muslim
Languages: Arabic, Kurdish, Turkic, Aramaic
Political system: Republic
Economy: Oil, collapsed due to UN sanctions
GNP per capita: US$1,800
Currency: Dinar

Israel
Area: 8,130 sq. mi.
Population: 7,020,000
Capital: Jerusalem
(*pop:* 662,700)
Religions: Jewish, Muslim
Languages: Hebrew, Arabic
Political system: Republic
Economy: Industry, agriculture
GNP per capita: US$15,900
Currency: Shekel

Japan
Area: 145,870 sq. mi.
Population: 126,281,000
Capital: Tokyo (*pop:* 11,927,457)
Religions: Shinto, Buddhism
Main language: Japanese
Political system: Constitutional monarchy
Economy: Electronics
GNP per capita: US$37,850
Currency: Yen

Jordan
Area: 37,738 sq. mi.
Population: 6,304,000
Capital: Amman
(*pop:* 1,270,000)
Religions: Muslim, Christian
Languages: Arabic, English, French
Political system: Constitutional monarchy
Economy: Phosphates, chemicals
GNP per capita: US$1,570
Currency: Jordanian dinar

© Copyright AND Cartographic Publishers Ltd.

Kazakhstan

Area: 1,049,156 sq. mi.
Population: 16,319,000
Capital: Astana (*pop:* 292,000)
Religions: Muslim, Russian Orthodox
Languages: Kazakh, Russian
Political system: Republic
Economy: Gas, oil, coal, uranium
GNP per capita: US$1,340
Currency: Tenge

Maldives
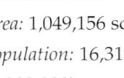
Area: 115 sq. mi.
Population: 271,000
Capital: Male (*pop:* 62,973)
Religion: Sunni Muslim
Main language: Maldivian
Political system: Republic
Economy: Tourism, fishing
GNP per capita: US$1,150
Currency: Rufiyaa

Pakistan

Area: 307,374 sq. mi.
Population: 148,166,000
Capital: Islamabad (*pop:* 350,000)
Religions: Sunni Muslim, Hindu
Languages: Punjabi, Urdu, Sindi, Pushto
Political system: Republic
Economy: Cotton, rice, oil
GNP per capita: US$490
Currency: Pakistan rupee

Sri Lanka

Area: 25,332 sq. mi.
Population: 18,455,000
Capital: Colombo (*pop:* 615,000)
Religions: Buddhist, Hindu, Christian
Languages: Sinhala, Tamil, English
Political system: Republic
Economy: Tea, tourism
GNP per capita: US$800
Currency: Sri Lankan rupee

Kuwait

Area: 6,880 sq. mi.
Population: 1,811,000
Capital: Kuwait (*pop:* 400,000)
Religions: Muslim, Christian
Languages: Arabic, English
Political system: Constitutional monarchy
Economy: Oil, gas
GNP per capita: US$17,390
Currency: Kuwaiti dinar

Mongolia
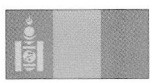
Area: 604,829 sq. mi.
Population: 2,579,000
Capital: Ulan Bator (*pop:* 515,100)
Religions: Buddhist, Muslim
Languages: Mongolian, Kazakh
Political system: Republic
Economy: Agriculture, oil, coal
GNP per capita: US$390
Currency: Tugrik

Philippines

Area: 115,831 sq. mi.
Population: 72,944,000
Capital: Manila (*pop:* 8,594,150)
Religions: Roman Catholic, Protestant
Languages: Filipino, English
Political system: Republic
Economy: Agriculture
GNP per capita: US$1,220
Currency: Philippine peso

Syria

Area: 71,498 sq. mi.
Population: 15,333,000
Capital: Damascus (*pop:* 1,549,000)
Religions: Sunni Muslim, Christian
Languages: Arabic, Kurdish, Turkish
Political system: Republic
Economy: Oil
GNP per capita: US$1,150
Currency: Syrian pound

Kyrgyzstan

Area: 76,641 sq. mi.
Population: 4,643,000
Capital: Bishkek (*pop:* 627,800)
Religions: Muslim, Russian Orthodox
Languages: Kirghiz, Russian
Political system: Republic
Economy: Collective farming, coal
GNP per capita: US$440
Currency: Som

Myanmar (Burma)

Area: 261,228 sq. mi.
Population: 44,497,000
Capital: Rangoon (*pop:* 2,513,023)
Religions: Buddhist, Muslim
Languages: Burmese, English, Shan, Karen
Political system: Republic
Economy: Teak, rice
GNP per capita: US$1,000
Currency: Kyat

Qatar

Area: 4,247 sq. mi.
Population: 579,000
Capital: Doha (*pop:* 217,294)
Religions: Sunni Muslim, Hindu
Languages: Arabic, English
Political system: Absolute monarchy
Economy: Oil, gas
GNP per capita: US$11,600
Currency: Qatar riyal

Taiwan

Area: 13,800 sq. mi.
Population: 21,700,000
Capital: Taipei (*pop:* 2,607,010)
Religions: Buddhist, Confucian, Taoist
Languages: Mandarin Chinese, Taiwanese
Political system: Republic
Economy: Manufacturing, electronics
GNP per capita: US$12,000
Currency: New Taiwan dollar

Laos

Area: 91,429 sq. mi.
Population: 5,163,000
Capital: Vientiane (*pop:* 120,000)
Religions: Buddhist, Christian
Languages: Lao, French
Political system: Republic
Economy: Timber, mining
GNP per capita: US$400
Currency: Kip

Nepal

Area: 56,827 sq. mi.
Population: 22,847,000
Capital: Kathmandu (*pop:* 419,073)
Religions: Hindu, Buddhist
Main language: Nepali
Political system: Constitutional monarchy
Economy: Agriculture
GNP per capita: US$210
Currency: Nepalese rupee

Saudi Arabia
Area: 830,000 sq. mi.
Population: 20,181,000
Capital: Riyadh (*pop:* 1,800,000)
Religions: Sunni Muslim
Languages: Arabic, English
Political system: Absolute monarchy
Economy: Oil, gas
GNP per capita: US$7,040
Currency: Saudi riyal

Tajikistan

Area: 55,251 sq. mi.
Population: 6,015,000
Capital: Dushanbe (*pop:* 602,000)
Religion: Sunni Muslim
Languages: Tajik, Uzbek, Russian
Political system: Republic
Economy: Carpet-making
GNP per capita: US$330
Currency: Tajik rouble

Lebanon

Area: 4,015 sq. mi.
Population: 3,191,000
Capital: Beirut (*pop:* 1,500,000)
Religions: Muslim, Christian
Languages: Arabic, French, English
Political system: Republic
Economy: Banking, services
GNP per capita: US$3,350
Currency: Lebanese pound

North Korea
Area: 46,540 sq. mi.
Population: 23,348,000
Capital: Pyongyang
(*pop:* 2,000,000)
Religions: Traditional beliefs, Buddhist
Main language: Korean
Political system: Republic, one-party state
Economy: Manufacturing, agriculture
GNP per capita: US$1,000
Currency: Won

Singapore
Area: 239 sq. mi.
Population: 3,476,000
Capital: Singapore
Religions: Buddhist, Christian, Muslim
Languages: Malay, Mandarin, Tamil, English
Political system: Republic
Economy: Finance, banking
GNP per capita: US$32,940
Currency: Singapore dollar

Thailand

Area: 198,115 sq. mi.
Population: 60,300,000
Capital: Bangkok (*pop:* 5,876,000)
Religions: Buddhist, Muslim
Languages: Thai, Chinese, Khmer, Malay
Political system: Constitutional monarchy
Economy: Manufacturing, rice, rubber
GNP per capita: US$2,800
Currency: Baht

Malaysia

Area: 127,320 sq. mi.
Population: 21,410,000
Capital: Kuala Lumpur
(*pop:* 1,145,075)
Religions: Muslim, Buddhist
Languages: Malay, English, Chinese, Tamil
Political system: Constitutional monarchy
Economy: Electronics, cars
GNP per capita: US$4,680
Currency: Malaysian dollar

Oman
Area: 82,030 sq. mi.
Population: 2,382,000
Capital: Muscat
(*pop:* 400,000)
Religions: Ibadi Muslim, Hindu
Languages: Arabic, Qarra, Mahra
Political system: Absolute monarchy
Economy: Oil, gas
GNP per capita: US$4,820
Currency: Rial

South Korea

Area: 38,330 sq. mi.
Population: 46,109,000
Capital: Seoul (*pop:* 10,776,201)
Religions: Mahayana Buddhist, Protestant
Main language: Korean
Political system: Republic
Economy: Ship-building, cars
GNP per capita: US$10,550
Currency: Won

Turkey
Area: 299,158 sq. mi.
Population: 64,479,000
Capital: Ankara (*pop:* 3,103,000)
Religion: Muslim
Main language: Turkish
Political system: Republic
Economy: Textiles, manufacturing
GNP per capita: US$3,130
Currency: Turkish lira

Turkmenistan

Area: 188,456 sq. mi.

Population: 4,309,000

Capital: Ashkhabad (*pop:* 407,000)

Religion: Muslim

Languages: Turkmenian, Russian, Uzbek

Political system: Republic

Economy: Cotton, gas

GNP per capita: US$630

Currency: Manat

United Arab Emirates

Area: 32,278 sq. mi.

Population: 2,353,000

Capital: Abu Dhabi (*pop:* 450,000)

Religion: Sunni Muslim

Languages: Arabic, English

Political system: Federation of absolute monarchies

Economy: Oil, gas

GNP per capita: US$17,400

Currency: Dirham

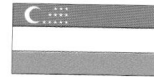

Uzbekistan

Area: 172,742 sq. mi.

Population: 23,574,000

Capital: Tashkent (*pop:* 2,094,000)

Religions: Muslim

Languages: Uzbek, Russian

Political system: Republic

Economy: Agriculture, oil, gas

GNP per capita: US$1,010

Currency: Sum

Vietnam

Area: 128,066 sq. mi.

Population: 77,562,000

Capital: Hanoi (*pop:* 3,056,146)

Religions: Buddhist, Roman Catholic

Languages: Vietnamese, French, English

Political system: Republic

Economy: Steel, gas, oil

GNP per capita: US$320

Currency: Đông

Yemen

Area: 203,850 sq. mi.

Population: 16,887,000

Capital: San'a (*pop:* 926,595)

Religion: Sunni Muslim

Main language: Arabic

Political system: Republic

Economy: Oil, gas

GNP per capita: US$270

Currency: Riyal

AUSTRALIA AND OCEANIA

Australia

Area: 2,988,902 sq. mi.

Population: 18,520,000

Capital: Canberra (*pop:* 307,100)

Religions: Protestant, Roman Catholic

Main Language: English

Political system: Constitutional monarchy

Economy: Mining, agriculture

GNP per capita: US$20,540

Currency: Australian dollar

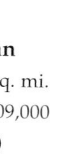

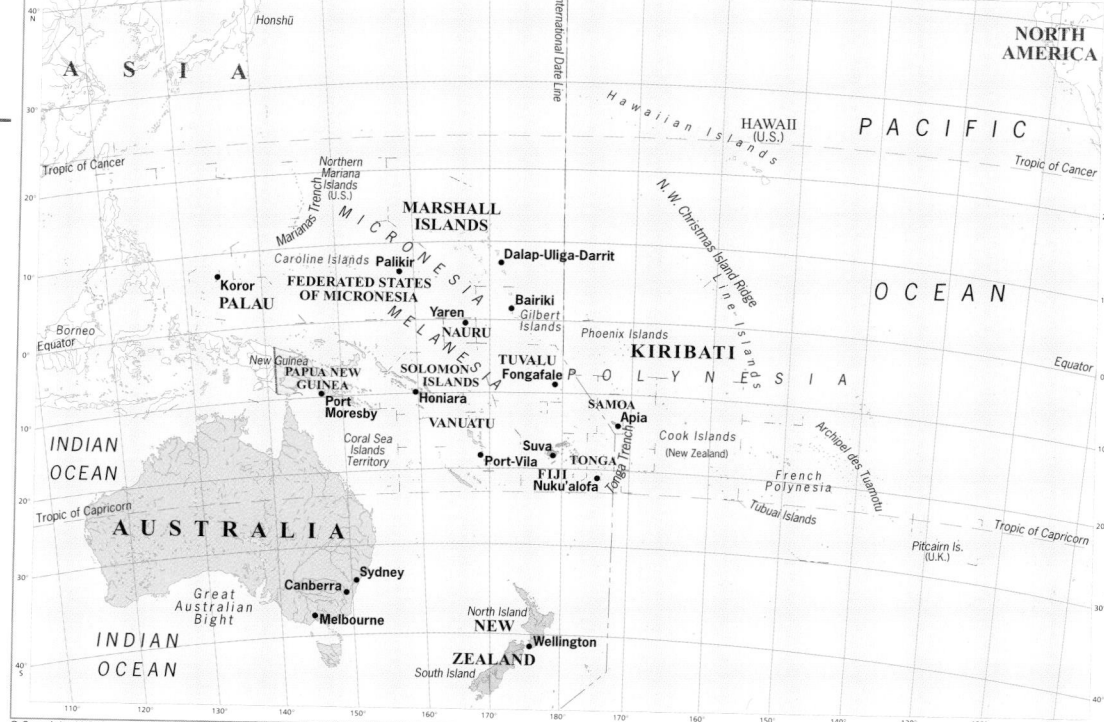

Fiji

Area: 7,056 sq. mi.

Population: 796,000

Capital: Suva (*pop:* 141,273)

Religions: Christian, Hindu, Muslim

Languages: Fijian, Hindi

Political system: Republic

Economy: Sugar, gold, timber

GNP per capita: US$2,470

Currency: Fiji dollar

Kiribati

Area: 280 sq. mi.

Population: 81,000

Capital: Bairiki (*pop:* 17,921)

Religions: Roman Catholic, Protestant

Languages: I-Kiribati, English

Political system: Republic

Economy: Coconuts, copra

GNP per capita: US$910

Currency: Australian dollar

Marshall Islands

Area: 70 sq. mi.

Population: 60,000

Capital: Dalap-Uliga-Darrit (*pop:* 20,000)

Religions: Protestant, Roman Catholic

Languages: Marshallese, English

Political system: Republic

Economy: Copra, tuna-fishing

GNP per capita: US$1,770

Currency: US dollar

Micronesia, Federated States of

Area: 271 sq. mi.

Population: 114,000

Capital: Palikir

Religions: Roman Catholic, Protestant

Languages: English, Yapese, Ulithian, Woleaian

Political system: Republic

Economy: Fishing, US aid

GNP per capita: US$1,980

Currency: US dollar

Nauru

Area: 8 sq. mi.

Population: 11,000

Capital: Yaren

Religions: Christian, others

Languages: Nauruan, English

Political system: Republic

Economy: Phosphate

GNP per capita: US$10,000

Currency: Australian dollar

New Zealand

Area: 104,454 sq. mi.

Population: 3,796,000

Capital: Wellington (*pop:* 326,900)

Religions: Protestant, Roman Catholic

Languages: English, Maori

Political system: Constitutional monarchy

Economy: Agriculture, wool

GNP per capita: US$16,480

Currency: New Zealand dollar

Palau

Area: 177 sq. mi.

Population: 19,000

Capital: Koror (*pop:* 10,493)

Religions: Christian, traditional beliefs

Languages: Palauan, English

Political system: Republic

Economy: Coconuts, US aid

GNP per capita: US$2,260

Currency: US dollar

Papua New Guinea

Area: 178,704 sq. mi.

Population: 4,600,000

Capital: Port Moresby (*pop:* 173,500)

Religions: Christian, others

Languages: English, Pidgin English

Political system: Constitutional monarchy

Economy: Gold, copper, oil

GNP per capita: US$940

Currency: Kina

Samoa

Area: 1,093 sq. mi.

Population: 174,000

Capital: Apia (*pop:* 36,000)

Religions: Protestant, Roman Catholic

Languages: Samoan, English

Political system: Constitutional monarchy

Economy: Agriculture, banking

GNP per capita: US$1,150

Currency: Tala

Solomon Islands

Area: 11,157 sq. mi.

Population: 417,000

Capital: Honiara (*pop:* 40,000)

Religions: Christian, others

Main language: English

Political system: Constitutional monarchy

Economy: Palm oil, copra, cocoa

GNP per capita: US$900

Currency: Solomon Islands dollar

Tonga

Area: 288 sq. mi.

Population: 98,000

Capital: Nuku'alofa (*pop:* 29,018)

Religions: Protestant, Roman Catholic

Languages: Tongan, English

Political system: Constitutional monarchy

Economy: Cash crops

GNP per capita: US$1,830

Currency: Pa'anga

Tuvalu

Area: 10 sq. mi.

Population: 11,000

Capital: Fongafale (*pop:* 2,856)

Religions: Protestant, others

Languages: Tuvaluan, English

Political system: Constitutional monarchy

Economy: Fishing, foreign aid

GNP per capita: US$600

Currency: Australian dollar

Vanuatu

Area: 4,706 sq. mi.

Population: 182,000

Capital: Port-Vila (*pop:* 26,100)

Religions: Protestant, Roman Catholic

Languages: Bislama, English, French

Political system: Republic

Economy: Copra, cocoa

GNP per capita: US$1,310

Currency: Vatu

INDEX

How to use the index

This is an alphabetically arranged index of the places and features that can be found on the maps in this atlas. Each name is generally indexed to the largest scale map on which it appears.

Names composed of two or more words are alphabetised as if they were one word.

All names appear in full in the index, except for "St." and "Ste.", which although abbreviated, are indexed as though spelled in full.

Where two or more places have the same name, they can be distinguished from each other by the country or province name which immediately follows the entry. These names are indexed in the alphabetical order of the country or province.

Alternative names, such as English translations, can also be found in the index and are cross-referenced to the map form by the "=" sign. In these cases the names also appear in brackets on the maps.

Settlements are indexed to the position of the symbol, all other features are indexed to the position of the name on the map.

Abbreviations used in this index are explained in the list on page 159.

Finding a name on the map

Each index entry contains the name, followed by a symbol indicating the feature type (see below), a page reference and a grid reference:

The grid reference locates a place or feature within a rectangle formed by the network of lines of longitude and latitude. A name can be found by referring to the red letters and numbers placed around the maps. First find the letter, which appears along the top and bottom of the map, and then the number, down the sides. The name will be found within the rectangle uniquely defined by that letter and number.

A number in brackets preceding the grid reference indicates that the name is to be found within an inset map.

Name	Owosso	99	D2
	Owyhee	97	C2
	Owyhee	97	C2
Symbol	Oxford, New Zealand	89	D6
	Oxford, United Kingdom	27	A3
	Oxnard	101	C2
Page reference	Oyama	**81**	K5
	Oyapock	109	G3
	Oyem	63	G4
Grid reference	Oyen	95	D1

Symbols

X	Continent name	▲	Mountain, volcano, peak	◣	Sea, ocean
A	Country name	▲▲	Mountain range	▷	Cape, point
a	State or province name	⬭	Physical region or feature	⬚	Island or island group, rocky or
■	Country capital	⌇	River, canal		coral reef
▢	State or province capital	♪	Lake, salt lake	✳	Place of interest
●	Settlement	◥	Gulf, strait, bay	⬚	Historical or cultural region

158

Abbreviations

A

Name		Page	Grid
Aachen	●	59	J4
Aalen	●	67	F8
Aalst	●	59	G4
Aarau	●	75	D3
Aare	✦	75	C3
Aarschot	●	59	G4
Aba	●	95	F3
Ābādān	●	87	C1
Ābādeh	●	87	E1
Abadla	●	91	E2
Abaji	●	95	F3
Abakaliki	●	95	F3
Abakan	▫	103	S7
Abancay	●	141	C6
Abano Terme	●	75	G5
Abarqū	●	87	E1
Abashiri	●	113	N1
Abava	✦	61	M8
Ābaya Hāyk'	✦	97	F2
Abay Wenz	✦	93	G5
Abbeville, France	●	59	D4
Abbeville, United States	●	135	C4
Abd al Kūrī	◳	85	F7
Abéché	●	93	D5
Abengourou	●	95	D3
Abenójar	●	73	F6
Åbenrå	●	67	E1
Abensberg	●	67	G8
Abeokuta	●	95	E3
Aberaeron	●	69	H9
Aberdeen, South Africa	●	99	C6
Aberdeen, United Kingdom	●	69	K4
Aberdeen, Miss., United States	●	135	D3
Aberdeen, S.D., United States	●	129	G1
Aberdeen, Wash., United States	●	129	B1
Aberdeen Lake	✦	125	M4
Aberystwyth	●	69	H9
Abez'	●	63	M1
Abhā	●	93	H4
Abhar	●	83	N5
Abidjan	●	95	D3
Abilene	●	133	G2
Abiline	●	123	M6
Abingdon, United Kingdom	●	59	A3
Abingdon, United States	●	135	E2

Name		Page	Grid
Abnûb	●	93	F2
Aboisso	●	95	D3
Abomey	●	95	E3
Abong Mbang	●	95	G4
Abou Déia	●	93	C5
Abqaiq	●	87	C4
Abrantes	●	73	B5
Absaroka Range	▲	129	E1
Abū al Abayḍ	●	87	E4
Abu Aweigîla	●	86	B6
Abu Ballâs	▲	93	E3
Abu Dhabi = Abū Ẓabī	■	87	F4
Abu Hamed	●	93	F4
Abuja	●	95	F3
Ābune Yosēf	▲	93	G5
Abū Nujaym	●	93	C1
Abu Qarin	●	93	C1
Aburo	▲	97	E3
Abu Simbel	●	93	F3
Abut Head	⊠	121	B6
Abuye Meda	▲	97	F1
Abū Ẓabī	■	87	F4
Abv Nujaym	●	91	J2
Acaponeta	●	127	E7
Acapulco	●	137	E5
Acará	●	141	H4
Acarigua	●	141	D2
Accra	■	95	D3
Achaguas	●	137	L7
Achayvayam	●	105	W4
Acheng	●	111	H1
Achenkirch	●	75	G3
Achen See	✦	75	G3
Achill Island	◳	69	B8
Achim	●	67	E3
Achinsk	●	103	S6
Achit	●	63	L3
Aci Göl	✦	81	M7
A Cihanbeyli	●	81	Q6
Acireale	●	77	K11
Acklins Island	◳	137	K4
Aconcagua	▲	139	D7
Açores	◳	91	(1)B2
A Coruña	●	73	B1
Acqui Terme	●	75	D6
Acre	ⓐ	141	C5
Acri	●	77	L9
Ada	●	65	K12
Ada	●	135	B3

Name		Page	Grid
Adak Island	◳	133	(3)C1
Adam	●	85	G5
Adams Island	◳	121	(2)B1
'Adan	●	85	E7
Adana	●	83	F5
Adda	✦	75	E5
Ad Dafrah	◎	87	E5
Ad Dahnā	◎	87	B3
Ad Dakhla	●	91	B4
Ad Dammām	●	87	D3
Ad Dawādimī	●	85	D5
Ad Dawḩah	●	87	D4
Ad Dilam	●	87	B5
Ad Dir'īyah	●	87	B4
Addis Ababa = Ādīs Ābeba	■	97	F2
Ad Dīwānīyah	●	85	D3
Adel	●	131	B2
Adelaide	▫	119	G6
Adelaide Peninsula	◎	125	M3
Adelaide River	●	119	F2
Aden = Adan	●	85	E7
Aderbissinat	●	95	F1
Adh Dhayd	●	87	F4
Adi	◳	115	(2)D3
Adige	✦	75	G5
Adīgrat	●	93	G5
Adilabad	●	107	C5
Adin	●	129	B2
Adīrī	●	93	B2
Ādīs Ābeba	■	97	F2
Adi Ugri	●	93	G5
Adıyaman	●	85	C2
Adjud	●	79	Q3
Adler	●	83	H2
Admiralty Island	◳	125	E5
Admiralty Islands	◳	117	E6
Adoni	●	107	C5
Adour	✦	71	F10
Adra	●	73	H8
Adrano	●	77	J11
Adrar	●	91	E3
Adrar des Ifôghas	◎	91	F5
Adrar Tamgak	▲	91	G5
Adria	●	75	H5
Adriatic Sea	▱	77	H4
Adycha	✦	105	P3
Adygeya	ⓐ	83	J1
Adygeysk	●	83	H1
Adz'vavom	●	63	L1

Name		Page	Grid
Aegean Sea	▱	81	H5
A Estrada	●	73	B2
Afghanistan	Ⓐ	85	H3
'Afīf	●	93	H3
Afikpo	●	95	F3
Afognak Island	◳	133	(1)G4
A Fonsagrada	●	73	C1
Afragóla	●	77	J8
'Afrīn	●	83	G5
Afuá	●	141	G4
'Afula	●	86	C4
Afyon	●	81	N6
Agadez	●	91	G5
Agadir	●	91	D2
Agadyr'	●	103	N8
Agalega Islands	◳	89	J7
Agan	✦	105	B4
Āgaro	●	97	F2
Agartala	●	107	F4
Agathonisi	◳	81	J7
Agattu Island	◳	105	W6
Agde	●	71	J10
Agen	●	71	F9
Ağın	●	83	H4
Aginskoye	●	103	S6
Agios Efstratios	◳	81	H5
Agios Georgios	◳	81	F7
Agios Nikolaos	●	81	H9
Agnita	●	79	M4
Agra	●	107	C3
Agrakhanskiy Poluostrov	◎	83	M2
Agri	✦	77	L8
Ağrı	●	83	K4
Agrigento	●	77	H11
Agrinio	●	81	D6
Agrópoli	●	77	K8
Agryz	●	63	K3
Agua Prieta	●	133	E2
Aguascalientes	●	137	D4
A Gudiña	●	73	C2
Aguelhok	●	91	F5
Águilas	●	73	J7
Agulhas Negras	▲	141	H8
Ağva	●	81	M3
Ahar	●	83	M4
Ahaura	●	121	C6
Ahaus	●	59	K2
Ahititi	●	121	E4
Ahlen	●	59	K3

Legend:
- ⊠ Continent name
- Ⓐ Country name
- ⓐ State or province name
- ■ Country capital
- ▫ State or province capital
- ● Settlement
- ▲ Mountain, volcano, peak
- ▲ Mountain range
- ◎ Physical region or feature
- ✦ River, canal
- ✦ Lake, salt lake
- ▱ Gulf, strait, bay
- ▱ Sea, ocean
- ⊠ Cape, point
- ◳ Island or island group, rocky or coral reef
- ✳ Place of interest
- ◳ Historical or cultural region

Name	Page	Ref
Ahmadabad	107	B4
Ahmadnagar	107	B5
Ahmadpur East	107	B3
Ahr	67	B6
Ahram	87	D2
Ahrensburg	67	F3
Ahvāz	85	E3
Aichach	67	G8
Aigialousa	83	F6
Aigina	81	F7
Aigio	81	E6
Aigosthena	81	F6
Aihui	105	M6
Aim	105	N5
Ain	71	L7
Aïn Beïda	91	G1
'Aïn Ben Tili	91	D3
Aïn Bessem	73	P8
Aïn el Hadjel	73	P9
Ain Oussera	91	F1
Ainsa	73	L2
Aïn Sefra	91	E2
Ain Taya	73	P8
Aïn-Tédélès	73	L8
Aïn Témouchent	73	J9
Airão	141	E4
Aire	69	L8
Air Force Island	125	S3
Airolo	75	D4
Airpanas	115	(2)C4
Aisne	59	F5
Aitape	115	(2)F3
Aitkin	131	B1
Aitutaki	117	K7
Aiud	79	L3
Aix-en-Provence	71	L10
Aix-les-Bains	71	L8
Aizawl	107	F4
Aizkraukle	61	N8
Aizpute	61	L8
Aizu-wakamatsu	113	K5
Ajaccio	77	C7
Aj Bogd Uul	111	B2
Ajdābiyā	93	D1
Ajigasawa	113	L3
Ajka	65	G10
Ajlun	86	C4
Ajmān	87	F4
Ajmer	107	B3
Ajo	133	D2
Akanthou	86	A1
Akaroa	121	D6
Akasha	93	F3
Akashi	113	H6
Akbalyk	103	P8
Akçakale	83	H5
Akçakoca	81	P3
Aken	67	H5
Aketi	97	C3
Akhalk'alak'i	83	K3
Akhisar	81	K6
Akhmīm	93	F2
Akhty	83	M3
Akimiski Island	125	Q6
Akita	113	L4
Akjoujt	91	C5
Akka	91	D3
Akkajaure	61	J3
Akkeshi	113	N2
'Akko	86	C4
Akmeqit	85	L2
Aknanes	61	(1)B2
Akobo	97	E2
Akola	107	C4
Akonolinga	95	G4
Akordat	93	G4
Akpatok Island	125	T4
Akqi	103	P9
Akra Drepano	81	G5
Akra Sounio	81	F7
Akra Spatha	81	F9
Akra Trypiti	81	G9
Åkrehamn	61	C7
Akron	131	D2
Aksaray	83	E4
Aksarka	103	M4
Akşehir	81	P6
Akseki	81	P7
Aksha	105	J6
Akshiy	103	P9
Aksu	103	Q9
Aksuat	103	Q8
Aktuma	103	M8
Āksum	93	G5
Aktau, Kazakhstan	57	K3
Aktau, Kazakhstan	103	N7
Aktogay	103	N8
Aktogay	103	P8
Aktuma	103	M8
Aktyubinsk	63	L4
Akula	97	C3
Akune	113	F8
Akure	95	F3
Akureyri	61	(1)E2
Akwanga	95	F3
Alabama	135	D3
Alaçam	83	F3
Alagoas	141	K5
Alagoinhas	141	K6
Alagón	73	J3
Al Ahmadi	87	C2
Al 'Amārah	85	E3
Alaminos	109	F3
Alamo	129	C3
Alamogordo	133	E2
Alamo Lake	133	D2
Åland	61	K6
Alanya	83	E5
Alappuzha	107	C7
Al Arṭāwīyah	85	E4
Alaşehir	81	L6
Al 'Ashurīyah	93	H1
Alaska	133	(1)F2
Alaska Peninsula	133	(1)E4
Alaska Range	133	(1)G3
Alassio	75	D6
Alatri	77	H7
Alatyr'	63	J4
Alaverdı	83	L3
Alavus	61	M5
Alaykuu	103	N9
Al 'Ayn	87	F4
Alazeya	105	S2
Alba, Italy	75	D6
Alba, Spain	73	E4
Albacete	73	J5
Alba Iulia	79	L3
Albania	81	B3
Albany	125	Q6
Albany, Australia	119	C6
Albany, Ga., United States	135	E3
Albany, Ky., United States	135	E2
Albany, N.Y., United States	131	F2
Albany, Oreg., United States	129	B2
Albardão do João Maria	143	L4
Al Başrah	85	E3
Albatross Bay	119	H2
Albatross Point	121	E4
Al Baydā'	93	D1
Albenga	75	D6
Albert	59	E4
Alberta	125	H6
Albertirsa	65	J10
Albert Kanaal	59	G3
Albert Lea	131	B2
Albert Nile	97	E3
Albertville	71	M8
Albi	71	H10
Albina	141	G2
Albino	75	E5
Albion	129	F1
Ålborg	61	E8
Ålborg Bugt	61	F8
Albox	73	H7
Albstadt	67	E8
Albufeira	73	B7
Āl Bū Kamāl	83	J6
Albuquerque	133	E1
Al Buraymī	85	G5
Alburquerque	73	D5
Albury	119	J7
Al Buşayyah	87	B1
Alcácer do Sal	73	B6
Alcala de Guadaira	73	E7
Alcala de Henares	73	G4
Alcalá la Real	73	G7
Alcamo	77	G11
Alcañiz	73	K3
Alcantarilla	73	J7
Alcaraz	73	H6
Alcaudete	73	F7
Alcazar de San Juan	73	G5
Alcobendas	73	G4
Alcoi	73	K6
Alcolea del Pinar	73	H3
Alcorcón	73	G4
Alcoutim	73	C7
Aldabra Group	99	(2)A2
Aldan	105	M5
Aldan	105	N5
Aldeburgh	59	D2
Alderney	71	C4
Aldershot	59	B3
Aleg	91	C5
Aleksandrov-Sakhalinskiy	105	Q6
Aleksandrovskiy Zavod	105	K6
Aleksandrovskoye	63	Q2
Alekseyevka	103	N7
Aleksinac	79	J6
Alençon	71	F5
Aleppo = Ḩalab	83	G5
Aléria	77	D6
Alès	71	K9
Aleşd	65	M10
Alessándria	75	D6
Ålesund	61	D5
Aleutian Islands	133	(3)B1
Aleutian Range	133	(1)F4
Aleutian Trench	101	W5
Alexander Archipelago	133	(1)K4
Alexander Bay	99	B5
Alexander City	135	D3
Alexandra	121	B7
Alexandreia	81	E4
Alexandria = El Iskandarīya, Egypt	93	E1
Alexandria, Romania	79	N6
Alexandria, La., United States	135	C3
Alexandria, Minn., United States	131	A1
Alexandria, Va., United States	131	E3
Alexandroupoli	81	H4
Alexis Creek	125	G6
'Āley	86	C3
Aley	103	Q7
Aleysk	103	Q7
Al Farwāniyah	87	B2
Al Fāw	87	C2
Alfeld	67	E5
Alföld	79	H2
Alfonsine	75	H6
Alfreton	59	A1
Al Fuḩayḩil	87	C2
Al-Fujayrah	87	G4
Algeciras	73	E8
Algemes	73	K5
Algena	93	G4
Alger	91	F1
Algeria	91	E3
Al Ghāṭ	87	A3
Al Ghaydah	85	F6
Alghero	77	C8
Algiers = Alger	91	F1
Algona	131	B2
Al Hadīthah	86	E5
Alhama de Murcia	73	J7
Al Ḩamar	87	B5
Al Ḩamīdīyah	86	C2
Al Ḩammādah al Ḩamrā'	91	G3
Al Harūj al Aswad	93	C2
Al Ḩasakah	83	J5
Alhaurmín el Grande	73	F8
Al Ḩijāz	93	G2
Al Ḩillah	85	D3
Al Ḩilwah	87	B5
Al Hoceima	91	E1
Al Ḩudaydah	93	H5
Al Hufūf	87	C4
Al Ḩumaydah	85	C4
Aliabad	87	F2
Aliağa	81	J6
Aliakmonas	81	E4
Äli Bayramlı	83	N4
Alicante	73	K6
Alice	135	B4
Alice Springs	119	F4
Alicudi	77	J10
Aligarh	107	C3
Alindao	97	C2
Alingås	61	G8
Alisos	133	D2
Aliwal North	99	D6
Al Jabal al Akhḍar	93	D1
Al Jaghbūb	93	D2
Al Jālamīd	93	G1
Al Jarah	87	B2
Al Jawf	93	G2
Aljezur	73	B7
Al Jifārah	87	A5
Al Jubayl	87	C3
Aljustrel	73	B7
Al Kāmil	85	G5
Al Khābūrah	87	G5
Al Kharj	87	B4
Al Khaşab	87	G3
Al Khawr	87	D4
Al Khubar	87	D3
Al Khums	91	H2
Al Khuwayr	87	D3
Alkmaar	59	G2
Al Küt	85	E3
Al Kuwayt	87	C2
Al Lādhiqīyah	83	F6
Allahabad	107	D3
Allakh-Yun'	105	P4
Alldays	99	D4
Allen	109	G4
Allendale	135	E3
Allentown	131	E2
Aller	67	E4
Aller = Cabañquinta	73	E1
Alliance	129	F2
Allier	71	J8
Allinge	65	D2
Al Lith	93	H3
Alma, Canada	131	F1
Alma, Nebr., United States	129	G2
Alma, Wis., United States	131	B2
Almada	73	A6
Almadén	73	F6
Al Madīnah	93	G3
Al Majma'ah	85	E4
Almalyk	103	M9
Al Manāmah	87	D3
Almansa	73	J6
Al Marj	93	D1
Almaty	103	P9
Al Mawşil	83	K5
Al Mazāhumīyah	87	B4
Almazán	73	H3
Almeirim	141	G4
Almelo	59	J2
Almendralejo	73	D6
Almería	73	H8
Al'met'yevsk	103	J7
Almiros	81	E5
Al Mish'āb	87	C2

✕ Continent name
Ⓐ Country name
ⓐ State or province name
■ Country capital
▣ State or province capital
● Settlement
▲ Mountain, volcano, peak
⬭ Mountain range
⬭ Physical region or feature
◪ River, canal
◪ Lake, salt lake
⬭ Gulf, strait, bay
⬭ Sea, ocean
▷ Cape, point
▣ Island or island group, rocky or coral reef
✳ Place of interest
▣ Historical or cultural region

Name	Page	Grid
Almonte	73	D7
Almora	107	C3
Almosa	129	E3
Al Mubarraz	87	C4
Al Mudawwara	86	D7
Al Mukallā	85	E7
Al Mukhā	93	H5
Almuñécar	73	G8
Al Muqdādīyah	83	L7
Al Nu'ayrīyah	87	C3
Alnwick	69	L6
Alonnisos	81	F5
Alor	115	(2)B4
Alor Setar	109	C5
Alotau	119	K2
Alpena	131	D1
Alphen	59	G2
Alpi Lepontine	75	D4
Alpine	133	E2
Alpi Orobie	75	E4
Alps	75	B5
Al Qadmūs	86	D1
Al Qāmishlī	83	J5
Al Qar'ah	87	B3
Al Qaryāt	93	B1
Al Qaryatayn	86	E2
Al Qaţrūn	93	B3
Al Qunayţirah	86	C3
Al Qunfudhah	93	H4
Al Qurayyāt	93	G1
Al Qurnah	87	B1
Al Quşayr	87	A1
Al Quţayfah	86	D3
Als	67	E1
Alsask	125	K6
Alsasua	73	H2
Alsfeld	67	E6
Altaelva	61	M2
Altai Mountains	111	A1
Altamira	141	G4
Altamura	77	L8
Altanbulag	105	H6
Altay	103	R7
Altay, China	103	R8
Altay, Mongolia	111	B1
Altdorf	75	D4
Alte Mellum	67	D3
Altenburg	67	H6
Altenkirchen	67	J2
Altkirch	75	C3
Alto Garças	141	G7
Alto Molócuè	99	F3
Alton, United Kingdom	59	B3
Alton, United States	131	B3
Altoona	131	E2
Alto Parnaíba	141	H5
Altötting	75	H2
Altun Shan	103	S10
Alturas	129	B2
Altus	135	B3
Al 'Ubaylah	85	F5
Alūksne	61	P8
Alupka	83	E1
Alushta	83	F1
Al 'Uwayqīlah	93	H1
Al 'Uzayr	87	B1
Alva	135	B2
Alvarães	141	E4
Älvdalen	61	H6
Älvsbyn	61	L4
Al Wafrā'	87	B2
Al Wajh	93	G2
Alwar	107	C3
Al Wari'ah	87	B3
Alytus	65	P3
Alzey	67	D7
Alzira	73	K5
Amadi	97	E2
Amādīyah	83	K5
Amadjuak Lake	125	S4
Amadora	73	A6
Amahai	115	(2)C3
Amakusa-Shimo-shima	113	E7
Amaliada	81	D7
Amalner	107	C4
Amamapare	115	(2)E3
Amami-Ōshima	101	S7
Amanab	115	(2)F3
Amándola	77	H6
Amantéa	77	L9
Amapá	141	G3
Amapá	141	G3
Amarante	141	J5
Amarapura	109	B2
Amarillo	133	F1
Amasya	81	F3
Amay	59	H4
Amazar	105	L6
Amazon = Amazonas	139	F4
Amazonas	141	D4
Amazonas	141	E4
Ambala	107	C2
Ambanjä	99	H2
Ambarchik	105	U3
Ambato	141	B4
Ambato Boeny	99	H3
Ambatondrazaka	99	H3
Amberg	67	G7
Ambikapur	107	D4
Ambilobe	99	H2
Amboise	71	G6
Ambon	115	(2)C3
Ambositra	99	H4
Ambovombe	99	H5
Amchitka Island	133	(3)B1
Amderma	103	L4
Amdo	107	F2
Ameland	59	H1
Amengel'dy	103	M7
American Falls	129	D2
American Samoa	117	J7
Americus	135	E3
Amersfoort	59	H2
Amery	125	N5
Amery Ice Shelf	144	(2)M2
Ames	131	B2
Amfilochia	81	D6
Amfissa	81	E6
Amga	105	L5
Amga	105	N4
Amgun'	105	P6
Amherst	125	U7
Amiens	59	E5
Amirante Islands	99	(2)B2
Amistad Reservoir	133	F3
Amlekhganj	107	D3
Âmli	61	E7
'Ammān	86	C5
Ammerland	59	K1
Ammersee	75	F2
Ammochostos	83	E6
Ammochostos Bay	86	A1
Amo	109	C2
Amol	85	F2
Amorgos	81	H8
Amos	131	E1
Ampana	115	(2)B3
Ampanihy	99	G4
Amparai	107	D7
Ampezzo	75	H4
Amposta	73	L4
Amrān	85	D6
Amravati	107	C4
Amritsar	107	B2
Amroha	107	C3
Amrum	67	D2
Amsterdam, Netherlands	59	G2
Amsterdam, United States	131	F2
Amstetten	75	K2
Am Timan	93	D5
Amudar'ya	103	L9
Amundsen Gulf	125	G2
Amundsen Sea	144	(2)GG3
Amungen	61	H6
Amuntai	115	(1)F3
Amur	105	P6
Amursk	105	P6
Amvrakikos Kolpos	81	C6
Anabar	105	J2
Anaconda	129	D1
Anacortes	129	B1
Anadarko	129	G3
Anadolu Dağları	83	H3
Anadyr'	105	X4
Anadyrskaya Nizmennost'	105	X3
Anadyrskiy Zaliv	105	Y3
Anafi	81	H8
'Ānah	83	J6
Anaheim	133	C2
Anáhuac	133	F3
Analalava	99	H2
Anamur	83	E5
Anan	113	H7
Anantapur	107	C6
Anan'yiv	79	T2
Anapa	83	G1
Anápolis	141	H7
Anār	87	F1
Anārak	85	F3
Anardara	85	H3
Anatolia	81	M6
Añatuya	143	J4
Anchorage	133	(1)H3
Ancona	77	H5
Ancud	143	G7
Anda	111	H1
Andalgalá	143	H4
Åndalsnes	61	D5
Andalusia	135	D3
Andaman Islands	109	A4
Andaman Sea	109	A4
Andapa	99	H2
Andarāb	85	J2
Andenne	59	H4
Andernach	59	K4
Anderson	125	F3
Anderson	135	E3
Andes	139	D5
Andfjorden	61	J2
Andipsara	81	H6
Andizhan	103	N9
Andkhvoy	85	J2
Andoas	141	B4
Andong	113	E5
Andorra	73	L2
Andorra la Vella	73	M2
Andover	59	A3
Andøya	61	H2
Andradina	143	L3
Andreanof Islands	133	(3)C1
Andrews	133	F2
Andria	77	L7
Andros	81	G7
Andros, Greece	81	G7
Andros, The Bahamas	135	F5
Andros Town	135	F5
Andrott	107	B6
Andrychów	65	J8
Andújar	73	F6
Andulo	99	B2
Aneto	73	L2
Angara	105	G5
Angarsk	105	G6
Ånge	61	H5
Angel de la Guarda	133	D3
Angeles	109	G3
Ängelholm	61	G8
Angeln	67	E2
Angermünde	67	K4
Angers	71	E6
Anglesey	69	H8
Angmagssalik = Tasiilaq	125	Z3
Ango	97	D3
Angoche	99	F3
Angol	143	G6
Angola	89	E7
Angola	131	D2
Angostura Reservoir	129	F2
Angoulême	71	F8
Angren	103	M9
Anguilla	137	M5
Aniak	133	(1)F3
Anina	79	J4
Anıyaman	83	H5
Ankang	111	D4
Ankara	83	E4
Ankazoabo	99	G4
Anklam	67	J3
Ankpa	95	F3
Ånn	61	G5
Anna	63	H4
Annaba	91	G1
Annaberg-Buchholz	67	H6
An Nabk, Saudi Arabia	86	E5
An Nabk, Syria	86	D2
An Nafud	93	G2
An Nāirīyah	85	E3
An Najaf	85	D3
Annapolis	131	E3
Annapurna	107	D3
Ann Arbor	131	D2
An Nāşirīyah	93	J1
Annecy	75	B5
Annemasse	75	B4
Anniston	135	D3
Annobón	95	F5
Annonay	71	K8
An Nukhayb	85	D3
Anqing	111	F4
Ansbach	67	F7
Anshan	113	B3
Anshun	111	D5
Ansley	129	G2
Anson	135	B3
Ansongo	91	F5
Antakya	83	G5
Antalaha	99	J2
Antalya	81	N8
Antalya Körfezi	81	N8
Antananarivo	99	H3
Antarctic Peninsula	144	(2)LL3
Antequera	73	F7
Anti-Atlas	91	D3
Antibes	75	C7
Antigo	131	C1
Antigua	137	M5
Antigua and Barbuda	137	M5
Antikythira	81	F9
Antiparos	81	G7
Antipaxoi	81	C5
Antipayuta	103	P4
Antipodes Islands	121	(3)A1
Antlers	135	B3
Antofagasta	143	G3
Antonito	129	E3
Antrim	69	F7
Antropovo	63	H3
Antsalova	99	G3
Antsirabe	99	H3
Antsirañana	99	H2
Antu	113	E2
Antwerp = Antwerpen	59	G3
Antwerpen	59	G3
Anuradhapura	107	D7
Anxi	111	B2
Anyang, China	111	E3
Anyang, South Korea	113	D5
Anyuysk	105	U3
Anzhero-Sudzhensk	103	R6
Anzio	77	G7
Aoga-shima	113	K7
Aomori	113	L3
Aosta	75	C5

Name	Page	Ref.	Name	Page	Ref.	Name	Page	Ref.	Name	Page	Ref.
Aoukâr	91	C5	Arcos de la Frontera	73	E8	Arnprior	131	E1	Ashland, *Wis., United States*	131	B1
Aoukoukar	95	C1	Arctic Bay	125	P2	Arnsberg	59	L3	Ashqelon	86	B5
Apalachee Bay	135	E4	Arctic Ocean	144	(1)A1	Arnstadt	67	F6	Ash Shadādah	83	J5
Apalachicola	135	D4	Arctic Red River	125	E3	Arolsen	67	E5	Ash Shāriqah	87	F4
Aparri	109	G3	Arda	81	H3	Arorae	117	H6	Ash Shiḩr	85	E7
Apatin	79	F4	Ardabīl	83	N4	Arquipélago dos Bijagós	95	A2	Ash Shu'bah	87	A2
Apatity	63	F1	Ardahan	83	K3	Ar Ramādī	85	D3	Ash Shurayf	93	G2
Ape	61	P8	Årdalstangen	61	D6	Ar Ramlah	86	C7	Ash Shuwayrif	91	H3
Apeldoorn	59	H2	Ardas	81	J3	Arran	69	G6	Ashtabula	131	D2
Api	107	D2	Ardatov	63	J4	Ar Raqqah	83	H6	Ashuanipi	125	T6
Apia	117	J7	Ardennes	59	G4	Arras	59	E4	Ashuanipi Lake	125	T6
Apoera	141	F2	Ardestān	85	F3	Arrasate	73	H1	Asia	117	B2
Apolda	67	G5	Ardila	73	C6	Ar Rastan	86	D2	Āsika	107	D5
Apollo Bay	119	H7	Ardmore	127	G5	Ar Rawḍah	85	E7	Asilah	91	D1
Aporé	141	G7	Aredo	115	(2)D3	Ar Rayn	87	A5	Asinara	77	C7
Apostle Islands	131	B1	Areia Branca	141	K5	Arrecife	91	C3	Asino	103	R6
Apoteri	141	F3	Arendal	61	E7	Ar Riyāḍ	85	E5	Asīr	93	H3
Appalachian Mountains	135	E3	Arenys de Mar	73	N3	Arrow Lake	129	C1	Aşkale	83	J4
Appennino	77	G5	Arequipa	141	C7	Arroyo Grande	133	B1	Askim	61	F7
Appennino Abruzzese	77	H6	Arere	141	G4	Ar Ruşāfah	83	H6	Askot	107	D3
Appennino Calabro	77	K10	Arévalo	73	F3	Ar Rustāq	85	G5	Asmara	93	G4
Appennino Lucano	77	K8	Arezzo	77	F5	Ar Ruţba	85	D3	Āsnen	61	H8
Appennino Tosco-Emiliano	75	E6	Argan	103	R9	Ar Ruways	85	F5	Aso	75	J7
Appennino Umbro-Marchigiano	77	H6	Argenta	75	G6	Ārsandøy	61	G4	Āsosa	97	E1
Appleton	131	C2	Argentan	59	B6	Arsiè	75	G5	Aspang Markt	75	M3
Aprília	77	G7	Argentina	143	H6	Arta, *Greece*	81	C5	Aspe	73	K6
Apure	141	D2	Argenton-sur-Creuse	71	G7	Arta, *Mallorca*	73	P5	Aspermont	133	C1
Apurimac	141	C6	Argeş	79	N5	Artem	113	G2	As Pontes de Garcia Rodriguez	73	E1
Āqā	85	H3	Argolikos Kolpos	81	E7	Artemovsk	103	S7	As Sa'an	86	E1
'Aqaba	86	C7	Argos	81	E7	Artemovskiy	105	K5	Assab	93	H5
Aquidauana	141	F8	Argos Orestiko	81	D4	Artesia	133	F2	As Şalīf	85	D6
Ara	107	D3	Argostoli	81	C6	Arthur	129	F2	As Salmān	85	E3
Arabian Sea	85	H6	Argun'	105	K6	Arthur's Town	135	F5	As Salwā	87	D4
Aracaju	141	K6	Argungu	95	E2	Artigas	143	K5	Assamakka	91	G5
Aracati	141	K4	Argunsk	105	L6	Artillery Lake	125	J4	As Samāwah	93	J1
Araçatuba	141	G8	Argyll	69	G5	Artsyz	79	S4	Aş Şanamayn	86	D3
Aracuca	137	L7	Århus	61	F8	Artux	103	P10	As Sarīr	93	D2
Arad	79	J3	Ariano Irpino	77	K7	Artvin	83	J3	Asse	59	G4
Arādah	85	F5	Ari Atoll	107	B8	Artyk	105	Q4	Assen	59	J2
Arafura Sea	115	(2)D5	Arica	141	C7	Aru	117	D6	Assens	67	E1
Aragarças	141	G7	Ariège	71	G11	Arua	97	E3	As Sīb	87	H5
Araguaia	139	F4	Arihge	73	M2	Aruba	137	K6	As Sidrah	93	C1
Araguaína	141	H5	Arinos	141	F6	Arumã	141	E4	Assiniboia	125	K7
Araguari	141	H7	Aripuanã	141	E5	Arusha	97	F4	Assiniboine	125	M7
Araguatins	141	H5	Aripuanã	141	E5	Arvayheer	111	C1	Assis	143	L3
Arāk	85	E3	Ariquemes	141	E5	Arviat	125	N4	Assisi	77	G5
Arak	91	F3	Arizona	133	D2	Arvidsjaur	61	K4	As Sukhnah	83	H6
Aral Sea	103	K8	Arjäng	61	G7	Arvika	61	G7	As Sulaymānīyah	83	L6
Aral'sk	63	M5	Arka	105	Q5	Ary	103	Y3	As Sulayyil	85	E5
Aranda de Duero	73	G3	Arkadak	63	H4	Aryta	105	M4	Assumption Island	97	H5
Aranđjelovac	79	H5	Arkadelphia	135	C3	Arzamas	63	H3	Astana	103	N7
Aran Island	69	D6	Arkalyk	103	M7	Arzew	73	K9	Astara	85	E2
Aran Islands	69	B8	Arkansas	135	C3	Arzignano	75	G5	Asti	75	D6
Aranjuez	73	G4	Arkansas	135	C3	Asahi-dake	113	M2	Astorga	73	D2
Aranos	99	B4	Arkansas City	135	B2	Asahikawa	113	M2	Astoria	129	B1
Aranyaprathet	109	C4	Arkhalts'ikhe	83	K3	Āsalē	93	G5	Astove Island	97	H6
Araouane	91	E5	Arkhangel'sk	63	H2	Asansol	107	E4	Astrakhan'	63	J5
Arapahoe	129	G2	Arkhipelag Nordenshel'da	103	R2	Asarum	65	D1	Astypalaia	81	J8
Arapiraca	141	K5	Arklow	69	F9	Asbest	63	M3	Asunción	143	K4
'Ar'ar	85	D3	Arkoudi	81	C6	Ascension	89	B6	Aswān	93	F3
Araras	141	G5	Arles	71	K10	Ascensión	141	E7	Aswân Dam	93	F3
Ararat	83	L4	Arlington, *Oreg., United States*	129	B1	Aschaffenburg	67	E7	Asyût	93	F2
Arauca	141	D2	Arlington, *Tex., United States*	135	B3	Aschersleben	67	G5	As Zaydīyah	93	H4
Araxá	141	H7	Arlington, *Va., United States*	131	E3	Áscoli Piceno	77	H6	Ata	117	J8
Araz	83	L4	Arlit	91	G5	Āsela	97	F2	Atafu	117	J6
Arbīl	83	K5	Arlon	59	H4	Åsele	61	J4	Atakpamé	95	C3
Arbon	75	E3	Armagh	69	F7	Asenovgrad	81	G3	Atâr	91	C4
Arbre du Ténéré	91	G5	Armavir	83	J1	Asha	63	L3	Atasu	103	N8
Arbroath	69	K5	Armenia	83	K3	Ashburton	121	C6	Atbara	93	F4
Arcachon	71	D9	Armenia	141	B3	Asherton	135	B4	Atbasar	63	N4
Arcadia	135	E4	Armentières	59	E4	Asheville	131	D3	Atchison	135	B2
Arcata	129	B2	Armidale	119	K6	Ashford	59	C3	Aterno	77	H6
Archidona	73	F7	Armstrong	125	P6	Ash Fork	133	D1	Ath	59	F4
Archipelago of the Recherche	119	D6	Armyans'k	63	F5	Ashgabat	85	G2	Athabasca	125	J5
Archipel de la Société	117	L7	Arnedo	73	H2	Ashington	69	L6	Athens = Athina	81	F7
Archipel des Tuamotu	117	M7	Arnett	135	B2	Ashizuri-misaki	113	G7	Athens, *Al., United States*	135	D3
Archipiélago de Camagüey	137	J4	Arnhem	59	H3	Ashkhabad = Ashgabat	85	G2	Athens, *Ga., United States*	135	E3
Archipiélago de la Reina Adelaida	143	F9	Arnhem Land	119	F2	Ashland, *Kans., United States*	129	G3	Athens, *Oh., United States*	135	E2
Archipiélago de los Chonos	143	F7	Arno	75	F7	Ashland, *Ky., United States*	131	D3			
Arco	129	D2	Arnøy	61	G3	Ashland, *Mont., United States*	129	E1			
			Arnøya	61	L1	Ashland, *Oreg., United States*	129	B2			

Name	Page	Grid
Athens, *Tenn., United States*	135	E2
Athens, *Tex., United States*	135	B3
Athina	81	F7
Athlone	69	E8
Ath Thāyat	86	D7
Athy	69	F8
Ati	93	C5
Atiamuri	121	F4
Atico	141	C7
Atikokan	131	B1
Atka	105	S4
Atka Island	133	(3)C1
Atlanta	135	E3
Atlantic, *Ia., United States*	135	B1
Atlantic, *N.C., United States*	135	F3
Atlantic City	131	F3
Atlantic Ocean	57	C3
Atlas Bogd	111	B2
Atlas Mountains	73	N9
Atlasovo	105	T5
Atlas Saharien	91	E2
Atlin	125	E5
Atmakur	107	C5
Atmore	135	D3
Atoka	135	B3
Atokos	81	C6
Atol das Rocas	141	L4
Aţ Ţā'if	85	D5
Attapu	109	D4
Attawapiskat	125	Q6
Attersee	75	J3
Attica	131	C2
Attu Island	133	(3)A1
At Turbah	93	H5
Atyrau	63	K5
Aubagne	71	L10
Aubange	59	H5
Aube	71	K5
Aubenas	71	K9
Aubry Lake	125	F3
Auburn, *Al., United States*	135	D3
Auburn, *Calif., United States*	129	B3
Auburn, *Nebr., United States*	129	G2
Auburn, *Wash., United States*	129	B1
Aubusson	71	H8
Auce	65	M1
Auch	71	F10
Auchi	95	F3
Auckland	121	E3
Auckland Island	121	(2)B1
Aude	71	H10
Aue	67	H6
Auerbach	67	H6
Augathella	119	J5
Augsburg	75	F2
Augusta, *Australia*	119	C6
Augusta, *Italy*	77	K11
Augusta, *Ga., United States*	135	E3
Augusta, *Me., United States*	131	G2
Augustów	65	M4
Aulla	75	E6
Aurangābād	107	C5
Auray	71	C6
Aurich	59	K1
Aurillac	71	H9
Aurora, *Colo., United States*	129	F3
Aurora, *Ill., United States*	131	C2
Aurora, *Mo., United States*	135	C2
Aurukun	119	H2
Aus	99	B5
Auschwitz = Oświęcim	65	J7
Austin, *Minn., United States*	131	B2
Austin, *Nev., United States*	129	C3
Austin, *Tex., United States*	135	B3
Australia	119	E4
Australian Alps	117	E9
Australian Capital Territory	119	J7
Austria	75	J3
Autun	71	K7
Auxerre	71	J6
Avallon	71	J6
Avam	105	E2
Āvārsin	83	M4
Aveiro	73	B4
Avellino	77	J8
Averøya	61	D5
Avesnes-sur-Helpe	59	F4
Avesta	61	J6
Avezzano	77	H6
Aviemore	69	J4
Avignon	71	K10
Ávila	73	F4
Avilés	73	E1
Avion	59	E4
Avola	77	K12
Avon, *United Kingdom*	59	A2
Avon, *United Kingdom*	59	A3
Avranches	71	D5
Avrig	79	M4
Awaji-shima	113	H6
Awanui	121	D2
Awat	103	Q9
Awatere	121	D5
Awbārī	93	B2
Awjilah	93	D2
Awka	95	F3
Ax-les-Thermes	71	G11
Ayacucho	141	C6
Ayaguz	103	Q8
Ayakkuduk	103	M9
Ayamonte	73	C7
Ayan	105	E3
Ayan	105	P5
Aya Napa	86	A2
Ayancık	83	F3
Ayanka	105	V4
Ayaviri	141	C6
Aydin	83	B5
Aydıncık	81	R8
Aykhal	105	J3
Aykino	103	H5
Aylesbury	59	B3
Aylmer Lake	125	K4
Ayní	85	J2
Ayní	103	M10
Ayn 'Isá	83	H5
Ayoûn el 'Atroûs	91	D5
Ayr, *Australia*	119	J3
Ayr, *United Kingdom*	69	H6
Aytos	79	Q7
Ayutthaya	109	C4
Ayvalik	81	J5
Azaila	73	K3
Azaouâd	91	E5
Āzārān	83	M5
Azare	95	G2
A'zāz	83	G5
Azdavay	81	R3
Azerbaijan	83	M3
Azogues	141	B4
Azores = Açores	91	(1)B2
Azov	63	G5
Azpeitia	73	H1
Azrou	91	D2
Aztec	129	E3
Azuaga	73	E6
Azul	143	K6
Az Zabadānī	86	D3
Az̧ Z̧ahrān	87	D3
Az Zāwīyah	93	B1
Az Zubayr	87	B1

B

Name	Page	Grid
Ba'albek	86	D2
Baardheere	97	G3
Babadag	79	R5
Babaeski	81	K3
Bāb al Mandab	85	D7
Babanusa	97	D1
Babar	115	(2)C4
Babayevo	63	G3
Babayurt	83	M2
Babo	115	(2)D3
Bābol	85	F2
Babruysk	63	E4
Babura	95	F2
Babushkin	105	H6
Babuyan Islands	109	G3
Bacabal	141	J4
Bacan	115	(2)C3
Bacău	79	P3
Baccarat	75	B2
Bachu	85	L2
Back	125	M3
Bačka Palanka	79	G4
Bačka Topola	79	G4
Backnang	75	E2
Bac Liêu	109	D5
Bacolod	109	G4
Badajós	141	H4
Badajoz	73	D6
Bad al Milḥ	83	K7
Badalona	73	N3
Bad Ausee	75	J3
Bad Bentheim	59	K2
Bad Berleburg	67	D5
Bad Doberan	67	G2
Bad Dürkheim	67	D7
Bad Ems	59	K4
Baden	65	F9
Baden-Baden	75	D2
Bad Freienwalde	67	K4
Badgastein	75	J3
Badgingarra	119	C6
Bad Harzburg	67	F5
Bad Hersfeld	67	E6
Bad Homburg	67	D6
Bad Honnef	59	K4
Badin	107	A4
Bad Ischl	75	J3
Bādiyat ash Shām	86	D4
Bad Kissingen	67	F6
Bad Kreuznach	59	K5
Bad Langensalza	67	F5
Bad Lauterberg	67	F5
Bad Liebenwerda	67	J5
Bad Mergentheim	67	E7
Bad Nauheim	67	D6
Bad Neuenahr-Ahrweiler	59	K4
Bad Neustadt	67	F6
Bad Oeynhausen	67	D4
Badong	111	E4
Bad Reichenhall	75	H3
Bad Säckingen	67	C9
Bad Salzuflen	67	D4
Bad Salzungen	67	F6
Bad Schwartau	67	F3
Bad Segeberg	67	F3
Bad Sobemheim	59	K5
Bad Urach	75	E2
Bad Vöslau	79	D2
Bad Waldsee	75	E3
Bad Wilbad	75	D2
Bad Wildungen	67	E5
Bad Windsheim	67	F7
Bad Wurzach	75	E3
Baena	73	F7
Bærum	61	F7
Baeza	73	G6
Baffin Bay	123	J2
Baffin Island	125	R2
Bafia	95	G4
Bafoulabé	95	B2
Bafoussam	95	G3
Bāfq	85	G3
Bafra	83	F3
Bafra Burun	83	G3
Bāft	87	G2
Bafwasende	97	D3
Baga	93	B5
Bagani	99	C3
Bagaroua	95	E2
Bagdad	133	D2
Bagdarin	105	J6
Bagé	143	L5
Baggs	129	E2
Baghdād	85	D3
Bagheria	77	H10
Baghlān	85	J2
Bagnères-de-Bigorre	71	F10
Bagno di Romagna	75	G7
Bagnols-sur-Cèze	71	K9
Baguio	109	G3
Bagun Datuk	115	(1)C2
Baharampur	107	E4
Bahawalnagar	107	B3
Bahawalpur	107	B3
Bahçe	83	G5
Bahia	141	J6
Bahía Blanca	143	J6
Bahía Blanca	143	J6
Bahía de Banderas	137	C4
Bahía de Campeche	137	F4
Bahía de Manta	141	A4
Bahía de Petacalco	137	D5
Bahía de Pisco	141	B6
Bahía de Santa Elena	141	A4
Bahía de Sechura	141	A5
Bahía Grande	143	H9
Bahia Kino	127	D6
Bahía Negra	143	K3
Bahía Samborombón	143	K6
Bahir Dar	93	G5
Bahraich	107	D3
Bahrain	87	D4
Baḩrat Ḩimş	86	D2
Bahr el Abiad	93	F5
Bahr el Azraq	93	F5
Bahr el Ghazal	93	C5
Bahr el Ghazal	97	D2
Bahr el Jebe	97	E2
Bahr el Nîl = Nile	93	F4
Baía de Marajó	141	H4
Baía de Todos os Santos	141	K6
Baía do Bengo	95	G6
Baia Mare	79	L2
Baião	141	H4
Baia Sprie	79	L2
Baïbokoum	97	B2
Baicheng, *China*	103	Q9
Baicheng, *China*	111	G1
Baie Comeau	131	G1
Baie de la Seine	59	B5
Baie de la Somme	59	D4
Baie du Poste	125	S6
Baie St. Paul	131	F1
Baiji	83	K6
Baile Átha Cliath = Dublin	69	F8
Bailén	73	G6
Bailleul	59	E4
Bailundo	99	B2
Bainbridge	135	E3
Bairiki	117	H5
Bairin Yuoqi	111	F2
Bairin Zuoqi	111	F2
Bairnsdale	119	J7
Bais	109	G5
Baja	79	F3
Baja California	127	C5
Bakchar	103	Q6
Bakel	95	B2
Baker	117	J5
Baker, *Calif., United States*	129	C3
Baker, *Mont., United States*	129	F1
Baker, *Oreg., United States*	129	C2
Baker Lake	125	M4
Baker Lake	125	N4
Bakersfield	133	C1
Bakhta	105	D4
Baki	85	E1
Bakkafjörður	61	(1)F1

Legend

✖	Continent name
A	Country name
	State or province name
	Country capital
	State or province capital
	Settlement
▲	Mountain, volcano, peak
	Mountain range
	Physical region or feature
	River, canal
	Lake, salt lake
	Gulf, strait, bay
	Sea, ocean
	Cape, point
	Island or island group, rocky or coral reef
	Place of interest
	Historical or cultural region

Name	Page	Grid
Bakkaflói	61	(1)F1
Baku = Baki	85	E1
Balâ	83	E4
Balabac	109	F5
Balabac Strait	109	F5
Balagansk	105	G6
Balaghat	107	D4
Balaguer	73	L3
Balakhta	103	S6
Balaklava	83	E1
Balakovo	63	J4
Bālā Morghāb	103	L10
Bālan	79	N3
Balāngīr	107	D4
Balashov	63	H4
Balassagyarmat	79	G1
Balaton	79	E3
Balatonfüred	79	E3
Balatonlelle	79	E3
Balchik	83	C2
Balclutha	121	B8
Bald Knob	131	B3
Baldwin	135	E3
Balearic Islands = Islas Baleares	73	N5
Bāleshwar	107	E4
Baley	105	K6
Baléyara	95	E2
Balguntay	103	R9
Bali	115	(1)F4
Balige	115	(1)B2
Balıkesir	81	K5
Balikpapan	115	(1)F3
Balimo	115	(2)F4
Balingen	75	D2
Balintang Channel	109	G3
Balkhash	103	N8
Ballarat	119	H7
Balleny Island	144	(2)Y3
Ballina, Australia	119	K5
Ballina, Republic of Ireland	69	C7
Ballinasloe	69	D8
Ballinger	133	G2
Ball's Pyramid	119	L6
Ballymena	69	F7
Balmazújváros	79	J2
Balotra	107	B3
Balranald	119	H6
Balş	79	M5
Balsas	137	D5
Balsas	141	H5
Balta	79	S2
Bălţi	79	Q2
Baltic Sea	61	J8
Baltijsk	65	J3
Baltimore	131	E3
Baltrum	67	C3
Balvi	61	P8
Balykchy	103	P9
Balykshi	63	K5
Bam	85	G4
Bamaga	119	H2
Bamako	95	C2
Bamba	91	E5
Bambari	97	C2
Bamberg	67	F7
Bambesa	97	D3
Bambouk	91	C6
Bambouk Kaarta	95	B2
Bamda	111	B4
Bamenda	95	G3
Bāmīān	85	J3
Banaba	117	G6
Bañados del Izozog	141	E7
Banalia	97	D3
Banana, Australia	119	K4
Banana, Dem. Rep. of Congo	97	A5
Banaz	81	M6
Ban Ban	109	C3
Banbury	69	L9
Banda	107	D3
Banda Aceh	109	B5
Bandama	95	C3
Bandar-e 'Abbās	87	G3
Bandar-e Anzalī	85	E2
Bandar-e Deylam	87	D1
Bandar-e Ganāveh	87	D2
Bandar-e Khoemir	87	F3
Bandar-e Lengeh	87	F3
Bandar-e Ma'shur	87	C1
Bandar-e Torkeman	85	F2
Bandar Khomeynī	87	C1
Bandar Seri Begawan	115	(1)E2
Banda Sea	115	(2)C3
Band-e Moghūyeh	87	F3
Bandirma	81	K4
Bandundu	97	B4
Bandung	115	(1)D4
Bāneasa	79	Q5
Bāneh	83	L6
Banff, Canada	125	H6
Banff, United Kingdom	69	K4
Bangalore	107	C6
Bangangté	95	G3
Bangassou	97	C3
Bangbong	115	(2)B3
Banggi	115	(1)F1
Banghāzī	93	D1
Bangka	115	(1)D3
Bangkok = Krung Thep	109	C4
Bangladesh	107	E4
Bangor, N.Ire., United Kingdom	69	G7
Bangor, Wales, United Kingdom	69	H8
Bangor, United States	131	G2
Bang Saphan Yai	109	B4
Bangui	97	B3
Ban Hat Yai	109	C5
Ban Hua Hin	109	B4
Bani-Bangou	95	E1
Banī Walīd	91	H2
Bāniyās	83	F6
Banja Luka	79	E5
Banjarmasin	115	(1)E3
Banjul	95	A2
Ban Khemmarat	109	D3
Banks Island = Moa, Australia	119	H2
Banks Island, B.C., Canada	125	E6
Banks Island, N.W.T., Canada	125	G2
Banks Lake	129	C1
Banks Peninsula	121	D6
Banks Strait	119	J8
Bannerman Town	135	F5
Bannu	107	B2
Bánovce	65	H9
Banská	65	J9
Banská Štiavnica	65	H9
Bansko	81	F3
Bantry	69	C10
Banyo	95	G3
Banyoles	73	N2
Banyuwangi	115	(1)E4
Baode	111	E3
Baoding	111	F3
Baoji	111	D4
Bao Lôc	109	D4
Baoro	97	B2
Baoshan	109	B1
Baotou	111	E2
Baoying	111	F4
Bapaume	59	E4
Ba'qūbah	85	D3
Baquedano	143	H3
Bar	79	G7
Barabai	115	(1)F3
Baraboo	131	C2
Barakaldo	73	H1
Baramati	107	B5
Baramula	107	B2
Baran	107	C3
Baranavichy	63	E4
Baraolt	79	N3
Barbados	141	F1
Barbastro	73	L2
Barbate	73	E8
Barbuda	137	M5
Barcaldine	119	J4
Barcău	79	K2
Barcellona Pozzo di Gotto	77	K10
Barcelona, Spain	73	N3
Barcelona, Venezuela	137	M6`
Barcelos, Brazil	141	E4
Barcelos, Spain	73	B3
Barco de Valdeorras = O Barco	73	D2
Barcs	79	E4
Bārda	83	M3
Bardai	93	C3
Barddhamān	107	E4
Bardejov	65	L8
Bareilly	107	C3
Barents Sea	103	E3
Barentu	93	G4
Bareo	115	(1)F2
Barga	107	D2
Bargaal	97	J1
Barguzin	105	H6
Bar Harbor	131	G2
Bari	77	L7
Barikot	107	B1
Barinas	141	C2
Bārīs	93	F3
Barisal	107	F4
Barito	115	(2)A3
Barkam	111	C4
Barkava	61	P8
Barkly Tableland	119	F3
Barkol	103	S9
Bârlad	79	Q3
Bârlad	79	Q3
Bar-le-Duc	59	H6
Barletta	77	L7
Barmer	107	B3
Barmouth Bay	69	H9
Barnaul	103	Q7
Barnsley	69	L8
Barnstaple	69	H10
Barnstaple Bay	69	H10
Barpeta	107	F3
Barquisimeto	141	D1
Barr	75	C2
Barra, Brazil	141	J6
Barra, United Kingdom	69	E4
Barracão do Barreto	141	G5
Barra do Bugres	141	F7
Barra do Corda	141	H5
Barra do Garças	141	G7
Barra do São Manuel	141	G5
Barragem de Santa Clara	73	B7
Barragem de Sobradinho	141	J5
Barragem do Castelo de Bode	73	B5
Barragem do Maranhão	73	C6
Barranca, Peru	141	B4
Barranca, Peru	141	B6
Barranquilla	137	K6
Barreiras	141	H6
Barreiro	73	A6
Barretos	141	H8
Barrie	131	E2
Barron	131	B1
Barrow	133	(1)F1
Barrow-in-Furness	69	J7
Barrow Island	119	B4
Barrow Strait	125	N2
Barshatas	103	P8
Barsi	107	C5
Barstow	133	C2
Bar-sur-Aube	71	K5
Barth	67	H2
Bartın	83	E3
Bartle Frere	117	E7
Bartlesville	135	B2
Bartlett	129	G2
Bartoszyce	65	K3
Barus	115	(1)B2
Baruun Urt	111	E1
Barwani	107	B4
Barysaw	63	E4
Basaidu	87	F3
Basankusu	97	B3
Basarabeasca	79	R3
Basarabi	79	R5
Basca	77	C2
Basel	75	C3
Bashkiriya	63	K4
Bāsht	87	D1
Basilan	115	(2)B1
Basildon	59	C3
Basiluzzo	77	K10
Basingstoke	69	L10
Başkale	83	K4
Basoko	97	C3
Bassano	127	D1
Bassano del Grappa	75	G5
Bassar	95	E3
Bassas da India	99	F4
Basse Santa Su	91	C6
Basse Terre	137	M5
Bassett	129	G2
Bass Strait	119	H7
Bassum	67	D4
Bastak	87	F3
Bastānābād	83	M5
Basti	107	D3
Bastia	77	D6
Bastogne	59	H4
Bastrop, La., United States	135	C3
Bastrop, Tex., United States	135	B3
Bata	95	F4
Batagay	105	N3
Batak	81	G3
Batamay	105	M4
Batangas	109	G4
Batan Islands	109	G2
Batanta	115	(2)C3
Batemans Bay	119	K7
Batesville	135	D3
Bath, United Kingdom	69	K10
Bath, United States	131	E2
Bathinda	107	B2
Bathurst, Australia	119	J6
Bathurst, Canada	125	T7
Bathurst Inlet	125	K3
Bathurst Island, Australia	119	E2
Bathurst Island, Canada	125	M1
Batman	85	D2
Batna	91	G1
Baton Rouge	135	C3
Bátonyterenye	79	G2
Batroûn	86	C2
Battipaglia	77	J8
Battle	125	J6
Battle Creek	131	C2
Battle Harbour	125	V6
Battle Mountain	129	C2
Batu	97	F2
Batui	115	(2)B3
Bat'umi	83	J3
Batu Pahat	115	(1)C2
Baturino	103	R6
Baubau	115	(2)B4
Bauchi	95	F2
Baudette	131	B1
Baukau	115	(2)C4
Baume-les-Dames	71	M6
Bauru	143	M3
Bauska	61	N8
Bautzen	65	D6
Bawean	115	(1)E4
Bawiti	93	E2
Bawku	95	D2
Bayamo	137	J4
Bayanaul	103	P7
Bayandelger	105	H7
Bayan Har Shan	111	B4
Bayanhongor	111	C1
Bayan Mod	111	C2

Name	Page	Grid
Bayan Obo	111	D2
Bayansumküre	103	Q9
Bayburt	83	J3
Bay City, *Mich., United States*	131	D2
Bay City, *Tex., United States*	135	B4
Baydhabo	97	G3
Bayerische Alpen	75	G3
Bayeux	59	B5
Bayfield	131	B1
Bayindir	81	K6
Bāyir	86	D6
Baykit	103	T5
Baykonur	103	M8
Bay Minette	135	D3
Bay of Bengal	107	E5
Bay of Biscay	71	C9
Bay of Fundy	125	T8
Bay of Islands	121	E2
Bay of Plenty	121	F3
Bayonne	71	D10
Bayramaly	85	H2
Bayramiç	81	J5
Bayreuth	67	G7
Baysun	85	J2
Bayt al Faqīh	93	H5
Bay View	121	F4
Baza	73	H7
Bazas	71	E9
Bazdar	85	J4
Beach	129	F1
Beachy Head	59	C4
Beagle Gulf	119	E2
Bealanana	99	H2
Bear Island	69	B10
Bear Island = Bjørnøya	103	B3
Bear Lake	129	D2
Beasain	73	H1
Beas de Segura	73	H6
Beatrice	135	B1
Beatty	133	C1
Beaufort, *Malaysia*	115	(1)F1
Beaufort, *N.C., United States*	135	F3
Beaufort, *S.C., United States*	135	E3
Beaufort Sea	123	Q2
Beaufort West	99	C6
Beaumont	135	C3
Beaune	71	K6
Beauvais	59	E5
Beaver	129	D3
Beaver Creek	133	(1)J3
Beaver Dam	131	C3
Beaver Falls	131	D2
Beawar	107	B3
Beazley	143	H5
Bebra	67	E6
Bečej	79	H4
Béchar	91	E2
Beckley	135	E2
Becks	121	B7
Beckum	59	L3
Beclean	79	M2
Bedford, *United Kingdom*	69	M9
Bedford, *United States*	135	D2
Bedworth	59	A2
Beenleigh	119	K5
Beer Menuha	86	C6
Be'ér Sheva'	86	B5
Beeville	135	B4
Behbehān	87	D1
Bei'an	105	M7
Beihai	109	D2
Beijing	111	F3
Beipan	111	D5
Beipiao	111	G2
Beira	99	E3
Beirut = Beyrouth	86	C3
Beiuş	79	K3
Beizhen	113	A3
Béja	91	G1
Bejaïa	91	G1
Béjar	73	E4
Bekdash	85	F1
Békés	65	L11
Békéscsaba	79	J3
Bekily	99	H4
Bela	85	J4
Bela Crkva	79	J5
Belaga	115	(1)E2
Belarus	57	G2
Bela Vista	99	E5
Belaya	63	K3
Belaya Gora	105	R3
Bełchatów	65	J6
Belcher Islands	125	Q5
Beledweyne	97	H3
Belém	141	H4
Belen	137	C2
Belfast	69	G7
Belfield	129	F1
Belfort	75	B3
Belgazyn	103	T7
Belgium	59	G4
Belgorod	63	G4
Belgrade = Beograd	79	H5
Beli	95	G3
Belice	77	H11
Beli Manastir	79	F4
Belinyu	115	(1)D3
Belitung	115	(1)D3
Belize	137	G5
Belize	137	G5
Bellac	71	G7
Bella Coola	125	F6
Bellary	107	C5
Bellefontaine	131	D2
Belle Fourche	129	F2
Belle Glade	135	E4
Belle Île	71	B6
Belle Isle	125	V6
Bellême	71	F5
Belleterre	131	E1
Belleville, *Canada*	131	E2
Belleville, *United States*	131	C2
Bellingham	129	B1
Bellingshausen Sea	144	(2)JJ4
Bellinzona	75	E4
Bello	141	B2
Belluno	75	H4
Bellyk	105	E6
Belmont	131	E2
Belmonte, *Brazil*	141	K7
Belmonte, *Spain*	73	H5
Belmopan	137	G5
Belmullet	69	B7
Belogorsk	105	M6
Belogradchik	79	K6
Belo Horizonte	141	J7
Beloit, *Kans., United States*	135	B2
Beloit, *Wis., United States*	131	C2
Belomorsk	63	F2
Belorechensk	83	H1
Beloretsk	63	L4
Belo Tsiribihina	99	G3
Belovo	103	R7
Beloyarskiy	103	M5
Beloye More	63	G1
Belozersk	63	G2
Belozerskoye	63	N3
Belye Vody	103	M9
Belyy Yar	103	Q6
Belzig	67	H4
Bembibre	73	D2
Bemidji	131	A1
Bena Dibele	97	C4
Benavente	73	E3
Benbecula	69	E4
Bend	129	B2
Bender-Bayla	97	J2
Bender Qaasim	97	H1
Bendorf	59	K4
Bene	99	E3
Benešov	65	D8
Benevento	77	J7
Bengbu	111	F4
Bengkulu	115	(1)C3
Benguela	99	A2
Benguerir	91	D2
Benha	93	F1
Beni	97	D3
Beni	141	D6
Beni Abbès	91	E2
Benicarló	73	L4
Benidorm	73	K6
Benî Mazâr	93	F2
Beni Mellal	91	D2
Benin	95	E2
Benin City	95	F3
Beni Saf	73	J9
Beni Slimane	73	P8
Beni Suef	93	F2
Benito Juaréz	143	K6
Benjamin Constant	141	D4
Benkelman	129	F2
Benkovac	75	L6
Ben More Assynt	69	H3
Ben Nevis	69	H5
Bennington	131	F2
Benoud	91	F2
Bensheim	67	D7
Benson, *Ariz., United States*	133	D3
Benson, *Minn., United States*	127	G2
Benteng	115	(2)B4
Bentinck Island	119	G3
Bentonville	135	C2
Bentung	115	(1)C2
Benue	95	G3
Benxi	111	G2
Beograd	79	H5
Bepazarı	83	D3
Berat	81	B4
Beravina	99	H3
Berber	93	F4
Berbera	93	H5
Berbérati	97	B3
Berchtesgaden	75	J3
Berck	59	D4
Berdigestyakh	105	M4
Berdyans'k	63	G5
Berdychiv	63	E5
Bereeda	97	J1
Berehove	79	K1
Bererreá	73	C2
Berettyóújfalu	79	J2
Berettys	65	L10
Bereznik	63	H2
Berezniki	63	L3
Berezovo	63	N2
Berezovyy	105	P6
Berga	73	M2
Bergama	81	K5
Bérgamo	75	E5
Bergara	73	H1
Bergedorf	67	F3
Bergen, *Germany*	67	E4
Bergen, *Germany*	67	J2
Bergen, *Netherlands*	59	G2
Bergen, *Norway*	61	C6
Bergen op Zoom	59	G3
Bergerac	71	F9
Bergheim	59	J4
Bergisch Gladbach	67	C6
Bergsfjordhalvøya	61	L1
Beringen	59	H3
Beringovskiy	105	X4
Bering Sea	133	(1)C4
Bering Strait	133	(1)C2
Berkeley	133	B1
Berkner Island	144	(2)A2
Berkovitsa	79	L6
Berlin, *Germany*	67	J4
Berlin, *United States*	131	F2
Bermejillo	133	F3
Bermejo	143	K4
Bermeo	73	H1
Bermuda	123	H6
Bern	75	C4
Bernado	133	E2
Bernau	67	J4
Bernay	59	C5
Bernburg	67	G5
Berner Alpen	75	C4
Beroun	65	D8
Berounka	67	J7
Berovo	81	E3
Berrouaghia	73	N8
Berry Islands	135	F4
Bertoua	95	G4
Bertram	131	D1
Beruni	103	L9
Berwick-upon-Tweed	69	L6
Besalampy	99	G3
Besançon	71	M6
Beshneh	87	F2
Bessemer	135	D3
Bestamak	103	P8
Bestuzhevo	63	H2
Bestyakh, *Russia*	105	L3
Bestyakh, *Russia*	105	M4
Betanzos	73	B1
Bětdâmbâng	109	C4
Bethany	131	B2
Bethel, *Ak., United States*	133	(1)E3
Bethel, *Pa., United States*	131	F2
Bethlehem, *Israel*	86	C5
Bethlehem, *South Africa*	99	D5
Béthune	59	E4
Betioky	99	G4
Betoota	119	H5
Betpak-Dala	103	M8
Betroka	99	H4
Bet-She'an	86	C4
Bettiah	107	D3
Betul	107	C4
Betzdorf	67	C6
Beulah	131	C2
Beverley	69	M8
Beverungen	67	E5
Bexhill	59	C4
Bey Dağlari	81	M8
Beyla	95	C3
Beyneu	103	J8
Beypazarı	81	P4
Beyrouth	86	C3
Beyşehir	81	P7
Beyşehir Gölü	81	P7
Bezhetsk	63	G3
Béziers	71	J10
Bhadgaon	107	E3
Bhadrakh	107	E4
Bhadravati	107	C6
Bhagalpur	107	E3
Bhairab Bazar	107	F4
Bhakkar	107	B2
Bhamo	109	B2
Bharuch	107	B4
Bhatpara	107	E4
Bhavnagar	107	B4
Bhawanipatna	107	D5
Bhilai	107	D4
Bhilwara	107	B3
Bhīmavaram	107	D5
Bhind	107	C3
Bhiwandi	107	B5
Bhopal	107	C4
Bhubaneshwar	107	E4
Bhuj	107	A4
Bhusawal	107	C4
Bhutan	107	E3
Biak	115	(2)E3
Biak	115	(2)E3
Biała	65	K8
Biała Podlaska	65	N5
Białogard	65	F3
Białystok	65	N4

Name	Page	Grid	Name	Page	Grid	Name	Page	Grid	Name	Page	Grid
Biarritz	71	D10	Bï'r Bazïrï	86	E2	Blanco	141	E6	Bo Hai	111	F3
Biasca	75	D4	Birdsville	119	G5	Blanding	133	E1	Bohmerwald	67	H7
Bibbiena	75	G7	Bireun	115	(1)B1	Blankenberge	59	F3	Bohol	109	G5
Biberach	75	E2	Bîr Gifgâfa	86	A6	Blankenburg	67	F5	Bohumin	65	H8
Bicaz	79	P3	Birhan	93	G5	Blankenheim	59	J4	Boiaçu	141	E4
Bickerton Island	119	G2	Bîr Hasana	86	A6	Blantyre	99	F3	Boise	129	C2
Bicske	79	F2	Bīrjand	85	G3	Blasket Islands	69	B9	Boise City	133	F1
Bida	95	F3	Birkenfeld	59	K5	Blaubeuren	75	E2	Bojnürd	103	K10
Bidar	107	C5	Birmingham, *United Kingdom*	69	L9	Blaye-et-Sainte-Luce	71	E8	Bokatola	97	B4
Bidbid	87	H5	Birmingham, *United States*	135	D3	Bled	75	K4	Boké	95	B2
Biddeford	131	F2	Bîr Mogreïn	91	C3	Blenheim	121	D5	Bokspits	99	C5
Bideford	69	H10	Birnie	117	J6	Blevands Huk	67	D1	Bokungu	97	C4
Biedenkopf	67	D6	Birnin-Gwari	95	F2	Blida	91	F1	Bolbec	59	C5
Biel	75	C3	Birnin Kebbi	95	E2	Blind River	127	K2	Bole, *China*	103	Q9
Bielefeld	67	D4	Birnin Konni	95	F2	Bloemfontein	99	D5	Bole, *Ghana*	95	D3
Biella	75	D5	Birnin Kudu	95	F2	Bloemhof	99	D5	Bolechiv	65	N8
Bielsko-Biała	65	J8	Birobidzhan	105	N7	Blois	71	G6	Bolesławiec	65	E6
Bielsk Podlaski	65	N5	Birsk	63	L3	Blönduós	61	(1)C2	Bolgatanga	95	D2
Biên Hoa	109	D4	Biržai	65	P1	Błonie	65	K5	Bolhrad	79	R4
Bietigheim-Bissingen	75	E2	Bi'r Zaltan	93	C2	Bloomfield	135	D2	Bolintin-Vale	79	N5
Big	125	G2	Bisbee	133	E2	Bloomington, *Ill., United States*	131	C2	Bolivar	131	B3
Biga	81	K4	Biscéglie	77	L7	Bloomington, *Ind., United States*	131	C3	Bolivia	141	D7
Bigadiç	81	L5	Bischofshofen	75	J3	Bludenz	75	E3	Bollène	71	K9
Big Desert	119	H7	Bischofswerda	65	D6	Blue Earth	131	B2	Bollnäs	61	J6
Big Falls	131	B1	Biševo	77	L6	Bluefield	131	D3	Bolmen	61	G8
Bighorn	127	E2	Bishkek	103	N9	Bluefields	137	H6	Bolnisi	83	L3
Bighorn Lake	129	E1	Bishop	129	C3	Blue Mountain Lake	131	F2	Bolobo	95	H5
Bighorn Mountains	129	E2	Bishop Auckland	69	L7	Blue Mountains	129	C2	Bologna	75	G6
Bight of Bangkok	109	C4	Bishop's Stortford	59	C3	Blue Nile = Bahr el Azraq	93	F5	Bolognesi	141	J6
Bight of Benin	95	E3	Biskra	91	G2	Bluenose Lake	125	H3	Bolomba	95	H4
Bight of Biafra	95	F4	Bislig	109	H5	Bluff, *New Zealand*	121	B8	Bolotnoye	103	Q6
Big Lake	133	(1)H2	Bismarck	127	F2	Bluff, *United States*	133	E1	Bol'shaya Pyssa	63	J2
Bignona	91	B6	Bismarck Sea	117	E6	Blumenau	143	M4	Bol'sherech'ye	103	P3
Big Pine	135	E5	Bissau	91	B6	Blythe	133	D2	Bol'shezemel'skaya Tundra	103	J4
Big Rapids	131	C2	Bistcho Lake	125	H5	Blytheville	135	D2	Bol Shirta	105	C4
Big River	125	K6	Bistriţa	79	M2	Bo	95	B3	Bolshoy Atlym	63	N2
Big Sandy	129	D1	Bistriţa	79	P3	Boac	109	G4	Bol'shoy Osinovaya	105	W3
Big Sioux	129	G2	Bitburg	59	J5	Boa Vista, *Brazil*	141	E3	Bol'shoy Vlas'evo	105	Q6
Big Spring	133	F2	Bitche	67	C7	Boa Vista, *Cape Verde Islands*	95	(1)B1	Bol'shoy Yuga	63	P2
Big Sur	133	B1	Bitkine	93	C5	Bobbili	107	D5	Bolsover	59	A1
Big Trout Lake	125	P6	Bitlis	83	K4	Bóbbio	75	E6	Bolton	69	K8
Bihać	75	L6	Bitola	81	D3	Bobigny	59	E6	Bolu	83	D3
Bijapur	107	C5	Bitonto	77	L7	Bobingen	75	F2	Bolvadin	81	P6
Bījār	83	M6	Bitterfeld	67	H5	Boblingen	75	E2	Bolzano = Bozen	75	G4
Bijeljina	79	G5	Bitterroot Range	129	C1	Bobo Dioulasso	95	D2	Boma	95	G6
Bijelo Polje	79	G6	Bitti	77	D8	Bobr	65	E6	Bombala	119	J7
Bijie	111	D5	Bitung	115	(2)C2	Bobrov	63	H4	Bombay = Mumbai	107	B5
Bikanar	107	B3	Biu	95	G2	Bôca do Acre	141	D5	Bomili	97	D3
Bikin	105	N7	Biwa-ko	113	H6	Boca Grande	137	M7	Bom Jesus da Lapa	141	J6
Bikini	117	G4	Bixby	131	B3	Boca Grande	139	E3	Bømlo	61	C7
Bilaspur	107	D4	Biyāvra	107	C4	Bocaiúva	141	J7	Bomnak	105	M6
Biläsuvar	83	N4	Biysk	103	R7	Bocaranga	97	B2	Bonāb	83	M5
Bila Tserkva	63	F5	Bizerte	91	G1	Bochart	131	F1	Bonaparte Archipelago	119	B2
Bilbao	73	H1	Bjelovar	79	D4	Bochnia	65	K8	Bonavista Bay	125	W7
Bileća	79	F7	Bjørnøya	103	B3	Bocholt	67	B5	Bondeno	75	G6
Bilecik	81	M4	B-Köpenick	67	J4	Bochum	67	C5	Bondo	97	C3
Bilećko Jezero	79	F7	Blackburn	69	K8	Bodaybo	105	J5	Bondokodi	119	C1
Biled	79	H4	Blackfoot	129	D2	Bode	67	G4	Bondoukou	95	D3
Biłgoraj	65	N7	Blackfoot Reservoir	129	D2	Bodélé	93	C4	Bondowoso	115	(1)E4
Bilhorod-Dnistrovs'kyy	63	F5	Black Hills	129	F2	Boden	61	L4	Bonganga	97	C3
Bilina	67	J6	Blackpool	69	J8	Bodham	107	C5	Bongao	115	(2)A1
Billings	129	D1	Black Range	133	E2	Bodmin	69	H11	Bongor	95	H2
Bill of Portland	69	K11	Black River Falls	131	B2	Bodø	61	H3	Bonifacio	77	D7
Bilma	93	H3	Black Rock Desert	129	C2	Bodrog	65	L9	Bonn	67	C6
Biloxi	135	D3	Blacksburg	131	D3	Bodrum	81	K7	Bonners Ferry	129	C1
Bimini Islands	135	F4	Black Sea	83	D2	Boe	129	D2	Bonorva	77	C8
Binche	59	G4	Blacks Harbour	131	G1	Boende	97	C4	Bonthe	95	B3
Bindi Bindi	119	C6	Black Sugarloaf	119	K6	Bogale	109	B3	Bontoc	109	G3
Bindura	99	E3	Black Volta	95	D3	Bogalusa	135	D3	Bonyhád	79	F3
Bingen	67	C7	Blackwater	69	D9	Boggabilla	119	K5	Boone	131	D3
Binghamton	131	E2	Blagny-sur-Bresle	59	D5	Boghni	73	P8	Boonville	135	C2
Bingöl	83	J4	Blagodarnyy	83	K1	Bognor Regis	59	B4	Boorama	97	G2
Binongko	115	(2)B4	Blagoevgrad	81	F3	Bogo	109	G4	Boosaaso	85	E7
Bintulu	115	(1)E2	Blagoveshchenka	103	P7	Bogor	115	(1)D4	Boothia Peninsula	125	M2
Bintuni	115	(2)D3	Blagoveshchensk	105	M6	Bogorodskoye	105	Q6	Boué	95	G5
Binyang	109	D2	Blain	71	D6	Bogotá	141	C3	Boppard	67	C6
Binzhou	111	F3	Blair	131	A2	Bogotol	103	R6	Bor, *Russia*	105	D4
Biograd	75	L7	Blairsden	129	B3	Bogra	107	E4	Bor, *Sudan*	97	E2
Birāk	91	H3	Blairsville	135	E3	Boguchany	105	F5	Bor, *Turkey*	81	S7
Birao	93	D5	Blaj	79	L3	Bogué	91	C5	Bor, *Yugoslavia*	79	K5
Biratnagar	107	E3	Blakely	135	E3				Borah Peak	129	C3

Name	Page	Grid
Borås	61	G8
Borāzjān	87	D2
Bordeaux	71	E9
Borden Peninsula	125	Q2
Border Town	119	H7
Bordj Bou Arréridj	91	F1
Bordj Bounaam	73	M9
Bordj Flye Sante Marie	91	E3
Bordj Messaouda	91	G2
Bordj Mokhtar	91	F4
Bordj Omar Driss	91	G3
Borgarnes	61	(1)C2
Borger	133	F1
Borgomanero	75	D5
Borgo San Dalmazzo	75	C6
Borgo San Lorenzo	75	G7
Borgosésia	75	D5
Borgo Val di Taro	75	E6
Bori Jenein	91	H2
Borislav	65	N8
Borisoglebsk	63	H4
Borjomi	83	K3
Borken	59	J3
Borkou	93	C4
Borkum	59	J1
Borlänge	61	H6
Bórmida	75	D6
Bormio	75	F4
Borna	67	H5
Borneo	115	(1)E3
Bornholm	61	H9
Borodino	103	R5
Borodinskoye	61	Q6
Boromo	95	D2
Borovichi	63	F3
Borovskoy	63	M4
Borriana	73	K5
Borroloola	119	G3
Borşa	79	M2
Borshchiv	79	P1
Borshchovochnyy Khrebet	105	J7
Borðeyri	61	(1)C2
Borūjerd	85	E3
Borzya	105	K6
Bosa	77	C8
Bosanska Dubica	79	D4
Bosanska Gradiška	79	E4
Bosanska Kostajnica	75	M5
Bosanska Krupa	79	D5
Bosanski Brod	79	F4
Bosanski Novi	79	D4
Bosanski Petrovac	79	D5
Bosansko Grahovo	75	M6
Boşca	79	J4
Bose	109	D2
Bosilegrad	79	K7
Boskovice	65	F8
Bosna	79	F5
Bosnia-Herzegovina	79	E5
Bosobolo	97	B3
Bosporus = İstanbul Boğazı	81	M3
Bosporus	85	A1
Bossámbélé	97	B2
Bossangoa	97	B2
Bossier City	135	C3
Bosten Hu	103	R9
Boston, United Kingdom	69	M9
Boston, United States	131	F2
Botevgrad	79	L7
Botlikh	85	E1
Botna	79	R3
Botoşani	79	P2
Botou	111	F3
Botrange	59	J4
Botswana	99	C4
Bottrop	59	J3
Bou Ahmed	73	F9
Bouaké	95	C3
Bouar	97	B2
Bouârfa	91	E2
Boufarik	73	N8
Bougainville Island	117	F6
Bougainville Reef	119	J3
Bougouni	95	C2
Bougzoul	73	N9
Bouira	91	F1
Bou Ismaïl	73	N8
Bou Izakarn	91	D3
Boujdour	91	C3
Bou Kadir	73	M8
Boulder	129	E2
Boulder City	133	D1
Boulia	119	G4
Boulogne-sur-Mer	59	D4
Bounty Islands	117	H10
Bourem	91	E5
Bourg-de-Piage	71	L9
Bourg-en-Bresse	71	L7
Bourges	71	H6
Bourgoin-Jallieu	71	L8
Bourke	119	J6
Bournemouth	69	L11
Bou Saâda	91	F1
Bousso	93	C5
Boussu	59	F4
Boutilimit	91	C5
Bouzghaïa	73	M8
Bowbells	129	F1
Bowen	119	J4
Bowie, Ariz., United States	133	E2
Bowie, Tex., United States	133	G2
Bowkan	83	M5
Bowling Green, Fla., United States	135	E4
Bowling Green, Ky., United States	135	D2
Bowling Green, Mo., United States	135	C2
Bowman	129	F1
Bowman Bay	125	R3
Bo Xian	111	F4
Boxwood Hill	119	C6
Boyabat	83	F3
Boyang	111	F5
Boyarka	105	F2
Boysen Reservoir	129	E2
Boyuibe	143	J3
Bozcaada	81	H5
Boz Dağ	81	M7
Bozeman	129	D1
Bozen	75	G4
Bozkır	81	Q7
Bozoum	97	B2
Bozüyük	81	N5
Bra	75	C6
Brač	79	D6
Bracciano	77	G6
Bräcke	61	H5
Brad	79	K3
Brádano	77	L8
Bradford	69	L8
Brady	135	B3
Braga	73	B3
Bragança, Brazil	141	H4
Bragança, Portugal	73	D3
Brahmapur	107	D5
Brahmaputra	107	F3
Brăila	79	Q4
Brainerd	131	B1
Braintree	59	C3
Brake	67	D3
Bramming	67	D1
Brampton	131	E2
Bramsche	67	D3
Branco	141	E3
Brandberg	99	A4
Brandenburg	67	H4
Brandenton	135	E4
Brandon	125	M7
Brandvlei	99	C5
Brandýs	65	D7
Braniewo	65	J3
Brasileia	141	D6
Brasília	141	H7
Braslaw	61	P9
Braşov	79	N4
Bratislava	65	G9
Bratsk	105	G5
Bratskoye Vodokhranilishche	105	G5
Brattleboro	131	F2
Braţul	79	R4
Braunau	75	J2
Braunschweig	67	F4
Brawley	133	C2
Bray	69	F8
Brazil	139	F4
Brazzaville	97	B4
Brčko	79	F5
Brda	65	G4
Bream Bay	121	E2
Breckenridge	133	G2
Břeclav	65	F9
Breda	59	G3
Bredasdorp	99	C6
Bredstedt	67	E2
Bredy	63	M4
Bree	59	H3
Bree	71	L2
Bregenz	75	E3
Breiðafjörður	61	(1)A2
Bremangerlandet	61	B6
Bremen, Germany	67	D3
Bremen, United States	135	D3
Bremerhaven	67	D3
Bremerton	129	B1
Bremervörde	67	E3
Brenham	135	B3
Brennero	75	G4
Breno	75	F5
Brentwood	59	C3
Bréscia	75	F5
Breslau = Wrocław	65	G6
Bressanone = Brixen	77	F2
Bressay	69	M1
Bressuire	71	E7
Brest, Belarus	63	D4
Brest, France	71	A5
Breteuil	59	E5
Bretten	67	D7
Breves	141	G4
Brewarrina	119	J5
Brewton	135	D3
Brežice	79	C4
Brézina	91	F2
Brezno	65	J9
Bria	97	C2
Briançon	75	B6
Briceni	79	Q1
Bridgend	69	J10
Bridgeport, Calif., United States	133	C1
Bridgeport, Conn., United States	131	F2
Bridgeport, Nebr., United States	129	F2
Bridgetown	141	F1
Bridgewater	125	U8
Bridgwater	69	J10
Bridlington	69	M7
Brienzer See	75	D4
Brig	75	C4
Brigham City	129	D2
Brighton, United Kingdom	59	B4
Brighton, United States	129	F3
Brignoles	75	B7
Brikama	95	A2
Brilon	67	D5
Bríndisi	77	M8
Brinkley	135	C3
Brisbane	119	K5
Bristol, United Kingdom	69	K10
Bristol, United States	135	E2
Bristol Bay	133	(1)E4
Bristol Channel	69	H10
British Columbia	125	F5
Britstown	99	C6
Brive-la-Gaillarde	71	G8
Briviesca	73	G2
Brixen	75	G4
Brixham	69	J11
Brlik	103	N9
Brno	65	F8
Broad Sound	119	J4
Broadus	129	E1
Brockton	131	F2
Brockville	131	E2
Brod	79	J9
Brodeur Peninsula	125	P2
Brodick	69	G6
Brodnica	65	J4
Broken Arrow	137	E1
Broken Bow	135	C3
Broken Hill	119	H6
Brokopondo	141	F2
Bromölla	65	D1
Bromsgrove	69	K9
Brønderslev	61	E8
Brooke's Point	109	F5
Brookhaven	127	H5
Brookhaven	135	C3
Brookhaven	137	F2
Brookings, Oreg., United States	129	B2
Brookings, S.D., United States	129	G2
Brooks	125	J6
Brooks Range	133	(1)F2
Brooksville	135	E4
Broome	119	D3
Brösarp	61	H9
Brovary	63	F4
Brownfield	133	F2
Browning	129	D1
Brownsville, Tenn., United States	135	D2
Brownsville, Tex., United States	135	B4
Brownwood	135	B3
Bruchsal	67	D7
Bruck, Austria	75	L3
Bruck, Austria	75	M2
Bruck an der Mur	79	C2
Brugge	59	F3
Brühl	59	J4
Bruint	107	G3
Brumado	141	J6
Brumath	75	C2
Bruneau	129	C2
Bruneck	75	G4
Brunei	115	(1)E2
Brunico = Bruneck	77	F2
Brunflo	61	H5
Brunsbüttel	67	E3
Brunswick, Ga., United States	135	E3
Brunswick, Me., United States	131	G2
Bruntál	65	G8
Brush	129	F2
Brussels = Bruxelles	59	G4
Bruxelles	59	G4
Bryan	135	B3
Bryanka	103	S6
Bryansk	63	F4
Brzeg	65	G7
Brzeg Dolny	65	F6
Brzeziny	65	J6
B-Spandau	65	C5
Bubi	99	E4
Bucak	83	D5
Bucaramanga	141	C2
Buchanan	95	B3
Buchan Gulf	125	S2
Bucharest = Bucureşti	79	P5
Buchen	67	E7
Buchholz	67	E3
Buchy	71	M5
Bückeburg	67	E4
Bucureşti	79	P5
Budapest	79	G2
Budennovsk	83	L1

Legend

- ◪ Continent name
- Ⓐ Country name
- Ⓐ State or province name
- ■ Country capital
- ◻ State or province capital
- ◉ Settlement
- ▲ Mountain, volcano, peak
- ▬ Mountain range
- ⌀ Physical region or feature
- ◿ River, canal
- ◪ Lake, salt lake
- ◡ Gulf, strait, bay
- ⊟ Sea, ocean
- ⊳ Cape, point
- ◳ Island or island group, rocky or coral reef
- ✳ Place of interest
- ◱ Historical or cultural region

Symbol	Meaning		Symbol	Meaning		Symbol	Meaning
⊠	Continent name		▲	Mountain, volcano, peak		⬛	Sea, ocean
▲	Country name		⬔	Mountain range		⬔	Cape, point
⬚	State or province name		⬚	Physical region or feature		⬚	Island or island group, rocky or coral reef
■	Country capital		✈	River, canal		✳	Place of interest
□	State or province capital		✈	Lake, salt lake		⬚	Historical or cultural region
●	Settlement		⬛	Gulf, strait, bay			

Name	Page	Grid
Çamiçigölü	81	K7
Caminha	73	B3
Camiranga	141	H4
Camocim	141	J4
Camooweal	119	G3
Camopi	141	G3
Campbell Island	121	(2)C2
Campbell River	125	F7
Campbellsville	131	C3
Campbellton	131	G1
Campbeltown	69	G6
Campeche	137	F5
Câmpeni	79	L3
Câmpia Turzii	79	L3
Câmpina	79	N4
Campina Grande	141	L5
Campinas	143	M3
Campobasso	77	J7
Campo de Criptana	73	G5
Campo de Diauarum	141	G6
Campo Gallo	143	J4
Campo Grande	143	L3
Campo Maior	141	J4
Campo Mourão	143	L3
Campos	143	N3
Câmpulung	79	N4
Câmpulung Moldovenesc	79	N2
Cam Ranh	109	D4
Çan	81	K4
Canada	123	M4
Canadian	133	F1
Canadian	133	F1
Çanakkale	81	J4
Çanakkale Boğazı	81	J4
Canal de Panamá	137	J7
Cananea	133	D2
Canary Islands = Islas Canarias	89	A3
Canary Islands = Islas Canarias	91	B3
Cañaveras	73	H4
Canberra	119	J7
Cancún	137	G4
Çandarli Körfezi	81	J6
Candelaro	79	C8
Candlemas Island	139	J9
Cangamba	99	B2
Cangas	73	B2
Cangas de Narcea	73	D1
Cangyuan	109	B2
Cangzhou	111	F3
Canicatti	77	H11
Canindé	141	K4
Çankiri	83	E3
Canna	69	F4
Cannanore	107	B6
Cannanore	107	C6
Cannes	75	C7
Cannock	59	A2
Canon City	133	E1
Cantanduanes	109	G4
Canterbury	59	D3
Canterbury Bight	121	C7
Canterbury Plains	121	C6
Cân Tho	109	D5
Canto do Buriti	141	J5
Canton, Miss., United States	135	D3
Canton, Oh., United States	135	E1
Canton, S.D., United States	129	G2
Canumã	141	F4
Canumã	141	F5
Canutama	141	E5
Canyon	133	F1
Canyon Ferry Lake	129	D1
Cao Băng	109	D2
Caorle	75	H5
Cap Blanc	77	D11
Cap Bon	91	H1
Cap Corse	77	D5
Cap d'Agde	71	J10
Cap d'Antifer	59	C5
Cap de Fer	91	G1
Cap de Formentor	73	P5
Cap de la Hague	71	D4
Cap-de-la-Madeleine	131	F1
Cap de Nouvelle-France	125	S4
Cap de ses Salines	73	P5
Cap des Trois Fourches	73	H9
Cape Agulhas	99	C6
Cape Alexandra	143	P9
Cape Andreas	85	B2
Cape Apostolos Andreas	83	F6
Cape Arid	119	D6
Cape Arnaoutis	83	D6
Cape Arnhem	119	G2
Cape Barren Island	119	J8
Cape Bauld	125	V6
Cape Blanco	129	B2
Cape Borda	119	G7
Cape Breton Island	125	U7
Cape Brett	121	E2
Cape Byron	119	K5
Cape Campbell	121	E5
Cape Canaveral	135	E4
Cape Canaveral	135	E4
Cape Carnot	119	F6
Cape Charles	131	E3
Cape Chidley	125	U4
Cape Christian	125	T2
Cape Churchill	125	N5
Cape Clear	69	C10
Cape Cleare	133	(1)H4
Cape Coast	95	D3
Cape Cod	131	G2
Cape Colville	121	E3
Cape Columbine	99	B6
Cape Comorin	107	C7
Cape Constantine	133	(1)E4
Cape Coral	135	E4
Cape Crawford	119	G3
Cape Croker	119	F2
Cape Dalhousie	133	(1)L1
Cape Direction	119	H2
Cape Disappointment	143	P9
Cape Dominion	125	R3
Cape Dorchester	125	Q3
Cape Dorset	125	R4
Cape Dyer	125	U3
Cape Egmont	121	D4
Cape Eleaia	86	B1
Cape Farewell, Greenland	123	F4
Cape Farewell, New Zealand	121	D5
Cape Fear	135	F3
Cape Finisterre = Cabo Fisterra	73	A2
Cape Flattery, Australia	119	J2
Cape Flattery, United States	129	A1
Cape Forestier	119	J8
Cape Foulwind	121	C5
Cape Fria	99	A3
Cape Girardeau	131	C3
Cape Greko	83	F6
Cape Grenville	119	H2
Cape Grim	119	H8
Cape Harrison	125	V6
Cape Hatteras	135	F2
Cape Henrietta Maria	125	Q5
Cape Horn = Cabo de Hornos	143	H10
Cape Howe	119	K7
Cape Inscription	119	B5
Cape Jaffa	119	G7
Cape Karikari	121	D2
Cape Kellett	125	F2
Cape Kidnappers	121	F4
Cape Leeuwin	119	B6
Cape Lévêque	119	D3
Cape Londonderry	119	E2
Cape Lookout	137	J2
Cape May	131	F3
Cape Melville	119	H2
Cape Mendenhall	133	(1)D4
Cape Mendocino	129	A2
Cape Mercy	125	U4
Cape Meredith	143	J9
Cape Naturaliste	119	B6
Capenda-Camulemba	99	B1
Cape Negrais	109	A3
Cape Nelson	119	H7
Cape Newenham	133	(1)E4
Cape of Good Hope	99	B6
Cape Palliser	121	E5
Cape Palmas	95	C4
Cape Parry	125	G2
Cape Providence	121	A8
Cape Race	123	G5
Cape Ray	125	V7
Cape Reinga	121	D2
Cape Romanzof	133	(1)D3
Cape Runaway	121	G3
Cape Sable	125	T8
Cape St. Elias	133	(1)J4
Cape St. Francis	99	C6
Cape San Agustin	109	H5
Cape San Blas	135	D4
Cape Saunders	121	C7
Cape Scott	119	E1
Cape Stephens	121	D5
Cape Terawhiti	121	E5
Cape Three Points	95	D4
Cape Town	99	B6
Cape Turnagain	121	F5
Cape Verde	95	(1)B2
Cape Wessel	119	G2
Cape Wrangell	105	W6
Cape Wrath	69	G3
Cape York	119	H2
Cape York Peninsula	119	H2
Cap Figalo	73	J9
Cap Fréhel	71	C5
Cap Gris-Nez	59	D4
Cap-Haïtien	137	K5
Cap Juby	91	C3
Cap Lopez	95	F5
Cap Negro	73	E9
Capo Carbonara	77	D10
Capo Colonna	77	M9
Capo Gallo	77	H10
Capo Granitola	77	G11
Capo Murro di Porco	77	K11
Capo Palinuro	77	J8
Capo Passero	77	K12
Capo Santa Maria di Leuca	77	N9
Capo San Vito	77	G10
Capo Spartivento	77	C10
Capo Vaticano	77	K10
Capraia	77	D5
Cap Rhir	91	C2
Capri	77	J8
Capricorn Group	119	K4
Cap Rosa	77	C11
Cap Serrat	77	D11
Cap Spartel	73	E9
Cap Timiris	91	B5
Capua	77	J7
Cap Verga	95	B2
Cap Vert	95	A2
Caquetá	141	C4
Caracal	79	M5
Caracarai	141	E3
Caracas	141	D1
Caransebeş	79	K4
Carauari	141	D4
Caravaca de la Cruz	73	J6
Caravelas	141	K7
Carazinho	143	L4
Carballiño	73	B2
Carballo	73	B1
Carbondale, Ill., United States	135	D2
Carbondale, Pa., United States	135	F1
Carboneras	73	J7
Carbónia	77	C9
Carcar	109	G4
Carcassonne	71	H10
Cardiff	69	J10
Cardigan Bay	69	H9
Cardston	129	D1
Carei	79	K2
Carentan	71	D4
Cariacica	143	N3
Cariati	77	L9
Caribbean Sea	137	J6
Carlet	73	K5
Carleton Place	131	E1
Carlisle, United Kingdom	69	K7
Carlisle, United States	131	E2
Carlow	69	F9
Carlsbad	133	F2
Carlyle	129	F1
Carmacks	125	C4
Carmagnola	75	C6
Carmarthen	69	H10
Carmarthen Bay	69	G10
Carmaux	71	H9
Carmen	137	F5
Carmona	73	E7
Carnarvon, Australia	119	B4
Carnarvon, South Africa	99	C6
Car Nicobar	107	F7
Carnot	97	B2
Carnsore Point	69	F9
Carolina	141	H5
Carolina Beach	135	F3
Caroline Island	117	L6
Caroline Islands	117	E5
Carpathian Mountains	65	J8
Carpatii Meridionali	79	K4
Carpentras	71	L9
Carpi	75	F6
Carrabelle	135	E4
Carrara	75	F6
Carrickfergus	69	G7
Carrick-on-Suir	69	E9
Carrington	129	G1
Carrizozo	133	E2
Carroll	131	B2
Carrollton, Ky., United States	131	D3
Carrollton, Mo., United States	135	C1
Çarşamba	83	G3
Carson City	129	C3
Cartagena, Colombia	141	B1
Cartagena, Spain	73	K7
Carthage	135	C3
Cartwright	125	V6
Caruaru	141	K5
Carúpano	141	E1
Casablanca	91	D2
Casa Grande	133	D2
Casale Monferrato	75	D5
Casalmaggiore	75	F6
Casarano	77	N9
Cascade, Id., United States	129	C2
Cascade, Mont., United States	129	C1
Cascade Range	129	B2
Cascade Reservoir	129	C2
Cascais	73	A6
Cascavel	143	L3
Caserta	77	J7
Cashel	99	E3
Casino	119	K5
Ácsma	75	M5
Caspe	73	K3
Casper	129	E2
Caspian Sea	57	J3
Cassiar	125	F5
Cassino	77	H7
Castanhal	141	H4
Castelbuono	77	J11
Castel di Sangro	77	J7
Castellamare del Golio	77	G10
Castellane	75	B7
Castellaneta	77	L8
Castelli	143	J4
Castelló de la Plana	73	K5
Castelnaudary	71	G10
Castelo Branco	73	C5
Castelsarrasin	71	G10
Castelvetrano	77	G11

Legend:

- ⊠ Continent name
- Ⓐ Country name
- ▣ State or province name
- ■ Country capital
- ▢ State or province capital
- ● Settlement
- ▲ Mountain, volcano, peak
- ▰▰ Mountain range
- Physical region or feature
- River, canal
- Lake, salt lake
- ◣ Gulf, strait, bay
- ▭ Sea, ocean
- ⊠ Cape, point
- Island or island group, rocky or coral reef
- Place of interest
- Historical or cultural region

⊠	Continent name	▲	Mountain, volcano, peak
▲	Country name	▬	Mountain range
▣	State or province name	⬡	Physical region or feature
■	Country capital	∕	River, canal
□	State or province capital	∕	Lake, salt lake
●	Settlement	▬	Gulf, strait, bay

▬	Sea, ocean
⬡	Cape, point
🗺	Island or island group, rocky or coral reef
✳	Place of interest
⬡	Historical or cultural region

Name	Page	Grid
Ch'ew Bahir	97	F3
Cheyenne	129	F2
Cheyenne	129	F2
Cheyenne Wells	133	F1
Cheyne Bay	119	C6
Chhatarpur	107	C4
Chhindwara	107	C4
Chhuka	107	E3
Chia-i	111	G6
Chiang Khan	109	C3
Chiang-Mai	109	B3
Chiang Rai	109	B3
Chiavari	75	E6
Chiavenna	75	E4
Chiba	113	L6
Chibougamau	125	S6
Chibuto	99	E4
Chicago	131	C2
Chicapa	97	C5
Chichagof Island	133	(1)K4
Chichaoua	91	D2
Chichester	59	B4
Chickasha	135	B3
Chiclana de la Frontera	73	D8
Chiclayo	141	B5
Chico	143	H8
Chicopee	131	F2
Chicoutimi	125	S7
Chicualacuala	99	E4
Chiemsee	75	H3
Chieri	75	C5
Chiese	75	F5
Chieti	77	J6
Chifeng	111	F2
Chiganak	103	N8
Chigubo	99	E4
Chihuahua	133	E3
Chiili	103	M9
Chikwa	99	E2
Chilas	107	B1
Childress	133	F2
Chile	139	D8
Chile Chico	143	G8
Chilik	103	P9
Chilika Lake	107	D4
Chillán	143	G6
Chillicothe, Mo., United States	131	B3
Chillicothe, Oh., United States	131	D3
Chilliwack	129	B1
Chiloquin	129	B2
Chilpancingo	137	E5
Chi-lung	111	G5
Chimbay	103	K9
Chimborazo	141	B4
Chimbote	141	B5
Chimchememel'	105	V3
Chimec	79	J1
Chimoio	99	E3
China	101	N6
Chincha Alta	141	B6
Chincilla de Monte-Aragón	73	J6
Chinde	99	F3
Chin do	113	C6
Chindwin	109	A2
Chingola	99	D2
Chinhoyi	99	E3
Chiniot	107	B2
Chinju	113	E6
Chinmen	109	F2
Chinnur	107	C5
Chióggia	75	H5
Chios	81	H6
Chios	81	J6
Chipata	99	E2
Chippewa Falls	131	B2
Chipping Norton	59	A3
Chirchik	103	M9
Chirikof Island	133	(1)F5
Chiromo	99	F3
Chirpan	81	H2
Chirripo	137	H7
Chişinău	79	R2
Chişineu-Criş	79	J3
Chita	105	J6
Chitato	97	C5
Chitembo	99	B2
Chitipa	97	E5
Chitradurga	107	C6
Chitral	107	B1
Chitré	137	H7
Chittagong	107	F4
Chittaurgarh	107	B4
Chittoor	107	C6
Chitungwiza	99	E3
Chiume	99	C3
Chivasso	75	C5
Chizha	63	H1
Chodov	67	H6
Choiseul	117	F6
Chojnice	65	G4
Chokurdakh	105	R2
Chókwé	99	E4
Cholet	71	E6
Choma	99	D3
Chomutov	65	C7
Chona	105	H4
Chonan	113	D5
Chone	141	A4
Ch'ŏngjin	113	E3
Ch'ŏngju	113	D6
Chŏngp'yŏng	113	D4
Chongqing	101	P7
Chŏngŭp	113	D6
Ch'ŏnju	113	D5
Chonogol	111	F1
Chon Thanh	109	D4
Chop	65	M9
Chornobyl'	63	F4
Chornomors'ke	63	F5
Ch'osan	113	C3
Chōshi	113	L6
Choszczno	65	E4
Choteau	129	D1
Chott el Hodna	91	F1
Chott el Jerid	91	G2
Chott Melrhir	91	G2
Choybalsan	105	J7
Choyr	111	D1
Chre	71	H9
Christchurch	121	D6
Christiansburg	131	D3
Christiansø	65	E2
Christmas Island	115	(1)D5
Chrudim	65	E8
Chrysi	81	H10
Chu	103	N9
Chubut	143	H7
Chugach Mountains	125	B4
Chūgoku-sanchi	111	J3
Chugwater	129	F2
Chukchi Sea	133	(1)C2
Chukotskiy Khrebet	105	W3
Chukotskiy Poluostrov	105	Z3
Chula Vista	133	C2
Chulucanas	141	A5
Chulym	103	R6
Chum	63	M1
Chumikan	105	P6
Chum Phae	109	C3
Chumphon	109	B4
Ch'unch'ŏn	113	D5
Chunchura	107	E4
Chundzha	103	P9
Ch'ungju	113	D5
Chur	75	E4
Churapcha	105	N4
Churchill	125	N5
Churchill, Man., Canada	125	M5
Churchill, Nfld., Canada	125	U6
Churchill Falls	125	U6
Churchill Peak	125	F5
Churu	107	B3
Chuska Mountains	133	E1
Chusovoy	63	L3
Chute des Passes	125	S7
Chuuk	117	F5
Chuvashiya	63	J3
Chuxiong	109	C2
Chuya	105	J5
Ciadîr-Lunga	79	R3
Cide	83	E3
Ciechanów	65	K5
Ciego de Avila	137	J4
Cienfuegos	137	H4
Cieza	73	J6
Cihanbeyli	83	E4
Cijulang	115	(1)D4
Cilacap	115	(1)D4
Cili	111	E5
Cimarron	135	B2
Cimişlia	79	R3
Cîmpeni	65	N11
Cinca	73	L3
Cincinnati	131	D3
Çine	81	L7
Ciney	59	H4
Cintalapa	137	F5
Circle, Ak., United States	133	(1)J2
Circle, Mont., United States	129	E1
Circleville	131	D3
Cirebon	115	(1)D4
Cirò Marina	77	M9
Cisco	135	B3
Cistierna	73	E2
Citronelle	135	D3
Cittadella	75	G5
Città di Castello	75	H7
Ciucea	79	K3
Ciudad Acuña	133	F3
Ciudad Bolívar	141	E2
Ciudad Camargo	133	E3
Ciudad del Carmen	137	F5
Ciudad del Este	143	L4
Ciudad Delicias	133	E3
Ciudad del Maíz	133	G4
Ciudad de México	137	E5
Ciudad de Valles	137	E4
Ciudad Guayana	141	E2
Ciudad Juárez	133	E2
Ciudad Madero	133	G4
Ciudad Mante	137	E4
Ciudad Obregón	137	C3
Ciudad Real	73	G6
Ciudad-Rodrigo	73	D4
Ciudad Valles	133	G4
Ciudad Victoria	127	G7
Ciutadella	73	P4
Cividale del Friuli	75	J4
Cívita Castellana	77	G6
Civitanova Marche	77	H5
Civitavécchia	77	F6
Cizre	83	K5
Clacton-on-Sea	59	D3
Clair Engle Lake	129	B2
Clairview	119	J4
Clamecy	71	J6
Clare Island	69	B8
Clarence	121	D6
Clarence Strait	119	E2
Clarendon	133	F2
Clarkdale	133	D2
Clarksburg	135	E2
Clarksdale	135	C3
Clarks Junction	121	C7
Clarkston	129	C1
Clarksville, Ark., United States	135	C2
Clarksville, Tenn., United States	135	D2
Claro	141	G7
Clausthal-Zellerfeld	67	F5
Claveria	109	G3
Clayton	133	F1
Clear Island	69	C10
Clear Lake	131	B2
Clear Lake Reservoir	129	B2
Clearwater	129	C1
Clearwater	135	E4
Clearwater Mountains	129	C1
Cleburne	135	B3
Clermont, Australia	119	J4
Clermont, France	59	E5
Clermont-Ferrand	71	J8
Cles	75	F4
Cleveland, Oh., United States	131	D2
Cleveland, Tenn., United States	135	E2
Cleveland, Tex., United States	135	B3
Clifden	121	A7
Clifton	133	E2
Climax	129	E1
Clines Corners	133	E2
Clinton, Canada	125	G6
Clinton, New Zealand	121	B8
Clinton, Ark., United States	131	B3
Clinton, Ia., United States	127	H3
Clinton, Miss., United States	135	C3
Clinton, Mo., United States	131	B3
Clinton, N.C., United States	135	F3
Clinton, Okla., United States	135	B2
Clipperton Island	137	C6
Clonmel	69	E9
Cloppenburg	67	D4
Cloquet	131	B1
Cloud Peak	129	E2
Clovis, Calif., United States	129	C3
Clovis, N.Mex., United States	133	F2
Cluj-Napoca	79	L3
Cluny	71	K7
Cluses	75	B4
Clyde	69	H6
Clyde River	125	T2
Coaldale	129	C3
Coalville	129	C2
Coari	141	E4
Coast Mountains	125	E5
Coast Range	129	B3
Coatbridge	69	J6
Coats Island	125	Q4
Coatzacoalcos	137	F5
Cobalt	125	R7
Cobán	137	F5
Cobija	141	D6
Cobourg	127	L3
Cobourg Peninsula	119	F2
Cóbuè	99	E2
Coburg	67	F6
Cochabamba	141	D7
Cochin = Kochi	107	C7
Cochrane	131	D1
Cockburn Town	135	G5
Coco	137	H6
Cocoa	135	E4
Cocobeach	95	F4
Coco Channel	109	A4
Coco Island	109	A4
Codajás	141	E4
Codigoro	75	H6
Cod Island	125	U5
Codlea	79	N4
Codó	141	J4
Codogno	75	E5
Codroipo	75	J5
Cody	129	E2
Coesfeld	67	C5
Coëtivy Island	89	J6
Coeur d'Alene	129	C1
Coeur d'Alene Lake	129	C1
Coevorden	59	J2
Coffs Harbour	119	K6
Cofrents	73	J5
Cognac	71	E8
Cogne	75	C5
Coiba	139	C3
Coihaique	143	G8
Coimbatore	107	C6
Coimbra	73	B4

Symbol legend:

- ✖ Continent name
- ▲ Country name
- ◼ State or province name
- ◼ Country capital
- ◻ State or province capital
- ◼ Settlement
- ▲ Mountain, volcano, peak
- ◣ Mountain range
- ⬙ Physical region or feature
- ◿ River, canal
- ◪ Lake, salt lake
- ◤ Gulf, strait, bay
- ◪ Sea, ocean
- ▷ Cape, point
- ▦ Island or island group, rocky or coral reef
- ✳ Place of interest
- ◨ Historical or cultural region

Name	Page	Grid
Colchester	59	C3
Colebrook	131	F1
Coleman	135	B3
Coleraine	69	F6
Colesberg	99	D6
Colfax	129	C1
Colibaşi	79	M5
Colico	75	E4
Coll	69	F5
Collado-Villalba	73	F4
College Station	135	B3
Collier Bay	119	D3
Collingwood	131	E2
Collins	135	D3
Colmar	75	C2
Colmenar Viejo	73	G4
Colombia	141	C3
Colombo	107	C7
Colonia Las Heras	143	H8
Colonial Heights	131	E3
Colonsay	69	F5
Colorado	129	E3
Colorado, Colo., United States	133	E1
Colorado, Tex., United States	133	G2
Colorado Plateau	133	D1
Colorado Springs	129	F3
Columbia	129	C1
Columbia, La., United States	135	C3
Columbia, Md., United States	135	F2
Columbia, Mo., United States	135	C2
Columbia, S.C., United States	135	E3
Columbia, Tenn., United States	135	D2
Columbia Mountains	125	G6
Columbus, Ga., United States	135	E3
Columbus, Ind., United States	135	D2
Columbus, Miss., United States	135	D3
Columbus, Mont., United States	129	E1
Columbus, Nebr., United States	129	G2
Columbus, N.Mex., United States	133	E2
Columbus, Oh., United States	135	E1
Columbus, Tex., United States	135	B4
Colville	133	(1)G2
Colville Lake	133	(1)M2
Comacchio	75	H6
Comăneşti	79	P3
Comarnic	79	N4
Combarbalá	143	G5
Combeaufontaine	71	M6
Comilla	109	A2
Comino = Kemmuna	77	J12
Commentry	71	H7
Commercy	59	H6
Como	75	E5
Comoé	95	D3
Comondú	127	D6
Comoros	99	G2
Compiègne	59	E5
Comrat	79	R3
Comstock	133	F3
Conakry	95	B3
Concarneau	71	B6
Conceição do Araguaia	141	H5
Concepción, Bolivia	141	E7
Concepción, Chile	143	G6
Conches-en-Ouche	59	C6
Conchos	137	C3
Concord, Calif., United States	133	B1
Concord, N.H., United States	131	F2
Concord, N.C., United States	135	E2
Concordia, Argentina	143	K5
Concordia, United States	135	B2
Condé-sur-Noireau	59	B6
Condobolin	119	J6
Condom	71	F10
Conegliano	75	H5
Conggar	107	F3
Congo	89	E6
Congo	95	G5
Connecticut	131	F2

Name	Page	Grid
Connemara	69	C8
Conrad	129	D1
Côn Son	109	D5
Constanţa	83	C1
Constantina	73	E7
Constantine	91	G1
Consul	129	E1
Contact	129	D2
Contamana	141	B5
Contwoyto Lake	125	J3
Convay	135	F3
Conway	135	C2
Conwy	69	J8
Conwy Bay	69	H8
Coober Pedy	119	F5
Cookeville	131	C3
Cook Inlet	133	(1)A2
Cook Islands	117	K7
Cook Strait	121	E5
Cooktown	119	J3
Coolabah	119	J6
Coolgardie	119	D6
Cooma	119	J7
Coonabarabran	119	J6
Coon Rapids	131	B1
Coopers Town	135	F4
Coorabie	119	F6
Coos Bay	129	B2
Cootamundra	119	J6
Copenhagen = København	61	G9
Copiapó	143	G4
Copper Harbor	131	C1
Côqen	107	E2
Coquille	129	B2
Coquimbo	143	G4
Corabia	79	M6
Coral	127	K1
Coral Sea	119	K2
Coral Sea Islands Territory	117	F7
Coral Sea Islands Territory	119	J2
Coral Springs	135	E4
Corantijn	141	F3
Corbeil-Essonnes	71	H5
Corbigny	71	J6
Corby	59	B2
Cordele	135	E3
Cordillera Cantábrica	73	D2
Cordillera Central	139	E5
Cordillera del Condor	141	B5
Cordillera de Mérida	139	D3
Cordillera de Oliva	143	G4
Cordillera Isabella	137	G5
Cordillera Occidental	139	E5
Cordillera Oriental	139	D5
Cordillera Penibética	73	F8
Cordillera Vilcabamba	141	C6
Córdoba, Argentina	143	J5
Córdoba, Spain	73	F7
Corfu = Kerkyra	81	B5
Coria	73	D5
Corigliano	77	L9
Corinth	135	D3
Corinto	141	H7
Cork	69	D10
Cork Harbour	69	D10
Corleone	77	H11
Çorlu	81	K3
Corn Islands	139	C2
Cornwall	127	M2
Cornwallis Island	125	M2
Coro	141	D1
Corocoro	141	D7
Coromandel	121	E3
Coromandel Coast	107	D6
Coromandel Peninsula	121	E3
Coron	109	G4
Coronation Gulf	125	J3
Coronel Oviedo	143	K4
Coronel Pringles	143	J6
Coronel Suárez	143	J6
Corpus Christi	135	B4

Name	Page	Grid
Corrientes	143	K4
Corrigan	135	C3
Corriverton	141	F2
Corse	77	D6
Corsica = Corse	77	D6
Corsicana	135	B3
Corte	77	D6
Cortegana	73	D7
Cortez	133	E1
Cortina d'Ampezzo	75	H4
Cortland	131	E2
Cortona	77	F5
Coruche	73	B6
Çorum	83	F3
Corumbá	141	F7
Corvallis	129	B2
Corvo	91	(1)A2
Cosenza	77	L9
Cosmoledo Group	99	(2)A2
Cosne-sur-Loire	71	H6
Cossato	75	D5
Costa Blanca	73	K7
Costa Brava	73	P3
Costa del Sol	73	F8
Costa de Mosquitos	137	H6
Costa Dorada	73	M4
Costa de Sol	73	A6
Costa Rica	137	G7
Costa Smeralda	77	D7
Costa Verde	73	D1
Costeşti	79	M5
Coswig	67	H5
Cotabato	109	G5
Cotonou	95	E3
Cottage Grove	129	B2
Cottbus	65	D6
Cotulla	135	B4
Couhe	71	F7
Coulommiers	59	F6
Council Bluffs	129	F2
Courland Lagoon	65	L2
Courtacon	59	F6
Courtenay	127	B2
Coushatta	135	C3
Coutances	71	D4
Couvin	59	G4
Covasna	79	P4
Coventry	69	L9
Covilhã	73	C4
Covington, Ga., United States	135	E3
Covington, Ky., United States	135	E2
Covington, Va., United States	131	D3
Cowell	119	G6
Cowes	59	A4
Cowra	119	J6
Cox's Bazar	107	F4
Cradock	99	D6
Craig	129	E2
Crailsheim	67	F7
Craiova	79	L5
Cranbrook, Australia	119	C6
Cranbrook, United States	127	C2
Crater Lake	129	B2
Crato	141	K5
Crawford	129	F2
Crawfordsville	131	C2
Crawley	59	B3
Cree Lake	125	K5
Creil	59	E5
Crema	75	E5
Cremona	75	F5
Crépy-en-Valois	59	E5
Cres	75	K6
Cres	75	K6
Crescent City	129	B2
Crest	71	L9
Creston	131	B2
Crestview	127	J5
Crestview	137	G2
Crete = Kriti	81	H10
Créteil	59	E6

Name	Page	Grid
Creuse	71	G7
Crevillent	73	K6
Crewe	69	K8
Crianlarich	69	H5
Criciúma	143	M4
Cristalina	141	H7
Cristóbal Colón	123	J8
Crna Gora	79	F7
Croatia	79	C4
Crockett	135	B3
Croker Island	119	F2
Cromer	69	P9
Cromwell	121	B7
Crooked Island	137	K4
Crookston	127	G2
Cross City	135	E3
Cross Lake	125	M6
Crossville	131	C3
Crotone	77	M9
Crowley	135	C3
Crownest Pass	127	D2
Crown Point	131	C2
Cruz Alta	143	L4
Cruz del Eje	143	J5
Cruzeiro do Sul	141	C5
Crvenka	79	G4
Crystal City	135	B4
Crystal Falls	131	C1
Crystal River	135	E4
Crystal Springs	135	C3
Csorna	79	E2
Csurgó	75	N4
Cuamba	99	F2
Cuando	99	C3
Cuangar	99	B3
Cuango	97	B5
Cuanza	97	B5
Cuatro Ciénegas	133	F3
Cuauhtémoc	133	E3
Cuba	129	E3
Cuba	137	H4
Cubal	97	A6
Cubali	99	A2
Cubango	99	B3
Çubuk	81	R4
Cucuí	141	D3
Cúcuta	141	C2
Cuddalore	107	C6
Cuddapah	107	C6
Cuemba	99	B2
Cuenca, Ecuador	141	B4
Cuenca, Spain	73	H4
Cuernavaca	137	E5
Cuero	135	B4
Cuiabá	141	F7
Cuilo	97	B5
Cuito	99	B3
Cuito Cuanavale	99	B3
Culbertson	129	E1
Culfa	83	L4
Culiacán	137	C4
Cullera	73	K5
Cullman	135	D3
Culpepper	141	(1)A1
Culuene	141	G6
Culverden	121	D6
Cumaná	141	E1
Cumberland	131	E3
Cumberland Peninsula	125	T3
Cumberland Sound	125	T3
Cummings	129	B3
Cumpas	133	E3
Çumra	81	Q7
Cunderdin	119	C6
Cunene	99	A3
Cuneo	75	C6
Cunnamulla	119	J5
Čuprija	79	J6
Cure	71	J6
Curicó	143	G5
Curitiba	143	M4

Name	Page	Ref.
Currais Novos	141	K5
Curral Velho	95	(1)B1
Currie	119	H7
Curtea de Argeş	79	M4
Curtici	79	J3
Curtis Island	119	K4
Curuá	141	G5
Curup	115	(1)C3
Curuzú Cuatiá	143	K4
Curvelo	141	J7
Cusco	141	C6
Cuthbert	135	E3
Cutro	77	L9
Cuttack	107	E4
Cuvier Island	121	E3
Cuxhaven	67	D3
Cuya	141	C7
Cuyuni	141	F2
Cwmbran	69	J10
Cyclades = Kyklades	81	G7
Cypress Hills	127	D2
Cyprus	83	E6
Czarnków	65	F5
Czech Republic	65	C8
Częstochowa	65	J7
Człuchów	65	G4

D

Name	Page	Ref.
Da'an	111	G1
Daaquam	131	F1
Dab'a	86	D5
Dabas	79	G2
Dabat	93	G5
Dabola	95	B2
Dąbrowa Górnicza	65	J7
Dăbuleni	79	M6
Dachau	75	G2
Daet	109	G4
Dagana	91	B5
Dagestan	83	M2
Dagupan	109	G3
Da Hinggan Ling	111	G1
Dahlak Archipelago	93	H4
Dahlonega	135	E3
Dahn	59	K5
Dahod	107	B4
Dahongliutan	85	L2
Dahūk	83	K5
Daimiel	73	G5
Dai Xian	111	E3
Dakar	95	A2
Dakoro	95	F2
Dakota City	129	G2
Dakovica	79	H7
Dakovo	79	F4
Dalai Nur	111	F2
Dalälven	61	H6
Dalaman	83	C5
Dalandzadgad	111	C2
Dalap-Uliga-Darrit	117	H5
Da Lat	109	D4
Dalbandin	85	H4
Dalby	119	K5
Dalgān	85	G4
Dalhart	133	F1
Dalhousie	107	C2
Dali	109	C1
Dalian	111	G3
Dalizi	113	D3
Dallas	135	B3
Daloa	95	C3
Dalry	69	H6
Dāltenganj	107	D4
Dalton	135	E3
Dalvík	61	(1)D2
Daly Waters	119	F3
Daman	107	B4
Damanhûr	93	F1
Damar	115	(2)C4

Name	Page	Ref.
Damara	95	H3
Damasak	95	G2
Damascus = Dimashq	86	D3
Damaturu	95	G2
Damoh	107	C4
Damqawt	85	F6
Danau Poso	115	(2)A3
Danau Toba	115	(1)B2
Danau Towuti	115	(2)B3
Danba	111	C4
Dandeldhura	107	D3
Dandong	113	C3
Da Nĕng	109	D3
Dangara	85	J2
Danger Islands	117	K7
Danghe Nanshan	111	B3
Daniel	129	D1
Danilov	63	H3
Dank	87	G5
Dankov	63	G4
Dannenberg	67	G3
Dannevirke	121	F5
Dansville	131	E2
Danube	57	F3
Danville, Ill., United States	135	D1
Danville, Ky., United States	135	E2
Danville, Va., United States	135	F2
Dan Xian	109	D3
Dao Phu Quôc	109	C4
Dapa	109	H5
Dapaong	95	E2
Da Qaidam	111	B3
Daqing	105	M7
Dar'ā	86	D4
Dārāb	87	F2
Darabani	79	P1
Daraj	93	B1
Darazo	95	G2
Darbhanga	107	E3
Dardanelles = Çanakkale Boğazı	81	J4
Darende	83	G4
Dar es Salaam	97	F5
Darfo	75	F5
Dargaville	121	D2
Darham	105	H7
Darjeeling	107	E3
Darling	119	H6
Darlington	69	L7
Darłowo	61	J9
Dărmănești	79	P3
Dar Mazār	87	G2
Darmstadt	67	D7
Darnah	93	D1
Darnley Bay	125	G3
Daroca	73	J3
Darß	67	H2
Dartmouth	125	U8
Daru	115	(2)F4
Daruba	115	(2)C2
Daruvar	75	N5
Darvaza	103	K9
Darwin	119	F2
Daryācheh-ye Bakhtegan	87	E2
Daryācheh-ye Orūmīyeh	83	L5
Daryācheh-ye Tashk	87	E2
Dārzīn	87	H2
Dashkhovuz	103	K9
Dasht-e Kavir	85	F3
Dasht-e Lut	87	H1
Datça	81	K8
Datça	83	B5
Date	113	L2
Datong	111	C3
Datong	111	E2
Daugava	63	E3
Daugavpils	63	E3
Daun	59	J4
Dauphin	125	M6
Dausa	107	C3
Dāvāci	83	N3

Name	Page	Ref.
Davangere	107	C6
Davao	109	H5
Davenport	131	B2
Daventry	59	A2
David	137	H7
Davis Sea	144	(2)Q3
Davis Strait	125	V3
Davlekanovo	103	J7
Davos	75	E4
Dawa	111	G2
Dawqah	85	F6
Dawson	133	(1)K3
Dawson Creek, B.C., Canada	125	G5
Dawson Creek, Y.T., Canada	125	D4
Dawu	111	C4
Dax	71	D10
Daxian	111	D4
Dayong	111	E5
Dayr az Zawr	83	J6
Dayton, Oh., United States	131	D3
Dayton, Tenn., United States	131	C3
Dayton, Tex., United States	135	C4
Dayton, Wash., United States	129	C1
Daytona Beach	135	E4
De Aar	99	C6
Dead Sea	86	C5
Deakin	119	E6
Deal	59	D3
De'an	111	F5
Deán Funes	143	J5
Dease Lake	133	(1)M4
Dease Strait	125	J3
Death Valley	129	C3
Deba Habe	95	G2
Debar	81	C3
Dębica	65	L7
Debin	105	S4
Dęblin	65	L6
Dębno	65	D5
Debre Birhan	97	F2
Debrecen	79	J2
Debre Markos	93	G5
Debre Tabor	93	G5
Decatur, Al., United States	131	C4
Decatur, Ill., United States	131	C3
Decazeville	71	H9
Deccan	107	C5
Děčín	65	D7
Decize	71	J7
Decorah	131	B2
Dedoplis	83	M3
Dédougou	95	D2
Dedza	99	E2
Dee, Scot., United Kingdom	69	K4
Dee, Wales, United Kingdom	69	J9
Deering	133	(1)E2
Deer Lake	125	V7
Deer Lodge	129	D1
Deer Park	129	C1
De Funiak Springs	135	D3
Degeh Bur	97	G2
Deggendorf	75	J2
Dehaj	87	F1
Dehalak Desët	85	D6
Deh Bid	87	E1
Deh-Dasht	87	D1
Dehkūyeh	87	F3
Dehlonān	85	E3
Dehra	85	L3
Dehra Dun	107	C2
Dehri	107	D4
Deh Shū	85	H3
Deinze	59	F4
Dej	79	L2
De Kalb	135	C3
De-Kastri	105	Q6
Dekese	97	C4
Delano	133	C1
Delaware	131	D2
Delaware	135	F2
Delbrück	67	D5

Name	Page	Ref.
Delémont	75	C3
Delfoi	81	E6
Delft	59	G2
Delfzijl	59	J1
Delgo	93	F3
Delhi, India	107	C3
Delhi, United States	131	F2
Delitzsch	67	H5
Dellys	73	P8
Delmenhorst	67	D3
Delnice	75	K5
Delray Beach	135	E4
Del Rio	133	F3
Delta, Colo., United States	129	E3
Delta, Ut., United States	129	D3
Delta del Orinoco	141	E2
Delta Junction	133	(1)H3
Deming	133	E2
Demirci	81	L5
Demmin	67	J3
Democratic Republic of Congo	97	C4
Demopolis	135	D3
Demyanka	63	P3
Dem'yanskoye	63	N3
Denain	59	F4
Denau	85	J2
Denbigh	131	E1
Den Burg	59	G1
Dender	59	F4
Dendi	97	F2
Denham	119	B5
Den Helder	59	G2
Dénia	73	L6
Deniliquin	119	H7
Denio	129	C2
Denison, Ia., United States	131	A2
Denison, Tex., United States	135	B3
Denizli	83	C5
Denmark	57	E2
Denmark	119	C6
Denmark Strait	123	D3
Denpasar	115	(1)E4
Denton	133	G2
D'Entrecasteaux Islands	119	K1
Denver	129	F3
Deogarh, India	107	B3
Deogarh, India	107	D4
Deoghar	107	E4
De Panne	59	E3
Depok	115	(1)D4
Dépression du Mourdi	93	D4
Deputatskiy	105	P3
Dêqên	109	B1
Dera Ghazi Khan	85	K3
Dera Ismail Khan	85	K3
Derbent	85	E1
Derby, Australia	119	D3
Derby, United Kingdom	69	L9
De Ridder	135	C3
Dermott	135	C3
Derventa	79	E5
Desē	93	G5
Deseado	143	H8
Deseado	143	H8
Desert Center	133	C2
Des Moines, Ia., United States	127	H3
Des Moines, N.Mex., United States	133	F1
Desna	63	F4
Dessau	67	H5
Desvres	59	D4
Deta	79	J4
Detmold	67	D5
Detroit	127	K3
Detroit Lakes	131	A1
Det Udom	109	C4
Detva	65	J9
Deurne	59	H3
Deva	79	K4
Deventer	59	J2
Devil's Lake	125	L7

Name	Page	Grid
Dumbarton	69	H5
Ďumbier	65	J9
Dumboa	95	G2
Dumfries	69	J6
Dümmer	67	D4
Dumont d'Urville Sea	144	(2)U3
Dumyât	93	F1
Duna = Danube	79	E2
Dunaj = Danube	65	G10
Dunajská Streda	79	E2
Dunakeszi	79	G2
Dunărea = Danube	79	K5
Dunaújváros	79	F3
Dunav = Danube	79	J5
Dunayivtsi	63	E5
Dunbar, Australia	119	H3
Dunbar, United Kingdom	69	K6
Duncan	129	B1
Duncan Passage	109	A4
Dundaga	61	M8
Dundalk	69	F7
Dundalk Bay	69	F8
Dundee, South Africa	99	E5
Dundee, United Kingdom	69	K5
Dunedin	121	C7
Dunfermline	69	J5
Dungarvan	69	E9
Dungeness	59	C4
Dungu	97	D3
Dungun	109	C6
Dunhua	113	E2
Dunhuang	111	A2
Dunkerque	59	E3
Dunkirk	131	E2
Dunkwa	95	D3
Dun Laoghaire	69	F8
Dunnet Head	69	J3
Dunseith	129	G1
Dunsmuir	129	B2
Duque de Caxias	143	N3
Du Quoin	135	D2
Durance	71	L10
Durango, Mexico	133	F4
Durango, Spain	73	H1
Durango, United States	129	E3
Durant	135	B3
Durazno	143	K5
Durban	99	E5
Düren	59	J4
Durgapur	107	E4
Durham, Canada	131	D2
Durham, United Kingdom	69	L7
Durham, United States	135	F2
Duri	115	(1)C2
Durmã	87	B4
Durmanec	79	C3
Durmitor	79	G6
Durrës	81	B3
Dursey	69	B10
Dursunbey	81	L5
D'Urville Island	121	D5
Dushanbe	85	J2
Düsseldorf	59	J3
Duvno	75	N7
Duyun	111	D5
Düzce	81	P4
Dvina	57	H2
Dvinskaya Guba	63	G1
Dwarka	107	A4
Dworshak Reservoir	129	C1
Dyat'kovo	63	F4
Dyersburg	135	D2
Dyje	75	M2
Dzavhan	103	S8
Dzerzhinsk	63	H3
Dzhalinda	105	L6
Dzhambeyty	63	K4
Dzhankoy	63	F5
Dzhardzhan	105	L3
Dzharkurgan	85	J2
Dzhetygara	63	M4
Dzhezkazgan	63	N5
Dzhigudzhak	105	T4
Dzhizak	103	M9
Dzhusaly	63	M5
Działdowo	65	K4
Dzüünbulag	111	F1

E

Name	Page	Grid
Eads	129	F3
Eagle	133	(1)J3
Eagle Lake	129	B2
Eagle Pass	133	F3
East Antarctica	144	(2)P2
East Cape	121	G3
East China Sea	111	H4
East Dereham	59	C2
Easter Island	117	Q8
Eastern Cape	99	D6
Eastern Ghats	107	C6
Easter Ross	69	H4
East Falkland	143	K9
East Grinstead	59	C3
East Kilbride	69	H6
Eastleigh	59	A4
East Liverpool	135	E1
East London	99	D6
Eastmain	125	R6
Eastmain	125	S6
East Point	135	E3
East Retford	59	B1
East St. Louis	131	B3
East Siberian Sea = Vostochno-Sibirskoye More	105	U2
Eatonton	135	E3
Eau Claire	131	B2
Ebbw Vale	69	J10
Ebensee	75	J3
Eberbach	67	D7
Ebersbach	65	D6
Ebersberg	75	G2
Eberswalde	67	J4
Ebinur Hu	103	Q9
Éboli	77	K8
Ebolowa	95	G4
Ebro	73	K3
Eceabat	81	J4
Ech Chélif	91	F1
Echinos	81	G3
Echo Bay	125	H3
Écija	73	E7
Eckernförde	67	E2
Ecuador	141	B4
Ed	93	H5
Edam	59	H2
Eday	69	K2
Ed Da'ein	93	E5
Ed Damazin	93	F5
Ed Debba	93	F4
Ed Dueim	93	F5
Ede, Netherlands	59	H2
Ede, Nigeria	95	E3
Edéa	95	G4
Edelény	65	K9
Eden, Australia	119	J7
Eden, United States	133	G2
Edendale	121	B8
Eder	67	D5
Edersee	67	E5
Edessa	81	E4
Edgecumbe	121	F3
Edinburgh	69	J6
Edineţ	79	Q1
Edirne	81	J3
Edmonds	129	B1
Edmonton	125	J6
Edmundson	127	N2
Edmundston	131	G1
Edolo	75	F4
Edremit	81	J5
Edremit Körfezi	81	H5
Edwards	133	C2
Edwards Plateau	133	F2
Eemshaven	59	J1
Éfaté	117	G7
Eferding	65	D9
Effingham	135	D2
Eganville	131	E1
Eger	67	G6
Eger	79	H2
Egersund	61	D7
Eggenfelden	75	H2
Egilsstaðir	61	(1)F2
Eğridir	81	N7
Eğridir Gölü	81	N6
Egvekinot	105	Y3
Egypt	93	E2
Ehingen	75	E2
Eibar	73	H1
Eichstätt	75	G2
Eider	67	D2
Eidsvold	119	K5
Eidsvoll	61	F6
Eifel	59	J4
Eigg	69	F5
Eight Degree Channel	107	B7
Eilenburg	67	H5
Einbeck	67	E5
Eindhoven	59	H3
Eirunepé	141	D5
Eiseb	99	C4
Eisenach	67	F6
Eisenerz	75	K3
Eisenhüttenstadt	65	D5
Eisenstadt	75	M3
Eisleben	67	G5
Eivissa	73	M5
Eivissa	73	M6
Ejea de los Caballeros	73	J2
Ejido Insurgentes	127	D6
Ejin Horo Qi	111	D3
Ejin Qi	111	C2
Ejmiadzin	83	L3
Ekalaka	129	F1
Ekenäs	61	M7
Ekibastuz	103	P7
Ekimchan	105	N6
Ekonda	103	V4
Eksjo	61	H8
Ekwan	125	Q6
El Aaiún	91	C3
Elafonisos	81	E8
El 'Alamein	93	E1
El Amria	73	J9
El 'Arîsh	86	A5
Elat	86	B7
Elazığ	83	H4
El Azraq	86	D5
Elba	77	E6
El Banco	141	C2
Elbasan	81	C3
El Baúl	141	D2
Elbe	67	F3
Elbeuf	59	D5
Elbistan	83	G4
Elblag	65	J3
El Borj	73	E9
Elbow	127	E1
Elbrus	83	K2
El Burgo de Ebro	73	K3
El Burgo de Osma	73	G3
El Cajon	133	C2
El Callao	141	E2
El Campo	135	B4
El Centro	133	C2
El Cerro	141	E7
Elch	73	K6
Elda	73	K6
El'dikan	105	P4
Eldorado	143	L4
El Dorado, Mexico	127	E7
El Dorado, Ark., United States	135	C3
El Dorado, Kans., United States	135	B2
El Dorado, Venezuela	141	E2
Eldoret	97	F3
Elefsína	81	F6
Elektrėnai	65	P3
El Encanto	141	C4
Elephant Butte Reservoir	133	E2
Eleuthera	127	L6
El Fahs	77	D12
El Faiyûm	93	F2
El Fasher	93	E5
El Geneina	93	D5
Elgin, United Kingdom	69	J4
Elgin, Ill., United States	131	C2
Elgin, N.D., United States	129	F1
El'ginskiy	105	Q4
El Gîza	93	F1
El Goléa	91	F2
El Iskandarîya	93	E1
Elista	63	H5
Elizabeth	131	F2
Elizabeth City	135	F2
Elizabethton	135	E2
El Jadida	91	D2
El Jafr	86	D6
El Jafr	86	D6
Ełk	65	M4
Ełk	65	M4
El Kala	77	C12
Elk City	133	G1
El Kef	77	C12
El Kelaâ des Srarhna	91	D2
El Khârga	93	F2
Elkhart, Ind., United States	131	C2
Elkhart, Kans., United States	135	A2
El Khartum	93	F4
El Khartum Bahri	93	F4
Elkhorn	129	G2
Elkhorn	131	C2
Elkhovo	81	J2
Elkins	131	E3
Elko, Canada	129	C1
Elko, United States	129	C2
Elk River	131	B1
El Kuntilla	86	B7
Ellendale	127	G2
Ellensburg	129	B1
Ellesmere Island	123	K1
Ellice Islands	117	H6
Elliot	99	D6
Ellis	125	J8
Ellisras	99	D4
Elliston	119	F6
Ellsworth	131	G2
Ellwangen	75	F2
Elmadağ	81	R5
Elmali	81	M8
El Mansûra	93	F1
El Minya	93	F2
Elmira	131	E2
Elmshorn	67	E3
El Muglad	93	E5
El Nido	109	F4
El Obeid	93	F5
El Odaiya	93	E5
El Oued	91	G2
El Paso	133	E2
El Portal	133	C1
El Potosi	133	F4
El Prat de Llobregat	73	N3
El Puerto de Santa María	73	D8
El Qâhira	93	F1
El Reno	135	B2
El Sahuaro	133	D2
El Salvador	137	F6
Elster	67	H5
Elsterwerda	67	J5
El Sueco	133	E3
El Suweis	93	F2

Legend:

- ✕ Continent name
- Ⓐ Country name
- ⓐ State or province name
- ■ Country capital
- □ State or province capital
- ● Settlement

- ▲ Mountain, volcano, peak
- ▬ Mountain range
- ◫ Physical region or feature
- ⤢ River, canal
- Lake, salt lake
- Gulf, strait, bay

- Sea, ocean
- Cape, point
- Island or island group, rocky or coral reef
- ✳ Place of interest
- Historical or cultural region

Name	Page	Ref.
Eltanin Bay	144	(2)JJ2
El Tarf	77	C12
El Thamad	86	B7
El Tigre	141	E2
El Turbio	143	G9
Eluru	107	D5
Elvas	73	C6
Elverum	61	F6
Elvira	141	C5
El Wak	97	G3
Ely, *United Kingdom*	69	N9
Ely, *United States*	129	D3
Emajõgi	61	P7
Emämrüd	85	F2
Emba	63	L5
Emba	63	L5
Embalse de Alarcon	73	H5
Embalse de Alcántara Uno	73	D5
Embalse de Almendra	73	D3
Embalse de Contreras	73	J5
Embalse de Gabriel y Galán	73	D4
Embalse de Garcia Sola	73	E5
Embalse de Guadalhorce	73	F8
Embalse de Guadalmena	73	G6
Embalse de Guri	141	E2
Embalse de la Serena	73	E6
Embalse de la Sotonera	73	K2
Embalse del Bembézar	73	E6
Embalse del Ebro	73	G1
Embalse del Río Negro	139	F7
Embalse de Negratmn	73	G7
Embalse de Ricobayo	73	E3
Embalse de Santa Teresa	73	E4
Embalse de Yesa	73	J2
Embalse Toekomstig	141	F3
Embarcación	143	J3
Emden	67	C3
Emerald	119	J4
Emi Koussi	93	C4
Emin	103	Q8
Emirdağ	81	P5
Emmeloord	59	H2
Emmen	59	J2
Emmendingen	75	C2
Emmerich	59	J3
Emory Peak	133	F3
Empalme	133	D3
Empangeni	99	E5
Empoli	75	F7
Emporia	135	B2
Empty Quarter = Rub' al Khālī	85	E6
Ems	59	J1
Ems-Jade-Kanal	67	C3
Enafors	63	B2
Encarnación	143	K4
Encs	79	J1
Ende	115	(2)B4
Enderby Island	121	(2)B1
Energetik	63	L4
Enewetak	117	F4
Enez	81	J4
Enfida	77	E12
Engel's	63	J4
Enggano	115	(1)C4
Enghien	59	G4
England	69	L9
English Channel	69	J12
Engozero	61	S4
'En Hazeva	86	C6
Enid	135	B2
Enkhuizen	59	H2
Enköping	61	J7
Enna	77	J11
En Nahud	93	E5
Enngonia	119	J5
Ennis, *Republic of Ireland*	69	D9
Ennis, *United States*	129	D1
Enniscorthy	69	F9
Enniskillen	69	E7
Enns	75	K2
Enns	75	K3
Enschede	59	J2
Ensenada	133	C2
Enshi	111	D4
Entebbe	97	E3
Enterprise	129	C1
Entrevaux	75	B7
Entroncamento	73	B5
Enugu	95	F3
Enurmino	105	Z3
Envira	141	C5
Enz	75	D2
Enza	75	F6
Epanomi	81	E4
Epéna	97	B3
Épernay	71	J4
Épinal	75	B2
Epsom	59	B3
Eqlīd	87	E1
Equatorial Guinea	95	F4
Erbach	67	D7
Erçek	83	K4
Erciş	83	K4
Ercolano	77	J8
Érd	79	F2
Erdek	81	K4
Erdemli	81	S8
Erdenet	105	G7
Erding	75	G2
Erechim	143	L4
Ereğli, *Turkey*	83	D3
Ereğli, *Turkey*	83	F5
Ereikoussa	81	B5
Erenhot	111	E2
Erfurt	67	G6
Ergani	83	H4
Erg Chech	91	D4
Erg du Ténéré	91	H5
Ergel	111	D2
Erg Iguidi	91	D3
Erie	131	D2
Erimo-misaki	113	M3
Eriskay	69	E4
Eritrea	93	G4
Erlangen	67	G7
Ermenek	83	E5
Ermoupoli	81	G7
Erode	107	C6
Er Rachidia	91	E2
Er Renk	97	E1
Errol	131	F2
Er Ruseifa	86	D4
Ersekë	81	C4
Erskine	131	A1
Ertai	103	S8
Ertix	103	R8
Erzgebirge	67	H6
Erzin	103	S7
Erzincan	83	H4
Erzurum	83	J4
Esan-misaki	113	L3
Esashi, *Japan*	113	L3
Esashi, *Japan*	113	M1
Esbjerg	61	E9
Escanaba	131	C1
Escárcega	137	F5
Esch	59	J5
Eschwege	67	F5
Eschweiler	59	J4
Escondido	133	C2
Eséka	95	G4
Eşfahān	85	F3
Eskifjöður	61	(1)G2
Eskilstuna	61	J7
Eskimo Lakes	133	(1)L2
Eskişehir	83	D4
Esla	73	E3
Eslāmābād e Gharb	83	M6
Eslamshahr	85	F2
Esler Dağ	81	M7
Eslö	65	C2
Esmeraldas	141	B3
Esneux	59	H4
Espalion	71	H9
Espanola, *Canada*	131	D1
Espanola, *United States*	129	E3
Espelkamp	67	D4
Esperance	119	D6
Esperance Bay	119	D6
Espinho	73	B4
Espírito Santo	141	J7
Espíritu Santo	117	G7
Esplanada	141	K6
Espoo	61	N6
Espungebera	99	E4
Essaouira	91	D2
Es Semara	91	C3
Essen, *Belgium*	59	G3
Essen, *Germany*	59	K3
Essequibo	141	F2
Esslingen	75	E2
Eştahbānāt	87	F2
Este	75	G5
Estella	73	H2
Estepona	73	E8
Esteros	143	J3
Estevan	127	F2
Estonia	61	M7
Estoril	73	A6
Estrecho de Le Maire	143	H10
Estrecho de Magallanes	143	G9
Estrela	73	C4
Estremoz	73	C6
Estuário do Rio Amazonaz	141	H3
Esztergom	79	F2
Étain	59	H5
Étampes	71	H5
Étang de Berre	71	L10
Étaples	59	D4
Etawah	107	C3
Ethiopia	89	G5
Etolin Strait	133	(1)D3
Etosha Pan	99	B3
Étretat	59	C5
Ettelbruck	67	B7
Ettlingen	67	D8
Eucla	119	E6
Euclid	131	D2
Eufala	135	B2
Eufaula Lake	135	B2
Eugene	129	B2
Eupen	67	B6
Euphrates = Firat	83	H4
Euphrates	85	D3
Eure	59	D6
Eureka, *Calif., United States*	129	B2
Eureka, *Mont., United States*	129	C1
Eureka, *Nev., United States*	133	C1
Eureka, *Ut., United States*	129	D3
Europoort	59	F3
Euskirchen	67	B6
Eutin	67	F2
Eutsuk Lake	125	F6
Evans Strait	125	Q4
Evanston, *Ill., United States*	131	C2
Evanston, *Wyo., United States*	129	D2
Evansville	135	D2
Evaz	87	F3
Everett	129	B1
Everglades City	135	E4
Evergreen	135	D3
Evesham	59	A2
Évora	73	C6
Évreux	59	D5
Evron	71	E5
Evros	81	J3
Evvoia	81	F6
Ewo	95	G5
Exaltación	141	D6
Exe	69	J11
Exeter	69	J11
Exmouth, *Australia*	119	B4
Exmouth, *United Kingdom*	69	J11
Exuma Sound	127	L7
Eyl	97	H2
Eyre Peninsula	119	G2
Ezine	81	J5

F

Name	Page	Ref.
Faadippolu Atoll	107	B8
Fåborg	67	F1
Fabriano	75	H7
Fada	93	D4
Fada Ngourma	95	E2
Faenza	75	G6
Færingehavn = Kangerluarsoruseq	125	W4
Faeroes	57	D1
Făgăraş	79	M4
Fagernes	61	E6
Fagersta	61	H6
Fagurhólsmýri	61	(1)E3
Fahraj	87	H2
Faial	91	(1)B2
Fairbanks	133	(1)H3
Fair Isle	69	L2
Fairlie	121	C7
Fairmont	131	B2
Faisalabad	107	B2
Faith	129	F1
Faizabad	107	D3
Fakfak	115	(2)D3
Fakse	67	H1
Fakse Bugt	61	G9
Faku	111	G2
Falaise	59	B6
Falaise de Tiguidit	91	G5
Falconara Maríttima	75	J7
Falcon Lake	135	B4
Fălești	79	Q2
Falfurrias	135	B4
Falkenberg	61	G8
Falkensee	67	J4
Falkland Islands	143	K9
Falkland Sound	143	J9
Falköping	61	G7
Fallingbostel	67	E4
Fallon	129	C3
Fall River	131	F2
Falls City	127	G3
Falmouth, *United Kingdom*	69	G11
Falmouth, *United States*	131	F2
Falster	67	H2
Fălticeni	79	P2
Falun	61	H6
Famagusta = Ammochostos	86	A1
Fanchang	111	F4
Fandriana	99	H4
Fangzheng	111	H1
Fannūj	85	G4
Fanø	67	D1
Fano	75	J7
Fanø Bugt	67	D1
Faradje	97	D3
Farafangana	99	H4
Farāh	85	H3
Farah Rud	85	H3
Faranah	95	B2
Fareham	59	A4
Farewell Spit	121	D5
Fargo	127	G2
Faribault	131	B2
Faridabad	107	C3
Farihy Alaotra	99	H3
Färjestaden	65	F1
Farmington, *Me., United States*	131	F2
Farmington, *N.Mex., United States*	133	E1
Farnborough	59	B3
Farne Islands	69	L6
Fårö	61	K8
Faro, *Brazil*	141	F4

Symbol	Meaning		Symbol	Meaning		Symbol	Meaning
⊠	Continent name		▲	Mountain, volcano, peak		⬱	Sea, ocean
Ⓐ	Country name		◭	Mountain range		⊵	Cape, point
ⓐ	State or province name		⊘	Physical region or feature		🔲	Island or island group, rocky or coral reef
◼	Country capital		⊿	River, canal		✳	Place of interest
◻	State or province capital		⬓	Lake, salt lake		⊞	Historical or cultural region
●	Settlement		⬛	Gulf, strait, bay			

Name		Page	Ref.
Faro, *Portugal*	⊙	73	C7
Farquhar Group	🏝	99	(2)B3
Farrāshband	⊙	87	E2
Farson	⊙	129	E2
Fasā	⊙	87	E2
Fasano	⊙	77	M8
Fategarh	⊙	107	C3
Fatehpur	⊙	107	D3
Făurei	⊙	79	Q4
Fauske	⊙	61	H3
Fauville-en-Caux	⊙	59	C5
Favara	⊙	77	H11
Faversham	⊙	59	C3
Favignana	⊙	77	G11
Faxaflói	🌊	61	(1)B2
Faya	⊙	93	C4
Fayette	⊙	135	D3
Fayetteville, *Ark., United States*	⊙	135	C2
Fayetteville, *N.C., United States*	⊙	131	E3
Fayetteville, *Tenn., United States*	⊙	135	D2
Faylakah	🏝	87	C2
Fdérik	⊙	91	C4
Featherston	⊙	121	E5
Fécamp	⊙	59	C5
Federated States of Micronesia	A	117	E5
Fedorovka	⊙	63	M4
Fehmarn	🏝	67	G2
Feijó	⊙	141	C5
Feilding	⊙	121	E5
Feira de Santana	⊙	141	K6
Feistritz	⟋	75	L3
Fejø	🏝	67	G2
Feldbach	⊙	75	L4
Feldkirch	⊙	75	E3
Feldkirchen	⊙	75	K4
Felidu Atoll	🏝	107	B8
Felixstowe	⊙	59	D3
Feltre	⊙	75	G4
Femø	🏝	67	G2
Femund	⟋	61	F5
Fengcheng	⊙	113	C3
Fenghua	⊙	111	G5
Fengning	⊙	111	F2
Feng Xian	⊙	111	D4
Feni	⊙	107	F4
Fenyang	⊙	111	E3
Feodosiya	⊙	83	F1
Fergana	⊙	85	K1
Fergus Falls	⊙	127	G2
Ferkessédougou	⊙	95	C3
Ferlach	⊙	75	K4
Fermo	⊙	77	H5
Fernandina Beach	⊙	135	E3
Fernandópolis	⊙	143	L3
Ferrara	⊙	75	G6
Ferreira do Alentejo	⊙	73	B7
Ferrol	⊙	73	B1
Ferry Lake	⟋	135	C2
Fès	⊙	91	E2
Festus	⊙	131	B3
Feteşti	⊙	79	Q5
Fethiye	⊙	81	M8
Fetisovo	⊙	85	F1
Fetlar	🏝	69	M1
Feucht	⊙	67	G7
Feuchtwangen	⊙	67	F7
Feyzābād	⊙	85	K2
Fianarantsoa	⊙	99	H4
Fianga	⊙	97	B2
Fichě	⊙	97	F2
Fidenza	⊙	75	F6
Fieni	⊙	79	N4
Fier	⊙	81	B4
Figeac	⊙	71	G9
Figline Valdarno	⊙	75	G7
Figueira da Foz	⊙	73	B4
Figueres	⊙	73	N2
Figuig	⊙	91	E2
Figuil	⊙	95	G3
Fiji	A	117	H8
Filadélfia	⊙	143	J3
Fil'akovo	⊙	65	J9
Filiaşi	⊙	79	L5
Filicudi	🏝	77	J10
Finale Ligure	⊙	75	D6
Findlay	⊙	131	D2
Fingoè	⊙	99	E3
Finike	⊙	81	N8
Finland	A	61	P3
Finlay	⟋	125	F5
Finley	⊙	119	J7
Finnsnes	⊙	61	K2
Finsterwalde	⊙	67	J5
Firat	⟋	83	H4
Firenze	⊙	75	G7
Firminy	⊙	71	K8
Firozabad	⊙	107	C3
Firozpur	⊙	107	B2
Firth of Clyde	🌊	69	G6
Firth of Forth	🌊	69	K5
Firth of Lorn	🌊	69	G5
Firth of Thames	🌊	121	E3
Fish	⟋	99	B5
Fisher Strait	🌊	125	Q4
Fishguard	⊙	69	H9
Fiskenæsset = Qeqertarsuatsiaat	⊙	125	W4
Fismes	⊙	59	F5
Fitzroy Crossing	⊙	119	E3
Fivizzano	⊙	75	F6
Fizi	⊙	97	D4
Flaming Gorge Reservoir	⟋	129	E2
Flamingo	⊙	135	E4
Flannan Islands	🏝	69	E3
Flåsjön	⟋	61	H4
Flateyri	⊙	61	(1)B1
Flathead Lake	⟋	129	D1
Flensburg	⊙	67	E2
Flensburg Fjorde	🌊	67	E2
Flers	⊙	59	B6
Flinders Island	🏝	119	J7
Flinders Ranges	⛰	119	G6
Flinders Reefs	🏝	119	J3
Flin Flon	⊙	125	L6
Flint	⊙	131	D2
Flint Island	🏝	117	L7
Flirey	⊙	75	A2
Flöha	⊙	67	J6
Florac	⊙	71	J9
Florence = Firenze, *Italy*	⊙	75	G7
Florence, *Al., United States*	⊙	135	D3
Florence, *S.C., United States*	⊙	135	F3
Florencia	⊙	141	B3
Florennes	⊙	59	G4
Florenville	⊙	59	H5
Flores, *Azores*	🏝	91	(1)A2
Flores, *Indonesia*	🏝	115	(2)B4
Flores Sea	🌊	115	(2)A4
Floreşti	⊙	79	R2
Floriano	⊙	141	J5
Florianópolis	⊡	143	M4
Florida	ⓐ	135	E4
Florida	⊙	143	K5
Florida Keys	🏝	123	K7
Florina	⊙	81	D4
Florissant	⊙	131	B3
Florø	⊙	61	C6
Floydada	⊙	133	F2
Flumendosa	⟋	77	D9
Fly	⟋	115	(2)F4
Foča	⊙	79	F6
Foça	⊙	81	J6
Focşani	⊙	79	Q4
Fóggia	⊙	77	K7
Fogo	🏝	95	(1)B1
Fogo Island	🏝	125	W7
Fohnsdorf	⊙	75	K3
Föhr	🏝	67	D2
Foix	⊙	71	G11
Folegandros	🏝	81	G8
Foleyet	⊙	131	D1
Foligno	⊙	77	G6
Folkestone	⊙	59	D3
Folkston	⊙	135	E3
Follónica	⊙	77	E6
Fond du Lac	⊙	131	C2
Fondi	⊙	77	H7
Fongafale	■	117	H6
Fontainebleau	⊙	71	H5
Fonte Boa	⊙	141	D4
Fontenay-le-Comte	⊙	71	E7
Fontur	🌊	61	(1)F1
Fonyód	⊙	77	M2
Forbach, *France*	⊙	59	J5
Forbach, *Germany*	⊙	59	L6
Forchheim	⊙	67	G7
Førde	⊙	61	C6
Fordyce	⊙	135	C3
Forest, *Canada*	⊙	131	D2
Forest, *United States*	⊙	135	D3
Forestville	⊙	131	G1
Forfar	⊙	69	K5
Forges-les-Eaux	⊙	59	D5
Forks	⊙	129	B1
Forli	⊙	75	H6
Formazza	⊙	75	D4
Formentera	🏝	73	M6
Fórmia	⊙	77	H7
Formiga	⊙	143	M3
Formosa, *Brazil*	⊙	141	H7
Formosa, *Paraguay*	⊙	143	K4
Fornovo di Taro	⊙	75	F6
Forssa	⊙	61	M6
Forst	⊙	67	K5
Forsyth	⊙	129	E1
Fort Abbas	⊙	107	B3
Fort Bayne	⊙	99	D6
Fort Benton	⊙	129	D1
Fort Bragg	⊙	133	B1
Fort Chipewyan	⊙	125	J5
Fort Cobb Reservoir	⟋	135	B2
Fort Collins	⊙	129	E2
Fort-de-France	■	137	M6
Fort Dodge	⊙	131	B2
Forte dei Marmi	⊙	75	F7
Fort Frances	⊙	131	B1
Fort George	⊙	125	R6
Fort Gibson Lake	⟋	135	B2
Fort Good Hope	⊙	125	F3
Forth	⟋	69	H5
Fort Hope	⊙	125	P6
Fortín Coronel Eugenio Garay	⊙	143	J3
Fort Kent	⊙	131	G1
Fort Lauderdale	⊙	135	E4
Fort Liard	⊙	125	G4
Fort Mackay	⊙	125	J5
Fort Macleod	⊙	129	D1
Fort McMurray	⊙	125	J5
Fort McPherson	⊙	133	(1)L2
Fort Munro	⊙	85	J4
Fort Myers	⊙	135	E4
Fort Nelson	⊙	125	G5
Fort Norman	⊙	133	(1)M3
Fort Payne	⊙	135	D3
Fort Peck Reservoir	⟋	129	E1
Fort Pierce	⊙	135	E4
Fort Pierre	⊙	129	F2
Fort Portal	⊙	97	E3
Fort Providence	⊙	125	H4
Fort Rupert	⊙	125	R6
Fort St. John	⊙	125	G5
Fort Saint Lucie	⊙	135	E4
Fort Scott	⊙	135	C2
Fort Severn	⊙	125	P5
Fort Shevchenko	⊙	103	J9
Fort Simpson	⊙	125	G4
Fort Smith, *Canada*	⊙	125	J4
Fort Smith, *United States*	⊙	135	C2
Fort Stockton	⊙	133	F2
Fort Summer	⊙	133	F2
Fortuna	⊙	129	F1
Fortune Bay	🌊	125	V7
Fort Vermilion	⊙	125	H5
Fort Wayne	⊙	135	D1
Fort William	⊙	69	G5
Fort Worth	⊙	135	B3
Fort Yates	⊙	129	F1
Foshan	⊙	109	E2
Fosna	⟋	61	F5
Fossano	⊙	75	C6
Fossombrone	⊙	75	H7
Fougamou	⊙	95	G5
Fougères	⊙	71	D5
Foula	🏝	69	K1
Foulness	🏝	59	C3
Foumban	⊙	95	G3
Fourmies	⊙	59	G4
Fournoi	🏝	81	J7
Fouta Djallon	🗺	95	B2
Foveaux Strait	⟋	121	A8
Foxe Basin	🌊	125	R3
Foxe Channel	🌊	125	R4
Foxe Peninsula	🌊	125	R4
Fox Islands	🏝	133	(1)D5
Foz do Cunene	⊙	99	A3
Foz do Iguaçu	⊙	143	L4
Fraga	⊙	73	L3
Franca	⊙	143	M3
Francavilla	⊙	77	M8
Francavilla al Mare	⊙	77	J6
France	A	71	G7
Franceville	⊙	95	G5
Francisco I. Madero	⊙	133	F4
Francistown	⊙	99	D4
Francs Peak	⛰	129	E2
Frankenberg	⊙	67	D5
Frankenthal	⊙	67	D7
Frankfort, *Ind., United States*	⊙	135	D1
Frankfort, *Ky., United States*	⊡	135	D2
Frankfurt, *Germany*	⊙	67	K4
Frankfurt, *Germany*	⊙	67	D6
Franklin, *N.C., United States*	⊙	131	D3
Franklin, *Tenn., United States*	⊙	131	C3
Franklin Bay	🌊	125	F2
Franklin D. Roosevelt Lake	⟋	129	C1
Franklin Mountains	🗺	125	F3
Franklin Strait	🌊	125	M2
Franz Josef Glacier	⊙	121	C6
Franz Josef Land = Zemlya Frantsa-Iosifa	🏝	103	J2
Fraser	⟋	125	G6
Fraserburg	⊙	99	C6
Fraserburgh	⊙	69	L4
Fraser Island	🏝	119	K5
Frater	⊙	131	D1
Frauenfeld	⊙	75	D3
Fredensborg	⊙	65	B2
Frederick, *Md., United States*	⊙	131	E3
Frederick, *Okla., United States*	⊙	135	B3
Fredericksburg, *Tex., United States*	⊙	135	B3
Fredericksburg, *Va., United States*	⊙	131	E3
Fredericktown	⊙	131	B3
Fredericton	⊡	125	T7
Frederikshåb = Paamiut	⊙	125	X4
Frederikshavn	⊙	61	F8
Frederikssund	⊙	65	B2
Frederiksværk	⊙	61	G9
Fredrikstad	⊙	61	F7
Freeport, *Ill., United States*	⊙	131	C2
Freeport, *Tex., United States*	⊙	135	B4
Freeport City	⊙	135	F4
Freer	⊙	135	B4
Free State	ⓐ	99	D5
Freetown	■	95	B3
Fregenal de la Sierra	⊙	73	D6
Freiberg	⊙	67	J6
Freiburg	⊙	75	C3
Freilassing	⊙	75	H3
Freising	⊙	75	G2
Freistadt	⊙	75	K2

G

Name	Type	Page	Grid
Fréjus	settlement	71	M10
Fremantle	settlement	119	C6
Fremont, *Calif., United States*	settlement	133	B1
Fremont, *Nebr., United States*	settlement	127	G3
Frenchglen	settlement	129	C2
French Guiana	state/province	141	G3
French Polynesia	island group	117	L7
Frenda	settlement	91	F1
Fresnes-sur-Apances	settlement	75	A3
Fresnillo	settlement	137	D4
Fresno	settlement	133	C1
Fresno Reservoir	lake	129	E1
Freudenstadt	settlement	75	D2
Freyung	settlement	67	J8
Frias	settlement	143	H4
Fribourg	settlement	75	C4
Friedburg	settlement	75	G2
Friedrichshafen	settlement	75	E3
Friesach	settlement	75	K4
Friesoythe	settlement	67	C3
Frisian Islands	island group	59	H1
Fritzlar	settlement	67	E5
Frobisher Bay	gulf	125	T4
Frolovo	settlement	63	H5
Frome	settlement	69	K10
Frontera	settlement	137	F5
Frontignan	settlement	71	J10
Frosinone	settlement	77	H7
Frøya	island	61	D5
Fruges	settlement	59	E4
Frýdek Místek	settlement	65	H8
Fudai	settlement	113	L4
Fuding	settlement	111	G5
Fuengirola	settlement	73	F8
Fuentesauco	settlement	73	E3
Fuerteventura	island	91	C3
Fugu	settlement	111	E3
Fuhai	settlement	103	R8
Fujieda	settlement	113	K6
Fujin	settlement	105	N7
Fuji-san	mountain	113	K6
Fukuchiyama	settlement	113	H6
Fukue	settlement	113	E7
Fukue-jima	island	113	E7
Fukui	settlement	113	J5
Fukuoka	settlement	113	F7
Fukushima	settlement	113	L5
Fukuyama	settlement	113	G6
Fulda	settlement	67	E6
Fulda	river	67	E6
Fuling	settlement	111	D5
Fulton	settlement	135	D2
Funabashi	settlement	113	L6
Funafuti	island group	117	H6
Funchal	settlement	91	B2
Fundão	settlement	73	C4
Funing	settlement	109	D2
Funtua	settlement	95	F2
Furano	settlement	113	M2
Fürg	settlement	87	F2
Furmanovka	settlement	103	N9
Furmanovo	settlement	63	J5
Furneaux Group	island group	119	J8
Furqlus	settlement	86	E2
Fürstenberg	settlement	67	J3
Fürstenfeldbruck	settlement	75	G2
Fürstenwalde	settlement	67	K4
Fürth	settlement	67	F7
Furukawa	settlement	113	L4
Fushun	settlement	113	B3
Fusong	settlement	113	D2
Füssen	settlement	75	F3
Futog	settlement	79	G4
Fuxhou	settlement	111	F5
Fu Xian	settlement	111	D3
Fuxin	settlement	111	G2
Fuyang	settlement	111	F4
Fuyu	settlement	111	G1
Fuyun	settlement	103	R8
Fuzhou	settlement	109	F1
Fyn	island	67	F1
Fynshav	settlement	67	F2
Gaalkacyo	settlement	97	H2
Gabès	settlement	91	H2
Gabon	country	95	G5
Gaborone	country capital	99	D4
Gabrovo	settlement	79	N7
Gacé	settlement	59	C6
Gacko	settlement	79	F6
Gäddede	settlement	61	H4
Gadsden	settlement	135	D3
Găeşti	settlement	79	N5
Gaeta	settlement	77	H7
Gafsa	settlement	91	G2
Gaggenau	settlement	75	D2
Gagnoa	settlement	95	C3
Gagra	settlement	83	J2
Gaildorf	settlement	75	E2
Gaillac	settlement	71	G10
Gainesville, *Fla., United States*	settlement	135	E4
Gainesville, *Ga., United States*	settlement	135	E3
Gainesville, *Mo., United States*	settlement	135	C2
Gainesville, *Tex., United States*	settlement	135	B3
Gai Xian	settlement	113	B3
Gala	settlement	107	E3
Galana	river	97	F4
Galanta	settlement	75	N2
Galapagos Islands = Islas Galápagos	island group	141	(1)B1
Galashiels	settlement	69	K6
Galaţi	settlement	79	R4
Galdhøpiggen	mountain	61	D6
Galena	settlement	133	(1)F3
Galesburg	settlement	131	B2
Galich	settlement	63	H3
Gallabat	settlement	93	G5
Galle	settlement	107	D7
Gallipoli	settlement	77	N8
Gallipolis	settlement	135	E2
Gällivare	settlement	61	L3
Gallup	settlement	133	E1
Galtat Zemmour	settlement	91	C3
Galveston Bay	gulf	127	G6
Galway	settlement	69	C8
Galway Bay	gulf	69	C8
Gambēla	settlement	97	E2
Gambier Islands	island group	117	N8
Gamboma	settlement	97	B4
Gamboula	settlement	97	B3
Gan	river	105	L7
Ganado	settlement	133	E1
Gäncä	settlement	83	M3
Gandajika	settlement	97	C5
Gander	settlement	125	W7
Ganderkesee	settlement	67	D3
Gandesa	settlement	73	L3
Gāndhīdhām	settlement	107	B4
Gandhinagar	settlement	107	B4
Gandia	settlement	73	K6
Gandu	settlement	141	K6
Ganganagar	settlement	107	B3
Gangara	settlement	95	F2
Gangdise Shan	mountain range	107	D2
Ganges	settlement	71	J10
Ganges	river	107	E3
Gangi	settlement	77	J11
Gangtok	settlement	107	E3
Gannett Peak	mountain	129	E2
Ganta	settlement	95	C3
Ganye	settlement	95	G3
Ganzhou	settlement	111	E5
Gao	settlement	91	E5
Gaoual	settlement	91	C6
Gap	settlement	75	B6
Garanhuns	settlement	141	K5
Garbsen	settlement	67	E4
Gardelegen	settlement	67	G4
Garden City	settlement	129	F3
Gardēz	settlement	85	J3
Gardone Val Trómpia	settlement	75	F5
Gargždai	settlement	65	L2
Gariau	settlement	115	(2)D3
Garissa	settlement	97	F4
Garland	settlement	135	B3
Garlasco	settlement	75	D5
Garliava	settlement	65	N3
Garmisch-Partenkirchen	settlement	75	G3
Garnett	settlement	135	B2
Garonne	river	71	E9
Garoowe	settlement	97	H2
Garoua	settlement	95	G3
Garoua Boulaï	settlement	95	G3
Garry Lake	lake	125	L3
Garut	settlement	115	(1)D4
Garwolin	settlement	65	L6
Gary	settlement	127	J3
Garyarsa	settlement	107	D2
Garzê	settlement	111	B4
Gasan Kuli	settlement	85	F2
Gasht	settlement	85	H4
Gashua	settlement	95	G2
Gastonia	settlement	135	E2
Gastre	settlement	143	H7
Gatchina	settlement	63	F3
Gateshead	settlement	69	L7
Gatesville	settlement	135	B3
Gatineau	settlement	131	E1
Gatrūyeh	settlement	87	F2
Gauja	river	61	N8
Gaula	river	61	F5
Gauteng	settlement	99	D5
Gava	settlement	73	N3
Gāvbandī	settlement	87	E3
Gavdos	island	81	G10
Gävle	settlement	61	J6
Gawler	settlement	119	G6
Gawler Ranges	mountain range	119	G6
Gaxun Nur	lake	111	C2
Gaya, *India*	settlement	107	E4
Gaya, *Niger*	settlement	95	E2
Gaylord	settlement	131	D1
Gayndah	settlement	119	K5
Gayny	settlement	63	K2
Gaza	settlement	86	B5
Gaz-Achak	settlement	103	L9
Gazandzhyk	settlement	103	K10
Gaza Strip	state/province	86	B5
Gaziantep	settlement	83	G5
Gazipaşa	settlement	81	Q8
Gazli	settlement	103	L9
Gbaaka	settlement	95	C3
Gbarnga	settlement	95	C3
Gdańsk	settlement	65	H3
Gdov	settlement	61	P7
Gdyel	settlement	73	K9
Gdynia	settlement	65	H3
Gebel el Tîh	physical region	86	A7
Gebel Halâl	mountain	86	A6
Gebel Katherina	mountain	93	F2
Gebel Yi'allaq	mountain	86	A6
Gebze	settlement	81	M4
Gedaref	settlement	93	G5
Gediz	river	81	K6
Gediz	settlement	81	M6
Gedser	settlement	67	G2
Geel	settlement	59	H3
Geelong	settlement	119	H7
Geesthacht	settlement	67	F3
Gê'gvai	settlement	107	D2
Geidam	settlement	95	G2
Geilenkirchen	settlement	59	J4
Geilo	settlement	61	E6
Geinhausen	settlement	67	E6
Geislingen	settlement	75	E2
Geita	settlement	97	E4
Gejiu	settlement	109	C2
Gela	settlement	77	J11
Geladī	settlement	97	H2
Geldern	settlement	59	J3
Geleen	settlement	59	H4
Gelendzhik	settlement	83	H1
Gelibolu	settlement	81	J4
Gelibolu Yarimadasi	cape/point	81	J4
Gelsenkirchen	settlement	59	K3
Gembloux	settlement	59	G4
Gembu	settlement	95	G3
Gemena	settlement	97	B3
Gemlik	settlement	81	M4
Gemlik Körfezi	gulf	81	L4
Gemona del Friuli	settlement	75	J4
Genalē Wenz	river	97	G2
General Acha	settlement	143	J6
General Alvear	settlement	143	H6
General Pico	settlement	143	J6
General Pinedo	settlement	143	J4
General Roca	settlement	143	H6
General Santos	settlement	109	H5
Geneva	settlement	131	E2
Genève	settlement	75	B4
Gengma	settlement	109	B2
Genil	river	73	F7
Genk	settlement	59	H4
Genoa = Genova	settlement	75	D6
Genova	settlement	75	D6
Gent	settlement	59	F3
Genteng	settlement	115	(1)D4
Genthin	settlement	67	H4
Geographe Bay	gulf	119	B6
George	settlement	99	C6
George	river	125	T5
George Town, *Australia*	settlement	119	J8
George Town, *Malaysia*	settlement	115	(1)C1
George Town, *United States*	settlement	135	F5
Georgetown, *Gambia*	settlement	95	B2
Georgetown, *Guyana*	country capital	141	F2
Georgetown, *Ky., United States*	settlement	135	E2
Georgetown, *S.C., United States*	settlement	135	F3
Georgetown, *Tex., United States*	settlement	135	B3
George West	settlement	135	B4
Georgia	country	83	K2
Georgia	state/province	135	E3
Georgian Bay	gulf	131	D1
Gera	settlement	67	H6
Geraldine	settlement	121	C7
Geraldton, *Australia*	settlement	119	B5
Geraldton, *Canada*	settlement	127	J2
Gérardmer	settlement	75	B2
Gerāsh	settlement	87	F3
Gerede	settlement	83	E3
Gerefsried	settlement	75	G3
Gereshk	settlement	85	H3
Gérgal	settlement	73	H7
Gerik	settlement	109	C5
Gerlach	settlement	129	C2
Germantown	settlement	131	C3
Germany	country	67	E6
Germencik	settlement	81	K7
Germering	settlement	75	G2
Germersheim	settlement	59	L5
Gernika	settlement	73	H1
Gerolzhofen	settlement	67	F7
Gêrzê	settlement	107	D2
Geser	settlement	115	(2)D3
Getafe	settlement	73	G4
Gettysburg	settlement	129	F2
Getxo	settlement	73	H1
Geugnon	settlement	71	K7
Gevaş	settlement	83	K4
Gevgelija	settlement	81	E3
Gewanē	settlement	93	H5
Geyik Dağ	mountain	81	Q8
Geyser	settlement	129	D1
Geyve	settlement	81	N4
Ghadāmis	settlement	91	G2
Ghadīr Minqār	lake	86	E3
Ghana	country	95	D3
Ghanzi	settlement	99	C4
Gharandal	settlement	86	C5
Ghardaïa	settlement	91	F2
Gharo	settlement	85	J5

Legend

Symbol	Meaning		Symbol	Meaning		Symbol	Meaning
X	Continent name		▲	Mountain, volcano, peak		⌣	Sea, ocean
A	Country name		⌢	Mountain range		⊿	Cape, point
a	State or province name		⊘	Physical region or feature		⬚	Island or island group, rocky or coral reef
■	Country capital		✓	River, canal		✳	Place of interest
□	State or province capital		◣	Lake, salt lake		⬒	Historical or cultural region
●	Settlement		⌐	Gulf, strait, bay			

Name	Page	Ref		Name	Page	Ref
Gharyān	91	H2		Golfo de Fonseca	137	G6
Ghāt	93	B2		Golfo de Guayaquil	141	A4
Ghazaouet	91	E1		Golfo de Honduras	137	G5
Ghaziabad	107	C3		Golfo del Darién	141	B2
Ghazipur	107	D3		Golfo dell' Asinara	77	C7
Ghazn	85	J3		Golfo de los Mosquitos	141	A2
Gheorgheni	79	N3		Golfo de Mazarrón	73	J7
Gherla	79	L2		Golfo de Morrosquillo	141	B1
Ghizar	107	B1		Golfo de Panamá	137	J7
Ghotāru	107	B3		Golfo de Penas	143	F8
Giannitsa	81	H4		Golfo de San Jorge	143	H8
Giannutri	77	F6		Golfo de Santa Clara	133	D2
Giarre	77	K11		Golfo de Tehuantepec	137	E5
Gibraltar	73	E8		Golfo de Valéncia	73	L5
Gibson Desert	119	D4		Golfo de Venezuela	141	C1
Gideån	61	K5		Golfo di Augusta	77	K11
Gien	71	H6		Golfo di Catánia	77	K11
Gießen	67	D6		Golfo di Gaeta	77	H7
Gifhorn	67	F4		Golfo di Gela	77	J11
Gifu	113	J6		Golfo di Genova	77	C4
Gigha	69	G6		Golfo di Manfredonia	77	L7
Giglio	77	E6		Golfo di Ólbia	77	D8
Gijón	73	E1		Golfo di Oristano	77	C9
Gila	133	E2		Golfo di Orosei	77	D8
Gila Bend	133	D2		Golfo di Palmas	77	C10
Gilan Garb	83	L6		Golfo di Policastro	77	K9
Gilazi	83	N3		Golfo di Salerno	77	J8
Gilbert Islands	117	H5		Golfo di Sant'Eufemia	77	K10
Gilbués	141	H5		Golfo di Squillace	77	L10
Gilching	75	G2		Golfo di Taranto	77	L8
Gilf Kebir Plateau	93	E3		Golfo di Trieste	75	J5
Gilgandra	119	J6		Golfo San Matías	143	J6
Gilgit	85	K2		Gölhisar	81	M8
Gilgit	107	B1		Golin Baixing	113	A1
Gillam	125	N5		Gölköy	83	G3
Gillette	129	E2		Gölmarmara	81	K6
Gillingham	59	C3		Golyshmanovo	103	M6
Gills Rock	131	C1		Goma	97	D4
Gilroy	129	B3		Gombe	95	G2
Gīmbī	97	F2		Gombi	95	G2
Gimli	125	M6		Gomera	91	B3
Gimol'skoe Ozero	61	R5		Gómez Palacio	133	F3
Gīnīr	97	G2		Gonam	105	M5
Gióia del Colle	77	L8		Gonbad-e Kavus	85	G2
Gióia Tauro	77	K10		Gonda	107	D3
Gioura	81	F5		Gonder	93	G5
Giresun	83	H3		Gondia	107	D4
Girga	93	F2		Gondomar	73	B3
Girona	73	N3		Gönen	81	K4
Gironde	71	E8		Gongga Shan	111	C5
Girvan	69	H6		Gonghe	111	C3
Gisborne	121	G4		Gongliu	103	Q9
Gisenyi	97	D4		Gongpoquan	111	B2
Gitega	97	D4		Gongshan	109	B1
Giurgiu	79	N6		Gonzáles	127	G7
Givet	59	G4		Gonzales	135	B4
Givors	71	K8		González	133	G4
Giyon	97	F2		Goodland	129	F3
Gizhiga	105	U4		Goolgowi	119	J6
Gizhiginskaya Guba	105	T4		Goomalling	119	C6
Giżycko	65	L3		Goondiwindi	119	K5
Gjiri i Vlorës	81	B4		Goose Lake	129	B2
Gjirokaster	81	C4		Göppingen	75	E2
Gjøvik	61	F6		Góra	65	F6
Glacier Peak	129	B1		Gora Bazardyuzi	83	M3
Gladstone	119	K4		Gora Kamen	103	S4
Glamoč	79	D5		Gorakhpur	107	D3
Glan	67	C7		Gora Ledyanaya	105	W4
Glan	115	(2)C1		Gora Pobeda	105	R4
Glarner Alpen	75	D4		Gora Yenashimskiy Polkan	103	S6
Glasgow, United Kingdom	69	H6		Goražde	79	F6
Glasgow, Ky., United States	131	C3		Gorbitsa	105	K6
Glasgow, Mont., United States	129	E1		Gore	95	H3
Glauchau	67	H6		Goré	97	F2
Glazov	103	J6		Gore	121	B8
Gleisdorf	75	L3		Gorgān	85	F2
Glendale, Ariz., United States	133	D2		Gorgona	75	E7
Glendale, Calif., United States	133	C2		Gori	83	L2
Glendambo	119	G6		Gorinchem	59	H3
Glendive	129	F1		Goris	83	M4
Glennallen	133	(1)H3		Gorizia	75	J5
Glenn Innes	119	K5		Gorki	63	N1
Glenrothes	69	J5		Gorlice	65	L8
Glens Falls	131	F2		Görlitz	65	D6
Glenwood, Ark., United States	131	B4		Gorna Oryakhovitsa	79	N6
Glenwood, Minn., United States	131	A1		Gornji Milanovac	79	H5
Glenwood, N.Mex., United States	133	E2		Gorno-Altaysk	103	R7
Glenwood Springs	129	E3		Gorno Oryakhovitsa	81	H1
Glidden	131	B1		Gorodets	63	H3
Glina	75	M5		Gorontalo	115	(2)B2
Gliwice	65	H7		Goryachiy Klyuch	83	H1
Głogów	65	F6		Gory Belukha	103	R8
Glomfjord	61	H3		Gory Ulutau	63	N5
Glomma	61	F5		Gorzów Wielkopolski	65	E5
Glorieuses	89	H7		Goslar	67	F5
Gloucester, United Kingdom	69	K10		Gospić	77	K4
Gloucester, United States	131	F2		Gosport	71	D3
Głowno	65	J6		Gostivar	81	C3
Głuchołazy	65	G7		Gostyń	65	G6
Glückstadt	67	E3		Gostynin	65	J5
Gmünd, Austria	75	J4		Göteborg	61	F8
Gmünd, Austria	75	L2		Gotha	67	F6
Gmunden	75	J3		Gothèye	95	E2
Gniezno	65	G5		Gotland	61	K8
Gnjilane	81	D2		Gotō-rettō	113	E7
Gnoien	67	H3		Gotse Delchev	81	F3
Goalpara	107	F3		Gotska Sandön	61	K7
Goba	97	F2		Göttingen	67	E5
Gobabis	99	B4		Gouda	59	G2
Gobernador Gregores	143	G8		Gough Island	89	B10
Gobi Desert	111	C2		Goundam	91	E5
Gobustan	85	E1		Gouraya	73	M8
Goch	59	J3		Gourdon	71	G9
Godbout	131	G1		Gournay-en-Bray	59	D5
Godé	97	G2		Governador Valadares	141	J7
Goderich	131	D2		Governor's Harbour	135	F4
Godhra	107	B4		Govorovo	105	M3
Gödöllő	79	G2		Gowārān	85	J4
Gods Lake	125	N6		Goya	143	K4
Godthåb = Nuuk	125	W4		Gozha Co	107	D1
Goeree	59	F3		Gozo = Gwardex	77	J12
Goes	59	F3		Graaff-Reinet	99	C6
Gogama	131	D1		Grabovica	79	K5
Goiânia	141	H7		Gračac	75	L6
Goiás	141	G6		Gračanica	79	F5
Goiás	141	G7		Gradačac	79	F5
Gökçeada	81	H4		Gräfenhainichen	67	H5
Gökova Körfezi	81	K8		Grafton, Australia	119	K5
Göksun	83	G5		Grafton, United States	129	G1
Golaghat	107	F3		Graham Island	133	(1)L5
Golan Heights	86	C3		Grajaú	141	H5
Golbāf	87	G2		Grajewo	65	M4
Gölbasi	83	G5		Gram	67	E1
Gol'chikha	103	Q3		Grampian Mountains	69	H5
Gölcük	81	K5		Granada, Nicaragua	137	G6
Goldap	65	M3		Granada, Spain	73	G7
Gold Coast	119	K5		Granby	131	F1
Golden Bay	121	D5		Gran Canaria	91	B3
Goldendale	129	B1		Grand Bahama	135	F4
Golden Gate	133	B1		Grand Ballon	71	N6
Goldfield	129	C3		Grand Bank	125	V7
Goldsboro	131	E3		Grand Canyon	129	D3
Göle	83	K3		Grande, Bolivia	141	E7
Goleniów	65	D4		Grande, Brazil	141	J6
Golestānak	87	F1		Grande Cache	125	H6
Golfe d'Ajaccio	77	C7		Grande Prairie	125	H5
Golfe de Gabès	91	H2		Grand Erg de Bilma	91	H5
Golfe de Hammamet	91	H1		Grand Erg Occidental	91	E3
Golfe de Porto	77	C6		Grand Erg Oriental	91	F3
Golfe de Sagone	77	C6		Grand Falls, N.B., Canada	131	G1
Golfe de Saint-Malo	71	C5		Grand Falls, Nfld., Canada	125	V7
Golfe de Tunis	77	E11		Grand Forks, Canada	127	C2
Golfe de Valinco	77	C7		Grand Forks, United States	129	G1
Golfe du Lion	71	J10		Grand Haven	131	C2
Golfo de Almería	73	H8		Grand Island	129	G2
Golfo de Batabanó	137	H4		Grand Junction	129	E3
Golfo de Cádiz	73	C7		Grand Marais, Mich., United States	131	C1
Golfo de California	137	B3		Grand Marais, Minn., United States	131	B1
Golfo de Chiriquí	137	H7		Grand-Mère	131	F1
Golfo de Corcovado	143	F7		Grândola	73	B6
Golfo de Cupica	141	B2		Grand Portage	131	C1
				Grand Rapids, Canada	125	M6

Legend:

- ✕ Continent name
- △ Country name
- ⓐ State or province name
- ■ Country capital
- ▣ State or province capital
- ● Settlement

- ▲ Mountain, volcano, peak
- ▬ Mountain range
- ⊘ Physical region or feature
- ╱ River, canal
- ◪ Lake, salt lake
- ► Gulf, strait, bay

- ▭ Sea, ocean
- ▷ Cape, point
- ▨ Island or island group, rocky or coral reef
- ✳ Place of interest
- ▨ Historical or cultural region

Name	Page	Ref.
Grand Rapids, *Mich.*, United States	131	C2
Grand Rapids, *Minn.*, United States	131	B1
Grand Teton	129	D2
Grangeville	129	C1
Granite Falls	131	A2
Granollers	73	N3
Gran Paradiso	75	C5
Grantham	69	M9
Grants	133	E1
Grants Pass	129	B2
Granville	71	D5
Granville Lake	125	M5
Gräsö	61	K6
Grasse	75	B7
Grassrange	129	E1
Grass Valley	129	B3
Graulhet	71	G10
Gravelines	59	E3
Gravenhurst	131	E2
Gravesend	59	C3
Gravina in Puglia	77	L8
Gray	71	L6
Grayling	131	D2
Grays	59	C3
Grays Lake	129	D2
Grayville	131	C3
Graz	75	L3
Great Abaco	135	F4
Great Artesian Basin	119	H4
Great Australian Bight	119	E6
Great Bahama Bank	137	J4
Great Barrier Island	121	E3
Great Barrier Reef	119	J2
Great Basin	129	C3
Great Bear Lake	133	(1)M2
Great Bend	133	G1
Great Dividing Range	119	J4
Greater Antilles	137	J5
Greater Sunda Islands	117	B6
Great Exhibition Bay	121	D2
Great Exuma	127	L7
Great Falls	129	D1
Great Inagua	137	K4
Great Karoo	99	C6
Great Malvern	69	K9
Great Nicobar	107	F7
Great Ouse	69	N9
Great Plains	129	F2
Great Rift Valley	97	E5
Great Salt Lake	129	D2
Great Salt Lake Desert	129	D2
Great Sand Sea	93	D2
Great Sandy Desert	119	D4
Great Slave Lake	123	N3
Great Victoria Desert	119	E5
Great Wall	111	C3
Great Yarmouth	69	P9
Greece	81	D5
Greeley	129	F2
Green	129	D3
Green Bay	131	C2
Greenfield	135	D2
Greenland	123	G2
Greenland Sea	123	B2
Greenock	69	H6
Green River, *Wyo.*, United States	129	E2
Green River, *Ut.*, United States	129	D3
Greensboro	135	F2
Greensburg, *Ind.*, United States	135	D2
Greensburg, *Pa.*, United States	135	E2
Greenvale	119	J3
Green Valley	137	B2
Greenville, *Liberia*	95	C3
Greenville, *Al.*, United States	135	D3
Greenville, *Fla.*, United States	135	E3
Greenville, *Miss.*, United States	135	C3
Greenville, *N.C.*, United States	131	E3
Greenville, *S.C.*, United States	135	E3
Greenwood, *Miss.*, United States	135	C3
Greenwood, *S.C.*, United States	135	E3
Gregory	129	G2
Gregory Lake	119	E4
Greifswald	67	J2
Greifswalder Bodden	67	J2
Greiz	67	H6
Grenada	127	J5
Grenada	141	E1
Grenchen	75	C3
Grenoble	71	L8
Gretna	135	C4
Greve in Chianti	75	G7
Greven	59	K2
Grevena	81	D4
Grevenbroich	59	J3
Grevesmühlen	67	G3
Greybull	129	E2
Greymouth	121	C6
Grey Range	119	H5
Griesheim	67	D7
Grieskirchen	75	J2
Grigoriopol	79	S2
Grimma	67	H5
Grimmen	67	J2
Grimsby	69	M8
Grimsey	61	(1)D1
Grimsstaðir	61	(1)E2
Grímsvötn	61	(1)E2
Grindsted	61	E9
Grobina	65	L1
Gröbming	75	J3
Grodekovo	111	J2
Grodzisk Wielkopolski	65	F5
Grójec	65	K6
Gronau	67	C4
Groningen	67	B3
Groote Eylandt	119	G2
Grootfontein	99	B3
Großenhain	67	J5
Großer Arber	67	J7
Grosser Beerberg	67	F6
Grosseto	77	F6
Groß-Gerau	67	D7
Großglockner	75	H3
Groswater Bay	125	V6
Grottaglie	77	M8
Groupe Actéon	117	N8
Grove Hill	135	D3
Groznyy	83	L2
Grubišno Polje	79	E4
Grudovo	81	K2
Grudziądz	65	H4
Grünberg	67	D6
Gryazi	63	G4
Gryazovets	63	H3
Gryfice	65	E4
Gryfino	67	K3
Grytøya	61	J2
Grytviken	143	P9
Gstaad	75	C4
Guadalajara, *Mexico*	137	D4
Guadalajara, *Spain*	73	G4
Guadalcanal	117	F7
Guadalquivir	73	E7
Guadalupe	137	A3
Guadalupe	137	E3
Guadeloupe	139	E2
Guadiana	73	C7
Guadix	73	G7
Guaíra	143	L3
Guajará Mirim	141	D6
Guam	117	E4
Guanambi	141	J6
Guanare	141	D2
Guane	137	H4
Guangshui	111	E4
Guangyuan	111	D4
Guangzhou	109	E2
Guanipa	141	E2
Guanling	111	D5
Guantánamo	137	J4
Guanyun	111	F4
Guaporé	141	E6
Guaqui	141	D7
Guarabira	141	K5
Guarda	73	C4
Guardo	73	F2
Guasave	127	E6
Guastalla	75	F6
Guatemala	137	F5
Guatemala	137	F6
Guaviare	141	D3
Guayaquil	141	B4
Guayaramerín	141	D6
Guaymas	133	D3
Guba, *Democratic Republic of Congo*	97	D6
Guba, *Ethiopia*	93	G5
Guba Buorkhaya	105	N2
Gubakha	63	L3
Guban	97	G2
Gubbi	107	C6
Gúbbio	75	H7
Guben	67	K5
Gubin	65	D6
Gudaut'a	83	J2
Gudbransdalen	61	E6
Gudermes	83	M2
Gudvangen	61	D6
Guebwiller	67	C9
Guéckédou	95	B3
Guelma	91	G1
Guelph	131	D2
Guéret	71	B7
Guernsey	71	C4
Guernsey	129	F2
Guerrero Negro	133	D3
Gugē	97	F2
Gūh Küh	85	G4
Guiana	137	L7
Guiana Highlands	141	F3
Guider	95	G3
Guiglo	95	C3
Guildford	69	M10
Guilianova	77	H6
Guilin	109	E1
Guillaumes	75	B6
Guillestre	75	B6
Guimarães	73	B3
Guinea	95	B2
Guinea-Bissau	95	A2
Güines	137	H4
Guingamp	71	B5
Güiria	141	E1
Guise	59	F5
Guitiriz	73	C1
Guiyang	111	D5
Gujranwala	107	B2
Gujrat	107	B2
Gulang	111	C3
Gulbarga	107	C5
Gulbene	61	P8
Gulf of Aden	85	E7
Gulf of Alaska	133	(1)H4
Gulf of Aqaba	85	B4
Gulf of Boothia	125	N2
Gulf of Bothnia	61	K6
Gulf of Carpentaria	119	G2
Gulf of Finland	61	M7
Gulf of Gdansk	65	J3
Gulf of Guinea	95	D4
Gulf of Mannar	107	C7
Gulf of Martaban	109	B3
Gulf of Mexico	137	F3
Gulf of Oman	87	G4
Gulf of Riga	61	M8
Gulf of St. Lawrence	125	U7
Gulf of Santa Catalina	133	C2
Gulf of Thailand	109	C4
Gulf of Tongking	109	D3
Gulf of Venice	75	H5
Gulfport	135	D3
Gulistan	103	M9
Gülşehir	81	S6
Gulu	97	E3
Gülübovo	81	H2
Gumdag	85	F2
Gumel	95	F2
Gumla	107	D4
Gummersbach	59	K3
Gummi	95	F2
Gümüşhane	83	H3
Guna	107	C4
Guna Terara	93	G5
Gungu	97	B5
Gunib	83	M2
Gunnbjørns Fjeld	144	(1)U2
Gunnedah	119	K6
Gunnison, *Colo.*, United States	129	E3
Gunnison, *Ut.*, United States	129	D3
Gunong Kinabalu	115	(1)F1
Guntakal	107	C5
Guntur	107	D5
Gunung Kerinci	115	(1)C3
Gunung Korbu	115	(1)C2
Gunung Kwoka	115	(2)D3
Gunung Leuser	115	(1)B2
Gunung Mekongga	115	(2)B3
Gunung Mulu	115	(1)E2
Gunung Pangrango	115	(1)D4
Gunungsitoli	115	(1)B2
Gunung Togwomeri	115	(2)D3
Günzburg	75	F2
Gunzenhausen	67	F7
Guoyang	111	F4
Gura Humorului	79	N2
Gurk	75	K4
Gurskoye	105	P6
Gürün	83	G4
Gurupi	141	H4
Gusau	95	F2
Gusev	65	M3
Gushgy	85	H2
Gusinoozersk	105	H6
Gúspini	77	C9
Güssing	75	M3
Güstrow	65	B4
Gütersloh	67	D5
Guthrie, *Okla.*, United States	129	G3
Guthrie, *Tex.*, United States	133	F2
Gutsuo	107	E3
Guttenberg	131	B2
Guwahati	107	F3
Guyana	141	F2
Guyang	111	E2
Guymon	133	F1
Guyuan	111	D3
Guzar	85	J2
Gvardejsk	65	L3
Gwadar	85	H4
Gwalior	107	C3
Gwanda	99	D4
Gwardex	77	J12
Gwda	65	F4
Gweebarra Bay	69	C7
Gweru	99	D3
Gyangzê	107	E3
Gyaring Hu	111	B4
Gyaros	81	G7
Gyda	103	P3
Gydanskiy Poluostrov	103	P3
Gyirong	107	E3
Gyldenløues Fjord	125	Y4
Gympie	119	K5
Gyomaendrőd	79	H3
Gyöngyös	79	G2
Győr	79	E2
Gypsumville	125	M6
Gytheio	81	E8
Gyula	79	J3
Gyumri	83	K3

Legend

- ✕ Continent name
- Ⓐ Country name
- State or province name
- Country capital
- State or province capital
- Settlement
- Mountain, volcano, peak
- Mountain range
- Physical region or feature
- River, canal
- Lake, salt lake
- Gulf, strait, bay
- Sea, ocean
- Cape, point
- Island or island group, rocky or coral reef
- Place of interest
- Historical or cultural region

Name	Page	Grid
Gyzylarbat	85	G2

H

Name	Page	Grid
Haapajärvi	61	N5
Haapsalu	61	M7
Haar	75	G2
Haarlem	59	G2
Haast	121	B6
Habahe	103	R8
Habarūt	85	F6
Habaswein	97	F3
Habbān	85	E7
Habbānīyah	83	K7
Habirag	111	F2
Habomai-Shoto	105	R8
Haboro	113	L1
Hachijō-jima	113	K7
Hachinohe	113	L3
Hachiōji	113	K6
Hadadong	103	Q9
Haddunmahti Atoll	107	B8
Hadejia	95	F2
Hadejia	95	G2
Hadera	86	B4
Haderslev	67	E1
Ḥaḑramaut	85	E6
Hadilik	103	R10
Hadjout	73	N8
Haeju	113	C4
Haenam	113	D6
Ḥafar al Bāṭin	87	A2
Hafnarfjördur	61	(1)C2
Haft Gel	87	C1
Hagen	59	K3
Hagenow	67	G3
Hägere Hiywet	97	F2
Hagerstown	131	E3
Haguenau	59	K6
Haicheng	113	B3
Haifa = Ḥefa	86	B4
Haikou	109	E3
Hä'il	85	D4
Hailar	105	K7
Hailey	129	D2
Hailong	113	C2
Hailuoto	61	N4
Hainan	109	D3
Haines Junction	133	(1)K3
Haining	111	G4
Hai Phong	109	D2
Haiti	137	K5
Haiya	93	G4
Hajdúböszörmény	79	J2
Hajdúhadház	65	L10
Hajdúnánás	65	L10
Hajdúszoboszló	65	L10
Hajipur	107	E3
Hajmah	85	G6
Hajnówka	65	N5
Haka	107	F4
Hakkâri	83	K5
Hakodate	113	L3
Ḥalab	83	G5
Ḥalabān	93	H3
Ḥalabja	83	L6
Halaib	93	G3
Halba	86	D2
Halberstadt	67	G5
Halden	61	F7
Haldensleben	67	G4
Halifax	125	U8
Halifax Bay	119	J3
Hall	75	G3
Hall Beach	125	Q3
Halle	59	G4
Hallein	75	J3
Halligen	67	D2
Hallock	129	G1
Hall Peninsula	125	T4
Halls Creek	119	E3
Halmahera	115	(2)C2
Halmahera Sea	115	(2)C3
Halmstad	65	B1
Haltern	59	K3
Hamada	113	G6
Hamadān	85	E3
Hamāh	83	G6
Hamamatsu	113	J6
Hamar	61	F6
Hamarøy	61	H2
Hamatonbetsu	113	M1
Hambantota	107	D7
Hamburg, Germany	67	E3
Hamburg, Ark., United States	135	C3
Hamburg, N.Y., United States	131	E2
Hämeenlinna	61	N6
Hameln	67	E4
Hamersley Range	119	C4
Hamhŭng	113	D3
Hami	103	S9
Hamilton, Australia	119	H7
Hamilton, Bermuda	137	M2
Hamilton, Canada	131	E2
Hamilton, New Zealand	121	E3
Hamilton, Al., United States	135	D3
Hamilton, Mont., United States	129	D1
Hamilton, Oh., United States	131	D3
Hamina	61	P6
Hamirpur	107	D3
Hamm	67	C5
Hammada du Drâa	91	D3
Hammam Bou Hadjar	73	K9
Hammamet	77	E12
Hammam Lif	91	H1
Hammelburg	67	E6
Hammerfest	61	M1
Hammer Springs	121	D6
Hampden	121	C7
Hāmūn-e Jaz Mūrīān	87	H3
Hanamaki	113	L4
Hanau	67	D6
Hâncești	79	R3
Hancheng	111	E3
Hancock	131	C1
Handan	111	E3
Handeni	97	F5
Handerslev	61	E9
Handlová	65	H9
Hanford	129	C1
Hangayn Nuruu	103	T8
Hangu	111	F3
Hangzhou	111	F4
Hanīdh	87	C3
Hanko	61	M7
Hanksville	129	D3
Hanna	125	K6
Hannibal	135	C2
Hannover	67	E4
Hanö	65	D2
Hanöbukten	65	D2
Ha Nôi	109	D2
Hanoi = Ha Nôi	109	D2
Hanover	131	F2
Han Shui	111	D4
Hanson Bay	121	(1)B1
Hanumangarh	107	B3
Hanzhong	111	D4
Hao	117	M7
Hāora	107	E4
Haparanda	61	N4
Hāpoli	107	F3
Hapur	107	C3
Ḥaraḍ, Saudi Arabia	85	E5
Ḥaraḍ, Yemen	93	H4
Haramachi	113	L5
Harare	99	E3
Harbin	111	H1
Harbour Breton	125	V7
Harburg	67	F3
Hardangerfjorden	61	C7
Hardangervidda	61	D6
Hardenberg	59	J2
Harderwijk	59	H2
Hardin	129	E1
Hardy	135	C2
Haren	59	K2
Härer	97	G2
Hargeysa	97	G2
Har Hu	111	B3
Haridwar	107	C3
Harihari	121	C6
Harima-nada	113	H6
Hari Rud	85	H3
Harlan	131	A2
Härläu	79	P2
Harlem	129	E1
Harlingen, Netherlands	59	H1
Harlingen, United States	135	B4
Harlow	69	N10
Harlowtown	129	E1
Harney Basin	127	B3
Harney Lake	129	C2
Härnösand	61	J5
Har Nuur	103	S8
Haro	73	H2
Harricanaw	125	R6
Harrisburg, Ill., United States	131	C3
Harrisburg, Pa., United States	135	F1
Harrison	131	B3
Harrison Bay	133	(1)G1
Harrisville	131	D2
Harrogate	69	L8
Har Saggi	86	B6
Harsin	83	M6
Hârșova	79	Q5
Harstad	61	J2
Hartberg	75	L3
Hartford	131	F2
Hartland Point	69	H10
Hartlepool	69	L7
Har Us Nuur	103	S8
Harvey	129	G1
Harwich	59	D3
Harz	67	F5
Hāsā	86	C6
Haselünne	67	C4
Hashtpar	83	N5
Hāsik	85	G6
Haskell	135	B3
Haslemere	59	B3
Hassan	107	C6
Hasselfelde	67	F5
Hasselt	59	H4
Haßfurt	67	F6
Hassi Bel Guebbour	91	G3
Hässleholm	61	G8
Hastings, New Zealand	121	F4
Hastings, United Kingdom	59	C4
Hastings, Minn., United States	131	B2
Hastings, Nebr., United States	129	G2
Haṭeg	79	K4
Hatgal	105	G6
Ha Tinh	109	D3
Hatteras	135	F2
Hattiesburg	135	D3
Hatvan	79	G2
Haud	93	H6
Haud Ogadēn	97	G2/H2
Haugesund	61	C7
Hauraki Gulf	121	E3
Haut Atlas	91	D2
Hauts Plateaux	91	E2
Havana	135	C1
Havana = La Habana	137	H4
Havant	69	M11
Havel	65	C5
Havelock, New Zealand	121	D5
Havelock, United States	135	F3
Havelock North	121	F4
Havenby	67	D1
Haverfordwest	69	H10
Havlíčkův Brod	65	E8
Havre	129	E1
Havre-St-Pierre	125	U6
Havrylivtsi	79	P1
Havza	83	F3
Hawaii	133	(2)E2
Hawaii	133	(2)E4
Hawaiian Islands	117	J3
Hawera	121	E4
Hawi	133	(2)F3
Hawick	69	K6
Hawke Bay	121	F4
Hawker	119	G6
Hawr al'Awdah	87	B1
Hawr al Ḥammar	87	B1
Hawthorne	129	C3
Hay	119	H6
Hay	125	H5
Hayange	59	J5
Haydarābad	83	L5
Hayden	133	D2
Hayrabolu	81	K3
Hay River	125	H4
Hays	135	B2
Hazard	131	D3
Hazārībāg	107	E4
Hazebrouck	59	E4
Hazelton, Canada	125	F5
Hazelton, United States	131	E2
Head of Bight	119	F6
Hearne	135	B3
Hearst	131	D1
Hebbronville	133	G3
Hebgen Lake	129	D2
Hebi	111	E3
Hebron, Canada	125	U5
Hebron, Israel	86	C5
Hebron, Nebr., United States	129	G2
Hebron, N.D., United States	129	F1
Hecate Strait	125	E6
Hechi	109	D2
Hechingen	75	D2
Hede	61	G5
Heerenveen	59	H2
Heerlen	59	J4
Ḥefa	86	B4
Hefei	111	F4
Hegang	111	J1
Hegura-jima	113	J5
Hegyfalu	75	M3
Heide	67	E2
Heidelberg	67	D7
Heidenheim	75	F2
Heilbad Heiligenstadt	67	F5
Heilbronn	67	E7
Heimaey	61	(1)C3
Heinola	61	N6
Hejing	103	R9
Hekla	61	(1)D3
Helagsfjället	61	G5
Helena, Ark., United States	135	C3
Helena, Mont., United States	129	D1
Helen Reef	115	(2)D2
Helensville	121	E3
Helgea	65	D1
Helgoland	67	C2
Helgoländer Bucht	67	D2
Hellín	73	J6
Helmand	85	H3
Helmond	59	H3
Helmsdale	69	J3
Helmstedt	67	G4
Helodrano Antongila	99	H3
Helong	113	E2
Helsingborg	61	G8
Helsinge	65	B1
Helsingør	61	G8
Helsinki	61	N6
Helston	69	G11
Helwan	93	F2
Hemel Hempstead	69	M10

Continent name
Country name
State or province name
Country capital
State or province capital
Settlement

Mountain, volcano, peak
Mountain range
Physical region or feature
River, canal
Lake, salt lake
Gulf, strait, bay

Sea, ocean
Cape, point
Island or island group, rocky or coral reef
Place of interest
Historical or cultural region

Name	Page	Grid
Henashi-zaki	113	K3
Henderson, *Ky., United States*	131	C3
Henderson, *Nev., United States*	129	D3
Henderson, *N.C., United States*	135	F2
Henderson Island	117	P8
Hendersonville	131	C3
Hendijarn	87	C1
Hengelo	59	J2
Hengyang	111	E5
Henichesk	63	F5
Hénin-Beaumont	59	E4
Hennebont	71	B6
Hennigsdorf	67	J4
Henryetta	131	A3
Henzada	109	B3
Heppenheim	67	D7
Heppner	129	C1
Hepu	109	D2
Héradsflói	61	(1)F2
Herald Cays	119	J3
Herät	85	H3
Herbert	121	C7
Herborn	67	D6
Herceg-Novi	79	F7
Hereford, *United Kingdom*	69	K9
Hereford, *United States*	137	D2
Herentals	59	G3
Herford	67	D4
Herisau	75	E3
Herlen Gol	111	E1
Hermagor	75	J4
Herma Ness	69	M1
Hermel	86	D2
Hermiston	129	C1
Hermosillo	127	D6
Hernád	65	L9
Herne	67	C5
Herne Bay	59	D3
Herning	61	E8
Herrenberg	75	D2
Hersbruck	67	G7
Herstat	59	H4
Hertlay	59	E6
Hervey Bay	119	K5
Herzberg	67	F5
Hesdin	59	E4
Heshan	109	D2
Hesselø	65	A1
Hessisch-Lichtenau	67	E5
Hettstedt Lutherstadt	67	G5
Heves	65	K10
He Xian	109	E2
Hexigten Qi	111	F2
Heze	111	F3
Hialeah	135	E4
Hiawatha	135	B2
Hibbing	131	B1
Hickory	131	C3
Hidaka-sammyaku	113	M2
Hidalgo del Parral	137	C3
Hiddensee	67	H2
Hierro	91	B3
Higashi-suidō	113	E7
High Point	131	E3
High Wycombe	59	B3
Hiiumaa	61	M7
Hikurangi	121	E2
Hikurangi	121	G3
Hikutaia	121	E3
Hildburghausen	67	F6
Hildesheim	67	E4
Hillsboro, *Oh., United States*	135	E2
Hillsboro, *Oreg., United States*	129	B1
Hillsboro, *Tex., United States*	133	G2
Hillsville	131	D3
Hillswick	69	L1
Hilo	133	(2)F4
Hilton Head Island	135	E3
Hilva	83	H5
Hilversum	59	H2
Himalayas	101	L6
Himarë	81	B4
Himatnagar	107	B4
Himeji	113	H6
Himora	93	G5
Ḥimṣ	86	D2
Hindu Kush	107	A1
Hindupur	107	C6
Hinesville	135	E3
Hingoli	107	C5
Hinnøya	61	H2
Hiroo	113	M2
Hirosaki	113	L3
Hiroshima	113	G6
Hirson	59	G5
Hirtshals	61	E8
Hisar	107	C3
Hisdal	61	C6
Hispaniola	139	D2
Hitachi	113	L5
Hitoyoshi	113	F7
Hitra	61	D5
Hiuchi-nada	113	G6
Hiva Oa	117	M6
Hjälmaren	61	H7
Hjalmar Lake	125	K4
Hjelmsøya	61	M1
Hlinsko	65	E8
Hlohovec	75	N2
Hlyboka	79	N1
Hlybokaye	63	E3
Ho	95	E3
Hobart, *Australia*	119	J8
Hobart, *United States*	133	G1
Hobbs	133	F2
Hobro	61	E8
Hobyo	97	H3
Hô Chi Minh	109	D4
Höchstadt	67	F7
Hockenheim	67	D7
Hódmezővásárhely	79	H3
Hodonin	65	G9
Hoek van Holland	59	G3
Hoeryŏng	113	E2
Hof	67	G6
Hofgeismar	67	E5
Höfn	61	(1)F2
Hofsjökull	61	(1)D2
Hōfu	113	F6
Hohe	75	H3
Hohe Dachstein	65	C10
Hohe Tauern	77	G1
Hohhot	111	E2
Hoh Xil Shan	107	E1
Hôi An	109	D3
Hoima	97	E3
Hokitika	121	C6
Hokkaidō	113	N2
Holbæk	65	A2
Holbrook	133	D2
Holdrege	129	G2
Holguín	137	J4
Holíč	75	N2
Hollabrunn	75	M2
Holland	131	C2
Hollis	133	G2
Hollywood	135	E4
Holman	125	H2
Hólmavík	61	(1)C2
Holmes Reefs	119	J3
Holstebro	61	E8
Holsteinische Schweiz	67	F2
Holsteinsborg = Sisimiut	125	W3
Holton	135	B2
Holyhead	69	H8
Holy Island, *Eng., United Kingdom*	69	L6
Holy Island, *Wales, United Kingdom*	69	H8
Holyoke	129	F2
Holzkirchen	75	G3
Holzminden	67	E5
Homa Bay	97	E4
Homberg	67	E5
Hombori	91	E5
Home Bay	125	T3
Homestead	135	E4
Homewood	135	D3
Homs = Ḥimṣ	86	D2
Homyel'	63	F4
Hondo, *N.Mex., United States*	133	E2
Hondo, *Tex., United States*	133	G3
Honduras	137	G6
Hønefoss	61	F6
Honey Lake	129	B2
Honfleur	59	C5
Hon Gai	109	D2
Hong Kong	109	E2
Hongliuyuan	111	B2
Hongor	111	E1
Honiara	117	F6
Honjō	113	K4
Honokaa	133	(2)F3
Honolulu	133	(2)D2
Honshū	113	L5
Hooge	67	D2
Hoogeveen	59	J2
Hoogezand-Sappemeer	59	J1
Hooper Bay	133	(1)D3
Hoorn	59	H2
Hoorn Islands	117	H7
Hopa	83	J3
Hope, *Canada*	129	B1
Hope, *Ak., United States*	125	B4
Hope, *Ark., United States*	135	C3
Hopedale	125	U5
Hopetoun	119	H7
Hopin	107	G4
Hopkinsville	131	C3
Hoquiam	129	B1
Horadiz	83	M4
Horasan	83	K3
Horgo	105	F7
Horizon Depth	117	D8
Hormak	85	H4
Hormoz	87	F3
Horn	75	L2
Hornavan	61	J3
Horncastle	59	B1
Horodenka	79	N1
Horodok	65	N8
Horqin Youyi Qianqi	105	L7
Horsens	61	E9
Horsham, *Australia*	119	H7
Horsham, *United Kingdom*	59	B3
Horten	61	F7
Hortiguela	73	G2
Horton	133	(1)N2
Ḥoseynābād	87	G2
Hoshab	85	H4
Hoshangabad	107	C4
Hospet	107	C5
Hosséré Vokre	95	G3
Hotan	103	Q10
Hotan	103	Q10
Hot Springs, *Ark., United States*	131	B4
Hot Springs, *N.C., United States*	131	D3
Hottah Lake	125	H3
Houdan	59	D6
Houdelaincourt	75	A2
Houghton	131	C1
Houlton	131	G1
Houma, *China*	111	E3
Houma, *United States*	127	H6
Houmt Souk	91	H2
Houston	127	G6
Hovd	103	S8
Hövsgöl Nuur	105	F6
Howard Junction	121	D5
Howland	117	J5
Hoxie	135	C2
Höxter	67	E5
Hoxud	103	R9
Hoy	69	J3
Høyanger	61	D6
Hoyerswerda	67	K5
Hradeç Králové	65	E7
Hranice	65	G8
Hrazdan	83	L3
Hrodna	65	N4
Hron	65	H9
Hrubieszów	65	N7
Hsin-chu	109	G2
Hsueh-Shan	109	G2
Hsweni	109	B2
Huacho	141	B6
Huade	111	E2
Huadian	113	D2
Huaibei	111	F4
Huaibin	111	F4
Huaihua	111	D5
Huainan	111	F4
Huaiyin	111	F4
Huaki	115	(2)C4
Huallaga	141	B5
Huambo	99	B2
Huancavelica	141	B6
Huancayo	141	B6
Huangchuan	111	F4
Huang	111	F3
Huangshan	111	F5
Huangshi	111	F4
Huang Xian	111	G3
Huangyan	111	G5
Huanren	113	C3
Huanuco	141	B5
Huaráz	141	B5
Huarmey	141	B6
Huasco	143	G4
Huashixia	111	B3
Huatabampo	127	E6
Hubli	107	C5
Huch'ang	113	D3
Huddersfield	69	L8
Huddinge	61	K7
Hudiksvall	61	J6
Hudson	131	F2
Hudson	131	F2
Hudson Bay	125	L6
Hudson Bay	125	P5
Hudson Strait	125	S4
Huê	109	D3
Huelva	73	D7
Huercal Overa	73	J7
Huesca	73	K2
Huéscar	73	H7
Huftaroy	61	C6
Hugo	135	B3
Hugo Lake	135	B3
Huia	121	E3
Huich'ŏn	113	D3
Huila Plateau	99	A3
Huinan	113	C2
Huinca Renancó	143	J5
Huizhou	109	E2
Hulin	105	N7
Hull	131	E1
Hulst	59	G3
Hulun Nur	105	K7
Huma	105	M6
Huma	105	M6
Humaitá	141	E5
Humbe	99	A3
Humboldt	125	L6
Humboldt	129	C2
Hümedān	85	G4
Humenné	65	L9
Humphrey	129	D2
Humpolec	65	E8
Hün	93	C2
Húnaflói	61	(1)C2
Hunchun	113	F2
Hunedoara	79	K4
Hünfeld	67	E6
Hungary	79	F3

Legend:
- Continent name
- Country name
- State or province name
- Country capital
- State or province capital
- Settlement
- Mountain, volcano, peak
- Mountain range
- Physical region or feature
- River, canal
- Lake, salt lake
- Gulf, strait, bay
- Sea, ocean
- Cape, point
- Island or island group, rocky or coral reef
- Place of interest
- Historical or cultural region

Name	Page	Grid
Hungen	67	D6
Hungerford	119	H5
Hüngnam	113	D4
Hunjiang	113	D3
Hunsrück	67	B7
Hunstanton	59	C2
Hunte	67	D4
Hunter Island	117	H8
Huntingburg	135	D2
Huntingdon, *United Kingdom*	59	B2
Huntingdon, *United States*	135	E2
Huntington	135	D1
Huntington Beach	133	C2
Huntly	121	E3
Huntsville, *Canada*	131	E1
Huntsville, *Al., United States*	135	D3
Huntsville, *Tex., United States*	137	E2
Hunyuan	111	E3
Ḥūr	87	G1
Hurdiyo	97	J1
Hurghada	93	F2
Huron	129	G2
Hürth	59	J4
Húsavík	61	(1)E1
Huşi	79	R3
Huslia	133	(1)F2
Husn	86	C4
Husum	67	E2
Hutag	105	G7
Hutanopan	115	(1)B2
Hutchinson	133	G1
Ḥüth	93	H4
Huttwil	75	C3
Huvadu Atoll	107	B8
Huy	59	H4
Huzou	111	G4
Hvannadalshnúkur	61	(1)E2
Hvar	79	D6
Hvar	79	D6
Hvolsvöllur	61	(1)C3
Hwange	99	D3
Hyak	129	B1
Hyannis	129	F2
Hyderabad, *India*	107	C5
Hyderabad, *Pakistan*	85	J4
Hyères	71	M10
Hyesan	113	E3
Hyndam Peak	129	D2
Hyūga	113	F7
Hyvinkää	61	N6

I

Name	Page	Grid
Iaco	141	D6
Ialomiţa	79	P5
Ianca	79	Q4
Iaşi	79	Q2
Ibadan	95	E3
Ibagué	141	B3
Ibar	79	H6
Ibb	93	H5
Ibbenbüren	67	C4
Iberia	141	C5
Ibiza = Eivissa	73	M5
Ibiza = Eivissa	73	M6
Ibotirama	141	J6
Ibrā'	85	G5
'Ibrī	87	G5
Ica	141	B6
İçel	83	F5
Iceland	57	C1
Ichalkaranji	107	B5
Ichinoseki	113	L4
Idabel	135	C3
Ida Grove	131	A2
Idah	95	F3
Idaho	129	D2
Idaho Falls	129	D2
Idar-Oberstein	67	C7
Idfu	93	F3
Idhān Awbārī	91	H3
Idhan Murzūq	91	H4
Idiofa	97	C4
Idlib	83	G6
Idstein	67	D6
Ieper	59	E4
Ierapetra	81	H9
Ifanadiana	99	H4
Ife	95	E3
Igarka	103	R4
Iggesund	61	J6
Igizyar	85	L2
Iglésias	77	C9
Igloolik	125	Q3
Ignace	131	B1
İğneada	81	K3
Igoumenitsa	81	C5
Igra	63	K3
Igrim	63	M2
Igualada	73	M3
Iguatu	141	K5
Ilharaña	99	H2
Ihosy	99	H4
Ihtiman	81	F2
Iida	113	J6
Iim	75	G2
Iisalmi	61	P5
Iiulissat	125	W3
Ijebu Ode	95	E3
IJmuiden	59	G2
IJssel	59	J2
IJsselmeer	59	H2
Ikaria	81	J7
Ikeda	113	M2
Ikela	97	C4
Ikhtiman	79	L7
Iki	113	E7
Ikire	95	E3
Ikom	95	F3
Ikopa	99	H3
Ikorodu	95	E3
Ilagan	109	G3
Īlām	85	E3
Ilawa	65	J4
Ilbenge	105	L4
Ilebo	97	C4
Île d'Anticosti	125	U7
Île de Jerba	91	H2
Île de la Gonâve	137	K5
Île de Noirmoutier	71	C7
Île de Ré	71	D7
Île d'Oléron	71	D8
Île d'Yeu	71	C7
Île Europa	99	G4
Ilek	63	K4
Ilek	63	K4
Île Plane	77	E11
Îles Cani	77	D11
Îles Chesterfield	117	F7
Îles Crozet	89	J10
Îles de la Madeleine	125	U7
Îles Désappointement	117	M7
Îles d'Hyères	71	M11
Îles Duc de Gloucester	117	M7
Îles Glorieuses	99	H2
Ilesha	95	E3
Îles Kerkenah	91	H2
Îles Maria	117	L8
Îles Palliser	117	M7
Île Tidra	91	B5
Île Zembra	77	E11
Ilfracombe	69	H10
Ilha da Trindade	139	H6
Ilha de Marajó	141	H4
Ilha de São Luís	141	J4
Ilha do Bazaruto	99	F4
Ilha Fernando de Noronha	141	L4
Ilha Grande de Gurupa	141	G4
Ilhas Martin Vaz	143	Q3
Ilhéus	141	K6
Iliamna Volcano	133	(1)G4
Iligan	109	G5
Ilkal	107	C5
Iller	75	F3
Illertissen	75	F2
Illichivs'k	79	T3
Illinois	127	H3
Illinois	131	C2
Illizi	91	G3
Ilmenau	67	F6
Ilo	141	C7
Iloilo	109	G4
Ilorin	95	E3
Ilovlya	63	H5
Il'pyrskiy	105	U4
Ilwaco	129	B1
Ilych	63	L2
Imabari	113	G6
Imatra	61	Q6
Imeni-Babushkina	103	G6
Imeni Polinyosipenko	105	P6
Imese	97	B3
Imī	97	G2
İmişli	83	N4
Immeln	65	D1
Immenstadt	75	F3
Ímola	75	G6
Imotski	79	E6
Imperatriz	141	H5
Impéria	75	D7
Imperial	129	F2
Impfondo	97	B3
Imphal	107	F4
Imrali Adası	81	L4
Imroz	81	H4
Inambari	141	C6
In Aménas	91	G3
Inangahua	121	C5
Inanwatan	115	(2)D3
Iñapari	141	D6
Inarijärvi	61	P2
Inca	73	N5
İnce Burun	83	F2
Inch'ŏn	113	D5
Incirliova	81	K7
Indalsälven	61	H5
Independence, *Kans., United States*	135	B2
Independence, *Mo., United States*	131	B3
India	107	C4
Indiana	127	J3
Indiana	131	E2
Indianapolis	135	D2
Indian Ocean	107	D8
Indianola	131	B2
Indian Springs	129	C3
Indiga	63	J1
Indio	133	C2
Indonesia	115	(1)D3
Indore	107	C4
Indramayu	115	(1)D4
Indre	71	G6
Indre Sula	61	C6
Indus	85	K3
İnebolu	83	E3
İnecik	81	K4
İnegöl	83	C3
In Ekker	91	G4
Ineu	79	J3
Ingelheim	59	L5
Ingeniero Jacobacci	143	H7
Ingham	119	J3
Ingoda	105	J6
Ingolstadt	75	G2
Ingrāj Bāzār	107	E3
Ingushetiya	83	L2
Inhambane	99	F4
Inírida	141	D3
Inishmore	69	B8
Inkisi-Kisantu	95	H6
Inn	75	H2
Inner Hebrides	69	F5
Inner Mongolia = Nei Monggol	111	E2
Inneston	119	G7
Innisfail	119	J3
Innsbruck	75	G3
Inongo	97	B4
Inowrocław	65	H5
In Salah	91	F3
Insein	109	B3
Inta	103	K4
Interlaken	75	C4
International Falls	131	B1
Intsy	63	H1
Inubō-zaki	113	L6
Inukjuak	125	R5
Inuvik	133	(1)L2
Invercargill	121	B8
Inverness	69	H4
Inverway	119	E3
Investigator Group	119	F6
Investigator Strait	119	G7
Inya	103	R7
Inya	105	R4
Ioannina	81	C5
Iokanga	103	F4
Iola	135	B2
Iona	69	F5
Ionian Sea	81	B6
Ionioi Nisoi	81	B5
Ios	81	H8
Iowa	127	H3
Iowa City	131	B2
Iowa Falls	131	B2
Ipameri	141	H7
Ipatinga	143	N2
Ipatovo	63	H5
Ipiales	141	B3
Ipiaú	141	K6
Ipoh	115	(1)C2
Iporá	141	G7
Ippy	97	C2
İpsala	81	J4
Ipswich	69	P9
Iqaluit	125	T4
Iquique	143	G3
Iquitos	141	C4
Iracoubo	141	G2
Irakleia	81	F3
Irakleia	81	H8
Irakleio	81	H9
Iraklion = Irakleio	57	G4
Iran	85	F3
Irānshahr	85	H4
Irapuato	137	D4
Iraq	85	D3
Irbid	86	C4
Irbit	63	M3
Irecê	141	J6
Irgiz	63	M5
Irgiz	63	M5
Irhil M'Goun	91	D2
Irian Jaya	115	(2)E3
Iringa	97	F5
Iriri	141	G4
Irish Sea	69	G8
Irkutsk	105	G6
Iron Mountain	131	C1
Ironton	135	E2
Ironwood	131	B1
Irrawaddy	107	F5
Irshava	79	L1
Irta	63	J2
Irtysh	63	P3
Irtyshsk	103	P7
Irumu	97	D3
Irún	73	J1
Irving	69	H6
Irving	133	G2
Isabella	131	B1
Isabella Lake	133	C1
Isabela	115	(2)B1

Legend

- ✖ Continent name
- Ⓐ Country name
- State or province name
- ■ Country capital
- ◻ State or province capital
- ● Settlement
- ▲ Mountain, volcano, peak
- Mountain range
- Physical region or feature
- River, canal
- Lake, salt lake
- Gulf, strait, bay
- Sea, ocean
- Cape, point
- Island or island group, rocky or coral reef
- Place of interest
- Historical or cultural region

Name	Page	Grid
Kalyan	107	B5
Kalymnos	81	J7
Kalymnos	81	J8
Kama	57	K1
Kama	97	D4
Kamaishi	113	L4
Kamande	97	D4
Kamango	103	U6
Kambarka	63	K3
Kambo Ho	113	E3
Kamchatka	105	U6
Kamchatskiy Zaliv	105	U5
Kamenica	81	E2
Kamenka, *Russia*	63	H1
Kamenka, *Russia*	63	H4
Kamen'-na-Obi	103	Q7
Kamen'-Rybolov	113	F1
Kamensk-Shakhtinskiy	63	H5
Kamensk-Ural'skiy	63	M3
Kamenz	65	D6
Kamet	107	C2
Kamiiso	113	L3
Kamina	97	C5
Kamituga	97	D4
Kamiyaku	113	F8
Kamloops	125	G6
Kamoenai	113	L2
Kampala	97	E3
Kampen	59	H2
Kampong Cham	109	D4
Kam''yanets'-Podil's'kyy	63	E5
Kamyanyets	61	M10
Kamyshin	63	J4
Kamyzyak	63	J5
Kanab	133	D1
Kananga	97	C5
Kanazawa	113	J5
Kanbalu	107	G4
Kanchipuram	107	C6
Kandahār	85	J3
Kandalaksha	61	S3
Kandalakshskiy Zaliv	63	F1
Kandi	95	E2
Kandira	81	N3
Kandy	107	D7
Kane	131	E2
Kaneohe	133	(2)D2
Kang	99	C4
Kangaatsiaq	125	W3
Kangal	83	G4
Kangān, *Iran*	87	E3
Kangān, *Iran*	87	G4
Kangaroo Island	119	G7
Kangchenjunga	107	E3
Kangding	111	C4
Kangeq	125	Y4
Kangerluarsoruseq	125	W4
Kangersuatsiaq	125	W2
Kangetet	97	F3
Kangiqsualujjuaq	125	T5
Kangmar	107	E3
Kangnŭng	113	E5
Kango	95	G4
Kangping	111	G2
Kaniama	97	C5
Kanji Reservoir	89	D4
Kanjiža	79	H3
Kankaanpää	61	M6
Kankakee	131	C2
Kankan	95	C2
Kankossa	91	C5
Kannapolis	135	E2
Kano	95	F2
Kanoya	113	F8
Kanpur	107	D3
Kansas	135	A2
Kansas	135	B2
Kansas City, *Kans., United States*	135	C2
Kansas City, *Mo., United States*	135	C2
Kansk	103	T6
Kanta	97	F2
Kantchari	95	E2
Kantemirovka	63	G5
Kanye	99	C4
Kao-Hsiung	111	G6
Kaolack	91	B6
Kaoma	99	C2
Kapanga	97	C5
Kap Arkona	65	C3
Kapchagay	103	P9
Kap Cort Adelaer = Kangeq	125	Y4
Kap Farvel = Uummannarsuaq	125	Y5
Kapfenberg	75	L3
Kapidağı Yarimadası	81	K4
Kapiri Mposhi	99	D2
Kapit	115	(1)E2
Kapiti Island	121	E5
Kaplice	75	K2
Kapoeta	97	E3
Kaposvár	79	E3
Kappel	67	C6
Kappeln	67	E2
Kappl	75	F3
Kapsan	113	E3
Kapuskasing	127	K2
Kapuvár	79	E2
Kara	103	M4
Kara, *Russia*	103	M4
Kara, *Togo*	95	E3
Kara Ada	81	K8
Kara-Balta	103	N9
Karabekaul	85	H2
Kara-Bogaz-Gol	85	F1
Karabutak	63	M5
Karacabey	81	L4
Karacaköy	81	L3
Karacal Tepe	81	Q8
Karachayevo-Cherkesiya	83	J2
Karachayevsk	83	J2
Karachi	85	J5
Karaganda	103	N8
Karaginskiy Zaliv	105	V5
Karaj	85	F2
Karak	86	C5
Kara-Kala	85	G2
Kara-Köl	103	N9
Karakol	103	P9
Karakoram	101	L6
Karaksar	105	K6
Karam	105	H5
Karaman	83	E5
Karamay	103	R8
Karamea	121	D5
Karamea Bight	121	C5
Karamürsel	81	M4
Karaoy	103	N8
Karapinar	81	R7
Kara-Say	103	P9
Karasburg	99	B5
Kara Sea = Karskoye More	103	L3
Karasu	83	D3
Karasuk	103	P7
Karasuk	103	P7
Karatal	103	P8
Karataş	83	F5
Karatobe	63	K5
Karaton	63	K5
Karatsu	113	E7
Karazhal	63	P5
Karbalā'	85	D3
Karcag	79	H2
Karditsa	81	D5
Kärdla	61	M7
Kareliya	61	R4
Karepino	63	L2
Karesuando	61	M2
Kargalinskaya	83	M2
Kargasok	103	Q6
Kargat	103	P6
Kargil	107	C2
Kargopol'	63	G2
Kariba	99	D3
Kariba Dam	99	D3
Karibib	99	B4
Karimata	115	(1)D3
Karimnagar	107	C5
Karkaralinsk	103	P8
Karkinits'ka Zatoka	63	F5
Karlik Shan	111	A2
Karlovac	79	C4
Karlovasi	81	J7
Karlovo	81	G2
Karlovy Vary	67	H6
Karlshamn	65	D1
Karlskoga	61	H7
Karlskrona	61	H8
Karlsruhe	67	D8
Karlstad, *Norway*	61	G7
Karlstad, *United States*	131	A1
Karlstadt	67	E7
Karmala	107	C5
Karmi'el	86	C4
Karmøy	61	C7
Karnafuli Reservoir	107	F4
Karnal	107	C3
Karnische Alpen	75	H4
Karnobat	81	J2
Karodi	85	J4
Karonga	97	E5
Karpathos	81	K9
Karpathos	81	K9
Karpenisi	81	D6
Karpogory	63	H2
Karrabük	83	E3
Kars	83	K3
Karsakpay	63	N5
Kārsava	61	P8
Karshi	85	J2
Karskoye More	103	L3
Karslyaka	81	K6
Karstula	61	N5
Kartaly	63	M4
Kartayel'	63	K2
Kartuzy	65	H3
Karufa	115	(2)D3
Karumba	119	H3
Karur	107	C6
Karvina	65	H8
Karwar	107	B6
Karystos	81	G6
Kasai	97	B4
Kasaji	99	C2
Kasama	99	E2
Kasansay	103	N9
Kasba Lake	125	L4
Kasempa	99	D2
Kasenga	99	D2
Käshän	85	F3
Kashi	85	L2
Kashima	111	L3
Kashiwazaki	113	K5
Kāshmar	85	G2
Kashmor	85	J4
Kasimov	63	H4
Kasli	63	M3
Kasongo	97	D4
Kasos	81	K9
Kaspi	83	L3
Kaspiysk	83	M2
Kassala	93	G4
Kassandreia	81	F4
Kassel	67	E5
Kasserine	91	G1
Kastamonu	83	E3
Kastelli	81	F9
Kastoria	81	D4
Kasulu	97	E4
Kasumkent	83	N3
Kasur	107	B2
Kata	105	G5
Katchall	107	F7
Katerini	81	E4
Katete	99	E2
Katha	107	G4
Katherine	119	F2
Kathiawar	85	K5
Kathmandu	107	E3
Kati	95	C2
Katihar	107	E3
Katiola	95	C3
Kato Nevrokopi	81	F3
Katonga	97	E3
Katoomba	119	K6
Katowice	65	J7
Katrineholm	61	J7
Katsina	95	F2
Katsina-Ala	95	F3
Katsuura	113	L6
Kattakurgan	85	J2
Kattavia	81	K9
Kattegat	61	F8
Katun'	103	R7
Katwijkaan Zee	59	G2
Kauai	133	(2)B1
Kaufbeuren	75	F3
Kauhajoki	61	M5
Kaunas	65	N3
Kauno	65	P3
Kaunus	57	G2
Kaura Namoda	95	F2
Kavadarci	81	D3
Kavajë	81	B3
Kavala	81	G4
Kavār	87	E2
Kavaratti	107	B6
Kavarna	79	R6
Kawagoe	113	K6
Kawakawa	121	E2
Kawambwa	97	D5
Kawasaki	113	K6
Kawau Island	121	E3
Kaweka	121	F4
Kawhia	121	E4
Kawkareik	109	B3
Kawthaung	109	B4
Kaya	95	D2
Kayak	103	U3
Kaycee	129	E2
Kayenta	133	D1
Kayes	95	B2
Kaymaz	81	P5
Kaynar	103	P8
Kayseri	83	F4
Kazachinskoye	105	E5
Kazach'ye	105	P2
Kazakdar'ya	103	K9
Kazakhstan	103	L8
Kazan'	63	J3
Kazanlük	81	H2
Kazan-rettō	117	E3
Kazbek	83	L2
Kāzerūn	87	D2
Kazincbarcika	79	H1
Kazungula	99	D3
Kea	81	G7
Kearney	127	G3
Keban Barajı	83	H4
Kébémèr	91	B5
Kebkabiya	93	D5
Kebnekajse	61	K3
K'ebrī Dehar	97	G2
K'ech'a Terara	97	F2
Keçiborlu	81	N7
Kecskemet	79	G3
Kėdainiai	65	N2
Kedgwick	131	G1
Kédougou	95	B2
Kędzierzyn-Koźle	65	H7
Keele	133	(1)M3
Keene	131	F2
Keetmanshoop	99	B5
Keewatin	131	B1

Legend

- ⊠ Continent name
- A Country name
- a State or province name
- ■ Country capital
- ⬚ State or province capital
- ● Settlement

- ▲ Mountain, volcano, peak
- ▬ Mountain range
- ⊘ Physical region or feature
- ↗ River, canal
- ◪ Lake, salt lake
- ⊐ Gulf, strait, bay

- ▭ Sea, ocean
- ⊐ Cape, point
- ⊡ Island or island group, rocky or coral reef
- ✳ Place of interest
- ▦ Historical or cultural region

Name	Page	Grid
Kefallonia	81	C6
Kefamenanu	115	(2)B4
Keflavík	61	(1)B2
Kegen'	103	P9
Keg River	125	H5
Kehl	75	C2
Keila	61	N7
Keitele	61	N5
Kékes	79	H2
Kelai Thiladhunmathee Atoll	107	B7
Kelheim	75	G2
Kelibia	77	F12
Kelkit	83	G3
Kelmë	65	M2
Kélo	95	H3
Kelowna	125	H7
Kelso	129	B1
Keluang	115	(1)C2
Kem'	63	F2
Kemalpaşa	81	K6
Kemasik	115	(1)C2
Kemer, Turkey	81	M8
Kemer, Turkey	81	N8
Kemerovo	103	R6
Kemi	61	N4
Kemijärvi	61	P3
Kemijärvi	61	P3
Kemijoki	61	P3
Kemmerer	129	D3
Kemmuna	77	J12
Kemnath	67	G7
Kemp's Bay	135	F5
Kempten	75	F3
Kendal	69	K7
Kendall	135	E4
Kendari	115	(2)B3
Kendawangan	115	(1)E3
Kendégué	95	H2
Kendujhargarh	107	E4
Kenedy	135	B4
Kenema	95	B3
Keneurgench	85	G1
Kenge	97	B4
Kengtung	109	B2
Kenhardt	99	C5
Kénitra	91	D2
Kenmore	69	C10
Kennett	135	D2
Kennewick	129	C1
Keno Hill	133	(1)K3
Kenora	127	H2
Kenosha	131	C2
Kentau	103	M9
Kentucky	127	J4
Kentwood	135	C3
Kenya	89	G5
Keokuk	131	B2
Kępno	65	H6
Kepulauan Anambas	115	(1)D2
Kepulauan Aru	115	(2)E4
Kepulauan Ayu	115	(2)D2
Kepulauan Balabalangan	115	(1)F3
Kepulauan Banggai	115	(2)B3
Kepulauan Barat Daya	115	(2)C4
Kepulauan Batu	115	(1)B3
Kepulauan Bonerate	115	(2)A4
Kepulauan Kai	115	(2)D4
Kepulauan Kangean	115	(1)F4
Kepulauan Karimunjawa	115	(1)D4
Kepulauan Karkaralong	115	(2)B2
Kepulauan Laut Kecil	115	(1)F3
Kepulauan Leti	115	(2)C4
Kepulauan Lingga	115	(1)C2
Kepulauan Lucipara	115	(2)C4
Kepulauan Mentawai	115	(1)B3
Kepulauan Nanusa	115	(2)C2
Kepulauan Natuna	115	(1)D2
Kepulauan Riau	115	(1)C2
Kepulauan Sabalana	115	(1)F4
Kepulauan Sangir	115	(2)C2
Kepulauan Solor	115	(2)B4
Kepulauan Sula	115	(2)B3
Kepulauan Talaud	115	(2)C2
Kepulauan Tanimbar	115	(2)D4
Kepulauan Tengah	115	(1)F4
Kepulauan Togian	115	(2)B3
Kepulauan Tukangbesi	115	(2)B4
Kepulauan Watubela	115	(2)D3
Kerch	83	G1
Kerchevskiy	63	L3
Kerempe Burnu	81	R2
Keren	93	G4
Kericho	97	F4
Kerio	97	F3
Kerki	85	J2
Kerkrade	59	J4
Kerkyra	81	B5
Kerkyra	81	B5
Kerma	93	F4
Kermadec Islands	117	H8
Kermadec Trench	117	J9
Kermān	87	G1
Kermānshāh	85	E3
Kermānshāhān	87	F1
Keros	81	H8
Kerpen	59	J4
Kerrville	135	B3
Kerulen	105	J7
Keryneia	83	E6
Keşan	81	J4
Kesennuma	113	L4
Keşiş Dağları	85	C2
Keszthely	79	E3
Keta	95	E3
Ketapang	115	(1)D3
Ketchikan	133	(1)L4
Kétou	95	E3
Kętrzyn	65	L3
Kettering	69	M9
Kettle Falls	127	C2
Kewanee	131	C2
Keweenaw Peninsula	131	C1
Key Largo	135	E4
Keystone Lake	135	B2
Key West	135	E5
Kezhma	105	G5
Kežmarok	65	K8
Khabarovsk	105	P7
Khadyzhensk	83	H1
Khakasiya	103	R7
Khairwāra	107	B4
Khalíg el Suweis	93	F2
Khalīj Surt	93	C1
Khalūf	85	G5
Khamis Mushay	85	D6
Khamkkeut	109	C3
Khampa	105	L4
Khamrà	105	J4
Khān al Baghdād	83	K7
Khandagayty	103	S7
Khandwa	107	C4
Khanewal	107	B2
Khannya	103	X4
Khanpur	107	B3
Khān Shaykhūn	86	D1
Khantau	103	N9
Khantayka	105	D3
Khanty-Mansiysk	63	N2
Khān Yūnis	86	B5
Khapalu	107	C1
Kharabali	63	J5
Kharagpur	107	E4
Kharampur	105	B4
Kharan	85	J4
Khargon	107	C4
Kharkiv	63	G5
Kharlu	61	R6
Kharmanli	81	H3
Kharnmam	107	D5
Kharovsk	63	H3
Khartoum = El Khartum	93	F4
Khasavyurt	83	M2
Khāsh	85	H4
Khashgort	63	N1
Khashm el Girba	93	G4
Khashuri	83	K3
Khaskovo	81	H3
Khatanga	105	G2
Khātūnābād	87	F1
Khatyrka	105	X4
Khavda	85	J5
Khawr Fakkān	87	G4
Khaydarken	85	K2
Khayelitsha	99	B6
Khemis Miliana	91	F1
Khemisset	91	D2
Khenchela	91	G1
Kherämeh	87	E2
Kherson	63	F5
Kheta	103	T3
Kheta	103	T3
Kheygiyakha	63	P2
Khilok	105	J6
Khirbat Isrīyah	86	E1
Khīyāv	83	M4
Khmel'nyts'kyy	63	E5
Khodā Afarīn	83	M4
Kholmsk	105	Q7
Khonj	87	E3
Khon Kaen	109	C3
Khonuu	105	Q3
Khoper	63	H4
Khor	105	P7
Khor	105	P7
Khoreyver	63	L1
Khorinsk	105	H6
Khorramābād	85	E3
Khorramshahr	87	C1
Khorugh	85	K2
Khoseda Khard	63	L1
Khouribga	91	D2
Khrebet Cherskogo	105	P3
Khrebet Dzhagdy	105	N6
Khrebet Dzhugdzhur	105	N5
Khrebet Khamar Daban	105	G6
Khrebet Kolymskiy	101	U3
Khrebet Kopet Dag	85	G2
Khrebet Suntar Khayata	105	P4
Khrebet Tarbagatay	103	Q8
Khroma	105	Q2
Khudoseya	105	C3
Khudzhakh	105	R4
Khujand	85	J1
Khulna	107	E4
Khurayş	87	B4
Khushab	107	B2
Khust	79	L1
Khuzdar	85	J4
Khvormūj	87	D2
Khvoy	83	L4
Khyber Pass	85	K3
Kibaya	97	F4
Kibombo	97	D4
Kibondo	97	E4
Kibre Mengist	97	F2
Kičevo	81	C3
Kichmengskiy Gorodok	63	J3
Kicking Horse Pass	125	H6
Kidal	91	F5
Kidderminster	69	K9
Kidira	95	B2
Kiel	67	F2
Kielce	65	K7
Kieler Bucht	67	F2
Kiev = Kyyiv	63	F4
Kiffa	91	C5
Kigali	97	E4
Kigoma	97	D4
Kihnu	61	M7
Kıkıköy	81	L3
Kikinda	79	H4
Kikori	115	(2)F4
Kikwit	97	B5
Kilchu	113	E3
Kilifi	97	F4
Kilindoni	97	F5
Kilingi-Nõmme	61	N7
Kilis	83	G5
Kiliya	79	S4
Kilkenny	69	E9
Kilkis	81	E4
Killarney, Canada	131	D1
Killarney, Republic of Ireland	69	C9
Kilmarnock	69	H6
Kil'mez	63	K3
Kilosa	97	F5
Kilrush	69	C9
Kilttan	107	B6
Kilwa	97	D5
Kilwa Masoko	97	F5
Kimberley	99	C5
Kimberley Plateau	119	E3
Kimch'aek	113	E3
Kimolos	81	G8
Kimongo	95	G5
Kimry	63	G3
Kincardine	131	D2
Kinder	135	C3
Kindia	95	B2
Kindu	97	D4
Kineshma	63	H3
Kingaroy	119	K5
King City	129	B3
King George Islands	125	R5
Kingisepp	61	Q7
King Island, Australia	119	H7
King Island, Canada	105	AA3
Kingman	133	D1
Kingri	85	J3
Kingscote	119	G7
Kingsland	135	E3
King's Lynn	69	N9
King Sound	119	D3
Kings Peak	129	D2
Kingsport	135	E2
Kingston, Canada	131	E2
Kingston, Jamaica	137	J5
Kingston, United States	131	F2
Kingston-upon-Hull	69	M8
Kingston upon Thames	59	B3
Kingstown	141	E1
Kingsville	135	B4
King William Island	125	M3
King William's Town	99	D6
Kinik	81	K5
Kinka-san	113	L4
Kinna	61	G8
Kinsale	69	D10
Kinshasa	97	B4
Kinsley	135	B2
Kinston	131	E3
Kintampo	95	D3
Kintyre	69	G6
Kinyeti	97	E3
Kinzig	67	E6
Kipini	97	G4
Kipnuk	133	(1)E3
Kirchheim	75	E2
Kirchheimbolanden	59	L5
Kircudbright	69	H7
Kirenga	105	H5
Kirensk	105	H5
Kiribati	117	J6
Kırıkhan	83	G5
Kırıkkale	83	E4
Kirillov	63	G3
Kirinyaga	97	F4
Kirishi	63	F3
Kiritimati	117	L5
Kirkağaç	81	K5
Kirk Bulāg Dāgh	85	E2
Kirkcaldy	69	J5
Kirkjubæjarklaustur	61	(1)E3

Legend

- ☒ Continent name
- ▲ Country name
- ⓐ State or province name
- ■ Country capital
- ◻ State or province capital
- ● Settlement
- ▲ Mountain, volcano, peak
- ⛰ Mountain range
- ⬡ Physical region or feature
- ⟋ River, canal
- ◩ Lake, salt lake
- ◗ Gulf, strait, bay
- ⬓ Sea, ocean
- ◰ Cape, point
- ⬚ Island or island group, rocky or coral reef
- ✳ Place of interest
- ✳ Historical or cultural region

Symbol	Description		Symbol	Description		Symbol	Description
⊠	Continent name		▲	Mountain, volcano, peak		⊟	Sea, ocean
A	Country name		▬	Mountain range		⊳	Cape, point
a	State or province name		⊠	Physical region or feature		⊞	Island or island group, rocky or coral reef
■	Country capital		↗	River, canal		✳	Place of interest
□	State or province capital		◪	Lake, salt lake		⊡	Historical or cultural region
●	Settlement		◣	Gulf, strait, bay			

Name	Page	Grid
Krabi	109	B5
Kradeljevo	77	M5
Kragujevac	79	H5
Kraków	65	J7
Kraljeviča	75	K5
Kraljevo	79	H6
Kralovice	65	C8
Kramators'k	63	G5
Kramfors	61	J5
Kranj	79	B3
Krapina	77	K2
Krapinske Toplice	75	L4
Krasino	103	J3
Krāslava	61	P9
Kraśnik	65	M7
Krasnoarmeysk	63	N4
Krasnoborsk	63	J2
Krasnodar	63	G5
Krasnohrad	63	G5
Krasnokamensk	105	K6
Krasnosel'kup	105	C3
Krasnotur'insk	63	M3
Krasnoufimsk	63	L3
Krasnovishersk	63	L2
Krasnoyarsk	105	E5
Krasnoyarskoye Vodokhranilishche	103	S6
Krasnoznamensk	65	M3
Krasnystaw	65	N7
Krasnyy Chikoy	105	H6
Krasnyy Kut	63	J4
Krasnyy Yar	63	J5
Kratovo	81	E2
Kraynovka	83	M2
Krefeld	59	J3
Kremenchuk	63	F5
Kremmling	129	E2
Krems	75	L2
Kremsmünster	75	K2
Krestovka	63	K1
Krestyakh	105	K4
Kretinga	65	L2
Kribi	95	F4
Krichim	81	G2
Krishna	107	C5
Krishnagiri	107	C6
Kristiansand	61	E7
Kristianstad	61	H8
Kristiansund	61	D5
Kristinehamn	61	H7
Kristinestad	61	L5
Kriti	81	H10
Kriva Palanka	81	E2
Križevci	79	D3
Krk	75	K5
Krk	75	K5
Kroměříž	65	G8
Kronach	67	G6
Krŏng Kaôh Kŏng	109	C4
Kronotskiy Zaliv	105	U6
Kroonstad	99	D5
Kroper	77	H3
Kropotkin	63	H5
Krosno	65	L8
Krško	75	L5
Krugë	81	B3
Krui	115	(1)C4
Krumbach	75	F2
Krung Thep	109	C4
Kruså	67	E2
Kruševac	79	J6
Krychaw	63	F4
Krym'	83	E1
Krymsk	83	H1
Krynica	65	L8
Krytiko Pelagos	81	G9
Kryve Ozero	79	T2
Kryvyy Rih	63	F5
Krzna	65	N5
Ksar el Boukhari	73	N9
Ksen'yevka	105	K6
Ksour Essaf	91	H1
Kuala Kerai	115	(1)C1
Kuala Lipis	115	(1)C2
Kuala Lumpur	115	(1)C2
Kuala Terengganu	115	(1)C1
Kuandian	113	C3
Kuantan	115	(1)C2
Kuçadasi	81	K7
Kučevo	79	J5
Kuching	115	(1)E2
Kucovë	81	B4
Kudat	115	(1)F1
Kudus	115	(1)E4
Kudymkar	63	K3
Kufstein	75	H3
Kugmallit Bay	125	E2
Kühbonän	87	G1
Kühdasht	83	M7
Küh-e Alījuq	87	D1
Küh-e Bābā	85	J3
Küh-e Bül	87	E1
Küh-e Dīnār	87	D1
Küh-e Fürgun	87	G3
Küh-e Hazārān	87	G2
Küh-e Hormoz	87	F3
Küh-e Kalat	85	G3
Küh-e Kührän	87	H3
Küh-e Läleh Zär	87	G2
Küh-e Masähün	87	F1
Küh-e Safidär	87	E2
Kuh-e Sahand	83	M5
Kühestak	87	G3
Küh-e Taftän	85	H4
Kühhä-ye Bashäkerd	87	G3
Kühhä-ye Zägros	87	D1
Kuhmo	61	Q4
Kühpäyeh	87	G1
Kuito	99	B2
Kuji	113	L3
Kukës	79	H7
Kukhtuy	105	Q4
Kukinaga	113	F8
Kula	79	K6
Kulagino	63	K5
Kulandy	103	K8
Kuldīga	61	L8
Kulgera	119	F5
Kulmbach	67	G6
Külob	85	J2
Kul'sary	63	K5
Kultsjön	61	H4
Kulu	83	E4
Kulunda	103	P7
Kulynigol	105	C4
Kuma	63	N3
Kumamoto	113	F7
Kumanovo	79	J7
Kumara, *New Zealand*	121	C6
Kumara, *Russia*	105	M6
Kumasi	95	D3
Kumba	95	F4
Kumbakonam	107	C6
Kumeny	63	K3
Kumertau	63	L4
Kumla	61	H7
Kumluca	81	N8
Kummerower See	67	H3
Kumo	95	G3
Kumta	107	B6
Kumukh	83	M2
Kunene	99	A3
Kungrad	103	K9
Kungu	97	B3
Kungur	63	L3
Kunhing	109	B2
Kunlun Shan	107	D1
Kunming	111	C6
Kunsan	113	D6
Kunszetmarton	65	K11
Künzelsau	67	E7
Kuolayarvi	61	Q3
Kuopio	63	E2
Kupang	119	B2
Kupino	103	P7
Kupreanof Point	133	(1)F4
Kup''yans'k	63	G5
Kuqa	103	Q9
Kür	83	M3
Kura	85	E2
Kuragino	105	E6
Kurashiki	113	G6
Kurasia	107	D4
Kurchum	103	Q8
Kürdämir	83	N3
Kurduvadi	107	C5
Kürdzhali	81	H3
Kure	113	G6
Kure Island	117	J3
Kuressaare	61	M7
Kureyka	105	D3
Kureyka	105	E3
Kurgal'dzhinskiy	103	N7
Kurgan	63	N3
Kurikka	61	M5
Kuril Islands = Kuril'skiye Ostrova	105	S7
Kuril'skiye Ostrova	105	S7
Kuril Trench	101	V5
Kuripapango	121	F4
Kurmuk	93	F5
Kurnool	107	C5
Kuroiso	113	K5
Kurow	121	C7
Kuršėnai	65	M1
Kursk	63	G4
Kuršumlija	79	J6
Kurşunlu	83	E3
Kuruman	99	C5
Kurume	113	F7
Kurumkan	105	J6
Kushikino	113	F8
Kushimoto	113	H7
Kushir	105	H6
Kushiro	113	N2
Kushmurun	63	M4
Kushum	63	K4
Kuskokwim Bay	133	(1)E4
Kuskokwim Mountains	133	(1)F3
Kussharo-ko	113	N2
Kustanay	63	M4
Kütahya	83	C4
K'ut'aisi	83	K2
Kutan	83	M1
Kutchan	113	L2
Kutina	79	D4
Kutno	65	J5
Kutu	95	H5
Kutum	93	D5
Kuujjua	125	J2
Kuujjuaq	125	T5
Kuujjuarapik	125	R5
Kuusamo	63	E1
Kuvango	99	B2
Kuwait	87	B2
Kuwait = Al Kuwayt	87	C2
Kuya	63	H1
Kuybyshev	103	P6
Kuygan	103	N8
Kuytun	103	R9
Kuyumba	105	F4
Kuznetsk	63	J4
Kuzomen'	63	G1
Kvaløya, *Norway*	61	M1
Kvaløya, *Norway*	61	J2
Kvalynsk	103	H7
Kwale	97	F4
Kwangju	113	D6
Kwango	97	B5
Kwazulu Natal	99	E5
Kwekwe	99	D3
Kwidzyn	61	K10
Kwilu	95	H5
Kyakhta	105	H6
Kyancutta	119	G6
Kyaukse	107	G4
Kyeburn	121	C7
Kyeintali	107	F5
Kyjov	75	N2
Kyklades	81	G7
Kyle of Lochalsh	69	G4
Kyll	59	J4
Kyllini	81	D7
Kymi	81	G6
Kyŏngju	113	E6
Kyōto	113	H6
Kyparissia	81	D7
Kyperissiakos Kolpos	81	C7
Kyra Panagia	81	G5
Kyren	105	G6
Kyrgyzstan	103	N9
Kyritz	67	H4
Kyrta	63	L2
Kyshtovka	103	P6
Kystatyam	105	L3
Kytalyktakh	105	N3
Kythira	81	E8
Kythira	81	F8
Kythnos	81	G7
Kyūshū	113	F7
Kyūshū-sanchi	113	F7
Kyustendil	81	E2
Kyusyur	105	M2
Kyyiv	63	F4
Kyzyl	103	S7
Kyzyl-Dzhar	63	N5
Kyzyl-Orda	63	N6
Kzyltu	103	N7

L

Name	Page	Grid
Laascaanood	97	H2
Laatzen	67	E4
Laba	95	F2
La Banda	143	J4
La Bañeza	73	E2
La Baule	71	C6
Labbezenga	91	F5
Labe	65	E7
Labé	95	B2
Labin	75	K5
Labinsk	83	J1
Laboulaye	143	J5
Labrador	125	U6
Labrador City	125	T6
Labrador Sea	125	V4
Lábrea	141	E5
Labrieville	131	G1
Labuha	115	(2)C3
Labuhanbajo	115	(2)A4
Labytnangi	103	M4
Laç	79	G8
Lac à l'Eau Claire	125	R5
Lacanau	71	D8
La Carolina	73	G6
Lac Bienville	125	S5
Lac Brochet	125	L5
Laccadive Islands	107	B6
Lac d'Annecy	75	B5
Lac de Bizerte	77	D11
Lac Débo	91	E5
Lac de Kossou	95	C3
Lac de Lagdo	95	G3
Lac de Manantali	95	C2
Lac de Mbakaou	95	G3
Lac de Neuchâtel	75	B4
Lac de Retenue de la Lufira	97	D6
Lac de St-Croix	75	B7
Lac des Bois	125	G3
Lac de Sélingue	95	C2
Lac Do	91	E5
Lac du Bourget	75	A5
Lacedónia	77	K7

Legend

- X Continent name
- A Country name
- a State or province name
- Country capital
- State or province capital
- ● Settlement
- Mountain, volcano, peak
- Mountain range
- Physical region or feature
- River, canal
- Lake, salt lake
- Gulf, strait, bay
- Sea, ocean
- Cape, point
- Island or island group, rocky or coral reef
- Place of interest
- Historical or cultural region

Name	Page	Grid
Lacepede Bay	119	G7
Lac Evans	125	R6
Lac Faguibine	91	E5
Lac Fitri	93	C5
La Charité-sur-Loire	71	J6
La Chaux-de-Fonds	75	B3
La Chorrera	141	C4
Lac Ichkeul	77	D11
La Ciotat	71	L10
Lac La Biche	125	J6
Lac La Martre	125	H4
Lac Léman = Lake Geneva	75	B4
Lac Mai-Ndombe	97	B4
Lac-Mégantic	131	F1
Lac Minto	125	R5
Lac Nzilo	97	D6
Lac Onangué	95	F5
Láconi	77	D9
Laconia	131	F2
Lac Payne	125	S5
La Crosse	131	B2
La Cruz	127	E7
Lac St-Jean	131	F1
Lac St. Joseph	125	N6
Lac Seul	125	N6
Lac Tumba	97	B4
Lacul Brateş	79	Q4
Lacul Razim	79	R5
Lacul Sinoie	79	R5
Lac Upemba	97	D5
La Dorada	141	C2
Ladozhskoye Ozero	63	F2
Ladysmith, *South Africa*	99	D5
Ladysmith, *United States*	131	B1
Ladyzhenka	63	N4
La Esmeralda	141	D3
Læsø	61	F8
Lafayette, *Ind., United States*	131	C2
Lafayette, *La., United States*	135	C3
Lafia	95	F3
Lafiagi	95	F3
La Flèche	71	E6
Lafnitz	75	M3
Laft	87	F3
Lagan	61	G8
Lagan'	63	J5
Lage	59	L3
Lågen	61	E6
Lage's	129	D2
Laghouat	91	F2
Lagkadas	81	F4
Lagoa dos Patos	143	L5
Lagoa Mirim	143	L5
Lago Argentino	143	G9
Lago de Cahora Bassa	99	E3
Lago del Coghinas	77	C8
Lago del Flumendosa	77	D9
Lago de Maracaibo	141	C2
Lago de Nicaragua	137	G6
Lago de Poopó	141	D7
Lago di Caine	75	D5
Lago di Como	75	E4
Lago di Garda	75	F5
Lago di Lecco	75	E5
Lago di Lugano	75	E5
Lago d'Iseo	75	E5
Lago di Verano	77	K7
Lago Maggiore	75	D5
Lago Omodeo	77	C8
Lago Rogaguado	141	D6
Lagos, *Nigeria*	95	E3
Lagos, *Portugal*	73	B7
Lago Titicaca	141	D7
Lago Trasimeno	77	G5
La Goulette	77	E12
La Grand-Combe	71	K9
La Grande	129	C1
La Grange	135	E3
La Gran Sabana	141	E2
Laguna	143	M4
Laguna de Caratasca	137	H5
Laguna Madre	135	B4
Laguna Mar Chiquita	139	E7
Lagunillas	141	E7
La Habana	137	H4
Lahad Datu	109	F5
Lahat	115	(1)C3
La Haye-du-Puits	59	A5
Lāhījān	85	F2
Lahn	59	L4
Lahnstein	59	K4
Laholmsbukten	65	B1
Lahore	107	B2
Lahr	75	C2
Lahti	61	N6
Laï	97	B2
Laiagam	115	(2)F4
Lai Chau	109	C2
L'Aigle	59	C6
Laihia	61	M5
Laingsburg	99	C6
Laiwu	111	F3
Laiyuan	111	E3
Lajanurpekhi	83	K2
Lajes	143	L4
Lajosmizse	65	J10
La Junta	129	F3
Lake Abbe	97	G1
Lake Abitibi	131	E1
Lake Albert, *Democratic Republic of Congo/Uganda*	97	D3
Lake Albert, *United States*	129	B2
Lake Almanor	129	B2
Lake Amadeus	119	F4
Lake Andes	129	G2
Lake Argyle	119	E3
Lake Argyle Tourist Village	119	E3
Lake Athabasca	125	K5
Lake Austin	119	C5
Lake Balkhash = Ozero Balkhash	101	L5
Lake Bangweulu	99	E2
Lake Barlee	119	C5
Lake Benmore	121	C7
Lake Blanche	119	H5
Lake Buchanan	133	G2
Lake Callabonna	119	H5
Lake Carey	119	D5
Lake Carnegie	119	D5
Lake Chad	93	B5
Lake Charles	135	C3
Lake Chelan	129	B1
Lake Chilwa	99	F3
Lake City	135	E3
Lake Claire	125	J5
Lake Coleridge	121	C6
Lake Constance	75	E3
Lake Crowley	129	C3
Lake C. W. McConaughy	129	F2
Lake Diefenbaker	125	K6
Lake Disappointment	119	D4
Lake District	69	J7
Lake Dojran	81	E3
Lake Dora	119	D4
Lake Dundas	119	B6
Lake Edward	97	D4
Lake Elwall	129	D1
Lake Erie	131	D2
Lake Eyasi	97	E4
Lake Eyre	117	D8
Lake Eyre Basin	119	G5
Lake Eyre North	119	G5
Lake Eyre South	119	G5
Lake Francis Case	129	G2
Lake Frome	119	H6
Lake Gairdner	119	G6
Lake Geneva	75	B4
Lake Gordon	119	H8
Lake Grace	119	C6
Lake Harbour	125	T4
Lake Haroko	121	A7
Lake Havasu	133	C2
Lake Havasu City	133	D2
Lake Hopkins	119	E4
Lake Hudson	135	B2
Lake Huron	131	D1
Lake Jackson	135	B4
Lake Kariba	99	D3
Lake Kemp	135	B2
Lake Kerkinitis	79	L8
Lake Kivu	97	D4
Lake Kyoga	97	E3
Lake Ladoga = Ladozhskoye Ozero	63	F2
Lakeland	135	E4
Lake Lefroy	119	D6
Lake Louis	125	H6
Lake Macdonald	119	E4
Lake Mackay	119	E4
Lake Macleod	119	B4
Lake Manapouri	121	A7
Lake Manitoba	125	M6
Lake Manyara	97	F4
Lake Maurice	119	F5
Lake McDonald	129	D1
Lake McMillan	133	F2
Lake Mead	129	D3
Lake Melville	125	U6
Lake Michigan	131	C2
Lake Moore	119	C5
Lake Murray	115	(2)F4
Lake Mweru	97	D5
Lake Mweru Wantipa	97	E5
Lake Nash	119	G4
Lake Nasser	93	F3
Lake Natron	97	F4
Lake Neale	119	E4
Lake Nipigon	125	P6/7
Lake Nipissing	131	E1
Lake Nyasa	99	E2
Lake Oahe	129	F2
Lake of the Woods	131	B1
Lake Ohau	121	B7
Lake Ohrid	81	C4
Lake Okeechobee	135	E4
Lake Onega = Onezhskoye Ozero	57	H1
Lake Ontario	131	E2
Lake O' The Cherokees	131	B3
Lake O' The Pines	135	C3
Lake Paringa	121	B6
Lake Peipus	61	P7
Lake Placid	135	E4
Lakeport	129	B3
Lake Poteriteri	121	A8
Lake Powell	129	D3
Lake Prespa	81	D4
Lake Providence	135	C3
Lake Pskov	61	P7
Lake Pukaki	121	C7
Lake Rotorua	121	F4
Lake Rukwa	97	E5
Lake St. Lucia	99	E5
Lake Sakakawea	129	F1
Lake Scutari	79	G7
Lake Simcoe	131	E2
Lake Superior	131	C1
Lake Tahoe	129	B3
Lake Tanganyika	97	D5
Lake Taupo	121	E4
Lake Te Anau	121	A7
Lake Tekapo	121	C6
Lake Tekapo	121	C6
Lake Texoma	135	B3
Lake Torrens	119	G6
Lake Travis	133	G2
Lake Tschida	129	F1
Lake Turkana	97	F3
Lake Victoria	97	E4
Lakeview	129	B2
Lake Volta	95	D3
Lake Waikare	121	E3
Lake Waikaremoana	121	F4
Lake Wakatipu	121	B7
Lake Wanaka	121	B7
Lake White	119	E4
Lake Wills	119	E4
Lake Winnipeg	125	M6
Lake Winnipegosis	125	L6
Lakewood	129	E3
Lake Woods	119	F3
Lake Xau	99	C4
Lake Yamma Yamma	119	H5
Lakhdaria	73	P8
Lakhimpur	107	D3
Lakhpat	107	A4
Lakin	135	A2
Lakki	107	B2
Lakonikos Kolpos	81	E8
Lakota	129	G1
Lalín	73	B2
La Línea	73	E8
Lalitpur	107	C4
Lal-Lo	109	G3
La Loche	125	K5
La Louvière	59	G4
La Maddalena	77	D7
Lamar, *Colo., United States*	133	F1
Lamar, *Mo., United States*	135	C2
Lamard	87	E3
La Marsa	77	E12
Lambaréné	95	G5
Lambay Island	69	G8
Lam Chi	109	C3
Lamesa	133	F2
Lamia	81	E6
Lamone	75	G6
Lampang	109	B3
Lampasas	133	G2
Lampedusa	91	H1
Lamu	97	G4
Lanai	133	(2)D3
Lanai City	133	(2)E3
Lancang	109	B2
Lancaster, *United Kingdom*	69	K7
Lancaster, *Mo., United States*	131	B2
Lancaster, *N.H., United States*	131	F2
Lancaster, *Oh., United States*	131	D3
Lancaster, *Pa., United States*	131	E2
Lancaster, *S.C., United States*	135	E3
Lancaster Sound	125	Q2
Lanciano	77	J6
Landau, *Germany*	59	L5
Landau, *Germany*	75	H2
Landeck	75	F3
Lander	129	E2
Landerneau	71	A5
Landor	119	C5
Landsberg	75	F2
Land's End	69	F11
Landshut	75	H2
Landskrona	65	B2
Landstuhl	59	K5
Land Wursten	67	D3
La'nga Co	107	D2
Langarūd	83	N5
Langdon	129	G1
Langeland	67	F2
Langen	59	L5
Langenau	75	F2
Langenhagen	67	E4
Langeoog	67	C3
Langfang	111	F3
Langjökull	61	(1)C2
Langkawi	109	B5
Langkon	109	F5
Langon	71	E9
Langøya	61	H2
Langreo	73	E1
Langres	75	A3
Langsa	109	B6
Langtry	133	F3
Langvatnet	61	G3
Länkäran	83	N4
Lannion	71	B5

Name	Page	Grid
L'Anse	131	C1
Lansing	131	D2
Lanxi	111	H1
Lanya	97	E2
Lanzarote	91	C3
Lanzhou	111	C3
Laoag	109	G3
Lao Cai	109	C2
Laohekou	111	E4
Laon	59	F5
La Oroya	141	B6
Laos	109	C3
Laotougou	113	E2
Lapa	143	M4
La Palma	91	B3
La Palma	137	J7
La Paragua	141	E2
La Paz, *Argentina*	143	K5
La Paz, *Bolivia*	141	D7
La Paz, *Mexico*	137	B4
La Pedrera	141	D4
La Perla	133	F3
La Pérouse Strait	111	L1
La Pesca	135	B5
La Pine	129	B2
Lapithos	86	A1
La Plant	129	F1
La Plata	143	K5
Lappajärvi	61	M5
Lappeenranta	61	Q6
Lappland	61	M2
Laptev Sea = More Laptevykh	105	L1
Lapua	61	M5
Łapy	65	M5
La Quiaca	143	H3
L'Aquila	77	H6
Lār	87	F3
Larache	91	D1
Laramie	129	E2
Laramie Range	129	E2
Larantuka	115	(2)B4
Larat	115	(2)D4
Larba	73	P8
Laredo, *Spain*	73	G1
Laredo, *United States*	133	G3
Largo	135	E4
L'Ariana	77	E12
La Rioja	143	H4
Larisa	81	E5
Larkana	85	J4
Larnaka	86	A2
Larne	69	G7
La Rochelle	71	D7
La Roche-sur-Yon	71	D7
La Roda	73	H5
La Romana	137	L5
La Ronge	125	K5
Lar'yak	103	Q5
La Sarre	131	E1
Las Cabezas de San Juan	73	E7
Las Cruces	133	E2
La Serena	143	G4
La Seu d'Urgell	73	M2
La Seyne-sur-Mer	71	L10
Lashio	109	B2
Lashkar Gāh	85	H3
Łask	65	J6
Las Lomitas	143	J3
La Solana	73	G6
Las Palmas	91	B3
La Spézia	75	E6
Las Plumas	143	H7
Last Chance	129	F3
Lastoursville	95	G5
Lastovo	79	D7
Las Varas	127	E7
Las Varillas	143	J5
Las Vegas, *Nev., United States*	129	C3
Las Vegas, *N.Mex., United States*	133	E1
La Teste	71	D9

Name	Page	Grid
Latina	77	G7
Latisana	75	J5
La Toma	143	H5
La Tuque	131	F1
Latur	107	C5
Latvia	61	M8
Lauchhammer	67	J5
Lauenburg	67	F3
Lauf	67	G7
Lau Group	117	J7
Launceston, *Australia*	119	J8
Launceston, *United Kingdom*	69	H11
La Union	73	K7
Laupheim	75	E2
Laura	119	H3
Laurel	135	D3
Lauria	77	K8
Laurinburg	135	F3
Lausanne	75	B4
Laut, *Indonesia*	115	(1)F3
Laut, *Malaysia*	115	(1)D2
Lauter	59	K5
Lauterbach	67	E6
Lava	65	L3
Laval, *Canada*	131	F1
Laval, *France*	71	E5
La Vall d'Uixo	73	K5
Lavant	75	K4
La Vega	137	K5
Laviana	73	E1
La Vila Joiosa	73	K6
Lavras	143	N3
Lavrentiya	105	Z3
Lavrio	81	G7
Lawdar	93	J5
Lawra	95	D2
Lawrence, *New Zealand*	121	B7
Lawrence, *Kans., United States*	131	A3
Lawrence, *Mass., United States*	131	F2
Lawrenceville	135	D2
Lawton	133	B3
Laya	63	L1
Laylä	93	J3
Laysan Island	117	J3
Layton	129	D2
Lazarev	105	Q6
Lázaro Cárdenas	137	D5
Lazdijai	65	N3
Lazo	105	P3
Leadville	129	E3
Leamington	131	D2
Leavenworth, *Kans., United States*	131	A3
Leavenworth, *Wash., United States*	129	B1
Lebach	59	J5
Lebanon	86	C3
Lebanon, *Mo., United States*	131	B3
Lebanon, *N.H., United States*	131	F2
Lebanon, *Pa., United States*	131	E2
Lebanon, *Tenn., United States*	131	C3
Lebel-sur-Quévillon	131	E1
Lębork	65	G3
Lebrija	73	D8
Lebu	143	G6
Lecce	77	N8
Lecco	75	E5
Lech	75	F3
Leck	67	D2
Le Creusot	71	K7
Łeczna	65	M6
Łęczyca	65	J5
Ledmozero	61	R4
Lee	69	D10
Leech Lake	131	B1
Leeds	69	L8
Leek	59	A1
Leer	59	K1
Leesburg	135	E4
Leeston	121	D6
Leesville	135	C3

Name	Page	Grid
Leeuwarden	59	H1
Leeward Islands	137	M5
Lefkada	81	C6
Lefkada	81	C6
Lefkimmi	81	C5
Lefkonikon	86	A1
Lefkosia	81	R9
Legaspi	109	G4
Legionowo	65	K5
Legnago	75	G5
Legnica	65	F6
Leh	107	C2
Le Havre	59	C5
Lehrte	67	F4
Leiah	107	B2
Leicester	59	A2
Leiden	59	G2
Leie	59	F4
Leigh Creek	119	G6
Leighton Buzzard	59	B3
Leine	67	E4
Leinster	119	D5
Leipzig	67	H5
Leiria	73	B5
Leitrim	69	D8
Leiyang	111	E5
Lek	59	G3
Lelystad	59	H2
Le Mans	71	F6
Le Mars	131	A2
Lemberg	67	D8
Lemesos	81	Q10
Lemgo	59	L2
Lemieux Islands	125	U4
Lemmer	59	H2
Lemmon	129	F1
Le Muret	71	E9
Lena	73	E1
Lena	105	L4
Lendinare	75	G5
Lengerich	59	K2
Lengshuijiang	111	E5
Lengshuitan	111	E5
Leninsk-Kuznetskiy	103	R7
Leninskoye	63	J3
Lenmalu	115	(2)D3
Lenne	59	K3
Lennestadt	59	L3
Lens	59	E4
Lensk	105	K4
Lenti	75	M4
Lentini	77	J11
Léo	95	D2
Leoben	75	L3
León, *Mexico*	137	D4
León, *Nicaragua*	137	G6
León, *Spain*	73	E2
Leonberg	75	E2
Leonforte	77	J11
Leonidi	81	E7
Leonora	119	D5
Le Perthus	71	H11
Lepsy	103	P8
Le Puy	71	J8
Léré	95	G3
Lérici	75	E6
Lerik	83	N4
Lerma	73	G2
Leros	81	J7
Lerwick	69	L1
Lešak	79	H6
Les Andelys	59	D5
Lesbos = Lesvos	81	H5
Les Escaldes	71	G11
Les Escoumins	125	T7
Leshan	111	C5
Les Herbiers	71	D7
Leshukonskoye	63	J2
Leskovac	79	J7

Name	Page	Grid
Lesosibirsk	103	S6
Lesotho	99	D5
Lesozavodsk	113	G1
Les Sables-d'Olonne	71	D7
Les Sept Îles	71	B5
Lesser Antilles	137	L6
Lesser Slave Lake	125	J5
Lesvos	81	H5
Leszno	65	F6
Letaba	99	E4
Letchworth	59	B3
Letenye	75	M4
Lethbridge	129	D1
Lethem	141	F3
Leticia	141	D4
Letpadan	109	B3
Le Tréport	59	D4
Letterkenny	69	E7
Leutkirch	75	F3
Leuven	59	G4
Leuze	59	F4
Levadeia	81	E6
Lévanzo	77	G10
Levashi	83	M2
Levaya Khetta	63	P2
Leverkusen	59	J3
Levice	65	H9
Levico Terme	75	G4
Levin	121	E5
Lévis	131	F1
Levitha	81	J7
Levoča	65	K9
Levski	79	N6
Lewes	59	C4
Lewis	69	F3
Lewis and Clark Lake	129	G2
Lewis Range	125	J7
Lewiston, *Id., United States*	129	C1
Lewiston, *Me., United States*	131	F2
Lewistown, *Mont., United States*	129	E1
Lewistown, *Pa., United States*	131	E2
Lexington, *Ky., United States*	131	D3
Lexington, *Nebr., United States*	129	G2
Lexington, *Va., United States*	131	E3
Lexington Park	135	F2
Leyte	109	G4
Lezhë	79	G8
Lhari	107	F2
Lhasa	107	F3
Lhazà	107	E3
Lhokseumawe	109	B5
Lian Xian	109	E2
Lianyuan	109	E1
Lianyungang	111	F4
Liaocheng	111	F3
Liao He	113	B3
Liaoyang	113	B3
Liaoyuan	113	C2
Liard	125	F5
Liard River	125	F5
Libby	129	C1
Libenge	97	B3
Liberal	135	A2
Liberec	65	E7
Liberia	95	B3
Liberia	137	G6
Liberty	135	C1
Libjo	109	H4
Libourne	71	E9
Libreville	95	F4
Libya	93	C2
Libyan Desert	93	D2
Libyan Plateau	93	E1
Licata	77	H11
Lich	67	D6
Lichinga	99	F2
Lichtenfels	67	G6
Lida	61	N10
Lidköping	61	G7
Lido di Óstia	77	G7
Lidzbark Warmiński	65	K3

Legend

- X Continent name
- A Country name
- a State or province name
- Country capital
- State or province capital
- Settlement

- Mountain, volcano, peak
- Mountain range
- Physical region or feature
- River, canal
- Lake, salt lake
- Gulf, strait, bay

- Sea, ocean
- Cape, point
- Island or island group, rocky or coral reef
- Place of interest
- Historical or cultural region

Liebenwalde . . . . • 67 J4
Liechtenstein . . . . A 75 E3
Liège . . . . • 59 H4
Lieksa . . . . • 61 R5
Lienz . . . . • 75 H4
Liepāja . . . . • 65 L1
Lier . . . . • 59 G3
Liezen . . . . • 75 K3
Lifford . . . . • 69 E7
Lignières . . . . • 71 H7
Ligueil . . . . • 71 F6
Ligurian Sea . . . . ≈ 75 D7
Lihue . . . . • 133 B2
Lijiang . . . . • 109 C1
Likasi . . . . • 97 D6
Lilienfeld . . . . • 75 L2
Lille . . . . • 59 F4
Lillebonne . . . . • 59 C5
Lillehammer . . . . • 61 F6
Lillerto . . . . ⊿ 75 G3
Lilongwe . . . . ■ 99 E2
Liloy . . . . • 109 G5
Lima, *Peru* . . . . ■ 141 B6
Lima, *Mont., United States* . . . . • 129 D2
Lima, *Oh., United States* . . . . . . • 131 D2
Limanowa . . . . • 65 K8
Limassol = Lemesos . . . . • 81 Q10
Limbaži . . . . • 61 N8
Limburg . . . . • 59 L4
Limeira . . . . • 143 M3
Limerick . . . . • 69 D9
Limingen . . . . • 61 G4
Limni Kastorias . . . . ✒ 81 C4
Limni Kerkinitis . . . . ✒ 81 E3
Limni Koronia . . . . ✒ 81 F4
Limni Trichonida . . . . ✒ 81 D6
Limni Vegoritis . . . . ✒ 81 D4
Limni Volvi . . . . ⊿ 81 F4
Limnos . . . . ⬚ 81 H5
Limoges . . . . • 71 G8
Limon . . . . • 129 F3
Limón . . . . • 137 H7
Limoux . . . . • 71 H10
Limpopo . . . . ⊿ 99 D4
Linares, *Chile* . . . . • 143 G6
Linares, *Mexico* . . . . • 133 G4
Linares, *Spain* . . . . • 73 G6
Lincang . . . . • 109 C2
Linchuan . . . . • 111 F5
Lincoln, *United Kingdom* . . . . . . • 59 B1
Lincoln, *Ill., United States* . . . . . • 131 C2
Lincoln, *Me., United States* . . . . . • 131 G1
Lincoln, *Nebr., United States* . . . ◻ 129 G2
Lincoln, *N.H., United States* . . . . • 131 F2
Lindenow Fjord . . . . ≈ 125 Y4
Lindesnes . . . . • 61 D8
Lindi . . . . ⊿ 97 D3
Lindi . . . . • 97 F6
Lindos . . . . • 81 L8
Line Islands . . . . ⬚ 117 L5
Linfen . . . . • 111 E3
Lingen . . . . • 59 K2
Lingga . . . . ⬚ 115 (1)C3
Lingshui . . . . • 109 D3
Linguère . . . . • 95 A1
Lingyuan . . . . • 111 F2
Linhal . . . . • 111 G5
Linhares . . . . • 141 J7
Linhe . . . . • 111 D2
Linjiang . . . . • 113 D3
Linköping . . . . • 61 H7
Linkou . . . . • 113 F1
Linosa . . . . ⬚ 77 G13
Lins . . . . • 143 M3
Linton . . . . • 129 F1
Linxia . . . . • 111 C3
Lin Xian . . . . • 111 E3
Linyi . . . . • 111 F3
Linz . . . . • 75 K2
Liobomil' . . . . • 65 P6
Lipari . . . . • 77 J10

Lipari . . . . ⬚ 77 J10
Lipcani . . . . • 79 P1
Lipetsk . . . . • 63 G4
Lipin Bor . . . . • 63 G2
Lipno . . . . • 65 J5
Lipova . . . . • 79 J3
Lippe . . . . ⊿ 59 L3
Lippstadt . . . . • 59 L3
Lipsoi . . . . ⬚ 81 J7
Liptovský-Mikuláš . . . . • 65 J8
Lipu . . . . • 109 E2
Liqeni i Fierzës . . . . ✒ 79 H7
Liqeni Komanit . . . . ✒ 79 G7
Lira . . . . • 97 E3
Liri . . . . ⊿ 77 H7
Lisala . . . . • 97 C3
Lisboa . . . . ■ 73 A6
Lisbon = Lisboa . . . . ■ 73 A6
Lisburn . . . . • 69 G7
Liscannor Bay . . . . ≈ 69 C9
Lisieux . . . . • 59 C5
Liski . . . . • 63 G4
L'Isle-sur-la-Sorgue . . . . • 71 L10
Lisse . . . . • 59 G2
Lištica . . . . • 77 M5
Listowel . . . . • 69 C9
Listvyanka . . . . • 105 H6
Litang . . . . • 111 C5
Litani . . . . ⊿ 141 G3
Litava . . . . ⊿ 65 F8
Litchfield, *Ill., United States* . . . . • 131 C3
Litchfield, *Minn., United States* . . . • 131 B1
Lithgow . . . . • 119 K6
Lithuania . . . . A 61 L9
Litke . . . . • 105 Q6
Litomerice . . . . • 67 K6
Litomyši . . . . • 65 F8
Litovel . . . . • 65 G8
Litovko . . . . • 105 P7
Little Abaco . . . . ⬚ 135 F4
Little Andaman . . . . ⬚ 107 F6
Little Barrier Island . . . . ⬚ 121 E3
Little Current . . . . • 131 D1
Little Desert . . . . ⊘ 119 H7
Little Falls . . . . • 131 B1
Littlefield . . . . • 133 F2
Little Inagua . . . . ⬚ 137 K4
Little Karoo . . . . ⊘ 99 C6
Little Minch . . . . ≈ 69 E4
Little Nicobar . . . . ⬚ 107 F7
Little Ouse . . . . ⊿ 59 C2
Little Rock . . . . ◻ 135 C3
Littleton . . . . • 129 E3
Litvinov . . . . • 67 J6
Liupanshui . . . . • 111 C5
Liuzhou . . . . • 111 D6
Live Oak . . . . • 135 E3
Liverpool . . . . • 69 K8
Liverpool Bay . . . . ≈ 125 F2
Livingston, *United Kingdom* . . . . . • 69 J6
Livingston, *United States* . . . . . . • 129 D1
Livingstone . . . . • 99 D3
Livingstonia . . . . • 99 E2
Livno . . . . • 79 E6
Livny . . . . • 63 G4
Livonia . . . . • 131 D2
Livorno . . . . • 75 F7
Liwale . . . . • 97 F5
Lizard Point . . . . ⬒ 69 G12
Ljubljana . . . . ■ 75 K4
Ljugarn . . . . • 61 K8
Ljungan . . . . ⊿ 61 J5
Ljungby . . . . • 61 G8
Ljusdal . . . . • 61 J6
Ljusnan . . . . ⊿ 63 C2
Llandovery . . . . • 69 J9
Llandudno . . . . • 69 J8
Llanelli . . . . • 69 H10
Llanes . . . . • 73 F1

Llanos . . . . ⊘ 141 C2
Lleida . . . . • 73 L3
Lli . . . . ⊿ 103 P9
Lloret de Mar . . . . • 73 N3
Llucmajor . . . . • 73 N5
Loano . . . . • 75 D6
Lobatse . . . . • 99 D5
Löbau . . . . • 67 K5
Łobez . . . . • 65 E4
Lobito . . . . • 99 A2
Locarno . . . . • 75 D4
Lochboisdale . . . . • 69 E4
Lochinver . . . . • 69 G3
Loch Linnhe . . . . ✒ 69 G5
Loch Lomond . . . . ✒ 69 H5
Lochmaddy . . . . • 69 E4
Loch Ness . . . . ✒ 69 H4
Lockhart . . . . • 135 B4
Lock Haven . . . . • 131 E2
Lockport . . . . • 131 E2
Locri . . . . • 77 L10
Lodève . . . . • 71 J10
Lodeynoye . . . . • 63 F2
Lodge Grass . . . . • 129 E1
Lodi, *Italy* . . . . • 75 E5
Lodi, *United States* . . . . • 129 B3
Lodja . . . . • 97 C4
Lodwar . . . . • 97 F3
Łódź . . . . • 65 J6
Loei . . . . • 109 C3
Lofoten . . . . ⬚ 61 G3
Logan, *Ia., United States* . . . . . . • 131 A2
Logan, *N.Mex., United States* . . . . • 133 F1
Logan, *Ut., United States* . . . . . . • 129 D2
Logansport . . . . • 131 C2
Logatec . . . . • 75 K5
Logroño . . . . • 73 H2
Lohiniva . . . . • 61 N3
Lohr . . . . • 67 E7
Loikaw . . . . • 109 B3
Loir . . . . ⊿ 71 F6
Loire . . . . ⊿ 71 D6
Loja, *Ecuador* . . . . • 141 B4
Loja, *Spain* . . . . • 73 F7
Lokan tekojärvi . . . . ✒ 61 P3
Lokeren . . . . • 59 F3
Lokichar . . . . • 97 F3
Lokichokio . . . . • 97 E3
Lokoja . . . . • 95 F3
Lokosovo . . . . • 63 P2
Loks Land . . . . ≈ 125 U4
Lolland . . . . ⬚ 67 G2
Lollondo . . . . • 97 F4
Lolo . . . . • 129 D1
Lom . . . . • 79 L6
Lomami . . . . ⊿ 97 C4
Lomas . . . . • 141 C7
Lomas de Zamora . . . . • 143 K5
Lombadina . . . . • 119 D3
Lomblen . . . . ⬚ 115 (2)B4
Lombok . . . . ⬚ 115 (1)F4
Lomé . . . . ■ 95 E3
Lomela . . . . • 97 C4
Lomela . . . . ⊿ 97 C4
Lommel . . . . • 59 H3
Lomonosovka . . . . • 63 N4
Lompoc . . . . • 133 B2
Łomża . . . . • 65 M4
London, *Canada* . . . . • 131 D2
London, *United Kingdom* . . . . . . ■ 59 B3
London, *United States* . . . . • 135 E2
Londonderry . . . . • 69 E6
Londrina . . . . • 143 L3
Longarone . . . . • 75 H4
Long Bay . . . . ≈ 137 J2
Long Beach . . . . • 133 C2
Long Branch . . . . • 131 F2
Long Eaton . . . . • 59 A2
Longford . . . . • 69 E8
Long Island, *Canada* . . . . ⬚ 125 Q5
Long Island, *United States* . . . . . . ⬚ 131 F2

Longlac . . . . • 125 P7
Long Lake . . . . ✒ 129 F1
Longmont . . . . • 129 E2
Long Prairie . . . . • 131 B1
Long Range Mountains . . . . ⊘ 125 V6
Longueuil . . . . • 131 F1
Longview, *Tex., United States* . . . . • 135 C3
Longview, *Wash., United States* . . . • 129 B1
Longwy . . . . • 59 H5
Long Xuyên . . . . • 109 D4
Longyan . . . . • 109 F1
Löningen . . . . • 59 K2
Lönsdalen . . . . ⊿ 61 H3
Lons-le-Saunier . . . . • 75 A4
Lookout Pass . . . . ⊘ 129 C1
Loop Head . . . . ⬒ 69 B9
Lopez . . . . • 109 G4
Lop Nur . . . . ✒ 103 S9
Lopphavet . . . . ≈ 61 L1
Loptyuga . . . . • 63 J2
Lora del Rio . . . . • 73 E7
Lorain . . . . • 131 D2
Loralai . . . . • 107 A2
Lorca . . . . • 73 J7
Lordegān . . . . • 87 D1
Lord Howe Island . . . . ⬚ 119 L6
Lordsburg . . . . • 133 E2
Loreto . . . . • 137 B3
Lorient . . . . • 71 B6
Lörrach . . . . • 75 C3
Lorraine . . . . ⬚ 119 G3
Los Alamos . . . . • 133 E1
Los Angeles, *Chile* . . . . • 143 G6
Los Angeles, *United States* . . . . . • 133 C2
Los Banos . . . . • 129 B3
Los Blancos . . . . • 143 J3
Losheim . . . . • 59 J5
Lošinj . . . . ⬚ 75 K6
Los Mochis . . . . • 137 C3
Lospalos . . . . • 115 (2)C4
Los Telares . . . . • 143 J4
Los Teques . . . . • 141 D1
Lost Trail Pass . . . . ⊘ 129 D1
Los'va . . . . ⊿ 63 M2
Los Vientos . . . . • 143 H3
Lotta . . . . ⊿ 61 Q2
Lotte . . . . • 59 K2
Louang Namtha . . . . • 109 C2
Louangphrabang . . . . • 109 C3
Loubomo . . . . • 95 G5
Loudéac . . . . • 71 C5
Louga . . . . • 95 A1
Loughborough . . . . • 59 A2
Lough Conn . . . . ✒ 69 C7
Lough Corrib . . . . ✒ 69 C8
Lough Derg . . . . ✒ 69 D8
Lough Foyle . . . . ✒ 69 E6
Lough Leane . . . . ✒ 69 C9
Lough Mask . . . . ✒ 69 C8
Lough Neagh . . . . ✒ 69 F7
Lough Ree . . . . ✒ 69 E8
Louhans . . . . • 71 L7
Louisa . . . . • 131 D3
Louisiade Archipelago . . . . ⬚ 119 K2
Louisiana . . . . ▣ 135 C3
Louis Trichardt . . . . • 99 D4
Louisville, *Ga., United States* . . . . • 135 E3
Louisville, *Ky., United States* . . . . • 135 D2
Louisville, *Miss., United States* . . . • 135 D3
Loukhi . . . . • 61 S3
Loulé . . . . • 73 C7
Louny . . . . • 67 J6
Loup . . . . ⊿ 129 G2
Lourdes . . . . • 71 E10
Louth, *Australia* . . . . • 119 J6
Louth, *United Kingdom* . . . . • 59 C1
Loutra Aidipsou . . . . • 81 F6
Louviers . . . . • 59 D5
Lovech . . . . • 79 M6
Lovell . . . . • 129 E2
Lovelock . . . . • 129 C2

Legend

X	Continent name
A	Country name
a	State or province name
■	Country capital
◻	State or province capital
•	Settlement

▲	Mountain, volcano, peak
⬔	Mountain range
⊘	Physical region or feature
⊿	River, canal
✒	Lake, salt lake
≈	Gulf, strait, bay

◡	Sea, ocean
⬒	Cape, point
⬚	Island or island group, rocky or coral reef
✳	Place of interest
⬚	Historical or cultural region

Name	Page	Grid
Lovosice	67	K6
Lovran	75	K5
Lôvua	99	C2
Lowa	97	D4
Lowell	131	F2
Lower Hutt	121	E5
Lower Lake	129	B2
Lower Lough Erne	69	E7
Lower Post	125	F5
Lowestoft	59	D2
Lowville	131	F2
Loxstedt	67	D3
Loyalty Islands	117	G8
Loyno	63	K3
Loznica	79	G5
L-Travemünde	67	F3
Luama	97	D4
Luampa	99	C3
Lu'an	111	F4
Luanda	97	A5
Luangwa	99	E2
Luangwa	99	E3
Luanping	111	F2
Luanshya	99	D2
Luarca	73	D1
Luau	99	C2
Lubaczów	65	N7
Lubań	65	E6
Lubango	99	A2
Lubāns	61	P8
Lubao	97	D5
Lubartów	65	M6
Lübbecke	59	L2
Lübben	67	J5
Lübbenau	67	J5
Lubbock	133	F2
Lübeck	67	F3
Lubefu	97	C4
Lubero	97	D4
Lubilash	97	C5
Lubin	65	F6
Lublin	65	M6
Lubliniec	65	H7
Lubny	63	F4
Luboń	65	F5
Lubsko	65	D6
Lubudi	97	D5
Lubuklinggau	115	(1)C3
Lubumbashi	97	D6
Lubutu	97	D4
Lucala	97	B5
Lucca	75	F7
Luce Bay	69	H7
Lucedale	135	D3
Lucena, Philippines	109	G4
Lucena, Spain	73	F7
Lučenec	65	J9
Lucera	77	K7
Lucero	133	E2
Lucira	99	A2
Luckenwalde	67	J4
Lucknow	107	D3
Luçon	71	D7
Lucusse	99	C2
Ludden	129	G1
Lüdenscheid	59	K3
Lüderitz	99	B5
Ludhiana	107	C2
Ludington	131	C2
Ludlow	133	C2
Ludogori	79	P6
Luduş	79	M3
Ludvika	61	H6
Ludwigsburg	75	E2
Ludwigsfelde	67	J4
Ludwigshafen	59	L5
Ludwigslust	67	G3
Ludza	61	P8
Luebo	97	C5
Luena	99	B2
Lufeng	109	F2
Lufira	97	D6
Lufkin	135	C3
Luga	61	Q7
Luga	63	E3
Lugano	75	D4
Lugela	99	F3
Lugenda	99	F2
Luggate	121	B7
Lugo	75	G6
Lugoj	79	J4
Lugovoy	103	N9
Lugu	107	D2
Luhans'k	63	G5
Luhuo	111	C4
Lui	109	E2
Luilaka	97	B4
Luino	75	D4
Luis Moya	133	F4
Luiza	97	C5
Lukavac	79	F5
Lukovit	79	M6
Łuków	65	M6
Lukulu	99	C2
Lukumburu	97	F5
Lukuni	97	B5
Luleå	61	M4
Lüleburgaz	81	K3
Lulua	97	D5
Lumbala Kaquengue	99	C2
Lumberton	135	F3
Lumbrales	73	D4
Lumimba	99	E2
Lumsden	121	B7
Lund	65	C2
Lundazi	99	E2
Lundy	69	H10
Lüneburg	67	F3
Lüneburger Heide	67	F4
Lunel	71	K10
Lünen	59	K3
Lunéville	75	B2
Lungau	75	J3
Luntai	103	Q9
Luohe	111	E4
Luoyang	111	E4
Luozi	97	A4
Lupeni	79	L4
Lūrā Shīrīn	83	L5
Lure	75	B3
Luremo	97	B5
Lurgan	69	F7
Lurio	99	F2
Lusaka	99	D3
Lusambo	97	C5
Lushnjë	81	B4
Lushui	111	B5
Lüshun	111	G3
Lusk	129	F2
Lutembo	99	C2
Lutherstadt Wittenberg	67	H5
Luton	59	B3
Luts'k	63	E4
Lutto	61	P2
Lützow-Holmbukta	144	(2)J3
Luverne	131	A2
Luvua	97	D5
Luwuk	115	(2)B3
Luxembourg	59	H5
Luxembourg	59	J5
Luxeuil-les-Bains	75	B3
Luxor	93	F2
Luza	63	J2
Luza	63	J2
Luzern	75	D3
Luzhou	111	D5
Luzilândia	141	J4
Luznice	75	K1
Luzon	109	G3
Luzon Strait	109	G2
Luzy	71	J7
L'viv	65	N8
Lyady	61	Q7
Lyapin	63	M2
Lyckselle	63	C2
Lydenburg	99	E5
Lyme Bay	69	K11
Lymington	59	A4
Lynchburg	131	E3
Lynn	131	F2
Lynn Lake	125	L5
Lynx Lake	125	K4
Lyon	71	K8
Lys	59	E4
Lys'va	63	L3
Lysychans'k	63	G5
Lyttelton	121	D6

M

Name	Page	Grid
Maalosmadulu Atoll	107	B7
Ma'ān	86	C6
Maardu	61	N7
Ma'arrat an Nu'mān	83	G6
Maas	59	J3
Maasin	109	G4
Maastricht	59	H4
Mabalane	99	E4
Mabanza-Ngungu	95	G6
Mabein	109	B2
Mablethorpe	59	C1
Macapá	141	G3
Macas	141	B4
Macassar Strait	117	B6
Macau	109	E2
Macau	109	E2
Macau	141	K5
Macaúba	141	G6
Macclesfield	69	K8
Macdonnell Ranges	119	F4
Macedonia	81	C3
Maceió	141	K5
Macerata	75	J7
Machakos	97	F4
Machala	141	B4
Macheng	111	F4
Machilipatnam	107	D5
Machiques	141	C1
Macia	99	E4
Măcin	79	R4
Mack	133	E1
Mackay	119	J4
Mackay Lake	125	J4
Mackenzie	125	G4
Mackenzie Bay	125	D3
Mackenzie Mountains	125	E3
Mackinaw City	131	D1
Macmillan	125	E4
Macmillan Pass	125	F4
Macomb	131	B2
Macomer	77	C8
Macon, Ga., United States	135	E3
Macon, Mo., United States	135	C2
Mâcon	71	K7
Macuje	141	C3
Mādabā	86	C5
Madagascar	99	H3
Madan	79	M8
Madaoua	95	F2
Madeira	91	B2
Madeira	141	E5
Maden	83	H4
Madera	133	E3
Madikeri	107	C6
Madison	131	C2
Madison, Ind., United States	131	C3
Madison, Minn., United States	131	A1
Madison, S.D., United States	129	G2
Madisonville	131	C3
Madiun	115	(1)E4
Mado Gashi	97	F3
Madoi	111	B4
Madona	61	P8
Madras = Chennai, India	107	D6
Madras, United States	129	B2
Madre de Dios	141	C6
Madrid, Philippines	109	H5
Madrid, Spain	73	G4
Madridejos	73	G5
Madura	115	(1)E4
Madurai	107	C6
Maebashi	113	K5
Mae Hong Son	109	B3
Mae Nam Mun	109	C3
Mae Sariang	109	B3
Maevatanana	99	H3
Mafeteng	99	D5
Maffighofen	75	J2
Mafia Island	97	G5
Mafra	143	M4
Mafraq	86	D4
Magadan	105	S5
Magadi	97	F4
Magdagachi	105	M6
Magdalena	141	C2
Magdalena, Bolivia	141	E6
Magdalena, Mexico	133	D2
Magdalena, United States	133	E2
Magdeburg	67	G4
Magdelaine Cays	119	K3
Magelang	115	(1)E4
Magenta	75	D5
Magerøya	61	N1
Maglaj	79	F5
Máglie	77	N8
Magnitogorsk	63	L4
Magnolia	135	C3
Mago	105	P6
Magog	131	F1
Magu	97	E4
Magwe	109	A2
Mahābād	83	L5
Mahagi	97	E3
Mahajamba	99	H3
Mahajanga	99	H3
Mahalapye	99	D4
Mahān	87	G1
Mahanadi	107	D4
Mahanoro	99	H3
Mahasamund	107	D4
Mahavavy	99	H3
Mahbubnagar	107	D5
Maḩḍah	87	G4
Mahé Island	99	(2)C1
Mahenge	97	F5
Mahesāna	107	B4
Mahia Peninsula	121	F4
Mahilyow	63	F4
Mahnomen	131	A1
Mahón	73	Q5
Mahuva	85	K5
Maicao	141	C1
Maidenhead	59	B3
Maidstone	59	C3
Maiduguri	95	G2
Mai Gudo	97	F2
Maímédy	67	B6
Main	67	E7
Mainburg	75	G2
Main-Donau-Kanal	67	G7
Maine	131	G1
Maïné Soroa	95	G2
Maingkwan	109	B1
Mainland, Orkney Is., United Kingdom	69	J2
Mainland, Shetland Is., United Kingdom	69	L1
Maintirano	99	G3
Mainz	67	D6
Maio	95	(1)B1
Majene	115	(2)A3
Majicana	143	H4
Majuro	117	H5

Continent name
Country name
State or province name
Country capital
State or province capital
Settlement

Mountain, volcano, peak
Mountain range
Physical region or feature
River, canal
Lake, salt lake
Gulf, strait, bay

Sea, ocean
Cape, point
Island or island group, rocky or coral reef
Place of interest
Historical or cultural region

Name		Page	Grid
Makale	●	115	(2)A3
Makamba	●	97	D4
Makanza	●	97	B3
Makarora	●	121	B7
Makarov	●	105	Q7
Makarska	●	79	E6
Makar'yev	●	63	H3
Makat	●	63	K5
Makeni	●	95	B3
Makgadikgadi	◿	99	C4
Makhachkala	◻	83	M2
Makhorovka	●	103	M7
Makindu	●	97	F4
Makinsk	●	63	P4
Makiyivka	●	63	G5
Makkah	●	93	G3
Makó	●	79	H3
Makokou	●	95	G4
Makongolosi	●	97	E5
Makorako	▲	121	F4
Makoua	●	95	H4
Maków Mazowiecka	●	65	L5
Makran	▨	85	G4
Makronisi	▨	81	G7
Mākū	●	83	L4
Makumbako	●	97	E5
Makurazaki	●	113	F8
Makurdi	●	95	F3
Makūyeh	●	87	E2
Makuyuni	●	97	F4
Malabar Coast	▨	107	B6
Malabo	■	95	F4
Malack	●	65	F9
Malacky	●	75	M2
Malad City	●	129	D2
Maladzyechna	●	63	H4
Málaga	●	73	F8
Malaimbandy	●	99	H4
Malaita	▨	117	G6
Malakal	●	97	E2
Malakula	▨	117	G7
Malamala	●	115	(2)B3
Malang	●	115	(1)E4
Malanje	●	97	B5
Malanville	●	95	E2
Malaryta	●	65	P6
Malatya	●	83	H4
Malaut	●	107	B2
Mālavi	●	83	M7
Malawi	Ⓐ	99	E2
Malaya Baranikha	●	105	V3
Malaya Vishera	●	63	F3
Malaybalay	●	109	H5
Maläyer	●	85	E3
Malay Peninsula	▨	109	C6
Malay Reef	▨	119	J3
Malaysia	Ⓐ	115	(1)C2
Malbork	●	65	J3
Malchin, *Germany*	●	67	H3
Malchin, *Mongolia*	●	103	S8
Malden Island	▨	117	L6
Maldives	Ⓐ	107	B8
Maldonado	●	143	L5
Malé	●	75	F4
Male	■	107	B8
Male Atoll	▨	107	B8
Malegaon	●	107	B4
Malé Karpaty	▰	75	N2
Malesherbes	●	71	H5
Maleta	●	105	H6
Malheur	◿	129	C2
Malheur Lake	◿	129	C2
Mali	Ⓐ	91	E5
Malindi	●	97	G4
Malin Head	⊳	69	E6
Malkara	●	81	J4
Malko Tŭrnovo	●	79	Q8
Mallaig	●	69	G4
Mallawi	●	93	F2
Mallorca	▨	73	P5
Mallow	●	69	D9
Malmédy	●	59	J4
Malmesbury	●	99	B6
Malmö	●	65	C2
Malmyzh	●	63	K3
Malone	●	131	F2
Måløy	●	61	C6
Malozemel'skaya Tundra	▨	63	K1
Mălselv	◿	61	K2
Malta	Ⓐ	77	J13
Malta	●	129	E1
Malta Channel	⊵	77	J12
Maltahöhe	●	99	B4
Malvern	●	131	B4
Malý Dunaj	◿	75	N2
Malyy Uzen'	◿	63	J4
Mama	●	105	J5
Mamadysh	●	63	K3
Mambasa	●	97	D3
Mamburao	●	109	G4
Mamelodi	●	99	D5
Mammoth Hot Springs	●	129	D2
Mamonovo	●	65	J3
Mamoré	◿	141	D6
Mamou	●	95	B2
Mamoudzou	●	99	H2
Mamuju	●	115	(2)A3
Ma'mūl	●	85	G6
Mamuno	●	99	C4
Man	●	95	C3
Mana	●	133	(2)A1
Manacapuru	●	141	E4
Manacor	●	73	P5
Manado	●	115	(2)B2
Managua	■	137	G6
Manakara	●	99	H4
Manali	●	107	C2
Manananara	◿	99	H4
Mananara Avaratra	●	99	H3
Mananjary	●	99	H4
Manantenina	●	99	H4
Manassas	●	131	E3
Manaus	◻	141	E4
Manavgat	●	81	P8
Manbij	●	83	G5
Manchester, *United Kingdom*	●	69	K8
Manchester, *Ia., United States*	●	131	B2
Manchester, *Ky., United States*	●	131	D3
Manchester, *Tenn., United States*	●	131	C3
Manchester, *Vt., United States*	●	131	F2
Mand	●	85	H4
Mandabe	●	99	G4
Mandal	●	61	D7
Mandalay	●	109	B2
Mandalgovǐ	●	111	D1
Mandan	●	129	F1
Mandera	●	97	G3
Mandi	●	107	C2
Mandi Burewala	●	107	B2
Mandimba	●	99	F2
Manding	▰	91	D6
Mandla	●	107	D4
Mandø	▨	67	D1
Mandsaur	●	107	C4
Mandurah	●	119	C6
Mandúria	●	77	M8
Mandvi	●	107	A4
Mandya	●	107	C6
Manfredonia	●	77	K7
Manga	▨	95	G2
Manga	●	141	J6
Mangaia	▨	117	K8
Mangalia	●	79	R6
Mangalore	●	107	B6
Mangareva	▨	117	N8
Mangatupopo	●	121	E4
Mangaweka	▲	121	F4
Manggar	●	115	(1)D3
Mangit	●	85	H1
Mangnai	●	103	S10
Mango	●	95	E2
Mangoky	◿	99	G4
Mangole	▨	115	(2)C3
Mangonui	●	121	D2
Mangrove Cay	●	135	F5
Manhad	●	107	B5
Manhattan	●	135	B2
Manhuaçu	●	141	J8
Mania	◿	99	H3
Maniamba	●	99	F2
Manicoré	●	141	E5
Manicouagan	◿	125	T6
Manihiki	▨	117	K7
Maniitsoq	●	125	W3
Manila	■	109	G4
Manisa	●	81	K6
Manistee	●	131	C2
Manistique	●	131	C1
Manitoba	ⓐ	125	M6
Manitou	●	129	G1
Manitoulin Island	▨	131	D1
Manitouwadge	●	131	C1
Manitowoc	●	131	C2
Maniwaki	●	131	E1
Manizales	●	141	B2
Manja	●	99	G4
Manjimup	●	119	C6
Mankato	●	131	B2
Manley Hot Springs	●	125	A4
Manlleu	●	73	N3
Manna	●	115	(1)C3
Mannheim	●	59	L5
Manning, *Canada*	●	125	H5
Manning, *United States*	●	135	E3
Manokwari	●	115	(2)D3
Manono	●	97	D5
Manosque	●	71	L10
Manouane	●	131	F1
Manouane Lake	◿	125	S6
Manp'o	●	113	D3
Manra	▨	117	J6
Manresa	●	73	M3
Mansa	●	99	D2
Mansel Island	▨	125	Q4
Mansfield, *United Kingdom*	●	59	A1
Mansfield, *La., United States*	●	135	C3
Mansfield, *Oh., United States*	●	131	D2
Manta	●	141	A4
Manteo	●	135	F2
Mantes-la-Jolie	●	59	D5
Mántova	●	75	F5
Manturovo	●	63	H3
Manú	●	141	C6
Manuelzinho	●	141	G5
Manūjān	●	87	G3
Manukan	●	109	G5
Manukau	●	121	E3
Manukau Harbour	⊵	121	E3
Manyberries	●	129	D1
Manyinga	●	99	C2
Manyoni	●	97	E5
Manzanares	●	73	G5
Manzanillo	●	137	J4
Manzhouli	●	105	K7
Manzini	●	99	E5
Mao	●	93	C5
Maoming	●	109	E2
Mapam Yumco	◿	107	D2
Mapi	●	115	(2)E4
Mapinhane	●	99	F4
Maple Creek	●	127	E2
Mapuera	◿	141	E4
Maputo	●	99	E5
Maqueda	●	73	F4
Maquela do Zombo	●	97	B5
Maquinchao	●	143	H7
Maquoketa	●	131	B2
Maraba	●	141	F4
Maracaibo	●	141	C1
Maracay	●	141	D1
Marādah	●	93	C2
Maradi	●	95	F2
Marāgheh	●	83	M5
Maralal	●	97	F3
Marand	●	83	L4
Maranhão	ⓐ	141	H5
Marañón	◿	141	B4
Mărăşeşti	●	79	Q4
Marathon, *Canada*	●	131	C1
Marathon, *United States*	●	133	F2
Marbella	●	73	F8
Marburg	●	59	L4
Marcal	◿	75	N3
Marcali	●	75	N4
March	●	59	C2
Marche	●	59	H4
Marchena	●	73	E7
Mardan	●	107	B2
Mar del Plata	●	143	K6
Mardin	●	83	J5
Maré	▨	117	G8
Mareeba	●	119	J3
Marettimo	▨	77	F11
Marfa	●	133	F2
Margate	●	59	D3
Margherita di Savoia	●	77	L7
Marghita	●	79	K2
Margilan	●	85	K1
Marguerite Bay	⊵	144	(2)KK3
María Elena	●	143	H3
Marianas Trench	▨	117	E4
Marianna	●	135	D3
Mariánská Lázně	●	67	H7
Mariazell	●	75	L3
Mar'ib	●	93	J4
Maribo	●	67	G2
Maribor	●	75	L4
Maridi	●	97	D2
Marie Byrd Land	▨	144	(2)FF2
Marie Galante	▨	137	M5
Mariehamn	●	61	K6
Marienberg	●	67	J6
Mariental	●	99	B4
Marietta	●	135	E2
Marietta, *Oh., United States*	●	131	D3
Marietta, *Okla., United States*	●	135	B3
Mariinsk	●	103	R6
Marijampolė	●	65	N3
Marília	●	143	M3
Marín	●	73	B2
Marinette	●	131	C1
Maringá	●	143	L3
Marino	●	77	G7
Marion, *Ill., United States*	●	131	C3
Marion, *Ind., United States*	●	131	C2
Marion, *Oh., United States*	●	131	D2
Maripa	●	141	D2
Mariscal Estigarribia	●	143	J3
Maritime Alps	▰	75	C6
Marittimo	●	75	F7
Mariupol'	●	63	G5
Marīvān	●	83	M6
Mariy El	ⓐ	63	J3
Marjayoûn	●	86	C3
Marka	●	97	G3
Markam	●	111	B5
Markaryd	●	65	C1
Marked Tree	●	135	C2
Marken	⊵	59	H2
Markermeer	●	59	H2
Market Harborough	●	59	B2
Markham	●	131	E2
Marki	●	65	L5
Markit	●	103	P10
Markkleeberg	●	67	H5
Markovo	●	105	W4
Marktoberdorf	●	75	F3
Marktredwitz	●	67	H7
Marla	●	119	F5
Marle	●	59	F5
Marmande	●	71	F9
Marmara Adası	▨	81	K4
Marmara Denizi	⊟	81	L4

Legend

✕	Continent name
Ⓐ	Country name
ⓐ	State or province name
■	Country capital
◻	State or province capital
●	Settlement
▲	Mountain, volcano, peak
▰	Mountain range
▨	Physical region or feature
◿	River, canal
⊘	Lake, salt lake
⊵	Gulf, strait, bay
⊟	Sea, ocean
⊳	Cape, point
▨	Island or island group, rocky or coral reef
✳	Place of interest
⌘	Historical or cultural region

Name	Page	Grid
Marmaris	81	L8
Marmolada	75	G4
Marne	59	F5
Maroantsetra	99	H3
Marolambo	99	H4
Maroni	141	G3
Marotiri	117	M8
Maroua	95	G2
Marquesas Islands	117	M6
Marquette	131	C1
Marradi	75	G6
Marrakech	91	D2
Marra Plateau	93	D5
Marree	119	G5
Marrupa	99	F2
Marsa Alam	93	F2
Marsabit	97	F3
Marsala	77	G11
Marsberg	59	L3
Marsden	119	J6
Marseille	71	L10
Marseille-en-Beauvaisis	59	D5
Marshall, Ill., United States	135	D2
Marshall, Tex., United States	135	C3
Marshall Islands	117	G4
Marshalltown	131	B2
Marsh Harbour	135	F4
Marsh Island	135	C4
Martapura, Indonesia	115	(1)C3
Martapura, Indonesia	115	(1)E3
Martigny	75	C4
Martigues	71	L10
Martin, Slovakia	65	H8
Martin, United States	129	F2
Martina Franca	77	M8
Martinborough	121	E5
Martinique	137	M6
Martinsburg	131	E3
Martinsville, Ind., United States	131	C3
Martinsville, Va., United States	131	E3
Marton	121	E5
Martos	73	G7
Maruchak	85	H2
Mårvatn	61	E6
Mary	85	H2
Maryborough	119	K5
Maryland	131	E3
Marysville, Canada	131	G1
Marysville, Calif., United States	133	B1
Marysville, Kans., United States	135	B2
Maryville	131	B2
Masai Steppe	97	F4
Masaka	97	E4
Masalembu Besar	115	(1)E4
Masallı	83	N4
Masamba	115	(2)B3
Masan	113	E6
Masasi	97	F6
Masbate	109	G4
Masbate	109	G4
Mascara	91	F1
Maseru	99	D5
Mashhad	85	G2
Masi-Manimba	97	B4
Masindi	97	E3
Maşīrah	85	G5
Masjed Soleymān	85	E3
Maskanah	83	H5
Mason	135	B3
Mason Bay	121	A8
Mason City	131	B2
Masqaţ	87	H5
Massa	75	F6
Massachusetts	131	F2
Massachusetts Bay	131	G2
Massafra	77	M8
Massa Marittima	77	F6
Massawa	93	G4
Massena	131	F2
Masset	125	E6
Massif Central	71	H8
Massif de Guéra	93	C5
Massif de l'Aïr	91	G5
Massif des Écrins	75	B5
Massif du Chaillu	95	G5
Massif du Tsaratanana	99	H2
Massif Ennedi	93	D4
Massillon	131	D2
Massinga	99	F4
Masteksay	63	K5
Masterton	121	E5
Mastung	85	J4
Masty	61	N10
Masuda	113	F6
Masuguru	99	F2
Masvingo	99	E4
Maşyāf	86	D1
Matadi	97	A5
Matagami	131	E1
Matagorda Island	135	B4
Matakana Island	121	F3
Matakawau	121	E3
Matale	107	D7
Matam	95	B1
Matamoros, Mexico	133	F3
Matamoros, Mexico	133	G3
Matane	131	G1
Matanzas	127	K7
Matara	107	D7
Mataram	115	(1)F4
Mataranka	119	F3
Mataró	73	N3
Mataura	121	B8
Matawai	121	F4
Matehuala	133	F4
Matera	77	L8
Mátészalka	79	K2
Mateur	77	D11
Matheson	131	D1
Mathraki	81	B5
Mathura	107	C3
Mati	109	H5
Matlock	59	A1
Matmata	91	G2
Mato Grosso	141	F6
Mato Grosso	141	F6
Mato Grosso do Sul	141	F7
Matosinhos	73	B3
Maţraḩ	87	H5
Matrei	75	H4
Matrûh	93	E1
Matsiatra	99	H4
Matsu	111	G5
Matsue	113	G6
Matsumae	113	L3
Matsumoto	113	J5
Matsusaka	113	J6
Matsuyama	113	G7
Mattawa	131	E1
Matterhorn	75	C5
Matthews Ridge	141	E2
Mattighofen	67	J8
Mattoon	131	C3
Maturín	141	E2
Maubeuge	59	F4
Maui	133	(2)F3
Maullín	143	G7
Maun	75	K6
Maun	99	C3
Mauna Kea	133	(2)F4
Mauna Loa	133	(2)F4
Mauritania	91	C5
Mauritius	99	(1)B2
Mauron	71	C5
Mauthen	75	H4
Mavinga	99	C3
Mawlaik	109	A2
Max	129	F1
Maya	105	P5
Maya	115	(1)D3
Mayaguana	137	K4
Mayagüez	137	L5
Mayamba	97	B4
Maych'ew	93	G5
Maydh	97	H1
Mayenne	71	E5
Mayenne	71	E5
Mayer	133	D2
Maykamys	103	P8
Maykop	83	J1
Mayly-Say	85	K1
Maymecha	105	G3
Mayn	105	W4
Mayo	125	D4
Mayor Island	121	F3
Mayotte	99	H2
Mayrhofen	75	G3
Mayskiy	105	M6
Mayumba	95	G5
Mayya	105	N4
Mazagão	141	G4
Mazagran	71	K4
Mazama	129	B1
Mazamet	71	H10
Mazar	103	P10
Mazara del Vallo	77	G11
Mazār-e Sharīf	85	J2
Mazatlán	137	C4
Mažeikiai	65	M1
Mazocahui	133	D3
Mazomora	97	F5
Mazra	86	C5
Mazyr	63	E4
Mazzarino	77	J11
Mbabane	99	E5
Mbala	97	E5
Mbale	97	E3
Mbalmayo	95	G4
Mbamba Bay	99	E2
Mbandaka	97	B3
Mbanga	95	F4
M'banza Congo	97	A5
Mbarara	97	E4
Mbeya	97	E5
Mbomou	97	C3
Mbour	95	A2
Mbuji-Mayi	97	C5
Mbuyuni	97	F5
McAlester	135	B3
McBride	125	G6
McCamey	133	F2
McCammon	129	D2
McClintock	125	N5
McClintock Channel	125	L2
McComb	135	C3
McCook	129	F2
McDermitt	129	C2
McGehee	135	C3
McGrath	133	(1)F3
McKinlay	119	H4
McKinney	135	B3
McLaughlin	129	F1
McLennan	125	H5
McMinnville	131	C3
McPherson	135	B2
McRae	135	E3
Meadow Lake	125	K6
Meadville	131	D2
Meander River	125	H5
Meaux	59	E6
Mecca = Makkah	93	G3
Mechelen	59	G3
Mechernich	59	J4
Mecidiye	81	J4
Mecklenburger Bucht	67	G2
Mecula	99	F2
Meda	73	C4
Medak	107	C5
Medan	115	(1)B2
Médéa	73	N8
Medellín	141	B2
Medenine	91	H2
Medford	129	B2
Medgidia	79	R5
Mediaş	79	M3
Medicine Bow	129	E2
Medicine Hat	125	J7
Medicine Lodge	135	B2
Medina = Al Madīnah	93	G3
Medinaceli	73	H3
Medina de Campo	73	F3
Medina Sidonia	73	E8
Mediterranean Sea	57	E4
Mednogorsk	63	L4
Medveditsa	63	H4
Medvezh'yegorsk	63	F2
Meeker	129	E2
Meerane	67	H6
Meerut	107	C3
Mega	115	(2)D3
Megalopoli	81	E7
Meganisi	81	C6
Megara	81	F6
Megisti	81	M8
Mehrān	83	M7
Mehriz	85	F3
Meiktila	109	B2
Meiningen	67	F6
Meißen	67	J5
Meizhou	109	F2
Mejez El Bab	77	D12
Mékambo	95	G4
Mek'elē	93	G5
Meknès	91	D2
Mekong	109	D4
Melaka	115	(1)C2
Melanesia	117	F5
Melbourne, Australia	119	H7
Melbourne, United States	135	E4
Melchor de Mencos	137	G5
Meldrum Bay	131	D1
Meleuz	63	L4
Mélfi	93	C5
Melfi	77	K8
Melfort	125	L6
Melide	73	B2
Melilla	73	H9
Melita	129	F1
Melitopol'	63	G5
Melk	75	L2
Melkosopochnik	103	N8
Mělník	67	K6
Melo	143	L5
Melton Mowbray	59	B2
Melun	71	H5
Melut	93	F5
Melvern Lake	135	B2
Melville	125	L6
Melville Island, Australia	119	F2
Melville Island, Canada	123	N2
Melville Peninsula	125	P3
Memberamo	115	(2)E3
Memboro	115	(2)A4
Memmert	59	J1
Memmingen	75	F3
Mempawah	115	(1)D2
Memphis, Mo., United States	131	B2
Memphis, Tenn., United States	131	C3
Mena	135	C3
Menai Strait	69	H8
Ménaka	91	F5
Mendawai	115	(1)E3
Mende	71	J9
Menden	59	K3
Mendī	97	F2
Mendoza	143	H5
Menemen	81	K6
Menen	59	F4
Menfi	77	G11
Menggala	115	(1)D3
Meniet	91	F4
Menkere	105	L3
Menominee	131	C1
Menomonee Falls	131	C2

Legend

X	Continent name
A	Country name
a	State or province name
■	Country capital
□	State or province capital
●	Settlement
▲	Mountain, volcano, peak
▰	Mountain range
⊘	Physical region or feature
⟋	River, canal
◲	Lake, salt lake
◄	Gulf, strait, bay
▱	Sea, ocean
⟍	Cape, point
⊞	Island or island group, rocky or coral reef
*	Place of interest
⊠	Historical or cultural region

Name	Page	Grid
Menongue	99	B2
Menorca	73	Q4
Mentok	115	(1)D3
Menyuan	111	C3
Menzel Bourguiba	77	D11
Menzel Bouzelfa	77	E12
Menzel Temime	77	E12
Menzies	119	D5
Meppel	59	J2
Meppen	59	K2
Meran Merano	75	G4
Merauke	115	(2)F4
Mercato Saraceno	75	H7
Merced	129	B3
Mercedes, *Argentina*	143	H5
Mercedes, *Argentina*	143	K4
Mercedes, *United States*	135	B4
Mercedes, *Uruguay*	143	K5
Mercury Islands	121	E3
Mergenevo	63	K5
Mergui	109	B4
Mergui Archipelago	109	B4
Mérida, *Mexico*	137	G4
Mérida, *Spain*	73	D6
Mérida, *Venezuela*	137	K7
Meridian	135	D3
Merinha Grande	73	B5
Meriruma	141	G3
Merke	103	N9
Merkys	61	N9
Merowe	93	F4
Merredin	119	C6
Merrill	131	C1
Merriman	129	F2
Merritt	125	G6
Merseburg	67	H5
Mers el Kébir	73	K9
Mersey	69	J8
Mersin = İcel	81	S8
Mērsrags	61	M8
Merthyr Tydfil	69	J10
Méru	59	E5
Meru	97	F3
Merzifon	83	F3
Merzig	59	J5
Mesa	133	D2
Mesa de Yambi	141	C3
Mesagne	77	M8
Meschede	59	L3
Mesöaria Plain	86	A1
Mesolongi	81	D6
Mesopotamia	83	K6
Messaad	91	F2
Messina, *Italy*	77	K10
Messina, *South Africa*	99	D4
Messini	81	E7
Messiniakos Kolpos	81	D8
Mestre	75	H5
Meta	141	C2
Metairie	135	C4
Metaline Falls	129	C1
Metán	143	J4
Metangula	99	E2
Metema	93	G5
Meteor Depth	139	J9
Metković	79	E6
Metlika	75	L5
Metsovo	81	D5
Mettet	59	G4
Mettlach	59	J5
Metz	59	J5
Metzingen	75	E2
Meulaboh	109	B6
Meuse	59	G4
Mexia	135	B3
Mexicali	133	C2
Mexican Hat	133	E1
Mexico	131	B3
Mexico	137	D4
Meymaneh	85	H2
Mezdra	79	L6
Mezen'	63	H1
Mezenskaya Guba	63	H1
Mezhdurechensk	103	R7
Mezőberény	79	J3
Mezőkövesd	79	H2
Mezőtúr	79	H2
Mfuwe	99	E2
Miajadas	73	E5
Miami, *Fla., United States*	135	E4
Miami, *Okla., United States*	135	C2
Miandowāb	83	M5
Miandrivazo	99	H3
Mīāneh	83	M5
Miangyang	111	E4
Mianning	111	C5
Mianwali	107	B2
Mianyang	111	C4
Miaodao Qundao	111	G3
Miao'ergou	103	Q8
Miass	63	M4
Miastko	65	G4
Michalovce	65	L9
Michigan	131	C1
Michipicoten Island	131	C1
Michurinsk	63	H4
Micronesia	117	F4
Mid-Atlantic Ridge	139	G1
Middelburg, *Netherlands*	59	F3
Middelburg, *South Africa*	99	D6
Middelfart	67	E1
Middelkerke	59	E3
Middle America Trench	123	L8
Middle Andaman	109	A4
Middlebury	131	F2
Middle Lake	129	C2
Middlesboro	131	D3
Middlesbrough	69	L7
Middletown, *N.Y., United States*	131	F2
Middletown, *Oh., United States*	131	D3
Midland, *Canada*	131	E2
Midland, *Mich., United States*	131	D2
Midland, *Tex., United States*	133	F2
Midway Islands	117	J3
Midwest City	135	B2
Midzor	79	K6
Miechów	65	K7
Mielan	71	F10
Mielec	65	L7
Miembwe	97	F5
Mien	65	D1
Miercurea-Ciuc	79	N3
Mieres	73	E1
Miesbach	75	G3
Mī'ēso	97	G2
Miging	107	F3
Miguel Auza	133	F4
Mikhaylovka	63	H4
Mikhaylovskiy	103	P7
Mikino	105	U4
Mikkeli	61	P6
Mikulov	75	M2
Mikun'	63	K2
Mikuni-sammyaku	113	K5
Mikura-jima	113	K7
Mila	91	G1
Milaca	131	B1
Miladhunmadulu Atoll	107	B7
Milan = Milano, *Italy*	75	E5
Milan, *United States*	135	D2
Milano	75	E5
Milas	81	K7
Milazzo	77	K10
Miles	119	K5
Miles City	129	E1
Milford, *Del., United States*	131	E3
Milford, *Ut., United States*	129	D3
Milford Haven	69	G10
Milford Sound	121	A7
Miliana	73	N8
Milicz	65	G6
Milk	125	J7
Mil'kovo	105	T6
Millau	71	J9
Millbank	129	G1
Milledgeville	135	E3
Miller	129	G2
Millerovo	63	H5
Millington	131	C3
Millinocket	131	G1
Miloro	97	E5
Milos	81	G8
Milton, *New Zealand*	121	B8
Milton, *United States*	135	D3
Milton Keynes	59	B2
Miluo	111	E5
Milwaukee	131	C2
Mily	103	L8
Mimizan-Plage	71	D9
Mīnāb	87	G3
Mina Jebel Ali	87	F4
Minas	143	K5
Mīnā' Sa'ūd	87	C2
Minas Gerais	141	H7
Minas Novas	141	J7
Minatitián	137	F5
Minbu	109	A2
Minchinmávida	143	G7
Mincivan	83	M4
Mindanao	109	G5
Mindelheim	75	F2
Mindelo	95	(1)B1
Minden	59	L2
Mindoro	109	G4
Mindoro Strait	109	G4
Minehead	69	J10
Mineola	135	B3
Mineral'nyye Vody	83	K1
Minerva Reefs	117	J8
Minfeng	103	Q10
Minga	97	D6
Mingâçevir	83	M3
Mingâçevir Su Anbarı	83	M3
Mingulay	69	D5
Minicoy	107	B7
Minilya Roadhouse	119	B4
Minna	95	F3
Minneapolis	131	B2
Minnesota	131	A1
Minnesota	131	A2
Miño	73	C2
Minot	129	F1
Minsk	63	E4
Minturn	129	E3
Minusinsk	103	S7
Min Xian	111	C4
Min'yar	63	L3
Miquelon	131	E1
Miraflores	141	C3
Miramas	71	K10
Mirambeau	71	E8
Miranda	141	F8
Miranda de Ebro	73	H2
Miranda do Douro	73	D3
Mirandela	73	C3
Mirbāt	85	F6
Mīrjāveh	85	H4
Mirnyy	105	J4
Mirow	67	H3
Mirpur Khas	107	A3
Mirtoö Pelagos	81	F7
Mirzapur	107	D3
Miskolc	79	H1
Misoöl	115	(2)D3
Mişrātah	93	C1
Missinaibi	125	Q6
Missinipe	125	L5
Mission	129	F2
Mississippi	135	C3
Mississippi	135	D2
Mississippi River Delta	135	D4
Missoula	129	D1
Missouri	129	F1
Missouri	131	B3
Missouri City	135	B4
Mistassibi	125	S7
Mistelbach	75	M2
Mitchell	129	G2
Mithankot	85	K4
Mithaylov	63	G4
Mithymna	81	J5
Mito	113	L5
Mits'iwa	85	C6
Mittellandkanal	59	K2
Mittersill	75	H3
Mittweida	67	H6
Mitú	141	C3
Mitzic	95	G4
Miyake-jima	113	K6
Miyako	113	L4
Miyakonojō	113	F8
Miyazaki	113	F8
Miyoshi	113	G6
Mizdah	91	H2
Mizen Head	69	B10
Mizhhir''ya	79	L1
Mizil	79	P4
Mizpe Ramon	86	B6
Mjölby	61	H7
Mjøsa	61	F6
Mkuze	99	E5
Mladá Boleslav	65	D7
Mladenovac	79	H5
Mława	65	K4
Mljet	79	E7
Mmabatho	99	D5
Moa	119	H2
Moanda	95	G5
Moapa	129	D3
Moba	97	D5
Mobaye	97	C3
Mobayi-Mbongo	97	C3
Moberly	131	B3
Mobile	135	D3
Moçambique	99	G3
Môc Châu	109	C2
Mochudi	99	D4
Mocímboa da Praia	99	G2
Mocuba	99	F3
Modane	75	B5
Módena	75	F6
Modesto	129	B3
Módica	77	J12
Mödling	75	M2
Modowi	115	(2)D3
Modriča	79	F5
Moenkopi	133	D1
Moers	59	J3
Moffat	69	J6
Moffat Peak	121	B7
Mogadishu = Muqdisho	97	H3
Mogilno	65	G5
Mogocha	105	K6
Mogochin	103	Q6
Mogok	109	B2
Mohács	79	F4
Mohammadia	73	L9
Mohe	105	L6
Mohembo	99	C3
Mohoro	97	F5
Mohyliv-Podil's'kyy	79	Q1
Moi	61	D7
Moincêr	107	D2
Moineşti	79	P3
Mo i Rana	61	H3
Moissac	71	G9
Mojave	133	C1
Mojave Desert	133	C2
Mokau	121	E4
Mokohinau Island	121	E2
Mokolo	95	G2
Mokoreta	121	B8
Mokp'o	113	D6

X	Continent name
A	Country name
[a]	State or province name
■	Country capital
□	State or province capital
●	Settlement
▲	Mountain, volcano, peak
(mountain range)	Mountain range
(physical region)	Physical region or feature
(river)	River, canal
(lake)	Lake, salt lake
(gulf)	Gulf, strait, bay
(sea)	Sea, ocean
(cape)	Cape, point
(island)	Island or island group, rocky or coral reef
*	Place of interest
(historical)	Historical or cultural region

Legend:

X	Continent name
A	Country name
a	State or province name
■	Country capital
□	State or province capital
●	Settlement
▲	Mountain, volcano, peak
⬡	Mountain range
◉	Physical region or feature
Z	River, canal
⬛	Lake, salt lake
⬟	Gulf, strait, bay
▬	Sea, ocean
⬗	Cape, point
▢	Island or island group, rocky or coral reef
✳	Place of interest
▨	Historical or cultural region

Name	Type	Page	Grid
Mount Owen	▲	121	D5
Mount Paget	▲	143	P9
Mount Pleasant, *Ia.,* United States	◉	131	B2
Mount Pleasant, *Mich.,* United States	◉	131	D2
Mount Pleasant, *S.C.,* United States	◉	135	F3
Mount Pleasant, *Tex.,* United States	◉	135	B3
Mount Pleasant, *Ut.,* United States	◉	129	D3
Mount Pulog	▲	109	G3
Mount Rainier	▲	129	B1
Mount Ratz	▲	125	E5
Mount Richmond	▲	121	D5
Mount Roberts	▲	119	K5
Mount Robson	⬡	125	H6
Mount Roosevelt	▲	125	F5
Mount Roraima	▲	141	E2
Mount Ross	▲	121	E5
Mount Shasta	▲	129	B2
Mount Somers	▲	121	C6
Mount Stanley	▲	97	D3
Mount Tahat	▲	89	D3
Mount Travers	▲	121	D6
Mount Tuun	▲	113	D3
Mount Usborne	▲	143	K9
Mount Vernon, *Al.,* United States	◉	135	D3
Mount Vernon, *Ill.,* United States	◉	131	C3
Mount Vernon, *Oh.,* United States	◉	131	D2
Mount Vernon, *Wash.,* United States	◉	129	B1
Mount Victoria, *Myanmar*	▲	109	A2
Mount Victoria, *Papua New Guinea*	▲	117	E6
Mount Waddington	▲	125	F6
Mount Washington	▲	125	S8
Mount Whitney	▲	129	C3
Mount Wilson	▲	129	E3
Mount Woodroffe	▲	119	F5
Mount Ziel	▲	119	F4
Moura	◉	73	C6
Mousa	🝙	69	L2
Moussoro	◉	93	C5
Moutamba	◉	95	G5
Mouth of the Shannon	🝔	69	B9
Mouths of the Amazon	🝔	139	G3
Mouths of the Danube	⟋	79	S4
Mouths of the Ganges	🝔	107	E4
Mouths of the Indus	🝔	85	J5
Mouths of the Irrawaddy	🝔	109	A3
Mouths of the Krishna	🝔	107	D5
Mouths of the Mekong	🝔	109	D5
Mouths of the Niger	🝔	95	F4
Moûtiers	◉	75	B5
Moutong	◉	115	(2)B2
Moyale	◉	97	F3
Moyen Atlas	🝗	91	D2
Moyenvic	◉	59	J6
Moyeroo	⟋	103	U4
Moyynty	◉	103	N8
Mozambique	Ⓐ	99	E3
Mozambique Channel	🝔	99	F4
Mozdok	◉	83	L2
Mozhga	◉	63	K3
Mozirje	◉	75	K4
Mpanda	◉	97	E5
Mpika	◉	99	E2
Mporokoso	◉	97	E5
Mpumalanga	◩	99	D5
Mrągowo	◉	65	L4
Mrkonjić-Grad	◉	75	N6
M'Sila	◉	91	F1
Mtsensk	◉	63	G4
Mtwara	◉	97	G6
Muang Khammouan	◉	109	C3
Muang Không	◉	109	D4
Muang Khôngxédôn	◉	109	D3
Muang Khoua	◉	109	C2
Muang Pakxan	◉	109	C3
Muang Phin	◉	109	D3
Muang Sing	◉	109	C2
Muang Xai	◉	109	C2
Muar	◉	115	(1)C2
Muarabungo	◉	115	(1)C3
Muarawahau	◉	115	(1)F2
Mubarek	◉	103	M10
Mubende	◉	97	E3
Mubrani	◉	115	(2)D3
Muck	🝙	69	F5
Muckadilla	◉	119	J5
Muconda	◉	97	C6
Mucur	◉	81	S5
Mudanjiang	◉	113	E1
Mudanya	◉	81	L4
Muddy Gap	◉	129	E2
Mudurnu	◉	81	P4
Mufulira	◉	99	D2
Mughshin	◉	87	F6
Muğla	◉	81	L7
Mugodzhary	⬡	63	L5
Mühldorf	◉	75	H2
Mühlhausen	◉	67	F5
Muhos	◉	61	N4
Muhu	🝙	61	M7
Muhulu	◉	97	D4
Mukacheve	◉	65	M9
Mukdahan	◉	109	C3
Mukry	◉	85	J2
Mukuku	◉	99	D2
Mulaku Atoll	🝙	107	B8
Mulde	⟋	67	H5
Muleshoe	◉	133	F2
Mulgrave Island	🝙	119	H6
Mulhacén	▲	73	G7
Mülheim	◉	59	J3
Mulhouse	◉	75	C3
Muling	⟋	113	G1
Mull	🝙	69	G5
Mullaittivu	◉	107	D7
Mullewa	◉	119	C5
Müllheim	◉	75	C3
Mullingar	◉	69	E8
Mulobezi	◉	99	D3
Multan	◉	85	K3
Mumbai	◉	107	B5
Mumbwa	◉	99	D2
Muna	🝙	115	(2)B4
Münchberg	◉	67	G6
München	◉	75	G2
Münden	◉	67	E5
Mundo Novo	◉	141	J6
Mungbere	◉	97	D3
Munger	◉	107	E3
Munich = München	◉	75	G2
Münster, *Germany*	◉	59	K3
Munster, *France*	◉	75	C2
Munster, *Germany*	◉	67	F4
Munte	◉	115	(2)A2
Muojärvi	▨	61	Q4
Muonio	◉	61	M3
Muqdisho	■	97	H3
Mur	⟋	75	L4
Muradiye	◉	83	K4
Murang'a	◉	97	F4
Murashi	◉	63	J3
Murat	⟋	83	K4
Muratlı	◉	81	K3
Murchison	◉	121	D5
Murcia	◉	73	J7
Murdo	◉	129	F2
Mureş	⟋	79	J3
Muret	◉	71	G10
Murfreesboro, *N.C.,* United States	◉	135	F2
Murfreesboro, *Tenn.,* United States	◉	135	D2
Murghob	◉	85	K2
Muriaé	◉	141	J8
Müritz	▨	67	H3
Muriwai	◉	121	F4
Murmansk	◉	61	S2
Murnau	◉	75	G3
Murom	◉	63	H3
Muroran	◉	113	L2
Muros	◉	73	A2
Muroto	◉	113	H7
Murphy	◉	135	E2
Murray	⟋	119	H6
Murray	◉	131	C3
Murray Bridge	◉	119	G7
Murray River Basin	⬡	119	H6
Murska Sobota	◉	75	M4
Murter	🝙	75	L7
Murtosa	◉	73	B4
Murud	◉	107	B5
Murupara	◉	121	F4
Mururoa	🝙	117	M8
Murwara	◉	107	D4
Murzūq	◉	91	H3
Mürzzuschlag	◉	75	L3
Muş	◉	83	J4
Mūša	⟋	65	N1
Musala	▲	81	F2
Musandam Peninsula	⬡	87	G3
Musay'īd	◉	87	D4
Muscat = Masqaţ	■	87	H5
Musgrave Ranges	🝗	119	E5
Mushin	◉	95	E3
Muskegon	◉	131	C2
Muskogee	◉	135	B2
Musoma	◉	97	E4
Mustafakemalpaşa	◉	81	L4
Mut, *Egypt*	◉	93	E2
Mut, *Turkey*	◉	81	R8
Mutare	◉	99	E3
Mutarnee	◉	119	J3
Mutnyy Materik	◉	63	L1
Mutoray	◉	103	U5
Mutsamudu	◉	99	G2
Mutsu	◉	113	L3
Mutsu-wan	🝔	113	L3
Muttaburra	◉	119	H4
Muyezerskiy	◉	61	R5
Muyinga	◉	97	E4
Muynak	◉	103	K9
Muzaffarnagar	◉	107	C3
Muzaffarpur	◉	107	E3
Muzillac	◉	71	C6
Múzquiz	◉	133	F3
Muztagata	▲	103	N10
Mwali	🝙	99	G2
Mwanza	◉	97	E4
Mweka	◉	97	C4
Mwenda	◉	97	D6
Mwene-Ditu	◉	97	C5
Mwenezi	◉	99	E4
Mwenezi	⟋	99	E4
Mwinilunga	◉	99	C2
Myanmar	Ⓐ	109	B2
Myingyan	◉	109	B2
Myitkyina	◉	109	B1
Myjava	◉	75	N2
Myjava	⟋	75	N2
Mykolayiv	◉	65	N8
Mykonos	🝙	81	H7
Mymensingh	◉	107	F4
Mynbulak	◉	103	L9
Myndagayy	◉	105	N4
Myōjin	🝙	111	K4
Myonggan	◉	113	E3
Myrdalsjökull	⬡	61	(1)D3
Myrina	◉	81	H5
Myrtle Beach	◉	135	F3
Mys Alevina	⊐	105	S5
Mys Aniva	⊐	111	L1
Mys Buorkhaya	⊐	105	N2
Mys Dezhneva	⊐	105	Z3
Mys Elizavety	⊐	105	Q6
Mys Enkan	⊐	105	P5
Mys Govena	⊐	105	V5
Mys Kanin Nos	⊐	63	H1
Mys Kekurskij	⊐	61	S2
Mys Kril'on	⊐	111	L1
Myślenice	◉	65	J8
Myślibórz	◉	65	D5
Mys Lopatka, *Russia*	⊐	105	T6
Mys Lopatka, *Russia*	⊐	105	S2
Mys Navarin	⊐	105	X4
Mys Olyutorskiy	⊐	105	W5
Mysore	◉	107	C6
Mys Peschanyy	⊐	103	J9
Mys Povorotnyy	⊐	113	G2
Mys Prubiynyy	⊐	63	F5
Mys Shelagskiy	⊐	105	V2
Mys Sivuchiy	⊐	105	U5
Mys Terpeniya	⊐	105	Q7
Mys Tolstoy	⊐	105	T5
Mys Yuzhnyy	⊐	105	T5
Mys Zhelaniya	⊐	103	M2
Myszksw	◉	65	J7
My Tho	◉	109	D4
Mytilini	◉	81	J5
Mývatn	▨	61	(1)E2
Mže	⟋	67	H7
Mzimba	◉	99	E2
Mzuzu	◉	99	E2

N

Name	Type	Page	Grid
Naalehu	◉	133	(2)F4
Naas	◉	69	F8
Nabas	◉	109	G4
Naberezhnyye Chelny	◉	63	K3
Nabeul	◉	77	E12
Nabīd	◉	87	G2
Nabire	◉	115	(2)E3
Nablus	◉	86	C4
Nacala	◉	99	G2
Náchod	◉	65	F7
Nacogdoches	◉	135	C3
Nadiad	◉	107	B4
Nador	◉	91	E2
Nadvirna	◉	79	M1
Nadym	◉	63	F1
Nadym	⟋	63	P2
Næstved	◉	67	G1
Nafpaktos	◉	81	D6
Nafplio	◉	81	E7
Nagano	◉	113	K5
Nagaoka	◉	113	K5
Nagaon	◉	107	F3
Nagarzê	◉	107	F3
Nagasaki	◉	113	E7
Nagaur	◉	107	B3
Nagercoil	◉	107	C7
Nago	◉	111	H5
Nagold	◉	67	D8
Nagorsk	◉	63	K3
Nagoya	◉	113	J6
Nagpur	◉	107	C4
Nagqu	◉	107	F2
Nagyatád	◉	75	N4
Nagykállš	◉	79	J2
Nagykanizsa	◉	75	N4
Nagykáta	◉	65	J10
Nagykőrös	◉	79	G2
Naha	◉	111	H5
Nahanni	⟋	125	G4
Nahanni Butte	◉	125	G4
Nahr en Nile = Nile	⟋	93	F2
Naiman Qi	◉	111	G2
Nain	◉	125	U5
Nairn	◉	69	J4
Nairobi	■	97	F4
Naivasha	◉	97	F4
Naizishan	◉	113	D2
Najafābād	◉	85	F3
Nájera	◉	73	H2

Name	Page	Grid
Najibabad	107	C3
Najin	113	F2
Najrān	93	H4
Nakamura	113	G7
Nakatsu	113	F7
Nakhl	86	A7
Nakhodka, *Russia*	103	P4
Nakhodka, *Russia*	113	G2
Nakhon Ratchasima	109	C3
Nakhon Sawan	109	B3
Nakhon Si Thammarat	109	B5
Nakina	125	P6
Naknek	133	(1)F4
Nakonde	97	E5
Nakskov	67	G2
Nakten	61	H5
Nakuru	97	F4
Nal'chik	83	K2
Nallihan	81	P4
Nālūt	91	H2
Namagan	103	N9
Namakzar-e Shadad	87	G1
Namanga	97	F4
Namapa	99	F2
Namasagali	97	E3
Nam Can	109	C5
Nam Co	107	F2
Namdalen	61	G4
Nam Dinh	109	D2
Namib Desert	99	A4
Namibe	99	A3
Namibia	99	B4
Namlea	115	(2)C3
Namo	115	(2)A3
Nampa	129	C2
Nam Ping	109	B3
Namp'o	113	C4
Nampula	99	F3
Namsos	61	F4
Namtsy	105	M4
Namur	59	G4
Namwala	99	D3
Namwŏn	113	D6
Nan	109	C3
Nanaimo	129	B1
Nanao	113	J5
Nanchang	111	F5
Nanchong	111	D4
Nancy	75	B2
Nanda Devi	107	C2
Nānded	107	C5
Nandurbar	107	B4
Nangalala	119	G2
Nangapinoh	115	(1)E3
Nangatayap	115	(1)E3
Nangis	71	J5
Nangong	111	F3
Nang Xian	107	F3
Nanjing	111	F4
Nankoku	113	G7
Nannine	119	C5
Nanning	109	D2
Nanortalik	125	X4
Nanpan	109	D2
Nanping	111	F5
Nansei-shotō	113	H5
Nantes	71	D6
Nanton	127	D1
Nantong	111	G4
Nanumea	117	H6
Nanuque	141	J7
Nanyang	111	E4
Napa	129	B3
Napalkovo	103	N3
Napamute	133	(1)F3
Napas	105	C4
Napasoq	125	W3
Napier	121	F4
Naples = Napoli	77	J8
Naples	135	E4
Napo	141	C4
Napoli	77	J8
Naqb Ashtar	86	C6
Nara, *Japan*	113	H6
Nara, *Mali*	91	D5
Narathiwat	109	C5
Narbonne	71	H10
Nardò	77	N8
Nares Strait	123	J2
Narev	65	N5
Narew	65	L5
Narmada	107	C4
Narnaul	107	C3
Narni	77	G6
Narok	97	F4
Närpes	61	L5
Narrabri	119	J6
Narrandera	119	J6
Narsimhapur	107	C4
Nart	111	F2
Narva	61	P7
Narva	61	Q7
Narva Bay	61	P7
Narvik	61	J2
Nar'yan Mar	63	K1
Naryn	105	F6
Năsăud	79	M2
Nashua	131	F2
Nashville	135	D2
Našice	79	F4
Nasik	107	B4
Nasir	97	E2
Nassarawa	95	F3
Nassau	135	F4
Nässjö	61	H8
Nastapoka Islands	125	R5
Nasugbu	109	G4
Naswá	87	G5
Nata	99	D4
Natal	141	K5
Natara	105	L3
Natashquan	125	U6
Natchez	135	C3
Natchitoches	135	C3
National Park	121	E4
Natitingou	95	E2
Natuna Besar	115	(1)D2
Naujoji Akmenė	65	M1
Naumburg	67	G5
Na'ūr	86	C5
Nauru	117	G6
Nauta	141	C4
Nautonwa	107	D3
Navahermosa	73	F5
Navahrudak	61	N10
Navajo Reservoir	129	E3
Navalmoral de la Mata	73	E5
Navalvillar de Pela	73	E5
Navapolatsk	63	E3
Navlya	63	F4
Navoi	103	M9
Navojoa	127	E6
Navrongo	95	D2
Navsari	107	B4
Nawabshah	85	J4
Nāwah	85	J3
Naxçıvan	83	L4
Naxos	81	H7
Naxos	81	H7
Nayakhan	105	T4
Nāy Band, *Iran*	85	G3
Nāy Band, *Iran*	87	E3
Nayoro	113	M1
Nazaré	73	A5
Nazareth	86	C4
Nazarovo	103	S6
Nazca	141	C6
Nazca Ridge	143	E3
Naze	111	H5
Nazilli	81	L7
Nazino	103	P6
Nazran'	83	L2
Nazrēt	97	F2
Nazwá	85	G5
Nazyvayevsk	63	P3
Ndélé	97	C2
Ndjamena	93	B5
Ndjolé	95	G5
Ndola	99	D2
Neale Junction	119	E5
Neapoli	81	F8
Nea Zichni	81	F3
Nebbi	97	E3
Nebitdag	85	F2
Nebo	119	J4
Nebraska	129	G2
Neckar	67	D7
Neckar	67	D8
Neckarsulm	67	E7
Necker Island	117	K3
Necochea	143	K6
Nédély	93	C4
Needles	133	D2
Nefedovo	63	P3
Nefta	91	G2
Neftçala	83	N4
Neftekamsk	63	K3
Neftekumsk	83	L1
Nefteyugansk	63	P2
Nefza	77	D12
Negage	97	B5
Negār	87	G2
Negēlē	97	F2
Negele	97	F2
Negev	86	B6
Negomane	99	F2
Negombo	107	C7
Negotin	79	K5
Negotino	81	E3
Négrine	91	G2
Negro, *Argentina*	143	J7
Negro, *Brazil*	141	E4
Negros	109	G5
Negru Vodă	79	R6
Nehbandān	85	G3
Nehe	105	M7
Nehoiu	79	P4
Neijiang	111	C5
Nei Monggol	111	E2
Neiva	141	B3
Neixiang	111	E4
Nejanilini Lake	125	M5
Nek'emtē	97	F2
Nelidovo	63	F3
Neligh	129	G2
Nellore	107	C6
Nel'ma	105	P7
Nelson	125	N5
Nelson, *Canada*	129	C1
Nelson, *New Zealand*	121	D5
Nelspruit	99	E5
Nëma	91	D5
Nëman	61	N10
Neman	65	M2
Nemours	71	H5
Nemperola	115	(2)B5
Nemunas	65	P3
Nemuro	113	N2
Nen	105	L7
Nenagh	69	D9
Nenana	133	(1)H3
Nene	59	B2
Nenjiang	105	M7
Neosho	131	B3
Nepa	105	H5
Nepal	107	D3
Nepalganj	107	D3
Nepean	131	E1
Nepomuk	67	J7
Ner	65	H5
Nera	77	G6
Neratovice	67	K6
Neris	65	P2
Nerja	73	G8
Neryungri	105	L5
Nesebŭr	79	Q7
Ness City	135	B2
Netanya	86	B4
Netherlands	59	H2
Netherlands Antilles	137	L6
Nettilling Lake	125	S3
Neubrandenburg	67	J3
Neuburg	67	G8
Neuchâtel	75	B3
Neuenhagen	67	J4
Neufchâteau, *Belgium*	59	H5
Neufchâteau, *France*	71	L5
Neufchâtel-en-Bray	59	D5
Neuhof	67	E6
Neumarkt	67	G7
Neumünster	67	F2
Neunkirchen, *Austria*	75	M3
Neunkirchen, *Germany*	67	C7
Neuquén	143	H6
Neuruppin	67	H4
Neusiedler	65	F10
Neusiedler See	75	M3
Neuss	59	J3
Neustadt, *Germany*	59	L5
Neustadt, *Germany*	67	F2
Neustadt, *Germany*	67	F7
Neustadt, *Germany*	67	G6
Neustadt, *Germany*	67	G8
Neustadt, *Germany*	67	H7
Neustrelitz	67	J3
Neu-Ulm	67	F8
Neuwerk	67	D3
Neuwied	59	K4
Nevada	129	C3
Nevada	131	B3
Nevado Auzangate	141	C6
Nevado de Colima	137	D5
Nevado de Cumbal	141	B3
Nevado de Huascaran	141	B5
Nevado de Illampu	141	D7
Nevado Sajama	141	D7
Nevados de Cachi	143	H4
Never	105	L6
Nevers	71	J7
Nevesinje	79	F6
Nevėžis	61	M9
Nevinnomyssk	83	J1
Nevşehir	81	S6
Newala	97	F6
New Albany, *Ind., United States*	131	C3
New Albany, *Miss., United States*	135	D3
New Amsterdam	141	F2
Newark, *N.J., United States*	131	F2
Newark, *Oh., United States*	131	D3
Newark-on-Trent	59	B1
New Bedford	131	F2
Newberg	129	B1
New Bern	135	F2
Newberry	135	E3
New Braunfels	135	B4
New Britain	117	F6
New Brunswick	125	T7
Newburgh	131	F2
Newbury	59	A3
New Bussa	95	E3
Newcastle, *Australia*	119	K6
Newcastle, *United States*	129	F2
Newcastle-under-Lyme	69	K8
Newcastle-upon-Tyne	69	L6
Newcastle Waters	119	F3
New Delhi	107	C3
New England	129	F1
Newe Zohars	86	C5
Newfoundland	125	V5
Newfoundland	125	V7
New Georgia Island	117	F6
New Glasgow	125	U7
New Guinea	101	S10

Symbol	Meaning		Symbol	Meaning		Symbol	Meaning
⊠	Continent name		▲	Mountain, volcano, peak		▭	Sea, ocean
▲	Country name		△	Mountain range		▷	Cape, point
▫	State or province name		⊘	Physical region or feature		⊡	Island or island group, rocky or coral reef
■	Country capital		⟋	River, canal		✳	Place of interest
□	State or province capital		⬭	Lake, salt lake		▨	Historical or cultural region
•	Settlement		⊐	Gulf, strait, bay			

Name	Page	Ref
New Hampshire	131	F2
New Hampton	131	B2
New Hanover	117	F6
Newhaven	59	C4
New Haven	131	F2
New Iberia	135	C3
New Ireland	117	F6
New Jersey	131	F2
New Liskeard	131	E1
New London	131	F2
Newman	119	C4
Newmarket	59	C2
New Meadows	129	C2
New Mexico	133	E2
Newnan	135	E3
New Orleans	135	D4
New Plymouth	121	E4
Newport, *Eng., United Kingdom*	59	A4
Newport, *Wales, United Kingdom*	69	K10
Newport, *Ark., United States*	135	C2
Newport, *Oreg., United States*	129	B2
Newport, *R.I., United States*	131	F2
Newport, *Vt., United States*	131	F2
Newport, *Wash., United States*	129	C1
New Providence	135	F5
Newquay	69	G11
Newry	69	F7
New Siberia Islands = Novosibirskiye Ostrova	105	P1
New Smyrna Beach	135	E4
New South Wales	119	H6
Newton, *Ia., United States*	131	B2
Newton, *Kans., United States*	135	B2
Newtownards	69	G7
New Ulm	131	B2
New York	131	E2
New York	131	F2
New Zealand	121	B5
Neya	63	H3
Neyrīz	87	F2
Neyshābūr	85	G2
Ngabang	115	(1)D2
Ngalu	115	(2)B5
Ngaoundéré	95	G3
Ngara	97	E4
Ngawihi	121	E5
Ngo	95	H5
Ngoura	93	C5
Ngozi	97	D4
Nguigmi	95	G2
Nguru	95	G2
Nha Trang	109	D4
Nhulunbuy	119	G2
Niafounké	91	E5
Niagara Falls	131	E2
Niamey	95	E2
Niangara	97	D3
Nia-Nia	97	D3
Nias	115	(1)B2
Nicaragua	137	D3
Nicastro	77	L10
Nice	75	C7
Nicholls Town	135	F4
Nicobar Islands	109	A5
Nicosia = Lefkosia	81	R9
Nida	65	K7
Nidym	105	F4
Nidzica	65	K4
Niebüll	67	D2
Niedere Tauern	75	J3
Niefang	95	G4
Nienburg	67	E4
Niesky	67	K5
Nieuw Amsterdam	141	F2
Nieuw Nickerie	141	F2
Nieuwpoort	59	E3
Niğde	81	S7
Niger	91	G5
Niger	95	E2
Nigeria	95	F2
Nigoring Hu	111	B3
Niigata	113	K5
Niihau	133	(2)A2
Nii-jima	113	K6
Níjar	73	H8
Nijmegen	59	H3
Nikolayevsk-na-Amure	105	Q6
Nikol'sk	63	J3
Nikopol'	63	F5
Nik Pey	83	N5
Nikšić	79	F7
Nilande Atoll	107	B8
Nile	93	F3
Niles	131	C2
Nimach	107	B4
Nîmes	71	K10
Nimule	97	E3
Nin	75	L6
Nine Degree Channel	107	B7
9 de Julio	143	J6
Ning'an	113	E1
Ningbo	111	G5
Ningde	111	F5
Ninghai	111	G5
Ninh Hoa	109	D4
Ninohoe	113	L3
Niobrara	129	F2
Niobrara	129	G2
Nioro	91	D5
Nioro du Sahel	95	C1
Niort	71	E7
Nipigon	131	C1
Niquelândia	141	H6
Nirmal	107	C5
Niš	79	J6
Nisa	73	C5
Niscemi	77	J11
Nishinoomote	113	F8
Nisyros	81	K8
Niterói	143	N3
Nitra	65	H9
Nitra	65	H9
Nitsa	63	M3
Niue	117	K7
Nivelles	59	G4
Nizamabad	107	C5
Nizhnekamsk	63	K3
Nizhnekamskoye Vodokhranilishche	63	K3
Nizhneudinsk	105	F5
Nizhnevartovsk	63	Q2
Nizhneyansk	105	P2
Nizhniy Lomov	63	H4
Nizhniy Novgorod	63	H3
Nizhniy Tagil	63	M3
Nizhnyaya Tunguska	105	H4
Nizhyn	63	F4
Nizip	83	G5
Nizza Monferrato	75	D6
Njazidja	99	G2
Njombe	97	E5
Njombe	97	E5
Nkambe	95	G3
Nkhotakota	99	E2
Nkongsamba	95	F4
Noatak	133	(1)F2
Nobeoka	113	F7
Noci	77	M8
Nogales, *Mexico*	133	D2
Nogales, *United States*	133	D2
Nogat	65	J3
Nogent-le-Rotrou	71	F5
Noginsk	63	G3
Noginskiy	103	S5
Nogliki	105	Q6
Noheji	113	L3
Noia	73	B2
Noire	109	C2
Nojima-zaki	113	K6
Nok Kundi	85	H4
Nola, *Central African Republic*	97	B3
Nola, *Italy*	77	J8
Nolinsk	63	J3
Noma-misaki	113	F8
Nome	133	(1)D3
Nomoi Islands	117	F5
Nomo-saki	113	E7
Nong'an	113	C1
Nong Khai	109	C3
Noord-Beveland	59	F3
Noord-Oost-Polder	59	H2
Noordwijk aan Zee	59	G2
Norak	85	J2
Noranda	131	E1
Nordaustlandet	144	(1)L1
Norden	67	C3
Nordenham	67	D3
Norderney	67	C3
Norderstedt	67	F3
Nordfriesische Inseln	67	D2
Nordhausen	67	F5
Nordhorn	59	K2
Nordkapp	61	N1
Nordkinn	61	P1
Nordkinnhalvøya	61	P1
Nordkvaløya	61	J1
Nordli	61	G4
Nördlingen	67	F8
Nord-Ostsee-Kanal	67	E2
Nordstrand	67	D2
Nordvik	103	W3
Nore	69	E9
Norfolk, *Nebr., United States*	129	G2
Norfolk, *Va., United States*	131	E3
Norfolk Island	117	G8
Noril'sk	103	R4
Norman	135	B2
Normanton	119	H3
Norman Wells	125	F3
Nørre Åby	67	E1
Nørre Alslev	67	G2
Norristown	131	E2
Norrköping	61	J7
Norrtälje	61	K7
Norseman	119	D6
Norsk	105	N6
Northallerton	69	L7
Northam	119	C6
North America	117	P2
Northampton	59	B2
North Andaman	109	A4
North Battleford	125	K6
North Bay	131	E1
North Cape	121	D2
North Carolina	135	F2
North Channel	69	G6
North Charleston	135	F3
North Dakota	129	F1
Northeast Providence Channel	135	F4
Northeim	67	F5
Northern Cape	99	C5
Northern Ireland	69	E7
Northern Mariana Islands	117	E4
Northern Province	99	D4
Northern Territory	119	F4
North Foreland	59	D3
North Horr	97	F3
North Iberia	137	F2
North Island	121	D3
North Korea	113	C4
North Little Rock	135	C3
North Platte	127	F3
North Platte	129	F2
North Ronaldsay	69	K2
North Sea	69	N4
North Stradbroke Island	119	K5
North Taranaki Bight	121	D4
North Uist	69	E4
Northumberland Strait	125	U7
North Vancouver	129	B1
North West	99	C5
North West Basin	119	C4
North West Cape	119	B4
North West Christmas Island Ridge	117	K4
North West Highlands	69	G4
Northwest Territories	125	G4
Norton	135	B2
Norton Sound	133	(1)E3
Norway	61	F5
Norwegian Sea	61	B4
Norwich, *United Kingdom*	59	D2
Norwich, *United States*	131	F2
Nos	63	H1
Nos Emine	79	Q7
Nosevaya	63	K1
Noshiro	113	K3
Nos Kaliakra	79	R6
Noşratābād	85	G4
Nosy Barren	99	G3
Nosy Bé	99	H2
Nosy Boraha	99	J3
Nosy Mitsio	99	H2
Nosy Radama	99	H2
Nosy-Varika	99	H4
Notec	65	G4
Notia Pindos	81	D5
Notios Evvoïkos Kolpos	81	F6
Notre Dame Bay	125	V7
Notsé	95	E3
Nottingham	59	A2
Nottingham Island	125	R4
Nouâdhibou	91	B4
Nouakchott	91	B5
Nouméa	117	G8
Nouvelle Calédonie	117	G8
Nova Gorica	75	J5
Nova Gradiška	79	E4
Nova Iguaçu	143	N3
Nova Mambone	99	F4
Nova Pazova	79	H5
Novara	75	D5
Nova Scotia	125	T8
Novaya Igirma	105	G5
Novaya Karymkary	63	N2
Novaya Kasanka	63	J5
Novaya Lyalya	63	M3
Novaya Zemlya	103	J3
Nova Zagora	79	P7
Novelda	73	K6
Nové Město	65	F8
Nové Mesto	65	G9
Nové Zámky	65	H10
Novgorod	63	F3
Novi Bečej	79	H4
Novi Iskŭr	79	L7
Novi Ligure	75	D6
Novi Marof	75	M4
Novi Pazar, *Bulgaria*	79	Q6
Novi Pazar, *Yugoslavia*	79	H6
Novi Sad	79	G4
Novi Vinodolski	75	L5
Novoaleksandrovsk	63	H5
Novoalekseyevka	63	L4
Novoanninsky	63	H4
Novocheboksarsk	63	J3
Novocherkassk	63	H5
Novodvinsk	63	H2
Novo Hamburgo	143	L4
Novohrad-Volyns'kyy	63	E4
Novokazalinsk	63	M5
Novokutznetsk	103	R7
Novokuybyshevsk	63	J4
Novo Mesto	75	L5
Novomikhaylovskiy	83	H1
Novomoskovsk	63	G4
Novonazimovo	105	E5
Novorossiysk	83	G1
Novorybnoye	105	H2
Novoselivka	79	S2
Novosergiyevka	63	K4
Novosibirsk	103	Q6
Novosibirskiye Ostrova	105	P1

Legend

- ✖ Continent name
- ⬛ Country name
- ⬛ State or province name
- ■ Country capital
- □ State or province capital
- ● Settlement
- ▲ Mountain, volcano, peak
- ▲ Mountain range
- Physical region or feature
- River, canal
- Lake, salt lake
- Gulf, strait, bay
- Sea, ocean
- Cape, point
- Island or island group, rocky or coral reef
- Place of interest
- Historical or cultural region

Name	Page	Ref.
Novosil'	63	G4
Novotroitsk	63	L4
Novouzensk	63	J4
Novozybkov	63	F4
Nový Bor	67	K6
Nový Jičín	65	H8
Novyy Port	103	N4
Novyy Uoyan	105	J5
Novyy Urengoy	103	P4
Novyy Uzen'	103	J9
Nowa Ruda	65	F7
Nowata	135	B2
Nowogard	65	E4
Nowo Warpno	67	K3
Nowra	119	K6
Now Shahr	85	F2
Nowy Dwór Mazowiecki	65	K5
Nowy Sącz	65	K8
Nowy Targ	65	K8
Nowy Tomyśl	65	F5
Noyabr'sk	103	P5
Noyon	59	E5
Nsombo	99	D2
Ntem	95	G4
Ntwetwe Pan	99	C4
Nu	107	G2
Nuasjärvi	61	Q4
Nubian Desert	93	F3
Nudo Coropuna	141	C7
Nueltin Lake	125	M4
Nueva Rosita	133	F3
Nueva San Salvador	137	G6
Nuevo Casas Grandes	133	E2
Nuevo Laredo	133	G3
Nugget Point	121	B8
Nuhaka	121	F4
Nuku'alofa	117	J8
Nuku Hiva	117	M6
Nukumanu Islands	117	F6
Nukunonu	117	J6
Nukus	103	K9
Nullarbor Plain	119	E6
Numan	95	G3
Numazu	113	K6
Numbulwar	119	G2
Numfor	115	(2)E3
Numto	63	P2
Nunarsuit	125	X4
Nunavut	125	M3
Nuneaton	59	A2
Nunivak Island	133	(1)D3
Nunligran	105	Y3
Núoro	77	D8
Nuquí	141	B2
Nura	63	P4
Nurābād	87	D1
Nurata	85	J1
Nurmes	61	Q5
Nürnberg	67	G7
Nürtingen	75	E2
Nurzec	65	M5
Nushki	85	J4
Nutak	125	U5
Nuuk	125	W4
Nuussuaq	125	W2
Nyagan'	63	N2
Nyahururu	97	F3
Nyala	93	D5
Nyalam	107	E3
Nyamlell	97	D2
Nyamtumbo	97	F6
Nyandoma	63	H2
Nyantakara	97	E4
Nyborg	67	F1
Nybro	61	H8
Nyda	103	N4
Nyima	107	E2
Nyingchi	107	F3
Nyírbátor	79	K2
Nyíregyháza	65	L10
Nykarleby	61	M5

Name	Page	Ref.
Nykøbing	67	G2
Nyköping	61	J7
Nylstroom	99	D4
Nymburk	65	E7
Nynäshamn	61	J7
Nyngan	119	J6
Nyon	75	B4
Nysa	65	D6
Nysa	65	G7
Nyukhcha	63	J2
Nyunzu	97	D5
Nyurba	105	K4
Nyuya	105	K4
Nzega	97	E4
Nzérékoré	95	C3
N'zeto	97	A5
Nzwami	99	G2

O

Name	Page	Ref.
Oaho	133	(2)D2
Oahu	117	L3
Oakdale	135	C3
Oakham	59	B2
Oak Lake	129	F1
Oakland	129	B3
Oak Lawn	131	C2
Oakley	135	A2
Oak Ridge	131	D3
Oamaru	121	C7
Oaxaca	137	E5
Ob'	63	N2
Obama	113	H6
Oban	69	G5
O Barco	73	D2
Oberdrauburg	75	H4
Oberhausen	59	J3
Oberkirch	67	D8
Oberlin	135	A2
Oberndorf	75	H3
Oberstdorf	75	F3
Oberursel	67	D6
Obervellach	65	C11
Oberwart	75	M3
Obi	115	(2)C3
Obidos	141	F4
Obigarm	85	K2
Obihiro	113	M2
Obluch'ye	105	N7
Obninsk	63	G3
Obo, Central African Republic	97	D2
Obo, China	111	C3
Oborniki	65	F5
Obouya	95	H5
Oboyan'	63	J2
Obskaya Guba	103	N4
Obuasi	95	D3
Ob'yachevo	63	J2
Ocala	135	E4
Ocaña, Colombia	141	C2
Ocaña, Spain	73	G5
Ocean City	131	E3
Ocean Falls	125	F6
Oceanside	133	C2
Och'amch'ire	83	J2
Ochsenfurt	67	E7
Oconto	131	C2
Oda	95	D3
Ōda	113	G6
Ōdate	113	L3
Odda	61	D6
Odemira	73	B7
Ödemiş	81	L6
Odense	67	F1
Oder = Odra	65	F6
Oderzo	75	H5
Odesa	63	F5
Odessa = Odesa, Ukraine	63	F5
Odessa, United States	133	F2
Odienné	95	C3

Name	Page	Ref.
Odorheiu Secuiesc	79	N3
Odra	65	F6
Odžaci	79	G4
Oeiras	141	J5
Oelrichs	129	F2
Oelsnitz	67	H6
Oeno	117	N8
Oestev	143	H7
Ofaqim	86	B5
Offenbach	67	D6
Offenburg	75	C2
Ōgaki	113	J6
Ogasawara-shotō	101	T7
Ogbomosho	95	E3
Ogden	129	D2
Ogdensburg	125	R8
Ogilvie Mountains	125	C4
Oglio	75	E5
Ogosta	79	L6
Ogre	61	N8
Ogre	61	N8
O Grove	73	B2
Ogulin	75	L5
Ohai	121	A7
Ohio	131	C3
Ohio	131	D2
Ohre	67	J6
Ohrid	81	C3
Ohura	121	E4
Oiapoque	141	G3
Oil City	131	E2
Oise	59	E5
Ōita	113	F7
Ojinaga	133	F3
Ojos del Salado	143	H4
Oka	105	G6
Okaba	115	(2)E4
Okahandja	99	B4
Okanagan Lake	127	C2
Okano	95	G4
Okanogan	129	C1
Okara	107	B2
Okarem	85	F2
Okato	121	D4
Okavango Delta	99	C3
Okaya	113	K5
Okayama	113	G6
Okene	95	F3
Oker	67	F4
Okha, India	85	J5
Okha, Russia	105	Q6
Okhansk	63	L3
Okhotsk	105	Q5
Okhtyrka	63	F4
Okinawa	111	H5
Okinawa	111	H5
Oki-shotō	113	G5
Okitipupa	95	E3
Oklahoma	135	B2
Oklahoma City	135	B2
Okoppe	113	M1
Okoyo	95	H5
Okranger	61	E5
Oksino	63	K1
Oktinden	61	H4
Oktyabr'sk	63	L5
Oktyabr'skiy	63	K4
Okurchan	105	S5
Okushiri-tō	113	K2
Olancha	129	C3
Öland	61	J8
Olanga	61	Q3
Olathe	135	C2
Olava	67	J7
Olavarría	143	J6
Oława	65	G7
Ólbia	77	D8
Olching	75	G2
Old Crow	133	(1)K2
Oldenburg, Germany	67	D3
Oldenburg, Germany	67	F2

Name	Page	Ref.
Oldenzaal	59	J2
Oldham	69	L8
Old Head of Kinsale	69	D10
Olean	131	E2
Olekma	105	L5
Olekminsk	105	L4
Oleksandriya	63	F5
Olenegorsk	61	S2
Olenek	105	J3
Olenëk	105	L2
Olenëkskiy Zaliv	105	L2
Olhão	73	C7
Olib	75	K6
Olinda	141	L5
Oliva	73	K6
Olivet	129	G2
Olivia	131	B2
Olmos	141	B5
Olney	135	B3
Olochi	105	K6
Olonets	63	F2
Olongapo	109	G4
Oloron-Ste-Marie	71	E10
Olot	73	N2
Olovyannaya	105	K6
Olpe	59	K3
Olsztyn	65	K4
Olt	79	M4
Olten	75	C3
Oltenița	79	P5
Oltu	83	K3
Oluan-pi	109	G2
Olvera	73	E8
Olympia	129	B1
Olympos	81	E4
Olympus	81	Q10
Olyutorskiy	105	W4
Olyutorskiy Zaliv	105	V4
Om'	103	N6
Oma	107	D2
Omae-saki	113	K6
Omagh	69	E7
Omaha	129	G2
Omak	129	C1
Omakau	121	B7
Oman	85	G5
Omapere	121	D2
Omarama	121	B7
Omaruru	99	B4
Omba	107	E2
Ombrone	77	F6
Omdurman = Umm Durman	93	F4
Omegna	75	D5
Omeo	119	J7
Om Hajer	93	G5
Omīdeyeh	87	C1
Omis	75	M7
Ommen	59	J2
Omolon	105	T3
Omoloy	105	N3
Omo Wenz	97	F2
Omsk	103	N6
Omsukchan	105	S4
Ōmū	113	M1
Omulew	65	L4
Omuta	113	F7
Onda	73	K5
Ondangwa	99	B3
Ondjiva	99	B3
Ondo	95	E3
Ondörhaan	111	E1
One and a Half Degree Channel	107	B8
Onega	63	G2
O'Neill	129	G2
Oneonta	131	F2
Onești	79	P3
Onezhskoye Ozero	63	F2
Ongjin	113	C5
Ongole	107	D5
Onguday	103	R7
Oni	83	K2

X Continent name
A Country name
a State or province name
■ Country capital
□ State or province capital
● Settlement

▲ Mountain, volcano, peak
▬ Mountain range
⊘ Physical region or feature
◪ River, canal
◢ Lake, salt lake
◣ Gulf, strait, bay

▱ Sea, ocean
▷ Cape, point
▨ Island or island group, rocky or coral reef
✳ Place of interest
▨ Historical or cultural region

Name	Page	Grid		Name	Page	Grid		Name	Page	Grid		Name	Page	Grid
Onilahy	99	G4		Ormoc	109	G4		Ostrov Bol'shoy Begichev	105	J2		Oulx	75	B5
Onitsha	95	F3		Ormos Almyrou	81	G9		Ostrov Bol'shoy Lyakhovskiy	105	Q2		Oum-Chalouba	93	D4
Ono	113	J6		Ormos Mesara	81	G9		Ostrov Bol'shoy Shantar	105	P6		Oum-Hadjer	93	C5
Onon	105	J7		Ornans	71	M6		Ostrov Chechen'	83	M2		Ounarjoki	61	N3
Onon	105	J7		Ornö	61	K7		Ostrov Iturup	113	P1		Our	59	J4
Onslow Bay	137	J2		Örnsköldsvik	61	K5		Ostrov Kil'din	61	T2		Ouray	129	E3
Onsong	113	E2		Orocué	141	C3		Ostrov Kolguyev	103	H4		Ourense	73	C2
Ontario	125	N6		Orofino	129	C1		Ostrov Komsomolets	103	T1		Ouricuri	141	J5
Ontinyent	73	K6		Oromocto	131	G1		Ostrov Kotel'nyy	105	P1		Ourthe	59	H4
Ontonagon	131	C1		Orona	117	J6		Ostrov Kunashir	113	P1		Oustreham	59	B5
Onyx	133	C1		Oronoque	141	F3		Ostrov Mednyy	105	V6		Outer Hebrides	69	D4
Oodnadatta	119	G5		Oroqen Zizhiqi	105	L6		Ostrov Mezhdusharskiy	103	H3		Outjo	99	B4
Oologah Lake	135	B2		Orosei	77	D8		Ostrov Novaya Sibir'	105	S2		Outokumpu	61	Q5
Oostburg	59	F3		Orosháza	79	H3		Ostrov Ogurchinskiy	85	F2		Out Skerries	69	M1
Oostelijk-Flevoland	59	H2		Oroszlany	65	H10		Ostrov Oktyabr'skoy	103	S2		Ouyen	119	H7
Oostende	59	E3		Orotukan	105	S4		Ostrov Onekotan	105	S7		Ovacık	81	R8
Oosterhout	59	G3		Oroville	129	B3		Ostrov Paramushir	105	T6		Ovada	75	D6
Oosterschelde	59	F3		Orroroo	119	G6		Ostrov Rasshua	105	S7		Ovalle	143	G5
Ootsa Lake	125	F6		Orsay	71	H5		Ostrov Shiashkotan	105	S7		Ovareli	83	L3
Opala	97	C4		Orsha	63	F4		Ostrov Shumshu	105	T6		Overflakkee	59	G3
Oparino	63	J3		Orsk	63	L4		Ostrov Simushir	105	S7		Overlander Roadhouse	119	B5
Opava	65	G8		Orşova	79	K5		Ostrov Urup	105	S7		Overland Park	135	C2
Opelika	135	D3		Ørsta	61	D5		Ostrov Ushakova	103	Q1		Overton	129	D3
Opelousas	135	C3		Ortaklar	81	K7		Ostrov Vaygach	103	K3		Övertorneå	61	M3
Opheim	129	E1		Orthez	71	E10		Ostrov Vise	103	P2		Ovidiopol'	79	T3
Opochka	63	E3		Ortigueira	73	C1		Ostrov Vosrozhdeniya	103	K9		Oviedo	73	E1
Opoczno	65	K6		Ortisei	75	G4		Ostrov Vrangelya	105	W2		Owaka	121	B8
Opole	65	G7		Ortles	75	F4		Ostrowiec Świętokrzyski	65	L7		Owando	95	H5
Opornyy	103	J8		Ortona	77	J6		Ostrów Mazowiecka	65	L5		Owase	113	J6
Opotiki	121	F4		Ortonville	131	A1		Ostrów Wielkopolski	65	G6		Owatonna	131	B2
Opp	135	D3		Orümīyeh	83	L5		Ostuni	77	M8		Owensboro	131	C3
Opunake	121	D4		Oruro	141	D7		Osum	81	C4		Owens Lake	129	C3
Opuwo	99	A3		Orvieto	77	G6		Ōsumi-shotō	113	F8		Owen Sound	131	D2
Oradea	79	J2		Orville	71	L6		Osuna	73	E7		Owerri	95	F3
Orahovac	79	H7		Ōsaka	113	H6		Oswego	131	E2		Owo	95	F3
Orai	107	C3		Osăm	79	M6		Oświęcim	65	J7		Owosso	131	D2
Oran	73	K9		Osceola	131	B2		Otago Peninsula	121	C7		Owyhee	129	C2
Orán	143	C3		Oschatz	67	J5		Otaki	121	E5		Owyhee	129	C2
Orange	99	C5		Oschersleben	67	G4		Otaru	113	L2		Oxford, New Zealand	121	D6
Orange, Australia	119	J6		Osh	103	N9		Othonoi	81	B5		Oxford, United Kingdom	59	A3
Orange, France	71	K9		Oshamambe	113	L2		Oti	95	E3		Oxnard	133	C2
Orange, United States	135	C3		Oshawa	131	E2		Otjiwarongo	99	B4		Oyama	113	K5
Orangeburg	135	E3		Oshkosh, Nebr., United States	129	F2		Otočac	75	L6		Oyapock	141	G3
Orangeville	131	D2		Oshkosh, Wis., United States	131	C2		Otog Qi	111	D3		Oyem	95	G4
Orango	95	A2		Oshogbo	95	E3		Otoineppu	113	M1		Oyen	127	D1
Oranienburg	67	J4		Osijek	79	F4		Otorohanga	121	E4		Oyonnax	75	A4
Orapa	99	D4		Ósimo	75	J7		Ótranto	77	N8		Ózd	65	K9
Orăştie	79	L4		Oskaloosa	131	B2		Otrøy	61	D5		Ozernovskiy	105	T6
Oraviţa	79	J4		Oskarshamn	61	J8		Ōtsu	113	H6		Ozero Alakol'	103	Q8
Orbetello	77	F6		Oslo	61	F7		Otta	61	E6		Ozero Aralsor	63	J5
Orco	75	C5		Oslofjorden	61	F7		Ottawa	131	E1		Ozero Aydarkul'	103	M9
Ordes	73	B1		Osmancık	83	F3		Ottawa, Canada	131	E1		Ozero Balkhash	103	N8
Ordes Santa Comba	73	B1		Osmaniye	83	G5		Ottawa, Ill., United States	131	C2		Ozero Baykal	105	H6
Ordu	83	G3		Osnabrück	59	L2		Ottawa, Kans., United States	135	B2		Ozero Beloye	63	G2
Ordway	129	F3		Osor	75	K6		Ottawa Islands	125	Q5		Ozero Chany	103	P7
Öreälven	61	K4		Osorno	143	G7		Otterøy	61	F4		Ozero Chernoye	63	N3
Örebro	61	H7		Osprey Reef	119	J2		Ottobrunn	75	G2		Ozero Il'men'	63	F3
Oregon	129	B2		Oss	59	H3		Ottumwa	131	B2		Ozero-Imandra	61	R2
Oregon	131	A3		Osseo	131	B2		Otukpo	95	F3		Ozero Inder	103	J8
Orekhovo-Zuyevo	63	G3		Ossora	105	U5		Ouachita Mountains	135	C3		Ozero Janis'jarvi	61	R5
Orel	63	G4		Ostashkov	63	F3		Ouadâne	91	C4		Ozero Kamennoje	61	R4
Orem	129	D2		Oste	67	E3		Ouadda	97	C2		Ozero Kanozero	61	T3
Orenburg	63	L4		Osterburg	67	G4		Ouagadougou	95	D2		Ozero Karaginskiy	105	U5
Orestiada	81	J3		Osterdalen	61	F6		Oualàta	91	D5		Ozero Khanka	113	G1
Orford Ness	59	D2		Osterholz-Scharmbeck	67	D3		Ouargla	91	G2		Ozero Kolvitskoye	61	S3
Orhei	79	R2		Osterode	67	F5		Ouarzazate	91	D2		Ozero Kovdozero	61	S3
Orihuela	73	K6		Östersund	61	H5		Oudenaarde	59	F4		Ozero Kulundinskoye	103	P7
Orillia	131	E2		Ostfriesische Inseln	67	C3		Oudenbosch	59	G3		Ozero Kushmurun	63	N4
Orinoco	141	D2		Ostiglia	75	G5		Oudtshoorn	99	C6		Ozero Lama	105	D2
Orinoco Delta = Delta del Orinoco	141	E2		Ostrava	65	H8		Oued Medjerda	77	D12		Ozero Leksozero	61	R5
Orissaare	61	M7		Ostróda	65	K4		Oued Meliane	77	D12		Ozero Lovozero	61	T2
Oristano	77	C9		Ostrołęka	65	L4		Oued Tiélat	73	K9		Ozero Morzhovets	63	H1
Orivesi	61	Q5		Ostrov, Czech Republic	67	H6		Oued Zem	91	D2		Ozero Njuk	61	R4
Orkla	61	F5		Ostrov, Russia	63	E3		Ouésso	95	H4		Ozero Ozhogino	105	R3
Orkney Islands	69	K3		Ostrova Medvezh'I	105	T2		Ouezzane	91	D2		Ozero Pirenga	61	R3
Orlando	135	E4		Ostrov Atlasova	105	S6		Oujda	91	E2		Ozero Pyaozero	61	R3
Orléans	71	G6		Ostrova Vrangelya	123	V4		Oulainen	61	N4		Ozero Saltaim	63	P3
Orlik	105	F6		Ostrov Ayon	105	V2		Oulu	61	N4		Ozero Sarpa	63	J5
Orly	59	E6		Ostrov Belyy	103	N3		Oulujärvi	61	P4		Ozero Segozeroskoye	63	F2
Ormara	85	H4		Ostrov Beringa	105	V6		Oulujoki	61	P4		Ozero Seletyteniz	103	N7
				Ostrov Bol'shevik	103	V2						Ozero Sredneye Kuyto	61	R4

Ozero Taymyr	◪	**103**	U3
Ozero Teletskoye	◪	**103**	R7
Ozero Tengiz	◪	**63**	N4
Ozero Topozero	◪	**61**	R4
Ozero Umbozero	◪	**61**	T3
Ozero Vygozero	◪	**63**	G2
Ozero Yalpug	◪	**79**	R4
Ozero Zaysan	◪	**103**	Q8
Ozero Zhaltyr	◪	**63**	K5
Ozero Zhamanakkol'	◪	**63**	M5
Ozersk	⊡	**65**	M3
Ozhogina	⧄	**105**	R3
Ozhogino	⊡	**105**	R3
Ozieri	⊡	**77**	C8
Ozinki	⊡	**63**	J4
Ozona	⊡	**133**	F2
Ozurget'i	⊡	**83**	J3

P

Paamiut	⊡	**125**	X4
Paar	⧄	**67**	G8
Paarl	⊡	**99**	B6
Pabbay	⊞	**69**	E4
Pabianice	⊡	**65**	J6
Pabna	⊡	**107**	E4
Pacasmayo	⊡	**141**	B5
Pachino	⊡	**77**	K12
Pachuca	⊡	**137**	E4
Pacific Ocean	◛	**117**	M3
Pacitan	⊡	**115**	(1)E4
Packwood	⊡	**129**	B1
Padalere	⊡	**115**	(2)B3
Padang	⊡	**115**	(1)C3
Padangpanjang	⊡	**115**	(1)C3
Padangsidempuan	⊡	**115**	(1)B2
Paderborn	⊡	**67**	D5
Pádova	⊡	**75**	G5
Padre Island	⊞	**135**	B4
Padrón	⊡	**73**	B2
Paducah, *Ky., United States*	⊡	**131**	C3
Paducah, *Tex., United States*	⊡	**133**	F2
Padum	⊡	**107**	C2
Paekdu San	▲	**113**	D3
Paeroa	⊡	**121**	E3
Pafos	⊡	**81**	Q10
Pag	⊞	**75**	K6
Pag	⊡	**75**	L6
Pagadian	⊡	**109**	G5
Pagai Selatan	⊞	**115**	(1)B3
Pagai Utara	⊞	**115**	(1)B3
Pagalu = Annobón	⊞	**95**	F5
Pagan	⊞	**117**	E4
Pagatan	⊡	**115**	(1)F3
Page, *Ariz., United States*	⊡	**133**	D1
Page, *Okla., United States*	⊡	**135**	C3
Pagosa Springs	⊡	**129**	E3
Pagri	⊡	**107**	E3
Pahiatua	⊡	**121**	E5
Paia	⊡	**133**	(2)E3
Paide	⊡	**61**	N7
Päijänne	◪	**61**	N6
Painan	⊡	**115**	(1)C3
Painesville	⊡	**131**	D2
Paisley	⊡	**69**	H6
Paita	⊡	**141**	A5
Pakaraima Mountains	⛰	**141**	E2
Pakch'ŏn	⊡	**113**	C4
Paki	⊡	**95**	F2
Pakistan	Ⓐ	**85**	J4
Pakokku	⊡	**109**	A2
Pakotai	⊡	**121**	D2
Pakrac	⊡	**75**	N5
Paks	⊡	**79**	F3
Pakxé	⊡	**109**	D3
Pala	⊡	**93**	B6
Palafrugell	⊡	**73**	P3
Palagónia	⊡	**77**	J11
Palagruža	⊞	**77**	L6
Palamós	⊡	**73**	P3
Palana	⊡	**105**	U5
Palanga	⊡	**65**	L2
Palangkaraya	⊡	**115**	(1)E3
Palanpur	⊡	**107**	B4
Palantak	⊡	**85**	H4
Palatka, *Russia*	⊡	**105**	S4
Palatka, *United States*	⊡	**135**	E4
Palau	⊡	**77**	D7
Palau	Ⓐ	**117**	D5
Palau	⊞	**117**	D5
Palawan	⊞	**109**	F5
Palazzolo Arcéide	⊡	**77**	J11
Palembang	⊡	**115**	(1)C3
Palencia	⊡	**73**	F2
Paleokastritsa	⊡	**81**	B5
Palermo	⊡	**77**	H10
Palestine	⊡	**135**	B3
Palestrina	⊡	**77**	G7
Paletwa	⊡	**109**	A2
Palghat	⊡	**107**	C6
Pali	⊡	**107**	B3
Palikir	■	**117**	F5
Palimbang	⊡	**109**	G5
Palk Strait	⊳	**107**	C7
Palma	⊡	**73**	N5
Palma del Rio	⊡	**73**	E7
Palma di Montechiaro	⊡	**77**	H11
Palmanova	⊡	**75**	J5
Palmares	⊡	**141**	K5
Palmarola	⊞	**77**	G8
Palmas	▣	**141**	H6
Palmas	⊡	**143**	L4
Palm Bay	⊡	**135**	E4
Palmdale	⊡	**133**	C2
Palmerston	⊡	**121**	C7
Palmerston Island	⊞	**117**	K7
Palmerston North	⊡	**121**	E5
Palm Harbor	⊡	**135**	E4
Palmi	⊡	**77**	K10
Palmira	⊡	**141**	B3
Palmyra Island	⊞	**117**	K5
Palojärvi	⊡	**61**	M2
Palopo	⊡	**115**	(2)B3
Palu, *Indonesia*	⊡	**115**	(2)A3
Palu, *Turkey*	⊡	**83**	J4
Palyavaam	⧄	**105**	W3
Pama	⊡	**95**	E2
Pamhagen	⊡	**75**	M3
Pamiers	⊡	**71**	G10
Pamlico Sound	⊳	**135**	F2
Pampa	⊡	**133**	F1
Pampas	▨	**143**	J6
Pamplona, *Colombia*	⊡	**137**	K7
Pamplona, *Spain*	⊡	**73**	J2
Pana	⊡	**131**	C3
Panagyurishte	⊡	**79**	M7
Panaji	⊡	**107**	B5
Panama	Ⓐ	**137**	H7
Panamá	■	**141**	B2
Panama Canal = Canal de Panamá	⧄	**137**	J7
Panama City	⊡	**135**	D3
Panara	⧄	**75**	G6
Panaria	⊞	**77**	K10
Panarik	⊡	**115**	(1)D2
Panay	⊞	**109**	G4
Pančevo	⊡	**79**	H5
Panciu	⊡	**79**	Q4
Pandharpur	⊡	**107**	C5
Panevėžys	⊡	**65**	P2
Pangin	⊡	**107**	F3
Pangkajene	⊡	**115**	(2)A3
Pangkalpinang	⊡	**115**	(1)D3
Pangnirtung	⊡	**125**	T3
Panguitch	⊡	**129**	D3
Pangutaran Group	⊞	**109**	G5
Panhandle	⊡	**133**	F1
Panipat	⊡	**107**	C3
Panjāb	⊡	**85**	J3
Panjgur	⊡	**85**	H4
Pankshin	⊡	**95**	F3
Pantanal	▨	**141**	F7
Pantar	⊞	**115**	(2)B4
Pantelleria	⊞	**91**	H1
Páola	⊡	**77**	L9
Paoua	⊡	**97**	B2
Pápa	⊡	**79**	E2
Papa	⊡	**133**	(2)F4
Papakura	⊡	**121**	E3
Papantla	⊡	**137**	E4
Paparoa	⊡	**121**	E3
Papa Stour	⊞	**69**	L1
Papa Westray	⊞	**69**	K2
Papenburg	⊡	**67**	C3
Papey	⊞	**61**	(1)F2
Papua New Guinea	Ⓐ	**117**	E6
Papun	⊡	**109**	B3
Pará	ⓐ	**141**	G5
Para	⧄	**141**	H4
Parabel'	⊡	**103**	Q6
Paracatu	⊡	**141**	H7
Paracel Islands	⊞	**109**	E3
Paraćin	⊡	**79**	J6
Pará de Minas	⊡	**141**	J7
Paragould	⊡	**135**	C2
Paragua, *Bolivia*	⧄	**141**	E6
Paragua, *Venezuela*	⧄	**141**	E2
Paraguay	⧄	**139**	F6
Paraguay	Ⓐ	**143**	J3
Paraíba	ⓐ	**141**	K5
Parakou	⊡	**95**	E3
Paralimni	⊡	**86**	A1
Paramaribo	■	**141**	F2
Paranã	⊡	**141**	H6
Paranã	⧄	**141**	H6
Paraná	⊡	**143**	J5
Paraná	⧄	**143**	K4
Paraná	ⓐ	**143**	L3
Paranaguá	⊡	**143**	M4
Paranaíba	⊡	**141**	G7
Paranaíba	⧄	**141**	G7
Paranavaí	⊡	**143**	L3
Paranestio	⊡	**81**	G3
Paraparaumu	⊡	**121**	E5
Paray-le Monial	⊡	**71**	K7
Parbhani	⊡	**107**	C5
Parchim	⊡	**67**	G3
Pardo	⧄	**141**	J7
Pardubice	⊡	**65**	E7
Pareh	⊡	**83**	L4
Parepare	⊡	**115**	(2)A3
Parga	⊡	**81**	C5
Parigi	⊡	**115**	(2)B3
Parika	⊡	**141**	F2
Parintins	⊡	**141**	F4
Paris, *France*	■	**71**	H5
Paris, *Tenn., United States*	⊡	**135**	D2
Paris, *Tex., United States*	⊡	**135**	B3
Parkersburg	⊡	**131**	D3
Park Rapids	⊡	**131**	A1
Parla	⊡	**73**	G4
Parma	⧄	**75**	F6
Parma, *Italy*	⊡	**75**	F6
Parma, *United States*	⊡	**131**	D2
Parnaíba	⧄	**141**	J4
Parnassus	⊡	**121**	D6
Pärnu	⊡	**61**	N7
Pärnu	⧄	**61**	N7
Paros	⊡	**81**	H7
Paros	⊞	**81**	H7
Parry Bay	⊳	**125**	Q3
Parry Islands	⊞	**125**	L1
Parry Sound	⊡	**131**	D2
Parsons	⊡	**135**	B2
Parthenay	⊡	**71**	E7
Partinico	⊡	**77**	H10
Partizansk	⊡	**113**	G2
Paru	⧄	**141**	G4
Parvatipuram	⊡	**107**	D5
Paryang	⊡	**107**	D2
Pasadena, *Calif., United States*	⊡	**133**	C2
Pasadena, *Tex., United States*	⊡	**135**	B4
Paşalimani Adası	⊞	**81**	K4
Pasawng	⊡	**109**	B3
Paşcani	⊡	**79**	P2
Pasco	⊡	**129**	C1
Pasewalk	⊡	**67**	K3
Pasig	⊡	**109**	G4
Pasinler	⊡	**83**	J3
Pasłęk	⊡	**65**	J3
Pasłek	⧄	**65**	J3
Pasleka	⧄	**61**	L9
Pašman	⊞	**75**	L7
Pasni	⊡	**85**	H4
Paso de Hachado	▨	**143**	G6
Paso de Indios	⊡	**143**	H7
Paso de la Cumbre	▨	**143**	H5
Paso de San Francisco	▨	**143**	H4
Paso Río Mayo	⊡	**143**	G8
Paso Robles	⊡	**133**	B1
Passau	⊡	**67**	J8
Passo Fundo	⊡	**143**	L4
Passos	⊡	**141**	H8
Pastavy	⊡	**61**	P9
Pasto	⊡	**141**	B3
Pastos Bons	⊡	**141**	J5
Pásztó	⊡	**79**	G2
Patagonia	▨	**143**	G8
Patan, *India*	⊡	**107**	B4
Patan, *Nepal*	⊡	**107**	E3
Patea	⊡	**121**	E4
Pate Island	⊞	**97**	G4
Paterna	⊡	**73**	K5
Paterno	⊡	**77**	J11
Paterson	⊡	**131**	F2
Pathankot	⊡	**107**	C2
Pathein	⊡	**109**	A3
Pathfinder Reservoir	◪	**129**	E2
Patia	⧄	**141**	B3
Patiala	⊡	**107**	C2
Patmos	⊞	**81**	J7
Patna	⊡	**107**	E3
Patnos	⊡	**83**	K4
Patos de Minas	⊡	**141**	H7
Patra	⊡	**81**	D6
Patraikis Kolpos	⊳	**81**	D6
Patreksfjörđur	⊡	**61**	(1)B2
Pattani	⊡	**109**	C5
Pattaya	⊡	**109**	C4
Patti	⊡	**77**	J10
Paturau River	⊡	**121**	D5
Pau	⊡	**73**	K1
Pauini	⊡	**141**	D5
Pauini	⧄	**141**	D5
Paulatuk	⊡	**133**	(1)N2
Paulo Afonso	⊡	**141**	K5
Paul's Valley	⊡	**135**	B3
Pāveh	⊡	**83**	M6
Pavia	⊡	**75**	E5
Pāvilosta	⊡	**61**	L8
Pavlikeni	⊡	**79**	N6
Pavlodar	⊡	**103**	P7
Pavlohrad	⊡	**63**	G5
Pavlovsk	⊡	**63**	H4
Pavlovskaya	⊡	**63**	G5
Pavullo nel Frignano	⊡	**75**	F6
Paxoi	⊞	**81**	C5
Paxson	⊡	**133**	(1)H3
Payerne	⊡	**75**	B4
Payette	⊡	**129**	C2
Payne's Find	⊡	**119**	C5
Paysandu	⊡	**143**	K5
Payson	⊡	**133**	D2
Payturma	⊡	**103**	S3
Pazar	⊡	**83**	J3
Pazardzhik	⊡	**79**	M7
Pazin	⊡	**75**	J5
Peace	⧄	**125**	H5
Peace River	⊡	**125**	H5
Peach Springs	⊡	**133**	D1
Pearsall	⊡	**135**	B4
Pebane	⊡	**99**	F3
Pebas	⊡	**141**	C5

☒	Continent name	▲	Mountain, volcano, peak	◛	Sea, ocean
Ⓐ	Country name	⛰	Mountain range	⊿	Cape, point
ⓐ	State or province name	▨	Physical region or feature	⊞	Island or island group, rocky or coral reef
■	Country capital	⧄	River, canal	✳	Place of interest
▣	State or province capital	◪	Lake, salt lake	⊠	Historical or cultural region
⊡	Settlement	⊳	Gulf, strait, bay		

Name	Page	Ref.
Peć	79	H7
Pecan Island	135	C4
Pechora	63	K1
Pechora	63	L1
Pechorskoye More	103	J4
Pechory	61	P8
Pecos	133	F2
Pecos	133	F2
Pécs	79	F3
Pedja	61	P7
Pedra Azul	141	J7
Pedra Lume	95	(1)B1
Pedreiras	141	J4
Pedro Afonso	141	H5
Pedro Juan Caballero	143	K3
Pedro Luro	143	J6
Peel Sound	125	M2
Peene	67	J3
Peenemünde	67	J2
Pegasus Bay	121	D6
Pegnitz	67	G7
Pegu	109	B3
Pegunungan Barisan	115	(1)B2
Pegunungan Iban	115	(1)F2
Pegunungan Meratus	115	(1)F3
Pegunungan Schwaner	115	(1)E3
Pegunungan Maoke	115	(2)E3
Pegunungan Van Rees	115	(2)E3
Pehuajó	143	J6
Peine	67	F4
Peißenberg	75	G3
Peixe	141	H6
Pekalongan	115	(1)D4
Pekanbaru	115	(1)C2
Peking = Beijing	111	F3
Peleduy	105	J5
Peleng	115	(2)B3
Pelhřimov	65	E8
Pelješac	77	M6
Pello	61	N3
Pellworm	67	D2
Pelly Bay	125	P3
Peloponnisos	81	D7
Pelotas	143	L5
Pelym	63	M2
Pemangkat	115	(1)D2
Pematangsiantar	115	(1)B2
Pemba	99	G2
Pemba Island	97	F5
Pembina	129	G1
Pembine	131	C1
Pembroke, Canada	131	E1
Pembroke, United Kingdom	69	H10
Pembroke, United States	135	E3
Peñafiel	73	F3
Peñaranda de Bracamonte	73	E4
Peñarroya-Pueblonuevo	73	E6
Pendleton	129	C1
Pendolo	115	(1)G3
Pend Oreille Lake	129	C1
Pen Hills	131	E2
Peniche	73	A5
Península de Azuero	137	H7
Península de Guajira	137	K6
Península Valdés	143	J7
Péninsule de Gaspé	125	T7
Péninsule d'Ungava	125	R4
Penmarch	71	A6
Penne	77	H6
Pennines	69	K7
Pennsylvania	131	E2
Penrith	69	K7
Pensacola	137	G2
Penticton	129	C1
Penza	63	J4
Penzance	69	G11
Penzhina	105	V4
Penzhinskaya Guba	105	U4
Penzhinskiy Khrebet	105	V4
Peoria, Ariz., United States	133	D2
Peoria, Ill., United States	131	C2
Percival Lakes	119	D4
Peregrebnoye	63	N2
Pereira	141	B3
Pergamino	143	J5
Périgueux	71	F8
Peristera	81	G5
Perito Moreno	143	G8
Perleberg	67	G3
Perm'	63	L3
Përmet	81	C4
Pernambuco	141	K5
Pernik	79	L7
Péronne	59	E5
Perpignan	71	H11
Perrine	135	E4
Perry, Fla., United States	135	E3
Perry, Ga., United States	135	E3
Persepolis	87	E2
Persian Gulf	87	C2
Perth, Australia	119	C6
Perth, United Kingdom	69	J5
Pertuis Breton	71	D7
Peru	131	C2
Peru	141	C6
Peru-Chile Trench	139	D5
Perúgia	77	G5
Pervomays'k	63	F5
Pervoural'sk	63	L3
Pésaro	75	H7
Pescara	77	J6
Pescia	75	F7
Peshawar	107	B2
Peshkopi	81	C3
Peshtera	81	G2
Peski Karakumy	85	G2
Peski Kzyylkum	103	L9
Peski Priaral'skiye Karakumy	103	L8
Pesnica	75	L4
Pessac	71	E9
Petah Tiqwa	86	B4
Petalioi	81	G7
Petaluma	129	B3
Pétange	59	H5
Petare	137	L6
Petauke	99	E2
Peterborough, Canada	131	E2
Peterborough, United Kingdom	69	M9
Peterhead	69	L4
Peter I Øy	144	(2)JJ3
Petersburg	131	E3
Petersfield	59	B3
Petershagen	67	D4
Petilia	77	L9
Petit Mécatina	125	U6
Peto	137	G4
Petre Bay	121	(1)B1
Petrich	81	F3
Petrila	79	L4
Petrinja	75	M5
Petrolina	141	J5
Petropavlovka	105	H6
Petropavlovsk	63	N4
Petropavlovsk-Kamchatskiy	105	T6
Petrópolis	143	N3
Petroşani	79	L4
Petrovac	79	J5
Petrovsk-Zabaykal'skiy	105	H6
Petrozavodsk	63	F2
Petrun	63	M1
Petukhovo	63	N3
Pevek	105	W3
Pezinok	65	G9
Pfaffenhofen	67	G8
Pfarrkirchen	67	H8
Pflach	75	F3
Pforzheim	67	D8
Pfunds	75	F4
Pfungstadt	67	D7
Phalaborwa	99	E4
Phalodi	107	B3
Phan Rang	109	D4
Phan Thiêt	109	D4
Phatthalung	109	C5
Phet Buri	109	B4
Phichit	109	C3
Philadelphia, Miss., United States	135	D3
Philadelphia, Pa., United States	135	F2
Philippeville	59	G4
Philippines	109	G5
Philippine Trench	101	R8
Philips	125	K7
Phillipsburg	129	G3
Phitsanulok	109	C3
Phnum Penh	109	C4
Phoenix	133	D2
Phoenix Islands	117	J6
Phôngsali	109	C2
Phuket	109	B5
Piacenza	75	E5
Piádena	75	F5
Pianosa	77	E6
Piatra-Neamţ	79	P3
Piauí	141	J5
Piazza Armerina	77	J11
Pibor Post	97	E2
Picacho del Centinela	133	F3
Picayune	135	D3
Pichilemu	143	G5
Pico	91	(1)B2
Pico Almanzor	73	E4
Pico Cristóbal Colón	137	K6
Pico da Bandeira	143	N3
Pico da Neblina	141	D3
Pico de Itambé	143	N2
Pico de Teide	91	B3
Pico Duarte	137	K5
Picos	141	J5
Picton, New Zealand	121	D5
Picton, United States	131	E2
Pic Tousside	93	C3
Piedras Negras	133	F3
Pieksämäki	61	P5
Pielinen	61	Q5
Pierre	129	F2
Pierrelatte	71	K9
Piers do Rio	141	H7
Pieš'ťany	65	G9
Pietermaritzburg	99	E5
Pietersburg	99	D4
Pietrasanta	75	F6
Piet Retief	99	E5
Pieve di Cadore	75	H4
Pihlájavesi	61	P6
Pik Aborigen	105	R4
Piketberg	99	B6
Pik Kommunizma	85	K2
Pik Pobedy	103	P9
Piła	65	F4
Pilaya	143	H3
Pilcomayo	141	E8
Pilibhit	107	C3
Pilica	65	J7
Pimba	119	G6
Pimenta Bueno	141	E6
Pinamalayan	109	G4
Pinamar	143	K6
Pinang	109	B5
Pınarbası	83	G4
Pinar del Río	137	H4
Pinarhisar	81	K3
Pińczów	65	K7
Pindaré Mirim	141	H4
Pine Bluff	131	B4
Pine Bluffs	129	F2
Pine City	131	B1
Pine Creek	119	F2
Pine Creek Reservoir	131	A4
Pinega	63	H2
Pineios	81	E5
Pine Island Bay	144	(2)GG3
Pineland	135	C3
Pinerolo	75	C6
Pineville, Ky., United States	131	D3
Pineville, La., United States	135	C3
Pingdingshan	111	E4
Pingguo	109	D2
Pingle	109	E2
Pingliang	111	D3
P'ing-tung	109	G2
Pingxiang, China	109	D2
Pingxiang, China	109	E1
Pinhel	73	C4
Pini	115	(1)B2
Pinka	75	M3
Pink Mountain	125	G5
Pinneberg	67	E3
Pinsk	63	E4
Pioche	129	D3
Piombino	77	E6
Pioneer	133	D2
Pioneer Mountains	129	D1
Pionerskii	65	K3
Pionerskiy	63	M2
Piotrków Trybunalski	65	J6
Piove di Sacco	75	H5
Piperi	81	G5
Pipestone	131	A2
Pipiriki	121	E4
Piqua	131	D2
Piracicaba	143	M3
Pireas	81	F7
Pirin	81	F3
Piripiri	141	J4
Pirmasens	67	C7
Pirna	67	J6
Pirot	79	K6
Piru	115	(2)C3
Pisa	65	L4
Pisa	75	F7
Pisco	141	B6
Písek	65	D8
Pīshīn	85	H4
Pishin	85	J3
Piska	65	L4
Pisticci	77	L8
Pistóia	75	F7
Pisz	65	L4
Pitcairn Islands	117	P8
Piteå	61	L4
Piteälven	63	C1
Piteşti	79	M5
Pithara	119	C6
Pithiviers	71	H5
Pitkyaranta	63	F2
Pitlochry	69	J5
Pitlyar	63	N1
Pitt Island	121	(1)B2
Pittsburg	135	C2
Pittsburgh	131	D2
Pitt Strait	121	(1)B2
Piura	141	A5
Pivka	75	K5
Placer	109	G4
Placerville	133	B1
Plaiamonas	81	E5
Plains	133	F2
Plainview	133	F2
Planalto Central	141	H6
Planalto da Borborema	141	K5
Planalto do Mato Grosso	141	G6
Plankinton	129	G2
Plano	135	B3
Plasencia	73	D5
Plast	63	M4
Plateau du Djado	91	H4
Plateau du Limousin	71	F8
Plateau du Tademaït	91	F3
Plateau of Tibet = Xizang Gaoyuan	107	D2
Plateaux Batéké	95	G5
Platinum	133	(1)E4
Plato	137	K7

Legend

- ☒ Continent name
- ▣ Country name
- ▣ State or province name
- ■ Country capital
- ▣ State or province capital
- ● Settlement
- ▲ Mountain, volcano, peak
- ⏶ Mountain range
- ⬗ Physical region or feature
- ⬩ River, canal
- ⬩ Lake, salt lake
- ⬧ Gulf, strait, bay
- ⬛ Sea, ocean
- ⬒ Cape, point
- ⬕ Island or island group, rocky or coral reef
- ✳ Place of interest
- ⬔ Historical or cultural region

Name	Page	Grid
Plato Ustyurt	103	J9
Platte	135	B1
Platteville	131	B2
Plattling	67	H8
Plattsburgh	131	F2
Plattsmouth	135	B1
Plau	67	H3
Plauen	67	H6
Plavnik	75	K6
Plavsk	63	G4
Playas	141	A4
Plây Cu	109	D4
Pleasanton	133	G3
Pleiße	67	H5
Plentywood	129	F1
Plesetsk	63	H2
Pleven	79	M6
Pljevlja	79	G6
Płock	65	J5
Pločno	79	E6
Ploieşti	79	P5
Plomari	81	J6
Plön	67	F2
Płońsk	65	L5
Plovdiv	79	M7
Plumtree	99	D4
Plunge	65	L2
Plymouth, United Kingdom	69	H11
Plymouth, United States	131	C2
Plyussa	61	Q7
Plyussa	63	E3
Plzeň	65	C8
Po	75	E5
Pocahontas	137	F1
Pocatello	129	D2
Pochet	105	F5
Pochinok	63	F4
Pocking	75	J2
Pocomoke City	131	E3
Podgorica	79	G7
Podkamennaya Tunguska	105	F4
Podol'sk	63	G3
Podravska Slatina	79	E4
Poel	67	G2
Pofadder	99	B5
Poggibonsi	75	G7
Pogradec	81	C4
P'ohang	113	E5
Pohnpei	117	F5
Pohokura	121	F4
Pohořelice	75	M2
Point Arena	127	B4
Point Barrow	133	(1)F1
Point Conception	133	B2
Point Culver	119	D6
Point d'Entrecasteaux	119	B6
Pointe-Noire	95	G5
Point Hope	133	(1)D2
Point Hope	133	(1)D2
Point Pedro	107	D7
Point Sur	129	B3
Poitiers	71	F7
Pokaran	107	B3
Pokhara	107	D3
Poko	97	D3
Pokrovsk	105	M4
Pola de Siero	73	E1
Poland	65	G6
Polar Bluff	137	F1
Polatlı	81	Q5
Polatsk	63	E3
Police	67	K3
Polichnitos	81	J5
Poligny	71	L7
Poligus	103	S5
Polillo Islands	109	G4
Polis	81	Q9
Polistena	77	L10
Pollachi	107	C6
Pollença	73	P5
Polohy	63	G5
Polomoloc	109	H5
Polonnaruwa	107	D7
Poltava	63	F5
Poltavka	113	F1
Põltsana	61	N7
Poluostrov Shmidta	105	Q6
Poluostrov Taymyr	103	R3
Poluostrov Yamal	103	M3
Poluy	103	M4
Põlva	61	P7
Polyaigos	81	G8
Polyarnye Zori	61	S3
Polyarnyy	105	X3
Polykastro	81	E4
Polynesia	117	J6
Pombal	73	B5
Pomeranian Bay	65	D3
Pomeroy	129	C1
Pomorie	79	Q7
Pompano Beach	135	E4
Pompei	77	J8
Ponca City	135	B2
Ponce	137	L5
Pondicherry	107	C6
Pond Inlet	125	R2
Ponferrada	73	D2
Poniatowa	65	M6
Ponoy	63	H1
Pons	71	E8
Ponta Delgada	91	(1)B2
Ponta do Podrão	95	G6
Ponta do Sol	95	(1)B1
Ponta Grossa	143	L4
Ponta Khehuene	99	E5
Pont-à-Mousson	71	M5
Ponta Porã	143	K3
Pontarlier	71	M7
Pontassieve	75	G7
Ponta Zavora	99	F4
Pont-d'Alin	71	L7
Ponteareas	73	B2
Ponte da Barca	73	B3
Pontedera	75	F7
Ponte de Sor	73	C5
Pontevedra	73	B2
Pontiac	131	C2
Pontianak	115	(1)D3
Pontivy	71	C5
Pontoise	59	E5
Pontorson	71	D5
Pontrémoli	75	E6
Ponza	77	H8
Poogau	75	J3
Poole	69	L11
Poole Bay	69	L11
Pooncarie	119	H6
Poopó	141	D7
Poopó Challapata	143	H2
Popayán	137	J8
Poperinge	59	E4
Popigay	103	W3
Poplar Bluff	131	B3
Poplarville	135	D3
Popocatépetl	137	E5
Popokabaka	95	H6
Popovača	75	M5
Popovo	79	P6
Poprad	65	K8
Poprad	65	K8
Porangatu	141	H6
Porbandar	85	J5
Porcupine	133	(1)K2
Pordenone	75	H5
Poreč	75	J5
Poret	77	H3
Pori	61	L6
Porirua	121	E5
Porlamar	137	M6
Poronaysk	105	Q7
Poros	81	F7
Porosozero	63	F2
Porozina	75	K5
Porpoise Bay	144	(2)T3
Porriño	73	B2
Porsangen	61	N1
Porsgrunn	61	E7
Portadown	69	F7
Portage	131	C2
Portage la Prairie	129	G1
Port Alberni	129	B1
Port Albert	119	J7
Portalegre	73	C5
Portales	133	F2
Port Arthur, Australia	119	J8
Port Arthur, United States	135	C4
Port Augusta	119	G6
Port-au-Prince	137	K5
Port Austin	131	D2
Port Burwell	125	U4
Port Charlotte	135	E4
Port Douglas	119	J3
Portel, Brazil	141	G4
Portel, Portugal	73	C6
Port Elizabeth	99	D6
Port Ellen	69	F6
Porterville	133	C1
Port Fitzroy	121	E3
Port-Gentil	95	F5
Port Harcourt	95	F4
Port Hardy	125	F6
Port Hawkesbury	125	U7
Port Hedland	119	C4
Port Hope Simpson	125	V6
Port Huron	131	D2
Pórtici	77	J8
Portimão	73	B7
Port Jefferson	131	F2
Portland, Australia	119	H7
Portland, Ind., United States	131	D2
Portland, Me., United States	131	F2
Portland, Oreg., United States	129	B1
Portland Island	121	F4
Port Laoise	69	E8
Port Lavaca	135	B4
Port Lincoln	119	G6
Port Loko	95	B3
Port Louis	99	(1)B2
Port Macquarie	119	K6
Port-Menier	125	U7
Port Moresby	119	J1
Port Nolloth	99	B5
Porto, Corsica	77	C6
Porto, Portugal	73	B3
Porto Alegre	143	L5
Porto Amboim	99	A2
Porto do Son	73	A2
Pôrto Esperidião	141	F7
Portoferraio	77	E6
Pôrto Franco	141	H5
Port of Spain	141	E1
Pôrto Grande	141	G3
Portogruaro	75	H5
Porto Inglês	95	(1)B1
Portomaggiore	75	G6
Pôrto Murtinho	143	K3
Pôrto Nacional	141	H6
Porto-Novo	95	E3
Port Orford	129	B2
Porto San Giórgio	77	H5
Pôrto Santana	141	G3
Porto Santo	91	B2
Pôrto Seguro	141	K7
Porto Tolle	75	H6
Porto Tórres	77	C8
Porto-Vecchio	77	D7
Pôrto Velho	141	E5
Portoviejo	141	A4
Port Pire	119	G6
Port Renfrew	129	B1
Port Said = Bûr Sa'îd	93	F1
Port St. Johns	99	D6
Port Shepstone	99	E6
Portsmouth, United Kingdom	59	A4
Portsmouth, N.H., United States	131	F2
Portsmouth, Oh., United States	131	D3
Portsmouth, Va., United States	131	E3
Port Sudan = Bur Sudan	93	G4
Port Sulphur	135	D4
Port Talbot	69	J10
Portugal	73	B5
Portugalete	73	G1
Port-Vendres	71	J11
Port-Vila	117	G7
Port Warrender	119	E2
Posadas	143	K4
Poschiavo	75	F4
Poshekhon'ye	63	G3
Poso	115	(2)B3
Posŏng	113	D6
Posse	141	H6
Pößneck	67	G6
Post	133	F2
Postmasburg	99	C5
Postojna	75	K5
Posušje	79	E6
Potapovo	103	R4
Poteau	135	C2
Potenza	77	K8
P'ot'i	83	J2
Potiskum	95	G2
Potlatch	129	C1
Potosí	141	D7
Potsdam, Germany	67	J4
Potsdam, United States	131	F2
Pottuvil	107	D7
Poughkeepsie	131	F2
Pourerere	121	F5
Pouto	121	E3
Póvoa de Varzim	73	B3
Povorino	63	H4
Powder	129	E1
Powder River	129	E2
Powell River	125	G7
Poyang Hu	111	F5
Požarevac	79	J5
Poza Rica	137	E4
Požega	79	H6
Poznań	65	F5
Pozoblanco	73	F6
Prabumulih	115	(1)C3
Prachatice	65	D8
Prachuap Khiri Khan	109	B4
Prado	141	K7
Præstø	67	H1
Prague = Praha	65	D7
Praha	65	D7
Praia	95	(1)B2
Prainha	141	G4
Prairie du Chien	131	B2
Prapat	115	(1)B2
Praslin Island	99	(2)B1
Pratas = Dongsha Qundao	109	F2
Prato	75	G7
Pratt	129	G3
Prattville	135	D3
Praya	115	(1)F4
Preetz	67	F2
Preiļi	61	P8
Premnitz	67	H4
Premuda	75	K6
Prentice	131	B1
Prenzlau	65	C4
Preobrazhenka	105	H4
Preparis Island	109	A4
Preparis North Channel	109	A3
Preparis South Channel	109	A4
Přerov	65	G8
Presa de la Boquilla	133	G3
Presa de las Adjuntas	133	G4
Presa Obregón	133	E3

Legend

Symbol	Meaning	Symbol	Meaning	Symbol	Meaning
✗	Continent name	▲	Mountain, volcano, peak	⌐	Sea, ocean
Ⓐ	Country name	▬	Mountain range	⊵	Cape, point
⊡	State or province name	⊘	Physical region or feature	⊠	Island or island group, rocky or coral reef
■	Country capital	⊿	River, canal	✳	Place of interest
⊡	State or province capital	⊿	Lake, salt lake	⊠	Historical or cultural region
●	Settlement	⊳	Gulf, strait, bay		

Name	Page	Ref
Prescott	129	D4
Preševo	79	J7
Presho	129	G2
Presidencia Roque Sáenz Peña	143	J4
Presidente Prudente	143	L3
Presidio	133	F3
Preslav	79	P6
Presnogorkovka	63	N4
Prešov	65	L9
Presque Isle	131	G1
Přeštice	67	J7
Preston, United Kingdom	69	K8
Preston, Minn., United States	131	B2
Preston, Mo., United States	131	B3
Pretoria	99	D5
Preveza	81	C6
Priargunsk	105	K6
Pribilof Islands	133	(1)D4
Priboj	79	G6
Příbram	65	D8
Price	129	D3
Prichard	135	D3
Priego de Córdoba	73	F7
Priekule	61	L8
Prienai	65	N3
Prieska	99	C5
Priest Lake	129	C1
Prievidza	65	H9
Prijedor	79	D5
Prijepolje	79	G6
Prikaspiyskaya Nizmennost'	63	K5
Prilep	81	D3
Primorsk	61	Q6
Primorsko Akhtarsk	63	G5
Prince Albert	125	K6
Prince Albert Peninsula	125	H2
Prince Albert Sound	125	H2
Prince Charles Island	125	R3
Prince Edward Island	89	G10
Prince Edward Island	125	U7
Prince George	125	G6
Prince of Wales Island, Australia	119	H2
Prince of Wales Island, Canada	125	L2
Prince of Wales Island, United States	125	E5
Prince of Wales Strait	125	H2
Prince Patrick Island	123	Q2
Prince Regent Inlet	125	N2
Prince Rupert	125	E6
Princess Charlotte Bay	119	H2
Princeton, Canada	129	B1
Princeton, Ill., United States	131	C2
Princeton, Ky., United States	131	C3
Princeton, Mo., United States	131	B2
Prince William Sound	125	B4
Príncipe	95	F4
Prineville	129	B2
Priozersk	61	R6
Priština	79	J7
Pritzwalk	67	H3
Privas	71	K9
Privolzhskaya Vozvyshennost	63	H4
Prizren	79	H7
Probolinggo	115	(1)E4
Proddatur	107	C6
Progreso	137	G4
Prokhladnyy	83	L2
Prokop'yevsk	103	R7
Prokuplje	79	J6
Proletarsk	63	H5
Proliv Longa	105	X2
Proliv Vil'kitskogo	103	U2
Prophet	125	G5
Propriano	77	C7
Prorer Wiek	67	J2
Proserpine	119	J4
Prosna	65	G6
Prosperidad	109	H5
Prostojov	65	G8
Proti	81	D7
Provadiya	79	Q6
Prøven = Kangersuatsiaq	125	W2
Providence	131	F2
Providence Island	99	(2)B2
Provideniya	105	Z4
Provincetown	131	F2
Provins	71	J5
Provo	129	D2
Provost	125	J6
Prudhoe Bay	133	(1)H1
Prudnik	65	G7
Prüm	59	J4
Pruszków	65	K5
Prut	79	R4
Pružany	65	P5
Prvić	75	K6
Pryluky	63	F4
Prypyats'	57	G2
Przasnysz	65	K4
Przemyśl	65	M8
Przeworsk	65	M7
Psara	81	H6
Psebay	83	J1
Pskov	63	E3
Ptolemaïda	81	D4
Ptuj	75	L4
Pucallpa	141	C5
Pucheng	111	F5
Puch'ŏn	113	D5
Púchov	65	H8
Pucioasa	79	N4
Puck	65	H3
Pudasjärvi	61	P4
Pudozh	63	G2
Puebla	137	E5
Pueblo	129	F3
Puelches	143	H6
Puelén	143	H6
Puente-Genil	73	F7
Puerto Acosta	141	D7
Puerto Aisén	143	G8
Puerto Alegre	141	E6
Puerto Angel	137	E5
Puerto Ayacucho	137	L7
Puerto Barrios	137	G5
Puerto Berrío	141	C2
Puerto Cabezas	137	H6
Puerto Carreño	137	L7
Puerto del Rosario	91	C3
Puerto de Navacerrada	73	G4
Puerto Guarini	141	F8
Puerto Heath	141	D6
Puerto Inírida	141	D3
Puerto Leguizamo	141	C4
Puerto Libertad	133	D3
Puerto Limón	141	B3
Puertollano	73	F6
Puerto Maldonado	141	D6
Puerto Montt	143	G7
Puerto Nuevo	137	K7
Puerto Peñasco	133	D2
Puerto Princesa	109	F5
Puerto Real	73	D8
Puerto Rico	137	L5
Puerto Rico	141	D6
Puerto Rico Trench	139	E1
Puerto Santa Cruz	143	H9
Puerto Suárez	141	F7
Pukapuka	117	N7
Pukatawagen	125	L5
Pukch'ŏng	113	E3
Pukë	79	G7
Pula	75	J6
Pulaski	131	E2
Puławy	65	M6
Pullman	129	C1
Pułtusk	61	L10
Pulu	103	Q10
Pülümür	83	H4
Puncak Jaya	115	(2)E3
Puncak Mandala	115	(2)F3
Pune	107	B5
Punia	97	D4
Puno	141	C7
Punta Albina	99	A3
Punta Alice	77	M9
Punta Angamos	143	G3
Punta Arena	129	B3
Punta Arenas	143	G9
Punta Ballena	143	G4
Punta Dungeness	143	H9
Punta Eugenia	137	A3
Punta Galera	143	G6
Punta Gallinas	137	K6
Punta Gorda	135	E4
Punta La Marmora	77	D8
Punta Lavapié	143	G6
Punta Lengua de Vaca	143	G5
Punta Mala	141	B2
Punta Mariato	137	H7
Punta Medanosa	143	H8
Punta Negra	141	A5
Punta Norte, Argentina	143	J7
Punta Norte, Argentina	143	K6
Punta Pariñas	141	A5
Punta Rasa	143	J7
Puntarenas	137	H6
Punta San Gabriel	133	D3
Punta San Telmo	137	D5
Punta Sarga	91	B4
Puponga	121	D5
Puqi	111	E5
Puri	107	E5
Purmerend	59	G2
Purpe	105	B4
Purukcahu	115	(1)E3
Purus	141	E5
Puruvesi	61	Q6
Pusan	113	E6
Pushkin	63	F3
Püspökladany	65	L10
Putao	109	B1
Putaruru	121	E3
Putian	111	F5
Putna	79	P4
Puttalami	107	C7
Putten	59	G3
Puttgarden	67	G2
Putumayo	141	C4
Puuwai	133	(2)A2
Puy de Dôme	71	H8
Puy de Sancy	71	H8
Puysegur Point	121	A8
Pweto	97	D5
Pwllheli	69	H9
Pyal'ma	63	G2
Pyatigorsk	83	K1
Pyè	109	B3
Pyhäjärvi	61	M6
Pylos	81	D8
Pyŏktong	113	C3
P'yŏnggang	113	D4
P'yŏngyang	113	C4
Pyramid Island	121	(1)B2
Pyramid Lake	129	C2/3
Pyrenees	71	E11
Pyrgos	81	D7
Pyrzyce	65	D4
Pyshchug	63	J3
Pytalovo	61	P8

Q

Name	Page	Ref
Qadīmah	85	C5
Qādub	85	F7
Qagan Nur	111	F2
Qal'aikhum	85	K2
Qalamat Nadqān	87	D5
Qalāt	85	J3
Qal'at Bīshah	85	D5
Qal'eh-ye Now	85	H3
Qamdo	111	B4
Qamīnīs	93	C1
Qaraaoun	83	F7
Qardho	97	H2
Qartaba	86	C2
Qasr Farafra	93	E2
Qaţanā	86	D3
Qatar	87	D4
Qatrāna	86	D5
Qattâra Depression	93	E2
Qāyen	85	G3
Qazangöldag	83	M4
Qazax	83	L3
Qazımämmäd	83	N3
Qazvīn	85	E2
Qena	93	F2
Qeqertarsuatsiaat	125	W4
Qeqertarsuatsiaq	125	V2
Qeqertarsuup Tunua	125	V3
Qeshm	87	F3
Qeshm	87	G3
Qeys	87	E3
Qezel Owzan	83	N5
Qezi'ot	86	B6
Qianshanlaoba	103	Q8
Qiaowan	111	B2
Qidukou	107	G2
Qiemo	103	R10
Qijiang	111	D5
Qijiaojing	103	S9
Qila Saifullah	85	J3
Qilian	111	C3
Qilian Shan	111	B3
Qingdao	111	G3
Qinghai Hu	111	B3
Qinghai Nanshan	111	B3
Qingjiang	111	F4
Qingjiang	111	E3
Qingshuihe	111	E3
Qingyang	111	D3
Qingyuan, China	111	E6
Qingyuan, China	111	G2
Qinhuangdao	111	F3
Qinzhou	109	D2
Qionghai	109	E3
Qiqian	105	L6
Qiqihar	105	L7
Qira	103	Q10
Qiryat Ata	86	C4
Qiryat Motzkin	86	C4
Qiryat Shemona	86	C3
Qishn	85	F6
Qolleh-ye Damāvand	85	F2
Qom	85	F3
Qomisheh	85	F3
Qornet es Saouda	86	D2
Qorveh	83	M6
Qotūr	83	L4
Quang Ngai	109	D3
Quangolodougou	95	C3
Quang Tri	109	D3
Quanzhou	109	F2
Quaqtaq	125	T4
Quarto Sant'Elena	77	D9
Quba	83	N3
Quchan	85	G2
Québec	131	F1
Quedlinburg	67	G5
Queen Charlotte	125	E6
Queen Charlotte Islands	125	E6
Queen Charlotte Sound	125	E6
Queen Charlotte Strait	125	E6
Queen Elizabeth Islands	123	M2
Queen Maud Gulf	125	L3
Queensland	119	G4
Queenstown, Australia	119	J8
Queenstown, New Zealand	121	B7
Queenstown, South Africa	99	D6
Queets	129	B1
Quelimane	99	F3

✕	Continent name
Ⓐ	Country name
ⓐ	State or province name
■	Country capital
▫	State or province capital
●	Settlement
▲	Mountain, volcano, peak
▲	Mountain range
⬟	Physical region or feature
◿	River, canal
⬚	Lake, salt lake
⬎	Gulf, strait, bay
▬	Sea, ocean
⊳	Cape, point
⬚	Island or island group, rocky or coral reef
✳	Place of interest
⬚	Historical or cultural region

Name	Page	Ref.
Resolution Island, *New Zealand*	121	A7
Resovo	81	K3
Rethel	59	G5
Rethymno	81	G9
Réunion	99	(1)B2
Reus	73	M3
Reutlingen	67	E8
Revda	63	L3
Revillagigedo Island	133	(1)L4
Revin	59	G5
Revivim	86	B5
Revúca	65	K9
Rewa	107	D4
Rexburg	129	D2
Reykjanes	61	(1)B3
Reykjavík	61	(1)C2
Reynosa	135	B4
Rezat	67	F7
Rezé	71	D6
Rēzekne	61	P8
Rezina	79	R2
Rezovo	79	R8
Rheda-Wiedenbrück	67	D5
Rhein = Rhine	75	C2
Rheinbach	59	K4
Rheine	59	K2
Rheinfelden	75	C3
Rhin = Rhine	75	C2
Rhine	75	C2
Rhinelander	131	C1
Rho	75	E5
Rhode Island	131	F2
Rhodes = Rodos	81	L8
Rhondda	69	J10
Rhône	71	K9
Rhyl	69	J8
Ribadeo	73	C1
Ribas do Rio Pardo	143	L3
Ribe	61	E9
Ribeauville	71	N5
Ribeirão Prêto	143	M3
Ribeiria = Santa Eugenia	73	A2
Ribera	77	H11
Riberalta	141	D6
Ribnica	77	J3
Rîbnita	79	S2
Ribnitz-Damgarten	67	H2
Říčany	67	K6
Riccione	75	H7
Richardson Mountains	133	(1)K2
Richfield	129	D3
Richland	129	C1
Richlands	131	D3
Richmond, *Australia*	119	H4
Richmond, *New Zealand*	121	D5
Richmond, *Ky., United States*	131	D3
Richmond, *Va., United States*	131	E3
Ridgecrest	133	C1
Ridgway	131	E2
Ried	75	J2
Riesa	67	J5
Rieti	77	G6
Rifle	129	E3
Rīga	61	N8
Riggins	129	C1
Rigolet	125	V6
Rijeka	75	K5
Riley	129	C2
Rimava	65	J9
Rimavská Sobota	65	K9
Rímini	75	H6
Rimouski	131	G1
Rineia	81	H7
Ringe	67	F1
Ringkøbing	61	E8
Ringkøbing Fjord	61	D9
Ringsted	67	G1
Ringvassøya	61	J1
Rinteln	67	E4
Río Branco	141	D5
Río Colorado	143	J6
Río Cuarto	143	J5
Rio de Janeiro	143	N3
Rio de Janeiro	143	N3
Río de la Plata	143	K6
Río Gallegos	143	H9
Rio Grande	133	E2
Rio Grande	143	L5
Río Grande, *Argentina*	143	H9
Río Grande, *Mexico*	133	F4
Rio Grande City	135	B4
Rio Grande do Norte	141	K5
Rio Grande do Sul	143	L4
Ríohacha	137	K6
Río Largartos	137	G4
Riom	71	J8
Río Mulatos	141	D7
Rionero	77	K8
Rionero in Vulture	79	C9
Rio Tigre	141	B4
Rio Verde	141	G7
Rio Verde de Mato Grosso	141	G7
Ripley, *Oh., United States*	131	D3
Ripley, *Tenn., United States*	131	C3
Ripley, *W.Va., United States*	131	D3
Ripoll	73	N2
Ripon	69	L7
Rishiri-tō	105	Q7
Rishon le Ẕiyyon	86	B5
Ritchie's Archipelago	109	A4
Ritzville	129	C1
Rivadavia	143	G4
Riva del Garda	75	F5
Rivarolo	75	C5
Rivas	137	G6
Rivera, *Argentina*	143	J6
Rivera, *Uruguay*	143	K5
Riversdale	99	C6
Riversdale Beach	121	E5
Riverton, *Canada*	125	M6
Riverton, *New Zealand*	121	A8
Rivesaltes	71	H11
Rivière-du-Loup	131	G1
Rivne	63	E4
Rivoli	75	C5
Riwoqê	107	G2
Riyadh = Ar Riyāḍ	87	B4
Rize	83	J3
Rizhao	111	F3
Roanne	71	K7
Roanoke	131	D3
Roanoke Rapids	135	F2
Robe	119	G7
Robertsfors	61	L4
Robertval	131	F1
Roboré	141	F7
Robstown	135	B4
Roccastrada	77	F6
Rochefort, *Belgium*	59	H4
Rochefort, *France*	71	E8
Rochelle	131	C2
Rocher River	125	J4
Rochester, *United Kingdom*	59	C3
Rochester, *Minn., United States*	131	B2
Rochester, *N.H., United States*	131	F2
Rochester, *N.Y., United States*	131	E2
Rockall	57	C2
Rockefeller Plateau	144	(2)EE2
Rockford	131	C2
Rockhampton	119	K4
Rock Hill	131	D4
Rock Island	131	B2
Rocklake	129	G1
Rockport	129	B1
Rock Rapids	131	A2
Rock Springs	129	E2
Rocksprings	133	F3
Rocky Mount	131	E3
Rocky Mountains	125	F5
Rødby Havn	67	G2
Roddickton	125	V6
Rodez	71	H9
Rodi Gargánico	77	K7
Roding	67	H7
Rodney	131	D2
Rodopi Planina	79	M7
Rodos	81	B2
Rodos	81	L8
Roebourne	119	C4
Roermond	59	J3
Roeselare	59	F4
Roes Welcome Sound	125	P4
Rogers City	131	D1
Rogerson	129	D2
Rogliano	77	D6
Rogue	129	B2
Rohrbach	75	K2
Rohtak	107	C3
Roi Et	109	C3
Roja	61	M8
Rokiškis	61	N9
Rokycany	65	C8
Rolla	131	B3
Rolleston	121	D6
Rolvsøya	61	M1
Roma	115	(2)C4
Roma, *Australia*	119	J5
Roma, *Italy*	77	G7
Roman	79	P3
Romania	79	L4
Romans-sur-Isère	71	L5
Rombas	59	J5
Rome = Roma	77	G7
Rome, *Ga., United States*	135	D3
Rome, *N.Y., United States*	131	E2
Romney	131	E3
Romny	63	F4
Rømø	67	D1
Romorantin-Lanthenay	71	G6
Rona	69	G2
Ronan	127	D2
Roncesvalles	73	J2
Ronda	73	E8
Rondônia	141	E6
Rondônia	141	E6
Rondonópolis	141	G7
Rondu	85	L2
Rongcheng	111	G3
Rønne	65	D2
Ronneby	61	H8
Ronne Entrance	144	(2)JJ3
Ronne Ice Shelf	144	(2)MM2
Ronse	59	F4
Roosendaal	59	G3
Roper Bar	119	F2
Roraima	141	E3
Røros	61	F5
Rosário	141	J4
Rosario, *Argentina*	143	J5
Rosario, *Mexico*	127	D6
Rosario, *Mexico*	127	E7
Rosario, *Paraguay*	143	K3
Rosário Oeste	141	F6
Rosarito	127	C6
Rosarno	77	K10
Roscommon	69	D8
Roseau	137	M5
Roseburg	129	B2
Roseires Reservoir	93	F5
Rose Island	117	K7
Rosenburg	133	G3
Rosenheim	75	H3
Roses	73	P2
Rosetown	125	K6
Rosica	79	N6
Rosignano Solvay	75	F7
Roşiori de Vede	79	N5
Roskilde	61	G4
Roslavl'	63	F4
Rossano	77	L9
Ross Ice Shelf	144	(2)Z1
Ross Lake	129	B1
Roßlau	67	H5
Rosso	91	B5
Rossosh'	63	G4
Ross River	125	E4
Ross Sea	144	(2)AA2
Røssvatnet	61	G3
Røst	61	G3
Rostâq	87	E3
Rosthern	125	K6
Rostock	67	H2
Rostov	63	G3
Rostov-na-Donu	63	G5
Rostrenen	71	B5
Roswell	133	F2
Rota	117	E4
Rotarua	121	F4
Rote	115	(2)B5
Rotenburg, *Germany*	67	E3
Rotenburg, *Germany*	67	E5
Roth	67	G7
Rothenburg	67	F7
Roto	119	J6
Rott	75	H2
Rotterdam	71	K2
Rottnen	65	E1
Rottumeroog	59	J1
Rottumerplaat	59	J1
Rottweil	75	D2
Rotuma	117	H7
Roubaix	59	F4
Rouen	59	D5
Rouiba	73	P8
Round Mountain	119	K6
Round Rock	135	B3
Roundup	129	E1
Rousay	69	J2
Rouyn	131	E1
Rovaniemi	61	N3
Rovereto	75	G5
Rovigo	75	G5
Rovinj	75	J5
Rovuma	97	F6
Rowley Island	125	R3
Rowley Shoals	119	C3
Roxas	109	G4
Roxburgh	121	B7
Royal Leamington Spa	59	A2
Royal Tunbridge Wells	59	C3
Royan	71	D8
Roye	59	E5
Royston	59	C2
Rozdil'na	79	T3
Rožňava	65	K9
Rrëshen	81	B3
Rtishchevo	63	H4
Ruacana	99	A3
Ruahine Range	121	E5
Ruapehu	121	E4
Ruapuke Island	121	B8
Ruarkela	107	D4
Ruatahuna	121	F4
Ruatoria	121	G3
Ruawai	121	D3
Rub' al Khālī	85	E6
Rubi	97	C3
Rubtsovsk	103	Q7
Ruby	133	(1)F3
Rudan	87	G3
Ruda Śląska	65	H7
Rudbar	85	H3
Rüdersdorf	67	J4
Rudkøbing	67	F2
Rudnaya Pristan'	113	H2
Rudnyy	63	M4
Rudolstadt	67	G6
Rüdsar	83	P5
Rue	59	D4
Ruffec	71	F7
Rufiji	97	F5

Name	Page	Grid
Rugby, *United Kingdom*	59	A2
Rugby, *United States*	127	G2
Rügen	65	C3
Ruhnu	61	M8
Ruhr	59	L3
Rum	69	F5
Ruma	79	G4
Rumāh	87	B4
Rumaylah	87	B1
Rumbek	97	D2
Rum Cay	137	K4
Rumigny	59	G5
Rumoi	113	L2
Runanaga	121	C6
Rundu	99	B3
Ruoqiang	103	R10
Ruo Shui	111	C2
Rupa	75	K5
Rupat	115	(1)C2
Rupert	125	R6
Rupert	129	D2
Rurutu	117	L8
Ruse	79	N6
Rushon	107	G3
Rushville, *Ill., United States*	131	B2
Rushville, *Ind., United States*	131	C3
Rushville, *Nebr., United States*	129	F2
Russell	129	G3
Russellville, *Ark., United States*	135	C2
Russellville, *Ky., United States*	135	D2
Rüsselsheim	67	D7
Russia	61	L9
Russia	101	M3
Rust'avi	83	L3
Ruston	135	C3
Rutana	97	D4
Rute	73	F7
Ruteng	115	(2)B4
Rutland	131	F2
Rutog	107	C2
Ruvo di Puglia	77	L7
Ruvuma	97	F6
Ruzayevka	63	H4
Ružomberok	65	J8
Rwanda	97	D4
R-Warnemünde	67	H2
Ryazan'	63	G4
Ryazhsk	63	H4
Rybinsk	63	G3
Rybinskoye Vodokhranilishche	63	G3
Rybnik	65	H7
Rychnov	65	F7
Ryde	59	A4
Rye Patch Reservoir	129	C2
Ryki	65	L6
Ryl'sk	63	F4
Ryn-Peski	63	J5
Ryōtsu	113	K4
Rypin	65	J4
Ryukyu Islands = Nansei-shotō	111	H5
Rzeszów	65	M7
Rzhev	63	F3

S

Name	Page	Grid
Sa'ādatābād, *Iran*	87	E1
Sa'ādatābād, *Iran*	87	F2
Saale	67	G6
Saalfeld	67	G6
Saalfelden	75	H3
Saanen	77	B2
Saar	59	J5
Saarbrücken	59	J5
Saarburg	59	J5
Saaremaa	61	L7
Saarlouis	59	J5
Saatli	83	N4
Saatly	85	E2
Saba	137	M5

Name	Page	Grid
Sab' Ābār	86	E3
Šabac	79	G5
Sabadell	73	N3
Sabah	115	(1)F1
Sabang	109	B5
Sabhā	91	H3
Sabiñánigo	73	K2
Sabinas	133	F3
Sabinas Hidalgo	133	F3
Sabine	135	B3
Sabine Lake	135	C3
Sabinov	65	L8
Sabkhet el Bardawîl	86	A5
Sable Island	125	V8
Sablé-sur-Sarthe	71	E6
Sabôr	73	D3
Sabun	103	Q5
Sabzevār	85	G2
Săcele	79	N4
Sachanga	99	B2
Sachs Harbour	125	G2
Säckingen	75	C3
Sacramento	129	B3
Sacramento	129	B3
Şad'ah	85	D6
Sadiqabad	85	K4
Sadiya	107	G3
Sado	73	B6
Sadoga-shima	113	K4
Sadon	83	K2
Sado-shima	111	K3
Sa Dragonera	73	N5
Säffle	61	G7
Safford	133	E2
Safi, *Jordan*	86	C5
Safi, *Morocco*	91	D2
Safonovo, *Russia*	63	F3
Safonovo, *Russia*	63	J1
Safranbolu	81	Q3
Saga, *China*	107	E3
Saga, *Japan*	113	F7
Sagami-nada	113	K6
Sagar	107	C4
Sagastyr	103	Z3
Sage	129	D2
Saginaw	131	D2
Sagiz	63	K5
Sagiz	63	K5
Saguache	129	E3
Sagua la Grande	137	H4
Sagunt	73	K5
Sahāb	86	D5
Sahagún	73	E2
Sahara	89	C3
Saharah el Gharbîya	89	E2
Saharanpur	107	C3
Saharsa	107	E3
Şahbuz	83	L4
Sahel	89	C4
Sahiwal	85	K3
Sahuaripa	133	E3
Šahy	79	F1
Saïda, *Algeria*	91	F2
Saïda, *Lebanon*	86	C3
Sa'idābād	87	F2
Saidpur	107	E3
Saigo	113	G5
Saigon = Hô Chi Minh	109	D4
Saiha	107	F4
Saihan Toroi	111	C2
Saiki	113	F7
Saimaa	61	P6
Saimbeyli	83	G4
Sā'in	87	F1
Saindak	85	H4
St. Albans	59	B3
St-Amand-Montrond	71	H7
St. Andrä	75	K4
St. Andrews	69	K5
St. Anthony	125	V6
St. Arnaud	121	D5

Name	Page	Grid
St. Augustin	59	K4
St. Augustine	135	E4
St. Austell	69	H11
St-Avold	59	J5
St. Barthélémy	137	M5
St-Brieuc	71	C5
St. Catharines	127	L3
St-Chamond	71	K8
St-Claude	71	L7
St. Cloud	131	B1
St. David's	69	G10
St-Denis, *France*	59	E6
St-Denis, *Réunion*	99	(1)B2
St-Dié	75	B2
St-Dizier	71	K5
Ste-Anne-de-Beaupré	131	F1
Ste-Menehould	59	G5
Saintes	71	E8
Stes-Maries-de-la-Mer	71	K10
St-Étienne	71	K8
St-Étienne-du-Rouvray	59	D5
St-Félicien	131	F1
St-Florentin	71	J5
St-Flour	71	J8
St. Francis	129	F3
St. Gallen	75	E3
St-Gaudens	71	F10
St. George, *Australia*	119	J5
St. George, *United States*	129	D3
St. Georgen	75	D2
St. Georges	131	F1
St. George's	137	M6
St. George's Channel	69	F10
St-Germain-en-Laye	59	E6
St-Girons	71	G11
St. Helena	89	C7
St. Helena Bay	99	B6
St. Helens, *United Kingdom*	69	K8
St. Helens, *United States*	129	B1
St. Helier	71	C4
St-Hubert	59	H4
St. Ignace	131	D1
St. Ives	69	G11
St-Jean-d'Angely	71	E8
St-Jean-de-Luz	71	D10
St-Jean-de-Maurienne	75	B5
St-Jean-sur-Richelieu	131	F1
St. John	125	T7
St. John's	125	W7
St. Johnsbury	131	F2
St. Joseph	131	B3
St-Jovité	131	F1
St. Kilda	69	D4
St. Kitts-Nevis	137	M5
St-Laurent	141	G2
St-Laurent-en-Grandvaux	75	A4
St. Lawrence	131	G1
St. Lawrence Island	133	(1)C3
St-Léonard	131	G1
St-Lô	59	A5
St. Louis, *Senegal*	91	B5
St. Louis, *United States*	131	B3
St. Lucia	137	M6
St. Maarten	137	M5
St-Malo	71	D5
St. Marys	131	D2
St. Matthew Island	133	(1)C3
St-Mihiel	59	H6
St. Moritz	75	E4
St-Nazaire	71	C6
St-Nicolas-de-Port	75	B2
St. Niklaas	59	G3
St-Omer	59	E4
St-Palais	71	D10
St-Pamphile	131	G1
St. Paul	59	B6
St. Paul, *Minn., United States*	131	B2
St. Paul, *Nebr., United States*	129	G2
St. Peter	131	B2
St. Peter Ording	67	D2
St. Peter-Port	71	C4

Name	Page	Grid
St. Petersburg = Sankt-Peterburg	63	F3
St. Petersburg	135	E4
St-Pierre-et-Miquelon	125	V7
St. Pierre Island	99	(2)A2
St-Pol-de-Léon	71	A5
St-Pol-sur-Ternoise	59	E4
St. Pölten	75	L2
St-Quentin	59	F5
St-Raphaël	75	B7
St. Siméon	131	G1
St. Stephen	131	G1
St. Thomas	131	D2
St-Tropez	75	B7
St. Truiden	59	H4
St-Valéry-sur-Somme	59	D4
St. Veit	75	K4
St. Veit an der Glan	79	B3
St. Vincent and the Grenadines	137	M6
St-Vincent-les-Forts	75	B6
St-Vith	59	J4
Saipan	117	E4
Sajószentpéter	65	K9
Sākākah	85	D4
Sakaraha	99	G3
Sakarya	81	N4
Sakarya	81	N4
Sakata	113	K4
Sakchu	113	C3
Sakha	105	N3
Sakhalin	105	Q6
Sakhalinskiy Zaliv	105	Q6
Sakhon Nakhon	109	C3
Şäki	83	M3
Sakishima-shotō	111	H6
Saksköbing	67	G2
Sal	63	H5
Sal	95	(1)B1
Sala	61	J7
Šal'a	65	G9
Salacgrīva	61	N8
Sala Consilina	77	K8
Saladillo	143	K6
Salado	143	J4
Salālah	85	F6
Salamanca, *Mexico*	137	D4
Salamanca, *Spain*	73	E4
Salamanca, *United States*	131	E2
Salamina	81	F7
Salamīyah	86	E1
Salar de Uyuni	143	H3
Salawati	115	(2)D3
Salayar	115	(2)B4
Salbris	71	H6
Saldus	61	M8
Sale	119	J7
Salekhard	103	M4
Salem	129	B2
Salem, *India*	107	C6
Salem, *United States*	131	C3
Salerno	77	J8
Salgótarján	65	J9
Salida	129	E3
Salihli	81	L6
Salihorsk	63	E4
Salima	99	E2
Salina	77	J10
Salina, *Kans., United States*	129	G3
Salina, *Ut., United States*	129	D3
Salinas, *Brazil*	141	J7
Salinas, *Ecuador*	141	A4
Salinas, *Mexico*	133	F4
Salinas, *United States*	133	B1
Salinas Grandes	143	J4
Salinópolis	141	H4
Salisbury, *United Kingdom*	59	A3
Salisbury, *Md., United States*	131	E3
Salisbury, *N.C., United States*	131	D3
Salisbury Island	125	R4
Şalkhad	86	D4
Salla	61	Q3

✕		Continent name
Ⓐ		Country name
ⓐ		State or province name
■		Country capital
⊡		State or province capital
⊙		Settlement
▲		Mountain, volcano, peak
⛰		Mountain range
		Physical region or feature
		River, canal
		Lake, salt lake
		Gulf, strait, bay
		Sea, ocean
		Cape, point
		Island or island group, rocky or coral reef
✳		Place of interest
		Historical or cultural region

Continent name
Country name
State or province name
Country capital
State or province capital
Settlement

Mountain, volcano, peak
Mountain range
Physical region or feature
River, canal
Lake, salt lake
Gulf, strait, bay

Sea, ocean
Cape, point
Island or island group, rocky or coral reef
Place of interest
Historical or cultural region

Name	Page	Grid
Sapulpa	135	B2
Saqqez	83	M5
Sarāb	83	M5
Sara Buri	109	C4
Sarajevo	79	F6
Sarakhs	85	H2
Saraktash	63	L4
Saramati	107	G3
Saran	103	N8
Saranac Lake	131	F2
Sarandë	81	C5
Sarangani Islands	115	(2)C1
Saranpul	63	M2
Saransk	63	J4
Sarapul	63	K3
Sarapul'skoye	105	P7
Sarasota	135	E4
Sarata	79	S3
Saratoga	129	E2
Saratoga Springs	131	F2
Saratov	63	J4
Saravan	85	H4
Sarawak	115	(1)E2
Saray	81	K3
Sarayköy	81	L7
Sarayönü	81	Q6
Sarbāz	85	H4
Sarbīsheh	85	G3
Sárbogárd	79	F3
Sar Dasht	83	L5
Sardegna	77	E8
Sardinia = Sardegna	77	E8
Sardis Lake	135	B3
Sar-e Pol	85	J2
Sargodha	85	K3
Sarh	95	H3
Sārī	85	F2
Saria	81	K9
Sarıkamış	83	K3
Sarıkaya	83	F4
Sarikei	115	(1)E2
Sarina	119	J4
Sariñena	73	K3
Sarīr Tibesti	93	C3
Sariwŏn	113	C4
Sark	71	C4
Sarkad	79	J3
Sarkand	103	P8
Sarkikaraağaç	81	P6
Şarkışla	83	G4
Şarköy	81	K4
Sarmi	115	(2)E3
Särna	61	G6
Sarnia	131	D2
Sarny	63	E4
Sarolangun	115	(1)C3
Saronno	75	E5
Saros Körfezi	81	J4
Sárospatak	65	L9
Sarre	71	M5
Sarrebourg	71	N5
Sarreguemines	71	N4
Sarria	73	C2
Sartène	77	C7
Sartyn'ya	63	M2
Saruhanli	81	K6
Sārūr	83	L4
Sárvár	75	M3
Sarvestān	87	E2
Sarviz	79	F2
Sarykamyshkoye Ozero	103	K9
Saryozek	103	P9
Saryshagan	103	N8
Sarysu	103	M8
Sary-Tash	85	K2
Sarzana	75	E6
Sasaram	107	D4
Sasebo	113	E7
Saskatchewan	125	K6
Saskatchewan	125	L6
Saskatoon	125	K6
Saskylakh	103	W3
Sassandra	95	C4
Sassari	77	C8
Sassnitz	67	J2
Sassuolo	75	F6
Satadougou	95	B2
Satara	107	B5
Satna	107	D4
Sátoraljaújhely	65	L9
Satti	107	C2
Sättna	61	J5
Satu Mare	79	K2
Satun	115	(1)B1
Sauce	143	K5
Saudi Arabia	85	D4
Sauk Center	131	B1
Saulgau	75	E2
Saulieu	71	K6
Sault Ste. Marie, *Canada*	131	D1
Sault Ste. Marie, *United States*	131	D1
Saumlakki	115	(2)D4
Saumur	71	E6
Saunders Island	139	J9
Saurimo	97	C5
Sauđárkrókur	61	(1)D2
Sava	75	L5
Savaii	117	J7
Savalou	95	E3
Savannah	123	K6
Savannah, *Ga., United States*	135	E3
Savannah, *Tenn., United States*	135	D2
Savannakhet	109	C3
Savaştepe	81	K5
Savè	95	E3
Save	99	E4
Sāveh	85	F2
Saverne	67	C8
Savigliano	75	C6
Savona	75	D6
Savonlinna	61	Q6
Savu	115	(2)B5
Sawahlunto	115	(1)C3
Sawai Madhopur	107	C3
Sawqirah	85	G6
Sawu Sea	115	(2)B4
Sayanogorsk	103	S7
Sayansk	105	G6
Sayhūt	85	F6
Sāylac	93	H5
Saynshand	111	E2
Sayram Hu	103	Q9
Say'ūn	85	E6
Say-Utes	103	J9
Sazan	81	B4
Sazin	85	K2
Scafell Pike	69	J7
Scalea	77	K9
Scarborough	69	M7
Scarp	69	E3
Schaalsee	67	F3
Schaffhausen	75	D3
Schagen	59	G2
Scharbeutz	67	F2
Schärding	75	J2
Scharhörn	67	D3
Scheeßel	67	E3
Schefferville	125	T6
Scheibbs	75	L3
Schelde	59	F3
Schenectady	131	F2
Scheveningen	59	G2
Schiedam	59	G3
Schiermonnikoog	59	H1
Schio	75	G5
Schiza	81	D8
Schkeuditz	67	H5
Schlei	67	E2
Schleiden	59	J4
Schleswig	67	E2
Schlieben	67	J5
Schlüchtern	67	E6
Schneeberg	67	G6
Schneeberg	67	H6
Schönebeck	67	G4
Schongau	75	F3
Schöningen	67	F4
Schouwen	59	F3
Schramberg	75	D2
Schreiber	131	C1
Schrems	75	L2
Schull	69	C10
Schwabach	67	G7
Schwäbische Alb	75	E2
Schwäbisch-Gmünd	75	E2
Schwäbisch-Hall	67	E7
Schwalmstadt	67	E6
Schwandorf	67	H7
Schwarzenbek	67	F3
Schwarzenberg	67	H6
Schwarzwald	75	D3
Schwaz	75	G3
Schwechat	65	F9
Schwedt	65	D4
Schweich	59	J5
Schweinfurt	67	F6
Schwenningen	75	D2
Schwerin	67	G3
Schweriner See	67	G3
Schwetzingen	67	D7
Schwyz	75	D3
Sciacca	77	H11
Scicli	77	J12
Scobey	129	E1
Scotia Ridge	143	K9
Scotia Sea	144	(2)A4
Scotland	69	H5
Scott City	129	F3
Scott Inlet	125	T2
Scott Island	144	(2)Z3
Scott Reef	119	D2
Scottsbluff	129	F2
Scottsboro	131	C4
Scotty's Junction	133	C1
Scranton	131	E2
Scunthorpe	69	M8
Seal	125	M5
Sea of Azov	63	G5
Sea of Galilee	86	C4
Sea of Japan	113	G3
Sea of Marmara = Marmara Denizi	81	L4
Sea of Okhotsk	105	Q5
Sea of the Hebrides	69	E4
Searchlight	133	D1
Searcy	131	B3
Seaside	129	B1
Seattle	129	B1
Sebeş	79	L4
Sebkha Azzel Matti	91	F3
Sebkha de Timimoun	91	E3
Sebkha de Tindouf	91	D3
Sebkha Mekerrhane	91	F3
Sebkha Oum el Drouss Telli	91	C4
Sebkhet de Chemchâm	91	C4
Sebnitz	67	K6
Sebring	135	E4
Secchia	75	F6
Sechura	141	A5
Secretary Island	121	A7
Secunderabad	107	C5
Sécure	141	D7
Sedalia	131	B3
Sedan	59	G5
Sedano	73	G2
Seddonville	121	C5
Sede Boqer	86	B6
Sedeh	85	G3
Sederot	86	B5
Sédico	75	H4
Sedom	86	C5
Seeheim	99	B5
Seelow	67	K4
Seesen	67	F5
Seevetal	67	E3
Séez	75	B5
Seferihisar	81	J6
Segamat	115	(1)C2
Segezha	63	F2
Seghnän	85	K2
Ségou	95	C2
Segovia	73	F4
Segré	71	E6
Séguédine	91	H4
Seguin	135	B4
Segura	73	H6
Sehithwa	99	C4
Sehnde	67	E4
Seiland	61	M1
Seiling	135	B2
Seinäjoki	61	M5
Seine	71	F4
Sekondi	95	D3
Selassi	115	(2)D3
Selat Bangka	115	(1)D3
Selat Berhala	115	(1)C3
Selat Dampir	115	(2)D3
Selat Karimata	115	(1)D3
Selat Makassar	115	(1)F3
Selat Mentawai	115	(1)B3
Selat Sunda	115	(1)D4
Selawik	133	(1)F2
Selb	67	H6
Selby	129	G1
Selçuk	81	K7
Selebi-Phikwe	99	D4
Sélestat	75	C2
Selfoss	61	(1)C3
Seligman	133	D1
Seljord	61	E7
Selkirk	127	G1
Selkirk Mountains	127	C1
Sells	133	D2
Selm	59	K3
Selmer	131	C3
Selpele	115	(2)D3
Selvas	141	C5
Selwyn Lake	125	L5
Selwyn Mountains	133	(1)L3
Semanit	81	B4
Semarang	115	(1)E4
Sematan	115	(1)D2
Sembé	95	G4
Seminoe Reservoir	129	E2
Seminole, *Okla., United States*	129	G3
Seminole, *Tex., United States*	133	F2
Semiozernoye	103	L7
Semipalatinsk	103	Q7
Semiyarka	103	P7
Semois	59	H5
Semporna	115	(1)F2
Sena Madureira	141	D5
Senanga	99	C3
Senatobia	135	D3
Sendai	113	L4
Senec	75	N2
Seneca	135	E3
Senegal	95	A2
Sénégal	95	B1
Senftenberg	67	J5
Senhor do Bonfim	141	J6
Senica	65	G9
Senigallia	75	J7
Senj	75	K6
Senja	61	J2
Senlis	59	E5
Sennar	85	B7
Senneterre	131	E1
Sens	71	J5
Senta	79	H4
Seoni	107	C4
Seoul = Sŏul	113	D5
Separation Point	121	D5
Sept-Îles	125	T6

☒ Continent name	▲ Mountain, volcano, peak	▭ Sea, ocean
Ⓐ Country name	▬ Mountain range	⊳ Cape, point
ⓐ State or province name	⬖ Physical region or feature	⬚ Island or island group, rocky or coral reef
■ Country capital	↗ River, canal	✳ Place of interest
▣ State or province capital	◣ Lake, salt lake	⬔ Historical or cultural region
● Settlement	↘ Gulf, strait, bay	

211

Name	Type	Page	Grid
Seraing	●	59	H4
Serakhs	●	85	H2
Seram	🗺	115	(2)D3
Seram Sea	◪	115	(2)C3
Serang	●	115	(1)D4
Serbia = Srbija	[a]	79	H6
Serdobsk	●	63	H4
Serebryansk	●	103	Q8
Sered'	●	79	E1
Şereflikoçhisar	●	81	R6
Seregno	●	75	E5
Serein	◿	71	J6
Seremban	●	115	(1)C2
Serenje	●	99	E2
Sergelen	●	111	E1
Sergeyevka	●	63	N4
Sergipe	[a]	141	K6
Sergiyev Posad	●	63	G3
Seria	●	115	(1)E2
Serifos	🗺	81	G7
Serik	●	81	P8
Seringapatam Reef	🗺	119	D2
Sermata	🗺	115	(2)C4
Seronga	●	99	C3
Serov	●	63	M3
Serowe	●	99	D4
Serpa	●	73	C7
Serpukhov	●	63	G4
Serra Acari	▥	141	F3
Serra Curupira	▥	141	E3
Serra da Chela	▥	99	A3
Serra da Espinhaço	▥	141	J7
Serra da Ibiapaba	▥	141	J4
Serra da Mantiqueira	▥	143	M3
Serra de Maracaju	▥	143	K3
Serra do Cachimbo	▥	141	F5
Serra do Caiapó	▥	141	G7
Serra do Roncador	▥	141	G6
Serra dos Carajás	▥	141	G5
Serra dos Dois Irmâos	▥	141	J5
Serra dos Parecis	▥	141	E6
Serra do Tiracambu	▥	141	H4
Serra Estrondo	▥	141	H5
Serra Formosa	▥	141	F6
Serra Geral de Goiás	▥	141	H6
Serra Geral do Paraná	●	141	H7
Serra Lombarda	▥	141	G3
Serra Pacaraima	▥	141	E3
Serra Parima	▥	141	E3
Serra Tumucumaque	▥	141	F3
Serre da Estrela	●	73	C4
Serres, *France*	●	71	L9
Serres, *Greece*	●	81	F3
Serrinha	●	141	K6
Sertã	●	73	B5
Serui	●	115	(2)E3
Servia	●	81	D4
Sêrxü	●	111	B4
Sese Islands	🗺	97	E4
Sesfontein	●	99	A3
Sesheke	●	99	C3
Sessa Aurunca	●	77	H7
Sestri Levante	●	75	E6
Sestroretsk	●	61	Q6
Sestrunj	🗺	75	K6
Sesvete	●	75	M5
Setana	●	113	K2
Sète	●	71	J10
Sete Lagoas	●	141	J7
Setesdal	▨	61	D7
Sétif	●	91	G1
Settat	●	91	D2
Setúbal	●	73	B6
Sŏul	■	117	C2
Seurre	●	71	L7
Sevana Lich	◿	83	L3
Sevastopol'	●	83	E1
Seven Lakes	●	133	E1
Sevenoaks	●	59	C3
Severn, *Canada*	◿	125	P5
Severn, *United Kingdom*	◿	69	K10

Name	Type	Page	Grid
Severnaya Dvina	◿	63	H2
Severnaya Osetiya	[a]	83	L2
Severnaya Zemlya	🗺	103	U1
Severn Estuary	◿	69	J10
Severnoye	●	63	K4
Severnyy	●	103	L4
Severobaykal'sk	●	105	H5
Severodvinsk	●	63	G2
Severomorsk	●	61	S2
Severoural'sk	●	63	M2
Severo-Yeniseyskiy	●	103	S5
Sevier Lake	◿	129	D3
Sevilla	●	73	E7
Sevlievo	●	79	N7
Seward Peninsula	▨	133	(1)E2
Seyakha	●	103	N3
Seychelles	[A]	99	(2)B2
Seychelles Islands	🗺	89	J6
Seydişehir	●	81	P7
Seydisfjöður	●	61	(1)G2
Seyhan	◿	83	F5
Seymchan	●	105	S4
Seymour, *Australia*	●	119	J7
Seymour, *Ind., United States*	●	135	D2
Seymour, *Tex., United States*	●	135	B3
Sézanne	●	71	J5
Sezze	●	77	H7
Sfakia	●	81	G9
Sfântu Gheorghe	●	79	N4
Sfax	●	91	H2
's-Gravenhage	●	59	G2
Sha'am	●	87	G3
Shabunda	●	97	D4
Shabwah	●	85	E6
Shache	●	103	P10
Shādegān	●	87	C1
Shadehill Reservoir	◿	129	F1
Shagamu	●	95	E3
Shagonar	●	103	S7
Shag Rocks	🗺	143	N9
Shahbā'	●	86	D4
Shahdāb	●	87	G1
Shahdol	●	107	D4
Shah Fuladi	▲	85	J3
Shahjahanpur	●	107	C3
Shahrak	●	85	H3
Shahr-e Bābāk	●	87	F1
Shahrtuz	●	85	J2
Shakhrisabz	●	85	J2
Shakhtërsk	●	105	Q7
Shakhty	●	63	H5
Shakhun'ya	●	63	J3
Shaki	●	95	E3
Shakotan-misaki	◹	113	L2
Shama	◿	97	E5
Shamattawa	●	125	N5
Shamrock	●	133	F1
Shand	●	85	H3
Shandong Bandao	▨	111	G3
Shangani	◿	99	D3
Shangdu	●	111	E2
Shanghai	●	111	G4
Shangqui	●	111	F4
Shangrao	●	111	F5
Shangzhi	●	111	H1
Shangzhou	●	111	D4
Shantarskiye Ostrova	🗺	105	P5
Shantou	●	111	F6
Shanwei	●	109	F2
Shanyin	●	111	E3
Shaoguan	●	111	E6
Shaoxing	●	111	G5
Shaoyang	●	111	E5
Shapkina	◿	63	K1
Shaqrā'	●	87	A4
Sharga	●	103	T8
Sharjah = Ash Shāriqah	●	87	F4
Shark Bay	◿	117	B8
Shark Reef	🗺	119	J2
Sharm el Sheikh	●	93	F2
Sharūrah	●	85	E6

Name	Type	Page	Grid
Shashe	◿	99	D4
Shashi	●	111	E4
Shasta Lake	◿	129	B2
Shatsk	●	63	H4
Shats'k	●	65	N6
Shaubak	●	86	C6
Shawano	●	131	C2
Shcherbakove	●	105	U3
Shchigry	●	63	G4
* Shchuch'ye	●	103	L6
Shchuchyn	●	61	N10
Sheberghān	●	85	J2
Sheboygan	●	131	C2
Sheffield, *New Zealand*	●	121	D6
Sheffield, *United Kingdom*	●	69	L8
Sheffield, *Al., United States*	●	131	C4
Sheffield, *Tex., United States*	●	133	F2
Shegmas	●	63	J2
Shelburne	●	125	T8
Shelby	●	129	D1
Shelbyville	●	131	C3
Shelikof Strait	◿	133	(1)F4
Shenandoah	●	131	A2
Shendam	●	95	F3
Shendi	●	93	F4
Shenkursk	●	63	H2
Shenyang	●	113	B3
Shenzhen	●	111	E6
Shepetivka	●	63	E4
Shepparton	●	119	J7
Sherbro Island	🗺	95	B3
Sherbrooke	●	131	F1
Sheridan	●	129	E2
Sherkaly	●	63	N2
Sherlovaya Gora	●	105	K6
Sherman	●	135	B3
's-Hertogenbosch	●	59	H3
Shetland Islands	🗺	69	M1
Shetpe	●	103	J9
Sheyenne	●	129	G1
Sheykh Sho'eyb	🗺	87	E3
Shiant Islands	🗺	69	F4
Shibata	●	113	K5
Shibetsu, *Japan*	●	113	M1
Shibetsu, *Japan*	●	113	N2
Shibotsu-jima	🗺	113	P2
Shiderty	◿	103	N7
Shihezi	●	103	R9
Shijiazhuang	●	111	E3
Shikarpur	●	85	J4
Shikoku	🗺	113	G7
Shikoku-sanchi	▥	113	G7
Shikotan-tō	🗺	113	P2
Shikotsu-ko	◿	113	L2
Shiliguri	●	107	E3
Shilka	●	105	K6
Shilka	◿	105	K6
Shillong	●	107	F3
Shilovo	●	63	H4
Shimabara	●	113	F7
Shimla	●	107	C2
Shimoda	●	113	K6
Shimoga	●	107	C6
Shimo-Koshiki-jima	🗺	113	E8
Shimoni	●	97	F4
Shimonoseki	●	113	F7
Shinās	●	87	G4
Shīndan	●	85	H3
Shingū	●	113	H7
Shinjō	●	113	L4
Shinyanga	●	97	E4
Shiono-misaki	◹	113	H7
Shiprock	●	129	E3
Shiquan	●	111	D4
Shirakawa	●	113	L5
Shīrāz	●	87	E2
Shire	◿	99	E3
Shiretoko-misaki	◹	113	N1
Shiriya-zaki	◹	113	L3
Shır Küh	▲	85	F3
Shivpuri	●	107	C3

Name	Type	Page	Grid
Shiyan	●	111	E4
Shizuishan	●	111	D3
Shizuoka	●	113	K6
Shkodër	●	79	G7
Shomishko	●	103	K8
Shorap	●	85	J4
Shoreham	●	59	B4
Shoshone, *Calif., United States*	●	129	C3
Shoshone, *Id., United States*	●	129	D2
Shoshoni	●	129	E2
Shostka	●	63	F4
Show Low	●	133	E2
Shoyna	●	63	H1
Shreveport	●	135	C3
Shrewsbury	●	69	K9
Shuangliao	●	113	B2
Shuangyashan	●	105	N7
Shubarkuduk	●	103	K8
Shulan	●	113	D1
Shumagin Islands	🗺	133	(1)E5
Shumen	●	79	P6
Shumikha	●	63	M3
Shuqrah	●	85	E7
Shurchi	●	85	J2
Shūr Gaz	●	87	H2
Shurinda	●	105	J5
Shuryshkary	●	63	N1
Shuya	●	63	H3
Shuyang	●	111	F4
Shwebo	●	109	B2
Shymkent	●	103	M9
Sialkot	●	85	K3
Siatista	●	81	D4
Šiauliai	●	65	N2
Sibay	●	63	L4
Šibenik	●	79	C6
Siberia = Sibir	▨	101	N3
Siberut	🗺	115	(1)B3
Sibi	●	85	J4
Sibigo	●	115	(1)B2
Sibir	▨	101	N3
Sibiu	●	79	M4
Sibolga	●	115	(1)B2
Sibu	●	115	(1)E2
Sibuco	●	109	G5
Sibut	●	97	B2
Sicilia	🗺	77	G11
Sicilian Channel	◿	77	F11
Sicily = Sicilia	🗺	77	G11
Šid	●	79	G4
Siddipet	●	107	C5
Siderno	●	77	L10
Sidi Barrani	●	93	E1
Sidi Bel Abbès	●	91	E1
Sidi Kacem	●	91	D2
Sidirokastro	●	81	F3
Sidney	●	129	F2
Sidoan	●	115	(2)B2
Sidorovsk	●	103	Q4
Sieburg	●	59	K4
Siedlce	●	65	M5
Sieg	◿	59	K4
Siegen	●	59	L4
Siemiatycze	●	65	M5
Siĕmréab	●	109	C4
Siena	●	75	G7
Sierpc	●	65	J5
Sierra Blanca	●	133	E2
Sierra Colorada	●	143	H7
Sierra de Calalasteo	▥	143	H4
Sierra de Córdoba	▥	143	H5
Sierra de Gata	●	73	D4
Sierra de Gúdar	▨	73	K4
Sierra del Nevado	▥	143	H6
Sierra de Perija	▥	137	K7
Sierra Grande	●	143	H7
Sierra Leone	[A]	95	B3
Sierra Madre	▥	137	F5
Sierra Madre del Sur	▥	137	E5
Sierra Madre Occidental	▥	127	E6
Sierra Madre Oriental	▥	133	F3

Symbol	Meaning	Symbol	Meaning	Symbol	Meaning
☒	Continent name	▲	Mountain, volcano, peak	▥	Sea, ocean
Ⓐ	Country name	▨	Mountain range	◹	Cape, point
[a]	State or province name	▨	Physical region or feature	🗺	Island or island group, rocky or coral reef
■	Country capital	◿	River, canal	✳	Place of interest
□	State or province capital	◿	Lake, salt lake	⬚	Historical or cultural region
●	Settlement	◿	Gulf, strait, bay		

Legend:

- ☒ Continent name
- Ⓐ Country name
- ⓐ State or province name
- ■ Country capital
- □ State or province capital
- • Settlement
- ▲ Mountain, volcano, peak
- ▰ Mountain range
- ⬚ Physical region or feature
- ↗ River, canal
- ▱ Lake, salt lake
- ⬗ Gulf, strait, bay
- ▭ Sea, ocean
- ⬖ Cape, point
- ▦ Island or island group, rocky or coral reef
- ✳ Place of interest
- ▨ Historical or cultural region

Legend

- ☒ Continent name
- Ⓐ Country name
- ▣ State or province name
- ◼ Country capital
- ▢ State or province capital
- ● Settlement
- ▲ Mountain, volcano, peak
- ▰ Mountain range
- ⬮ Physical region or feature
- ◪ River, canal
- ◩ Lake, salt lake
- ◨ Gulf, strait, bay
- ⬓ Sea, ocean
- ⊵ Cape, point
- ⊡ Island or island group, rocky or coral reef
- ✳ Place of interest
- ⬚ Historical or cultural region

214

Name		Page	Grid
Strzelin	●	65	G7
Sturgeon Bay	●	131	C2
Sturgeon Falls	●	131	E1
Sturgis, *Ky., United States*	●	131	C3
Sturgis, *S.D., United States*	●	129	F2
Sturkö	⊠	65	E1
Štúrova	●	65	H10
Sturt Stony Desert	⊘	119	G5
Stuttgart, *Germany*	●	75	E2
Stuttgart, *United States*	●	135	C3
Stykkishólmur	●	61	(1)B2
Suai	●	115	(2)C4
Suakin	●	93	G4
Subcule	▲	93	H5
Subi Besar	⊠	115	(1)D2
Sublette	●	133	F1
Subotica	●	79	G3
Suceava	●	79	P2
Suck	◪	69	D8
Sucre	■	141	D7
Sudak	●	83	F1
Sudan	▣	93	E5
Sudan	⊘	95	D2
Suday	●	63	H3
Sudbury, *Canada*	●	131	D1
Sudbury, *United Kingdom*	●	59	C2
Sudd	⊘	97	E2
Sudová Vyshnya	●	65	N8
Suez = El Suweis	●	93	F2
Suez Canal	◪	93	F1
Suffolk	●	135	F2
Sugun	●	85	L2
Suhār	●	87	G4
Suhl	●	67	F6
Suide	●	111	E3
Suifenhe	●	113	F1
Suihua	●	105	M7
Suippes	●	59	G5
Suir	◪	69	E9
Suixi	●	111	E6
Suizhong	●	111	G2
Suizhou	●	111	E4
Sukabumi	●	115	(1)D4
Sukadana	●	115	(1)D3
Sukhinichi	●	63	G4
Sukhona	◪	63	H3
Sukkertoppen = Maniitsoq	●	125	W3
Sukkur	●	85	J4
Sula	●	63	K1
Sula	◪	63	K1
Sula Sgeir	⊠	69	F2
Sulawesi	⊠	115	(2)A3
Sulejówek	●	65	L5
Sule Skerry	⊠	69	H2
Sulgachi	●	105	N4
Sulina	●	79	S4
Sulingen	●	59	L2
Sullana	●	141	A4
Sullivan	●	135	C2
Sulmona	●	77	H6
Sulphur Springs	●	135	B3
Sultanhanı	●	81	R6
Sultanpur	●	107	D3
Sulu Archipelago	⊠	109	G5
Sulu Sea	⊟	109	F5
Sulzbach	●	59	K5
Sulzbach-Rosenberg	●	67	G7
Sulzberger Bay	⊟	144	(2)CC2
Sumatera	⊘	115	(1)C2
Sumatra = Sumatera	⊘	115	(1)C2
Sumba	⊠	115	(2)A5
Sumbawa	⊠	115	(2)A4
Sumbawabesar	●	115	(2)A4
Sumbawanga	●	97	E5
Sumbe	●	99	A2
Šumen	●	83	B2
Sumenep	●	115	(1)E4
Sumisu-jima	⊠	113	L8
Sumkino	●	63	N3
Summer Lake	◪	129	B2
Summerville	●	135	E3
Summit	●	125	B4
Šumperk	●	65	G8
Sumqayıt	●	83	N3
Sumter	●	135	E3
Sumy	●	63	F4
Sunbury	●	131	E2
Sunch'ŏn	●	113	D6
Sun City	●	99	D5
Sundance	●	129	F2
Sundarbans	⊘	107	E4
Sunday Strait	⊟	119	D3
Sunderland	●	69	L7
Sundridge	●	131	E1
Sundsvall	●	61	J5
Sundsvallsbukten	⊟	61	J5
Sungaipenuh	●	115	(1)C3
Sungei Petani	●	109	C5
Sunnyvale	●	129	B3
Sun Prairie	●	131	C2
Suntar	●	105	K4
Suntsar	●	85	H4
Sunwu	●	105	M7
Sunyani	●	95	D3
Suomussalmi	●	63	E2
Suō-nada	⊟	113	F7
Suonenjoki	●	61	P5
Suordakh	●	105	P3
Suoyarvi	●	63	F2
Superior	●	127	H2
Supetar	●	79	D6
Süphan Dağı	▲	83	K4
Sūqash Shuyūkh	●	87	B1
Suqian	●	111	F4
Suquţrā	⊠	85	F7
Sūr	●	85	G5
Sura	◪	63	J4
Surab	●	85	J4
Surabaya	●	115	(1)E4
Sūrak	●	87	H4
Surakarta	●	115	(1)E4
Šurany	●	79	F1
Surat	●	107	B4
Surat Thani	●	109	B5
Surdulica	●	79	K7
Sûre	◪	59	H5
Surfers Paradise	●	119	K5
Surgut	●	103	N5
Surgutikha	●	103	R5
Surigao	●	109	H5
Surin	●	109	C4
Surinam	▣	141	F3
Surkhet	●	107	D3
Sürmaq	●	87	E1
Surovikino	●	63	H5
Surskoye	●	63	J4
Surt	●	91	J2
Surtsey	⊠	61	(1)C3
Susa	●	75	C5
Şuşa	●	83	M4
Sušac	⊠	79	D7
Susak	●	75	K6
Susanville	●	129	B2
Suşehri	●	83	H3
Sušice	●	67	J7
Susitma	◪	133	(1)G3
Susuman	●	105	R4
Susurluk	●	81	L5
Sutherland	●	99	C6
Sutlej	◪	107	B3
Suusamyr	●	103	N9
Suva	●	117	H7
Suvorov Island	⊠	117	K7
Suwałki	●	65	M3
Suwannaphum	●	109	C3
Suweilih	●	86	C4
Suweima	●	86	C5
Suwŏn	●	113	D5
Suzak	●	63	N6
Suzhou, *China*	●	111	F4
Suzhou, *China*	●	111	G4
Suzuka	●	113	J6
Suzu-misaki	⊠	113	J5
Svalbard	⊠	144	(1)Q2
Svalyaya	●	79	L1
Svartenhuk Halvø	⊠	125	V2
Svatove	●	63	G5
Sveg	●	61	H5
Svendborg	●	61	F9
Šventoji	◪	61	N9
Sverdrup Islands	⊠	144	(1)DD2
Svetac	⊠	79	C6
Sveti Nikole	●	81	D3
Svetlaya	●	105	P7
Svetlogorsk	●	65	K3
Svetlograd	●	83	K1
Svetlyy, *Russia*	●	65	K3
Svetlyy, *Russia*	●	103	L7
Svidník	●	65	L8
Svilengrad	●	81	J3
Svishtov	●	79	N6
Svitava	◪	65	F8
Svitovy	●	65	F8
Svobodnyy	●	105	M6
Svratka	◪	65	F8
Svyetlahorsk	●	63	E4
Swain Reefs	⊠	119	K4
Swains Island	⊠	117	J7
Swakopmund	●	99	A4
Swale	◪	69	K7
Swan	⊠	139	C2
Swan Hill	●	119	H7
Swan Islands	⊠	137	H5
Swan River	●	125	L6
Swansea, *Australia*	●	119	J8
Swansea, *United Kingdom*	●	69	J10
Swaziland	▣	99	E5
Sweden	▣	61	H6
Sweetwater	●	133	F2
Swider	◪	65	L5
Swidnica	●	65	F7
Świdnik	●	65	M6
Świdwin	●	65	E4
Świebodzin	●	65	E5
Swift Current	●	127	E1
Swindon	●	59	A3
Świnoujście	●	61	H10
Switzerland	▣	75	C4
Syalakh	●	105	L3
Syamzha	●	63	H2
Sydney, *Australia*	⊡	119	K6
Sydney, *Canada*	●	125	U7
Syke	●	59	L2
Syktyvkar	⊡	63	K2
Sylacauga	●	135	D3
Sylhet	●	107	F4
Sylt	⊠	61	E9
Sylvania	●	131	D2
Sym	●	103	R5
Sym	◪	103	R5
Symi	⊠	81	K8
Synya	●	63	L1
Syracuse, *Kans., United States*	●	133	F1
Syracuse, *N.Y., United States*	●	131	E2
Syrdar'ya	●	85	J1
Syrdar'ya	◪	103	L8
Syria	▣	85	C3
Syrian Desert = Bādiyat ash Shām	⊘	86	D4
Syrna	⊠	81	J8
Syros	⊠	81	G7
Sytomino	●	63	P2
Syzran'	●	63	J4
Szamos	◪	79	K1
Szamotuły	●	65	F5
Szarvas	●	65	K11
Szczecin	●	65	D4
Szczecinek	●	65	F4
Szczytno	●	65	K4
Szeged	●	79	H3
Szeghalom	●	79	J2
Székesfehérvár	●	79	F2
Szekszárd	●	79	F3
Szentendre	●	79	G2
Szentes	●	79	H3
Szerencs	●	65	L9
Szigetvár	●	79	E3
Szolnok	●	79	H2
Szombathely	●	79	D2
Szprotawa	●	65	E6

T

Name		Page	Grid
Tab	●	79	F3
Tabarka	●	77	C12
Tabas	●	85	G3
Taber	●	129	D1
Table Cape	⊠	121	G4
Tabong	●	107	G3
Tábor	●	65	D8
Tabor	●	105	R2
Tabora	●	97	E5
Tabou	●	95	C4
Tabrīz	●	83	M4
Tabuaeran	⊠	117	K5
Tabūk	●	85	C4
Tacheng	●	103	Q8
Tachov	●	67	H7
Tacloban	●	109	H4
Tacna	●	141	C7
Tacoma	●	127	B2
Tacuarembó	●	143	K5
Tacurong	●	115	(2)B1
Tadjoura	●	93	H5
Tadmur	●	83	H6
Tadoussac	●	131	G1
Taech'ŏn	●	113	D5
Taegu	●	113	E6
Taejŏn	●	111	H3
Tafahi	⊠	117	J7
Tafalla	●	73	J2
Tafila	●	86	C6
Tafi Viejo	●	143	H4
Taganrog	●	63	G5
Taganrogskiy Zaliv	⊟	63	G5
Tagul	◪	105	F6
Tagum	●	109	H5
Tagus	◪	73	B5
Taharoa	●	121	E4
Tahiti	⊠	117	M7
Tahoe Lake	◪	125	K2
Tahoka	●	133	F2
Tahoua	●	95	F2
Tahrūd	●	87	G2
Tai'an	●	111	F3
T'ai-chung	●	111	G6
Taihape	●	121	E4
Taihe	●	111	E5
Taikeng	●	111	E4
Tailem Bend	●	119	G7
Tain	●	69	H4
T'ai-nan	●	111	G6
T'ai-Pei	■	111	G6
Taiping	●	115	(1)C1
Taipingchuan	●	113	B1
T'ai-tung	●	109	G2
Taivalkoski	●	61	Q4
Taiwan	▣	109	G2
Taiwan Strait	⊟	109	F2
Taiyuan	●	111	E3
Taizhou	●	111	F4
Ta'izz	●	85	D7
Tajikistan	▣	85	J2
Tajima	●	113	K5
Tajo	◪	57	D3
Tak	●	109	B3
Takaka	●	121	D5
Takamatsu	●	113	H6
Takaoka	●	113	J5
Takapuna	●	121	E3
Takasaki	●	113	K5
Takayama	●	113	J5

Legend:

▣	Continent name
▣	Country name
a	State or province name
■	Country capital
⊡	State or province capital
●	Settlement
▲	Mountain, volcano, peak
▬	Mountain range
⊘	Physical region or feature
◪	River, canal
◪	Lake, salt lake
⊟	Gulf, strait, bay
⊟	Sea, ocean
⊠	Cape, point
⊠	Island or island group, rocky or coral reef
✳	Place of interest
⊠	Historical or cultural region

Name	Page	Grid
Takefui	113	J6
Takengon	115	(1)B2
Takestän	85	E2
Takht	105	P6
Takhta-Bazar	85	H2
Takhtabrod	103	M7
Takhtakupyr	103	L9
Takijuq Lake	125	J3
Takikawa	113	L2
Takoradi	95	D4
Taksimo	105	J5
Takua Pa	109	B5
Takum	95	G3
Talak	91	F5
Talara	141	A4
Talas	103	N9
Tal'at Müsá	83	G6
Talavera de la Reina	73	F5
Talaya	105	S4
Talbotton	135	E3
Talca	143	G6
Talcahuano	143	G6
Taldykorgan	103	P9
Tälesh	85	E2
Taliabu	115	(2)B3
Talibon	109	G4
Talitsa	63	M3
Tall 'Afar	83	K5
Tallahassee	135	E3
Tallaimannar	107	C7
Tall al Laḥm	87	B1
Tallinn	61	N7
Tall Kalakh	86	D2
Tallulah	127	H5
Tall 'Uwaynāt	83	K5
Tălmaciu	79	M4
Tal'menka	103	Q7
Talon	105	R5
Tāloqān	103	N10
Taloyoak	125	N3
Talsi	61	M8
Taltal	143	G4
Tama	131	B2
Tamale	95	D3
Tamanrasset	91	G4
Tamanthi	107	G3
Tamási	79	F3
Tamazunchale	127	G7
Tambacounda	95	B2
Tambey	103	N3
Tambo	119	J4
Tambov	63	H4
Tambu	115	(2)A3
Tambura	97	D2
Tampa	135	E4
Tampere	61	M6
Tampico	137	E4
Tamsagbulag	111	F1
Tamsweg	75	J3
Tamworth, Australia	119	K6
Tamworth, United Kingdom	69	A2
Tana, Kenya	97	G4
Tana, Norway	61	P2
Tanabe	113	H7
Tanacross	133	(1)J3
Tanafjorden	61	Q1
Tanaga Island	133	(3)C1
T'ana Häyk'	93	G5
Tanahgrogot	115	(1)F3
Tanahjampea	115	(2)A4
Tanahmerah	115	(2)F4
Tanami	119	E4
Tanami Desert	119	F3
Tánaro	75	C6
Tandag	109	H5
Tăndărei	79	Q5
Tandil	143	K6
Tanega-shima	113	F8
Tanew	65	M7
Tanezrouft	91	E4
Tanga, Russia	105	J6
Tanga, Tanzania	97	F5
Tanger	91	D1
Tangermünde	67	G4
Tanggu	111	F3
Tangmai	107	G2
Tangra Yumco	107	E2
Tangshan	111	F3
Tanimbar	117	D6
Tanjona Ankaboa	99	G4
Tanjona Bobaomby	99	H2
Tanjona Masoala	99	H3
Tanjona Vilanandro	99	G3
Tanjona Vohimena	99	H5
Tanjung	115	(1)F3
Tanjungbalai	115	(1)B2
Tanjung Cangkuang	115	(1)C4
Tanjung Datu	115	(1)D2
Tanjung d'Urville	115	(2)E3
Tanjungkarang Telukbetung	115	(1)D4
Tanjung Libobo	115	(2)C3
Tanjung Mengkalihat	115	(1)F2
Tanjungpandan	115	(1)D3
Tanjung Puting	115	(1)E3
Tanjungredeb	115	(1)F2
Tanjung Selatan	115	(1)E3
Tanjungselor	115	(1)F2
Tanjung Vals	115	(2)E4
Tankovo	103	R5
Tankse	107	C2
Tanlovo	63	P1
Tanney	59	G5
Tanout	95	F2
Tanta	93	F1
Tan-Tan	91	C3
Tanzania	97	E5
Tao'an	111	G1
Taomasina	99	H3
Taongi	117	J4
Taormina	77	K11
Taos	133	E1
Taoudenni	91	E5
Taourirt	91	E2
T'ao-yuan	109	G2
Tapa	61	N7
Tapachula	137	F6
Tapajós	141	F4
Tapauá	141	E5
Tapolca	79	E3
Tappahannock	135	F2
Tapsuy	63	M2
Tapuaenuku	121	D6
Taquarí	141	F7
Tara	63	Q3
Tara	103	N6
Tarābulus	91	H2
Taracua	141	D3
Tarāghin	91	H3
Tarakan	109	F6
Taran	103	N3
Taranaki = Mount Egmont	121	E4
Tarancón	73	H5
Taranto	77	M8
Tarapoto	141	B5
Tarare	71	K8
Tarascon	71	K10
Tarauacá	141	C5
Tarauacá	141	C5
Tarawa	117	H5
Tarawera Lake	121	F4
Tarazona	73	J3
Tarbes	71	F10
Tarbet	69	F4
Tarcoola	119	F6
Taree	119	K6
Tarfaya	91	C3
Târgovişte	79	N5
Târgu Frumos	79	Q2
Târgu Jiu	79	L4
Târgu Lăpuş	79	L2
Târgu Mureş	79	M3
Târgu-Neamţ	79	P2
Târgu Ocna	79	P3
Târgu Secuiesc	79	P3
Tarhunah	91	H2
Tarif	87	E4
Tarifa	73	E8
Tarija	143	J3
Tarīm	85	E6
Tarim	103	Q9
Tarim Pendi	103	Q10
Tarīn Kowt	85	J3
Tariskay Shan	103	Q9
Taritatu	115	(2)E3
Tarkio	135	B1
Tarko Sale	103	P5
Tarlac	109	G3
Tarn	71	H10
Tarna	65	K10
Tärnaby	61	H4
Târnăveni	79	M3
Tarnogskiy Gorodok	63	H2
Tărnovo	81	K2
Tarnów	65	K7
Tarnowskie Góry	65	H7
Taro	75	E6
Taroom	119	J5
Taroudannt	91	D2
Tarquínia	77	F6
Tarragona	73	M3
Tarras	121	B7
Tàrrega	73	M3
Tarso Emissi	93	C3
Tarsus	83	F5
Tartagal	143	J3
Tartu	61	P7
Ţarţūs	86	C2
Tarutyne	79	S3
Tarvisio	75	J4
Tasbuget	63	N6
Tashigang	107	F3
Tashir	83	L3
Tashkent	103	M9
Tash-Kömür	103	N9
Tashtagol	103	R7
Tasiilaq	125	Z3
Tasikmalaya	115	(1)D4
Taskesken	103	Q8
Tasman Bay	121	D5
Tasmania	117	E10
Tasmania	119	H8
Tasman Mountains	121	D5
Tasman Sea	121	B3
Tăşnad	79	K2
Taşova	83	G3
Tassili du Hoggar	91	F4
Tassili-n'-Ajjer	91	G3
Tasty	103	M9
Tata, Hungary	79	F2
Tata, Morocco	91	D3
Tatabánya	79	F2
Tatarbunary	79	S4
Tatariya	63	J3
Tatarsk	103	P6
Tatarskiy Proliv	105	P7
Tateyama	113	K6
Tathlina Lake	125	H4
Tatta	85	J5
Tatvan	83	K4
Tauá	141	J5
Tauberbischofsheim	67	E7
Tauern	75	J4
Taumarunui	121	E4
Taungdwingyi	109	B2
Taung-gyi	107	G4
Taungup	107	F5
Taunsa	107	B2
Taunton, United Kingdom	69	J10
Taunton, United States	131	F2
Taunus	59	L4
Taunusstein	59	L4
Taupo	121	F4
Tauragė	65	M2
Tauranga	121	F3
Tauroa Point	121	D2
Tavda	63	N3
Tavda	63	N3
Tavira	73	C7
Tavoy	109	B4
Tavşanli	83	C4
Taw	69	J11
Tawas City	131	D2
Tawau	115	(1)F2
Tawitawi	115	(1)F1
Taxkorgan	103	P10
Tay	69	J5
Tayga	103	R6
Taylorville	135	D2
Taym	85	C4
Taymā'	93	G2
Taymura	105	F4
Taymylyr	105	L2
Tay Ninh	109	D4
Tayshet	105	F5
Tayuan	105	L6
Tayyebād	85	H3
Taza	91	E2
Tazeh Kand	83	M4
Tazenakht	91	D2
Tāzirbū	93	D2
Tazovskiy	103	P4
Tazovskiy Poluostrov	103	N4
Tazungdam	109	B1
T'bilisi	83	L3
Tchamba	95	G3
Tchibanga	95	G5
Tchin Tabaradene	91	G5
Tczew	65	H3
Te Anau	121	A7
Te Araroa	121	G3
Te Aroha	121	E3
Te Awamutu	121	E4
Teberda	83	J2
Tébessa	91	G1
Tebingtinggi	115	(1)B2
Téboursouk	77	D12
Techa	63	M3
Techiman	95	D3
Tecuala	133	C4
Tecuci	79	Q4
Tedzhen	85	H2
Tees	69	L7
Tegal	115	(1)D4
Tegernsee	75	G3
Tegina	95	F3
Tegucigalpa	137	G6
Tegul'det	103	R6
Te Hapua	121	D2
Te Haroto	121	F4
Tehek Lake	125	M3
Teheran = Tehrān	85	F2
Tehrān	85	F2
Teignmouth	69	J11
Tejo = Tagus	73	B5
Te Kaha	121	F3
Tekirdağ	81	K4
Teknaf	107	F4
Teku	115	(2)B3
Te Kuiti	121	E4
T'elavi	83	L3
Tel Aviv-Yafo	86	B4
Telegraph Creek	133	(1)L4
Telén	143	H6
Teles Pires	141	F5
Telford	69	K9
Telfs	75	G3
Teller	133	(1)D2
Telsen	143	H7
Telšiai	65	M2
Teltow	67	J4
Teluk Berau	115	(2)D3
Teluk Bone	115	(2)B3
Teluk Cenderawasih	115	(2)E3
Telukdalem	115	(1)B2

⊠ Continent name
Ⓐ Country name
▣ State or province name
■ Country capital
▣ State or province capital
◉ Settlement

▲ Mountain, volcano, peak
▰ Mountain range
⌾ Physical region or feature
↗ River, canal
▱ Lake, salt lake
◗ Gulf, strait, bay

▱ Sea, ocean
⌐ Cape, point
▤ Island or island group, rocky or coral reef
✳ Place of interest
⌖ Historical or cultural region

Legend

- Continent name
- Country name
- State or province name
- Country capital
- State or province capital
- Settlement

- Mountain, volcano, peak
- Mountain range
- Physical region or feature
- River, canal
- Lake, salt lake
- Gulf, strait, bay

- Sea, ocean
- Cape, point
- Island or island group, rocky or coral reef
- Place of interest
- Historical or cultural region

Name	Page	Coord.
Tolmezzo	75	J4
Tolmin	75	J4
Tolna	79	F3
Tolosa	73	H1
Tol'yatti	63	J4
Tolybay	103	L7
Tom'	103	R6
Tomah	131	B2
Tomakomai	113	L2
Tomar	73	B5
Tomari	105	Q7
Tomaszów Lubelski	65	N7
Tomaszów Mazowiecki	65	K6
Tombouctou	91	E5
Tombua	99	A3
Tomé	143	G6
Tomelloso	73	H5
Tomini	115	(2)B2
Tommot	105	M5
Tomo	141	D2
Tompo	105	P4
Tom Price	119	C4
Tomra	107	E2
Tomsk	103	Q6
Tomtor	105	Q4
Tomu	115	(2)D3
Tonalá	137	F5
Tondano	115	(2)B2
Tønder	67	D2
Tonga	97	E2
Tonga	117	J7
Tonga Islands	117	J8
Tongareva	117	K6
Tonga Trench	117	J8
Tongbai	111	E4
Tongchuan	111	D4
Tongduch'ŏn	113	D5
Tongeren	59	H4
Tonghae	113	E5
Tonghua	113	C3
Tongliao	111	G2
Tongling	111	F4
Tongshi	109	D3
Tongue	129	E1
Tongyu	111	G2
Tónichi	127	E6
Tonj	97	D2
Tonk	107	C3
Tonkābon	85	F2
Tônlé Sab	109	C4
Tonnay-Charente	71	E8
Tönning	67	D2
Tonopah	129	C3
Tooele	129	D2
Toora-Khem	103	T7
Toowoomba	119	K5
Topeka	127	G4
Topki	103	R6
Topliţa	79	N3
Topock	133	D2
Topol'čany	65	H9
Topolobampo	127	E6
Torbali	81	K6
Torbat-e Heydarīyeh	85	G2
Torbat-e Jām	85	H2
Tordesillas	73	F3
Torells	73	N2
Torgau	67	H5
Torgelow	65	C4
Torhout	59	F3
Torino	75	C5
Tori-shima	113	L8
Torneälven	61	L3
Torneträsk	61	K2
Tornio	61	N4
Toro	73	E3
Toronto	131	E2
Tororo	97	E3
Toros Dağları	83	E5
Torquay	69	J11
Torrance	133	C2
Torreblanca	73	L4
Torre de Moncorvo	73	C3
Torrejón de Ardoz	73	G4
Torrelavega	73	F1
Torremolinos	73	F8
Torrent	73	K5
Torreón	133	F3
Torres Strait	119	H2
Torres Vedras	73	A5
Torrevieja	73	K6
Torrington	129	F2
Tortol	77	D9
Tortona	75	D6
Tortosa	73	L4
Tortum	83	J3
Torūd	85	G2
Toruń	65	H4
Tory Island	69	D6
Torzhok	63	G3
Tosa-wan	113	G7
Tostedt	67	E3
Tosya	81	S3
Totaranui	121	D5
Tôtes	59	D5
Tot'ma	63	H3
Totora	141	D7
Tottori	113	H6
Touba, Ivory Coast	95	C3
Touba, Senegal	95	A2
Tougan	95	D2
Touggourt	91	G2
Toul	71	L5
Toulépleu	95	C3
Toulon	71	L10
Toulouse	71	G10
Toummo	91	H4
Toungoo	109	B3
Tourcoing	59	F4
Tournai	59	F4
Tours	71	F6
Touws River	99	C6
Tovuz	83	L3
Towanda	131	E2
Towari	115	(2)B3
Towcester	59	B2
Towner	129	F1
Townsend	129	D1
Townshend Island	119	K4
Townsville	119	J3
Toxkan	103	P9
Toyama	113	J5
Toyohashi	113	J6
Toyooka	113	H6
Toyota	113	J6
Tozeur	91	G2
Trâblous	86	C2
Trabzon	83	H3
Tracy	131	A2
Trail	129	C1
Traiskirchen	75	M2
Trakai	61	N9
Tralee	69	L3
Tralee Bay	69	B9
Tramán Tepuí	141	E2
Tranås	61	H7
Trancoso	73	C4
Trang	109	B5
Trangan	115	(2)D4
Transantarctic Mountains	144	(2)B1
Trapani	77	G11
Trappes	59	E6
Traun	75	K2
Traunreut	75	H3
Traunsee	75	J3
Traversay Islands	139	H9
Traverse City	131	C2
Travnik	79	E3
Trbovlje	75	L4
Trébbia	75	E6
Třebíč	65	E8
Trebinje	79	F7
Trebišov	79	J1
Trebnje	75	L5
Trebon	75	K1
Tregosse Islets	119	K3
Trelew	143	H7
Trelleborg	61	G9
Tremonton	129	D2
Tremp	73	L2
Trenčín	65	H9
Trent	69	M8
Trento	75	G4
Trenton, Canada	131	E2
Trenton, United States	131	F2
Trepassey	125	W7
Tres Arroyos	143	J6
Três Corações	141	H8
Tres Esquinas	141	B3
Tres Lagos	143	G8
Trespaderne	73	G2
Treuchtlingen	75	F2
Treviglio	75	E5
Treviso	75	H5
Triangle	99	E4
Tricase	77	N9
Trichur	107	C6
Trier	59	J5
Trieste	75	J5
Triglav	75	J4
Trikala	81	D5
Trikomon	86	A1
Trilj	75	M7
Trincomalee	107	D7
Trinidad	141	E1
Trinidad, Bolivia	141	E6
Trinidad, United States	133	F1
Trinidad, Uruguay	143	K5
Trinidad and Tobago	141	E1
Trinity Islands	133	(1)G4
Trino	75	D5
Trion	135	D3
Tripoli, Greece	81	E7
Tripoli = Trâblous, Lebanon	86	C2
Tripoli = Tarābulus, Libya	91	H2
Trischen	67	D2
Tristan da Cunha	89	B9
Trivandrum = Thiruvananthapuram	107	C7
Trjavna	83	A2
Trnava	79	E1
Trogir	79	D6
Troina	77	J11
Troisdorf	67	C6
Trois Rivières	131	F1
Troitsk	63	M4
Troitsko-Pechorsk	63	L2
Trojan	81	G2
Trollhättan	61	G7
Trombetas	141	F4
Tromsø	61	K2
Trona	129	C3
Trondheim	61	F5
Trondheimsfjörden	61	E5
Troodos	83	E6
Trotuş	79	P3
Trout Lake, N.W.T., Canada	125	G4
Trout Lake, Ont., Canada	125	N6
Troy, Al., United States	135	D3
Troy, N.Y., United States	131	F2
Troyan	79	M7
Troyes	71	K5
Trstenik	79	J6
Trudovoye	113	G2
Trujillo, Peru	141	B5
Trujillo, Spain	73	E5
Truro, Canada	125	U7
Truro, United Kingdom	69	G11
Trusovo	103	J4
Truth or Consequences	133	E2
Trutnov	65	E7
Tryavana	81	H2
Trzcianka	65	F4
Trzebnica	65	G6
Tsetserleg	105	G7
Tshabong	99	C5
Tshane	99	C4
Tshikapa	97	C5
Tshuapa	97	C4
Tsiafajavona	99	H3
Tsimlyanskoy Vodokhranilishche	63	H5
Tsiroanomandidy	99	H3
Ts'khinvali	83	K2
Tsuchiura	113	L5
Tsugaru-kaikyō	113	L3
Tsumeb	99	B3
Tsumkwe	99	C3
Tsuruga	113	J6
Tsuruoka	113	K4
Tsushima	113	E6
Tsuyama	113	H6
Tua	73	C3
Tual	115	(2)D4
Tuấn Giao	109	C2
Tuapse	83	H1
Tubarão	143	M4
Tübingen	75	E2
Tubize	59	G4
Tubruq	93	D1
Tubuai	117	M8
Tubuai Islands	117	L8
Tucano	141	K6
Tuchola	65	G4
Tucson	133	D2
Tucumcari	133	F1
Tucupita	141	E2
Tucuruí	141	H4
Tudela	73	J2
Tuguegarao	109	G3
Tugur	105	P6
Tui	73	B2
Tuktoyaktuk	133	(1)L2
Tula, Mexico	133	G4
Tula, Russia	63	G4
Tulare	129	C3
Tulcea	79	R4
Tulkarm	86	B4
Tullamore	69	E8
Tulle	71	G8
Tulln	75	M2
Tuloma	61	S2
Tulsa	127	G4
Tulsequah	133	(1)L4
Tulun	105	G6
Tulung La	107	F3
Tulu Weiel	97	E2
Tumaco	141	B3
Tumān	85	H2
Tumen	113	E2
Tumereng	141	E2
Tumkur	107	C6
Tumut	119	J7
Tunca	81	J3
Tunceli	83	H4
Tunduru	99	F2
Tundzha	79	P8
Tungir	105	L5
Tungku	115	(1)F1
Tungsten	133	(1)M3
Tungusk	103	S5
Tunis	91	H1
Tunisia	91	E2
Tunja	141	C2
Tupelo	135	D3
Tupik	105	L6
Tupiza	143	H3
Tupper Lake	131	F2
Tuquan	111	G1
Tura, India	107	F3
Tura, Russia	105	J3
Turan	103	S7
Turangi	121	E4
Turayf	93	G1

Name	Page	Ref
Turbat	85	H4
Turbo	141	B2
Turda	79	L3
Turek	65	H5
Turgay	103	L8
Turgay	103	L8
Turgayskaya Stolovaya Strana	103	L7
Türgovishte	79	P6
Turgutlu	81	K6
Turhal	83	G3
Turin = Torino	75	C5
Turinsk	63	M3
Turiy Rog	113	F1
Turka	105	H6
Türkeli Adası	81	K4
Turkestan	103	M9
Turkey	83	D4
Turkmenbashi	85	F1
Turkmenistan	85	G2
Turks and Caicos Islands	137	K4
Turks Islands	137	K4
Turku	61	M6
Turma	105	N6
Turnhout	59	G3
Turnov	65	E7
Turnu Măgurele	79	M6
Turpan	103	R9
Turpan Pendi	103	S9
Turquino	139	D2
Turtas	63	N3
Turtkul'	85	H1
Turtle Island	119	K3
Turu	103	U5
Turugart Pass	103	P9
Turukhan	105	C3
Turukhansk	103	R4
Turukta	105	K4
Tuscaloosa	135	D3
Tuscola	135	D2
Tuticorin	107	C7
Tutonchany	105	E4
Tutrakan	79	P5
Tuttle Creek Reservoir	135	B2
Tuttlingen	75	D3
Tutuila	117	K7
Tuvalu	117	H6
Tuxpan, *Mexico*	127	E7
Tuxpan, *Mexico*	127	G7
Tuxtla Gutiérrez	137	F5
Tuyên Quang	109	D2
Tuy Hoa	109	D4
Tuymazy	63	K4
Tuz Gölü	83	E4
Tuz Khurmātū	83	L6
Tuzla	79	F5
Tver'	63	G3
Tweed	69	K6
Twentynine Palms	133	C2
Twilight Cove	119	E6
Twin Buttes Reservoir	133	F2
Twin Falls	129	D2
Twizel	121	C7
Two Harbors	131	B1
Tyachiv	79	L1
Tygda	105	M6
Tyler	127	G5
Tylkhoy	105	U4
Tym	103	Q6
Tynda	105	L5
Tyne	69	K6
Tynemouth	69	L6
Tynset	61	F5
Tyra	103	S7
Tyrifjorden	61	F6
Tyrnavos	81	E5
Tyrrhenian Sea	77	F8
Tyry	105	P4
Tysa	65	N9
Tyukyan	105	K4
Tyumen'	103	M6
Tyung	105	K3
Tyva	105	F6

U

Name	Page	Ref
Uaupés	141	D3
Ubá	141	J8
Ubaitaba	141	K6
Ubangi	97	B3
Ube	113	F7
Úbeda	73	G6
Uberaba	141	H7
Uberlândia	141	H7
Überlingen	75	E3
Ubon Ratchathani	109	C3
Ubrique	73	E8
Ucayali	141	B5
Uchami	103	T5
Ucharal	103	Q8
Uchiura-wan	113	L2
Uchkuduk	103	L9
Uckermark	67	J3
Ucluelet	129	A1
Uda, *Russia*	105	F5
Uda, *Russia*	105	N6
Udachnyy	105	J3
Udagamandalam	107	C6
Udaipur	107	B4
Uddevalla	61	F7
Uddjaure	63	C1
Uddjaure Storavan	61	K4
Udine	75	J4
Udmurtiya	63	K3
Udon Thani	109	C3
Udupi	107	B6
Ueda	113	K5
Uele	97	C3
Uelen	105	AA3
Uel'kal	105	Y3
Uelzen	67	F4
Ufa	63	L3
Ufa	63	L4
Uganda	97	E3
Ugep	95	F3
Ugine	75	B5
Uglegorsk	105	Q7
Uglich	63	G3
Ugljan	75	K6
Ugol'nyye Kopi	105	X4
Ugulan	105	S4
Uh	79	K1
Uherské Hradiště	65	G8
Uherský Brod	65	G8
Uiju	113	C3
Uil	63	K5
Uil	63	K5
Uinta Mountains	129	D2
Uitenhage	99	D6
Újfehértó	79	J2
Ujiji	97	D4
Ujjain	107	C4
Ujung Pandang	115	(2)A4
Ukerewe Island	97	E4
Ukhta	103	J5
Ukiah	129	B3
Ukkusissat	125	W2
Ukmergė	65	P2
Ukraine	57	G3
Ulaanbaatar	105	H7
Ulaangom	103	S8
Ulan	111	B3
Ulan Bator = Ulaanbaatar	111	D1
Ulan-Ude	105	H6
Ulchin	113	C5
Uldz	105	J7
Ulety	105	J6
Ulhasnagar	107	B5
Uliastay	103	T8
Ulindi	97	D4
Ullapool	69	G4
Ullŭng do	113	F5
Ulm	75	F2
Ulog	79	F6
Ulongue	99	E2
Ulsan	113	E6
Ulu	105	M4
Ulubat Gölü	81	L4
Ulugqat	85	K2
Ulukışla	83	F5
Ulungur Hu	103	R8
Ulunkhan	105	J5
Uluru	119	F5
Ulu-Yul	105	D5
Ulva	69	F5
Ulverston	69	J7
Ulya	105	Q5
Ul'yanovsk	63	J4
Ulytau	103	M8
Uman'	63	F5
Umarkot	85	J4
Umba	63	F1
Umeå	61	L5
Umeälven	61	J4
Umfolozi	99	E5
Ummal Arānib	91	H3
Umm al Jamājim	87	A3
Umm Durman	93	F4
Umm Keddada	93	E5
Umm Lajj	93	G3
Umm Qaşr	87	B1
Umm Ruwaba	93	F5
Umnak Island	133	(1)E5
Umtata	99	D6
Umuarama	143	L3
Unalakleet	133	(1)E3
Unalaska Island	133	(1)E5
'Unayzah	86	C6
Underberg	99	D5
Ungava Bay	125	T5
Ungheni	79	Q2
Ungwana Bay	97	G4
União da Vitória	143	L4
Unije	75	K6
Unimak Island	133	(1)D5
Unim Bāb	87	D4
Unini	141	E4
Union	131	B3
Union City	137	G1
Union Springs	135	D3
United Arab Emirates	85	F5
United Kingdom	69	G6
United States	123	M5
Unna	59	K3
Unraven	133	E1
Unst	69	M1
Unstrut	67	G5
Unzha	63	H3
Upernavik	125	W2
Upernavik Kujalleq	125	V2
Upington	99	C5
Upolu	117	J7
Upper Hutt	121	E5
Upper Klamath Lake	129	B2
Upper Lough Erne	69	E7
Upper Sandusky	131	D2
Uppsala	61	J7
Upsala	131	B1
'Uqlat al 'Udhaybah	87	B2
Urad Houqi	111	D2
Urakawa	113	M2
Ural	63	K5
Ural Mountains = Ural'skiy Khrebet	57	L1
Ural'sk	63	K4
Ural'skiy Khrebet	57	L1
Urambo	97	E5
Uranium City	125	K5
Uraricoera	141	E3
Uray	63	M2
Urbana, *Ill.*, United States	131	C2
Urbana, *Oh.*, United States	131	D2
Urbania	75	H7
Urbino	75	H7
Urdzhar	103	Q8
Uren'	63	J3
Urengoy	103	P4
Urgench	85	H1
Urho	103	R8
Uritskiy	63	N4
Urla	81	J6
Urlaţi	79	P5
Uroševac	79	J7
Uro-teppa	85	J2
Urt	111	C2
Uruaçu	141	H6
Uruapan	137	D5
Urucurituba	141	F4
Uruguaiana	143	K4
Uruguay	143	K5
Uruguay	143	K5
Ürümqi	103	R9
Urus Martan	83	L2
Uryupino	105	L6
Ur'yupinsk	63	H4
Urzhum	63	K3
Urziceni	79	P5
Usa	103	L4
Uşak	83	C4
Usedom	67	J3
Useless Loop	119	B5
Usfān	85	C5
Ushtobe	103	P8
Usingen	67	D6
Usk	69	J10
Usman'	63	G4
Usol'ye Sibirskoye	105	G6
Ussel	71	H8
Ussuri	113	G1
Ussuriysk	111	J2
Usta	63	J3
Ust'-Alekseyevo	63	J2
Ust'-Barguzin	105	H6
Ust' Chaun	105	W3
Ústí	65	F8
Ústica	77	H10
Ust'-Ilimsk	105	G5
Ústí nad Labem	65	D7
Ust'-Ishim	103	N6
Ustka	65	F3
Ust'-Kamchatsk	105	U5
Ust'-Kamenogorsk	103	Q8
Ust'-Kamo	103	T5
Ust'-Karenga	105	K6
Ust'-Khayryuzovo	105	T5
Ust'-Kulom	63	K2
Ust'-Kut	105	G5
Ust'-Kuyga	105	P3
Ust'-Labinsk	83	H1
Ust'-Maya	105	N4
Ust'-Mukduyka	103	R4
Ust'-Muya	105	K5
Ust' Nem	63	K2
Ust'-Nera	105	Q4
Ust'-Nyukzha	105	L5
Ust'-Olenek	105	K2
Ust'-Omchug	105	R4
Ust' Ozernoye	105	D5
Ust' Penzhino	105	V4
Ust'-Pit	105	E5
Ustrem	63	N2
Ust'-Sopochnoye	105	T5
Ust' Tapsuy	63	M2
Ust'-Tarka	103	P6
Ust'-Tatta	105	N4
Ust'-Tsil'ma	103	J4
Ust' Un'ya	63	L2
Ust'-Urkima	105	L5
Ust' Usa	63	L1
Ust'-Uyskoye	103	L7
Usu	103	Q9

Legend

- ⊠ Continent name
- Ⓐ Country name
- ⓐ State or province name
- ■ Country capital
- ⊡ State or province capital
- ⊙ Settlement
- ▲ Mountain, volcano, peak
- ⌂ Mountain range
- ⊘ Physical region or feature
- ⟋ River, canal
- ⬙ Lake, salt lake
- ⊵ Gulf, strait, bay
- ⬛ Sea, ocean
- ⊳ Cape, point
- ⬚ Island or island group, rocky or coral reef
- ✳ Place of interest
- ⬚ Historical or cultural region

☒	Continent name
Ⓐ	Country name
▣	State or province name
■	Country capital
▣	State or province capital
●	Settlement
▲	Mountain, volcano, peak
⌂	Mountain range
⌾	Physical region or feature
◪	River, canal
◲	Lake, salt lake
◿	Gulf, strait, bay
⎋	Sea, ocean
⊟	Cape, point
⊡	Island or island group, rocky or coral reef
✳	Place of interest
⊞	Historical or cultural region

Name	Page	Grid
Vigévano	75	D5
Vigia	141	H4
Vigo	73	B2
Viho Valentia	77	L10
Vijaywada	107	D5
Vik	61	(1)D3
Vikna	61	E4
Vila de Conde	73	B3
Vilafranca del Penedäs	73	M3
Vila Franca de Xira	73	A6
Vila Nova de Gaia	73	B3
Vilanova y la Geltru	73	M3
Vila Real	73	C3
Vila-real	73	K5
Vilhelmina	61	J4
Vilhena	141	E6
Vilija	61	N9
Viljandi	61	N7
Vilkaviškis	65	N3
Villa Ahumada	137	C2
Villablino	73	D2
Villacarrillo	73	G6
Villach	75	J4
Villacidro	77	C9
Villa Constitución	127	D7
Villa de Cos	137	D4
Villafranca	75	F5
Villafranca de los Barros	73	D6
Villagarcia	73	B2
Villagrán	133	G4
Villahermosa	137	F5
Villa Huidobro	143	J5
Villalba	73	C1
Villaldama	133	F3
Villalpando	73	E3
Villamartín	73	E8
Villa Montes	143	J3
Villanueva	133	F4
Villanueva de Cordoba	73	F6
Villa Ocampo	133	E3
Villaputzu	77	D9
Villarrobledo	73	H5
Villa San Giovanni	77	K10
Villavelayo	73	H2
Villavicencio	141	C3
Villaviciosa	73	E1
Villedieu-les-Poëles	59	A6
Villefranche-de-Rouergue	71	H9
Villefranche-sur-Saône	71	K8
Villena	73	K6
Villeneuve-sur-Lot	71	F9
Villers-Bocage	59	B5
Villers-Cotterêts	59	F5
Villerupt	59	H5
Villeurbanne	71	K8
Villingen	75	D2
Vilnius	61	N9
Vilsbiburg	75	H2
Vilshofen	75	J2
Vilvoorde	59	G4
Vilyuy	105	L4
Vilyuysk	105	L4
Vilyuyskoye Vodokhranilishche	105	J4
Vimoutiers	59	C6
Vimperk	75	J1
Viña del Mar	143	G5
Vinaròs	73	L4
Vincennes	135	D2
Vineland	131	F3
Vinh	109	D3
Vinkovci	79	F4
Vinnytsya	63	E5
Vinson Massif	144	(2)JJ2
Vinstri	61	E6
Vinzili	63	N3
Vioolsdrift	99	B5
Vipava	75	J5
Vipiteno	75	G4
Vir	75	L6
Virac	109	G4
Viranşehir	83	H5
Virawah	107	B4
Virden	129	F1
Vire	59	B6
Virginia	127	L4
Virginia	131	B1
Virginia Beach	131	E3
Virgin Islands, *United Kingdom*	139	E2
Virgin Islands, *United States*	139	E2
Virihaure	61	J3
Virôchey	109	D4
Virovitica	79	E4
Virton	59	H5
Virtsu	61	M7
Virudunagar	107	C7
Vis	79	D6
Visalia	129	C3
Visby	61	K8
Viscount Melville Sound	125	J2
Viseu, *Brazil*	141	H4
Viseu, *Portugal*	73	C4
Vişeu de Sus	79	M2
Vishakhapatnam	107	D5
Vishera	103	K5
Vishnevka	103	N7
Visoko	79	F6
Visp	75	C4
Visselhövede	67	E4
Vistula = Wisła	57	F2
Viterbo	77	G6
Viti Levu	117	H7
Vitim	105	J5
Vitolište	81	D3
Vitória	143	N3
Vitória da Conquista	141	J6
Vitoria-Gasteiz	73	H2
Vitré	71	D5
Vitry-le-François	59	G6
Vitsyebsk	63	F3
Vitteaux	71	K6
Vittel	75	A2
Vittória	77	J12
Vittório Véneto	75	H5
Viveiro	73	C1
Vivi	103	T4
Vize	81	K3
Vizhas	63	J1
Vizianagaram	107	D5
Vizinga	103	H5
Vizzini	77	J11
Vjosë	81	C4
Vladikavkaz	83	L2
Vladimir	63	H3
Vladivostok	113	F2
Vlasotince	79	K7
Vlasovo	105	N2
Vlieland	59	G1
Vlissingen	59	F3
Vlorë	81	B4
Vltava	65	D8
Vöcklabruck	75	J2
Vodice	75	L7
Vodnjan	75	J6
Vogelsberg	67	E6
Voghera	75	D6
Vohipeno	99	H4
Vöhringen	75	F2
Voi	97	F4
Voinjama	95	C3
Voiron	71	L8
Voitsberg	75	L3
Vojens	67	E1
Vojmsjön	61	J4
Vojvodina	79	G4
Volary	67	J8
Volcán Antofalla	143	H4
Volcán Barú	137	H7
Volcán Cayambe	141	B3
Volcán Citlaltépetl	123	L7
Volcán Corcovado	143	G7
Volcán Cotopaxi	141	B4
Volcán Domuyo	143	G6
Volcán Lanin	143	G6
Volcán Llullaillaco	143	H3
Volcán San Pedro	143	H3
Volcán Tajumulco	137	F5
Volga	63	J5
Volgodonsk	63	H5
Volgograd	63	H5
Völkermarkt	75	K4
Volkhov	63	F3
Völklingen	59	J5
Volksrust	99	D5
Volochanka	103	S3
Volodarskoye	63	N4
Vologda	63	H3
Volonga	63	J1
Volos	81	E5
Volosovo	61	Q7
Volta Redonda	141	J8
Volterra	75	F7
Volti	75	D6
Volzhskiy	63	H5
Voorne	59	F3
Voranava	61	N9
Vorderrhein	75	E4
Vordingborg	67	G1
Voreios Evvoïkos Kolpos	81	E6
Voreria Pindos	81	C4
Vorkuta	63	M1
Vormsi	61	M7
Vorona	63	H4
Voronezh	63	G4
Vorstershoop	99	C5
Võru	61	P8
Vosges	75	C2
Voss	61	D6
Vostochno-Sibirskoye More	105	U2
Vostochnyy Sayan	103	T7
Vostok Island	117	L6
Votkinsk	103	J6
Vozhgora	63	J2
Vranje	79	J7
Vranov	65	L9
Vranov nad Toplau	79	J1
Vratsa	79	L6
Vrbas	79	E5
Vrbas	79	G4
Vrbovsko	75	L5
Vrendenburg	99	B6
Vryburg	99	C5
Vryheid	99	E5
Vsetín	65	G8
Vučitrn	79	J7
Vukovar	79	G4
Vuktyl'	63	L2
Vulcăneşti	79	R4
Vulcano	77	J10
Vung Tau	109	D4
Vuollerim	61	L3
Vuotso	61	P2
Vyatka	63	K3
Vyazemskiy	105	N7
Vyaz'ma	63	F3
Vyborg	61	Q6
Vychegda	63	K2
Vyksa	63	H3
Vylkove	79	S4
Vynohradiv	65	N9
Vyshniy Volochek	63	F3
Vyškov	65	G8
Vytegra	63	G2

W

Name	Page	Grid
Wa	95	D3
Waal	59	H3
Waalwijk	59	H3
Wabē Shebelē Wenz	97	G2
Waco	135	B3
Wad Banda	93	E5
Waddān	93	C2
Waddeneilanden	59	G1
Waddenzee	59	H1
Wadena	131	A1
Wādī al Fārigh	93	C1
Wādī al Hamīm	93	D1
Wadi Halfa	93	F3
Wādī Mūsā	86	C6
Wad Medani	93	F5
Wadsworth	133	C1
Wafangdian	111	G3
Wafangdian	113	A4
Wagga Wagga	119	J7
Wahai	115	(2)C3
Wahiawa	133	(2)C2
Wahpeton	129	G1
Waiau	121	D6
Waiblingen	75	E2
Waidhofen	75	K3
Waidhofen an der Ybbs	79	B2
Waigeo	115	(2)D3
Waiheke Island	121	E3
Waihi	121	E3
Waikabubak	115	(2)A4
Waikaia	121	B7
Waikaremoana	121	F4
Waikato	121	E4
Waikawa	121	B8
Wailuku	133	(2)E3
Waimate	121	C7
Waingapu	119	B1
Wainwright	133	(1)F1
Waiouru	121	E4
Waipara	121	D6
Waipawa	121	F4
Waipiro	121	G4
Waipukurau	121	F5
Wairoa	121	F4
Waitakaruru	121	E3
Waitaki	121	C7
Waitangi	121	(1)B1
Waitara	121	E4
Waiuku	121	E3
Wajima	113	J5
Wajir	97	G3
Wakasa-wan	113	H6
Wakayama	113	H6
Wakeeney	133	G1
Wakefield	69	L8
Wake Island	117	G4
Wakkanai	113	L1
Waku-Kungo	99	B2
Wałbrzych	65	F7
Walcheren	59	F3
Wałcz	65	F4
Waldmünchen	67	H7
Waldshut-Tiengen	75	D3
Walen See	75	E3
Wales	69	J9
Wales Island	125	P3
Walgett	119	J6
Walker Lake	133	C1
Walkerville	119	J7
Wall	129	F2
Wallaceburg	131	D2
Walla Walla	129	C1
Wallis et Futuna	117	J7
Walpole	119	C6
Walsall	69	L9
Walsenburg	129	F3
Walsrode	67	E4
Waltershausen	67	F6
Walvis Bay	99	A4
Wamba	97	D3
Wana	85	J3
Wanaaring	119	H5
Wanaka	121	B7
Wandel Sea	123	A1
Wandingzhen	109	B2
Wanganui	121	E4
Wanganui	121	E4

Legend

- ⊠ Continent name
- Ⓐ Country name
- ⒜ State or province name
- ■ Country capital
- ▣ State or province capital
- ● Settlement
- ▲ Mountain, volcano, peak
- Mountain range
- Physical region or feature
- River, canal
- Lake, salt lake
- Gulf, strait, bay
- Sea, ocean
- Cape, point
- Island or island group, rocky or coral reef
- Place of interest
- Historical or cultural region

Name	Page	Ref
Wangen	75	E3
Wangerooge	67	D3
Wangiwangi	115	(2)B4
Wan Hsa-la	109	B2
Wanxian	111	D4
Wanyuan	111	D4
Warangal	107	C5
Warburg	67	D5
Ward	121	E5
Wardha	107	C4
Waregem	59	F4
Waremme	59	H4
Waren	67	H3
Warendorf	59	K3
Warka	65	L6
Warla	65	H6
Warmandi	115	(2)D3
Warminster	69	K10
Warm Springs	129	C3
Warren, Mich., United States	131	D2
Warren, Oh., United States	131	D2
Warren, Pa., United States	131	E2
Warrensburg	131	B3
Warrenton	99	C5
Warri	95	F3
Warrington, United Kingdom	69	K8
Warrington, United States	135	D3
Warrnambool	119	H7
Warroad	131	A1
Warsaw = Warszawa	65	K5
Warstein	67	D5
Warszawa	65	K5
Warta	65	F5
Warwick	69	L9
Wasatch Range	133	D1
Wasco	133	C1
Washap	85	H4
Washburn Lake	125	K2
Washington	129	B1
Washington, N.C., United States	131	E3
Washington, Pa., United States	131	D2
Washington, Ut., United States	129	D3
Washington D.C.	123	J6
Wassenaar	59	G2
Wasserburg	75	H2
Watampone	115	(2)B3
Waterbury	131	F2
Waterford	69	E9
Waterloo	131	B2
Watersmeet	131	C1
Watertown, N.Y., United States	131	E2
Watertown, S.D., United States	129	G1
Watertown, Wis., United States	131	C2
Waterville	131	G2
Watford	59	B3
Watford City	129	F1
Watmuri	115	(2)D4
Watrous	125	K6
Watsa	97	D3
Watseka	135	D1
Watson Lake	133	(1)M3
Wau	97	D2
Waubay Lake	129	G1
Waukegan	131	C2
Waukesha	131	C2
Waurika	135	B3
Wausau	127	J3
Waverly	131	C3
Wavre	59	G4
Wawa	131	D1
Wāw al Kabīr	93	C2
Waxxari	103	R10
Waycross	135	E3
Waynesboro, Ga., United States	135	E3
Waynesboro, Miss., United States	135	D3
Waynesville	131	D3
Weaverville	129	B2
Weber	121	F5
Webi Shaabeelle	97	G3
Webster	129	G1
Weddell Island	143	J9
Weddell Sea	144	(2)A2
Wedel	67	E3
Weed	129	B2
Weert	59	H3
Wei	111	D4
Weichang	111	F2
Weida	67	H6
Weiden	67	H7
Weifang	111	F3
Weihai	111	G3
Weilburg	67	D6
Weilheim	75	G3
Weimar	67	G6
Weinan	111	D4
Weinheim	67	D7
Weining	111	C5
Weipa	119	H2
Weiser	129	C2
Weißenburg	67	F7
Weißenfels	67	G5
Weißwasser	67	K5
Weixi	109	B1
Wejherowo	65	H3
Welkom	99	D5
Welland	59	B2
Wellesley Islands	119	G3
Wellingborough	71	E1
Wellington, New Zealand	121	E5
Wellington, Colo., United States	129	F2
Wellington, Kans., United States	135	B2
Wells	129	C2
Wellsboro	131	E2
Wellsford	121	E3
Wellton	133	D2
Wels	75	K2
Welwyn Garden City	59	B3
Wenatchee	129	B1
Wenchang	109	E3
Wenga	97	B3
Wenman	141	(1)A1
Wentworth	119	H6
Wen Xian	111	C4
Wenzhou	111	G5
Werder	67	H4
Werdēr	97	H2
Werl	59	K3
Werneck	67	F7
Wernigerode	67	F5
Werra	67	F6
Wertheim	67	E4
Wesel	59	J3
Wesel Dorsten	67	B5
Weser	67	E4
Wessel Islands	119	G2
West Antarctica	144	(2)GG2
West Bank	86	C4
West Branch	131	D2
West Cape	117	G10
West End	135	F4
Western Australia	119	D5
Western Cape	99	B6
Western Ghats	107	B5
Western Reef	121	(1)B1
Western Sahara	91	C4
Wester Ross	69	G4
Westerschelde	59	F3
Westerstede	59	K1
Westerwald	59	K4
West Falkland	143	J9
West Frankfort	135	D2
West Glacier	129	D1
West Lunga	99	C2
West Memphis	135	C2
Weston	131	D3
Weston-super-Mare	69	K10
West Palm Beach	135	E4
West Plains	131	B3
Westport, New Zealand	121	C5
Westport, Republic of Ireland	69	C8
Westray	69	J2
West Siberian Plain = Zapadno-Sibirskaya Ravnina	101	L3
West Virginia	131	D3
West Wendover	129	D2
West Yellowstone	129	D2
Wetar	115	(2)C4
Wetaskiwin	125	J6
Wete	97	F5
Wetumpka	135	D3
Wetzlar	67	D6
Wewak	115	(2)F3
Wexford	69	F9
Wexford Harbour	69	F9
Weyburn	127	F2
Weymouth	69	K11
Whakatane	121	F3
Whale Cove	125	N4
Whalsay	69	M1
Whangarei	121	E2
Wharfe	69	L7
Wheeler Peak	133	E1
Wheeler Ridge	133	C2
Wheeling	135	E1
Whitby	69	M7
White, Nev., United States	129	C3
White, S.D., United States	125	L8
White Bay	125	V6
White Cliffs	119	H6
Whitecourt	125	H6
Whitefish Point	131	C1
Whitehaven	69	J7
Whitehorse	133	(1)L3
White Island	121	F3
Whitemark	119	J8
White Mountain Peak	129	C3
White Mountains	125	S8
Whitemouth	129	G1
White Nile = Bahr el Abiad	93	F5
White River, Canada	131	C1
White River, United States	129	F2
White Sea = Beloye More	63	G1
White Sulphur Springs	129	D1
Whiteville	135	F3
White Volta	95	D3
Whitney	131	E1
Whyalla	119	G6
Wichita	135	B2
Wichita Falls	135	B3
Wick	69	J3
Wickenburg	133	D2
Wicklow Mountains	69	F8
Widawka	65	J6
Wieluń	65	H6
Wien	75	M2
Wiener Neustadt	75	M3
Wieringermeer Polder	59	G2
Wiesbaden	67	D6
Wiesloch	67	D7
Wiesmoor	67	C3
Wigan	69	K8
Wiggins	129	F2
Wil	75	E3
Wilbur	129	C1
Wilcannia	119	H6
Wildeshausen	67	D4
Wilhelmshaven	67	D3
Wilkes-Barre	131	E2
Wilkes Land	144	(2)U2
Willapa Bay	129	B1
Willemstad	141	D1
Williams, Australia	119	C6
Williams, Ariz., United States	129	D3
Williams, Calif., United States	129	B3
Williamsburg	131	E3
Williams Lake	125	G6
Williamson	135	E2
Williamsport	131	E2
Willis Group	119	K3
Williston, Fla., United States	135	E4
Williston, N.D., United States	129	F1
Williston Lake	125	G5
Willmar	131	A1
Willow	133	(1)H3
Willowmore	99	C6
Willow River	131	B1
Willow Springs	131	B3
Wilmington, Del., United States	131	E3
Wilmington, N.C., United States	135	F3
Wilson	131	E3
Wilson Reservoir	135	B2
Wilson's Promontory	119	J7
Wiluna	119	D5
Winamac	131	C2
Winchester, United Kingdom	69	L10
Winchester, Ky., United States	131	D3
Winchester, Va., United States	131	E3
Windhoek	99	B4
Windischgarsten	75	K3
Windom	131	A2
Windorah	119	H5
Windsor, Canada	131	D2
Windsor, United Kingdom	59	B3
Windsor, United States	135	F2
Windward Islands	137	N6
Windward Passage	139	D2
Winfield, Al., United States	135	D3
Winfield, Kans., United States	133	G1
Wingate Mountains	119	E2
Winisk	125	P5
Winisk	125	P6
Winisk Lake	125	P6
Winnemucca	129	C2
Winner	129	G2
Winnfield	127	H5
Winnipeg	125	M7
Winona, Minn., United States	131	B2
Winona, Miss., United States	135	D3
Winschoten	59	K1
Winsen	67	F3
Winslow	133	D1
Winston-Salem	131	D3
Winterberg	67	D5
Winter Harbour	125	J2
Winterswijk	59	J3
Winterthur	75	D3
Winton, Australia	119	H4
Winton, New Zealand	121	B8
Wisbech	59	C2
Wisconsin	127	H2
Wisconsin	131	B2
Wisconsin Dells	131	C2
Wisconsin Rapids	131	C2
Wisła	65	H4
Wisła	65	H8
Wisłoka	65	L8
Wismar	67	G3
Wissembourg	67	C7
Witney	59	A3
Witten	59	K3
Wittenberge	67	G3
Wittenoom	119	C4
Wittingen	67	F4
Wittlich	59	J5
Wittmund	67	C3
Wittstock	67	H3
Witzenhausen	67	E5
W. J. van Blommesteinmeer	141	G2
Wkra	65	K5
Władysławowo	65	H3
Włocławek	65	J5
Włodawa	65	N6
Wodzisław Śląski	65	H7
Wohlen	75	D3
Wokam	115	(2)D4
Woking	69	M10
Wolf Creek	129	D1
Wolfen	67	H5
Wolfenbüttel	67	F4
Wolf Point	129	E1
Wolfratshausen	75	G3
Wolfsberg	75	K4
Wolfsburg	67	F4

Continent name
Country name
State or province name
Country capital
State or province capital
Settlement

Mountain, volcano, peak
Mountain range
Physical region or feature
River, canal
Lake, salt lake
Gulf, strait, bay

Sea, ocean
Cape, point
Island or island group, rocky or coral reef
Place of interest
Historical or cultural region

Name		Page	Ref
Wolgast	●	67	J2
Wollaston Lake	✦	125	K5
Wollaston Peninsula	⬡	125	H3
Wollongong	●	119	K6
Wołomin	●	65	L5
Wolsztyn	●	65	F5
Wolverhampton	●	69	K9
Wŏnju	●	113	D5
Wŏnsan	●	113	D4
Woodbridge	●	59	D2
Woodburn	●	129	B1
Woodland	●	129	B3
Woodstock, Canada	●	131	G1
Woodstock, United Kingdom	●	59	A3
Woodstock, United States	●	131	C2
Woodville, New Zealand	●	121	E5
Woodville, Miss., United States	●	135	C3
Woodville, Tex., United States	●	135	C3
Woodward	●	129	G3
Woody Head	▷	121	E3
Woonsocket, R.I., United States	●	131	F2
Woonsocket, S.D., United States	●	129	G2
Worcester, South Africa	●	99	B6
Worcester, United Kingdom	●	69	K9
Worcester, United States	●	127	M3
Wörgl	●	75	H3
Workington	●	69	J7
Worksop	●	59	A1
Worland	●	129	E2
Worms	●	67	D7
Wörth	●	67	D7
Worthing	●	69	M11
Worthington	●	127	G3
Wosu	▣	115	(2)B3
Wotu	●	115	(2)B3
Wowoni	🝙	115	(2)B3
Wrangell	●	125	E5
Wrangell Mountains	▲	125	C4
Wray	●	127	F3
Wrexham	●	69	K8
Wrigley	●	125	G4
Wrocław	●	65	G6
Września	●	65	G5
Wu	↗	111	D5
Wubin	●	119	C6
Wubu	●	111	E3
Wuchang	●	111	H2
Wuchuan	●	111	E2
Wuday'ah	●	85	E6
Wudu	●	111	C4
Wuhai	●	111	D3
Wuhan	●	111	E4
Wuhu	●	111	F4
Wüjang	●	107	C2
Wukari	●	95	F3
Wuli	●	107	F2
Wunsiedel	●	67	G6
Wunstorf	●	67	E4
Wuppertal	●	67	C5
Würzburg	●	67	E7
Wurzen	●	67	H5
Wushi	●	103	P9
Wusuli	↗	111	J1
Wutach	↗	75	D3
Wuwei	●	111	C3
Wuxi	●	111	G4
Wuxu	●	109	D2
Wuyuan	●	111	D2
Wuzhong	●	111	D3
Wuzhou	●	109	E2
Wye	↗	69	J9
Wyndham	●	119	E3
Wynniatt Bay	◿	125	J2
Wyoming	▣	127	E3
Wyszków	●	65	L5
Wytheville	●	135	E2

X

Name		Page	Ref
Xaafuun	●	97	J1

Name		Page	Ref
Xàbia	●	73	L6
Xaçmaz	●	83	N3
Xaidulla	●	103	P10
Xainza	●	107	E2
Xai-Xai	●	99	E4
Xam Nua	●	109	C2
Xankändi	●	83	M4
Xanten	●	59	J3
Xanthi	●	81	G3
Xapuri	●	141	D6
Xar Moron	↗	105	K8
Xàtiva	●	73	K6
Xiahe	●	111	C3
Xiamen	●	109	F2
Xi'an	●	111	D4
Xiangcheng	●	111	E4
Xiangfan	●	111	E4
Xianghoang	●	109	C3
Xianghuang Qi	●	111	E2
Xiangtan	●	111	E5
Xianning	●	111	E5
Xianyang	●	111	D4
Xiaogan	●	111	E4
Xiao Hinggan Ling	▰	105	M7
Xiaonanchuan	●	107	F1
Xichang	●	109	C1
Xigazê	●	107	E3
Xi Jiang	↗	111	E6
Xilinhot	●	111	F2
Xincai	●	111	E4
Xingcheng	●	111	G2
Xinghua	●	111	F4
Xingtai	●	111	F3
Xingu	↗	141	G5
Xingyi	●	109	C1
Xinhe	●	103	Q9
Xining	●	111	C3
Xinjin	●	111	G3
Xinmin	●	113	B2
Xintai	●	111	E3
Xinxiang	●	111	E3
Xinyang	●	111	E4
Xinyu	●	111	F5
Xinyuan	●	103	Q9
Xinzhou	●	111	E3
Xinzo de Limia	●	73	C2
Xique Xique	●	141	J6
Xi Ujimqin Qi	●	111	F2
Xiushu	●	111	E5
Xiwu	●	107	G2
Xixia	●	111	E4
Xi Xiang	●	111	D4
Xizang	⬡	107	E2
Xizang Gaoyuan	⬡	107	D2
Xuanhua	●	111	E3
Xuchang	●	111	E4
Xuddur	●	97	G3
Xuwen	●	109	E2
Xuzhou	●	111	F4

Y

Name		Page	Ref
Ya'an	●	111	D3
Yabassi	●	95	F4
Yabělo	●	97	F3
Yablonovyy Khrebet	▰	105	J6
Yabrūd	●	86	D3
Yabuli	●	113	E1
Yacuma	↗	141	D6
Yadgir	●	107	D5
Yagodnyy	●	63	N3
Yahk	●	125	H7
Yakima	●	129	B1
Yako	●	95	D2
Yakoma	●	97	C3
Yaksha	●	63	L2
Yakumo	●	113	L2
Yaku-shima	🝙	113	F8
Yakutat	●	133	(1)K4
Yakutsk	◻	105	M4

Name		Page	Ref
Yala	●	109	C5
Yalova	●	81	M4
Yalta	●	83	F1
Yalu	↗	113	D3
Yalutorovsk	●	63	N3
Yamagata	●	113	L4
Yamaguchi	●	113	F6
Yamarovka	●	105	J6
Yambio	●	97	D3
Yambol	●	79	P7
Yamburg	●	103	P4
Yamdena	🝙	115	(2)D4
Yamoussoukro	■	95	C3
Yampa	↗	129	E2
Yampil'	●	79	R1
Yamsk	●	105	S5
Yan'an	●	111	D3
Yanbu'al Baḩr	●	85	C5
Yancheng	●	111	G4
Yandun	●	111	A2
Yangambi	●	97	C3
Yangbajain	●	107	F2
Yangdok	●	113	D4
Yangi Kand	●	83	N5
Yangjiang	●	109	E2
Yangon	■	109	B3
Yangquan	●	111	E3
Yangshuo	●	109	E2
Yangtze = Chang Jiang	↗	111	D4
Yangzhou	●	111	F4
Yanhuqu	●	107	D2
Yani-Kurgan	●	103	M9
Yanji	●	113	E2
Yankton	●	129	G2
Yano-Indigirskaya Nizmennost'	⬡	105	N2
Yanqi	●	103	R9
Yanqing	●	111	F2
Yanshan	●	109	C2
Yanskiy Zaliv	◣	105	N2
Yantai	●	111	G3
Yaoundé	■	95	G4
Yap	🝙	117	D5
Yapen	🝙	115	(2)E3
Yaqui	↗	127	E6
Yaransk	●	63	J3
Yardımcı Burnu	▷	81	E8
Yare	↗	59	D2
Yaren	■	117	G6
Yarensk	●	63	J2
Yari	↗	141	C3
Yarkant	↗	85	L2
Yarkovo	●	63	N3
Yarlung Zangbo	↗	107	F3
Yarmouth	●	125	T8
Yaroslavl'	●	63	G3
Yar Sale	●	63	P1
Yartsevo	●	63	F3
Yashkul'	●	63	J5
Yasnyy	●	63	L4
Yāsūj	●	87	D1
Yatağan	●	81	L7
Yathkyed Lake	✦	125	M4
Yatsushiro	●	113	F7
Yavari	↗	141	C5
Yawatongguzlangar	●	103	Q10
Yaya	●	103	R6
Yayladağı	●	83	F6
Yazd	●	85	F3
Yazdān	●	85	H3
Yazd-e Khvāst	●	87	E1
Yazoo City	●	135	C3
Ydra	🝙	81	F7
Ye	●	109	B3
Yea	●	119	J7
Yecheng	●	85	L2
Yecla	●	73	J6
Yefremov	●	63	G4
Yegendybulak	●	103	P8
Yei	●	97	E3
Yekaterinburg	●	63	M3
Yelets	●	63	G4

Name		Page	Ref
Yell	🝙	69	L1
Yellowknife	◻	125	J4
Yellow River = Huang He	↗	111	C3
Yellow Sea	▬	111	G3
Yellowstone	↗	129	E1
Yellowstone Lake	✦	129	D2
Yeloten	●	85	H2
Yelva	↗	103	J5
Yelwa	●	95	E2
Yemen	[A]	85	D7
Yemetsk	●	63	H2
Yenakiyeve	●	63	G5
Yengisar	●	85	L2
Yenihisar	●	81	K7
Yenisey	↗	103	S6
Yeniseysk	●	103	S6
Yeniseyskiy Kryazh	▲	103	S5
Yeo Lake	✦	119	D5
Yeovil	●	69	K11
Yeppoon	●	119	K4
Yeraliyev	●	103	J9
Yerbogachen	●	105	H4
Yerevan	■	83	L3
Yerington	●	129	C3
Yerkov	●	81	S5
Yerkoy	●	83	F4
Yermak	●	103	P7
Yermitsa	●	63	K1
Yernva	↗	103	J5
Yershov	●	63	J4
Yerupaja	▲	141	B6
Yerushalayim	■	86	C5
Yesil'	●	63	N4
Yeşilhisar	●	83	F4
Yeşilköy	●	81	L4
Yessey	●	103	U4
Yevlax	●	83	M3
Yevpatoriya	●	63	F5
Yeyik	●	103	Q10
Yeysk	●	63	G5
Yibin	●	111	C5
Yichang	●	111	E4
Yichun, China	●	111	E5
Yichun, China	●	111	H1
Yilan	●	111	H1
Yıldız Dağları	▰	81	K2
Yıldızeli	●	83	G4
Yinchuan	●	111	D3
Yingcheng	●	111	E4
Yingkou	●	111	G2
Yining	●	103	Q9
Yirga Alem	●	97	F2
Yitomio	●	61	M3
Yitulihe	●	105	L6
Yiyang	●	111	E5
Yli-Kitka	✦	61	Q3
Ylivieska	●	61	N4
Ylöjärvi	●	61	M6
Yoakum	●	135	B4
Yoboki	●	93	H5
Yogyakarta	●	115	(1)E4
Yokadouma	●	95	G4
Yoko	●	95	G3
Yokohama, Japan	●	113	K6
Yokohama, Japan	●	113	L3
Yokosuka	●	113	K6
Yokote	●	113	L4
Yola	●	95	G3
Yonago	●	113	G6
Yonezawa	●	113	L5
Yong'an	●	109	F1
Yongdeng	●	111	C3
Yŏnghŭng	●	113	D4
Yongren	●	109	C1
Yongxiu	●	111	F5
Yonkers	●	131	F2
York, United Kingdom	●	69	L8
York, Nebr., United States	●	129	G2
York, Pa., United States	●	131	E3
Yorkton	●	125	L6
Yoshkar Ola	◻	63	J3

Name	Page	Grid
Yōsu	113	D6
Yotvata	86	C7
You	109	D2
Youghal	69	E10
Youghal Bay	69	E10
Youngstown	131	D2
Yozgat	83	F4
Yreka	129	B2
Ystad	65	C2
Ysyk-Köl	103	P9
Ytre Sula	61	B6
Ytyk-Kyuyel'	105	N4
Yu	109	D2
Yuan	109	C2
Yuanjiang	109	C2
Yuanmou	109	C1
Yuanping	111	E3
Yucatán	137	F5
Yucatan Channel	137	G4
Yuci	111	E3
Yudoma	105	Q4
Yuendumu	119	F4
Yueyang	111	E5
Yugorenok	105	P5
Yugoslavia	79	H6
Yugo-Tala	105	S3
Yukagirskoye Ploskogor'ye	105	S3
Yukon	133	(1)E3
Yukon Territory	133	(1)K2
Yukorskiy Poluostrov	103	L4
Yüksekova	83	L5
Yukta	105	H4
Yuli	103	R9
Yulin, *China*	109	E2
Yulin, *China*	111	D3
Yuma	133	C2
Yumen	111	B3
Yumin	103	Q8
Yuncheng	111	E3
Yun Xian	109	C2
Yuogi Feng	103	R8
Yurga	103	Q6
Yurimaguas	141	B5
Yurla	63	K3
Yuroma	63	J1
Yur'yevets	63	H3
Yu Shan	109	G2
Yushkozero	61	S4
Yushu, *China*	111	B4
Yushu, *China*	111	H2
Yusufeli	83	J3
Yutian	103	Q10
Yuyao	111	G4
Yuzhno Kuril'sk	113	N1
Yuzhno-Sakhalinsk	105	Q7
Yuzhno-Sukhokumsk	83	L1
Yuzhnoural'sk	63	M4
Yverdon-les-Bains	75	B4
Yvetot	59	C5

Z

Name	Page	Grid
Zaanstad	59	G2
Ząbkowice Śląskie	65	F7
Zabok	75	L4
Zābol	85	H3
Zabrze	65	H7
Zacatecas	133	F4
Zadar	75	L6
Zadonsk	63	G4
Zafora	81	J8
Zafra	73	D6
Zāgheh-ye-Bālā	83	M6
Zagora	91	D2
Zagreb	75	L5
Zagyva	65	K10
Zāhedān	85	H4
Zahirabad	107	C5
Zahlé	86	C3
Zahrān	85	D6
Zaječar	79	K6
Zakamensk	105	G6
Zākhō	83	K5
Zakopane	65	J8
Zakynthos	81	C7
Zakynthos	81	C7
Zala	75	M4
Zalaegerszeg	75	M4
Zalari	105	G6
Zalaszentgrót	75	N4
Zalău	79	L2
Zalim	85	D5
Zaliv Aniva	105	Q7
Zaliv Kara-Bogaz Gol	85	F1
Zaliv Kresta	105	Y3
Zaliv Paskevicha	63	L5
Zaliv Shelikhova	105	T5
Zaliv Terpeniya	105	Q7
Zamakh	85	E6
Zambezi	99	C2
Zambezi	99	E3
Zambia	99	D2
Zamboanga	109	G5
Zambrów	65	M5
Zamora	73	E3
Zamość	65	N7
Zanda	107	C2
Zandvoort	59	G2
Zanesville	135	E2
Zangguy	85	L2
Zanjān	83	N5
Zannone	77	H8
Zanzibar	97	F5
Zanzibar Island	97	F5
Zaozernyy	103	S6
Zapadnaya Dvina	63	E3
Zapadno-Sibirskaya Ravnina	103	L5
Zapadnyy Sayan	103	S7
Zapata	133	G3
Zaporizhzhya	63	G5
Zaprešić	75	L5
Zaqatala	83	M3
Zara	83	G4
Zarafshan	103	L9
Zaragoza	73	K3
Zarand	87	G1
Zaranj	85	H3
Zarasai	61	P9
Zaraza	141	D2
Zarechensk	61	R3
Zaria	95	F2
Zărneşti	79	N4
Zarqā'	86	D4
Zarqān	87	E2
Žary	65	G6
Zarzadilla de Totana	73	J7
Žatec	65	C7
Zavetnoye	63	H5
Zavidovići	79	F5
Zavitinsk	105	M6
Zayarsk	103	U6
Zaysan	103	Q8
Zayü	109	B1
Zbraslav	65	D8
Zēbāk	85	K2
Zēbār	83	L5
Zeebrugge	59	F3
Zefat	86	C4
Zeilona Góra	65	E6
Zeist	59	H2
Zeitz	67	H5
Zelenoborskiy	61	S3
Zelenograd	63	G3
Zelenogradsk	65	K3
Zelenokumsk	83	K1
Zella-Mehlis	67	F6
Zell am See	75	H3
Zémio	97	D2
Zemlya Alexsandry	103	G1
Zemlya Frantsa-Iosifa	103	J2
Zemlya Vil'cheka	103	L1
Zempoalteptl	137	E5
Zenica	79	E5
Zerbst	67	H5
Zermatt	75	C4
Zeta Lake	125	K2
Zeulenroda	67	G6
Zeven	67	E3
Zevenaar	59	J3
Zeya	105	M6
Zeya	105	M6
Zeydābād	87	F2
Zeyskoye Vodokhranilishche	105	M5
Zgharta	86	C2
Zgierz	65	J6
Zgorzelec	65	E6
Zhailma	103	M4
Zhaksy	63	N4
Zhaksykon	63	N5
Zhaltyr	63	N4
Zhambyl	103	N9
Zhanatas	103	M9
Zhangbei	111	E2
Zhangguangcai Ling	111	H2
Zhangjiakou	111	E2
Zhangling	105	L6
Zhangwu	111	G2
Zhangye	111	B3
Zhangzhou	109	F2
Zhanjiang	109	E2
Zhaodong	105	M7
Zhaoqing	109	E2
Zhaosu	103	Q9
Zhaoyuan	111	H1
Zharkamys	103	K8
Zharkent	103	P9
Zharma	103	Q8
Zharyk	103	N8
Zhaxigang	107	C2
Zheleznogorsk	63	G4
Zhengzhou	111	E4
Zhenjiang	111	F4
Zherdevka	63	H4
Zhetybay	103	J9
Zhezkazgan	103	M8
Zhigalovo	105	H5
Zhigansk	105	L3
Zhilinda	105	J2
Zhob	85	J3
Zholymbet	103	N7
Zhongba	107	D3
Zhongdian	111	B5
Zhongning	111	D3
Zhongshan	109	E2
Zhongze	111	G5
Zhoukou	111	E4
Zhuanghe	111	G3
Zhucheng	111	F3
Zhumadian	111	E4
Zhuo Xian	111	F3
Zhytomyr	63	E4
Žiar	65	H9
Zibo	111	F3
Zichang	111	D3
Zieriksee	59	F3
Ziesar	67	H4
Zigong	111	C5
Ziguinchor	91	B6
Zikhron Ya'aqov	86	B4
Žilina	65	H8
Zillah	93	C2
Zima	105	G6
Zimbabwe	99	D3
Zimmi	95	B3
Zimnicea	79	N6
Zinder	95	F2
Zinjibār	93	J5
Zirc	65	G10
Žirje	77	K5
Zistersdorf	75	M2
Zitava	65	H9
Zittau	67	K6
Ziway Häyk'	97	F2
Zixing	109	E1
Zlaté Moravce	65	H9
Zlatoust	63	L3
Zlín	65	G8
Zliţan	91	H2
Złotów	65	G4
Zmeinogorsk	103	Q7
Znamenskoye	103	N6
Žnin	65	G5
Znojmo	75	M2
Zoigê	111	C4
Zomba	99	F3
Zongo	97	B3
Zonguldak	81	P3
Zouar	93	C3
Zouérat	91	C4
Žovka	65	N7
Zrenjanin	79	H4
Zschopau	67	J6
Zug	75	D3
Zugdidi	83	J2
Zuger See	75	D3
Zugspitze	67	F9
Zuid-Beveland	59	F3
Zuni	133	E1
Zunyi	111	D5
Županja	79	F4
Zürich	75	D3
Zuru	95	F2
Žut	77	K5
Zutphen	59	J2
Zuwārah	93	B1
Zuyevka	63	J6
Zvishavane	99	E4
Zvolen	65	J9
Zvornik	79	G5
Zwedru	95	C3
Zweibrücken	59	K5
Zwettl	75	L2
Zwickau	67	H6
Zwiesel	67	J7
Zwolle	59	J2
Zyryanka	105	S3
Zyryanovsk	103	Q8
Żywiec	65	J8

Legend:

- Continent name
- Country name
- State or province name
- Country capital
- State or province capital
- Settlement
- Mountain, volcano, peak
- Mountain range
- Physical region or feature
- River, canal
- Lake, salt lake
- Gulf, strait, bay
- Sea, ocean
- Cape, point
- Island or island group, rocky or coral reef
- Place of interest
- Historical or cultural region

World Political

Equatorial Scale 1 : 78 000 000

ARCTIC OCEAN

Ellesmere Island

GREENLAND
(Denmark)

Greenland
Sea

Baffin Bay

Victoria
Island

Beaufort Sea

Baffin Island

Norwegian
Sea

ICELAND

Nuuk
(Godthåb)

Reykjavík

Arctic Circle

ALASKA
(U.S.)

Yukon

Anchorage

Mackenzie

Hudson
Bay

REPUBLIC OF
IRELAND

UNITED
KINGDOM

NETHER-
LANDS

Bering
Sea

Gulf of
Alaska

CANADA

Dublin

London

BEL.

60°

Edmonton

Calgary

Winnipeg

Lake Superior

ROCKY MOUNTAINS

Vancouver

Seattle

Missouri

Lake
Michigan

Lake
Huron

St Lawrence

Ottawa

Québec

Montréal

Paris

FRANCE

ANDORRA

MONACO

Denver

Chicago

Detroit

Toronto

UNITED STATES

San Francisco

Kansas City

New York

Philadelphia

Washington D.C.

PORTUGAL

Açores
(Portugal)

Lisboa

SPAIN

Madrid

Los Angeles

San Diego

Phoenix

Dallas

Houston

Atlanta

Bermuda
(U.K.)

ATLANTIC
OCEAN

Madeira
(Portugal)

Rabat

Casablanca

Alger

Tropic of Cancer

Rio Grande

New Orleans

MEXICO

Gulf of
Mexico

THE
BAHAMAS

Islas Canarias
(Spain)

MOROCCO

ALGERIA

SAHARA

30°

HAWAII
(U.S.)

Monterrey

Guadalajara

Ciudad
de México

La Habana

CUBA

HAITI

DOMINICAN REP

Santo
Domingo

PUERTO RICO (U.S.)

ANTIGUA & BARBUDA

WESTERN
SAHARA
(Morocco)

MAURITANIA

MALI

GUATE-
MALA

BELIZE

JAMAICA

DOMINICA

Nouakchott

Niger

Guatemala

HONDURAS

Caribbean Sea

ST LUCIA

CAPE
VERDE

Dakar

SEN.

N

Niamey

EL SALVADOR

NICARAGUA

ST KITTS-NEVIS

ST VINCENT &
THE GRENADINES

BARBADOS

THE GAMBIA

Banjul

Bamako

BURKINA

Managua

San José

COSTA
RICA

Panama

GRENADA

TRINIDAD & TOBAGO

GUINEA-BISSAU

Bissau

Conakry

GUINEA

NIG

PANAMA

Georgetown

Caracas

VENEZUELA

GUYANA

SURINAM

FRENCH
GUIANA (Fr.)

SIERRA LEONE

Freetown

Monrovia

LIBERIA

IVORY
COAST

Yamous-
soukro

GHANA

TOGO

BENIN

Accra

Porto-
Novo

PACIFIC
OCEAN

Islas Galápagos
(Ecuador)

COLOMBIA

Bogotá

EQUAT. GUINEA

SÃO TOMÉ
& PRÍNCIPE

KIRIBATI

Quito

ECUADOR

Iquitos

Amazon

Manaus

Belém

Fortaleza

Equator

0°

French
Polynesia

Lima

PERU

BRAZIL

Recife

Arequipa

La Paz

BOLIVIA

Sucre

Brasília

Salvador

Belo Horizonte

Tropic of Capricorn

Pitcairn Is.
(U.K.)

PARAGUAY

Rio de Janeiro

São Paulo

Curitiba

Asunción

Córdoba

CHILE

Santiago

Porto Alegre

URUGUAY

30°

ARGENTINA

Buenos
Aires

Montevideo

Punta
Arenas

Falkland
Islands
(U.K.)

South Georgia
(U.K.)

South Sandwich
Islands
(U.K.)

60°

Antarctic Circle

Bellinghausen
Sea

Weddell Sea

Ross Sea

© Copyright AND Cartographic Publishers Ltd.